■ **e-Flashcards** that you can use to review key terms and concepts

■ **Web links** to professional music organizations

DATE ~~~~~~~ to prepare you for your future in the industry

■ **Links to online videos, RSS Feeds, and other interactive material** to bring you up-to-date music business information, including Billboard's RSS feed

www.sagepub.com/baskerville9e

MUSIC
BUSINESS
HANDBOOK
AND CAREER GUIDE

edition 9

*To my family, and to those in the business
who care about the music, too*

DAVID BASKERVILLE

University of Colorado, Denver

TIM BASKERVILLE

MUSIC
BUSINESS
HANDBOOK
AND CAREER GUIDE

edition
9

Los Angeles | London | New Delhi
Singapore | Washington DC

For information:

SAGE Publications, Inc.
2455 Teller Road
Thousand Oaks,
  California 91320
E-mail: order@sagepub.com

SAGE Publications Ltd.
1 Oliver's Yard
55 City Road
London EC1Y 1SP
United Kingdom

SAGE Publications India Pvt. Ltd.
B 1/I 1 Mohan Cooperative
  Industrial Area
Mathura Road, New Delhi 110 044
India

SAGE Publications Asia-Pacific Pte. Ltd.
33 Pekin Street #02-01
Far East Square
Singapore 048763

Printed in the United States of America.

Library of Congress Cataloging-in-Publication Data

Baskerville, David.
Music business handbook and career guide/David Baskerville; editor,
Tim Baskerville. — 9th ed.
   p. cm.
Includes bibliographical references and index.
ISBN 978-1-4129-7679-4 (cloth)
  1. Music—Vocational guidance—United States—Handbooks, manuals, etc.
2. Music trade—Vocational guidance—United States—Handbooks, manuals, etc.
I. Baskerville, Tim. II. Title.

ML3795.B33 2010
780.23′73—dc22   2009035802

This book is printed on acid-free paper.

09 10 11 12 13 10 9 8 7 6 5 4 3 2 1

This publication is designed to provide accurate and authoritative information in regard to the subject matter covered. It is sold with the understanding that the publisher is not engaged in rendering legal, accounting, or other professional service. If legal advice or other expert assistance is required, the services of a competent professional person should be sought.

From the *Declaration of Principles* jointly adopted by a committee of the American Bar Association and a committee of publishers and associations.

Staff for the Ninth Edition

Editor:	Tim Baskerville
Project Managers:	Lynnette Pennings
	Deborah Sourgen
Senior Contributing Editors:	Robert Clarida, Esq., Dan Daley, Catherine Fitterman-Radbill, Richard Flohil, Marilyn Gillen, Phil Hardy, Robert Marich, Michael Sigman, Kim Wangler
Photo Editor:	Deborah Sourgen
Editorial Consultant:	Roberta Baskerville

Sage Staff for the Ninth Edition

Acquisitions Editor:	Lisa Cuevas Shaw
Editorial Assistant:	MaryAnn Vail
Production Editor:	Karen Wiley
Typesetter:	C&M Digitals (P) Ltd.
Proofreader:	Jennifer Gritt
Indexer:	Diggs Publishing Services
Cover Designer:	Janet Kiesel
Marketing Manager:	Christy Guilbault

Contents

Foreword

Nile Rodgers

Artists Need to Be Good Listeners, Too

Photo by Roy Cox.

I'll never forget what David Bowie told me was his objective when I produced his album "Let's Dance." He said, "Nile, darling, what we've got to do is come up with something that's the same but really quite different."

Don't laugh, because David is the consummate artist with an impresario's keen sense of the market. He knows the audience wants new musical sensations, but not so new that they are completely alien. Keeping your eye on the audience has been my philosophy ever since I was a skinny kid with glasses from the streets of New York, a musician who broke into the business playing in the house band at the Apollo Theater in Harlem.

My advice to the next generation of musical talent is to explore with an open mind and discover the musical world that's out there.

Don't assume that you are so smart and talented that the world is absolutely going to find you on your terms.

The music business, after all, is business. And business requires focus. I make my songs for the specific gatekeeper that I see just in front of me. The gatekeeper could be an A&R dude, who I know will then take my song to the label boss. I'm not looking way down the road like when I drive a car. This philosophy focuses creativity on a simple and achievable objective.

I've never had a manager because I always want to figure out the marketplace myself and then plot my next move (although not having a manager is right for me, it may not be right for others). When I started out, it was the age of the rock star—the Rolling Stones, Yes, and Jimi Hendrix. I knew that I'd never make it as a rock star because I didn't look the type. So I wrote songs that were catchier and more commercial than theirs.

When I broke into the business, all we could hope for was that our records would get on the radio and land on the *Billboard* charts. The business was like a distant fortress with high walls and just a few gatekeepers. As artists—the musicians, producers, and songwriters—we had to figure out how to get over that fortress wall.

In today's digital age, music is everywhere, creating a flat, wide landscape with many points of entry. It's not just record labels and radio stations anymore. In recent years, retailers ranging from coffee shops to clothing stores have sold select CDs, giving them national distribution. Clothing manufacturers, liquor marketers, tobacco companies, electronics companies, and other consumer product outfits sell and sponsor music in deals with artists, creating whole new classes of music financiers and enablers.

James Taylor, who is a friend of mine, made one of the single smartest moves of his entire career—and he has an incredible career going—when he did a Christmas album distributed through Hallmark Cards stores. This album sold over a million copies; Hallmark covered the cost of the recording and James kept ownership of the master. Now that's what I call knowing the audience and working the system!

Years ago, the business was more combative and appeared punctuated with endless battles between artists and labels. Today, the environment is much more collaborative, with fewer battles. That transformation requires listening with an open mind, but doesn't mean agreeing to what doesn't sound right. Once, I was in a disagreement with a label over one of my songs. The label was slow to come around to my view but finally agreed to destroy hundreds of thousands of singles that were just about to ship, and replaced them with *Good Times*, the song my band CHIC wanted. It ultimately went on to become one of our most influential songs and No. 1 on the *Billboard* chart.

That incident illustrates the big stick of leverage that the artist—who often is portrayed as powerless—actually wields in dealing with labels and other big entities that are partners in the music industry. Despite their armies of executives and their mounds of corporate money, the big companies know deep down that they don't *really* know. It's the artist who has a feel for the music, and—if listening to my advice—it's the artist who makes the effort to understand the audience.

The late Ahmet Ertegun—the legendary label executive known for his eye for up-and-coming talent—confided this little secret when I first met him. He told me, "Kid, the reason I'm letting you do whatever you want to do is because I learned early on that *I* am not the ultimate consumer."

The lesson: Listen to the audience, and the audience will listen to you.

Nile Rodgers is a recording artist, songwriter, video game scorer, and record producer who has collaborated with David Bowie, Eric Clapton, Madonna, and Diana Ross. His guitar-driven CHIC funk recording "Le Freak" is Atlantic Record's biggest single of all time. He is a trustee of The Recording Academy and founder of the We Are Family Foundation.

Preface

We all know the story of the frog that is placed in a pot of cold water and becomes somewhat uncomfortable as the burner ignites and the water gradually warms to the point of boiling. The question researchers keep testing: Does the frog realize its likely fate and jump to safety, or does its frog brain figure, "This is my environment, and I should sit still and tolerate it—even to the point of death."

The boiled-frog syndrome is the one we observers have been studying in the music industry since digital technology began to heat up toward the end of the last century.

It was all very easy when the first edition of this book rolled off the press in the cold-water era decades ago:

- the U.S. commanded the majority of global music sales,
- radio was the engine driving buying behavior,
- physical media (of various shapes and sizes) was a healthy growing business,
- what was to become the Internet was an experimental program of the U.S. Defense Department, and
- violation of copyright was a cultural oddity, not a rallying cry of respectable citizens.

Well, you don't need to read the next 30 chapters to gain this insight: The world has changed. The water has gotten awfully hot.

The questions we explore here are about how everyone in the business of making and selling music is adapting. It's a tale of what they're doing to avoid becoming frog soup.

Despite the headlines of woe and the legendary missteps of well-financed entities, our story is actually a hopeful one. By trial-and-error, with fits and starts, the stakeholders in music are figuring it out. Not all of them, of course. But enough of them to help chart a course for the rest of us seeking to identify lessons, to make decisions, and to forge careers and businesses that have genuine promise.

Some highlights from the frog pot as portrayed in this ninth edition:

- Individual musicians are discovering new ways to build serial careers, adjusting to the always-shifting demands of a multifaceted industry. Veterans like journeyman Gene Perla and aspiring newcomers like Katie Vogel show us how they do it. (For case studies see Chapters 2 and 22.)
- Changes in performance royalties in sound recordings have opened up entirely new revenue streams for record labels and artists, promising a lifeline for part of the business gasping for relief (Chapter 5).

- Increasingly common "360 deals" enable big labels to grab an ever-bigger share of overall artist revenues—but they are also spurring labels to align more precisely with the economic interests of their creative engines (Chapter 8).
- Plummeting record production costs and the ubiquitous Web have allowed Do-It-Yourself artists to write, record, and distribute their own music. A panacea of creative freedom for the creator, or an economic trap for the unwary (Chapter 11)?
- The concert business, once considered an ancillary activity requiring support by subsidies generated from record sales, has seen the tables turned. Concert ticket sales (combining box office and the resale ticket business) now rival the recorded music revenue stream (Chapter 12).
- Record promotion and distribution has had a rough ride. The decades-long strategy of using radio airplay to drive teenagers to a neighborhood record store has been hit with a triple whammy: Radio is weakened, and the neighborhood record store has faded or disappeared—not to mention that many music lovers don't need CDs anymore. What alternatives are emerging in this new world (Chapter 16)?
- The consumer click paths of the digital age are enabling a new level of insight into buying behavior, demographics, and shifting tastes. The once all-important record charts have given way to a panoply of market research tools, all in aid of better monetization of consumer desires (Chapter 17).
- Social networking has established its place in the music-marketing playbook, ceding some control to the audience while finding new and inexpensive ways to cash in on intellectual property (Chapter 18).
- Video games, once belittled as inconsequential toys, are now major economic platforms serving as customers for original and licensed-in music and as vehicles to promote artists and their work (Chapter 21).
- Throughout much of the last century the multinational music industry, in dollar terms, was largely an American affair. U.S. companies spread American culture to the mostly developed world and made a nice profit doing so. Today, the U.S. share of the world business is down sharply from its apogee, and the "American majors" in most cases aren't even U.S. companies anymore. Chronicling this change is an entirely new chapter about the globe's shift on its business axis (Chapter 29).

Change, then, is our theme. From Hollywood to Nashville. From New York to Hong Kong. From Miami to London. It is change that both threatens the established, known order and also offers possible escape hatches for those within the bedeviled music industry.

Those in the business, and those aspiring to get into the business, must calculate when and how to jump out of the frog pot.

Tim Baskerville
Los Angeles

Acknowledgments

We wish to thank those people who were helpful in generously sharing their knowledge of many facets of the music and entertainment business during the preparation of this ninth edition and its predecessors.

Substantial contributions for this edition came from Robert Marich, a veteran entertainment journalist (*The Hollywood Reporter, Variety Deal Memo*), and Michael Sigman, editor and music publisher (*Record World*, MajorSongs). They co-anchored our coverage of the domestic music industry and their insights are reflected throughout many chapters. Musician and journalist Dan Daley turned the spotlight to the digital age, illuminating a theme which necessarily shines throughout the book. Former *Billboard* editor Marilyn Gillen employed her razor-sharp pen to improve both our ideas and their expression.

Special thanks go to Kim Wangler of Appalachian State University for crafting the chapter on starting your own business, a topic also informed by insights from NYU Steinhardt's Catherine Fitterman Radbill. Wangler also brought our treatment of arts administration up to date, a subject additionally reflecting the knowledge of arts management consultant Nancy Hytone Leb and Ava Lawrence of Northeastern University.

Over the years a number of entertainment and music attorneys have kept us up to date with the shifting sands of law and regulation. Among the key contributors this time around were New York-based Robert Clarida of Cowan, Liebowitz & Latman, and Susan Rabin, Los Angeles-based entertainment attorney. In prior editions major contributions on copyright, publishing, and licensing were made by Alan S. Bergman, Bergman & Associates, Inc., and Dr. Janet Nepkie of State University of New York, College of Oneonta.

Abroad, we turned once again to UK-based Phil Hardy of The View for his tracking of the global scene, with Richard Flohil bringing us up to date on the unique world of Canadian music.

The U.S. performance rights organizations were generous with their help, particularly Mark Palermo of ASCAP, David Sanjek of BMI, and William Velez of SESAC.

The music business associations, unions, and guilds also offered helpful reviews and clarifications. Our appreciation goes to Jacqueline Charlesworth of HFA, Inc.; Christopher de Haan, AFTRA National Manager of Communications; Steve Rosen, AGVA West Coast Representative; Terry O'Neal, SAG; Maria Somma, Actors' Equity; Suzanne Hatcher, SLFA; Neill Dixon, CMW; Leslie Lashinsky, AFM Local 47; Liz Kennedy, Deputy Director, Communications, RIAA; Jim Donio, President of NARM; Clinton Billups, National President of the National Conference of Personal Managers; and Melanie Ripley, NAMM Member Contact Center Manager.

Warner Music Group was extremely helpful in sharing its publicly available information about various aspects of the music business. We also benefited from reviews and information from Sound Scoop, NielsenSoundScan, and the Recording Academy.

Other professionals, educators, and experts were generous with their time. Heartfelt thanks go to all of them:

David Card, VP and Principal Analyst at Forrester Research (acquirer of JupiterResearch), provided data and insight into digital music.

Laurie Soriano, Steve Winogradsky, and Howard Levitt for their contributions on songwriting.

Heather McBee, Vice President of Digital for Sony Music Nashville, contributed significant insight on the evolution of digital marketing.

Coleen Haynes, Executive Producer: Music Videos at HSI Productions, for her valuable help on music videos.

Don Leeds, who introduced us to foreword author Nile Rodgers.

Kate Wallace graciously contributed the reflections of a successful songwriter.

Frank Macchia and Craig Safan contributed significant insight on dramatic scoring.

Denis M. Hannigan, film and TV composer, and Steve Schnur, Worldwide Executive of Music and Marketing and President of Artwerk Music Group at Electronic Arts, provided expertise on scoring films, TV, and video games.

Thom Mocarsky, VP of Communications at Arbitron, lent his expertise to the subject of music in radio.

Gary Paticoff, Sr. VP and Executive Producer for Rubin Postaer and Associates, gave wise counsel on advertising.

David Hazan, music marketing executive, and John Rarrick, President of Bullseye Public Relations, provided insights on distribution and marketing.

Melville J. Noriega, music distribution executive, shared his knowledge about retailing and distribution.

Gene Perla was especially helpful with studio information, so much so that we urged him to let us describe the arc of his own career in Chapter 2.

Paul Christensen offered valuable information on record production.

Dan Del Fiorentino, NAMM historian, for providing an overview of the musical instruments business and Paul J. Ash, President of Sam Ash Music, for assistance in music instrument retailing and mail order.

Stephen Marcone of William Paterson College gave wise counsel on artist management.

Richard McIlvery of University of Southern California was immensely helpful with dramatic scoring.

James F. Slutz, retired from Indiana State University, lent his expert and extensive contribution in the area of music merchandising, along with intriguing insight on developments in China.

Barry Freeman, a record and radio industry veteran, was generous with his help, as was Lark Baskerville, Vice President, Director, Human Resources, of Rubin Postaer and Associates.

For help with careers in the music business, we thank the following reviewers: Brian Berge, Alf Claussen, Rick Fleishman, David Hamilton, Andrew Kaye, Willow Pearson, and Mary Salciccia.

Special thanks go to the many friends who gave us advice and information used throughout the book. We are especially grateful to Ira Mayer, Paul Sweeting, Lynne Dundas, Joe Diamond, Cathy Karol Crowther, and Tee Bosustow. Educators who have helped along the way include Rey Sanchez of the University of Miami; Tim Hays of Elmhurst College; Kristel Kemmerer and Robin Zaremski of Albright College, Pennsylvania; and Carole Knisely of York College of Pennsylvania.

Many people have contributed to the development of this book in earlier editions, including Dr. Alfred Reed, who, along with Dr. William Lee, established the first university degree program in music merchandising at the University of Miami.

Always helpful was attorney Jay L. Cooper, in addition to David Ludwick, Mike Milom, Craig Hayes, and Jeffrey Cunard.

Educators who offered useful suggestions include Geoffrey P. Hull, Richard Barnet, Dr. Newton J. Collins, Don Gorder, and David P. Leonard.

Insights of Patrick Williams, Tom Scott, Brian Ingoldsby, Dave Grusin, Bones Howe, and the late Nelson Riddle are reflected here, as are those of critic Henry Pleasants, Robert Young, Adam Somers, Mickey Granberg, John Devarion, Ralph Peer II, and Jay Morgenstern.

Among others who have been helpful over the years are Dave Dannheiser, John Fagot, Janet Bozeman, John Dobel, Walt Love, B. Aaron Meza, and David Bosca, as well as Bruce Stevens, Harley Drew, Monica Logan, Norm Visger, Al Tavera, Jim Taber, Chris Kershaw, Alan Ett, and Gail Kantor.

We're grateful to those educators who have labored for decades to enhance scholarship and curricula in the field of music business education, notably Bruce Ronkin of Northeastern University and Jim Progris, retired from the University of Miami.

To all of those mentioned here and to many other friends who have shared their knowledge of the music business with us—thank you.

—The Editors

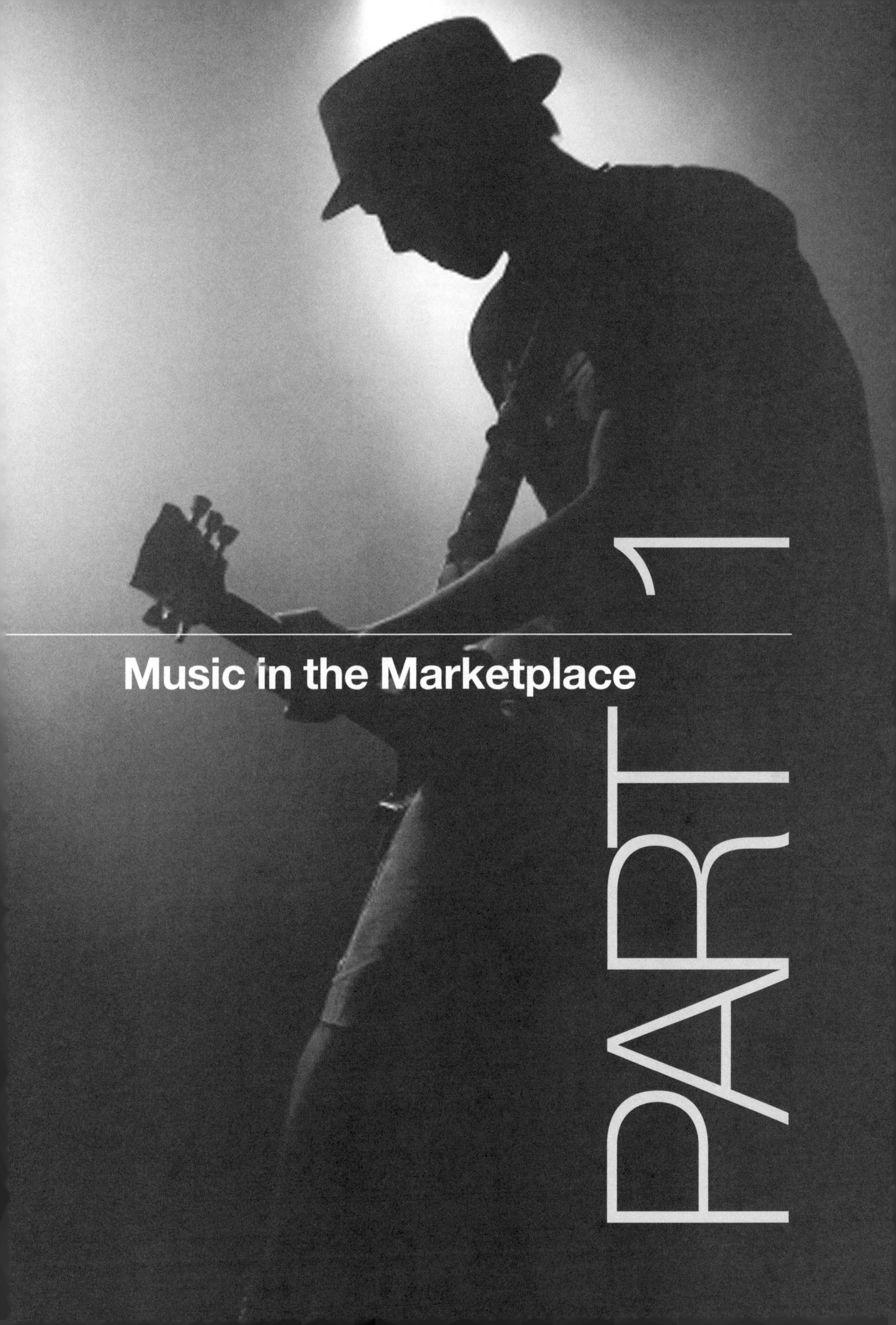

Music in the Marketplace

PART 1

CHAPTER 1

Overview

Did someone say "music business"? What happened to the *art* of music? The shortest possible answer is, "Billions!"—the windstorm of money swirling around the art and business of music. But the question of what is happening to musical art in the modern marketplace calls for a serious answer, particularly when that marketplace is changing so rapidly. That is what this book is all about.

> *"I never cared much for poverty."*
>
> —Igor Stravinsky

How much has the music business changed since the 20th century gave way to the 21st? More than many could have imagined only a few beats back. What remains the same? More than you might expect, given the chorus of questions about its future direction and shape. Yes, the music industry looks radically different today, having been reshaped by a still-evolving digital landscape, but the fundamentals of the business—the creation, publishing, packaging, marketing, distribution, and sale of music—are constant. Creators still create at one end, artists and merchants continue to "monetize" a music product at the other, and an array of equally passionate, talented individuals— agents, managers, producers, sound engineers, **label**[1] executives, bookers, promoters, broadcasters, business advisers, lawyers, accountants—perform their vital roles throughout the process. The differences, of course, are in the details.

That, then, is what will be laid out in the following chapters: the core fundamentals of the *music business* (the term is used here to include the art, the profession, and the business of music), along with the industry's current state of the art (those 21st century details). Not only do we examine the major changes in music and its audiences, we also set forth in detail just who produces the music, who "consumes"

Left: Sun Studio, Memphis, where Elvis Presley, Johnny Cash, Roy Orbison, and Jerry Lee Lewis recorded for Sun Records.

Photo © Gavin Hellier/Getty Images Entertainment.

it, and how the artists, merchants and others in that long music chain divvy up the billions of dollars that the industry produces. Armed with a thorough understanding of both, a music-industry hopeful will be well prepared not only for a career in today's music business, but also in the music business of tomorrow—one in which the next seismic shifts are surely only a few more beats away.

Music and Society: We've Got Music in Us

Prepare for some surprises: Perceptions of the profession and business of music are usually at wide variance from reality. This is partly because the field is so diverse and changes so rapidly, but it is also because its public face—the major record label and chart-topping superstar—reveals such a small piece of the whole picture. But it *can* be understood. It is argued that the music business, particularly the recording industry, is fundamentally irrational. But most of what really goes on in the business and the profession does submit to rational analysis.

We can begin to understand the music business, or any large and diverse activity, once we examine each of its components. That is our method here. But before we do this, let's consider the overall magnitude of the music business today. These facts can provide some perspective:

- More than 200 billion CDs have been sold worldwide since the format's introduction.
- Well over a *billion* digital music tracks are sold annually—compared with the 19 *million* bought as recently as 2003.
- Almost half of all American homes (45%) boast at least one digital portable music player, according to the Consumer Electronics Association.
- One of five Americans plays a musical instrument. These musicians spend more than $8 billion a year on instruments, accessories, and sheet music.
- Mobile music revenues (including ringtones) passed $1.3 billion in trade value in 2007, according to the International Federation of the Phonographic Industry (IFPI).

The love affair starts young—listening to music is cited as the most popular activity among teens—and it's not exactly monogamous: Our passion for music is not limited to any one genre, although a cursory glance through the major-media pop-culture lens might suggest so. The American Symphony Orchestra League reports that approximately 38,000 symphony concerts are given every year. This particular audience now numbers around 30 million patrons each season. Opera continues to attract its loyal audience, now being served by more than 300 professional and semiprofessional companies in this country.

Nor is the desire strong only in the U.S.: Recorded music is one of the primary mediums of entertainment for consumers worldwide, ringing up nearly $30 billion in retail sales in 2007, according to global music body IFPI.

Meanwhile, ever-cheaper digital production tools, along with the wide-open world of the Web, have combined to spark an explosion of choices for every possible music taste (or lack thereof), and those options are often only a click away from being pumped into the pocket-size digital media players attached to eager ears around the globe. Musicians are no longer restricted in their expression by the laws of acoustics—new electronic ways to make music are invented every year, offering a composer or video producer more controls than 10 fingers can handle. The people with access to newer technology are limited in their expressive capacities only by their imaginations.

In short, the *music* side of the music business is booming.

Art Versus Commerce: Music Changes Everything

What about the *business* side of the music business? A straight line between a strong consumer appetite for music and a fat, happy music industry is perhaps less certain than it once was. The early explosive—and initially largely unchecked[2]—growth of peer-to-peer file sharing in the 1990s, a shift toward nontraditional and online retail, and a recent sales skew toward single-track downloads rather than full (more expensive) albums has begun to alter the old equation. These new realities have spurred (some would say forced) new ways of thinking about how to connect "making music" with "making money."

Art and commerce, of course, have always made very strange bedfellows. This ever-present linkage is inherently contradictory, for musicians and merchants are, in many respects, natural enemies. They seem to hold generally conflicting views on what music should be and do. Musicians want their music to break creative boundaries and to be heard and appreciated by as many people as possible; they want to "connect" with an audience. Music merchants and businesspeople want music to fit the mainstream sales taste of the moment and to make as much money as possible; they want to "connect" with an audience's wallets. This art/commerce divide is often evident on the retail and radio side: "Good" does not necessarily equal "popular." Perhaps the reason so many hit songs sound bad is that they are. (One irony of the opening up of the creative process through cheaper digital tools and the Web is that there is more bad music being made than ever before—and more that is mind-blowingly good.)

Great music does still break through, as it always has, and great business is still being done. It is simply being done somewhat differently. The major music companies that continue to control the lion's share of the U.S. market—Universal Music Group, Sony Music Entertainment, Warner Music Group, and EMI—are exploring new business models and alliances, different types of artist contracts (including so-called "**360 deals**," which cut labels in on ancillary artist revenue), and previously untapped licensing opportunities for current hits and their all-important catalog titles. Musicians and recording artists—newcomers and veterans alike—are discovering that there are more ways than ever to "do-it-yourself": build a fan base, book shows, record music, and support themselves by selling it on the Web. Many artists are picking and choosing those areas where they need or desire professional muscle and those segments of their art or business that can be done better or cheaper with some **DIY** sweat.

Indeed, the very definitions of artist, label, merchant/retailer, and even "music product" are blurring and changing. An "artist" increasingly may be his own label—and his own retailer. A "composer" might compose music for a symphony, a commercial, a film, and a videogame. A "music store" might be a location in a local strip mall,[3] a merchandising section in a big-box retailer, a site on the Web, or an application on a cell phone. These "stores" may sell music in the form of albums or singles, physically or digitally, or they may sell access to it for a fee. The "product"— the recorded music itself—can be a direct source of revenue for artists and labels, or it might be viewed more as a method of promotion for bringing in revenue from touring and merchandise (it's hard to download and "share" a T-shirt).

The positives for the music business in this latest reinvention—for those already in it and those just starting out—are many. New technologies naturally equal new challenges. But, as the music industry has shown from its infancy, they also bring vast new opportunities to evolve, expand, and prosper—whether the technology in question is the Web, music-video channels, CDs, TV, radio, or the LP.

Historical Development

Finding a Paying Audience

History books provide only spotty information on how the musician fared in earlier times as a professional. Music historians, most of them tenured behind the protective walls of universities, have rarely shown concern for the bread-and-butter needs of the working musician. This traditional lack of concern for the professional status and financial condition of musicians dates from earliest times. We can assume that in the beginning, music making was undertaken by individuals and groups simply for their own pleasure. The performer was also the composer. If there was an audience, it was a social or religious gathering; it did not occur to the early musicians that they might develop an audience that would pay to hear them sing their songs.

Among the first important professional musicians in Western civilization were the mimes of the Greek and Roman theater. They were singing-dancing actors. Roman law held them to be disreputable types, calling them *infami* (outlaws). In the Middle Ages, the minstrels of Germany and the jongleurs of France were the first professionals. Accounts of their activities read like a review from *Variety*. These musicians were actually vaudevillians, and their acts might include not only singing and dancing but also juggling, card tricks, even knife throwing and trained animals. Show business had begun—in the Middle Ages.

A handful of musicians involved in secular music managed to earn at least part of their livelihood during the Middle Ages and Renaissance. But in the religious sector, almost no musicians enjoyed real professional status. The choirboys and men of the Western church performed in the cathedral choirs as just another part of their Christian service. Professional composers in the religious field seem to have first appeared in Paris around 1100 A.D. at Notre Dame cathedral. But musicologists cannot provide a satisfactory account of how the profession of composing music took shape in the following centuries. To this day, church musicians in most communities are either unpaid or paid below professional rates.

Conditions for the working musician were somewhat better in Germany in the 15th and 16th centuries. The tradition of guilds included the music trade. Musicians' guilds influenced not only working conditions but also creative and artistic standards. These early guilds were active in organizing composition and singing contests and formulated elaborate rules for them (an accurate account of these proceedings may be found in Richard Wagner's opera, *Die Meistersinger Von Nürnberg*).

In the following period in Europe, increasing numbers of artists were employed by the nobility as house musicians. Composers and performers were put on the royal payroll to make music in the salons, ballrooms, and chapels for their wealthy patrons. But nobility looked on these artists as servants, and they were expected to use the rear entrances to royal buildings. In addition, musicians' royal patrons would frequently pay them later than promised or not at all. Despite some advances in status, modern-day musicians sometimes complain that they still do not receive appropriate respect for their talents and professional stature.

In our own time and place, the champion for elevating the status of the music profession has been the American Federation of Musicians (AFM) of the United States and Canada. AFM **locals** receive requests regularly from sponsors of civic events, political rallies, and community benefits. These requests are usually sung in the same key: "Please, would you just send over some musicians for our event? They'll really enjoy it and, of course, we'll have some nice refreshments for them." Most musicians have been willing to play benefits, but they have also been exploited by those who would have them "share their art" just for the inherent pleasure of it (an echo heard all too often today). AFM locals have developed an effective response for unreasonable requests of this kind: They offer to supply union musicians without fee, provided the other trades and professions—stagehands, waiters, teamsters, bartenders—also work without pay. It is a fair offer; there are few takers.

Gradually, musicians acquired recognition as professionals with the development of a new phenomenon, the paying audience. This first occurred in the musical theater and opera, particularly in Italy and England. When the public began to pay its way into a room to hear music, the *music business* had begun. By the 1800s, the public had accepted the idea that you had to buy a ticket to hear a professional. Increasing numbers of paid concerts developed, not only in European cities such as Vienna, London, and Paris but also in New York, Philadelphia, and Boston.

We lack reliable accounts of who organized and promoted the earliest paid employment for professional musicians. Perhaps the earliest notable artist's manager or agent was Mozart's father, Leopold Mozart, who discovered his son's talent before the youngster had barely graduated from diapers. When Wolfgang was 6 years old, father Leopold started presenting his son to all of Europe. But Mozart's father did not teach his son much about career management. Mozart junior earned considerable sums in his short lifetime but seems to have died a pauper. Mismanagement of money and careers is not unique to recent decades.

A more recent ancestor of today's music entrepreneur was the circus genius, P. T. Barnum. In 1850, when Jenny Lind, "The Swedish Nightingale," came to America, Barnum presented her around the country as if she were a star acrobat. Barnum's bookings earned the artist $150,000 in her American tour, big money indeed in those days.

Barnum understood that the public likes a good show, and the music business grew, even in the classical field, in a razzle-dazzle, show-biz atmosphere. At the same time Barnum was touring opera star Jenny Lind, other entrepreneurs were developing enthusiastic audiences for that unique American contribution to theater—the minstrel show. This is not the place to treat the racist aspects of that phenomenon; our interest in minstrelsy here must be limited to how it fostered the development of the popular music business. As early as the Middle Ages, musicians from Africa were in Europe entertaining whites. But it was not until the mid-19th century, with the development of the minstrel show, that blacks began to find a place in the white musical world as full professionals. Although most of the performers were white, increasing numbers of blacks began to take part. This development turned out to be of historical significance, for it would be impossible even to conceive of music in the 20th century without the pervasive influence of black musicians.

The increasing popularity of minstrelsy in the 1850 to 1900 period enlarged public awareness and appreciation of popular music and the entertainment business. Near the end of the Reconstruction period, the size and affluence of the middle class grew. By the 1890s, the piano was a standard adornment in the parlors of upper-middle-class families. On thousands of piano racks across the land, one would probably find, in addition to some Stephen Foster songs and a hymnal, a copy of

After the Ball. The year was 1892, and this song was the first million-seller (in a 12-month period). It eventually sold 10 million copies of sheet music.

By this time, a number of large publishing houses had developed, such as E. B. Marks, Witmark Bros., T. B. Harms, Leo B. Feist, Mills Music, and Shapiro, Bernstein & Co. Some of these firms remain active and prosperous today. These popular music publishers took pride in being able to spot potential hits. When they couldn't find them, the publishers wrote the songs themselves or put composers on weekly salaries to work **in-house.**

These late-19th-century publishers developed the merchandising methods that prevailed until radio came on strong in the 1920s. Songs were introduced in a number of ways. In the final days of minstrelsy (which died around 1900), song pluggers would attempt to persuade performers to use material coming off the presses. When vaudeville and burlesque began to displace minstrel shows, pluggers contacted headliners and even lesser acts to try to get them to use the songs their firms were pushing at the time. A publisher who could come up with a piece of material that some vaudeville headliner like Al Jolson or Eddie Cantor would sing was almost ensured a hit, for these were the superstars of their day.

At this point in the music-business story, technology stepped in to play a starring role, not unlike the one it occupies today. And also not unlike today, many in the industry first feared that it might be more villain than hero. That hot new innovation? Radio.

Mass Media: Yesterday, Today, and Tomorrow

The world has always been full of music lovers, but it was not until the development of mass communication technology that so many "new" audiences were discovered. Until the 1920s, most professional music making was addressed to a small, elite audience that was accustomed to buying tickets to attend the opera, the symphony, perhaps a Broadway musical. When radio (and later, records and television) came along, that elite audience not only continued, it grew. But now it was joined and immeasurably augmented by whole new audiences for folk music, country and western songs, blues, and jazz. Mass media forever changed the size and composition of the music audience, and merchants were quick to respond to the new millions of paying customers.

Not that this tremendous upside was clear from the start. Industry leaders misjudged radio broadcasting: When it started in the 1920s, the publishers fought it, believing that "giving music away" through this medium would hurt sheet music sales. Overexposure via radio broadcasting, they argued, was killing songs in six weeks; potential customers could not get down to the store to make a purchase before the song's popularity had waned. It should be pointed out that publishers' income from broadcast performances at that time was zero.

Another significant technological development in the entertainment field occurred in 1927 when the "talkies" began. Movie producers discovered, with the very first sound film (a musical titled *The Jazz Singer,* starring Al Jolson), that audiences would buy a lot of theater tickets to hear songs sung on "the silver screen." The major studios began scrambling for **synchronization rights** to enable them to add music to films and turn out musical films in rapid succession.

During the Great Depression of the 1930s, million-selling records disappeared, and sales of sheet music collapsed. Attendance at vaudeville theaters dropped, too, with the growing popularity of the movie musical. Concurrent with these depressions in the music market, radio broadcasting grew rapidly. Music publishers now shifted their attention from plugging vaudeville performers to the new stars of radio. The network broadcasts at that time emanated mostly from New York, Chicago, and Los Angeles. Publishers closed their regional offices across the land and focused their plugging efforts on these new broadcasting centers. It worked. The publishers quickly discovered that they should point their promotional efforts toward the big bands and their singers who had weekly, sometimes nightly, radio broadcasts (which, at that time, were referred to as "remotes"). Song-plugging had grown from a local to a national enterprise with the development of network radio.

Publishers were not the only ones to benefit from the coming of network broadcasting. Big bands became name bands because of network radio. Then the name bands became the record stars. Management noticed that the best-selling big band records featured the band's singer. Alert talent handlers pulled the singers off the bandstand (Frank Sinatra, Doris Day, Ella Fitzgerald, etc.) and started them working alone—for much more money. This was the beginning of the present era of the dominance of the popular singer; they became the new stars and superstars, with the help of recordings and films.

During World War II, the whole world seemed to discover the appeal of America's popular music. Much of this worldwide popularity was fostered by the Armed Forces Radio network. With over 90 stations broadcasting American-made records around the world, millions of listeners, not just the G.I.s for whom the broadcasts were intended, heard the great entertainment available from this kind of music. By the late 1940s, the American style had become a world style.

When the G.I.s returned home, they bought large quantities of records. Music instrument factories, which had been shut down earlier to produce weapons, were now spewing out guitars, organs, pianos, and wind and percussion instruments in quantity. The music industry was reaching a mass market.

Record companies were moving millions of singles in the 1940s. When Columbia came out with the long-playing record, the music business again experienced a development of overwhelming significance. Now, instead of two songs per record, songwriters and publishers could place 12 songs on each release. Income could thus be increased by 600%. On the new LP, record buyers could hear an entire Broadway show; opera buffs could carry home an entire opera in a box; complete symphonies could easily fit on one LP. The dollar volume of classical records grew to 10% of the market.

Concurrent with the growing popularity of LPs was the increasing availability of low-cost tape recorders. Add to this the boom in high-fidelity sound. For a relatively low cost, consumers could hear recorded or broadcast music with a quality of sound that was better, audiophiles believed, than that offered at their local concert halls.

The music business began to attract not only new capital but also a new breed of merchants, some of whom were quite savvy. New distribution and merchandising methods developed. The most significant marketing development at the time was the discovery that people would buy records wherever they shopped. Enter the **rack jobber**. This new kind of music merchant set up record racks in supermarkets, variety stores, department stores—anywhere shoppers passed by.

Large corporations began to notice that people in the music publishing and record business were making lots of money. They decided to buy in. By the 1970s, even conservative bankers got the message: Music enterprise was now an acceptable risk. They began making loans to music publishers, record producers, and artists' managers—types of people they used to classify with street vendors. The main attraction to these new investors was record production. In what other kind of business enterprise could an individual or a bank invest, say, $20,000 in a master tape, then receive from it royalties one hundred times that amount, if the record hit? To the inexperienced investor, the music business began to look like a money tree. By the 1970s, the buying and selling of music companies resulted in the majority of industry revenue becoming controlled by a handful of giant corporations (to become the longtime "Big 6," since recombined into the Big 4).

This belief in a "money tree" seemed almost justified when another game-changing innovation was introduced in 1982: the compact disc. Labels shook their analog catalogs, and out poured dollars as consumers replaced their record collections with the digital discs and then scooped up new CD-only releases. Although audiophiles initially balked, the CD soon overtook both the LP and the previously unveiled "new" format, the music cassette; that complete symphony now fitted on *one side* of one disc. Music television was simultaneously taking root—having become a cultural force with the debut of MTV in 1981—and the two together helped usher in a period of creative and business growth.

Cue new technology once more, and underscore the arrival of the MP3 format onto the scene in the 1990s with a somewhat unsettling composition. When digital music was further compressed into files that could be distributed over the Internet freely (in every sense of the word), a new form of mass media became, in part, a medium controlled by the masses. The most fervent of music fans were now tastemakers, although not yet hit-makers, as they sought out, chatted up, and "distributed" songs online. Musicians were fast to tap into this newfound promotional base, and record labels followed.

The Internet, vast and far-reaching as it is, allowed a direct, intimate, and interactive connection with fans in ways never before possible outside of a small concert venue. It was mass media reimagined on a micro level. If the 20th century was about discovering new audiences, the 21st may prove to be about finding new, better, and—here is the still-open billion-dollar question—*profitable* ways to connect with them wherever they are and through whatever medium they desire—venues, music stores, TV, radio, film, the Web, social-networking sites, cellular phones, videogames, and whichever *next* new thing is just over the horizon.

Tools of the Trade: Everybody's Gotta Learn Sometime

Although being—and staying—informed has always been important in the music industry (or any industry, for that matter), in times of rapid change it is vital. A new trend, technology, or development that seemingly has little to do with a particular segment of the business may well suggest a new means of promotion, a potentially profitable new partnership, or an additional income stream to pursue. (Savvy composers and musicians, for example, recognized early on the growing—and lucrative—role that music might play in videogames.) New types of licensing deals and previously unheard-of music distribution methods bring with them new twists and turns on **copyright** and royalties issues—issues that could mean money in (or out of) the pockets of numerous music-business players. And, of course, job seekers looking for an "in" will need to know what new doors might be open to them and how best to educate and market themselves.

It is one of the great mysteries of the contemporary music scene, then, that many of those involved in it—composers, performers, businesspeople, educators—do not understand how it really works. Many artists and music merchants lack even basic information. Worse yet, much of what they believe they "know" is either out of date or incorrect. The result of this pervasive ignorance about the business and the profession has been tragic. Only about 15% of the AFM members work steadily in music. Top graduates of our conservatories fail to get their careers even started. Aspiring business-side candidates lack the big-picture smarts and specialized savvy to succeed in a competitive label environment. Musicians navigating the DIY waters fall victim to sharks.

So what does the artist or the business executive do to get the information needed to function effectively in this field? Start by reading the "trades," the music business magazines and papers. Rarely does a music business office not have these publications in evidence. Who reads the trades? Everybody, from interns and assistants to executives and presidents. They are an indispensable source of current information. Another source is the various professional meetings. These national (and international) affairs are sponsored by industry associations and trade magazines and sometimes by artists' unions. Most have Web sites (you'll find a listing of the major associations and their sites in Appendix C), offering industry overviews, news, and information, along with current research and publications to download or request (some free of charge, others for a fee). Specialized information can also be found in books on subjects such as copyright and pop songwriting; many of the industry associations' sites offer sector-specific suggestions.

The Web offers a wealth of information, although you'll need to wade through a lot of junk to find the truly helpful gems (something to which anyone who has gone trolling for music online can attest). The best bets are a handful of well-respected blogs, some of which focus on the creative and others on the business side of music. Because Web sites come and go, asking around for recommendations—from fellow musicians, instructors, industry-connected friends of friends—can point to the cream of the current crop.

The most reliable sources of information for the serious student can be found in a select group of colleges and universities. Following the leadership of the University of Miami in the mid-1960s, increasing numbers of accredited institutions are offering courses and degrees in the music business field. And then there is the option of *going to* the source. Qualified professionals in the business can be found throughout North America, although many are concentrated in one of the three major recording centers—New York, Nashville, or Los Angeles—where the big music companies have their U.S. headquarters. Most of the music business, even today, is based on the star system—specifically, the recording star system—and these cities remain the high-powered nexus.

Only a limited number of performers can attain star status, of course, so it is fortunate that the music business system offers many opportunities for individuals needed to help make the system function. No performer today can ascend to stardom or hang there in orbit without an array of qualified supporting satellites. As this book unfolds, we shall examine how stars and their satellites make the music business work.

But it is not only these breakthrough stars and *their* satellites who can earn a living in music, as shall also be detailed in these pages. While there are no guarantees—that, too, is one of the music-industry fundamentals—the 21st century changes already in motion mean that there are today more possible points of entry than ever before, at all levels, for people with a passion for music and the businesses that support and surround it—both major-label superstars and DIY working musicians, in-house engineers and home-studio entrepreneurs, big-label execs and savvy online startups. Provided, of course, that they learn their trade. *That* is something that will never change.

Notes

1. Words in **boldface** type indicate inclusion in the glossary section.

2. This trend is continuing. About 95% of the massive amount of music downloaded worldwide in 2008, more than 40 billion files, was "illegal" and not paid for, according to IFPI.

3. Traditional "record stores"—the name itself suggests a nostalgic past—now claim less than a third of U.S. music sales.

Chapter Takeaways

- Despite the upheavals of transformational change, global recorded music sales remain impressive, topping $30 billion.

- Tensions have always persisted between artists who want to connect with audiences and business enablers who want to connect to an audience's wallets.

- The rise of the middle class in the late 19th century made possible the first blockbuster music publishing hit, Stephen Foster's *After the Ball.*

- Technology, in its many forms, has been a consistent driver of the changing business—from the invention of radio, to movies, to TV, to vinyl LPs, to CDs, to the Web.

Key Terms

- 360 deals (p. 5)
- *infami* (p. 6)
- LP (p. 6)
- MP3 (p. 10)
- rack jobber (p. 9)
- synchronization rights (p. 8)

CHAPTER 2

The Music Business System

The music industry can be described as having two essential elements: the musician and the audience. Drawing them together is the business of music. Despite the distracting spotlight of changing technology, the music industry continues to operate much like other large, multifaceted commercial activities. A main difference between the music business and most other industries is, of course, its artistically driven "product" and the constant tug of hair-trigger cultural shifts. In examining the business aspects of music, it is the rapid change of product that makes this business almost unique.

> *"I would rather play 'Chiquita Banana' and have my swimming pool than play Bach and starve."*
>
> *—Xavier Cugat*

Getting Through the Maze

To analyze key industry interrelationships in detail, let's consider two different ways of viewing the industry as a whole. First, study the flowchart shown in Figure 2.1. It graphically illustrates the music business system and its principal subsystems. This flowchart can serve as a framework on which to hang additional subsystems.

A second way of grasping the big picture is to examine the sequence of events that often occurs as a new song finds its way to market. As you will observe, the following list sets forth much of the same information appearing on the flowchart in Figure 2.1.

Left: A student in the iPhone Music Programming Class, Music Engineering Technology Department, Frost School of Music, University of Miami.

Photo by John Zillioux courtesy University of Miami.

Figure 2.1   The Music Business System and Selected Principal Subsystems

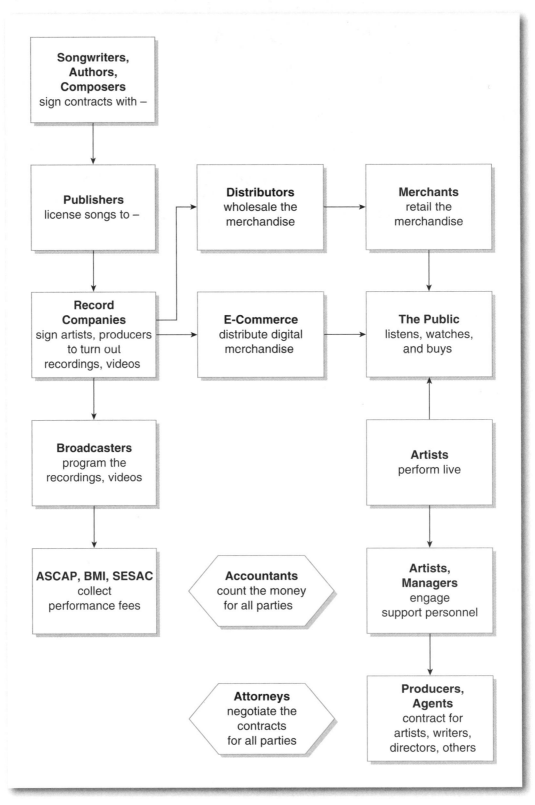

1. The composer—who sometimes is also the performing artist—writes a song and signs with a publisher.

2. The publisher persuades an artist (or that artist's producer) to record the song.

3. **Lawyers** (at several stages) negotiate contracts between parties and specify terms for varying forms of usage and exploitation, such as mechanical rights and synchronization licenses.

4. The record company produces a recording and, possibly, a video version of the song.

5. Promoters persuade programmers to broadcast the audio recording and the video.

6. The record company uploads the song for online sale and ships the merchandise to **distributors**, who sell it to retailers.

7. If the song becomes popular, a second wave of exploitation can occur—licensing of ringtones and merchandise connected to the song and/or artist.

8. A talent agency contacts promoters and books a concert tour.

9. Concert promoters enlist cosponsors and sell the tickets.

10. The road manager moves the people and the equipment.

11. The concert production manager dresses the stage, lights it, reinforces the sound.

12. The artists perform.

13. The performing rights organizations collect performance royalties.

14. The accountants count the money; the participants pay their bills.

15. The government collects the taxes.

Show Me the Money

Many people would say the making of music hasn't changed much in centuries—it's still all about a catchy tune performed by talented artists. But that's not the case. The music industry has mushroomed into an interconnected series of segmented multi-billion-dollar businesses in the United States (not even counting the intertwining of business abroad!). These businesses range from traditional recorded music to live concerts to sale of musical instruments and equipment to cell phone ring tones. Figure 2.2 shows just a sampling of the scores of segmented businesses. Many billions of dollars flow from business to business, as one sector's revenue (such as a composer's royalty receipts) is another sector's expense (a publisher's royalty expense). Thus the same "music dollar" may at one time or another end up in the pockets of multiple industry participants.

Figure 2.2   U.S. Music Industry Revenue: Select Segments (Estimate of Billions of Dollars Annually)

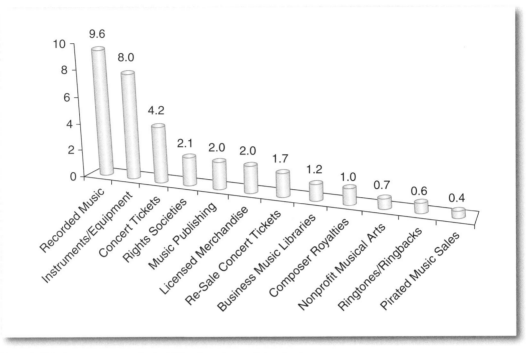

Recorded Music encompasses physical CDs, streaming, and downloads.
Rights Societies are ASCAP, BMI, and SESAC.
Nonprofit Musical Arts are independent music and dance entities.
Pirated Music Sales is money changing hands in sales to consumers mainly for physical CDs, excludes free peer transfers and estimated losses for legitimate sales.

Source: Various industry sources.

Note: Many categories double count revenue.

Music Business Studies in Higher Education

The rapid growth of the music industry after World War II resulted in a shortage of qualified people to handle its affairs. Most engaged in the music business learned on the job. But as the music business became larger and much more complex, it required a new kind of leadership: individuals possessing competence in diverse fields such as music, business administration, accounting, and law. The only places such a broad education can be acquired are colleges, universities, and certain specialized institutes.

Pressure for new curricula in the music business came from several sources. The students observed the burgeoning business of music and started asking their instructors how they might prepare themselves for jobs in fields such as recording, broadcasting, or music **publishing.** Most college faculty lacked experience in the "commercial" side of the profession. But a handful of their colleagues did have backgrounds in areas such as music merchandising, recording, and performance. Some were jazz educators who knew the "gigging" side of the music profession. This group of college teachers heard the students' concerns, perceived the need, and began to develop music business courses, then complete degree programs. Local music merchants, broadcasters, and sometimes, entertainment lawyers often assisted these on-campus instructors.

Thus, music business studies in higher education were born. After a slow start, hundreds of universities, institutes, and colleges now offer educational programs designed to prepare the new professionals for positions of leadership in the music and entertainment industry.[1] Course offerings include studies in music, certainly, but also in areas as diverse as business administration, accounting, marketing, business law, copyright, and recording technology. Graduates of these programs cannot know it all, of course. But they are far better prepared than anyone else to meet the wide-ranging demands of today's music industry.

The Musician-Entrepreneur: Prospering by Constantly Adapting

Gene Perla

While our analysis of the music business necessarily presents a close-up view of the many specializations—from songwriting, to producing concerts to monetizing downloads—the untold story of the industry is that sustained career success often is *not* due to mastery of one specialized garden of knowledge. Frequently, success over the years and decades comes from an adaptability to hop from specialty to specialty. That adaptability is fueled by a diverse base of knowledge, a curiosity for what is new, and a can-do attitude in navigating the many twists and turns in a fast-changing industry.

That's the case for Gene Perla, who has made a living in the many nooks and crannies of the music industry available to a jazz bassist throughout his career—Broadway show sound designer, music publishing company founder, recording studio entrepreneur, songwriter, studio musician, and music teacher.

"Sure, I like to sit back and come up with the 'grand concepts,'" he says of what drove him to work in so many music segments. "But I like to deal with the nuts and bolts as well. I like to do the futzing and fudging about with things so I really understand them."

After several years of musical instrument higher education, Perla broke onto the New York jazz scene as a bass player in the 1960s. Hoping to distribute the music of friends who could not get a record deal, he decided he needed to know how albums are made, so he enrolled in a technical school in Manhattan to study recording engineering. One night after class while relaxing in a night club where he sometimes performed, a stranger who recognized him from club performances offered him a job at Todd Rundgren's famous Secret Sound studio. It was at Secret Sound, not formal classes, that Perla really learned recording through a series of from-the-ground-up jobs.

Years later, another chance meeting with a stranger led to a teaching job at another New York multimedia school, where Perla took advantage of a faculty perk that allowed teachers to take other classes free of charge. He learned video production and computer graphics, among many skills.

(Continued)

(Continued)

Still a performing musician making contacts in gigs around town, Perla eventually played bass and had two of his songs recorded for the Blue Note jazz album, *Genesis,* by Elvin Jones (famous as the drummer in the band of the late John Coltrane). Perla had already registered those songs with the U.S. Copyright Office—which was and remains a simple process—but then went the extra step of creating his own publishing company to license the songs. Today, his Perla Music is a money-maker and has a catalog with 100 compositions, for which he sells sheet music at $3 a PDF download from his Web site. ASCAP administers other aspects of Perla Music.

Along the way, with skills learned in jobs, schools, and from personal contacts as a working musician, Perla established the Red Gate recording facility just outside of New York. His partner in this venture was Jan Hammer, keyboardist for the Mahavishnu Orchestra and composer of the *Miami Vice* theme song. Perla also established a small music label, PM Records. After another chance meeting, he was called to make an emergency rescue of a Broadway production just hours before show time. His tech knowledge enabled him to untangle a musical instrument digital interface (MIDI) setup whose otherwise bright software engineer messed up with improper cabling.

With that experience, he and partner Bernard Fox started their own sound design business for other stage productions such as *Beauty and the Beast, The Lion King,* and *City of Angels.* Sound designers provide equipment, billing shows weekly for service. Some $125,000 of microphones were purchased to service a show which promptly closed after just seven performances, but Perla wasn't fazed. "It worked out all right because we were doing other shows," he says.

He left Broadway for a lucrative business rerecording dialog in a studio for prime time network TV series, fixing street scenes with audio problems in what is known as automatic dialog replacement (ADR).

Today, Perla operates a computer services consultancy from his home in Easton, PA, from where he commutes to New York to teach and perform. He teaches music business and bass at Lehigh University and still plays gigs locally, regionally, and sometimes internationally (Europe, Mexico, and elsewhere).

Perla is nonchalant about his dizzyingly diverse career, saying only, "I am persistent," while also crediting education and some chance meetings.

Comparing the music landscape today versus when he broke in, Perla says that universities are churning out so many skilled jazz bassists that the competition for live gigs—where he got his start and made a living—is intense and the pay is therefore miserable. His advice to freshly graduated jazz musicians is not to be afraid to take jobs on the technological edge of music—such as telecom and multimedia companies—which are the Wild West frontier for music today. The graduates "may not be performing, but they will still be connected to the music," he says.

Help Wanted!

Over the years, transformational technology has reshaped the way people in the music business organize themselves to make a living. A century ago, a music publisher manufactured and shipped vast quantities of paper to retail stores throughout the land. Today, a publisher might be the part-time vocation of a songwriter, whose assets reside entirely on a hard drive. A half-century ago, a record company exploited just about the only path to putting recorded music, for a fee, in the hands of consumers. Today, some idiosyncratic artists—either with no recording contract in the offing or disenchanted with their last contract—might record in a home studio, manufacture on a **CD** burner, and sell the resulting handiwork via download or mail order through their own Web site. A few decades ago the nuanced performance of a large ensemble required having dozens of musicians on the payroll. Today, one or only a handful of musicians and **MIDI** controllers might provide a similar performance. The economists call this trend increased productivity. The old guard fears it, for jobs are jeopardized and investors traumatized. But with change also comes opportunity.

Even if aided by semiconductors and the Internet, a human being must still make the music, a human being must market and promote it, and human talent is the key ingredient all along the value chain between the original creative idea and the ears and eyes of a fan.

The reason some aspirants fail to achieve their goal is not so much a shortage of opportunity as a lack of sufficient talent and an understanding of how the music business system works. But many (although not all) ambitious newcomers do make it. Why: Luck? Timing? Education? Networking skills? These factors have helped launch many successful careers in both the creative and business ends of

Music business students' band, The Motion Sick, presents an annual concert at SXSW in Austin, Texas, to showcase acts on their label, Heavy Rotation Records.

Photo courtesy of Berklee College of Music.

the field. Four other factors contribute to the success of those who "win" in the music business:

1. They are strongly motivated; they really want to win.

2. They are talented—and they surround themselves with talented associates.

3. They persevere; they hang in there until they succeed.

4. They get the important information.

The first three items depend totally on you. This book deals only with Item 4. The music business offers excellent career opportunities for the really talented individual, provided that individual gets the important information—and acts on it. The essential core of that information is offered here.

Note

1. See *Index of Majors and Graduate Degrees* or *The College Blue Book*, both available at your local library or bookstore.

Chapter Takeaways

- The insatiable need for new product distinguishes the music business from most other industries.

- The music industry can be viewed as a series of sectors, distinct types of businesses that feed off each other, such as record labels and concert promoters.

- The same "music dollar" often passes from one industry participant to another.

- Over the course of a career people in the business often move back and forth from one work category (composer) to another (publisher).

Songwriting, Publishing, Copyright, and Licensing

PART 2

CHAPTER 3

Professional Songwriting

Everything begins with the songwriter. Before anyone else in the music business can make a sound—or a dollar—the songwriter must create a unique melody and lyrics. No songwriters, no music industry—it's that simple. Songs are the fuel that powers the global music business machine, and frequent fill-ups are essential. The great standards of the past—songs that have stood the test of time—are always there to be mined, but a steady stream of new works is also crucial. Over the decades, the relentless rise of new forms of media—from radio to films to video games to the Internet to satellite radio to cell phone ringtones—has expanded both the audience for music and the commercial demand for new "product" to supply new business niches. Great songs, and the writers who create them, will always be the foundation of the music industry.

> *"I've outdone anyone you can name— Mozart, Beethoven, Bach, Strauss. Irving Berlin, he wrote 1,001 tunes. I wrote 5,500."*
>
> *—James Brown*

That, of course, is the good news. The bad news is that only a fraction of aspiring songwriters will ever find commercial acceptance for their material, and fewer still will be able to build sustainable songwriting careers. This is partly a matter of ability (some talent, after all, is required) and partly of desire—an unwillingness to work at songwriting as a serious business enterprise. But it is also a matter of math: Music publishers are inundated with submissions, their mailrooms littered with thousands of unsolicited songs each week. Eager young songwriters descend on the recording

Left: Radio City Music Hall, New York.

Photo © Jeff Hunter.

centers like locusts. Probably 10% of the people flowing through the Greyhound stations in Nashville and Hollywood are carrying a suitcase full of **demos,** while countless iPods and hard drives in New York and Miami are stuffed with original songs, raps, or beats, all competing for the limited attention of executives who are in a position to turn dreams into reality. Add in the networking angle—preferential treatment for the lead singer's cousin, the band manager's neighbor, or the label VP's friend of a friend, all with songs "perfect for Big Label Act's new album"—and the difficulty getting a hearing increases exponentially.

That doesn't mean that there isn't a hearty appetite among labels and publishers for new songs from newcomers, but it does mean that finding a way to stand out amid the **clutter** to connect—to actually catch the eye and the ear of the person who can move one's work from a song on paper to a record on the **charts**—is a game of long odds. The payoff can be enormous, however, for everyone concerned. To achieve it, a person must know the craft and the business, both the art and the commerce, of songwriting.

Predictors of Success

Is it possible to define a "good" song? Yes—if you know what to look for. Can anyone predict professional acceptance? Sometimes—if you know how. Does anyone know which songs will become lasting hits? Not on this earth. In a perfect world, a good song and a hit song would be one and the same. Good songs would become hits, and hits would be good songs. That's not always the case (just ask any songwriter), so it is perhaps easier to look at the two concepts separately.

A hit song is one that gets significant radio **airplay** and sales. Hits are easily quantifiable through sales charts and airplay monitors. A good song is harder to define, but at a minimum it must be well crafted musically and, if it's not an instrumental, lyrically as well.

How far can we go in predicting how any song will fare in the marketplace? Until The Beatles came along and turned the world on its ear, musicians and merchants had a working understanding of what a "popular song" was. They knew what made a C&W (**country** and western) song or an R&B (rhythm and blues) song. A certain set of songwriting criteria—this type of lyric, that type of beat—could be counted on to resonate with a certain segment of the music-buying audience when matched up with the right artist. Today, these tidy classifications don't serve nearly as well, because many songs incorporate various styles and straddle multiple **genres.** Tastes are not easily predictable and trends can be born fast (and die faster). One thing, at least, has stayed constant through the centuries: From 11th-century chansons to this week's charts, the all-time favorite is the love song. So *that's* a good bet for success, right? But even within the love song genre, it's difficult to classify songs or to predict what might be successful. Hits come from everywhere. This unpredictability both frustrates and encourages writers. Sometimes you know you've nailed it, and sometimes you just get lucky.

There *are* some patterns to be found, however—some lessons to be learned from the past that can help predict what might work in the future. Although it is difficult to identify specific ingredients that might bring a song artistic or commercial success, we *can* critically examine great songs and see what they have in common. What makes a Franz Schubert, a Richard Rodgers, a Duke Ellington, or a John Lennon stand out above the rest? Is there a common denominator to be discovered in the works of Joni Mitchell, Randy Newman, Billy Joel, Diane Warren, and the creative team of Holland-Dozier-Holland? Can we identify the elements in their songs that make us love them?

Consider these general criteria and you'll begin to see that all good songs tend to exhibit the following characteristics:

1. The song is memorable; it sticks in the mind. This is often accomplished by use of a **hook**—a catchy phrase or refrain that repeats several times during the song.

2. The song has immediate appeal.

3. The lyrics contain an overall theme and employ vivid phrases or imagery. For example, not "Your beauty makes me love you," but perhaps, "Your touch makes me tremble."

4. The song is well crafted and exhibits an arc: It has a discernable beginning, middle, and end.

Even if a song has these basic characteristics of a *good* song, it still has only the potential to become a *hit* song. Achieving that breakthrough will involve a number of other elements beyond the songwriter's control. These include the following:

1. The song gets an appealing initial performance, hopefully by a well-known performer, that is captured in a recording session.

2. The record company gets behind the project and promotes strong airplay for the recording.

3. The song and the recording suit the taste of the current market.

4. The recording is distributed effectively throughout the country.

The Craft

OK, so now you have a general idea of what a good song is. How do you go about writing one? Not all songwriters are endowed with creative gifts, and there is little evidence that *creativity* can be taught. But the *craft* of songwriting can be learned through formal study and/or private instruction. All colleges accredited by the National Association of Schools of Music (NASM) offer at least 2 academic years of theory study—harmony, ear training, music reading, orchestration, and counterpoint. Some colleges offer composition classes that teach popular songwriting as well as classical fare. These are good options to explore. What about the various "how-to" books addressed to songwriters? Many contain useful information. Some are lightweight, get-rich-quick publications. And what about private instruction? Excellent, if you can find good teachers and can afford it.

Perhaps nothing could be more useful to a songwriter, amateur or pro, than to select 100 of the leading standards and then study them—phrase by phrase, line by line, chord by chord. To guide you in this kind of analysis, you might study Alec Wilder's excellent book *American Popular Song: The Great Innovators, 1900–1950*. Wilder, himself a first-rate songwriter, theorist, and contemporary music historian, studied not just 100 songs, but several thousand. Borrow Wilder's technique: If you can examine the internal workings of 100 great melodies, 100 great lyrics, you will have at least begun a serious study of the songwriting craft. If you lean more in the pop or rock and roll direction, do a similar analysis of the masterpieces of Lennon and McCartney, Bob Dylan and Paul Simon. For country, choose Willie Nelson or Merle Haggard; for soul or R&B, Smokey Robinson or Holland-Dozier-Holland. Talk to songwriters and read interviews with writing legends in books, magazines, and online songwriter forums, and you will likely get the same message from them: Serious songwriters never stop studying their craft.

Songwriters, particularly those just starting out, will also do well to open themselves up to all the advice and feedback they can get on their early writing efforts, which might not exactly be world-class right off the bat (they may, for instance, include lyrical clichés such as "right off the bat."). Here again, listen and learn. Don't become discouraged and don't take any one opinion as gospel—remember that The Beatles were turned down by every label in America before finally getting a deal—but keep an eye out for patterns: Are there particular points of criticism that keep coming up? Are your lyrics confusing to people, your hooks not snagging attention? Address those shortcomings via rewrites and new songs.

Collaboration

Some of the most creative artists in the history of popular music have managed to write both brilliant words and hummable music. If you can do this as well as Irving Berlin, Cole Porter, Bob Dylan, and Paul Simon, the world awaits. But if your strong point is melody, find yourself a lyricist. If you are good at lyrics and lack musical talent, don't try to fake it as a composer. If you write only words or only music, join the club that includes Rodgers and Hammerstein, George and Ira Gershwin, Lennon and McCartney, and so many others. In most cases two complementary talents can be greater than the sum of their parts.

There are no formulas for locating a collaborator. Try hanging out with other writers and performers. Get the word out around town that you are looking. Contact the regional offices of performing rights organizations (ASCAP, BMI, or SESAC), or call their headquarters for suggestions on regional workshops and other sources. Check local clubs for songwriting nights. Some good writing teams got started through placement of classified ads in trade papers or online, or on social networking sites. Whatever you do, don't pay someone to be your collaborator. Don't respond to ads soliciting song poems. Don't give money to any so-called publisher to "publish" your songs or add music or add words. *Legitimate publishers never charge writers a dime.* They pay *you.*

When coauthors are ready to approach publishers, they should have worked out a clear understanding, preferably in writing, of the terms of their relationship. The agreement should provide answers to these questions: Is all income generated by the collaboration to be shared equally? May one writer make changes in the material unilaterally? Under what conditions may one writer withdraw the words or music from the collaborative work if the work remains unpublished or otherwise unsuccessful? Under what circumstances will the collaborative relationship terminate? May the writers concurrently write alone or with a different collaborator? If a potential collaborator refuses to discuss these issues or does not show an interest in compromising, consider this an early warning sign of impending partnership problems.

A special kind of working relationship exists between a composer who doesn't read or write music and a chosen arranger. Some naturally gifted songwriters get by with their intuitive talent for inventing appealing, commercially viable melodies. They usually sing their tunes into a recorder, then hire an arranger to clean up the rhythm, fix the phrasing, add the harmony, and transcribe the results onto **lead-sheets.** (Be very clear on the copyright issues in these cases; such a relationship may be viewed as a cowriting arrangement, and some are indeed set up this way.) Such a composer should, however, endeavor to gain command of the songwriting craft, thus legitimizing the claim to be a professional composer. Computer "notation" software also is available that can help writers who haven't learned that skill.

Copyright Registration

Whether it is a solo or joint effort, a finished song raises a question for its creator(s): Should it be registered with the U.S. Copyright Office? Some writers file an application only when a song is ready to be used on an album or in another public forum, when such registration becomes necessary for the collection of royalties. Many other writers exercise caution and register all their songs upon completion. The only downside to this is the fee. Details of the latest fees and forms are on the Copyright Office's Web site (www.copyright.gov).

The Business of Writing

An ability to write good songs is only part of what it takes to make it as a professional songwriter. Anyone who aspires to a songwriting career must treat the job as a *business,* which of course it is. The details of the business will vary depending on the type of writer one is (for instance, a singer/songwriter vs. a "pure" songwriter) and the type of publishing arrangement one has (e.g., staff writer vs. single-song contractor vs. publishing company owner). The one constant is that a writer can expect to spend as much time and energy promoting his or her product as was devoted to creating it. Writing and promoting, promoting and writing: This is the professional songwriter's life. A writer will be successful only if those songs he or she creates are **exploited**—published, licensed, recorded, aired, and performed. A commitment to ensuring that this happens—and that the resulting royalty revenue streams keep flowing in—is what separates a songwriting hobby from a songwriting career.

From Tin Pan Alley to the Brill Building . . .

In the earlier days of the record industry—when, indeed, music was actually released on black-vinyl records—songwriting was very much a job, in the more traditional 9-to-5 sense. In fact, songwriters were in great demand as workers well before records existed, hired by publishing companies to create popular songs for sale as sheet music. These were the heady days of Tin Pan Alley, a nickname given to the New York City street where many music publishers worked from the late 1800s into the early 1950s and in whose offices many of the greatest standards were created by composers and lyricists.

By the 1950s, the music business was changing, and the concurrent rise of radio's popularity and expanding record sales put the focus on writing hit songs to feed to recording artists, largely targeted at the fast-growing teenage market. The roles remained highly compartmentalized, however: Songwriters wrote; artists performed. The legendary Brill Building, on Broadway in Manhattan, became the epicenter of this vital new songwriting scene—a virtual "hit factory" where prolific and talented songwriters all but punched a clock. Their output—from teams such as Goffin & King, Barry & Greenwich, and Mann & Weil—was staggering, and their songs remain classics of that era.

The mid-1960s saw another change in the songwriter's role, as Bob Dylan and The Beatles led a new generation of artists—from folk troubadours to soul singers to rock bands—who increasingly wrote their own material. The solid wall between the songwriter and the performer was breached. As the 1960s ended, Carole King, one of the most brilliant of the Brill Building composers, led the way by embracing the new singer/songwriter concept, reveling in the freedom to write more personal material.

. . . To the Home Studio

Today, of course, the singer/songwriter is an industry mainstay and few songwriters toil away in offices, cranking out tunes on demand (the commercial jingle business excepted). The job description of a songwriter is now a highly flexible one, encompassing diverse working styles, business affiliations, and creative approaches. In addition to writing songs for the record industry, songwriters can be found plying their trade for the film industry, TV shows, video games, Web sites, and advertising agencies.

Where a writer actually writes is a matter of personal preference. The key is to find an environment that works for you—whether that is completely away from distractions in a quiet home studio, perhaps, or surrounded by fellow scribes in a convivial workshop setting.

The Brill Building, New York.
Photo by Robert P. Marich.

Pace, too, is an individual decision. Most successful songwriters write all the time. They write not dozens, but hundreds of songs. Many professionals like to work out a schedule, perhaps setting aside every morning for creative work. They isolate themselves for several hours, not permitting anything or anybody to distract them. Others are more productive working in spurts. They might stay away from their studio for days or weeks. Then they get inspired or have to meet a deadline and work around the clock.

When not writing, the creator is working at promoting what has been written. Some professionals divide their work week nearly equally between writing and selling. Professional songwriters not only help their publishers and recording companies push their material, they are on the street and in the studios, and around the watering holes where the pros gather. They spread the good word. If they don't, who will know what they have written lately? And how will the writer learn what people are looking for?

The Performer's Dual Role

One whose "business" comprises performing as well as songwriting will have a somewhat different job focus. Many writers begin as performers, particularly in the fields of rock, folk, and country music. In the rock field especially, almost every successful group includes instrumentalists and singers who also write for the act. Although this would seem to limit opportunities for writers, many aspiring writers have made initial inroads by cowriting with members of bands already under label contract.

Not all singer/songwriters draw the line between the two disciplines in exactly the same place. Some see their performing careers in nightclubs and on independent label releases primarily as a valuable showcase for their songs—and as an additional revenue source. Others are performers first and foremost, and write solely with their own label deals and recordings in mind. Still others move seamlessly between the two sides, actively writing hits for others even as they score with their own releases. Where you draw the line will affect how you spend your time and how you juggle your writing and performing workloads.

Income Sources

The type of writer one is—whether a sole songwriter, a cowriter, or an artist/songwriter—will naturally have an impact on the bottom line. Table 3.1 gives a concise summary of the various revenue streams that flow to writers, and Figure 3.1 shows how writers' and publishers' incomes are related.

Income From a Recording

One of the main sources of income for a writer is mechanical royalties, which is keyed to the sale and distribution of recorded music. Another source of income is performance royalties. These and other terms relating to a writer's licensing royalties are defined in the chapters that follow, but it's helpful here to keep in mind that a writer always gets 50% of the mechanical royalties ("the writer's share"); the other 50%, "the publisher's share," may sometimes be shared with the writer, depending on the writer's publishing arrangement and the contract in effect.

Table 3.1   Writer's Potential Income Sources

Type of Music Use	Who Pays the Writer
Broadcast performances (TV—commercial and noncommercial)	Writer's performing rights organization
Nonbroadcast performance (clubs, hotels, stadiums, business music, in-flight music, aerobic and dance studios, etc.)	Writer's performing rights organization
Mechanical royalties (tape and CD sales)	Recording company pays publisher, which shares 50–50 with writer
Sheet music sales	Publisher pays pennies per song or percentage on "paper" sales
Synchronization of music to film or tape (movies, videos)	Publisher shares 50% of fees received with writer
Special permission, licenses (merchandising deals)	Users pay publisher, who shares with writer
Jukeboxes	Performing rights organization pays publisher, who shares 50–50 with writer
Dramatic (or grand) rights	Publisher shares with writer (unless writer or agent retains dramatic rights)
Digital MP3 downloads, cell phone ringtones, streaming interactive subscription services, satellite radio, Internet radio stations, and other Webcasts	Varies. Licensees pay writer's performing rights organization, or licensees pay publisher directly, which shares with writer

Note: All these uses are for *nondramatic* music, except dramatic (or grand) rights.

Here is a preview of what a songwriter might earn from just mechanicals on a hit record. Assume the following: (a) The recorded song is on an album that goes "gold," sells 500,000 copies; (b) the writer in question is the composer of two songs on the album, each under 5 minutes in length; and (c) the statutory mechanical royalty rate (it changes from time to time) is 9.10 cents per song for songs 5 minutes or less or 1.75 cents per minute or fraction thereof over 5 minutes.

500,000 albums sold × 9.10 cents per song × two songs = $91,000.
50–50 split between publisher and writer = $45,500 each.

If this same writer wrote all 10 songs on an album that went gold (500,000 copies sold), the math dictates that $455,000 would be earned from that hit album. Don't start seeing big dollar signs, however. Writers, and singer/songwriters in particular, routinely negotiate a rate lower than the statutory figure with their labels, which also often contractually "cap" the total mechanicals that will be paid on any one album (more on this later). Such categories of releases as "budget lines" and compilations may also carry reduced rates. The bottom line, then, is more like this: To generate a steady living wage, the writer must write and write and then write some more—and must find ways to get the material published and recorded on as regular a basis as possible.

Figure 3.1 Songwriters' and Publishers' Income Sources

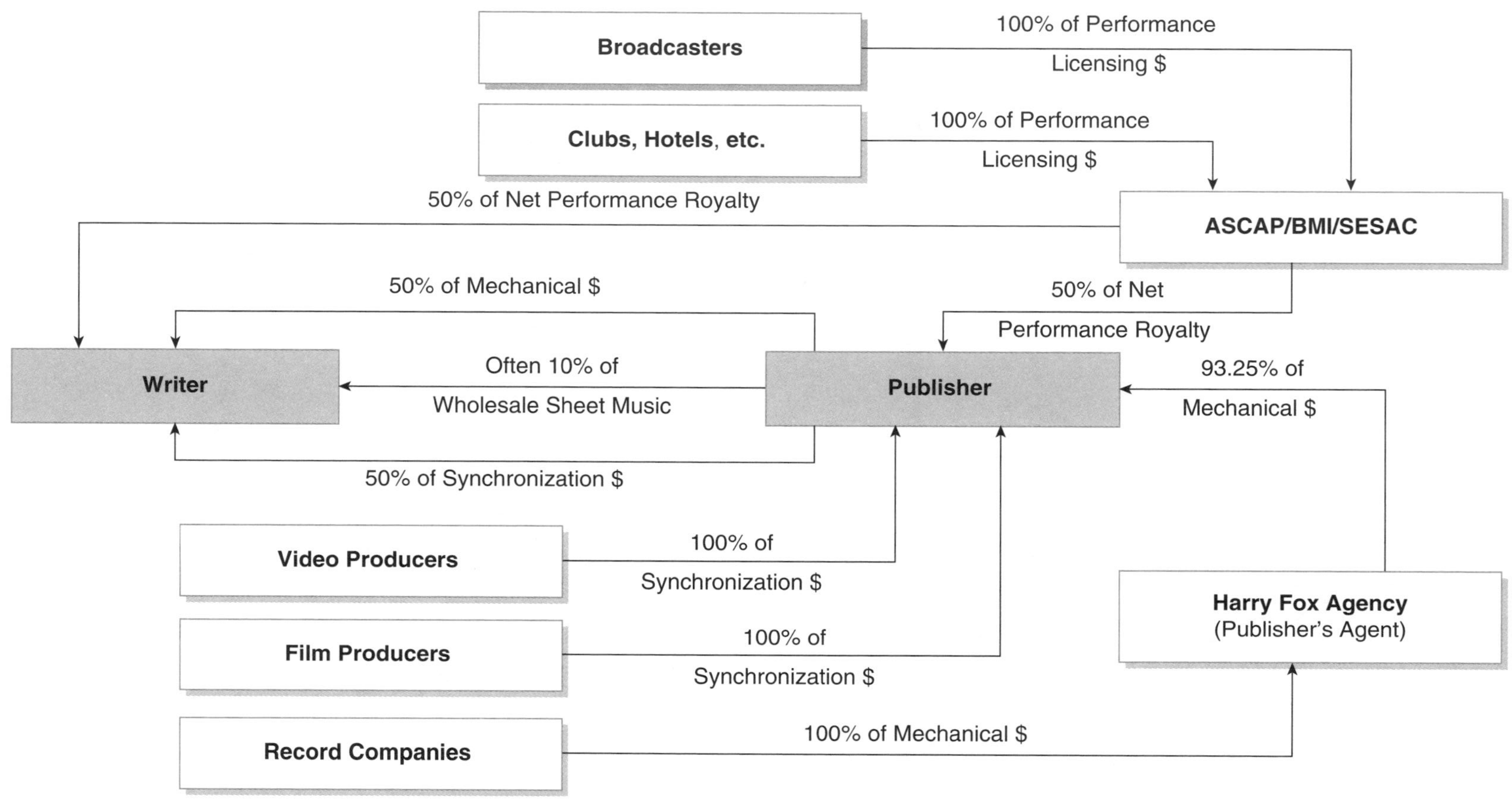

Performance Royalties and New Revenue Streams

The other main source of income for songwriters is performance royalties, which are generated by the broadcast or performance of a writer's works. This income can equal or surpass that of mechanicals; a hot single, for instance, may receive tremendous radio airplay even when the album it is drawn from rings up only lackluster sales. This royalty is collected by the writer's affiliated performing rights organization (ASCAP, BMI, or SESAC), which issues blanket licenses to broadcasters and others for the performance of music from its catalog and then remits monies collected to the writer based on his or her songs' use in the marketplace. In addition, a writer may collect income from a variety of other music uses, ranging from the old standard of sheet music and folio sales to the newer arena of digital MP3 downloads, video downloads, satellite radio, Internet radio, and digital subscription services. Some unusual technological tie-ins—such as licensing music for use as cell phone ringtones—have proved an out-of-the-blue boon for music creators; others will arise rapidly as technology and globalization create more opportunities.

Publishing Options

Before a writer can begin collecting any income, he or she must first get some songs published. A writer with a portfolio of marketable material has a number of options to consider. These are among the most common publishing arrangements:

1. *The writer can search out an established publisher and sign a contract with that firm.* Here, the writer participates only in writer's income. An unknown writer may begin with a single-song contract.

2. *The writer can negotiate a contract with a publisher in which the writer gets a piece of the publisher's share of the income.* This kind of deal is often called **copublishing** or "splitting the publishing"—the two parties usually share equally in the publisher's income. This option is obviously more appealing to the writer, and thus it generally takes a strong writer track record or a performer/writer's clout—such as having an existing album deal with a label—to negotiate this arrangement.

3. *The writer can set up a publishing company.* This option is often appealing to singer/songwriters who will record their own material. The writer will then own the copyrights and may make an agreement with an established publisher to administer his or her copyrights, for a fee.

4. *If the writer is also a recording artist, the personal manager under contract (or an attorney) might set up a publishing company owned by the writer and administered by the manager for a commission.*

5. *The writer might enter into a partnership or set up a corporation with others to operate a publishing company.* If the writer in a corporate structure is a full-time professional writer, the corporation might pay the writer as a regular employee. Whether the writer also receives a salary "override" on writer's royalties is determined by the provisions of the employment contract.

6. *The writer might be offered a staff job by a publisher.*

Staff Writers

A small and decreasing number of publishers will sometimes place promising writers on staff and demand their exclusive services on a full-time basis. Most staff writers receive a weekly salary; it may be just a token payment or a living wage. Whatever its size, the payment is treated as an advance on the writer's future royalty earnings. Remember, the bigger the advance, the more may have to be paid back or done without when the royalties start coming in—*it's not free money.*

Another kind of staff writer is also on salary, often full-time, for exclusive services. But the big difference here is that the writer is engaged to perform "work made for hire" for the publisher—meaning that the songs remain the exclusive property of the employer, and the writer can never claim copyright. The writer still receives the standard writer royalty from all sources of income, but cannot benefit from the copyright reversion provisions in the Copyright Act. If any work-for-hire songs become standards, this forfeiture of the right to recapture could represent a substantial financial loss for the writer and the writer's heirs.

Still another "staff" position at some publishing companies is that of a "song doctor." These writers rearrange and fix songs that the publisher owns an interest in to make the work more palatable to a certain audience. For example, the song doctor would rearrange a song to sound "modern country" in order to present it to a Nashville producer. The song doctor also makes small adjustments in the work to improve its overall condition. These positions are often salaried.

Early in a career, a writer might be so hungry that accepting a work-made-for-hire job is the only option. But it would be wise to seek a more attractive long-term alternative as soon as possible.

It's important to note that the above-described positions are becoming rarer and rarer in today's marketplace. But there are still a few mid-size publishers that engage writers in these kinds of roles.

Label-Affiliated Deals

As shown, multitalented songwriters can boost their marketability and their income by presenting themselves not just as writers but as performing artists. The monetary upside is easy to see: Singer-songwriters can earn both writer's royalties and artist's royalties. In addition, performing artists who write their own songs may be viewed as more attractive prospects by publishers, because they eliminate one of the efforts publishers must make with a "pure" songwriter—convincing a recording artist to use one of the writer's songs. An artist with an album deal already lined up is a particularly hot property.

Because of this potential for big earnings, everybody in the business wants a piece of that pie. A small label will pressure, sometimes coerce, a prospective writer-performer to assign some or all the publishing rights to the label's publishing arm. If the writer declines to share at least administration rights, the firm may **pass** on that writer—decline to sign a recording contract. Similar pressure on the singer-songwriter comes from many independent production companies. Typical dialogue: "Hey kid, we're gonna make you a big star, but it'll be expensive. We must have your publishing rights to help us recoup our recording costs and promotion expenses." The aspiring singer-songwriter has been cautioned to "hang on to your publishing" but may have to choose between signing it away to a production company or not getting signed as a recording artist.

There *is* a royalty downside to being a performer who writes one's own songs. As noted earlier, record companies generally include a *controlled composition clause* in their artists' agreements. This states that the recording company will pay only a percentage (typically, 75%) of the current mechanical royalty rate to the composer and publisher for any song written or coauthored by that artist/composer. In addition, a contractual "cap" on total mechanicals payable on an album (such as, 10 times 75% of the statutory rate) may require the artist to further lower his or her rate—for instance, if the album contains more than that number of **cuts**; alternately, the performer who uses both controlled and outside writers' songs may ask outside writers to reduce their rates in return for being included on the album.

In recent years, some publishers in Nashville have also been successful in contractually drawing from a songwriter's performance royalty, as well as from mechanical royalties, to recoup advance money. This point can be negotiable, if the writer is willing to take less in the way of an advance.

Evaluating Publishers

A writer who does not sign with the publishing arm of a record label or a production company, or who is not a recording artist, needs to pursue another business model, either by setting up a publishing company, or by locating a publisher independent of affiliation with a record company or production company.

How does a thoughtful writer evaluate a prospective publisher? Very carefully. Sharks and wolves abound where big dollars are available. Let us assume the writer is unknown. If there has been a struggle to gain the interest of a publisher, the writer may be tempted to sign on any terms with just about any firm that shows interest. An unpublished writer should think twice before rushing to sign the first contract offered.

The following questions can help inexperienced composers judge a prospective publisher:

1. What is the publisher's reputation for integrity? Is your information objective, trustworthy, and current?

2. How good is the firm's leadership? How competent? How stable?

3. What is the firm's long-term track record? Is it coasting on its catalog of golden oldies, or is it currently active with contemporary material?

4. Is the company making money? Says who?

5. Who in the company cares about you and your material? Do you know the professional manager, or are you dealing with a subordinate person in the firm? Is there at least one individual in the firm who likes your songs enough personally to exert real effort on your behalf? This kind of personal enthusiasm, rare in today's market, is sometimes the key to successful promotion.

6. What are the firm's resources? Do the professional manager and field promoters have valuable contacts with record producers and other important people in the business, such as film and TV music supervisors? Does the company agree to produce high-quality demos of your songs? Does the company have enough working capital to carry it over lean periods?

7. If your songs hit, does the company understand the print business and the income available from licensing for sale a variety of different editions?

8. If your songs hit, does the company know how to set up licensing arrangements abroad to maximize foreign income?

9. If your songs hit, does the company have experience in negotiating the whole range of digital uses, such as ringtones?

An unknown writer on the verge of signing a first contract with a publisher may be afraid to pose such pointed questions for fear of blowing the deal. But the writer risks being taken advantage of if the questions aren't asked and answered.

Whatever publishing arrangement the writer ultimately pulls together, the decision should be based on which person or firm can best exploit the music over the long term. Is the publisher a genuine professional with the know-how and contacts to exploit those copyrights internationally? Or are they only posing as a publisher, functioning merely as a collection agency for the writer's royalties? These days, a high percentage of so-called publishers function primarily as banks, collecting and disbursing money with little commitment to the writer or the music.

Henry Mancini.
Photo courtesy of Mancini Family.

The Songwriters Guild of America

One of the veteran organizations representing the songwriting community is the Songwriters Guild of America (SGA). The organization bearing this name was originally formed in 1931 as the Songwriters Protective Association. For many years, it was called the American Guild of Authors and Composers (AGAC); it changed to its current name in the 1980s.

The organization provides a variety of useful services to its members: (a) offers a standard writers' publishing contract; (b) collects royalties; (c) reviews members' publishing contracts, free of charge; (d) audits publishers; (e) maintains a copyright renewal service; (f) administers writer-publishers' catalogs (CAP, the Catalog Administration Plan); (g) provides a collaboration service; (h) maintains the Songwriters Guild Foundation; (i) operates an estates administration service; (j) provides financial evaluation of songs and catalogs to members and nonmembers; (k) offers workshops for writers; and (l) lobbies in Washington, D.C., on behalf of songwriters.

The Songwriters Guild of America Contract

The guild urges its members to attempt to negotiate acceptance of its Popular Songwriters Contract. As one would assume, it is heavily weighted in favor of the writer. Many publishers refuse to sign it. But writers can use it at least as a negotiating document. These provisions should be studied in tandem with the draft contract provisions in Chapter 4.

The agreement's main features are the following:

1. The writer warrants that the composition is the writer's "sole, exclusive, and original work" and that the writer has the right and power to make the contract and that "there exists no adverse claim to or in the composition."

2. If the publisher agrees to pay an advance, it will be provided in the agreement, and the advance will be recoupable from the writer's royalties.

3. Royalties on printed editions are not less than 10% of the wholesale selling price on the first 200,000 copies sold in the United States and Canada, not less than 12% on sales in excess of 200,000, and not less than 15% on sales in excess of 500,000.

4. The publisher pays the writer 50% of the publisher's receipts from all sources outside the United States and Canada.

5. The writer shares 50–50 with the publisher on income derived from all other sources—for example, mechanical royalties, synchronization rights, transcriptions, and block licenses. The publisher may discount any payments made to a collecting agent, such as the Harry Fox Agency, Inc.

6. The publisher must obtain the writer's consent before granting use of the composition in a movie, broadcast commercial, or dramatico-musical presentation or for any other new use, such as on the Internet.

7. The writer's royalties must be held in trust by the publisher and not used for any other purpose.

8. If the publisher fails to get a commercial recording of the composition within 1 year, the contract terminates. But the writer may grant an extension of 6 months, providing the publisher pays the writer $250.

9. The publisher must print and offer for sale regular piano copies or provide such copies or leadsheets to the writer.

10. The publisher must pay the writer 50% of foreign advances received by the publisher on a single song or a group of songs by the same writer.

11. The term (length) of the contract may be for any number of years but not more than 40 years "or 35 years from the date of first release of a commercial sound recording of the composition, whichever term ends earlier, unless this contract is sooner terminated in accordance with the provisions hereof."

12. When the contract terminates, the publisher revests in the writer all rights in the composition.

13. The publisher supplies a royalty statement at least every 6 months. The writer may demand an audit of the publisher's books upon supplying appropriate notice.

14. All disputes between the parties are to be submitted to arbitration under the rules of the American Arbitration Association, and the parties agree "to abide by and perform any award rendered in such arbitration."

15. The publisher may not assign (transfer or sell to another publisher) the contract without the writer's consent (except on the sale of a full catalog).

16. The writer and publisher must agree on future use—the exploitation of a composition in a manner not yet contemplated and therefore not specifically covered by the contract.

Contract Reassignment or Default

The writer and publisher may negotiate at length to shape an equitable contract. The relationship may turn out to be mutually profitable, even congenial. But it is the nature of the business that writers and publishers frequently want to terminate contracts. This does not mean the songs under contract must then die for lack of promotion. Rather, the copyrights may be reassigned.

Reassignments are common and can be to the advantage of the writer even if the songs are included in a bona fide sale of the first publisher's catalog, in the event of a merger or if the **assignment** is to a subsidiary or affiliated company. In each of these circumstances, the writer should demand from the first publisher a written instrument that states that the assignee-publisher assumes all obligations of the original (first) publisher.

Songwriters must continually police their contracts to make sure all the terms are being carried out. **Default** is a common occurrence. Default does not always involve unfairness, dishonesty, or fraud. More likely, a publisher defaults for one of the following reasons: inability to get the song recorded, the royalty statements are incorrect or incomplete, the publisher can't come up with royalty payments when they are due, or the publisher becomes overburdened working on other properties. If the writer believes the publisher is guilty of default and if the publisher has been given the chance to **cure** the default if such cure was stipulated in the contract, whatever the reasons, there are several options. The first is to go to arbitration, if that option is provided for in the contract. Next is to break the contract unilaterally. Courts take a dim view of unilateral action of this kind, for it is the court that must determine if a contract **breach** is "material" and whether the publisher has flagrantly disregarded appeals from the writer for **remedy.** Third, a lawsuit can be filed asking to be released from the contract. Fourth, a letter of termination can be sent to the publisher, stating that the publisher is in default and that henceforth the rights to any songs that have not yet been delivered to the publisher (known as *future rights*) will go to another publisher.

Breaking In

By now, you are probably both excited and terrified at the prospect of embarking on a career as a professional songwriter. (Don't worry—the contracts arena gets less intimidating over time.) You're likely also *ready to begin.* Breaking into the field is not as mysterious as generally believed. Many unknown writers are discovered every year, but few make it on luck alone. When we dig in to the so-called overnight success stories, we learn that most of these individuals used certain promotion techniques. We cannot articulate a breaking-in "formula." But we can describe what works for many new writers (see Table 3.2).

To increase your chances of success, you should undertake four levels of self-promotion: (a) establish a local reputation and local contacts, (b) contact publishers by mail and/or e-mail, (c) meet with publishers directly, and (d) network, network, network.

But first, you will need to arm yourself with a demo.

Demonstration Recordings

If you are a writer looking to connect with a publisher, or simply to get feedback from local artists and professionals on your work, you will need to be able to present a demonstration recording (demo) showcasing your songs. This will be your calling card, perhaps your one chance to make a strong impression. Choose your best five

Table 3.2   Seven Steps to Success

1. The first step is the most critical. Before spending time and money seeking a professional career, first find out if the talent is there. Your songs may go over great with family and friends. These reactions can be heartwarming—and misleading. What you as an amateur need at this point is an objective appraisal of your creative talents.

2. Make certain you know your craft. A writer needn't be a creative genius but can learn to be a craftsman.

3. Arm yourself with professional leadsheets, lyric sheets, and demonstration recordings.

4. Focus your promotion efforts on the specific market your songs fit.

5. Promote your songs in your own locale before risking a trip to the "big city." But do plan to make forays into music city hubs once you have a strong portfolio of songs you are ready to showcase before industry professionals.

6. Employ the promotion techniques outlined in these pages; learn the business, and develop and nurture music industry contacts wherever you can find them. Network.

7. Be relentless. Most of your competition will become discouraged and give up. Don't take it personally if someone doesn't return your calls or e-mails. Try again, and then try some more. The persistent writer can beat the competition by hanging in there.

songs and spend what you can to present them in their best possible light. (Some publishers can hear a diamond in the rough, but it's best not to count on that.) The first requirement? The vocals must be clearly heard above the music. If you are a talented singer, you can take the vocal yourself; if you doubt your ability and can afford to hire a professional—hungry singers abound—by all means do. The minimum accompaniment is piano or guitar. The maximum appropriate accompaniment would include a rhythm section and one or two frontline players. The singing should be straightforward; with a songwriter's demo, the listener wants to judge the song. Of course, if you are also a recording artist seeking a label deal, your demo should convey a representative performance.

A demo can be produced in a home studio if one has access to good-quality recording equipment and knows how to use it. Professional demo producers are also available at recording studios in many cities, at reasonable rates. They provide a professional singer accompanied by piano or guitar. Rates rise for more backup musicians, but producers offer special rates for more than one song. (See Chapter 11 for more information on recording studios and production.)

Demos are most commonly recorded on CD-Rs, and some writers still use high-quality audiocassettes. Each demo should be clearly labeled, on the box as well as on the recording itself, with an accompanying log of songs: their sequence numbers, song titles, and full names of composers. Tape one copy of the log outside the case and fold another copy inside. Be sure your own name, address, and phone number are included on every piece of material you submit; often, these items get separated.

Demos may include two notices of copyright: the letter P in a circle (℗), to protect the phonorecord, and the letter C in a circle (©), to protect the music contained in the recording.[1] The demo should also contain language saying it is for demonstration purposes only and is not to be distributed, sold, or otherwise disseminated; and that it should be returned or destroyed if the recipient doesn't wish to make professional use of it. Such notices offer some protection from unauthorized use. Demos are frequently lost due to inadequate identification (e.g., complete return address) and careless handling. If you are mailing one to a publisher, send it first class. Send copies, of course, not the masters.

Demos will likely also be recorded again when the writer is further along in the publishing process. A publisher, for instance, may want to produce a demo to showcase the new work of a writer under contract to persuade an artist or producer to record the songs. These demos can be much more polished and expensive than an aspiring writer's efforts. The upside is that a publisher will often pay at least part of the demo's costs, or at least provide the money for it as an advance on the writer's future royalties.

Local Promotion

Demo in hand, you are now ready to take your first steps toward a professional song-writing career, and for this task there is no place like home. Prove yourself locally. The amateur needs a place to make mistakes, to experiment with different kinds of promotional efforts before moving into the harsher spotlight of a music industry hub.

Look within your own circle of family and friends for a connection to the music business, no matter how small. If you don't have one, start with professional performers in your area. Go to their gigs, visit their rehearsals. Hang out, get acquainted. If your songs suit their style, you may persuade them to try your material. At this stage, it doesn't matter whether these professionals are well-known. Making their acquaintance now may provide a contact that will bear fruit later.

Contact your local radio stations and try to persuade program directors, disc jockeys, and music librarians to listen to your demos. Because radio, like music publishing, has become increasingly corporatized, with programming decisions made in far-off cities, they almost certainly will be unable to use your songs, but their evaluations could be valuable.

Now might also be the time to promote yourself on the Internet. It's easy to post your music on social networking sites. You can also set up your own Web site, complete with blogs and sample songs. This is a helpful tool to which you can refer interested parties. Remember to include your Web site address on all correspondence and on your business cards. If you are a singer/songwriter, you can also use these sites to sell copies of your CDs and advertise upcoming club dates. Be sure to register your site with major search engines.

Keep an eye out for acts coming through town on tour. Traveling performers often pick up useful material on the road. With some performers, it is more effective to try to get your songs to people *around* the artist, such as the performer's musical director (**MD**), arranger, or manager, any of whom could be an influential song picker.

Some smaller cities are headquarters for publishing companies. Do not rule out small publishers—they may do more for you than the majors. If you evaluate them according to the guidelines listed in this chapter and if they measure up, go with them if you do not have a more attractive option at the time.

Contact local advertising agencies and commercial production companies. Communities with populations of 100,000 and up will generally have such firms. They are in constant need of melodies and musical ideas for broadcast commercials.

If you begin to receive favorable local reaction to your writing, you just might be ready for the next step in promoting your songs.

Promotion by Mail and E-Mail

Amateur songwriters have sometimes been successful in landing their first publishers through an initial mail contact. This is a special technique, however, and efforts of this kind often fail because they are not handled effectively. But the writer who follows the procedures outlined has a chance of getting songs heard. All it costs is the price of postage and a few demo CDs, or a few minutes at the computer. Here's how to proceed:

1. Study the record charts and find out the names of publishers who are currently active in handling the type of music you write.

2. Get the addresses and telephone numbers of these publishers. Google them or try your local telephone company or library. Another source is *Billboard's International Buyers Guide,* published annually.

3. Verify by phone the name of the appropriate contact person.

4. Write a letter or send an e-mail requesting *permission* to mail in some of your songs. The letter should be short, well written, and to the point. Briefly state what reception your songs have already experienced with professional performers. If permission is received, mail in only your three to five best songs. Your package should contain a demo recording of each song (put all of them on the same cassette or CD) *and* separate lyric sheets for each song,

with your name, address, and telephone number on each sheet. Inclusion of professionally prepared leadsheets is optional with some publishers, but play it safe and include them too. In addition to your cover letter, include a self-addressed, stamped postcard. Send your package by first-class mail, not by certified or registered mail; some publishers feel that accepting such mail could mean trouble. Wait 3 weeks. If you receive no reply, call or e-mail the publisher to confirm that your material has arrived. If your songs have been received but have not gained acceptance, continue the process with other publishers until you receive a favorable reaction.

Very few publishers today will open unsolicited mail; not only are they wary of being accused of stealing material, but a greater concern is that the vast majority of unsolicited songs and demos are mediocre or worse. Publishers cannot take time to dig through the piles of songs received every week in the hope that one in a hundred might be worth serious consideration. But when a writer has been professional enough to obtain permission from the publisher to submit material, whatever is mailed in is viewed differently. Take a look at the sample first-contact letter that follows:

Mr. John Doe, Professional Manager

XYZ Music Publishing Company

Address

Dear Mr. Doe: Date:

Please indicate your response to the following question and then mail this card back to me (it is already addressed and stamped).

Will you examine my songs for publication?

Yes _____   **No** _____

Your response will be sincerely appreciated.

Thank you.

(Signed here)

Austin Hopeful

Address/Telephone

A first-contact e-mail will be very similar:

Dear Mr. Doe,

Please reply by return e-mail your response to the following question.

Will you examine my songs for publication?

Your response will be sincerely appreciated.

Thank you.

Austin Hopeful

Address/Telephone

Direct Contact With Publishers

Even though some lucky amateur songwriters manage to create publisher interest through mail contacts, most songs get published following a direct, personal contact with the publisher.

Because popular music publishers have offices in the leading recording centers, the amateur writer who wants to go professional and doesn't live in New York, Nashville, or Los Angeles will need to spend time in one or more of these cities. Occasionally, publishers will see unknown songwriters, but it is unwise for the newcomer to walk directly from the bus station to the publisher's office. First, write a letter or send an e-mail requesting an appointment, or call the office and talk to the receptionist about setting up a meeting (*always* be polite to this gatekeeper). If you can drop a name of someone in the industry who has referred you, your chances will improve dramatically.

If you are fortunate enough to have been granted a meeting with a publisher, be sure to write a thank-you note afterward. Keep up that valuable contact even if you may not have new material. Then, when you are ready to submit more songs— whether in person or by mail—you will have an "in."

Network, Network, and Then Network Some More

If it hasn't become apparent by now, it's worth stating bluntly here: Industry connections and contacts, those all-important "ins," are the key to getting your songs noticed and, ultimately, recorded. Many publishers will take meetings based only on referrals by industry pros, for instance, and record producers heading into the studio with an artist will usually turn first to songwriters they know or who have been recommended to them.

The music industry is built on networking and relationships, and songwriting is no exception. The good news is that networking can be easy and fun. It simply means getting out there, getting involved, getting seen, and getting heard. A good place to start is by contacting your regional ASCAP or BMI membership representative, who may be open to reviewing and assessing your songs; if he or she likes them, the representative can provide that all-important referral to a music publisher or label contact. ASCAP and BMI also host workshops for young writers, as do many other songwriter, publisher, and music business organizations. Use an online search engine to find out what's happening, and attend as many events as you can; even if you are not (yet) invited to perform yourself—you can make invaluable introductions. The National Academy of Popular Music, based in New York, also offers showcases, workshops, and forums. Seek out other organizations in your area and explore the many online music forums for relevant information.

Contests offer another avenue to get your name and your songs in front of industry professionals; even if you don't win, you may make an impression and a connection. The performing rights organizations sponsor some of the major ones, but others abound. Read music publications, search Web sites, and talk to other industry professionals for information; but exercise caution in making sure any such contests are legitimate and not moneymaking schemes keyed to entry fees or demo production charges.

Finally, of course, you can take the ultimate networking plunge and choose to immerse yourself in a songwriting hub city such as New York, Los Angeles, or Nashville. Particularly in Nashville, you will find yourself rubbing shoulders constantly with music industry insiders and wannabes—everywhere from coffee shops to clubs. If you can afford it, such a move can prove invaluable in many ways, including finding new collaborators. Even if not, a serious songwriter will try to schedule regular visits to any (or all) of these cities to attend workshops, forums, and meetings.

▌ Note

1. Some attorneys have suggested not using the Ⓟ symbol on a demo for fear its presence would create the legal presumption that the recording is "published," thus leaving the composer vulnerable to an unwanted compulsory mechanical license.

Chapter Takeaways

- Songwriting is the essential ingredient of the music industry, but the crush of competition makes success challenging.

- Successful songs tend to exhibit similar characteristics, notably a hook—a repeated catchy phrase or refrain.

- A songwriter can expect to spend as much time promoting songs as writing them.

- Main sources of songwriting income include mechanicals, performance royalties, and synchronization fees.

- There are many ways to publish a song, ranging from signing as a singer-songwriter with the publishing affiliate of a label, to establishing a publisher sole proprietorship.

- Carefully prepare a demo recording to woo publishers to offer a songwriting contract.

- Networking in the music industry is essential, particularly in the profession of songwriting.

Key Terms

- controlled composition clause   (p. 37)
- cure   (p. 41)
- default   (p. 41)
- demos   (p. 28)

- exploited   (p. 31)
- frontline   (p. 43)
- hook   (p. 29)
- leadsheet   (p. 31)

- mechanicals   (p. 34)
- performance royalties   (p. 33)
- song doctor   (p. 37)
- Tin Pan Alley   (p. 31)

CHAPTER 4

Music Publishing

Decades ago, music publishers made a living by printing copies of sheet music and placing them in local music stores or the "five and dime" for sale to the public. Today, of course, few families spend their evenings singing songs around a piano, and the business of music publishing has responded to the changes and challenges wrought by radio, records, and a parade of ever-changing technologies—the new means of exposing music to the public. In the popular music field, the great majority of new songs are no longer printed commercially at all. When publishers believe that printing their copyrighted works for sale to consumers might prove profitable, they usually license that right to specialty print publishers whose sole function is to provide these services (see Chapter 5 for more information on copyrights).

"Music is everybody's possession. It's only publishers who think that people own it."

—John Lennon

Today, the heart of the music **publishing** industry lies not in the print business, but in the marketing and administration of rights to songwriters' compositions. For the contemporary music publisher, success is keyed directly to how well the publishing company exploits music and generates **mechanical** royalties (from recordings), **performance** royalties (from broadcast or live performance), and other licensing fees (such as using an already existing piece of music in a film or other visual work). In recent years, the Internet and digital revolutions have created a world of new opportunities for garnering royalties, both from the performance of compositions (e.g., digital subscription services) and the sale of recordings (e.g., via Web sites

Left: The Warner/Chappell Music building, Los Angeles.

Photo courtesy Warner/Chappell Music, Inc.

where consumers can purchase and instantly own anything from a single song to the complete works of a classical composer). Online vendors and subscription services pay publishers a fee for providing consumers access to copyrighted music made available through authorized streaming, downloading, and CD burning.

Those with long experience in the music business know publishing to be a lucrative and steady source of income which can bring in revenue long after a hit song has faded from the airwaves (or even when it doesn't "hit" at all). "Keep your publishing" has become a mantra for copyright owners all over the world, and just about everyone in the performing and recording fields is involved in music publishing in one way or another.

To gain a perspective on how this field has become such a colossus, Table 4.1 shows how the industry developed historically.

Table 4.1 Development of Music Publishing

1640:	The first book published in America—and it happens to be a music book—is *The Bay Psalm Book*, which first used musical notation in its 1698 edition.
1770:	The first native-born American composer, William Billings, gets his music published.
1790:	First U.S. Congress passes first copyright law.
1850–1900:	Minstrel shows are widely popular and increase public interest in popular music. Publishers begin to prosper.
1890s:	The player piano becomes popular, creating a demand for player piano rolls. Large music publishing firms are established in the last two decades of the 1800s. Merchandising methods develop, and publishers begin to discover that if enough people hear a good song, it will probably be a hit. The most effective song promoters now are the performers in various theaters and vaudeville houses that develop around the turn of the century.
1900:	Popular music publishing becomes big business, and for the next 40-plus years, music publishers are the most powerful people in the entire music industry. In this first decade of the 20th century, an estimated 100 songs each sell a million copies or more within a 1-year period, at a time when the population of the United States is about 90 million. The U.S. Congress passes the historic 1909 Copyright Law that provides publishers, for the first time, with mechanical rights in recorded music. Initially, this revenue derives largely from player piano rolls.
1920s:	The American Society of Composers, Authors and Publishers (ASCAP), established in 1914, becomes a major force as a performing rights organization. For the first time in this country, publishers and writers begin to receive income from performances of their music. Radio broadcasting begins and is initially fought by publishers who believe radio hurts sheet music sales. Sound movies ("talkies") begin. Film producers negotiate fees for music synchronization rights. The Harry Fox Agency is established. Sheet music sales drop with the rise of radio. Publishers close most of their branch offices to concentrate promotion efforts on the radio network broadcasting centers that, at this time, are New York City, Chicago, and Los Angeles.
1930s:	The Great Depression severely hurts the music publishing business but increasing income from movie producers helps. The "big bands" develop and become the most important source of plugs for new songs, particularly if the band has a remote wire for radio broadcasting. National Music Publishers' Association (NMPA) expands the Harry Fox Agency to include mechanical licensing of copyrights. SESAC is formed, with headquarters in New York City, in response to European publisher concerns about performance royalty income from the United States.
1940s:	During and after World War II, people spend more of their incomes on music, instruments, records, and movies. The LP record appears in 1948, now producing publishers' royalties on 10 to 12 songs per record, not just 2. National Association of Broadcasters (NAB) forms Broadcast Music Inc. (BMI) in reaction to increasing demands from ASCAP. The big band singers (Perry Como, Frank Sinatra, Doris Day, and others) go solo and become the dominant source for introducing new songs. American gospel music becomes a mainstay of SESAC's representation.

1950s:	Rapid growth of television kills live music on the radio. Disc jockeys become the new hit-makers. Rock and roll comes to dominate popular music, greatly expanding the market for records. BMI succeeds in capturing the majority of copyrights in the rock and country fields. SESAC's repertory expands to include country music.
1960s:	Increasing dependence of publishers to break new songs on radio. The Beatles and other pop groups begin recording mostly their own material. The print business improves, particularly editions for the amateur and the educational field. Harry Fox Agency becomes a wholly owned subsidiary of the NMPA.
1970s:	Radio broadcasters shorten their playlists below the Top 40, forcing companies to promote airplay in secondary and tertiary markets located in smaller cities. The print business in the pop song folio and educational field continues to grow, but inflating costs cause many publishers to quit all print activity and assign such rights to subpublishers and licensees here and abroad. Publishers' incomes from ASCAP and BMI continue to rise. Record sales boom, and so do publishing revenues. New musical genres continue to develop.
1980s:	Old copyrights enjoy financial boom due to widespread popularity of CDs. Huge mergers and acquisitions dominate the publishing business and the music industry in general. Music becomes an even more significant part of films, television programs, and commercials. MTV begins broadcasting music videos 24 hours a day and becomes a key promotional tool for increasing sales. Increased music use via new media, particularly home videocassettes, computer games, and video jukeboxes, increases publisher revenues.
1990s:	The beginning of the Internet revolution spurs publishers, recording companies, and other music users to contemplate new ways to exploit their product. The European Economic Community eases restrictions between its member countries, and the United States makes trade agreements to remain competitive and to update legislation. New musical genres, including rap and alternative, challenge rock and roll for market dominance. Success in foreign markets remains critical to the overall success of an artist as a performer or composer. Media and entertainment companies, including their music publishing arms, consolidate.
2000:	The industry enters the new millennium grappling with technological issues such as file sharing and complex transmission standards for delivering digital audio. Mechanical royalties decline significantly due to unauthorized file sharing and changes in consumer habits. Music rights revenue surges from sources such as video games, DVDs, film, TV, and commercial synchronizations. Digital opportunities such as Internet downloading, satellite radio, online subscriptions, microsubscription services, and cell phone ringtones open new vistas for publishers to expose their material and generate incremental revenues.

Types of Publishers

Like the topsy-turvy record industry, the music publishing business is a collection of enterprises that run the gamut from a few corporate behemoths to a large number of small and medium size independent companies. Within this universe, there are administered and administering companies, print licensees, manager-publishers, lawyer-publishers, multinational media conglomerates, and **subpublishers,** whose role will be explored in depth later in this chapter.

The term *music publisher* includes everything from the one-person company devoted to the writings of a single artist/writer to the multinational affiliates of record companies, film companies, and media giants. Publishing companies can be publicly owned, artist/writer owned, or owned or administered by managers, lawyers, or even songwriters' relatives or friends. Some publishers are "full service," with huge catalogs covering a broad range of music styles. Others restrict their business to single genres such as jazz or classical music, or deal only in educational, religious, or printed publications. All large music publishers have affiliates or licensees abroad, and these relationships afford opportunities for reciprocal sharing of royalties in foreign territories. Music publishers have learned a valuable lesson from movie producers, who discovered decades ago that foreign receipts may equal or even outstrip domestic revenues.

Not too many years ago, there were as many as 30 major music publishers. Today, there are only a handful, and they dominate the industry domestically and throughout most of the developed world. Through an unprecedented surge of mergers and acquisitions, a few companies currently boast catalogs of more than a million copyrights. Clearly, it takes vast resources to effectively administer these catalogs. At the same time, new markets around the world and new media like the Internet and the DVD have changed the face of the music publishing industry. All music publishers, both large and small, realize that their future depends not only on finding and publishing new material but also on growth in new markets and effective administration and exploitation of rights in existing catalogs.

Major Companies

Prior to the great expansion of the recording industry in the 1960s and 1970s, many of the older music publishers included a wide range of musical styles in their catalogs—classical, educational, movie, pop, and show music. Today, new firms with this broad a repertoire are scarce, but a few major publishers are still active in multiple genres. Some are affiliated with record labels and, in some cases, major media companies as well. Major publishers trace their origins to the music of Hollywood, Broadway, or the great pop writers of **Tin Pan Alley**. These companies provided a "full line" of services such as printing and selling copies of sheet music, "plugging" songs to recording and performing artists, and developing long-term relationships with writers. Each major firm has developed its own corporate structure, but Figure 4.1 shows a typical organization of this scope. Department names and reporting relationships vary from company to company.

Recording Company Affiliates

Full-line publishers affiliated with major labels generally have their own staff and budgets and operate independently of their affiliated labels, although it is not unusual for a label and its affiliated publisher to negotiate with an artist/writer simultaneously. Label publishing affiliates, many of which are among the largest publishers in the world, also acquire catalogs from other publishers or writers, which may be purchased outright for substantial payments. A recording artist may have an existing catalog of previously recorded compositions, which might be acquired by a label's publishing affiliate as part of an overall record/publishing deal. Linkages such as these can make it difficult for the independent label or publisher to compete for a sought-after artist/writer. Of course, the argument can be made that these interlocking companies create a conflict of interest or an unfair negotiating advantage. Artists/writers are sometimes required to place their copyrights with the label's affiliated publisher; those who refuse to do so sometimes find it more difficult to get recording deals.

Despite the reduced mechanical payments and potential conflict issues, publishing/recording deals, when fairly handled, are a way for a new artist to maximize advance income and marshal the publisher's (and label's) resources to establish a successful recording and writing career.

Figure 4.1   Major Music Publisher Departments and Their Functions

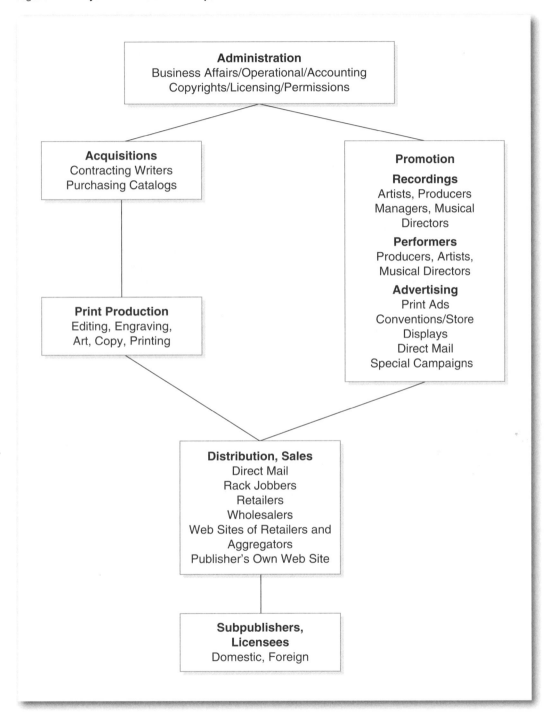

Independent Publishers

Firms not affiliated with either a multinational publishing organization or a record label are often referred to as independents. Independents range in size from the one-person operation to firms controlling multimillion-dollar catalogs. Many independents

Figure 4.2   **Writer-Owned Publishing Company**

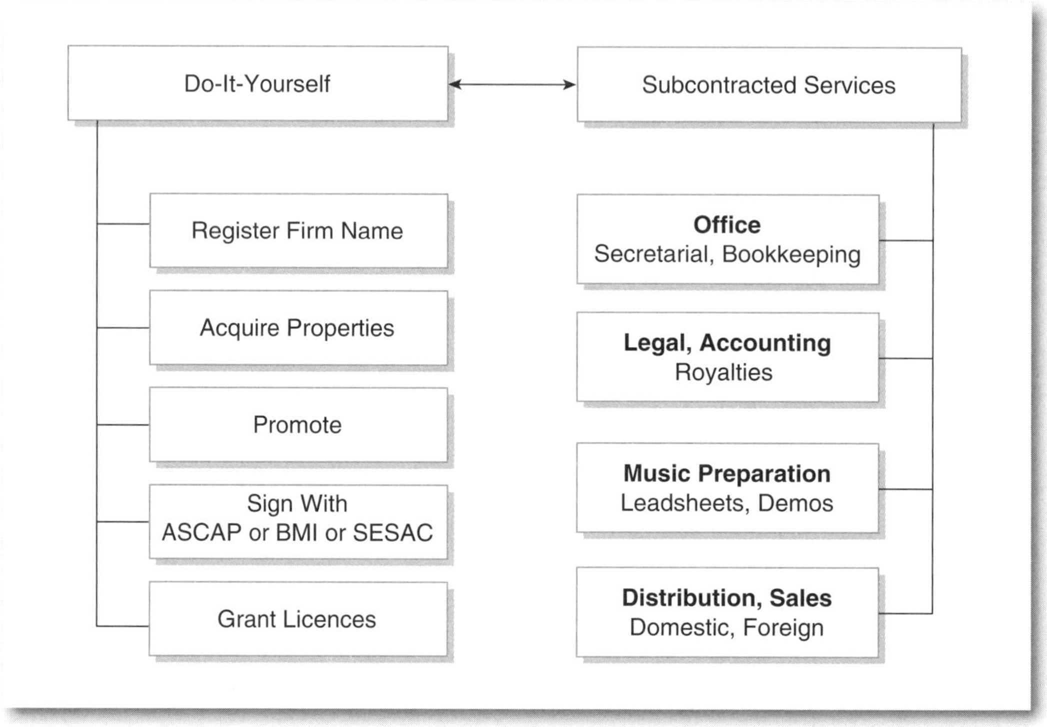

Do-It-Yourself	Subcontracted Services
Register Firm Name	**Office** Secretarial, Bookkeeping
Acquire Properties	**Legal, Accounting** Royalties
Promote	**Music Preparation** Leadsheets, Demos
Sign With ASCAP or BMI or SESAC	**Distribution, Sales** Domestic, Foreign
Grant Licences	

are members of the Association of Independent Music Publishers (AIMP). Some independent publishers perform only basic administrative duties in return for a percentage (often 10%) of the publishing income they administer. Responsibilities of such administrative publishers include registering new copyrights with performing rights societies and mechanical societies worldwide, licensing the use of copyrights, collecting and tracking royalties, and royalty accounting. They do little or no exploitation, which is not a problem for their clients, who are usually artists or writers who promote themselves. A significant number of independents offer more than administrative services, however. Some of these are based in Nashville, where old-style music publishing and songplugging still exists and indeed flourishes. The following are examples of functions that might be performed directly by an independent owner-publisher or subcontracted out to service providers.

Artist-Owned Companies

Many recording artists who write their own material form their own publishing companies. The reason is simple: They see no need to hand over the publishing income, especially when they themselves are the catalysts for the primary marketing tool, the record release. Royalties to the publisher of the copyrights accrue from record sales, so artists, usually with assistance from their managers and attorneys, set up publishing companies to keep control over their music and its proceeds. Because most artists are principally concerned with recording and performing, they generally publish only their own compositions. They rarely get involved in the print business. Once they achieve some international presence, they can arrange subpublishing deals abroad, usually negotiated by their attorneys or administrative publisher.

Writer-Owned Companies

A large number of very small publishing operations are owned by individual writers. These firms are set up either by writers who want to control their copyrights from the beginning, or by writers unable to get their music accepted by labels or other publishers. Some writer-owned firms have been established by composers who were previously under contract to a publisher but came to believe their material was not receiving sufficient promotion to justify the loss of a percentage of income and a degree of control required in a publishing deal. See Figure 4.2, which shows how very small music publishing firms can be structured.

Educational Publishing

Some publishers in the United States limit their catalogs primarily to music intended for use by students and schools from elementary grade levels through college. The biggest sellers are for piano and guitar, followed by strings and percussion. Part of these sales is known as bench packs—educational materials given by the equipment manufacturer to the customer upon sale of a new keyboard. The instrument manufacturer pays the copyright owners for these materials. The biggest-selling editions for schools are scored for choirs, marching bands, and concert bands.

Specialty Publishers

Many publishers limit their catalogs to one kind of music. Publishers active only in the country field, for example, are among the nation's largest independent publishers, although most major publishers also maintain active offices in Nashville. Most specialty houses are, however, relatively small, preferring to restrict their activities to the field they understand best, such as choral music, gospel, children's music, or so-called stage band (big bands in schools and colleges playing pop and jazz music). One example of this is the publisher devoted solely to what is called "Christian music." Many prosper not only through sales of their music on records but also from a good-sized print business.

Concert Music

Concert (or classical) music is that repertoire generally associated with opera, symphony, ballet, recital, choral, and religious music. Only a handful of publishers limit their catalogs to these fields. Representative concert music publishers include G. Schirmer, Peters, Boosey & Hawkes, Carl Fischer, and Theodore Presser.

Classical music publishers produce and distribute an array of special editions of the classics for school orchestras and choirs, as well as studies for keyboard, strings, solo instruments, and voice. Much of the income of classical publishers derives from the rental and licensing of scores and instrumental and vocal parts.

Besides maintaining catalogs of older music, nearly all of it from Europe, these houses provide a special service. They publish the works of 20th-century serious composers despite the lack of financial gain from this area of music. Some of these losses are offset by offering dramatic works and extended pieces through the rental of the parts rather than the sale of printed editions.

Some classical publishers emphasize contemporary serious (classical) and avant-garde music. Many of these publishers are subsidized by a foundation or university, and they may have sizable catalogs of foreign copyrights that they administer for the U.S. territory. Recordings of their music are also largely subsidized.

Print Licensees

Few popular music publishers in the United States print, market, or distribute printed editions of their copyrights; instead, they license this function to another company. Most print deals provide that the licensee (the print firm) will bear the full costs of preparing, printing, and distributing the printed edition; the licensee then pays the licensor (the publisher controlling the rights) a royalty on sales, often in the range of 20% of the wholesale price. In deals of this kind, the licensee is sometimes called a selling agent. A major publisher with deeper pockets, however, will probably insist on a different type of print deal in which it bears the full costs of preparing, printing, and distributing the printed edition in exchange for retaining a bigger chunk of the proceeds; the print licensee in these cases will get only a distribution fee, usually about 20% on sales.

Subpublishing

The publishing business is increasingly a global one, and many American publishers receive a large percentage of their income from foreign exploitation of their American catalogs. The foreign exploitation of copyrights via a license from the original publisher is referred to as subpublishing.

Subpublishing Agreements

Some large U.S. companies have branch offices in foreign countries that fill the subpublishing role for their affiliated publishers, functioning much like the American parent firm. First, they try to exploit the American catalog in their territory by promoting the original recording, getting cover records, selling printed editions, securing **synchronization licenses** for film, TV, and commercials, and collecting mechanical and performance royalties. As part of this effort, the branch office may arrange for translations of English lyrics into the local language. Second, branch offices often acquire compositions created in their own territories.

An independent American publisher lacking branch offices abroad may seek out licensees in those territories. Those subpublishers may be foreign independents or they may be affiliates of multinational companies that are seeking outside catalogs in addition to their own. The latter aggressively pursue successful U.S. catalogs.

Independent publishers lacking the resources to set up subpublishing deals can also choose to retain U.S. licensing firm The Harry Fox Agency to meet many of their basic needs for services in foreign territories through the agency's reciprocal agreements with foreign societies (see Chapter 30, Table 30.1., Foreign Affiliates).[1]

Although royalty splits vary from company to company and country to country, a common arrangement between the original publisher and a subpublisher is 80% to 90% of the gross earnings in the territory paid to the original publisher and 10% to 20% retained by the licensee. Advances are usually paid by the foreign subpublisher to the original publisher based on the projected success and U.S. activity of the song. Usually, the larger the advance, the larger the commission kept by the subpublisher. Most of these subpublishing deals are for at least 3 years. The American company will expect the subpublisher to exploit the American copyrights through securing release and handling promotion of the original recording, arranging cover records, providing printed editions, and collecting performance royalties. The performing rights organization functioning in a given territory will forward the writer's share to ASCAP, BMI, or SESAC, but the American firm's subpublisher is usually allowed to collect the publisher's share and apply that to outstanding advances. It is also an advantage for the original publisher to have the publisher's share collected by the subpublisher in the licensed territory because the periods of time otherwise involved with transmitting that payment from the local territory to ASCAP or BMI in the United States might involve a delay of up to 2 years. In addition, the subpublisher is in a better position to make sure the accountings are accurate based on activity of the catalog in that territory.

With regard to foreign collections, a distinction should be made between a collection deal and a subpublishing deal. In a collection deal, the subpublisher is merely expected to collect the income earned from the copyright, taking 10% or 15% as an administrative fee. In a subpublishing deal, the percentages are more favorable to the local publisher and usually involve advances to the original publisher supplying the catalog and more aggressive commitments for exploitation of that catalog in the territory, as outlined above.

A writer's decision about what kind of foreign deal to make can have far-reaching implications, especially because currency fluctuations in various territories can cause the percentage of foreign income to skyrocket or plummet.

At-Source Deals Versus Receipts-Basis Deals

In choosing a subpublisher, the original publisher (the company to which the writer originally assigned the copyright in the United States) can make a deal with independent subpublishers in various territories or with a multinational subpublisher for a group of territories.

While many factors will play into that decision, the choice of a multinational publisher offers an advantage to the original licensor's bottom line. The reason lies in the distinction between an "at-source" deal and a "receipts-based" agreement. Payment of royalties earned at the source is a concept more favorable to the original publisher and writer, and such setups are usually available only from publishers who have wholly-owned affiliates in foreign territories, such as multinational companies.

In an at-source deal, the publisher and writer's share is calculated on income earned in the foreign territory, or "at the source." The original publisher (who accounts to the writer) gets paid as if it were in the country where the money is earned without any deductions by the subpublisher. The writer, in turn, gets his or her 50% share (or more, depending on the deal in effect) of the income earned in the foreign territory, before deductions for subpublishers are made, no matter what money is eventually remitted to the United States. In an at-source deal, if $100 is earned in Australia, the writer's share would be $50.

In contrast, in a receipts-based agreement common among independent subpublishers, the publisher and writer's share is calculated only on income received by the publisher in the United States, *after* payments or deductions to a subpublisher have been made. In a receipts deal, the writer would get royalties based on monies received by the original publisher. If that same $100 is earned in Australia under this type of agreement and the publisher had a 75/25 deal with the Australian subpublisher, the American publisher would receive $75 and the writer's share would be $3,7.50 (half of that 75%).

On a positive note, independent subpublishers often give more attention to writers, have better contacts, and work harder to get covers and synch licenses than do the branch offices of multinational conglomerates.

Agreements for Multiple Territories

American firms usually contract with subpublishers to cover more than one country. For example, it is common for a subpublisher based in Germany to cover Germany, Austria, and German-speaking Switzerland, which makes up the territory of GEMA, the German performance rights society. French-based subpublishers would probably service the French-speaking territories in Africa and, quite possibly, the French-speaking radio stations in Luxembourg and Switzerland, which is the territory administered by the French performing rights society, SACEM. A Scandinavian subpublisher would probably have jurisdiction over Norway, Sweden, Denmark, Iceland, and Finland.

There is no one "right" deal for a U.S. publisher looking for overseas exploitation, since different approaches may suit different needs. Any subpublishing situation, however, should ideally include a person "on the ground" in the country who understands the language and knows the ways of the region's music business, especially with regard to registering copyrights with local societies and collecting performance royalties.

Administration

Administration of publishing companies varies greatly according to the size of the firm. Independent companies may have a small staff, with each individual performing a variety of tasks. In some cases, a small, independent publisher might have only one employee: the owner-songwriter. Contrast this type of operation with the management structure of a major publisher (see Figures 4.1 and 4.2).

Large publishers will have a central administration consisting of a president (or vice president in charge of administration), department heads, and support personnel. Firms vary in the names they apply to departments. What follows is a description of the administrative structure of a typical major publisher.

Royalty Department

The royalty department is managed by an individual, usually an accountant or finance person, who supervises assistants handling receipts, disbursements, and fields inquiries from writers, among other duties.

Copyright Department

Most publishers have at least one employee who handles copyrights. Larger firms have a copyright division, with a department head over a number of staff people. A qualified copyright department head must know the U.S. Copyright Laws of 1909, the 1976 revisions, and basic international laws and agreements ("conventions") covering foreign copyrights.

The firm's copyright department performs a number of essential tasks. Among the most important are the following:

1. Conducting title searches. The copyright department must first determine who really owns a work. The Library of Congress will assist in this research. Copyright ownership can get complicated. If the work has coauthors, what

are their claims of ownership and are the claims valid? Have the melody and/or the lyrics fallen into the public domain? What if the work was published before? What if the music or the lyrics have been revised? How does a publisher determine if some of the rights have been assigned to another firm or individual or estate? After the copyright department has performed this research, questions remaining unclear are referred to a copyright attorney, who may or may not be on the publisher's staff.

2. Registering claims of copyright.

3. Recording transfers of copyright ownership.

4. Forming a liaison with The Harry Fox Agency to issue and administer mechanical licenses. Publishing firms occasionally choose to issue their own mechanical licenses or to go through the American Mechanical Rights Agency, Inc. (AMRA).

5. Keeping records of **subsisting** copyrights and their pending expiration and termination dates. Recommending renewal, extension, sale, or abandonment of subsisting copyrights. Proper timing is essential as valuable rights could be forfeited. In matters of this importance, top management would, of course, be directly involved.

Legal and Business Affairs

Well-run music publishers must have lawyers who have expertise in both copyright law and music publishing. They also need to be versed in tax law, artist management, and the recording industry. Nearly all publishing transactions are based on contracts, and the ongoing services of qualified attorneys are essential in negotiating them. Small firms employ these specialists by the hour or on a monthly retainer basis. Larger firms not only retain counsel part-time, as needed, but also employ one or more lawyers as full-time staff. Attorneys from outside firms may also be employed for specific projects, such as litigation or to facilitate a major acquisition.

Print Publishing Operations

Print publishing requires additional resources. After a copyright title has been cleared and the author is signed to a contract, and after the arrangers and editors have performed their tasks, the music must go through a number of additional operations before it can be distributed and sold. Many firms group these activities, such as printing, warehousing, inventory control, and shipping, under an operations department.

Editing for Print Publications

Nearly all music submitted for print publication needs editing. Few composers, even those classically trained, know the proper way to prepare a manuscript for the printer. Even a simple leadsheet should be prepared by an arranger qualified in this specialized field. At the outset, the arranger-editor must correct errors in notation, and perhaps even rewrite portions that do not make good musical sense. In rare cases, editors may be called on to polish lyrics, though that task, when needed, is usually left to professional lyricists or "song doctors." Print publication has changed dramatically in recent years because of the introduction of computerized ordering, editing, and printing and the use of computerized graphics.

The Print Production Line

In the classical and specialty print business, once a publisher determines that a newly acquired piece of music should be offered for sale in printed form, the music goes down a production line, somewhat like other products, progressing from raw material to vendible commodity. Here is a typical line of production for a piece of printed music headed for the marketplace:

1. The publisher's acquisitions committee (or an authorized individual) determines that the piece of music or a specific arrangement, instruction book, or other proposed publication should be accepted for publication.

2. The publisher's copyright department determines that the title (ownership) of the music is clear (unencumbered).

3. The publisher registers a claim to copyright with the Copyright Office and places copies on file with the Library of Congress.

4. If the composition is an original composition or group of compositions, the publisher's arranger (or a freelance arranger) scores a piano-voice version of the music. The editor makes sure it is in acceptable form, then directs the preparation of digital files or camera-ready art. At some point, it is usually submitted to the writer for approval.

5. After proofreading, if the editor approves the completed work, the printer (in-house or external) prints the music. First printings in the educational field are normally 1,000 copies. In the case of popular song folios, a first printing may run 25,000 copies or more.

6. The printer (in-house or external) then ships and drop ships (ships directly to the customer but bills through the retailer) copies of the music according to instructions from the publisher. No set distribution patterns prevail, but two are fairly common: A publisher may ship directly to its rack jobbers and larger retail outlets or may assign to a subpublisher a license to promote, distribute, and sell the entire edition.

7. Meanwhile, the publisher's or licensee's promotion/advertising people try to generate sales both here and abroad. If they succeed, purchasers put down their money and everyone is happy.

8. The publisher pays the author royalties based on sales volume of the printed editions.

Distribution

Publishers vary in how they handle the distribution and sale of printed editions. As previously noted, most publishers sublicense the print area entirely and merely receive a royalty or share of income that they share with their writers under their overall agreement. The distribution trail generally goes from publisher to print publisher to rack jobber (the middle man between manufacturer and retailer) to retailer to customer, although some printed products are still sold via direct mail.

As consumers become increasingly Web-savvy, publishers are gradually selling more of their "print" products via the Internet. This is done either through online aggregators, the Web sites of music retailers, or through the Web sites of the

A delegate makes notes at the NAMM show.

Photo courtesy of NAMM.

publishers themselves. Consumers can search, listen, and sample everything from single sheets to choral arrangements to folios to **fake books** to piano and guitar books. If they like what they see, they can either order the music to be mailed to them or purchase and download their music on the spot.

Creative Department

There was a time when all publishers in the popular music field employed what were known in the late 1940s as "songpluggers." Their place in the world of show business has been portrayed colorfully in the movies and other media. Gradually, they came to be known as professional managers and later the terms **creative** or A&R (artist and repertoire) were used as well. Since World War II, the professional manager has had to assume a role much broader in scope than songplugging. Here are the principal responsibilities of the creative department:

1. Discover and sign new writers.

2. Maintain good working relationships with writers under contract.

3. Persuade artists and producers to record the writer's music.

4. Secure synch licenses for film, TV, and commercials; negotiate favorable rates when licensing uses of the copyrights.

5. Search out ancillary uses of those copyrights, such as jingles and merchandising tie-ins.

Acquiring New Material

The single most important enterprise of a music publisher is to locate new music and sign writers. The relentless search for new talent and new material is essential to the success of a publishing company, which cannot manufacture its own raw material. There is no shortage of new songs; the challenge for publishers is to discover talented writers among the thousands of composers who think their music is just what the market wants.

The most lucrative source of new material is from writers currently or recently hot on the charts. These writers can be as sought after as recording stars, and can pick and choose their own publishers. To persuade writers to place their new songs with them, publishers offer a variety of inducements. In fact, many successful writers change publishers frequently, ever seeking a better contract, stronger promotion, and more fruitful relationships.

A second source of good writers for publishers comes through the recommendation of those in the music business whose musical judgment appears trustworthy or whose track record in the field has been impressive. Producers, label A&R executives, and other writers are among the most frequently tapped insiders.

A third source of usable new material is writers already under contract, either on a work-made-for-hire basis or as writers paid a royalty advance in exchange for the rights to publish their output. (See Chapter 3 for more on publisher-songwriter working arrangements.) Professional managers often need to prod their own staff writers to keep turning out material for the insatiable market.

Often the recording company and publisher are seeking the same talent. Many new writers signed by publishers are potential recording artists who have not yet come to the attention of the label A&R staff. At this stage, the publisher can sign the artist or group to a publishing deal with the intent of then placing them with a label. This has two important advantages: (a) The publisher getting involved at this early stage usually pays less in advances, and (b) the artist/writer is getting some much needed money at a crucial time while establishing a relationship with an influential ally who can provide creative as well as business assistance. On the other hand, lawyers and managers usually prefer to sign an artist to a label first and then either make a bigger publishing deal for the now more valuable artist or have the artist retain the publishing, at least in the United States.

Some music publishers pride themselves on discovering raw talent and developing it, perhaps employing "song doctors" to work with young contract writers whose material may lack professional polish. Many publishers devote themselves to finding new artist/songwriters, making demos, and then "shopping" those demos in an effort to find a record deal.

Acceptance Criteria. Successful popular music publishers have developed criteria that often serve well to distinguish acceptable material. Most publishers, knowingly or intuitively, seem to judge material based on these criteria:

1. Does the demo hit you right off the bat? If the music doesn't appeal to you in the first eight bars, that demo probably will never be heard to its end.

2. What has the composer done lately? Audiences are more fickle than ever, so a publisher may have better odds going with a currently charted writer than with someone with an impressive history but no recent success.

3. Which artists might record the song? What projects are going on at the moment, and who are the right producers, managers, or other key decision makers to pitch?

4. Does the material fill a current need in the publisher's overall catalog? Most publishers seek, over a period of time, some kind of balance among the types of songs they accept. Someone might submit an attractive piece of material, but if that particular publisher is loaded with that kind of song, it may be rejected.

5. Does the material show inherent quality? Most of the decision makers in the business love music. Although they can go broke if they pander too often to their own personal tastes, many music publishers know that the best way to build a catalog of lasting value is to continue searching not just for the surface appeal of a new song but also for music that has inherent quality and might also appeal to listeners of the next generation.

Catalog Acquisitions. The purchase and sale of entire catalogs have always been common in the industry. If the firm on the block is small and headed by a successful writer or manager, the buyer may seek to contract for the ongoing services of the management team that developed the firm's early success. More often, the buyer has its own team in place and simply wants to own the copyrights. The price of an acquisition is usually based on a multiple of the average annual net publisher's share (NPS) over a 3- to 5-year period. This multiple is generally between 5 and 10, but it can be much lower—or in some cases higher—depending on the demand, the steadiness of earnings, and the remaining copyright life of the compositions being purchased. For instance, a catalog may have one hit song that made a huge amount of money in the two years prior to the acquisition, which would skew the 3- or 5-year average NPS in the seller's favor. In that case, the multiple would be significantly reduced.

When whole catalogs are bought, the seller normally assigns all rights of copyright and ownership, including subsisting contracts with writers. This means that if the first publisher has contracted with a composer to publish that composer's music for the next several years, the new publisher must honor that contract. The new publisher also, of course, assumes all obligations for payment of royalties.

Contracts With Writers

In the preceding chapter, we discussed the Songwriters Guild of America (SGA) contract, which is weighted in favor of the writer. In the past, at least, some publishers refused to sign it, insisting their writers sign a contract favoring the publisher. Although the SGA contract is a single-song agreement, it would be useful to bear in mind the issues presented in the SGA agreement when considering an exclusive-term contract between a writer and publisher.

In an ideal world, writer and publisher would work out a contract that balances the interests of both parties. The draft that follows might serve as a model for two parties coming to the table with comparable bargaining power. They give and take and just might end up with something like this draft agreement:

Assumptions

Any **consideration** of contract negotiations requires knowledge of the background of the parties and their relative bargaining strengths. In this draft contract, we make the following assumptions:

About the Writer: This is a creative person who writes both songs and instrumental pieces in the popular music genre. Prior to entering into these negotiations with our imaginary publisher, the writer enjoyed some publishing success through modest sales of recordings of music and has some music "in the trunk," compositions not yet copyrighted or published, that could be assigned to the publisher for the right kind of deal. Wanting to advance in this career, not only as a writer but also as a recording artist, the writer can be persuaded to assign copyrights in works covered by the contract to the publisher exclusively if the offer is good enough.

About the Publisher: The firm is well established and moderately successful, an ancillary operation of a parent recording company with multinational distribution. The label's publishing wing has not yet fully established its operations in foreign territories. The publisher farms out all its printed music activity. The publisher has strong faith in the potential earning power of the prospective writer and seeks the writer's exclusive services.

Draft Contract

This draft is for study purposes only. It covers the essentials of a hypothetical exclusive publishing agreement. It incorporates some of the language of the SGA Single Song agreement described in Chapter 3. We recommend that each party entering into contract negotiations retain legal counsel to recommend the actual language of any agreement.

AGREEMENT made (date) _____ by and between _____, the Writer, and _____, the Publisher

1.0. **Appointment**. The Publisher engages the Writer as a composer, lyricist, arranger, **orchestrator**, and/or music editor, and the Writer's services as a writer shall be rendered exclusively for the Publisher. Services performed under this agreement shall not be deemed to be work made for hire as defined under U.S. copyright law.

2.0. **Term**. This agreement starts on (date) _____ and ends on (date) _____.[2] The Publisher is granted options to extend this agreement, by 1-year increments of extension for additional years, but not to exceed an aggregate total of _____ years,[3] on the identical terms and conditions of the initial term. The foregoing notwithstanding, the Writer retains the option to deny these extension options unless the Publisher has obtained, directly or indirectly, _____[4] commercially released recordings of the Controlled Compositions during the time period of _____. This shall be referred to hereafter as The Recording Goal.[5]

The writer would not have the option to deny extensions of the initial term if advances had been paid and unrecouped. The same agreement could be negotiated to provide a reversion of copyright after a period of years but only if all advances have been recouped.

2.1. If the Publisher's affiliated recording company terminates the Writer's contract as a royalty artist, this Writer's contract shall be **coterminous** with that recording contract.[6]

In situations where there is an affiliated recording company, the publishing deal will often be a copublishing deal rather than the 50/50 writer-publisher split described below. Copublishing deals are explained later in this chapter.

3.0. **Assignment**. The Writer assigns to the Publisher all rights throughout the world in the compositions listed on Schedule A attached hereto (prior compositions).[7] Throughout this contract the word *composition* shall include music, words, and title. During the term of this agreement, the Writer agrees to deliver _____ songs a year.

The assignment language might require a portion of the songs delivered by the writer to be recorded on demos. This obligation of the writer is a different "recording requirement" than one the publisher might undertake elsewhere in the contract in order to demonstrate to the writer the eventual economic viability of the publishing deal.

3.1. The Writer also assigns to the Publisher all rights in the compositions created by the Writer during the term and under the conditions of this agreement. The foregoing notwithstanding, these works are offered to the Publisher on a first-refusal basis only. If the Publisher does not agree to accept them for publication and exploitation within 60 days of their being offered, the Writer reserves the right to assign them to any other publisher.

A first-refusal deal would be made only if no advances were paid. If the writer has been paid an advance by the publisher, the publisher will not allow the writer to sign with another publisher.

All works listed on Schedule A, together with all works described under 3.1 that the Publisher accepts, are referred to hereinafter as the Controlled Compositions.

4.0. **Warranty**. The Writer warrants that the Writer has the right to enter into this agreement and that the Controlled Compositions are original and that as the sole author and composer, the Writer has not paraphrased or otherwise used any other copyrighted material for them.

4.1. The Writer indemnifies the Publisher against loss or damage and attorney fees arising out of a breach of warranty, including a situation where any copyright infringement action is settled with the Writer's consent.

5.0. **Advances and Royalties.** In consideration of this agreement the Publisher agrees:

5.0-A. To pay the Writer $ _____ in twelve (12) equal monthly installments, and the receipt of the first installment is hereby acknowledged, as a nonreturnable advance against royalties, and these payments shall be deductible only from payments becoming due the Writer under this contract. Payment of such advances is dependent upon the Writer's prior delivery of the agreed-upon number of compositions, and in the event of nondelivery, Publisher shall have the right to suspend payment of advance installments hereunder.

Advances are a critical part of writer-publisher agreements. The publisher usually needs to provide a healthy enough advance for the writer to live while his works are in the initial stages of exploitation, but not so generous an amount that the publisher risks losing significant money if the advance is never recouped.

5.0-B. Subject to Paragraph 5.1 below, to pay the Writer one half of the Publisher's net receipts in the United States from all other licenses of Controlled Compositions under licenses relating to uses now known or hereafter developed.

5.1. The Writer shall not be entitled to receive any income from any performing rights organizations anywhere in the world designated as a Publisher's share nor shall the Publisher be entitled to receive any income from any performing rights organization anywhere in the world designated as a Writer's share.

5.2. The Publisher shall not grant any mechanical license at a rate lower than the prevailing statutory maximum to any individual or company with whom the Publisher has any affiliation or financial interest.[8]

If the artist has signed a recording contract that has record-contract controlled composition language, the lower mechanical rate might apply despite this prohibition in the publishing contract. The writer's attorney must reconcile this provision with that contract.

5.3. To pay the Writer 10% of the wholesale price on the sale of all printed editions in the United States and Canada.

5.4. No cross-collateralization is permitted the Publisher in respect to any royalties or other payments made to the Writer by the Publisher's affiliated recording company.

If limitations are not put on so-called cross-collateralization language, the recording company and the publishing company affiliate may treat advances under the publishing agreement as being recoupable from royalties payable from the publishing agreement and/or the recording agreement. It could even be extended to allow recoupment of recording costs and advances under the record agreement from royalties payable under the publishing agreement. This cross-collateralization is obviously extremely favorable to the publisher/record company and would be agreed to only by an artist/writer who had very little bargaining power and over the vehement protests of the artist's entertainment attorney.

5.5. Where a Controlled Composition has more than one author, the shares of royalties among them shall be apportioned in relation to the creative contributions of each Writer as these apportionments have been negotiated by the parties. The Writer will have final approval over which additional cowriters or arrangers are used.

5.6. If the Publisher engages the Writer as an arranger, orchestrator, editor, or copyist, the Writer, if a union member, will be paid the appropriate AFM union scale for such services, and such payments shall be over and above all other advances and royalties provided for in this contract and shall not be recoupable from royalties hereunder.[9]

6.0. **Foreign Rights.** Publisher shall have the right to designate subpublishers, foreign licensees, or affiliates outside the territory of the United States on such terms as the Publisher in its reasonable business judgment shall determine pursuant to **arm's length** negotiations, provided that in no event shall the percentage paid to the Publisher of income earned at the source be less than 75%.[10]

An arm's length agreement is negotiated between two unaffiliated parties acting in good faith to reach an understanding that benefits both parties. Such a stipulation would avoid the possibility of one party having an undue advantage over the other. An agreement between a parent company and its affiliate or a subsidiary company that favors the parent company at the expense of the subsidiary company is not an agreement negotiated at arm's length.

7.0. **Promotion Expense.** The Publisher shall be solely responsible for all promotion expense, including the production of audio and video demonstration tapes or discs.

The extent to which promotion expenses are recoupable is subject to negotiation. The demo costs are normally 50% recoupable.

7.1. If the ownership and copyright of any Controlled Composition should revert from the Publisher to the Writer, all demos on that composition shall also become the property of the Writer.

8.0. **Right to Audit.** The Publisher grants to the Writer the right to engage a qualified accountant to examine the Publisher's books and related financial documents, following receipt of reasonable notice. The cost of any such audit is to be borne entirely by the Writer except that if the Writer is found to be owed a sum equal to or greater than _____ %[11] of the sum shown on that royalty statement as being due the Writer, then the Publisher shall pay the entire cost of the audit, but not to exceed _____ %[12] of the amount shown to be due the Writer.

9.0. **Creative Rights.** The Publisher acknowledges that the Writer's reputation and potential income relate importantly to the originality and quality of the Controlled Compositions as well as to their use. The Writer acknowledges, however, that the Publisher has the right to make minimal changes in the compositions and has the day-to-day responsibility of determining the best way to exploit the compositions. To balance these interests of the parties in this respect, it is agreed that the Publisher has the right to do any or all of the following in this context only with the consent of the Writer:

9.0-A. Engage a lyricist to alter the Writer's lyrics materially or to write new lyrics.

9.0-B. Make substantive changes in the Writer's music.

9.0-C. Grant a synchronization license for a Controlled Composition when the usage does not comport with reasonable standards of taste and decorum, such as sexually explicit or violent content, or content offensive or demeaning to any race, class, or gender.

9.0-D. Use the Writer's likeness, photograph, or name to exploit a product or service, in respect to appropriateness and good taste, and without paying the Writer a royalty commensurate with the exploitation value.

9.0-E. License a Controlled Composition for use in connection with a broadcast commercial, print advertisement, or merchandising of a product or service.

9.0-F. Grant a Grand or Dramatic Right in connection with part of the production and performance of a Controlled Composition as a **dramatic musical** work.

Grand rights are often excluded in publishing contracts.

10.0. **Right of Assignment.** The Publisher reserves the right to assign this contract to another fully qualified publisher. The Writer consents to this right of assignment only if such assignment is part of a sale of a substantial portion of publisher assets and provided the assignee assumes all the responsibilities and obligations of the first publisher hereafter.

11.0. **Reversion.** If the Recording Goal is not reached, the Writer will grant the Publisher an extension period of six (6) months beyond the initial term set forth under Item 2.0 of this contract. If, by the end of the extension period, the Recording Goal has still not been reached, and if no advances have been paid by the Publisher to the Writer, or if paid, recouped or repaid to the Publisher, all rights in any Controlled Composition not released or recorded revert to the Writer.

12.0. **Default, Cure.** If either the Publisher or the Writer asserts that the other party is in default or breach of this contract, the aggrieved party shall provide written notice setting forth the nature of the default or breach. The accused party is then allowed 30 days to cure the alleged default, during which period no default or other grievances shall be deemed incurable.

13.0. **Arbitration.** The parties agree to submit all disputes to the American Arbitration Association and be bound by and perform any award rendered in such **arbitration.**

_____ Publisher _____ Writer

_____ Date _____ Date

County of _____ State of _____

Split Publishing, Copublishing

Nowadays many songs on the pop charts are copublished by two or more publishers. In reality, nearly all these **split publishing** deals are simply a number of persons or firms agreeing to share the publishing income, not the publishing responsibilities.

In a traditional arrangement, publishing money is divided equally between the artist/songwriter and the publisher; that is, the artist/songwriter gets 50% of the publishing income and the publisher gets the other 50%. In this case, the publisher usually owns all of the copyright.

If an artist who already has a record deal signs a publishing agreement, the publisher is often willing to give half of its publishing income and half of the copyright ownership to the artist/songwriter. In one kind of common copublishing deal, the parties are co-owners of the copyright, and the artist/songwriter receives 75% of the income (the writer's 50% plus 50% of the publisher's share). The administration of the copyright remains with the publisher.

When ownership of a copyright is split, administration of the property can be difficult. Where coauthors are involved, ASCAP, BMI, and SESAC will honor directions from the co-owners to divide performance royalties among the writers and publishers involved. With respect to mechanical royalties and synchronization fees, the Harry Fox Agency is accustomed to splitting monies in accordance with instructions it receives from **copyright proprietors.**

Joint administration of copyright requires specific contractual arrangements for sharing of synchronization fees. **Synchronization rights** apply worldwide, but differences of opinion prevail on how income from this source should be shared. In the past, most publishers have believed it equitable to attribute 50% of synchronization fee income to the United States and the balance to foreign sources. Administration of copyrights outside this country should be assigned entirely to one co-owner or the other, because sharing of the responsibility can lead to confusion and lack of control. This is particularly important because in some foreign countries a unilateral commitment by one co-owner may be binding on the other.

Where a work has two authors, and two publishers split the copyright, one writer's share comes from one publisher, the other writer's share from the other publisher. Unless otherwise provided in a joint administration agreement, mechanical royalties will be equally divided by the two publishers, and each publisher will then be able to pay its writer.

Sometimes the copyright proprietor does not split ownership. Instead, the copyright owner may offer someone an income participation or **cut-in** from the copyright. If a new artist/writer lacks the funds to rent a preferred studio or to hire a favored producer, the artist/writer may offer a cut-in to the studio or producer in place of, or in addition to, payment up front. Under controlled circumstances, the cut-in can be fair and work even better than joint administration; a single administration is generally preferable to one that is shared. But a cut-in agreement should specify certain limitations: It should be limited to payments on mechanicals derived from a particular record by a specified artist for a finite period. If a work is recorded but never commercially released, the cut-in deal should be automatically voided or the proprietorship and copyright income should return to the original owner.

In yet another kind of cut-in, some songwriters or publishers agree to add the name of a prominent recording artist to a song in exchange for the artist's recording the song.

Copyright Protection: Sampling

As new technologies come on the scene, new concerns about copyright protection inevitably arise. For example, anyone who has access to the appropriate technical equipment can easily make perfect digital copies of an entire recording or simply sample part of a song. Since copyrights are the lifeblood of music publishers, policing their use is a key business issue.

The word *sampling* is used in two different but related ways:

1. **Sampling** is the basis for how digital sound recording works. Imagine a 1-second visual event. If you were to take four evenly spaced photographs of that event, you would have specific details of how that event unfolded over time. If you were to take 40 photos, you could sequence them in your hand like a child's flip-picture book and see the event unfold as though it were happening, but you could stop it at any moment and examine any detailed point in the event. That is how digital audio recording works: Each second of a sound recording is "sampled" at a specific rate, known as the "sampling rate." More simply, sampling is the process by which the amplitude and frequency of some sound waves are measured and reproduced. The higher the sampling rate (the greater the number of samples taken), the truer the reproduction.

2. In the music business, the meaning of the term sampling has been broad-ened to include the digital copying of portions of existing recordings for use in other recordings. Anyone who's listened to a rap song has experienced this. The **new use** may be instantly recognizable to the listener, or it may be changed or altered to such an extent that it is very unlike the original.

No matter how previously recorded sounds are used, permission to sample must be sought from the publisher and the recording company of the original recording.

If music is sampled without the permission of the publisher and recording com-pany, the sampler is infringing the copyrights in the original work and in the sound recording. The sampler is then subject to various penalties, including payment of actual or statutory damages, impoundment of recordings, and an injunction against further release of the infringing recording.

Revenue from sampling has become a significant part of the earning power of many copyrights. The legitimate use of a sample can take the form of one-time, flat-fee licenses, royalty participation in the new recording and/or the new underly-ing composition (i.e., the copyright of the song), or a combination; there are no set standards. However, unauthorized use of samples in new recordings is even costlier when lawsuits ensue, and countless ones have. The clearance of sampled portions of recordings for use in other recordings has become a lucrative legal and administra-tive subsector of the music industry, one attributable largely to digital technology.

Promotion, Advertising

Popular Music

The main concern of a publisher of popular songs is getting music recorded and broadcast. Although the promotion methods discussed here are ultimately meant to encourage the public to consume more music, much of the promotion process is initially aimed at professionals who are already in the music business. Publishers generally persuade artists and record producers to record their music through direct, personal contacts. Even though the publishing and recording industries are huge, much of the power and control are in the hands of a relatively small number of insiders, including major recording artists, record producers, established writers, and important managers.[13]

Song Casting. A critical function of a publisher is to attempt to match songs with performers. Creative departments and staff analyze songs carefully and search out recording artists they believe have a performing style that matches the material. This is often called song casting; it is as crucial as casting a TV show or Broadway play. This matching of artist to repertoire used to be the principal concern of staff record producers—hence their appellation, **A&R producers**. Those who do this well are scarce, in high demand, and well paid.

One of the largest popular music publishers has said that the song-casting pro-cess often works in reverse for prestigious publishers: Recording producers will contact the publisher, listing their current needs, and ask the publisher to supply material the publisher believes right for a particular recording project. A publisher enjoying this kind of prestige has an edge with producers and artists who believe the firm has good casting judgment and strong material.

Experienced publishers understand that, at the outset, only a select number of recording artists will even consider their material because so many acts in popular music are *self-contained*—the individual performer or group uses only its own material. Rarely do self-contained acts accept outside songs.

Cover Records. The publisher who has a self-contained act under contract understands, or should understand, that once the material is initially recorded by that act, the publisher's job has only begun. A traditional major concern is getting cover records—inducing other artists to record the song. Whatever the size of a publisher's catalog, the long-range income of the firm is tied in part to the number of quality covers generated over the years.

Given the unending need for potential hit material, it might be assumed that getting cover records is relatively easy, but nothing could be further from the truth. In addition to the difficulty of getting self-contained artists to record covers, many acts who are open to cover material tend to make their own decisions about which songs they will record. In fact, as record sales have slowed and revenue from synch performances has increased, many publishers now devote only minimal time and energy to pursuing covers.

Because online sites have widened the opportunities for consumers to purchase one song at a time, song promoters seeking covers generally limit the material they submit to songs they believe might make it as singles. Most recording artists already have available, from their own hands or from insiders and friends, all the album-cut material they believe they can use. Of course, no one can consistently predict which songs will be hit singles, but the most talented publishers, especially in the country area, often have very good track records.

Another aspect of publisher promotion is offering services directly to recording companies, who share some of their economic interests. One manifestation of this is cooperative promotion campaigns for new material, frequently in connection with personal appearances of recording artists.

Digital Promotion. Electronic or digital exploitation has become a key promotional vehicle and income source for publishers. Record companies can promote, license, and sell CDs or enable downloading of music directly via the Internet, and independent labels and individual artists are able to bypass the major distribution companies to promote and distribute their own product. The National Music Publishers' Association (NMPA), the Recording Industry Association of America (RIAA), and other trade associations are trying to keep up with the technology by establishing sophisticated systems to monitor and administer digital music distribution and to compensate music owners for use of their music.

The Internet and other forms of digital delivery, such as cell phone ringtones, enhance the global market for publishers' catalogs, greatly increasing access to worldwide music and new genres that might remain unheard if dependent on the more traditional record company promotion. The Internet has thus created a more level playing field for artists trying to break into the music business.

Synchronization Promotion. As we noted earlier in this chapter, film, TV, and commercial synchs are bringing in a greater share of publishers' revenues than ever before, as much as doubling the percentage in the span of a few years. Large and mid-sized publishers have "synch experts" who pitch material to **music supervisors** and ad agencies. Smaller publishers may retain independent promoters to pitch their catalogs, generally paying these firms a monthly retainer and a percentage of synch revenues.

Educational Field

Publishers promote printed music intended for student and school use in several ways. The first is via direct mail campaigns. Music educators receive promotional mailings on a regular basis. Along with recordings of arrangements, printed samples of new releases are included in these mailings in the form of thematics—short samples of themes from complete works. The educator, when "sold" by such mailings, places an order through a store or by telephone, fax, mail, or the Internet.

A second promotional avenue involves publishers placing display advertisements in music education journals such as *Music Educators Journal*, the *Instrumentalist*, and *Down Beat.*

A unique promotional device used in the educational and church fields is the reading clinic. A large retailer or an educational group will cohost daylong readings of new publications. Educators attend these readings (school ensembles are commonly used) and subsequently place orders with their dealers to cover their needs for the school or church year.

In a very significant development, publishers are turning more and more to the Internet to promote their products. E-mail blasts, promotion on the Web sites of sheet music and songbook aggregators and retailers, and direct promotion on publishers' own Web sites are among the tools that have become commonplace.

Classical Field

Publishers of chamber music, art songs, operas, and ballets have their own ways of acquainting potential buyers with their music. Unlike the pop and educational fields that focus on new music, classical music publishers are usually engaged in reminding customers of, rather than promoting, the great music of the past. They periodically enliven their catalogs with new compositions and arrangements, but the bulk of their sales come from reprints and new editions of the classics.

New serious works of any length are rarely printed, because anticipated sales most often cannot produce enough money to cover costs of production. In lieu of direct sales, large-scale works such as new operas, ballets, and symphonic pieces are made available through rental of the scores and parts for performance and recording. With regard to dramatic musical works, publishers often get additional income by charging performance fees. Dramatic works by major contemporary composers can produce fairly good income for both publishers and writers.

Classical music is also promoted through display ads placed in music journals. A large part of the classical and semiclassical repertoire spills over into the educational field, and most publishers sell to schools and colleges either the original scores or parts or arrangements scored specifically for school use.

Income Sources

Publishing revenues continue to thrive because they are generated from so many diverse sources. The most important ones are shown in Table 4.2. The rise of new distribution technology has led to the shrinking of the revenue pie slice representing traditional mechanical royalties, as illustrated in Figure 4.3. Over the long term, one of the all-time money earners is probably the Broadway musical. If we were to aggregate the income of a dramatic musical work such as *South Pacific* or *A Chorus Line*—including **grand rights**, performance income of hits from the show, print rights, movie rights, mechanical royalties—these receipts would probably exceed all the money generated by the stage production at the box office. Not all publishers own these kinds of multimillion-dollar properties, but standards of lesser value and current hits are in demand for tie-ins for such diverse uses as computer software, cell phone ringtones, musical greeting cards, apparel, posters, and stationery. Licensing fees, individually considered, for uses of this kind will rarely be high, but when aggregated, money from these ancillary sources can generate a respectable share of a publisher's annual income.

Except where a **compulsory license** is involved (see Chapter 5), a publisher has the option of granting permissions-to-use either on a royalty basis (a percentage of sales) or for a one-time flat fee.

Table 4.2 Publisher's Potential Income Sources

Type of Music Use	Who Pays the Publisher
Broadcast performance (TV, radio, cable, Internet)	Publisher's performing rights organization, which collects from the broadcasters
Nonbroadcast performances (clubs, hotels, stadiums, environmental music, in-flight music, aerobic and dance studios, etc.)	Publisher's performing rights organization, which collects from the venues where the music is played
Mechanical royalties (disc, tape, and CD sales)	Recording company
Sheet music sales	Publisher's print music licensee
Synchronization of music (to films, videos, Internet, DVD, and computer games)	Movie, video, or game producers
Special permissions, licenses (merchandising deals such as musical greeting cards, toys and dolls, lyrics used in books and magazines, cell phone ringtones, etc.)	Publisher's licensee
Jukeboxes	Publisher's performing rights organization
Dramatic (or grand rights)	Producer of the dramatic performance
Foreign rights	Subpublishers, licensees abroad; reciprocating performing rights organizations (through ASCAP, BMI, and SESAC)

Figure 4.3   Publishing's Diverse Revenue Streams: Percent of Revenue by Type

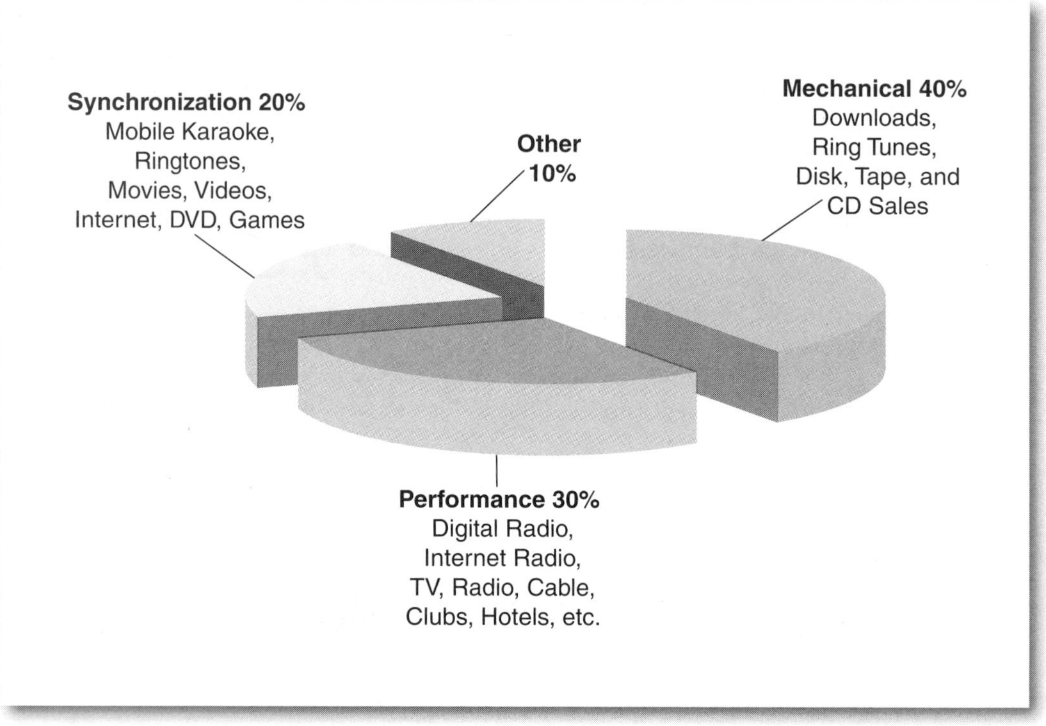

Synchronization 20%
Mobile Karaoke,
Ringtones,
Movies, Videos,
Internet, DVD, Games

Other
10%

Mechanical 40%
Downloads,
Ring Tunes,
Disk, Tape, and
CD Sales

Performance 30%
Digital Radio,
Internet Radio,
TV, Radio, Cable,
Clubs, Hotels, etc.

Source: EMI Music Publishing financial results, London, 2008.

Note: Not all publishers classify revenue sources the same way.

Trade Associations

National Music Publishers' Association

The trade association most representative of publishers in the popular music field is the National Music Publishers' Association (NMPA). The NMPA performs important services for thousands of American publishers through its licensing subsidiary, The Harry Fox Agency, which provides licensing services for its music publishing principals.

The NMPA is deeply immersed in the process of providing leadership for the music publishing/songwriting community and in helping to formulate policy regarding copyright infringement, the protection of copyrights in an age of advancing technology, and the payment of royalties for electronic delivery of music throughout the world.

Today, the NMPA/Harry Fox Agency licenses a large percentage of the uses of music in the United States on records, tapes, CDs, and imported **phonorecords,** as well as for new technology applications.

The Harry Fox Agency, Inc.

The NMPA established The Harry Fox Agency, Inc., in 1927 to provide an information source, clearinghouse, and monitoring service for licensing musical copyrights.

The Harry Fox Agency provides the following services in the United States on behalf of its publisher principals:

1. Mechanical Licensing: The licensing of copyrighted musical compositions for use on commercial CDs, records, and tapes.

2. Digital Licensing: The licensing of copyrighted musical compositions for use on the Internet as on-demand streaming and/or limited downloads with subscription-based services, among other applications. It also issues specialized ringtone licenses, and licenses for digital background music services.

3. Royalty Compliance: The periodic review and tracking of the books and records of licensees using copyrighted musical compositions based on the license issued, as well as the identification of unlicensed product.

4. Royalty Collection and Distribution: The collection of royalties from licensees using copyrighted musical compositions, and the distribution of these royalties to publishers.

The Harry Fox Agency does not act in the area of licensing public performance, grand and dramatic rights, print rights, and derivative uses (music arrangements). It discontinued synchronization licensing services in 2002. Further information on how the agency functions is found in Chapter 6.

Association of Independent Music Publishers

The Association of Independent Music Publishers (AIMP) was formed in 1977 by a group of Los Angeles music publishers and now has chapters in both Los Angeles and New York. The organization's primary focus is to educate and inform local music publishers about industry trends and practices via monthly meetings, forums, and workshops. The AIMP includes in its membership not only independent music publishers, but also publishers that are affiliated with record labels or motion picture and television production companies, as well as individuals from other areas of the entertainment community, such as songwriters, artist managers, and members of the legal and accounting professions.

Notes

1. Because certain foreign societies—Germany's GEMA, for instance—will not pay mechanical royalties directly to an American publisher, it is important in some countries to have a subpublisher or be affiliated with The Harry Fox Agency, which can collect these monies in most territories.

2. This kind of exclusive-term contract in earlier times was often limited to 1 year. Now, however, even enterprising publishers are often unable to develop acceptance of a composition in the first year of a contract.

3. In California, a contract for personal services cannot normally be enforced for a period longer than 7 years. Five-year-term contracts are probably the most common today, whatever statutory limitations might prevail.

4. The SGA contract allows the publisher 1 year to obtain a commercially released recording of the particular song under contract, unless the publisher pays the writer a sum of money to "buy" 6 additional months' time to attain that goal. Failing this, all rights to the song revert to the writer.

5. A reasonable "recording goal" might be getting recording deals for half the Controlled Compositions. See 11.0 for the consequences if the recording goal is not reached.

6. Although coterminous contracts are often inadvisable for the writer, in this instance the writer would want to be released from the publishing contract to be free to negotiate a new publishing deal with another recording company.

7. This list would probably include all the works the writer had in the trunk prior to signing this contract that had not been previously published or otherwise encumbered by prior commitment. Some lawyers recommend their clients grant only administrative rights to a writer's available works composed prior to a term contract.

8. This clause prevents the publisher from offering anyone a "sweetheart" deal and helps guard against the three-fourths statutory rate commonly found in controlled compositions clauses in artist recording contracts.

9. If the income of the writer under this contract fails to aggregate a reasonable amount, the contract may not be enforceable in some states in that the publisher has the writer completely tied up as exclusive writing "property," thus denying the writer the opportunity of finding additional outside writing income. California law makes personal service agreements unenforceable if the artist or writer has failed to achieve a certain minimum level of income from entertainment contracts.

10. The parent contract is left open-ended here to provide the parties an opportunity to remain flexible in response to rapidly changing foreign markets. Although the parties might agree on a worldwide 50–50 split of income, equity might be better served by negotiating deals territory by territory.

11. The SGA contract calls for 5% here. Between 10% and 15% might be reasonable, at least from the publisher's point of view.

12. The SGA contract calls for 50% here.

13. Publishers therefore employ promotion personnel who have strong relationships with these insiders—the power brokers—and who understand their needs, will keep track of market trends and changing tastes, and deliver the right material. This fact has been mitigated somewhat by the rise of the DIY (do-it-yourself) phenomenon made possible by technological advances that greatly reduce the cost of recording one's own music.

Chapter Takeaways

- In the early part of the 20th century music publishers were the most powerful people in the music industry—shaping tastes and reaping substantial revenues from printing sheet music.

- Today the heart of the music publishing business is exploiting rights in songs through mechanical, performance, and synchronization royalties and fees.

- Publishers range in size from multinational giants affiliated with large labels, to medium-size independent companies, to in-your-hat operations run by songwriters who want to control all forms of exploitation.

- Print publishing is a profitable niche business, but is less important than revenues from other forms of exploitation.

- Though there can be advantages in having one party administer exploitation of a copyright, it is commonplace for publishing royalties to be divided between one or more composers and one or more lyricists.

- Subpublishers in foreign territories help the original publisher (and songwriter) maximize royalties from overseas sources.

Key Terms

- at-source deal   (p. 57)
- bench pack   (p. 55)
- copublishing   (p. 68)
- cross-collateralize   (p. 66)
- cut-in   (p. 69)
- drop ship   (p. 60)

- grand rights   (p. 73)
- mechanicals   (p. 69)
- NPS   (p. 63)
- print licensee   (p. 56)
- sampling   (p. 69)
- self-contained act   (p. 71)

- songplugging   (p. 54)
- split publishing   (p. 68)
- subpublisher   (p. 51)
- subsisting copyright   (p. 59)

CHAPTER 5

Music Copyright

Every serious student of copyright should acquire a complete copy of the Copyright Act, together with other special publications and bulletins relating to copyright. In addition to the act, Circular 1 (Copyright Basics), and Circular 50 (Copyright Registration for Musical Compositions) are especially useful. These documents are available on the Copyright Office Web site at www.copyright.gov. The Copyright Office Public Information Office number is (202) 707–3000. If legal advice or other expert assistance is required, the services of a competent professional should be sought.

> "Music is spiritual.
> The music business
> is not."
> —Van Morrison

Background

A fundamental principle of American law is that an author of a work may reap the fruits of that work for a limited period of time. Copyright is a form of protection provided by the laws of the United States for works of literature, music, and other forms of creativity. Copyright literally means "the right to copy." The term has come to mean that body of exclusive rights granted by law to authors for protection of their work. Article I, Section 8 of the Constitution gives Congress the power to enact laws

Left: Congressman Sonny Bono. The singer-songwriter had a major change in copyright law named after him months after his death in 1998.

establishing a system of copyright in the United States, and Congress enacted the first U.S. copyright law in 1790. Comprehensive revisions were enacted in 1831, 1870, and 1909, and the current Copyright Act, enacted by Congress in 1976 (U.S. Code, Title 17, Copyrights), became generally effective on January 1, 1978.

As we've seen in previous chapters, copyright issues have an enormous effect on many of the essential components of the music business, including the writing, publishing, recording and/or performance of songs and other musical material. While no work can be automatically copyrighted worldwide, two international treaties have brought cooperation from countries on copyright matters. The United States became a party to the Universal Copyright Convention in 1955 and to the Berne Convention in 1989, both of which have greatly enhanced the protection of its copyrights internationally (see Chapter 30).

From the outset, the goal of Congress was to seek a balance of interests between copyright owners and users.[1] This search for fairness took place under the watchful eye and with the vigorous participation of a number of special interest groups representing the motion picture, music, radio, and TV industries as well as educators, librarians, the cable industry, and other public interest groups. When ultimately enacting the 1976 Copyright Act, Congress stated its intent that the implementation of the law "would minimize any disruptive impact on the structure of the industries involved and on generally prevailing industry practices."[2]

The 1976 act has been interpreted in widely varying ways by the different courts, and it is useful to remember that copyright law involves not only examining the "letter of the law" but also developing persuasive *interpretations* of the statute. Copyright law has also evolved through new statutes written by Congress and through interpretations by the courts in previous cases (legal precedent). The ultimate authority in all matters relating to copyright law is, of course, the U.S. Constitution.

To explore the broader landscape of copyright law, it is necessary to first become familiar with the law's basic terms and provisions.

Essential Provisions

Following are seven essential provisions of the 1976 act and subsequent amendments:

1. The statute preempts nearly all other copyright laws—both statutory and **common law.** Therefore, only the federal Copyright Act can provide protection for most types of works. One notable exception is pre-1972 sound recordings, which are still protected under state law.

2. The duration of copyright has been lengthened over the years, and now conforms closely to practices prevailing throughout most of the rest of the world: generally, life of the author plus 70 years.

3. For years following the 1976 act, performance royalties were not paid to copyright owners of sound recordings. The first crack in that longstanding principle occurred in the 1990s and involved initiating royalties for performances by digital transmission. However, musical works (the underlying song and lyrics) routinely earn performance royalties for broadcasts and live performances, in addition to digital transmissions.

4. Public broadcasters, cable systems, and jukebox operators were compelled to begin paying for the use of copyrighted music, as were schools and colleges. As a by-product of accession to the Berne Convention in 1989, the law was later amended to provide for **negotiated licenses** between jukebox operators and music copyright owners (through performing rights organizations) rather than statutorily mandated **compulsory licenses**.

5. Congress codified the principles previously enunciated in case law as to what constitutes the "fair use defense" to otherwise infringing activity. Four discrete factors (detailed later in this chapter) are to be considered by the courts in determining the applicability of the fair use defense, and courts may also look to other factors as appropriate to a particular case.

6. Policies and rates of music use licenses were to be periodically reexamined.

7. Some formal procedures, such as copyright notice and renewal, were treated more permissively, and others were eliminated.

Key Terms

An understanding of copyright depends on awareness of how the current law defines its terms. Most of the definitions that follow are quoted directly from Section 101 of the Copyright Act. (Language not relating to music has been deleted.)

"Audiovisual works" are works that consist of a series of related images intended to be shown via projectors, viewers, or electronic equipment, together with accompanying sounds, if any.

The **"best edition"** of a work is the edition, published in the United States at any time before the date of deposit, that the Library of Congress determines to be the most suitable for its purposes.

A **"collective work"** is a work, such as a periodical issue, anthology, or encyclopedia, in which a number of contributions, constituting separate and independent works in themselves, are assembled into a collective whole.

A **"compilation"** is a work formed by the collection and assembling of preexisting materials selected, coordinated, or arranged in such a way that the resulting work as a whole constitutes an original work of authorship. A compilation can also be a collective work.

"Copies" are material objects, other than phonorecords, in which a work is fixed, and from which the work can be perceived, reproduced, or otherwise communicated, either directly or with the aid of a machine or device.

"Copyright owner [proprietor]," with respect to any one of the exclusive rights comprised in a copyright, refers to the owner of that particular right.

A work is **"created"** when it is fixed in a copy or phonorecord for the first time; where a work is prepared over a period of time, the portion that has been fixed at any particular time constitutes the work as of that time, and where the work has been prepared in different versions, each version constitutes a separate work.

A **"derivative work"** is a work based on one or more preexisting works, such as a musical arrangement, dramatization, fictionalization, motion picture version, sound recording, or any other form in which a work may be recast, transformed, or adapted. A work consisting of editorial revisions, annotations, elaborations, or other modifications that, as a whole, represent an original work of authorship is a derivative work.

A **"device," "machine,"** or **"process"** is one now known or later developed.

A **"digital phonorecord delivery"**[3] is a delivery of the content of a phonorecord by digital transmission which results in an identifiable reproduction by any recipient, whether via a public performance of the recording or a nondramatic musical work. This does not include real-time subscription transmission of a recording where no reproduction is made.

To **"display"** a work means to show a copy of it, either directly or by means of a film, slide, television image, or any other device or process or, in the case of a motion picture or other audiovisual work, to show individual images nonsequentially.

An **"establishment"** is a store, shop, or any similar place of business open to the general public in which the majority of its nonresidential space is used for the primary purpose of selling goods or services, and in which nondramatic musical works are performed publicly.

A work is **"fixed"** in a tangible medium of expression when its embodiment in a copy or phonorecord, by or under the authority of the author, is sufficiently permanent or stable to permit it to be perceived, reproduced, or otherwise communicated for a period of more than transitory duration. A work consisting of sounds, images, or both that are being transmitted is "fixed" for purposes of this title if a fixation of the work is being made simultaneously with its transmission.

A **"food service or drinking establishment"** is a restaurant, inn, bar, tavern, or any other similar place of business in which the public or patrons assemble for the primary purpose of being served food or drink in which the majority of the gross square feet of space that is nonresidential is used for that purpose and in which nondramatic musical works are performed publicly.

To **"perform"** a work means to recite, render, play, dance, or act it, either directly or by means of any device or process,. or in the case of a motion picture or other audiovisual work, to show its images or to make the sounds accompanying it audible.

"Phonorecords" are material objects in which sounds, other than those accompanying a motion picture or other audiovisual work, are fixed by any method now known or later developed, and from which the sounds can be perceived, reproduced, or otherwise communicated, either directly or with the aid of a machine or device. The term phonorecord applies to the material object, such as a CD, in which the sounds are fixed.

A **"pseudonymous work"** is a work of which the author is identified under a fictitious name.

"Publication" is the distribution of copies or phonorecords of a work to the public by sale or other transfer of ownership, or by rental, lease, or lending.

Publication is also the *offering* to distribute copies or phonorecords to a group of persons for purposes of further distribution, public performance, or public display, although a public performance or display of a work does not constitute publication.

To perform or display a work **"publicly"** means:

1. To perform or display it at a place open to the public or at any place where a substantial number of persons outside of a normal circle of a family and its social acquaintances are gathered; or

2. To transmit or otherwise communicate a performance or display of the work to a place specified by clause (1) or to the public, by means of any device or process, whether the members of the public capable of receiving the performance or display receive it in the same place or in separate places and at the same time or at different times.

"Registration" means a registration of a claim in the original or the renewed and extended term of copyright.

"Sound recordings" are works that result from the fixation of a series of musical, spoken, or other sounds, but not including the sounds accompanying a motion picture or other audiovisual work, regardless of the nature of the material objects, such as discs, tapes, or other phonorecords, in which they are embodied.

A **"transfer of copyright ownership"** is any conveyance, such as an assignment or license, of the exclusive rights comprised in a copyright, whether or not it is limited in time or place of effect, but not including a nonexclusive license.

A **"transmission program"** is a body of material that has been produced for the sole purpose of transmission to the public in sequence and as a unit.

To **"transmit"** a performance or display is to communicate it by any device or process whereby images or sounds are received beyond the place from which they are sent.

A **"work made for hire"** is (a) a work prepared by an employee within the scope of his or her employment; or (b) a work specially ordered or commissioned for use as a contribution to a collective work, as a part of a motion picture or other audiovisual work, as a translation, as a supplementary work, as a compilation, as an instructional text, as a test, as answer material for a test, or as an atlas, if the parties agree in writing that the work shall be considered a work made for hire. A "supplementary work" is one prepared for publication as a secondary adjunct to a work by another author for the purpose of introducing, concluding, illustrating, explaining, revising, commenting upon, or assisting in the use of the other work, such as a musical arrangement.

Coverage

A key principle of copyright is that its protection does not extend to ideas themselves, but only to the expression of those ideas. For example, no one can copyright the idea of "reggae music," but a particular expression of that genre (say, a reggae song by Ziggy Marley) may be protected. The fact that no one can copyright an idea itself (the beat, the general concepts defining the genre, etc.) allows the normal development of musical forms, which always includes elements borrowed from other sources. It is the unauthorized exploitation of a particular artist's expression of an idea that is prohibited.

Copyright protection is granted to original works of authorship. As noted above, such works must be "fixed in any tangible medium of expression, from which they can be perceived, reproduced, or otherwise communicated, either directly or with the aid of a machine or device." Works of authorship include the following categories:[4]

- Literary works
- Musical works, including any accompanying words
- Dramatic works, including any accompanying music
- Pantomimes and choreographic works
- Pictorial, graphic, and sculptural works
- Motion pictures and other audiovisual works
- Sound recordings
- Architectural works

The works listed above are subject to protection under the law even if unpublished, without regard to the nationality or domicile of the author.

Copyright protection can also cover compilations and derivative works, but this protection does not extend to any part of a compilation or derivative work in which such material has been used unlawfully. Also, copyright in compilations and derivative works extends only to the material contributed by the author of such work (as distinguished from the preexisting material employed in the work) and does not imply any exclusive right in the preexisting material. The copyright in compilations and derivative works is independent of and does not affect or enlarge the scope, duration, ownership, or subsistence of any copyright protection in the preexisting material.

Copyright does not extend to publications of the U.S. government. An individual may reproduce or quote from such publications without concern for copyright infringement.

Exclusive Rights

Section 106 of the Copyright Act specifies six distinct exclusive rights vested in the author of a protected work. Subject to certain limitations,[5] the act states that the owner of copyright has the exclusive right to do and to authorize any of the following:

(1) to reproduce the copyrighted work in copies or phonorecords;

(2) to prepare derivative works based upon the copyrighted work;

(3) to distribute copies or phonorecords of the copyrighted work to the public by sale or other transfer of ownership, or by rental, lease, or lending;

(4) in the case of literary, musical, dramatic, and choreographic works, pantomimes, and motion pictures and other audiovisual works, to perform the copyrighted work publicly;

(5) in the case of literary, musical, dramatic, and choreographic works, panto-mimes, and pictorial, graphic, or sculptural works, including the individual images of a motion picture or other audiovisual work, to display the copyrighted work publicly; and

(6) in the case of sound recordings, to perform the copyrighted work publicly by means of a digital audio transmission.

These are often referred to as the **bundle of rights.**

Fair Use of Copyrighted Material

In passing the current legislation, Congress attempted to reconcile the rightful interests of the copyright owners with the legitimate, nonprofit interests of individuals, schools, libraries, religious houses of worship, and noncommercial broadcasters in using copyrighted material. Much of the act, particularly Sections 107 through 112, concerns the limitations of the bundle of rights.

Since the 19th century, the courts have held that certain uses of copyrighted material are "fair," within reason, and not an infringement or materially damaging to a copyright owner. This tradition was largely validated and codified in the 1976 law, which offers examples of what constitutes fair use.[6]

The fair use of a copyrighted work, including such use by reproduction in copies or phonorecords, or by any other means specified by Section 106 of the law, for purposes such as criticism, comment, news reporting, teaching (including multiple copies for classroom use), scholarship, or research, "is not an infringement of copyright." In determining whether the use made of a work in any particular case is a fair use, four criteria have been established by prior court actions and are incorporated in the new law:

1. The purpose or character of the use, including whether such use is of a commercial nature or is for nonprofit educational purposes

2. The nature of the copyrighted work

3. The amount and substantiality of the portion used in relation to the copyrighted work as a whole

4. The effect of the use on the potential market for or value of the copyrighted work

The **fair use doctrine,** a legal defense to a copyright infringement claim, essentially allows minimal takings of copyrighted material for purposes such as scholarship, research, and news reporting. However, any substantial taking is likely to be looked upon by the court as an infringement.

Some analysts point out a potential conflict between broad First Amendment free speech rights and the more limited fair use doctrine of copyright law. Although copyright law provides an incentive for authorship, some critics say it gives creators monopoly rights that may conflict with public interest in the dissemination of information. A counterargument runs that copyright protection extending only to the expression of ideas (as opposed to the ideas themselves) allows free speech to flourish. In addition to fair use, which requires a case-by-case analysis, the law also identifies certain kinds of performances that are always considered to be exceptions to the copyright owner's exclusive rights. These performances are not infringements:[7]

1. The performance or display of a work by instructors or pupils in the course of face-to-face teaching activities of a nonprofit educational institution

2. Performance of a nondramatic literary or musical work, display of a work, by or in the course of a transmission, if

   a. the performance or display is a regular part of the systematic instructional activities of a governmental body or a nonprofit educational institution

   b. the performance or display is directly related and of material assistance to the teaching content of the transmission

   c. the transmission is made primarily for reception in classrooms or similar places devoted to instruction

3. Performance of a nondramatic literary or musical work or of a **dramatico-musical** work of a religious nature in the course of religious services

4. Performance of a nondramatic literary or musical work (otherwise than in a transmission to the public) without any direct or indirect purpose of commercial advantage and without payment of any fee or other compensation for the performance to any of its performers, promoters, or organizers, if

   a. there is no direct or indirect admission charge; or

   b. the proceeds, after deducting reasonable costs of production, are used exclusively for educational, religious, or charitable purposes and not for private financial gain

5. Communication by an establishment of a transmission or retransmission embodying a performance or display of a nondramatic musical work intended to be received by the general public, originated by a radio or television broadcast station, or, if an audiovisual transmission, by a cable system or satellite carrier, if that establishment contains less than 3,750 gross square feet, or, for those establishments containing more than 3,750 gross square feet, if (1) their audio use is via six or fewer speakers with not more than four in any one room, or (2) their audio/visual use is via not more than four TVs, of which no more than one TV is in any room unless a direct charge is made to see or hear the transmission, or the transmission thus received is further transmitted to the public. Those non–food service and beverage establishments that contain more than 2,000 gross square feet must meet the requirements of (1) and (2) above in order to be exempt.

6. Performance of a nondramatic musical work by a vending establishment where the sole purpose of the performance is to promote the retail sale of copies or phonorecords of the work or of the devices used in performing the work

Copyright Ownership

Copyright ownership vests initially and exclusively in the author of the work,[8] and includes the six exclusive rights under copyright (the bundle of rights enumerated earlier).

Where there are multiple authors, ownership of the copyright is shared. In the popular song field, it is customary for the composer(s) of the music to share ownership equally with the lyricist(s). Multiple authors may, however, set up, through a written agreement, disproportionate shares of ownership in a work in which they collaborated. Examples:

Composers' Share (50%)	Lyricists' Share (50%)
Example 1. One composer and one lyricist, sharing equally:	
One composer: owns 50%	One lyricist: owns 50%
Example 2. Two composers splitting their share equally, three lyricists dividing their share unequally:	
First composer: owns 25%	First lyricist: owns 25%
Second composer: owns 25%	Second lyricist: owns 15%
	Third lyricist: owns 10%

Ownership Limitation

Ownership of copyright, or any of the exclusive rights under a copyright, is distinct from ownership of any material object in which the work may be embodied, such as sheet music, discs, or tapes. Transfer of ownership of any such material object does not convey any rights in the embodied copyrighted work. For example, the ownership of the physical master tapes on which a song is recorded does not carry with it any ownership of copyright in the underlying song (see First Sale Doctrine below).

Collective Works

Copyright in each separate contribution to a collective work (such as an album of songs) is distinct from copyright in the collective work as a whole and vests initially in the author of the contribution. In the absence of an express transfer of the copyright, the owner of the copyright in the collective work is presumed to have acquired only the privilege of reproducing and distributing the contribution as part of that particular collective work, any revision of that collective work, and any later collective work in the same series.

Film Music

Copyright in music, and accompanying words, written for theatrical films and TV movies is often covered by the overriding copyright in the movie itself as an audiovisual work; however, additional copyrights may preexist for music a film producer licenses for inclusion in this production. In this kind of situation, the two copyrights coexist. The film producer would be required to obtain a synchronization license for use of the preexisting copyrighted music. But even in this situation, the complete audiovisual work—the movie itself—could still be protected by a blanket copyright covering its particular combination of component parts.

Transfer or Assignment

Although all six exclusive rights of authorship vest initially in the author(s) of a work, the law states that any or all of these rights may be transferred or assigned to other persons. As a matter of fact, most original copyright owners find it necessary to transfer or assign some or all of their rights in order to generate income from their properties. Some writers own their own publishing companies and record labels, but the great majority assign publishing and recording rights to others, usually through the granting of exclusive licenses (see Chapter 6). Transfers must be in writing to be effective, but nonexclusive licenses may be oral, or even implied from conduct.

The law even permits subdivisions of individual rights. As explained elsewhere, this often occurs with publishing rights, where authors "split the publishing."

Recordation of Transfer

As just noted, when copyright owners assign or grant an exclusive license for any of their copyrights, the action does not become valid until the parties (or their agents) execute a written agreement confirming the transfer. This written instrument may then be filed with the Copyright Office in accordance with procedures set by that office, although such filing is not necessary for the transfer to be effective. Filers must also pay the specified fee (the latest forms and fees are available on the Copyright Office Web site, www.copyright.gov). Following these actions, the Copyright Office issues a Certificate of Recordation.

This recordation serves to provide all persons with what lawyers call "constructive notice" of the facts stated in the Certificate of Recordation.

Occasionally, a situation arises where two transfers are in conflict. In such instances, the first transfer to be properly executed prevails (see Title 17, Section 205 for instructions for proper recordation).

Termination or Recapture

In the case of any work other than a work made for hire, the exclusive or nonexclusive "grant of a transfer" or license of copyright or any right under a copyright, executed by the author on or after January 1, 1978, is subject to termination under the following essential conditions, cited in Section 203:

1. Termination of the grant may be effected at any time during a period of 5 years beginning at the end of 35 years from the date of execution of the grant; or

2. If the grant covers the right of publication of the work, the period begins at the end of 35 years from the date of publication of the work under the grant or at the end of 40 years from the date of execution of the grant, whichever term ends earlier.

3. Advance notice of intent to terminate must be in writing, signed by the number and proportion of owners of termination interests required under Section 203, or by their duly authorized agents, served upon the grantee or the grantee's successor in title. The notice shall state the effective date of the termination, which shall fall within the 5-year period specified in Section 203, and the notice shall be served not less than 2 or more than 10 years before that date. To be in effect, this notice must be recorded in the Copyright Office before the effective date of termination. An individual intending to file a

notice of termination must comply with the form, content, and manner of service prescribed by the Register of Copyrights.

4. Termination of a grant may be effected notwithstanding any agreement to the contrary, including an agreement to make a will or to make any further grant.

5. Upon the effective date of termination, all rights under this title that were covered by the terminated grant revert to the author(s).

6. Unless and until termination is effected under Section 203, the grant, if it does not provide otherwise, continues in effect for the term of copyright provided by law.

Section 203 thus establishes the outer limits of copyright assignability by providing statutory termination guidelines. In practice, however, writers and publishers may negotiate a shorter term (typically, 1 to 5 years) to balance the writer's interest in recapturing copyrights that have not been effectively "worked" by the publisher against the publisher's interest in controlling the property long enough to promote it.

In the case of any copyright subsisting in either its first or renewal term on January 1, 1978, other than a copyright in a work made for hire, the exclusive or nonexclusive grant of a transfer or license of the renewal copyright or any right under it, executed before January 1, 1978, by an author or any statutory successors, is also subject to termination.

The termination of the grant may be effected at any time during a period of 5 years beginning at the end of 75 years from the date copyright was originally secured. Termination of the grant may be effected notwithstanding any agreement to the contrary, including an agreement to make a will or to make any future grant.

Work Made for Hire

The term *work made for hire*[9] has special meaning under copyright law and is of great significance to composers, publishers, and movie producers. Whenever a composer is engaged on a work-made-for-hire basis, the employer is considered under the law as the author of any resulting creative work. And the "author," under copyright law, is the owner of the works.

In music, this arrangement was first fully developed in the 1920s and 1930s in the Tin Pan Alley days, when large publishing companies employed salaried songwriters to work in-house on a full-time basis. Songwriters today typically operate as independent contractors with much less supervision.

Occasionally, however, a music publisher will attempt to claim authorship rights in a work produced by a writer who is effectively working as an independent contractor. To protect against this kind of conflict, before signing a work-made-for-hire agreement, it's advisable to run it by an attorney.

Section 101 describes (but does not clearly define) conditions in which certain "creations" are to be considered works made for hire:

1. Work prepared by an employee within the scope of employment; or

2. Work specifically ordered or commissioned for use in one of several categories, the most relevant for composers being "as part of a motion picture or other audiovisual work." Even if the work falls into one of the defined categories, the parties must sign an agreement saying the work is made for hire.

Some disputes center on the language of the first condition. To resolve these disputes, bills are periodically introduced in Congress that attempt to clarify the meaning of "employee" by, for example, attaching social security benefits and withholding of taxes to the definition, as the courts have often required. In 1989, the Supreme Court spoke to the question of when a creative artist may be considered an employee, listing no less than 13 factors to be considered.[10] The case dealt with whether ownership of a sculpture rested with the sculptor or the group that commissioned its creation. Although the original court decision found for the organization, that decision was reversed on appeal and the Supreme Court affirmed the reversal, **finding** the sculptor to be the owner of copyright in the commissioned work.

Musical Arrangements

Copyright law provides that the original holder of the copyright has the exclusive right "to prepare derivative works based upon the copyrighted work." Because musical arrangements are usually considered derivative (or supplementary) works, arrangers must obtain permission of the copyright owner before scoring their own version of the material. In practice, this permission is sought and granted only under particular circumstances, especially when the proposed arrangement might substantially alter or distort the original. But music publishers are usually delighted that anyone is interested in recording one of their songs and welcome the potential exposure and income from a **cover record.** Most publishers issue a negotiated **mechanical license** (see Chapter 6) to record one of their properties. Implicit in this license is the understanding that the record producer may create a new arrangement consisting of minor changes that will suit the style of the recording artist. Copyright law provides that when a compulsory (mechanical) license is issued, that license "includes the privilege of making a musical arrangement of the work to the extent necessary to conform it to the style or manner of interpretation of the performance involved" for the recording. This industry practice is not so much a specific permission to create such an arrangement as it is a tacit agreement by the publisher not to raise any objection to it.

With respect to arrangements made primarily for educational use, many publishers give their approval by accepting the standard form, Request for Permission to Arrange, which states that the publisher owns the arrangement made and limits its use.

Arrangers' Rights

The role of the music arranger is often as creative as that of the original composer of the song. Arrangers usually create work for hire, receiving a flat, one-time fee based on the American Federation of Musicians (AFM) scale for "orchestration," or negotiating whatever the traffic will bear. Except for work on music in the public domain—when the underlying work is not owned or controlled by anyone— arrangers who work under such agreements generally enjoy no rights of copyright ownership and receive no royalties from record sales, nor do they share in income generated for composers and publishers from licensing of performances of their arrangements.

Public Domain

A different condition prevails when an arranger creates an original chart of a work in the **public domain**. The arranger's publisher of such material may demand and receive mechanical royalties from producers of recordings, then usually splits one half of such receipts with the arranger. In respect to performance income, ASCAP, BMI, and SESAC are accustomed to paying (often reduced) royalties to authors and publishers of arrangements based on works in the public domain. Arrangers of works in the public domain may also receive royalties from their publisher's sale of printed editions.

Arrangers are accorded more privileges in some European countries, where they are not always required to secure publishers' approval to render new arrangements of copyrighted material. Furthermore, arrangers are often accorded parallel rights, which provide a share of royalties derived from mechanical licensing and performances of their charts.

Sound Recordings

As noted at the beginning of this chapter, a potentially confusing aspect of the 1976 Copyright Act and subsequent amendments is that a musical work (the underlying song with lyrics) is categorically differentiated from a sound recording. The recording company typically holds the copyright in the sound recording, while the publishing company, which sometimes is a division of the same company, holds the copyright in the musical work.

The owner of a sound recording, under Section 114, has these exclusive rights:

1. To reproduce the copyrighted work to duplicate the sound recording in the form of phonorecords (or copies of motion pictures and other audiovisual works). Note that this right is limited to duplicating the actual sounds fixed in the recording.

2. To prepare derivative works based on the copyrighted material—to make and distribute phonorecords that are new arrangements or versions of the copyrighted work (sound recording).

3. To distribute phonorecords to the public by sale or other transfer of ownership, or by rental, lease, or lending, or by digital phonorecord delivery (downloading).

4. To perform by digital audio transmission.

Performance Right Exclusion

The 1976 law specifically excluded **performance rights** in sound recordings, and owners of sound recordings still do not enjoy the level of protection and relative economic return common in many other parts of the world, including more than 50 Western countries. From the standpoint of the music industry, progress in chipping away at this longstanding U.S. regulatory bulwark has been slow and patchy. It took years for the Recording Industry Association of America (RIAA) to achieve a partial victory when Congress passed The Digital Performance Right In Sound Recording Act (DPRA) in 1995, which provided to copyright holders in sound recordings the exclusive right "to perform the copyrighted work publicly by means of a digital audio transmission." This allowed record companies to collect a royalty on digital performances of the sound recording on digital cable and satellite television, the Internet, and satellite radio.

Except for this narrowly defined right, owners of sound recordings for many years did not receive performance royalties when music from these recordings was broadcast or otherwise performed. Congressional sparring over this policy has illuminated a long-standing battle between the intellectual property community (including labels and artists) and users of creative works (notably broadcasters).[11]

Imitation Exclusion

The exclusive rights of the owner of copyright in a sound recording with respect to the preparation and reproduction of derivative works do not extend to the making or duplicating of another sound recording that consists entirely of an independent fixation of other sounds, even though such sounds imitate or simulate those in the copyrighted sound recording. In other words, imitations that mimic the original recording are legally permissible, but the imitative recording cannot simply be a recorded copy of the original. Furthermore, it is not legal to market the mimicked recordings as if they feature the original artists or in any way that might confuse the public about who performed the song.

Compulsory Mechanical License

One of the most important copyright provisions concerns the conditions under which a person is permitted to produce and distribute phonorecords of nondramatic musical works. The law provides that copyright owners of nondramatic music have complete control over recording rights of their properties until they license the material for the first recording. But after this first recording is distributed to the public, they are compelled by law to license any other person to produce and distribute recordings of the copyrighted music in exchange for a fixed statutory royalty, which is adjusted periodically. This provision stems in part from an important goal in copyright law: the increased dissemination of works to the public.

According to Section 115, copyrighted songs become "subject to compulsory licensing" after they have been released on record for the first time. This kind of licensing requires special conditions, the most important of which are:

1. "A person may obtain a compulsory license only if the primary purpose in making phonorecords is to distribute them to the public for private use, including by means of a digital phonorecord delivery." This sentence is very significant and clearly excludes from compulsory licensing all recordings that are generally classified under the term **transcriptions.** In the music field, the term transcriptions is not applied to phonorecords intended for purchase and use by the public but to recordings sold for special uses, such as theme music for broadcast programs or wired music services such as Muzak.

2. "A person may not obtain a compulsory license for use of the work in the making of phonorecords duplicating a sound recording fixed by another, unless (i) such sound recording was fixed lawfully; and (ii) the making of the phonorecords was authorized by the owner of copyright in the sound

recording or, if the sound recording was fixed before February 15, 1972 [the date when sound recordings first became subjects of statutory copyright protection in this country], by any person who fixed the sound recording pursuant to an express license . . . for use of such work in a sound recording." (The purpose of this provision was to prevent pirates and counterfeiters from availing themselves of the compulsory license.)

3. "A compulsory license includes the privilege of making a musical arrangement of the work to the extent necessary to conform it to the style or manner of interpretation of the performance involved." But the law also states that the arranger shall not change the basic melody or fundamental character of the work. Furthermore, the new arrangement shall not be subject to protection as a derivative work, except with the express consent of the copyright owner.

4. The person planning to obtain a compulsory license must notify the copyright proprietor of this intention before or within 30 days after making, and before distributing, any phonorecords of the work. If the person cannot locate the owner of the work, "it shall be sufficient to file notice of intention in the Copyright Office." Failure to serve or file notice forecloses the possibility of a compulsory license and, in the absence of a negotiated license, renders the making and distribution of phonorecords actionable as acts of infringement.

Compulsory License Bypass

Compulsory mechanical license provisions in the copyright statute are so stringent, particularly in respect to notice and accounting requirements, that the industry typically uses an alternative, the negotiated mechanical license. This alternative kind of license is permitted by law and is explained in Chapter 6.

Royalty Payments (Section 115[c])

After permitting the initial recording of a song, publishers are limited as a practical matter by the statute as to what royalty rate they may charge record makers. The statutory rate provided in the 1976 act was "2.75 cents, or one-half of one cent per minute of playing time or fraction thereof, whichever amount is larger" for each work embodied in a phonorecord. By 2004, this "statutory rate" increased to 8.5 cents or 1.65 cents per minute, whichever amount is larger, and continues to rise periodically. The rates for 2006, for example, rose to 9.1 cents or 1.75 cents per minute.

To be entitled to receive royalty payments under a compulsory license, the copyright owner must be identified in the registration or other public records of the Copyright Office. The owner is entitled to royalties for phonorecords made and distributed after being so identified but is not entitled to recover for any phonorecords previously made and distributed.

Except as provided above, the royalty under a compulsory license shall be payable for every phonorecord made and distributed in accordance with the license. "For this purpose, . . . a phonorecord is considered 'distributed' if the person exercising the compulsory license has voluntarily and permanently parted with its possession." This language helps reduce the ambiguity prevalent until 1978 relative to liability for royalty payments. It appears that the manufacturer is not liable for royalty payments on records returned to it that have not been sold, for such records did not leave the manufacturer's possession permanently, as the law provides. "Giveaways" such as free goods and promotional copies do, however, trigger royalty payments, as the definition doesn't require a sale.

Duration of Copyright

Copyright protection obtained prior to enactment of the 1976 act could last no more than a total of 56 years: a 28-year initial term, followed by an optional 28-year renewal term. Under section 302 of the Copyright Act, this was changed so that copyright in a work created on or after January 1, 1978, was to last for 50 years from the author's death. But that did not settle the matter.

In 1998, the Sonny Bono Copyright Term Extension Act (named after singer-turned-congressman Sonny Bono) added 20 years to the term of protection of works protected by copyright. A song that had previously been protected for the life of the author plus 50 years was protected after 1998 for the life of the author plus 70 years. Works for hire receive even longer protection (see Table 5.1).

Table 5.1   Duration of Copyright Term After Sonny Bono Act

Date of Work	When Protection Attaches	Term of Protection
Created in 1978 or later	Upon fixation	Unitary term of life + 70 (or if anonymous or pseudonymous or work for hire, 95 years from publication or 120 years from creation, whichever is shorter)
Published[a] or registered 1964–1978	Upon registration or publication with notice	95 years (28 + automatic 67-year renewal)
Published or registered 1923–1963	Upon registration or publication with notice	28 years + 67 years renewal term, if renewal was made before end of first term
Published or registered before 1923	Upon registration or publication with notice	Work is now in the public domain; although term of protection is now at 85 years for works covered in the 1909 act, works made from 1922 and earlier were already public domain in 1998 when Sonny Bono Act was passed, and the act does not revive them. Thus, status cannot be determined simply by counting back 95 years from present date.
Created but never published before 1978	Upon creation	Unitary term of at least life + 70; earliest possible expiration is 12/31/2002, if work remains unpublished. If work is published prior to 12/31/2002, earliest possible expiration is 12/31/2047.

Source: Adapted by Robert Clarida, Partner, Cowan, Liebowitz, and Latman, from chart on p. 275 of Latman, A., Gorman, R. & Ginsburg, J. (1989). *Copyright for the Nineties.* Charlottesville, VA: Michie.

[a]To start the term running, the publication must be authorized by the copyright owner. An unauthorized publication, even with notice, has no legal effect.

Subsisting Copyrights in Their First Term on January 1, 1978 (Section 304)

Copyrights still in their first terms continue, under the 1976 law, for their original 28 years. At the expiration of the original term of copyright, the copyright shall endure for a renewed and extended further term of 67 years

1. if the application to register a claim to such further term has been made to the Copyright Office within 1 year before the expiration of the original term of copyright, and the claim is registered, shall vest in the proprietor of the copyright who is entitled to claim the renewal of copyright at the time the application is made; or

2. if no such application is made or the claim is not registered, shall vest, upon the beginning of such further term, in the person or entity that was the proprietor of the copyright as of the last day of the original term of copyright.

Renewal Registration

As the result of a 1992 renewal amendment to the Copyright Act, there is no longer a requirement to register a renewal of a pre-1978 copyright during the 28th year to keep the work from falling into the public domain. It is, however, advisable to make such renewal registration to enhance the enforceability of the copyright during its renewed and extended term. Renewal registration will also determine who has the right to use derivative works prepared under a grant of a transfer or license made before the expiration of the original term.

Subsisting Copyrights in Their Renewal Term

As Congress stated, the 1976 law creates an entirely new property right in the renewal term. The 1909 law provided a maximum of only 56 years of protection for pre-1978 works, which was later extended to 75 years by the original 1976 act. The current law provides, for these works, a total of 95 years of protection. The significant monetary value of many popular songs written before 1978—which have come to be known as "standards"—gives authors and publishers a strong incentive to establish claims on the additional 20 years of protection to which they are entitled.

After 75 Years

Properties whose 75-year protection would otherwise expire under the original 1976 act are, under the new amendments, automatically granted copyright protection for a total of 95 years. If a writer wants to recapture a composition from a publisher to whom the renewal term has been assigned, the writer may, within a 5-year period following the original 75-year protection, terminate the grant of renewal term to the publisher by serving a notice of termination. This notice of termination must be given to the publisher not less than 2 years or more than 10 years ahead of the termination date decided on by the author. Once an author has thus reclaimed the publisher-owned renewal copyright, ownership by the author is free and clear. Failure to exercise the option to terminate within the 5-year period will permit a copyright to remain with the publisher to the end of the renewal period.

After January 1, 1978

Copyright protection in works created on or after January 1, 1978, extends to a work from its creation and, except as provided under certain conditions, endures for a term consisting of the life of the author and 70 years after the author's death.

Joint Works. Where two or more authors prepared a joint work (and did not do the work for hire), they enjoy copyright for a term consisting of the life of the last surviving author and 70 years after such surviving author's death.

Work Made for Hire. In a work made for hire, copyright exists for 95 years from the date of its first publication, or a term of 120 years from the year of its creation, whichever expires first. Works made for hire are not included in the provisions concerning termination of grants for the 20-year extension period.

Works in the Trunk (Section 303)

Copyright in a work created before January 1, 1978, but not theretofore in the public domain or copyrighted, subsists from January 1, 1978, and endures for the life of the author and 70 years after the author's (or last surviving coauthor's) death. "In no case, however, shall the term of copyright in such a work expire before December, 2002; and, if the work is published on or before December 31, 2002, the term of copyright shall not expire before December 31, 2047."[12]

In summary, songwriters generally leave the task of taking care of renewals and terminations to their publishers, attorneys or administrators. But it's not infrequent that these representatives fail to act in a timely manner, resulting in headaches and lost income. Songwriters should therefore keep track of their copyrights as a check against such outcomes.

Formalities

The term *formalities* is used around the world in reference to the specific actions a claimant must take to validate claim to copyright.[13] These formalities include notice of copyright, deposit of copies, and registration of claim to copyright. The 1976 law is permissive in respect to some kinds of mistakes in following through on formalities. After March 1, 1989 (the effective date the United States joined the Berne Convention), these formalities for U.S. works became almost entirely optional. But to be on the safe side, claimants should put a proper notice on copyrighted material (see below).

Notice on Printed Music

The term "notice of copyright" refers to the public display of information concerning the date the work was published and who registered the claim. On printed editions, the law stipulates:

1. Notice may be placed on all publicly distributed copies. The notice imprinted should be the symbol © or the word *Copyright* or the abbreviation *Copr.* and the year of first publication of the work. The type of notice most often seen is this:

   © 2010 John Doe

Although not required by the Copyright Act, the language "All Rights Reserved" should also accompany the statutory notice to provide additional protection in some foreign countries under the Pan-American Convention.

2. In the case of compilations or derivative works incorporating previously published material, the year of the first publication of the compilation or derivative work is sufficient.

3. The notice must also include the name of the copyright owner. A recognizable abbreviation of the owner's name may be used.

4. The position of the notice shall be affixed to the copies so as to give reasonable notice of the claim to copyright.

Notice on Phonorecords (Section 402)

Whenever a sound recording protected under the 1976 law is published in the United States or elsewhere by authority of the copyright owner, a notice may be placed on all publicly distributed phonorecords of the sound recording. It is still prudent to do this. The form of the notice consists of three elements:

1. The symbol ℗

2. The year of the first publication of the sound recording, and

3. The name of the owner of the copyright in the sound recording. A recognizable abbreviation may be used. If the producer of the sound recording is named on the phonorecord labels or containers, and if no other name appears in conjunction with the notice, the producer's name shall be considered a part of the notice.

Position of Notice. The notice shall be placed on the surface of the phonorecord, or on the phonorecord label or container, in such a manner and location as to give reasonable notice of the claim to copyright. A typical notice for a phonorecord is:

℗ 2010 Smith Records

Audiovisual works do not require the symbol ℗ but rather the symbol ©, because they are not phonorecords.

Notice Errors or Omissions

For works first published between January 1, 1978, and March 1, 1989, as detailed in Sections 401, 402, and 403, omission of notice from copies or phonorecords does not invalidate the copyright in a work (Section 405) under any of the following conditions:

1. The notice has been omitted from no more than a relatively small number of copies or phonorecords distributed to the public.

2. Registration for the work has been made before or is made within 5 years after the publication without notice, and a reasonable effort is made to add notice to all copies or phonorecords that are distributed to the public in the United States after omission has been discovered.

3. The notice has been omitted in violation of an express requirement in writing that, as a condition of the copyright owner's authorization of the public distribution of copies or phonorecords, they bear the prescribed notice.[14]

Deposit (Section 407)

Deposit of works in the Library of Congress and registration of works are separate formalities. Neither action is a condition of copyright, yet both are important. With respect to published copies, Section 407 states that the copyright owner (or the publisher) must deposit, within three months after the date of publication, two complete copies of "the best edition" of the work. The deposit for sound recordings shall include two complete phonorecords of the best edition, together with any printed material or other visually perceptible material published with such phonorecords. Under the Berne Convention, notice of copyright is no longer required in deposit copies.

Under certain conditions, deposits made prior to any attempt to register the work may be used to satisfy the deposit requirements called for when the author (or the publisher) undertakes to register the work. If the author desires to have the initial deposit satisfy the deposit requirements specified on the registration forms, a letter must be enclosed with the initial deposit specifically directing the Library of Congress to hold those deposits for later connection with the author's registration application. If such a letter is not enclosed, the Copyright Office will require separate, additional deposits of a work, as specified on the registration form.

Congress has authorized modifications of deposit requirements from time to time, at the discretion of the Copyright Office. Although failure to deposit copies or phonorecords according to current regulations does not actually endanger the copyright, the Register of Copyrights does have the authority to demand copies and impose fines of up to $250 per work on laggards, and levy additional fines up to $2,500 for willful and repeated refusal to comply.

Registration (Section 408)

Although deposits and registration are referred to in the law as "separate formalities" and a deposit can be made independently of registration, it is important to note that registration of a claim to copyright must be accompanied by the deposit specified on the application form. The law also states that registration "is not a condition of copyright." But registration is strongly advised because, under certain conditions, an author's work left unregistered lacks certain advantages the work would otherwise enjoy. Most important, a work must be registered before the copyright owner can sue anyone for infringement.

A work may be registered at any time during the term of the copyright, whether it is published or unpublished. The registration may generally be made by the author as copyright owner or the publisher, as exclusive licensee.

The acceptance of sound recordings, not just sheet music, in claims to copyright the underlying music was a significant advance over the 1909 law. In the popular music field, many songwriters lack the ability to render their material in music notation. Now all they have to do is make a simple recording and submit it in lieu of sheet music. The acceptance of sound recordings also provides important advantages to persons desiring to copyright jazz improvisations, many of which are not easily transcribed into conventional music notation.

If the Register of Copyrights determines that all legal and formal requirements have been met, a certificate of registration will be sent to the applicant. If the claim is found invalid, the Register will refuse registration and notify the applicant in writing of the reasons for such refusal. (The Copyright Office has formulated an appeal procedure for applicants whose claims have been found invalid.) The effective date of copyright registration is the day on which an application, deposit, and fee have all been received in the Copyright Office.

If the author or the author's publisher made a mistake in an original registration of claim, or if either party wants to modify it, the Register of Copyright has established procedures and set fees to accommodate these matters.

Fees (Section 708)

The Copyright Office charges fees for certain services, such as registration of claims and recordation of transfers. For current rates, contact the Copyright Office, Library of Congress, Washington, D.C. 20559, or consult the Copyright Office Web site, www.copyright.gov.

Copyright Royalty Board

The 1976 Copyright Act provided for the establishment of an instrumentality of the Congress to serve that legislative body in matters concerning copyright. That instrumentality was the Copyright Royalty Tribunal (CRT). The CRT set and periodically adjusted compulsory royalty rates and held hearings to determine whether rates and royalty distribution were fair and equitable.

The CRT was abolished in 1993 and replaced with ad hoc Copyright Arbitration Royalty Panels (**CARP**s) administered by the Librarian of Congress and the Copyright Office. CARPs were phased out beginning in 2005, when the Copyright Royalty and Distribution Act of 2004 replaced them with the Copyright Royalty Board (**CRB**). CRB comprises three Copyright Royalty Judges who determine rates and terms for copyright **statutory licenses** and make determinations on distribution of statutory license royalties collected by the United States Copyright Office of the Library of Congress. Royalties within its jurisdiction include:

- cable and satellite retransmission,
- digital performance and phonorecord delivery,
- mechanicals, and
- educational broadcasting.

Infringement, Remedy

Copyright infringement is widespread, most of it going unnoticed and unpunished. Where infringement is "innocent" and of little or no financial consequence, courts may limit assessment of statutory damages (see below) to as little as $200. Where a library or school is involved with an infringement arising out of a lack of full understanding of the law, sometimes no damages at all are awarded.

Remedies. When infringements are not innocent offenses, the following remedies are available following a successful court action:

1. Injunction: A temporary or final injunction can be sought from any court having jurisdiction to prevent or restrain infringement of copyright.

2. Impoundment: The court may order impoundment of articles alleged to be involved with infringement. The impoundment can hold pending court determination of the merits of the claim of infringement. Impoundment could include printed copies, phonorecords, masters, even duplicating, manufacturing, and packaging equipment.

3. Destruction: The court could order, as part of a final judgment, destruction of inventories, such as printed copies and phonorecords.

4. Damages:

   a. The infringer is liable, except as the law otherwise provides, for (1) actual damages suffered by the copyright owner as a result of the infringement; and (2) any additional profits gained by the infringer as a result of acts of infringement.

   b. The copyright owner may elect, before final judgment is rendered, to seek statutory damages instead of actual damages and profits for all infringements in a sum not less than $750 or more than $30,000, "as the court considers just."

   c. In a case where the copyright owner sustains the burden of proving, and the court finds "that infringement was committed willfully, the court at its discretion may increase the award of statutory damages to a sum of not more than $150,000." Lesser awards are made where the court finds the infringer was not aware and had no reason to believe the actions constituted infringement, and even in cases of willful infringement, a statutory damage award is not supposed to provide a windfall for the copyright owner.

   d. Costs and attorneys' fees may be recovered by the prevailing party, at the court's discretion. At today's legal rates, this amount is usually substantial.

   e. Copyright owners may choose to sue for actual damages or statutory damages and may change to the latter course at any time before final judgment of the court. Successful artists with significant dollars at risk will often seek actual damages; multimillion-dollar cases are not uncommon.

Neither statutory damages nor attorneys' fees can be awarded, however, if the copyright was not registered before the infringement began. This is the most important reason to register copyright in a work before making it available to potential infringers, whether within the music industry or the public at large.

Record Counterfeiting, Penalties

The 1976 law imposed strong penalties for counterfeit use of the copyright symbol on phonorecords. Owners of copyrights in sound recordings complained that the threat of fines and imprisonment were not adequate deterrents. Violators seemed to view threatened sanctions simply as "the cost of doing business." Subsequently, Congress strengthened the penalties by passing the Piracy and Counterfeit Act of 1982. This law made both piracy and counterfeiting a felony. Among its other provisions, the 1982 law provided a maximum penalty of a $250,000 fine along with jail terms. A person would receive this maximum penalty if found guilty of illegally manufacturing or distributing within a 180-day period at least 10 copies or phonorecords or one or more copyrighted works with a retail value of more than $2,500.

The trend in the United States and abroad is toward increasing penalties for copyright infringers.

Changing Laws

Laws governing copyright have never been able to keep fully abreast of changes in the way music is produced, communicated, bought, and sold. This time lag is most damaging to copyright owners when it comes to matters of counterfeiting, home taping, direct satellite transmissions, or other alternative distribution via the Internet, cable, or cellular technology.

As technological change thrusts new issues into the spotlight, two economic coalitions traditionally line up against each other, trying to persuade Congress and the courts to rule in their favor. On one side is the creative community: authors, composers, filmmakers, and those who hold copyrights on their creations—publishers, recording companies, movie producers, and so on. On the opposite side are the users of copyrighted properties: broadcasters, hardware manufacturers, software merchants, and the consumer, who is understandably reluctant to pay for music uses and the royalties that may be demanded.

First Sale Doctrine

The principle of "first sale" was carried over from the 1909 statute to the 1976 copyright law (Section 109[a]). Simply stated, the first sale principle provides that the copyright owner is entitled to compensation for the first sale of the copy or phonorecord embodying the copyrighted work. Thereafter, the owner of the physical copy may dispose of it or transfer it as the owner sees fit, with only a few exceptions. This provision, developed to facilitate dissemination of creative works, prevents copyright holders from exercising control (other than control over duplicating) over the product once it has left the distributors. This doctrine became the legal basis for the video software rental business.

The Audio Home Recording Act of 1992 (AHRA)

In 1992, Congress enacted the Audio Home Recording Act, which amended the 1976 Copyright Act by allowing home audio taping and by implementing a royalty payment system and a serial copy management system for digital audio recordings. As a direct result of the passage of this act, home taping is no longer an infringement of copyright, and certain additional copyright infringement actions were prohibited.

The Digital Performance Right in Sound Recording Act of 1995 (DPRA)

As detailed earlier in this chapter, the DPRA, after years of fierce negotiations, gave record companies the exclusive right "to perform the copyrighted work publicly by means of a digital audio transmission," paving the way for them to collect audio-only digital performance royalties from digital cable and satellite television, Internet, and satellite radio providers.

The Digital Millennium Copyright Act of 1998 (DMCA)

Congress further explicated and extended the reach of copyright law by adopting the Digital Millennium Copyright Act of 1998. A key provision of the act requires that "Webcasters"—such as Internet radio stations and Webcasting services—pay licensing fees to record companies. It also criminalizes production and dissemination of technology, devices, or services intended to circumvent measures that control access to copyrighted works. This is commonly known as Digital Rights Management (DRM). (In certain circumstances, exemptions from anti-circumvention provisions are provided for nonprofit libraries, archives, and educational institutions.) The law also generally limits Internet service providers (ISPs) from copyright infringement liability for simply transmitting information over the Internet. However, ISPs are expected to remove material from users' Web sites that appears to constitute copyright infringement. In addition, the DMCA heightens the penalties for copyright infringement on the Internet.

Rights in Names and Trademarks

Rights in trade names and trademarks are not covered under copyright law in the United States, but such rights are related. Company names and professional names of performers cannot be protected under copyright law but are covered under a broader branch of law concerning unfair competition. In some states, it is a criminal offense to infringe on someone else's name or mark. (For more information, see the Federal Lanham Act, U.S. Code, Title 15.)

Individuals seeking federal registration of a name or mark must apply to the U.S. Patent and Trademark Office. Before proceeding, write to the Government Printing Office in Washington, D.C. (www.gpo.gov) for the pamphlet *General Information Concerning Trademarks,* and consult the Trademark Office Web site at www.uspto .gov. Table 5.2 provides a summary of information regarding trademarks, copyrights, and patents.

Selection of a Name

A new performing group should select its professional name with care to avoid duplication and possible confusion with another group using the same, or similar, name. Because most performing groups will have to register their professional names as "fictitious," they may discover at their own county and state government levels if any other group in that geographic area has already registered the same name or a similar one (for details, see Chapter 26, "Starting Your Own Business"). To confirm the uniqueness of the group's name on a national level, the group should inquire of organizations such as artists' unions, ASCAP, BMI, and SESAC. Libraries often have publications such as Index to the Trademark Register that can be consulted, as can the USPTO Web site. In addition, the group's attorney can provide the names of firms specializing in searches of this kind and can offer guidance on time restrictions for any filing that might be required under the Trademark Act.

Rights in a Name

Performing groups should, at the very outset, draw up a written agreement that explicitly states who owns the professional name, how the ownership is shared, and

Table 5.2 Summary Table Comparing Trademarks, Copyrights, and Patents

	Trademarks	*Copyrights*	*Patents*
Nature	Commercial identifications of source such as words, designs, slogans, symbols, trade dress	Original literary and artistic expressions such as books, paintings, music, records, plays, movies, software	New and useful inventions and configurations of useful articles
Scope	Protects against creating a likelihood of confusion or diluting a famous mark	Protects against unauthorized use or copying	Excludes others from making, using, offering for sale or selling the invention in the U.S. or by importation into the U.S.
Purpose	Protects owners and public from unfair competition	Encourages and rewards creative expression	Encourages and rewards innovation
How to obtain rights	Use mark in commerce or apply for federal registration	Create work and fix it in tangible form. Registration confirms rights	Apply for federal grant
Principal advantages of registration	Nationwide priority rights; possibly conclusive evidence of validity and ownership; U.S. Customs recordation; increased anti-counterfeiting remedies	Statutory damages and attorney's fees; prima facie evidence of validity; U.S. Customs recordation	Protection for nonsecret inventions
Basis for registration	(1) Bona fide intention to use in commerce followed by actual use; (2) non-U.S. owner's country of origin registration or application filed within 6 months prior to U.S. application, or extension to U.S. of international registration, plus bona fide intention to use in commerce; or (3) actual use in commerce	Originality	Novelty, unobviousness, utility
Notice requirements	Optional. "TM" or "SM" if unregistered; "®" or "Reg. U.S. Pat. & Tm. Off." if registered	Optional after March 1, 1989. © or "Copyright" with year of first publication and name of owner	Optional. "Patent applied for" or "Pat. Pending" after application; "Patent" or "Pat." plus registration number after grant
Term of rights	As long as used; registrations must be maintained by filing use declaration before each 6th and 10th anniversary; renewal required every 10 years	Creations after January 1, 1978: author's lifetime plus 70 years, or if anonymous or work made for hire, earlier of 95 years from publication or 120 years from creation	20 years from filing date (or sometimes 17 years from grant) for utility or plant patents, subject to periodic maintenance fees; 14 years from registration for design patents

(Continued)

Table 5.2 (Continued)

	Trademarks	*Copyrights*	*Patents*
Infringement prerequisites	Registration optional	Registration required for U.S. nationals; optional for foreign nationals	Issued patent required
Infringement standard	Likelihood of confusion, mistake or deception as to source or sponsorship; or dilution by blurring or tarnishment	Unauthorized use or copying (access plus substantial similarity)	Unauthorized manufacture, use, sale, or offer for sale of devices or processes embodying the invention
International protection	(1) Individual countries; (2) Community Trade Mark registration; or (3) Madrid Protocol centralized filing	Usually protected without registration through international treaties	Usually granted on a country-by-country basis with centralized filing available under the Patent Cooperation Treaty or European Patent Convention

Note: This summary is highly simplified and should be used only for a general comparison. A printed brochure including visual samples is available by snail mail. Please call (212) 790-9290 or e-mail info@cll.com © 2003 Cowan, Liebowitz & Latman, P.C.

under what circumstances shares of ownership end or are modified when individual performers join or leave the group. Signing a basic agreement of this kind should help the artists avoid the kinds of costly lawsuits that have hurt less organized groups.

A Final Note on Law

Just as knowing how the law protects you is vital to success in the music business, so is an understanding of when the law will not protect you. Copyright protection extends to "expressions" but not "ideas." Anyone who is considering entering the recording and publishing part of the music and entertainment industry should be familiar with the Copyright Act, the Lanham Act, and issues of unfair competition, rights of privacy, and First Amendment issues relating to free speech. Contract law provides for additional remedies in many circumstances. No matter how well you may understand the law, however, court delays and attorneys' fees may effectively prevent access to a judicial decision on your issue.

Notes

1. 1976 Copyright Act, Chapter 8. Section references throughout this chapter are from the 1976 act, unless otherwise noted.
2. 1976 Copyright Act, Chapter 8.
3. This definition from Section 115(d).
4. Section 102.
5. As laid out in sections 107 through 122.
6. Section 107.

7. Section 110.

8. Section 201.

9. Section 201(b).

10. Community for Creative Non-violence v. Reid, 490 U.S. 730, 109 S.Ct. 2166, 104 L.Ed.2d 811 (1989).

11. At this writing Congress is once again attempting to establish a broad-based performance right in sound recordings that would require broadcasters to pay royalties to labels and artists. Many previous such attempts have failed.

12. Section 303(a).

13. Chapter 4 of the 1976 Copyright Act.

14. For pre-Berne Convention works (prior to March 1, 1989), an error in the date appearing in the copyright notice does not invalidate the copyright. For example, when the year in the notice is earlier than the year in which the publication first occurred, any period computed from the year of first publication under Section 302 is to be computed from the year of the notice; or when the year is more than 1 year later than the year in which the publication first occurred, the work is considered to have been published without any notice and is governed by the provisions of Section 405.

Chapter Takeaways

- Beginning with the first U.S. copyright law of 1790, Congress has sought to balance the conflicting interests of creators with the rights of users of intellectual property.

- A bedrock principle is that copyright does not to extend to ideas themselves, but only to new specific expressions of ideas fixed in a tangible medium such as sheet music or sound recordings.

- With some exceptions, new copyrights remain in effect for the life of the author plus 70 years.

- The bundle of rights reserved to authors regarding their works generally include the exclusive right to reproduce, prepare derivations, distribute copies, perform, and display.

- Congress and the courts permit "fair use" of copyrighted works, particularly for some limited educational, nonprofit and scholarly activity.

- The copyright in a song (music and lyrics) is categorically different than a copyright of the recoding of the song—with different rights and benefits accruing through these distinct types of works.

- Copyrighted sound recordings typically do not generate performance royalties for exploitation in most media, such as radio and TV.

- By paying a compulsory license fee, anyone may make a cover record of a work that has been legitimately released.

Key Terms

- audiovisual work (p. 81)
- best edition (p. 81)
- Certificate of Recordation (p. 88)
- collective work (p. 81)
- compilation (p. 81)
- compulsory license (p. 92)
- copyright owner (proprietor) (p. 81)

- derivative work (p. 82)
- digital rights management (DRM) (p. 102)
- dramatico-musical work (p. 86)
- fair use (p. 85)
- first sale doctrine (p. 101)
- fixed (p. 82)

- formalities (p. 96)
- negotiated license (p. 81)
- phonorecord (p. 82)
- pseudonymous work (p. 82)
- public domain (p. 91)
- subsisting (p. 95)
- work made for hire (p. 89)

CHAPTER 6

Music Licensing

Music Rights: An Overview

Under U.S. copyright law, protected music generally can be used only after permission is obtained from the copyright owner. This consent is customarily given by the granting of a license, which usually involves the payment of a fee. That path from creation of copyright to collection of cash is the heartbeat of the business of music, and the *music licensing system* is a critical—and occasionally complex—part of the process.

It is also omnipresent: If you have listened to a song on the radio, hummed along to a familiar tune helping hawk a car on TV, tried to *avoid* humming along to a classic rock instrumental pumped into an elevator, plunked a couple of coins into a jukebox at a neighborhood restaurant, glared at a fellow diner whose blaring cell phone is repeating the melody of last week's chart-topper, melted to the strains of a favorite love song during a romantic movie scene, or ponied up a 20 for the film's soundtrack at the mall, you have brushed up against just a few of the many fruits of music licensing. Somewhere, money has probably changed hands before your quarters hit the slot, your hand touched the radio dial, or your movie ticket was collected; in some way, a songwriter,

"There should be a single Art Exchange in the world, to which the artist would simply send his works and be given in return as much as he needs. As it is, one has to be half a merchant on top of everything else, and how badly one goes about it!"

—Ludwig van Beethoven

Left: Ray Charles at the New Orleans Jazz Festival, 1980.

Photo © C. Fishman/Woodfin Camp/PNI.

music publisher, and/or recording artist is probably making money from the music that surrounds you every day and everywhere, whether or not you ever pay for a download or buy an album.

This is the highly lucrative world of music licensing, a system of permissions and payments keyed to copyrighted material.

What permissions are required, how *large* those payments will be, *with whom* the licenses must be negotiated, and *to whom* the license fees will be paid can vary widely depending on how the music will be used and how eager the licensee is to obtain it, among other factors. Some licensing deals are done for a flat fee, whereas others require the payment of royalties. (We told you it could be complex.) The everyday examples cited above, for instance, involve a host of different license requirements, including the big three of **performance, synchronization,** and **mechanical** (and various combinations thereof).

These and other common types of license agreements are addressed in Table 6.1 and will be explored in this chapter, but first it is important to establish a basic distinction between the two different types of *music copyright* that a music licensee might seek permission to use: the composition copyright, owned by the songwriter and/or music publisher, and the sound recording copyright, usually owned by the recording label. The former is the copyright in the song itself, encompassing the words and music; it's the © a songwriter affixes to the composition. The latter, which was established only in 1972, encompasses the actual recording of the song—the artist singing, the musicians playing, the entire production as put down on a CD or other recorded format. The label-owned recording copyright is reflected in a **master use license,** because it represents the licensee's right to use the recorded *master,* not just the song. Depending on the usage, this can take various forms, such as a master sample license or a master ringtone ("mastertone") license. This is the ℗ you'll see on your CDs.

An understanding of this distinction and its implications is crucial, because it determines the type(s) of licenses needed for various purposes. A master use license would come into play in the earlier example of the hit love song used in a movie. Use of a *preexisting recording* in a film, television show, commercial, and so on requires permission from both the music publisher *and* the record label—the appropriate © *and* ℗ owners. The music publisher will issue a synchronization license, and the record label will issue a master use license. A synchronization license gives permission for a composition to be used in synch with visual images. A master use license gives permission for a sound recording to be synched in the same manner. And here's a potential complication: For the resulting soundtrack album containing that previously released love song, the record company releasing it needs to go to the record label that owns the original recording copyright to obtain a master use license (if this was not negotiated as part of the original film license). It also needs to compensate the music publisher of the song via a mechanical license, giving the soundtrack label the right to reproduce the song in a record and sell it.

The level of permission involved in different kinds of licensing deals (in other words, the right to *refuse* to issue a license or to haggle over the terms of copyright use) is also a variable, depending on whether the licenses are designated as compulsory. Remember that mechanical licenses, as discussed in previous chapters, are *compulsory* after a song has been recorded once; that is, after the first recording, anyone can make a **cover** of a song and produce copies for sale by applying for a compulsory license and paying the statutory mechanical rate or negotiating a rate with the publisher. However, no one has the right to use copyrighted music in a movie or a commercial, for instance, without the express *permission* of the copyright holder, among others, for that particular use.

Table 6.1   Music Licenses

Type of Music Use	Type of License Required
Commercial radio broadcast of nondramatic music	Performance license and (often) transcription license
Nonbroadcast performance of nondramatic music	Performance license
Phonorecord (audiocassette, compact disc, LP)	Compulsory or negotiated mechanical license
DVR, videocassette, videodisc, AV downloads sold for private use	Negotiated synch license
Music video production used for broadcast or cable TV	Synch license by producer and performance license by broadcaster
Streaming downloads, online subscriptions	Statutory master-use performance license
Video (electronic) games	Negotiated fees
Motion picture for theatrical exhibition	Synch license that includes the right of U.S. theatrical exhibition[a]
Broadcast commercial	Performance license and, for some spots, synch license
Merchandising tie-ins, computer software applications, etc.	Negotiated fees
Business music (e.g., Muzak)	Transcription license that includes the right of performance
Dramatico-musical production (performed live)	Grand right or dramatic right
Public broadcasting station	Performance license and, for some shows, synch license
Jukebox	Negotiated license
Cable TV	Performance license and, for some shows, synch license. For digital audio channels, a compulsory performance license for recordings
Cell phone ringtone	Mechanical license if ringtone is a "mastertone," i.e., derived from the actual master recording of the song

a. Performing licenses for theaters outside the United States are often obtained by foreign performing rights organizations directly from movie theater operators. Costs of these licenses are scaled to a share of the box office receipts. ASCAP and BMI members sometimes share in this income through foreign performing rights organizations having reciprocal arrangements with ASCAP and/or BMI.

For the movie soundtrack album, that permission request would need to include information such as a royalty rate, SRLP (suggested retail list price), advance, territory, term, number of tracks, methods of sale, and release date to allow the record label that owns the recording copyright to decide if and on what terms it wants to take part in the project. (The same holds true for compilation albums.) Similarly, to obtain the synch and master use licenses for the *film's* use of the same love song, the film production company would be expected to detail in its permission requests the type of use (e.g., visual, vocal, background instrumental, instrumental), length of use (e.g., up to 30 seconds), territory (usually universal), term (length of time the resulting work will be distributed), a scene description, rights (e.g., free TV, basic cable, satellite, theatrical), and options. Recording artists, managers, and musicians unions may also be involved in these permission and payment processes for film music and soundtracks.

The permissions issue can be an especially thorny one in clearing music samples, because the copyright holders (the music publisher and record label) may insist on hearing how the sample of a preexisting recording is used in the new recording before considering the sample license request; that is, the artist has to record it before knowing if it can be used in the final recording. To clear a sample, one must send a copy of the new work to the music publisher that owns the copyright and the record label that owns the sampled track with an explanation of the proposed use. The rights requested typically cover inclusion of the song on an album and in a video, promotional uses, third-party uses (i.e., synchronization)—basically, whatever rights one would need to sell and promote the music. Once the publisher gives permission for the use, a copublishing deal can be negotiated and a mechanical license issued. Once the owner of the sound recording gives permission, a master sample use agreement can be negotiated.

The digital distribution of music online and certain types of Webcasting are two of the newer arenas where compulsory mechanical and master use performance licenses, respectively, have been established in recent years. These mandate writers and publishers to allow the use of their songs for sale as full digital downloads in exchange for payment of a statutory mechanical royalty rate; they also require labels to allow their masters to be used for Webcasting in exchange for payment of a statutory rate negotiated within the industry or decided by the Copyright Royalty Board (CRB). Webcasters must meet a set of requirements to be eligible for the statutory master-use performance license. The Digital Performance Right and Sound Recordings Act of 1995 extended the compulsory mechanical copyright license to include the digital distribution of records at the full statutory rate, i.e., no reductions due to controlled composition clauses. The Digital Millennium Copyright Act of 1998 provided a compulsory license for the Webcasting of masters.

Complicated enough for you? Fortunately, a fairly well-established and regulated system of licenses and use permits that covers most situations has evolved over the years, smoothing the process considerably. There also are a number of respected organizations whose sole focus is on issuing licenses, monitoring licensees, and collecting and distributing monies from these licenses to the appropriate copyright holders.

Performing Rights Organizations

One of the important rights granted writers under U.S. copyright law is the right to control the performance of one's compositions in public. In practice, this means that most any venue or broadcaster that exploits a copyrighted composition must obtain permission from the copyright holder in the form of a license and must generally pay a fee. (There are a few exceptions.) The largest source of income for many composers and publishers is from such licensed public performances of their music, including live concerts; broadcast over radio, TV, and the Internet; and other means of transmission.

In the United States, recording artists historically have not received performance royalties for most public performances of their recorded works, such as on radio broadcasts. But attitudes toward this historical precedent have shifted somewhat over the last couple of decades. The limitation on sound performance rights first changed in the digital domain, where a limited public performance right for masters—such as under the Webcast licenses mentioned earlier—was carved out. For writers and publishers—as distinct from labels and performers—the performing right has long been a bedrock of licensing income from a wide variety of sources.

From the beginning it became obvious that it was impractical for thousands of licensees to send separate payments to thousands of copyright holders. Not surprisingly, then, there are several performing rights organizations, or **PRO**s, whose express purpose is the issuing of performing rights licenses and collecting and distributing royalties generated by them to writers and publishers. In the United States, the performance rights for virtually every copyrighted musical work are handled by one of three PROs: the American Society of Composers, Authors and Publishers (ASCAP), Broadcast Music Inc. (BMI), and SESAC, Inc. SoundExchange, covered later in this chapter, collects and distributes digital performance royalties from statutory licenses on behalf of recording artists and sound recording copyright owners.

These organizations also lobby Congress on music-copyright concerns, promote music scholarship, enforce their members' rights through infringement litigation, and host awards events. They do not publish music[2] and they rarely promote individual copyrights.

ASCAP, BMI, and SESAC typically issue *blanket* performance licenses, which allow their entire repertoire (from all affiliated writers and publishers) to be used by broadcasters and others for a single, annual fee. Some entertainment companies that do not wish to pay for the complete catalog when they use only a small portion or have a limited need for music performances may seek licenses at the *source* (through the program provider) or *directly* (from the copyright owner), thus bypassing the PROs. For example, motion picture or TV producers may get source and direct licenses by negotiating a single fee for both performance and synchronization rights in the same transaction.

Although the Supreme Court's position on blanket licensing has traditionally been that the PROs offer the most efficient and economical way of handling the large flow of information, there is evidence that the courts and Congress may be becoming increasingly sympathetic to broadcasters' arguments against the practice and its inherent monopoly over song rights. In 1993, for instance, a lower federal court ruled that ASCAP must offer commercial television stations *per-program* licenses with surcharges for processing that approximate pro rata blanket licenses in cost. PROs typically offer per-program licenses or low-cost blanket licenses to radio stations that use little music, such as news/talk formats.

How much money do the U.S. PROs collect and distribute? Close to $2 billion a year from all sources, both foreign and domestic. This is fueled largely by the vast economic scale of broadcasting and cable television. Other factors also contribute: (a) increasing acceptance by music users that they must obey the copyright laws and pay up, (b) increasing efficiency of the collecting agencies, (c) rising licensing rates, and (d) more efficient, comprehensive collections from reciprocating foreign collecting organizations.

ASCAP and BMI, which operate on a nonprofit basis, both retain under 20% of their gross receipts for overhead, then distribute the rest to their members and affiliates. SESAC, a for-profit business, is privately held and does not publish its operating expenses or the amount of collections that it retains as profit, but SESAC maintains that its royalties to individual copyright holders are competitive with ASCAP and BMI.

Performance Licensing: The Nuts and Bolts

Each PRO negotiates license fees for its catalog of affiliated music writers and publishers with groups or entities that use music. The deals can take many forms and range widely in monetary terms from hundreds of dollars to hundreds of thousands and beyond. Some are based on a percentage of the user's revenue, others set a flat annual fee, others are keyed to the number of subscribers, and still others may be pegged to such factors as a venue's seating capacity or its weekly music budget.

The list of licensees is wide ranging. The PROs license practically all radio **stations** and most TV stations, as well as broadcast and cable **networks**, and satellite carrier systems. TV and radio generate the majority of PROs' total revenue from performances.

Between 10% and 15% of income from performances is generated by nonbroadcast sources that also are licensed by the rights organizations. These include clubs, hotels, arenas, airlines, colleges, restaurants, taverns, concert promoters, symphony orchestras, skating rinks, circuses, and theme and amusement parks. The PROs also license background music services, Web sites, and cell phone ringtone providers, among others. As noted earlier, if you are hearing music while you are out and about or surfing online, someone is probably paying a license fee to play or broadcast it.

Or, at least, someone *should* be! Prospective licensees—those who are legally obligated to take out a license—are initially contacted by a PRO's field representative who educates music users about the responsibilities that exist under U.S. copyright law. Most prospective licensees enter into licensing agreements at that time. If an agreement is not struck and the prospective licensee persists in using the music without permission, a lawsuit is brought by the licensing organization or by, and in, the names of specific members for specific infringements. Licensing organizations almost always win these legal battles, through persuasion or the courts, because copyright law is on their side.

Nonexempt[3] clubs, bars, and other such facilities which present live music performances are normally asked to sign a 1-year blanket license. Hotel and motel licenses cover a 5-year period. The setting of the license rate may take into account (a) the seating capacity of the **venue,** (b) whether it charges admission, (c) its live music weekly budget, and (d) the number of hours of musical entertainment provided. It may also factor in the estimated gross income of the facility or the amount the venue expends for entertainment.

Performing artists and their agents and managers normally are not expected to pay performance royalties to anyone. Rather, this responsibility and expense falls on either the venue owner or the entertainment promoter or producer.

When a venue, such as a stadium or arena, offers musical entertainment only occasionally, PROs attempt to collect performance fees from the promoter or producer renting the facility or sponsoring the event. When a facility offers entertainment on a regular basis, ASCAP, BMI, and SESAC will, however, normally look to the owner of the location to pay for the performance license.

Keeping Track of the Music

To monitor the use of their repertoire by licensees and to properly credit royalties to their affiliated writers and publishers, the PROs use a variety of techniques, including censuses and sample surveys of performances. A census refers to a complete count, whereas a sample looks at a statistically significant sampling of the whole.

ASCAP, BMI, and SESAC each have their own approaches to attaining this critical marketplace data, but common techniques include a review of cue sheets and program logs for movies and TV broadcasts obtained from program producers and broadcasters, a review of TV program guides obtained from various listings sources, random samples and censuses of radio broadcasts, reviews of radio logs, checks of actual programming recorded from TV and radio broadcasts, and censuses of performances transmitted by background music services or used online. The organizations also are increasingly using sophisticated technological means to track performances, such as Nielsen Broadcast Data Systems (BDS) or MEDIAGUIDE's computerized music-monitoring system, to monitor radio airplay (see Chapter 17 for more information).

Costs prohibit rights groups to directly survey performances in venues such as clubs, hotels, skating rinks, or dance schools. Rather, the revenue generated by licensing such venues is generally distributed to members based on surveyed radio and television performances as a proxy. Distributions are also made based on surveyed performances by commercial music services as well as for live concerts.

With respect to concert music, a census is used, drawing evidence of live performances of composers' works by scrutinizing printed concert programs or via performance activity reports received directly from the composer.

Royalty Distribution

Once a writer affiliates with a PRO and has his or her works performed, the next logical question is, "What is my fair share of the total royalties collected?"

While specifics vary depending on the rights organization, a member's or affiliate's share of the total royalties collected is determined broadly by the number and kind of performances of his or her music in the marketplace, as tracked by the rights group using the techniques laid out above.

Some songs have more than one writer, or even more than one publisher. If they do not all belong to the same PRO, the parties can earn differing amounts from their respective performing rights societies. This is because ASCAP, BMI, and SESAC use their own particular methods to determine royalty payments, which are usually paid quarterly.

Performing rights earnings vary tremendously for individual members and affiliates, depending on the popularity of their works in the marketplace and the types of uses for which the songs are licensed. But the composers, authors, and publishers of widely performed copyrights earn royalties year after year going into six figures and beyond.

Foreign Collections

Performance royalties generated outside the United States can add significantly to those total earnings, and have increased rapidly as additional foreign markets open up to Western music, and surveys and accounting procedures have made it easier to collect what is due. U.S. adherence to the Berne Convention, under which member countries treat foreigners as nationals for protection purposes, is a significant development which facilitates greater ease and accuracy in foreign copyright royalty collections (see Chapter 30).

The foreign subpublisher remains the dominant source of foreign collections. For those publishers who cannot depend on subpublishers to collect performance fees, ASCAP, BMI, and SESAC perform this service through reciprocal agreements with all the major music licensing organizations abroad (currently well in excess of 60 territories). They receive performance royalties from these foreign organizations and then pay members their share, withholding a small service fee.

With the exception of Brazil, ASCAP, BMI, and SESAC generally need to deal with only one licensing agency in each country. Among the most lucrative foreign sources of income at this time are Japan, the United Kingdom, Germany, France, Canada, Australia, Italy, Spain, and the Netherlands.

Membership Options

Songwriters can affiliate with only one PRO. So how does one choose among ASCAP, BMI, and SESAC? There is no right or wrong choice, but there are differences that, when explored, help writers find the best "fit" for their situation. These include the organizations' current license and royalty rates, policies on issues of particular concern, and service to members and affiliates. In general, once a member/affiliate strikes a relationship with a PRO, staying with that organization may be wise, as the disruption in income flow resulting from changing organizations can be costly. PROs have, from time to time, created policies that penalize catalog movement between societies. In its Amended Final Judgment of ASCAP's consent decree (see below for more on this), the Justice Department attempted to lay the foundation for a "level playing field" approach that would provide more flexibility to writers and publishers interested in exploring a change in affiliation. But for the most part, the PROs' gains in membership occur through attracting new writers and publishers, not from raiding each other's rosters.

Keep in mind, too, that ASCAP and BMI are open to all writers who meet a certain set of qualifications. SESAC uses a selective admissions process, whereby writers must pass a screening process before being invited to join.

There also are differences in the three groups' payment policies, organizational structures, ownership setup, member benefits, sampling and survey policies, and rules for termination, among other issues. Snapshots of the three leading organizations follow.

American Society of Composers, Authors and Publishers

ASCAP Voice of Music Award honoree Mary J. Blige gives her acceptance speech at the 20th Annual ASCAP Rhythm & Soul Music Awards.

Photo by Lester Cohen courtesy of ASCAP.

America's first PRO, ASCAP, was founded largely because of the passage of the U.S. Copyright Act of 1909. The act firmly established that the right to perform a copyrighted work belongs to the creator(s) of the work; others wishing to perform the work must obtain permission from the creator(s) or a designated representative. In 1914, a small number of the leading American music writers and publishers of the day convened to form ASCAP to license and collect fees for the public performances of their works and to distribute the fees as royalties to the writer and publisher members.

The organization had a difficult time in its early days. Not surprisingly, music users—typically restaurants, nightclubs, and hotels—were reluctant to start paying for music performances they had traditionally enjoyed free of charge. Today, after decades of educating music users and after numerous court decisions in favor of copyright holders, the concept of payment of performance fees through music licensing organizations is now broadly, if sometimes reluctantly, accepted.

Income, Royalty Distribution

In addition to being the oldest U.S. PRO, ASCAP is also the largest, collecting and distributing the most royalties. In 2007 alone, ASCAP's revenues exceeded $863 million. ASCAP also takes pride in its low operating expenses, which allows it to distribute more of its collections to its songwriter and publisher members.

Where does that money come from? According to the organization, some 20% to 25% of ASCAP's income derives from reciprocating foreign licensing organizations. Close to half of ASCAP's income from licensed performances comes from broadcast, cable, and satellite TV stations and networks. Radio generates about 25% of the total. The remainder of ASCAP's license fees is derived through the licensing of clubs, restaurants, hotels, and other venues and services, as well as the licensing of new media, such as Web sites, cell phone ringtones, and digital jukeboxes.

Membership

Until the mid-1940s, ASCAP's membership comprised mostly composers and lyricists of Broadway shows, movie musicals, and pop songs. Among the organization's charter members were Victor Herbert, John Philip Sousa, Jerome Kern, George M. Cohan, James Weldon Johnson, and Irving Berlin. Today, new members are admitted to ASCAP if they have at least one song published and distributed or one song commercially recorded, available on rental, or performed in media licensed by the society.

By the end of 2008, ASCAP's membership exceeded 340,000 songwriters, composers, and publishers. ASCAP's repertory, numbering in the millions, covers the entire spectrum of music—from Gershwin standards to Madonna pop, from the Beatles classics to Outkast hip-hop. ASCAP's members have won countless Grammy, Oscar, Emmy, and other awards and prizes. ASCAP members do not pay annual dues.

ASCAP is distinct among PROs in being governed by its members. ASCAP's board of directors is made up of 12 writer members and 12 publisher members, all elected by its membership. Many of the greatest names in American music have served on ASCAP's board, including Harold Arlen, Sammy Cahn, Aaron Copland, Oscar Hammerstein II, Morton Gould, Cy Coleman, Marilyn Bergman, and Virgil Thomson.

Music users have, from time to time, looked on the practices of music licensing organizations as monopolistic and in violation of antitrust law. Whatever the validity of that view, the U.S. Department of Justice, in actions in 1941, 1950, 1960, and 2001, agreed to a court-supervised control of ASCAP with ASCAP's consent. The arrangement is known legally as a *consent decree*.[4] To this day, a federal judge supervises a portion of ASCAP's affairs, mainly with respect to licensing music users.

ASCAP conducts a significant public relations campaign to create good will among its members and the music community. It offers prizes each year to composers and symphony orchestras. Its ASCAPLUS Awards Program provides cash and recognition for writer members whose performances are primarily in venues not surveyed, or whose catalogs have prestige value for which they would not otherwise be compensated. In addition to distribution of earned income, ASCAP has an extensive program of annual awards given to its most successful members.

ASCAP also hosts a variety of songwriter workshops and showcases across the country to help aspiring composers improve their writing, as well as their awareness of how the music business functions, and to bring these talents to the attention of the industry. Since 1968, ASCAP has given its Deems Taylor Award to authors and publishers for outstanding print, broadcast, and more recently, new media coverage of music. The second edition of this *Handbook* was honored with the award in 1980. ASCAP also has been active in exploring technological innovations and offers its members access to a variety of online benefits.

Weighting Performances

Licensing organizations use various formulas to calculate the relative value, or weight, of sampled performances of music in the marketplace. As part of its calculation, ASCAP takes into account, among other factors, the following:

1. The medium in which the performance takes place (e.g., local radio, local television, network television)

2. The weight of the station on which the performance is carried (each local radio and TV station has a weight that reflects its relative size in terms of the license fee it pays to ASCAP)

3. The weight of a TV network (the number of stations carrying a performance)

4. The time of day during which the performance occurs (e.g., prime-time network performances are accorded greater weight than performances earlier in the broadcast day or in the middle of the night)

5. The type of performance (whether it is a feature, theme, or background)

Background music underscoring a film is credited on a durational basis, and performances of serious works are also credited in this manner. More detailed information about ASCAP, as well as access to its online registration forms and other documents, is available on its Web site at www.ascap.com.

Broadcast Music Inc.

Broadcast Music Inc. (BMI) is owned by stockholders, originally some 475 broadcasters in this country. A select group of stockholders serve on the board of directors, which monitors overall performance of the company's management. When formation of BMI was first proposed in the late 1930s, the prospectus distributed to investors stated that stockholders could anticipate no dividends, and none have ever been paid. BMI is managed by its president and executive team, who design the company's strategy and run the day-to-day operations. BMI argues that this traditional business mode of operation is the most efficient and responsive way to serve its songwriters, publishers, and licensees.

Concerned with ASCAP's dominance, broadcasters created BMI to introduce competition into the field of music licensing, and it has a tradition of embracing songwriters of musical styles that may not have been previously represented by PROs. Its first affiliates worked in such genres as jazz, rhythm and blues (R&B), country, gospel, folk, and other indigenous American music. BMI was the representative of more than 90% of the composers in those genres whose work served as the foundation for the growth of the "Golden Age of Rock" that occurred in the 1950s and 1960s.

Membership

BMI has no "members"; instead, it has writer and publisher affiliates. BMI accepts a writer affiliate if that applicant has written a musical composition, alone or in collaboration with other writers, and the work is either commercially published or recorded or otherwise likely to be performed. As for admission of new publishers, BMI literature states, in part, that affiliation with BMI will be of practical benefit only to publishers who have the ability and financial resources to undertake broad-based exploitation of their works. BMI does not charge

Paul McCartney and BMI's Phil Graham celebrate more than 6 million broadcasts of "Yesterday" as the most performed song in BMI's catalog.

Photo courtesy of BMI.

its affiliated writers an application fee or dues. BMI publisher affiliates pay an application fee.

BMI describes its attitude toward bringing in new affiliates as "the open door," and it is active in promoting awareness of the organization. Among its outreach efforts, BMI offers awards to school composers, unknown writers, and arts organizations such as symphony orchestras.

BMI also sponsors a number of workshops in which seasoned composers and performers help train a new generation of creators. The workshops cover a range of music styles and include the Lehman Engel Musical Theatre Workshop; the Earle Hagen Workshop, for those pursuing a career in television and film music; and the Jazz Composers Workshop, which stresses the techniques of jazz composition and arrangement. The field of concert music is represented by the long-standing BMI Student Composers Awards competition.

The organization's BMI Foundation, a separate nonprofit entity, aims to encourage the creation of a broad spectrum of music and to nurture the talent of young composers, artists, conductors, and musicians through scholarship grants. The foundation's awards include, among others, the Charlie Parker Jazz Composition Prize, the BMI Student Composer Award, and the Jerry Bock Musical Theater Award.

Sampling, Accounting

To avoid separate dealings with the many thousands of music users, BMI conducts overall negotiations with established trade organizations. For example, it periodically negotiates industry-wide rates with the American Hotel and Motel Association. In the classical field, BMI negotiates with the League of American Orchestras. With respect to hotels, restaurants, and clubs, BMI works out license fees based in part on the establishment's weekly budget for music; the size of the orchestra, if any; the number of hours the business caters to the public; its seating capacity; and so forth. Licenses for venues such as theaters, concert halls, and stadiums are based largely on the frequency of their use and seating capacity.

BMI uses a combination of sampling and census techniques to track music usage across various licensing categories. The combined census and sample data brings the number of radio hours surveyed to over 4 million.

Following accumulation of data via logging, or census, procedures, the numbers are combined with information generated from the sampling process. These accumulated numbers are then used by BMI in a formula to determine royalty payments to its affiliated writers and publishers.

Income, Royalty Distribution

BMI's standard contract with writers and publishers (see Appendix A) does not cite payment rates, but BMI does make its *Royalty Information Booklet* available on its Web site.

Commercial radio royalty payments are based on the license fees that BMI collects from each station that performs a work. Payments are higher for performances of songs that air on stations paying higher license fees and lower for performances on stations paying lower license fees. BMI songwriters, composers, and publishers are paid on a scheduled basis. Statements and royalty checks for broadcast performances and commercials are distributed four times annually, while royalties from live pop concert performances and foreign performances are issued twice annually. Those pertaining to classical concert performances are distributed once a year.

Foreign collections are an important factor in BMI's total income, and it has reciprocal arrangements with the major music licensing organizations abroad. More information about BMI can be found on its Web site at www.bmi.com.

SESAC

SESAC, Inc., a third PRO, was founded in 1930 by Paul Heinecke, making it the second oldest performance licensing organization in the nation. Although the acronym originally stood for Society of European Stage Authors and Composers, the company has been known only as SESAC since the 1960s. Unlike ASCAP and BMI, SESAC is a closely held, for-profit corporation. It was purchased in 1992 by Freddie Gershon, Ira Smith, and Stephen Swid and the merchant banking house of Allen & Company. Also unlike ASCAP and BMI, SESAC does not operate under a court-supervised consent decree.

SESAC is the smallest U.S. performing rights society, by design. The company maintains that staying small allows it to provide more personal attention to its members, thereby giving them the greatest "bang for the buck" in exploiting both catalog acquisition and licensing opportunities.

Sampling, Accounting, Income, Royalty Distribution

In recent years, SESAC has established itself as the technological leader among U.S. PROs by being the first to embrace a variety of state-of-the-art tracking systems. In 1993, SESAC formed a division called SESAC Latina, dedicated to representing

SESAC office building in Nashville.

Photo courtesy of SESAC.

Spanish-language music. SESAC Latina formed an alliance with Nielsen Broadcast Data Systems (Nielsen BDS) to employ its monitoring system to track performances and distribute royalties based on the Nielsen BDS data. Two years later, SESAC expanded its Nielsen BDS usage to track affiliates' music across all other major radio formats.

For niche radio formats such as jazz and Americana, SESAC also uses digital pattern-recognition ("fingerprint") technology for tracking radio performances. A performance on a station paying a large blanket license fee is generally weighted more heavily than a performance on a smaller station.

SESAC also collects license fees from concert promoters and various "live" music venues as well as commercial music services, such as DMX, Music Choice, and Muzak.

Payment for performances from these sources is based on the license fees collected and the number of payable performances occurring in each quarter.

SESAC conducts periodic song seminars for writers and writers' showcases for its affiliates and helps pair up potential collaborators. It has agreements for foreign representation with more than 60 foreign PROs. More information is available on its Web site at www.sesac.com.

SoundExchange

SoundExchange was created in 2000 as a division of the Recording Industry Association of America (RIAA), and spun off in 2003 as an independent, nonprofit performance rights organization. It is the principal administrator designated by the U.S. Copyright Office to collect and distribute digital performance royalties from statutory licenses for featured recording artists and sound recording copyright owners (usually record labels) when their recordings are performed on digital cable and satellite-delivered television and radio services. (A performance right for sound recordings via **digital transmissions** was established in the 1995 and 1998 copyright law revisions.)

Though collections and distributions by SoundExchange are very small compared to those of ASCAP or BMI, the growth in this area is rapid and there is every reason to believe that artists and record labels will benefit greatly from digital performance payments in years to come. The members of SoundExchange include both signed and unsigned recording artists; small, medium, and large independent record companies; and major label groups and artist-owned labels. SoundExchange has built reciprocal relationships with collection societies around the world to receive royalties earned by U.S. artists and companies.[5]

Mechanical Licenses

A second significant source of licensing income for writers and publishers are mechanical royalties. As explained in Chapter 5, "Music Copyright," recording companies are required to obtain a mechanical license to manufacture and distribute phonorecords to the public. This type of license is limited to those who intend to make these recordings available only for private use—the kinds of recordings people buy and take home or, in the age of digital distribution, purchase and download.

The copyright law sets forth procedures and fees for record companies to obtain a compulsory mechanical license. The notion that music is "a business of pennies" likely has its roots in the statutory rate for mechanical licenses. The first change in that rate since 1909 occurred in 1978, when Congress implemented an increase from 2 cents to 2.75 cents for each work embodied in a phonorecord or one-half cent per minute of playing time or fraction thereof, whichever amount is larger. This rate has been periodically adjusted upward since then.[6]

In actual practice, however, most licenses of recordings for home use are *negotiated* mechanical licenses. Publishers and recording companies generally bypass the compulsory licensing route and work out their own terms, although the prevailing statutory rate is often used as a general benchmark in negotiating lower rates.

A negotiated mechanical license may differ from a statutory compulsory license in three ways:

1. The royalty rate may be lower.
2. Royalty accountings are usually quarterly rather than monthly as required under a statutory license.
3. The statutory requirement of "notice of intent" to record the copyrighted material is waived.

Most publishers use the Harry Fox Agency, Inc. (HFA), the mechanical collection arm of the National Music Publishers Association (NMPA), to issue mechanical licenses. After publishers instruct the HFA on the royalty to charge, the agency implements the license, collects the royalties, takes out a service fee of 6.75%, and forwards the balance to the publisher. The HFA has also been active in responding to the need for mechanical licenses in the digital and new media realms, such as ringtone licenses.

Many publishers are not large enough to support strong branch offices in foreign territories to license their works and collect their international royalties. The HFA has reciprocal arrangements with most foreign collecting agencies, which normally charge the HFA about 5% to 20% for their collecting service. The HFA takes off its own service fee, then forwards the balance to the publisher client.

Publishers choosing not to retain the HFA to collect royalties have a few alternatives. Publishers can arrange their own licenses—sometimes a publisher will license some material through HFA and issue their own licenses for other songs—or use the American Mechanical Rights Agency (AMRA). Another option is SESAC, which also licenses and collects mechanical royalties for an administration fee. SESAC "piggybacks" on its existing foreign public performance reciprocal contracts to form a network for collection of mechanicals in major foreign territories.

Synchronization Licenses

Music copyrights also play a starring—and lucrative—role in another primary arena of licensing: movies and television.

A producer of theatrical motion pictures must acquire two kinds of licenses in the United States. The first one, as touched on earlier in this chapter, is called a synchronization license. The term refers to the right to use music that is timed to synchronize with, or relate to, the action on the screen. Often as part of the same negotiation, film producers ordinarily also seek a performance license for theater exhibitions in the United States.[7]

The producer who wants new music composed expressly for a film will engage a film music composer to write the original score, often buying these creative services on a work-made-for-hire basis. In this circumstance the producer, or employer, not only owns all the rights to the original music but is considered, under copyright law, the author of the work and therefore does not require a license of any kind from the composer.

If the film producer does not obtain the musical score on a work-made-for-hire basis, the producer may engage a film composer as an independent contractor, pay a fee, then negotiate publishing rights to the music. If the composer retains all publishing rights, the film producer must then obtain from the composer a synchronization license to use the music in a film.

Another source for film music is music already copyrighted and published. A film producer who, for example, wants to use an established pop song must negotiate a synchronization license with the publisher. Movie synch revenues, as well as those for TV and commercials, have grown significantly over the past several decades.

Synchronization license fees vary and are largely determined by the market value of the music—whether the music is to be performed on camera or just underscored, whether it is to be sung, and the duration of the performance in the film. Record labels and publishers will likely also weigh the promotional upside of being featured in a particular motion picture in deciding on an acceptable fee (newer artists, for instance, may be willing to take less in exchange for a high-profile boost of exposure).

It is very important for the film producer to obtain the broadest possible synchronization license, because a movie originally planned for theatrical exhibition in this country will probably be used later in foreign theaters, television broadcasts here and abroad, cable TV, and home video. The publisher may try to grant the film producer a limited license to maximize profits later when the film is used in different media. (This can be a sore spot for movie companies and a boon to writers of standards. Because most licenses for old movies neglected to include a "universal" license, publishers and writers have been able to garner additional license fees when a new technology, such as DVDs, is introduced.)

With respect to performance licenses for film music, conditions in the United States differ from those in Europe. It is customary for film producers to acquire from publishers a performance license for theatrical exhibition of a film in this country. In most countries outside the United States, each country's own performance-licensing organization grants to theaters in that country a blanket license for the performance of music accompanying films. These organizations generally derive their income from film music by charging a small percentage of the net box office receipts. Nearly all PROs outside the U.S. grant licenses for music controlled by ASCAP, BMI, and SESAC through reciprocal agreements with these PROs. American composers sometimes receive substantial performance royalties from music they have scored for films that become popular in theaters abroad.

TV Movie Rights

A different set of licensing challenges arises when a film is originally produced for television broadcast. The producer will go for the broadest possible synchronization license—including downloads within the context of the program, streaming on the Internet, and wireless distribution to personal digital assistant (PDAs)—in anticipation that the production will eventually be aired in other media and possibly foreign territories. The producer will normally not need a performance license for television broadcasts, as TV stations and networks already have blanket performance licenses with ASCAP, BMI, and SESAC. Broadcasters may, however, seek to use direct or source licensing to avoid paying for both performance and synchronization licenses.

New Use Rights

A film producer or TV movie producer frequently wants to use music already existing in a commercially released recording. This can be attractive to the producer because it is already known how the music will sound and how it has been received by the public. But obtaining permission to use a recording in a film score can be a complicated, expensive process. Negotiations of this kind involve not only the recording company but also the performing artists, the artists' unions, and music publishers. The recording company contract with the artist may prohibit use of that artist's recordings in another medium. If so, special waivers and artist's compensation must be negotiated. Both artists' unions—the American Federation of Musicians (AFM) and the American Federation of Television and Radio Artists (AFTRA)—will require new use payments. The music publisher will require from the producer both a synchronization license and a performing license.

Cable Television Licenses

Cable television systems (which pick up TV stations' signals, boost them, and wire the pictures into homes) are described in the 1976 Copyright Act as being in the business of offering secondary transmissions of primary material. As such, cable operators are required to operate under a compulsory license. These licenses are issued and administered by the Copyright Office. Rates are determined by an elaborate set of guidelines, including reports from the cable TV companies on the number of channels transmitted, number of subscribers, and adjusted gross receipts. After deducting administrative expenses, the Copyright Office then distributes this money to copyright owners. Rates set by the 1976 Copyright Act are periodically reevaluated with the assistance of the Copyright Royalty Board (CRB), which is empowered by the Register of Copyrights to adjust them.

Individual members of the groups representing copyright owners, such as the three traditional American PROs, for example, are encouraged to negotiate among themselves for fair apportionments. When disputes arise (and they often do), the CRB is empowered to determine fair shares.

Other Cable TV Licenses

Almost all cable operators offer their subscribers not only relays of conventional over-the-air TV stations but also additional channels as part of their basic service, and yet more channels for a premium. (Cable TV operators are usually referred to as multiple system operators, or **MSOs**.) In addition to negotiating licenses with cable operators, PROs negotiate separate licensing arrangements with program *networks*— for example, MTV, HBO, and Showtime. These network agreements are distinct from the compulsory licenses the law requires for cable TV *operators*.

With respect to music bounced off satellites and picked up by earth stations, copyright laws were clarified in the Satellite Home Viewer Act of 1988. Section 119 of the Copyright Act generally requires a compulsory license for programming originating on superstations or network stations and distributed to the home by satellite.

Video Licenses

The music video market grew rapidly in the early 1980s with the launch of MTV and the increased availability and affordability of videocassette recorders and players. Initially, no industry standards were in place for licensing of these works, which was further complicated by the failure of the 1976 Copyright Act to address the question. Over the years, entertainment lawyers and industry leaders have gradually formed a consensus. Here is a summary of their views:

1. All videos, whether clips or albums, must be defined under copyright law as audiovisual works. As such, they are like small movies, and producers must acquire synchronization licenses from music publishers or their agents.

2. Performance rights in the musical portion of videos must be acquired from the publisher by the party who shows the videos to the public. When the video is shown through conventional (i.e., "free") TV or via cable (e.g., MTV, HBO), the broadcasters' blanket performance rights agreement is sufficient. If the video is shown in a club or other public venue, the venue's blanket performance license with ASCAP, BMI, or SESAC will suffice.

3. Video producers or manufacturers must pay publishers or their agents for the right to reproduce the videos as cassettes or discs for home use. Unless addressed explicitly in an agreement covering television rights, this right is not automatically considered part of a synchronization license but must be addressed specifically and negotiated separately. For newer motion pictures

and many television programs, these rights are now standard and included in the initial negotiation, but they can also be considered a separate right with separate payment. The parties or their agents can determine through negotiation whether the royalty is to be paid as a one-time flat fee or as a per-unit fee based on sales.

Transcription Licenses

The term *transcription license* is applied imprecisely to cover music used by syndicated programs, background music companies such as Muzak, in-flight entertainment, and music library services. It may not sound too sexy, but these various uses of music are a large and attractive source of generating income for one's copyrights. These kinds of music users require a mechanical license and a performance license. The two may be combined in one agreement or contracted separately.

A user seeking such licenses may negotiate directly with publishers, through the HFA or, in rare cases, SESAC. With respect to the collection of performance fees, users negotiate agreements with ASCAP, BMI, or SESAC.

Firms such as Muzak usually obtain a master license from the PROs with fixed annual fees based on their current number of franchised dealers. Other transcription licenses may call, for example, for a payment of 5 cents per selection for each copy of the tape that is sold to users. This nickel would include 2 cents for the mechanical license and 3 cents for the performance right.

A somewhat different kind of transcription license is obtained by program syndicators and broadcasters' library services such as those described elsewhere (see Chapters 19 and 24). The transcription licenses for these packages must be negotiated through the HFA or directly with the music publishers.

With respect to in-flight entertainment, the supplier of the tapes and films must obtain rights of synchronization and mechanical reproduction from copyright owners. Negotiations may be directly with publishers or through the HFA. In-flight program suppliers normally negotiate performance licenses directly with the PROs.

Special Use Permits

As explained in Chapter 4, "Music Publishing," music is often licensed for a wide range of applications, including broadcast commercials, video games, and various merchandising tie-ins, such as posters, apparel, and greeting cards. Licenses of this kind are referred to as permissions or special use permits. The music publisher will either negotiate a one-time fee or a royalty tied to sales.

Broadcast Commercials

For many publishers, the highest earnings from special use permits are generated from broadcast commercials. An advertising agency or sponsor who wants to use all or part of a pop standard is often willing to pay many thousands of dollars for the privilege. (Microsoft famously paid millions to use the Rolling Stones' "Start Me Up" in a commercial, although that's an extreme case.) These kinds of music licenses often include the right to alter the words and music to suit the needs of the advertisers—a prospect which can cause resistance from some songwriters who don't want their lyrics tampered with.

For music composed originally for broadcast commercials, the composer usually has the option of granting the advertiser a **buyout** deal or, more likely, permitting unlimited performances of the music if the usage is confined to advertising.

Video (Electronic) Games

Video games are a huge, multi-billion dollar industry unto themselves, and the music licensed for them has also become a tremendous revenue source for publishers and record labels. As with other special uses, the agreement for any particular game is negotiated on the basis of, among many factors, the software manufacturer's need for a certain track, the length of usage, the manufacturing run, and the projected earnings of the game.

Jukebox Licenses

Since 1978, jukebox owners have been required to obtain a public performance license for so-called nondramatic music played on their machines (before then, jukeboxes were legally considered "toys" under U.S. copyright law and were not liable for payment). These licenses are negotiated between the jukebox operator and the copyright owner, often with the involvement of a PRO.

In 1990, ASCAP, BMI, SESAC, and the Amusement and Music Operators Association (AMOA) created the Jukebox License Office (JLO), which contacts jukebox operators and offers them a blanket license to cover the use of music from all three PROs. This **joint venture** handles the rebates and new jukebox registrations. Licensing fees are negotiated based on standard rates recommended by the PROs.

Dramatic Music Rights

If you're wondering about that reference to "nondramatic" music above, you should be: It's an important point because U.S. copyright law makes sharp distinctions between dramatic music and nondramatic music. Accordingly, the licensing of rights differs markedly.

Despite the way it sounds, this has nothing to do with a particularly heartwrenching lyric or over-the-top vocal performance. The term *dramatic music* refers to compositions used in the context of a wider piece or in the telling of a larger story—including, for example, operas, musical shows and revues, in whole or in part. The term may also include music that did not originate in a theatrical production but was written as part of a TV or radio show where the music was integral to the plot and where it contributed to carrying the drama forward. It is customary to refer to performing rights in dramatic music as grand rights, and grand rights must be negotiated with copyright owners separately from nondramatic rights, which are sometimes termed **small rights.**

With respect to Broadway musicals and similar productions, rights of authors, composers, and lyricists are set forth in contracts recommended by the Dramatists Guild, Inc. Under the guild's Approved Production Contract (APC), the separate rights in music and lyrics that make up the dramatico-musical work are retained by the composers and lyricists and their publishers, sometimes with certain restrictions, as in the sale of movie rights. Also, there may be restrictions with respect to when the music and lyrics can be recorded (e.g., there may be a prohibition against releasing recordings of a show's songs on a single prior to the release of the original cast album).

A show's composers receive royalties from ASCAP, BMI, or SESAC for performances of individual songs on radio and TV or in clubs and restaurants, and so forth. But when a dramatic musical work is performed as a whole or a substantial portion of it is performed—a scene including music and dialogue, for example—grand rights must be licensed. ASCAP does not involve itself in licensing grand rights of any of its repertoire. Its members usually assign that responsibility to one of the firms involved in grand rights licensing and rental of scores and parts. BMI licenses with broadcasters also grant only nondramatic rights but do grant the right to perform up to 30 minutes of a full-length dramatic or dramatico-musical work or an insubstantial portion of a shorter dramatic or dramatico-musical work. SESAC's standard contract with broadcasters excludes dramatic music.

When a Broadway musical becomes a hit, its writers enjoy income from its performances long after its Broadway run. There are hundreds of regional theaters within the U.S. offering performances of these beloved shows. The author holds the so-called subsidiary rights to these shows, including motion pictures, band arrangements, live performance rights, TV usage, commercial jingle usage, and stage performance rights. Some companies act as agents that specialize in the licensing of subsidiary rights such as stock and amateur productions of musicals. Stock and amateur rights of a play are those rights reserved by the authors of the play and licensed to organizations such as Samuel French, Inc., Music Theatre International, R&H Theatricals, and Tams-Witmark. These companies, mostly based in New York City, represent authors for specific works rather than representing authors for every musical they write. The companies receive an agent's commission and handle the licensing of those shows to stock and amateur theaters around the country.

Each dramatic performance of this kind requires a license and royalty payment. Royalty rates are calculated on a percentage based on the seating capacity of the house, the number of performances, and the ticket prices. In addition to the license fee, the show's **book** (or script), score, and parts must be rented from the licensing agency. Professional performances of Broadway shows (following a Broadway run) require a license involving a weekly minimum guarantee against 6% to 14% of the box office receipts. Professional productions also must rent the show's book, score, and parts. The producers are generally charged higher rates than those for amateur groups.

Performance licenses for touring companies vary. Some touring companies are under the aegis of the original Broadway producer; others are mounted independently. The producer usually has many options and a period of time after the opening (or close) of the producer's production of the play in which to exercise them, such as the right to send out a touring company. If the producer doesn't send out a touring company, the rights to license a touring company revert to the authors (this is one of the subsidiary rights that include motion picture rights, touring rights, and foreign rights). If the original show has run long enough that the Broadway producer is entitled to a share of subsidiary rights, the authors would then pay the producer a portion of their receipts just as they do with stock and amateur rights.

Notes

1. Ringtones can also invoke another license requirement entirely—a mechanical, which grants the right to reproduce songs for sale or distribution.

2. BMI did publish music for a while in its early history (1940s) but no longer does so. Neither ASCAP nor SESAC has ever published music.

3. There are some exceptions to the license requirement. The Fairness in Music Licensing Act of 1998, an adjunct to the Sonny Bono Copyright Term Extension Act mentioned in Chapter 5, exempts smaller businesses such as restaurants, taverns, and mall shops from paying royalties for the use of background music if their square footage is below a certain threshold. (According to the World Trade Organization, this puts the United States in violation of the copyright protection rules it had agreed to as a signatory of the Berne Convention, an international treaty.)

4. BMI is also under a consent decree, but it sets forth a different set of constraints.

5. In addition, another fund administered jointly by AFM and AFTRA distributes 5% of digital performance royalties collected in the U.S. as well as other performance levies from some foreign territories. This fund pays nonfeatured musicians and vocalists, regardless of their union membership. (Current information is available on the group's site: www.raroyalties.org.)

6. In 2006, the rate was raised to 9.1 cents or 1.75 cents per minute, whichever amount is larger.

7. For this license, the film producer usually goes to the publisher (or the publisher's agent) because a court decree has denied, to ASCAP at least, the right to require a performance license directly from movie theaters in the United States.

Chapter Takeaways

- Compulsory licenses set a fee that the licensee can choose to pay the licensor (the copyright owner). Negotiated licenses require the two parties to agree on a flat fee or royalty.

- The largest source of income for many publishers and composers is broadcast public performance income paid through performance rights organizations. In the U.S. these PROs include ASCAP, BMI, and SESAC.

- Though a compulsory mechanical license is available to licensees who wish to distribute records, most such licenses are negotiated between labels and either publishers or their agent, such as the Harry Fox Agency (HFA).

- A synchronization license granted by a music publisher gives a producer the right to use a composition in an audiovisual work such as a movie or TV show.

- A large variety of licenses and special use permits can increase the revenue of music owners, ranging from jukeboxes to grand rights for mounting Broadway shows.

- Clearing rights to samples is thorny because the publisher and label licensors may insist on hearing how the sample is used before granting permission.

Key Terms

- blanket performance license (p. 111)

- buyout deal (p. 125)

- census (performance) (p. 112)

- compulsory license (p. 108)

- consent decree (p. 114)

- copublishing (p. 110)

- "fingerprint" technology (p. 119)

- grand rights (p. 125)

- Harry Fox Agency (HFA) (p. 120)

- master use license (p. 108)

- mechanical license (p. 120)

- Multiple System Operator (MSO) (p. 123)

- phonorecord (p. 120)

- small rights (p. 125)

- source (or direct) license (p. 111)

- SRLP (p. 109)

- subpublisher (p. 113)

- synchronization license (p. 121)

- transcription license (p. 124)

PART 3

Managing Artist Relationships

CHAPTER 7

Agents, Managers, and Attorneys

Many professional artists find it desirable, even imperative, to call on others to assist them in handling their business affairs and the development of their careers. Partly because of the glamour of the music and entertainment fields, performers of even moderate success find themselves surrounded by individuals who claim they can help the artist find the path to fame and fortune. Although some performers of modest gifts have been swept from the unemployment line to at least temporary success through the efforts of clever management, many others, obviously very talented, continue to flounder in the small time for want of someone competent enough to guide their careers upward.

"The first thing we do, let's kill all the lawyers."

—Shakespeare, Henry VI, Part 2, Act IV, Scene II

Artists have a long to-do list: Negotiate record deals and music publishing contracts, book concert venues and night clubs, arrange travel itineraries, license merchandise and product endorsements, maintain fan and press relations, and land movie and TV acting gigs. For all this, they engage a team of assistants and professionals, probably including a personal manager, agent, business manager, road manager, attorney, publisher, and publicist. The services that support personnel perform often overlap and intertwine.

In this chapter, the roles of agents, managers, and attorneys are defined and discussed as they relate to the arts and entertainment industry. Figures 7.1a, b, and c illustrate possible configurations of an artist's team of professional assistants.

Left: Norah Jones performs in Saratoga.

Photo © Tim Mosenfelder/Getty Images Entertainment.

Figure 7.1a   The Team

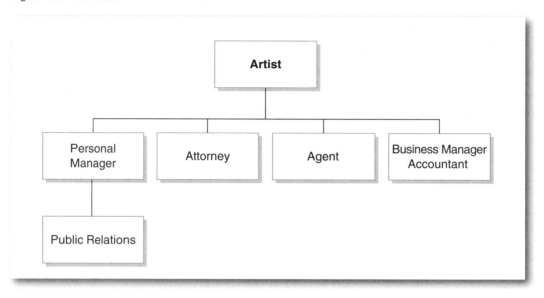

Figure 7.1b   The Team in the Studio

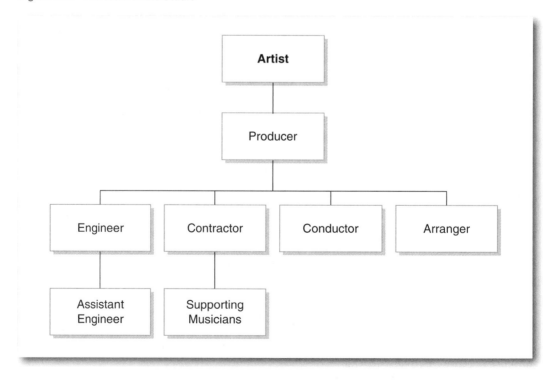

Figure 7.1c   The Touring Team

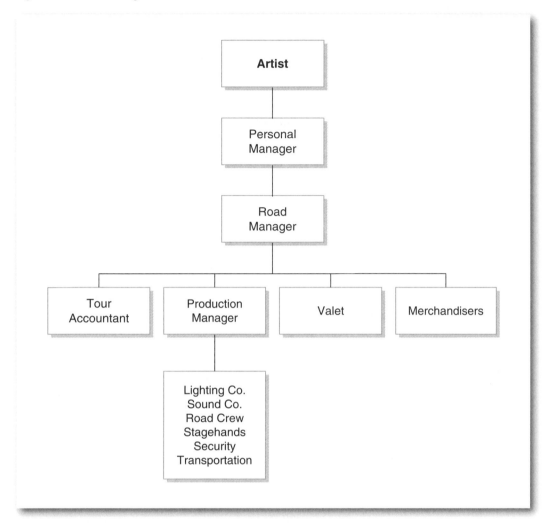

Agents

An agent represents clients by seeking employment for them, and as an employment agent, this person is subject to state laws.

Agents go by various names. Many people refer to them as *booking* agents, which most of them are. In California, they are known as *talent* agents. Sometimes people in and out of the business use the term *manager* or *artist's manager* interchangeably with *agent,* although these roles are separated by some state laws. A high percentage of agency work is conducted in California, so the word *agent* is used here the way California statutes define talent agent—that person who is in the full-time business of procuring employment primarily for performers, writers, producers, and directors. In the music industry, talent agents work primarily in booking live appearances of artists, whether at clubs or concerts. Music talent agents generally do not negotiate recording contracts (there are some exceptions) and are not particularly involved in overall career guidance (as are film and TV agents).

The talent agent has two kinds of clients. The first is a roster of artists. The other kind of client is the buyer of such talent—primarily producers, concert promoters, and club owners. The talent agent's job is to deliver artists to talent buyers, to serve as the middleman, the negotiator who knows, or should know, what an artist is worth and what the buyer is willing and able to pay. The agents who are most successful over the long run have earned the respect and confidence of both buyers and sellers. It is the agent's task to obtain the highest possible fees for clients and to work closely with an artist's manager. If an agent can attract a large number of major artists, commissions may place the agent in an income bracket comparable to that of a star performer, as agents generally receive 10% of an artist's income.

Regional and Boutique Agencies

An agent often starts out in a medium-sized city working alone, quickly discovers it is hard to be very effective that way, and connects with one or two other local agents. Perhaps three of them can afford to rent a modest office and hire a secretary. Agencies of this size handle most local bookings, attempting to persuade local club owners to try live music instead of recorded music. One of their greatest challenges is locating acts attractive enough to pull dancers and drinkers into local clubs. Most of the acts sending them demos are, at best, semiprofessional—clearly not strong enough to justify the club owner's paying them even union scale. So the agent keeps searching for buyers and qualified talent.

Until the agent can discover acts with some drawing power, there will rarely be a chance to build the booking business above a minimum survival level. But now and then, local acts create a following and start to command fees high enough to earn the agent a respectable income.

Agents with ambitions transcending the city limits search out contacts and joint bookings with national, and even international, agencies. Such deals ordinarily involve commission splits.

Another type of talent agency in this classification is the boutique, which is relatively small and specialized. Boutiques usually can be found in Los Angeles and New York, and confine themselves to just one aspect of entertainment—such as only booking music acts at live events (so no TV, film, etc.).

National Full-Service Agencies

National booking agencies—often called full-service agencies—employ hundreds of people and often operate with offices in the major cities of the world. Agencies such as William Morris Endeavor (WME) Entertainment, International Creative Management (ICM), Creative Artist's Agency (CAA), Paradigm, and United Talent Agency (UTA) handle hundreds of artists and gross hundreds of millions of dollars a year. Such agencies generally take commissions of 10% (and occasionally up to 15%) of the music artist's gross income from work generated by the agency or otherwise eligible for commission. These same full-service agencies also represent film and TV's biggest stars and major behind-the-camera talent. The big talent agencies try to represent artists in all fields of entertainment, including concerts, television, recordings, films, commercials, video games, publishing, licensed products, and product endorsements. A music artist signing with a national talent agency may negotiate for

carve outs, such as excluding music publishing, composing, and TV acting from the contract.

Major agencies rarely sign unknown talent; they are preoccupied booking their stars. Unknown acts must struggle along with local agents, usually until they achieve some success as recording artists.

In the process of signing an artist, a large agency may submit a package of 10 or more contracts for the signature of the new client. Some of these agreements are form contracts used by that particular agency. Of the many contracts submitted to prospective new clients, only a few are frequently used for contemporary recording artists or performing groups:

1. American Federation of Musicians (AFM) Exclusive Agent-Musician Agreement.

2. American Federation of Television and Radio Artists (AFTRA) Standard Exclusive Agency Contract.

3. The talent agency's own general services and materials agreement. This is a comprehensive agreement that covers creative materials, services, TV and movie packages, and other kinds of entertainment packages.

Altogether, the agreements generally provide that the agency serves as the artist's adviser and representative in respect to the artist's activity and participation in fields such as merchandising, testimonials, and commercial tie-ins. The standard contracts often used by talent agencies in California incorporate language of the union contracts stipulating that the artist's approval is required prior to the agency committing the artist. The parties also agree that the contract can be terminated if the agency can't find work for the artist for a specified number of consecutive months, that any disputes are to be referred to the Labor Commissioner of the State of California or binding arbitration, that the agreement shall not conflict with any union contracts involving the artist, and under what circumstances the agency has the right to assign the contract to a third party.

It is also possible for an artist to work with an agency on a nonexclusive basis, or even with no written agreement at all—a so-called handshake agreement. An agency might be hired to work with an artist in a limited or specific territory or kind of performance. An example of this kind of limited representation would be an artist who retains an agency to book live performance tours in a certain territory or for a specific tour but who does not use that agency for deals involving other territories, movie companies, or commercials. For rock tours, large agencies sometimes join forces with other agencies to package the tour.

Changing Representation. Artists frequently change agencies in the hope that new representation will further their careers. Large agencies are often criticized for neglecting the individual artist unless that person is a star of some magnitude. Many lesser names feel they get lost in the shuffle of a big company attempting to find work for its big earners. The major agencies are aware of these negative views of their operations and attempt to offer each of their clients the personal attention of at least one particular agent on their staff who is assigned to keep the artist working and happy. The AFM agency agreement, for example, requires that the firm name the specific individual agents who are to handle the affairs of the musician under contract.

On occasions when agents change companies or break off and set up their own firms, it is particularly disruptive to their artist clients. Often, personal relationships and confidences are built up between agent and artist. When the agent leaves, it is a common occurrence for those artists to seek relief from their contracts with the company, declaring their intention of following that agent. A court battle may ensue. In general, in these kinds of altercations the courts have tended to find for the artist, recognizing that in the employment field, the element of personal relationships is entitled to special consideration. Many artists insist on inserting **key man clauses** into their agency agreements, giving the artist the right to terminate the agreement if the "key man" is no longer present. While the key man's importance to the agency is cemented in such agreements, the agency as an institution may object to this clause.

Regulation of Agents

Some of the colorful characterizations of booking agents depicted in old movies might lead one to believe that the only qualifications needed by an agent are a tolerance for cigar smoke and a pair of alligator shoes. Although such images of unscrupulous agents may be interesting movie fiction, the modern talent agent is a professional whose success is measured, in large part, by the success of the talent or business entity represented.

Statutory Regulation. Agents and artist managers proliferated early in the last century with the rapid growth of the movie industry. In the early days of agents' abuses of performers, wages would be skimmed or never paid; collusion between agents and employers would occur. Artists would be dispatched long distances to jobs that never existed. Because agents became particularly active in the early days of the film industry, California was one of the first states to grapple with abuses. Following first attempts in 1913 to regulate employment agencies, California enacted its Labor Code in 1937. This code made a distinction between "motion picture employment agencies" and agents active primarily in booking vaudeville acts, circus performers, and actors for the legitimate stage.

In 1943, California added a new category, "artist's manager." In 1967, California repealed substantial portions of its Labor Code. "Theatrical employment agencies" and "motion picture employment agencies" were eliminated as separate categories. But the "artist's manager" category was retained and placed under the jurisdiction of the Labor Commissioner of the Department of Industrial Relations. "Employment agency" provisions were shifted to the jurisdiction of what is now the Department of Consumer Affairs.

In 1978, California altered its artist's manager statute, the principal change being one of nomenclature: Artist's managers were to be known as "talent agents." Because of widespread abuse of artists by agents in the past, California laws today severely limit the activities of all persons involved in artist representation. Procurement of employment for artists and entertainers in California is strongly regulated by two state statutes: the Talent Agencies Act of 1978 and the Employment Agency Act.

Simply stated, all persons engaged in the procurement, or attempt of procurement, of employment for an artist must be licensed by the state to do so. Any contract can be canceled by either party or the state where an individual engaged in procuring employment lacks the required state license.

In a landmark case, the agent regulations were cited by TV actress Rosa Blasi as justification to quit paying commissions to her management firm. She asserted that her entire contract was voided because the firm illegally served as an agent on some of her acting jobs. Her manager, Marathon Management, sued, which resulted in years of back-and-forth litigation. Hollywood watched on the edge because millions of dollars in commissions were at risk, as it is common from time to time for personal managers to step over the legal line into agenting—directly procuring and negotiating work for clients. Hollywood labor unions sided with Blasi. In the other corner, managers around Hollywood backed Marathon Management, saying an ungrateful client was trying to stiff the organization that engineered her career success. In 2008, the California Supreme Court ruled that Marathon's contract was not entirely nullified because of Marathon's limited violations of the Talent Agencies Act, and that "an isolated instance of procurement does not automatically bar a manager from collecting commissions." This was a partial victory for personal managers everywhere. The decision cooled interest of artists to invoke this justification when attempting to break contracts.

Union Regulation. In addition to state laws governing persons engaged in agency activity, talent agents representing union musicians are restricted severely on a national basis by the various performers' unions and **guilds.** The organizations most involved here are the AFM for instrumentalists, AFTRA for singers, the American Guild of Variety Artists (AGVA) and the American Guild of Musical Artists (AGMA) for opera/dance, and the Screen Actors Guild (SAG) for movies and some TV programs.

Artists' guilds and unions vary in what they require when they **franchise** or license a talent agent, but the following requirements are typical of most agreements:

1. Maximum allowable commissions are stipulated. For example, AFTRA and SAG apply only a 10% ceiling on commissions applied to the artist's gross compensation. Artists with those unions are not permitted to pay both an agent and a manager more than an aggregate total of 10%. The AFM requires that the company name the specific individual agents who are to handle the affairs of the musician under contract. The AFM allows a 20% commission on one-night gigs and 15% if the job runs 2 or more days per week for the same employer. In cases where AFM agents have a Federation Personal Management Agreement with AFM musicians, the AFM will allow an additional 5% commission.

2. AFTRA and SAG generally franchise only those agents who agree to limit their professional activity to procurement of employment for artists. This constraint is designed to protect the artist from paying superfluous or excessive commissions for other nonagent services. The disadvantage of this restriction is that some professionals are barred from acting as agents because they also participate in other entertainment industry enterprises such as management, production, publishing, and recording.

3. Lengths of contracts are limited. AFTRA allows a maximum term of 3 years. Under certain conditions, SAG limits its members to contracts of 1 year's duration.

Getting Started. Individuals wanting to get a career started in the talent agency field often find it daunting. Sometimes, students can enter a talent agency as apprentices. Perhaps, after a stint in the mail room or a short training period, they may be put on as assistant agents. Artists' unions license all owners of each franchised agency, then permit subagents to work under an individual owner's license.

Managers ▓▓▓▓▓▓▓▓▓▓▓▓▓▓▓▓▓▓▓▓▓▓▓▓▓▓▓▓▓▓▓

The arts and entertainment industry engages a number of different kinds of managers. The most influential among them is the artist's personal manager. Personal managers are expected to perform tasks ranging from negotiating multimillion-dollar contracts to checking on the star's wardrobe. Fees range from 10% to 25% of artists' deals. Managers of less famous stars earn a higher percentage, as they invest more effort in building a career at a time when the artist's earnings are low.

This chapter limits the discussion of personal managers to how they are regulated by state statutes and artists' unions. The manner in which management contracts are negotiated and how managers advance the careers of their clients is treated in Chapter 10.

Regulation of Managers

California regulates artists' personal managers quite strictly. Because many management contracts are negotiated with these professionals, an understanding of California's regulations is most useful.

Statutory Regulation. As mentioned above, in California the only person allowed to procure employment for an artist is one who is licensed as a talent agent. Personal managers are supposed to be principally concerned with advising and counseling their clients about their overall careers and longer-term objectives. But booking gigs is important to clients, so it is difficult for personal managers to completely separate themselves from that activity.

If the personal manager in California wants to stay within the law and remain in the management profession, he or she needs to obtain a talent agent's license. But then the individual would have to function under the constraints imposed by artists' unions on talent agents. If the manager decides against becoming a licensed talent agent, there are other options:

1. The manager may voluntarily forgo commissions on all employment procured by a talent agent. However, in various rulings, California's Labor Commission has frowned on this practice.

2. The manager may go into partnership with the artist. Both parties may find this unattractive, however, in that they are exposed to liability for their partner's actions.

3. The manager may employ the artist exclusively and supply the artist's services to third parties. This might serve the manager's interests, but it will seriously disadvantage the artist by imposing restrictions on the artist's activities that could go well beyond the terms normally encountered in a regular management agreement.

4. The personal manager might set up a corporation that would deliver the artist's services to third parties. Some lawyers believe this may offer the best insulation available from the constraints of talent agent licensing requirements.

Next to California, New York hosts the greatest number of personal management contract negotiations. That state offers a less restrictive regulatory framework than California. New York avoids the issue of licensing personal managers in that it defines theatrical agencies (booking agencies) as those that procure employment other than incidental to the manager-artist relationship. This would appear to exclude personal managers because most of their procurement activity is incidental.

Union Regulation. Personal managers of good reputation could obtain a franchise from an artists' union, but they would then fall under close regulations. The unions would impose a ceiling on their commissions, the term of their contracts with clients would be shorter, and they would probably be required by the franchise agreement to engage in employment procurement activity full-time and not engage in other business activities concurrently. Few managers could function under these restrictions; it is the very nature of the business for them to be involved at any given time in a number of entertainment business activities, particularly publishing and recording. Generally, managers in New York are not union affiliated.

The personal manager in California has one other option: to take out a union franchise, then ignore the union's restraints. This is a temptation because unions have rarely enforced these rules. But ignoring union rules can be risky: No one can predict when the union might start enforcing its franchising agreements. Also, clients could later cite the absence of a union franchise as justification for refusal to pay a manager's commission. The end result of statutory and union constraints on personal managers is that, in California at least, many established and respectable personal managers opt against both state licensing and union franchising.

Steely Dan (circa 1973). Artists, producer, publicist, booking agent, and managers show off the evidence of their collective success.

Photo © Tim Mosenfelder/Getty Images.

Assistants to Management

Most managers will try to accompany their artists to all performances or events that are important for the artist's career—the start of a long run in the main room of a Las Vegas casino, big city stops of national concert tours, and star performances on TV shows. Few artists' managers attempt to travel regularly with their clients, however, and assign such duties to a road manager. Road managers handle the transportation of people and equipment, arrange for meals and lodging, ensure that adequate security is provided, hire tour accountants, supervise sound reinforcement and lighting personnel, check box office receipts, and collect performance income. Road managers who learn the business and know how to hustle often graduate to artist management jobs. Some have become producers.

Many young people break into show business by signing on as *roadies,* the word often used to describe persons hired to move and help set up the performance. Even though some roadies have previous training in areas such as lighting or sound, others seem to learn what is expected of them on the job.

The people hired on as road crew members for lesser known acts usually earn minimum salaries plus their travel expenses; such acts have little difficulty locating an adequate supply of individuals willing to work for low wages and high adventure. In contrast, today's top acts tour with highly disciplined, well-paid crews.

Whether the individual is a recording artist or some other kind of professional in the field, when income reaches a respectable level, other support personnel will be required to advance that performer's career. This is treated in Chapter 10, Artist Management.

Attorneys

Entertainment business attorneys are greatly important due to the constant stream of transactions inherent in the music business. With the continuing transformation of existing entertainment companies, not to mention the frequent acquisitions and consolidations, the role of the entertainment attorney is more crucial today than ever before.

Law practices are often roughly divided into litigation services and transactional services. In litigation, attorneys press the rights of their clients in court cases (or threatened court cases) over copyright, contract issues, disputes over rights to names and rights to music. Relatively few disputes, of course, escalate to the point where litigation is required. The bulk of day-to-day legal work is performed by transactional attorneys who negotiate and draft contracts. Although some firms specialize in entertainment litigation, most entertainment practice falls into the transactional category. For the glamour fields of music, theater, movies, and TV, law schools are turning out at least twice as many interested graduates as seem to be needed. Despite the unemployment (or underemployment) among graduates now emerging from law schools, there is an actual shortage of lawyers fully qualified and experienced to practice in the entertainment field. Entertainment attorneys tend to specialize in chosen subareas of the business. Some work primarily with issues of intellectual property, including copyright and trademark. Some negotiate with recording and publishing companies; others work with clients who are involved with the theater or TV or movies. Law firms frequently employ a number of attorneys with different entertainment specialties and thus can move a given music client's business to specialists within the same law firm. Specialized attorneys have the advantage of drawing on past experience and thus understand what deal points the other party may concede, and what may be a line in the sand that can't be crossed. In fact, most attorneys would prefer to battle a knowledgeable adversary rather than a naïve newcomer.

The most experienced lawyers in copyright are found in Washington, D.C., New York City, Nashville, and the state of California. The best-qualified lawyers in general music business practice are found in the three recording centers in the United States. In Canada, a handful of entertainment and sports industry lawyers practice in Toronto and Montreal.

Retaining Legal Counsel

How can someone go about finding a qualified legal counselor? A good starting point is to check with colleagues in the business; send an e-mail to knowledgeable friends or use a professional social networking site. Attorney organizations also provide one-stop information. For example, the Beverly Hills Bar Association has a specialized entertainment section. Local chapters of the American Bar Association, a national organization, are another starting point.

These questions might be asked:

1. What is the prospective attorney's reputation, and what is the source of your information? Is it objective? The fact that a lawyer has passed the state bar examination and offers all the appearances of respectability is insufficient reason for complete trust. Read the music trade news, such as *Billboard,* to see who is active in the field; check online listings; and view individual law firm Web sites. Find out which attorneys already represent successful artists, managers, and companies in the business, since their preexisting contacts can open doors.

2. Is the prospective lawyer sufficiently experienced in the music field to look out for the musician's interests in publishing, recording, performance rights, and foreign rights?

3. Is the prospective lawyer well informed about the nuances of copyright protection?

Though a licensed music attorney could offer other legal services (such as real estate or tax advice), most music lawyers stick to their branch of specialization—which is challenging enough to master. For nonmusic issues, the client may be referred to another lawyer in the same firm or another firm altogether.

As the role of the music attorney has significantly expanded over the decades, some clients retain attorneys primarily for their inside-industry connections. It is now common for lawyers to perform tasks that seem more appropriately handled by managers, such as circulating demo tapes to labels: Established lawyers are highly respected by A&R (artist and repertoire) executives. Some law firms even have separate artist management departments, and some of the most successful managers are or were lawyers. Before employing an attorney, be sure to know precisely what services may be provided.

Payment Options. One of the universal complaints about lawyers is their cost. Attorney fees can easily exceed thousands of dollars per transaction, which might be greater than the revenue of a deal for a client at the bottom of the music industry ladder. But when legal services are imperative and the transaction involves enough revenue to justify professional fees, the client has a number of payment options.

The usual arrangement is paying an hourly fee. Before running up a bill, the prospective client should simply ask the lawyer, in an exploratory meeting, about the charges. If ongoing legal services are needed, the client may place the lawyer on a monthly retainer.

Another payment option is a fixed fee to complete a specific transaction, doing away with hourly billing. The third alternative is a **contingent** payment plan that is pegged to a percentage—typically 5% but sometimes higher—on specified aspects of the deal. For example, the percentage could be applied to the recording budget or artist advance. Such contingency arrangements may include a minimum fee specified by language such as "but, in no event, less than X dollars." When the client is a production company or film producer, the lawyer might *participate,* a term used in the industry to describe sharing in an investment in a project or a company. A participating attorney might charge no legal fee, but "take points" instead—receive a small percentage of specified deal elements being negotiated. The lawyer may have a central role in finding a deal for the artist by shopping the artist's demo tape to record and publishing companies. If that is the case, the lawyer deserves compensation for legal services that are contributing to the artist's success.

How much is a lawyer entitled to charge for services? State bar associations publish guidelines for their members.[1] Professional canons of ethics call for lawyers to follow them.

Form of Organization. When an attorney accepts a client, one of the first tasks in many entertainment industry situations is to determine the client's legal status. In business and legal relationships, will the client be best served by being self-employed, a partner, proprietor, or independent contractor—or would interests be better served by forming a corporation or taking part in joint ventures? The client (who may be a group of persons) will need the lawyer to explain the advantages and disadvantages of these options.

Contract Negotiations. As pointed out, nearly all significant events in the entertainment industry involve the negotiation of contracts. And that is the business of lawyers. The number and kinds of contracts commonly used in the industry are extensive. Typical agreements include the following:

- Composer with a publisher, coauthor
- Performer with employer, agent, promoter, producer, contractor, performing group, lawyer, broadcaster, merchandiser, advertising agency, recording company, publisher
- Producer with a recording company, performer, recording studio, production company, publisher, distributor, merchandiser, lawyer
- Talent agent with a performer, promoter, club owner, producer, production company, recording company, film company, lawyer
- Artist's personal manager with an artist, recording company, broadcaster, accountant, auditor, road manager

The Adversarial Relationship. Individuals entering into contract negotiations are, by definition, adversaries. They may be the best of friends, but once they start negotiating a legal agreement, the parties should seek every legitimate advantage available. Contract negotiations need not be unfriendly encounters, but the parties are advised by their attorneys, as a rule, to go for whatever they can rightly get. Having worked on many previous deals, knowledgeable attorneys representing each party start out with an idea of what all parties will get in the end—even if they don't volunteer this in back-and-forth negotiations.

Each party entering into contract negotiations should have separate legal counsel. When one lawyer attempts to represent both parties, there may be difficulty serving them impartially. The American Bar Association's Code of Professional Responsibility and most state bar associations' codes of ethics assert that in the absence of full disclosure and an agreement signed by all parties, lawyers should not represent adversaries and should urge prospective clients to retain their own attorneys.

Independent legal counsel is particularly important in situations where collateral contracts are entered into simultaneously—for example, an artist-manager contract and an artist-manager-publisher deal. If an attorney is involved in two or more of the collateral contracts, then that attorney faces the quandary of representing more than one side of interconnected deals and potential exposure to conflicts of interest. Disputes can arise about the legitimacy of transactions where conflict of interest by negotiating attorneys exists. Often, these conflicts are inadvertent. When conflicts occur, courts have sometimes found that a lawyer had taken advantage of the client's ignorance and subsequently determined that one or more of the contracts was unenforceable.

Extralegal Services. While clients may ask their attorneys to recommend agents and managers, frequently the attorney offers some of the same services. It is not unusual for a lawyer to agree to administer the client's publishing company, for example. In general, a lawyer attempting to provide a client with two different kinds of professional services is exposed to potential conflicts of interest, but this can be handled if discussed in depth in advance and the client provides a waiver. Some of the sharpest critics of conflicts of interest have been lawyers themselves.

Bar associations state that lawyers shall not enter into a business transaction with a client or knowingly acquire a financial interest in an artist's enterprise potentially adverse to the client unless the transaction

> is fair and reasonable to the client and fully disclosed and transmitted in writing to the client in a manner and terms which should have reasonably been understood by the client . . . and the client is given reasonable opportunity to seek advice of independent counsel of the client's choice on the transaction . . . and the client consents in writing thereto.[2]

If a lawyer provides extralegal services and enters into business or investment deals with a client, legal ethics demand that all conduct be in accordance with the ethical and legal constraints imposed on a licensed **attorney-at-law.**

Termination. The law provides that a client can discharge a lawyer at any time.[3] But some courts have held that the discharge of a lawyer does not necessarily discharge a former client's liability. For example, dismissing an attorney where a contingent fee arrangement is in place can become sticky for the client. In this kind of situation, the former client will probably have to continue paying the attorney, after disengagement, on earnings flowing from contracts negotiated before the parties went separate ways.

Whether or not a contingent fee is involved, a client who discharges a lawyer should send written notice of termination. Where the artist is retaining a new attorney, the former attorney should be asked, in the notice of termination, to forward all material in the client's file to the new lawyer. Bar associations view this kind of procedure as a matter of professional courtesy.

Notes

1. Language in the California Bar's *Rules of Professional Conduct* is typical: "A member of the State Bar shall not enter into an agreement for, charge or collect an illegal or unconscionable fee . . . when it is so exorbitant and wholly disproportionate to the service as to shock the conscience of lawyers of ordinary prudence practicing in the same community."

2. Quoted from p. 15 of "Ethical Constraints on Contingent Fee Arrangements" in Rules of Professional Conduct. Sacramento: California Bar Association.

3. Code of Civil Procedure, Section 284.

Chapter Takeaways

- Talent agents seek employment for music artists, primarily in the field of live performance.

- Managers guide careers and, depending on the jurisdiction and contractual obligations, are often restricted in negotiating specific employment for clients. This restriction is most prevalent in California because of historical abuses in the motion picture industry.

- Road managers oversee the complexities of touring operations.

- Attorneys negotiate the many contracts that undergird the business. Some attorneys are engaged as much for their "street credibility" and networking skills as they are for their legal knowledge.

Key Terms

- boutique agencies (p. 134)
- carve out (p. 135)
- collateral contracts (p. 143)
- conflict of interest (p. 143)
- franchise (p. 137)
- full-service agencies (p. 134)
- key man clause (p. 136)
- participate (p. 142)
- points (p. 142)

CHAPTER 8

Artists' Recording Contracts

To produce and distribute recorded music, a label must negotiate the acquisition of a variety of goods and services, all of which become part of the finished product. Among the most essential elements of this package are, of course, the services of musicians who perform on the recording. Some recorded works are by self-contained groups. Others use a mix of **sidemusicians** (instrumentalists employed for the session), background (or backup) vocalists, and a featured vocalist or vocal group. The services of backup performers are often controlled exclusively by the terms of the applicable union agreements. The featured artist may also be a union member, and as such, is also subject to the union agreements. However, contracts for featured artists go beyond the issues covered by union contracts; these artists negotiate separate agreements adding, among other terms, a royalty based on record sales. This chapter addresses both the standard union and royalty artist agreements.

> *"I don't know anything about music. In my line you don't have to."*
>
> —Elvis Presley

AFTRA Agreements

All the major recording labels and many independents enter into a labor contract with the American Federation of Television and Radio Artists (AFTRA) for the services of singers. This agreement, known as the AFTRA National Code of Fair Practice for Sound Recordings, covers all singers on a recording—from featured artists to

Left: Elvis Presley singing and playing the piano during a recording session for RCA.

Photo © by Hulton Archive/Getty Images.

backup vocalists, soloists to full choirs. The contract addresses wage **scales**, **overdubbing**, working conditions, **reuse** payments, and labels' contributions to AFTRA's Health & Retirement Funds.

Vocal Contractors

Where recording involves three or more AFTRA-covered singers, AFTRA requires the designation of a union contractor, who must be a singing member of the group. The AFTRA code defines contractors as "those artists who perform any additional services, such as contracting singers, prerehearsing, coaching singers, arranging for sessions or rehearsals, or any other similar or supervisory duties, including assisting with and preparation of production memoranda." AFTRA makes no distinction in this respect between a vocal contractor and a vocal director. The AFTRA contractor must be present at all recording sessions to supervise the adherence of the record producer to the terms of the AFTRA code. An AFTRA contractor is also required when the recording of a Broadway show involves three or more singers. In addition to compensation as a group singer, the contractor receives a fee per hour or per side of recording, whichever is higher.

One of the contractor's important responsibilities is to keep track of overdubbing, or reuse of a taped performance of voices. Voices are overdubbed either "live on tape" or through electronic means, such as tape delays. These techniques are sometimes used to change the **timbre,** resonance, or intensity of voices. Sometimes, through a process called **tracking**, a mixing engineer can cause one to four voices to sound as if many more singers are performing.

Because most tracking results in a net loss of employment for singers, and more work for the singers on any particular project, AFTRA endeavors to control its use through assessing extra charges for such services. The practice of tracking is almost universal today, and it is the task of the AFTRA contractor to log these events, then charge the producer for them. AFTRA requires that when its singers record additional tracks, they are to be paid for the session "as if each **overtracking** were an additional side." Producers sometimes find that extensive overdubbing can cost more than hiring additional singers in the first place.

An additional source of income for performers is a share in the fees paid by users of the sound recording copyright, a revenue stream that began as a trickle in the U.S. with the passage of the Digital Music Copyright Act of 1998. Historically, artists and labels in many other countries have enjoyed more significant income from this source.

For all sessions involving AFTRA-covered singing groups, the contractors, the producers, or the singers must render AFTRA's Sound Recording Sessions Report, which cites the record producer's name, hours of recording, the names of singers involved, and wages due them. The contractor has the producer sign this form, then turns it in to the AFTRA office.

Scale

The AFTRA code sets forth in detail its requirements regarding minimum wages. A producer or contractor should consult an AFTRA representative for current details. There are several common classifications of employment and wages, including the following:

1. Soloists or duos

2. Group singers

3. Soloists who "step out" of a group

4. Singers who record original cast albums (Broadway shows, etc.)

5. Choral singers recording classical music

A royalty artist may be given a recording fund or other advance to cover production costs, and will then earn royalties based on unit sales after production costs have been recouped. If the album is released by a record company signatory to an AFTRA or AFM (American Federation of Musicians) agreement, the company may be required to pay the royalty artist up to three times minimum scale per recorded side (regardless of the number of sessions required to make the recording).

It wasn't until 1974 that AFTRA managed to negotiate a contract incorporating the minimum royalty concept—a significant breakthrough in how extra wages were to be calculated for session singers. AFTRA singers who previously did not receive a royalty started receiving additional wages based on recordings sold. Prior to the contract this was not the case, no matter how successful a particular recording became. These extra payments became known as **contingent scale payments**. For example, under the current contract when an album reaches 157,500 in sales, nonroyalty AFTRA singers on that album receive a payment equal to 50% of their original scale for those particular sessions. There are 15 contingent scale plateaus, up to as high as 3 million in sales, totaling an additional 1,005% of scale. Other payment schedules apply to single recordings and original cast albums.

A recording generates these payments for a period of 10 years following its initial release, and payments are limited to sales in the United States that occur through normal retail channels. Sales through record clubs, premiums, and mail orders are excluded, as are recordings distributed for promotional purposes. In determining which releases are subject to these payments, only the initial release of a record side in album form is included, not any subsequent inclusions of that side in other albums. As for singles, only the initial release is eligible, but a single later included in an album also qualifies. A side first released in an album is eligible when it first reappears as a single.

AFTRA has also negotiated payments to nonroyalty singers for the sale of digital downloads, ringtones, and music video downloads. Permanent digital downloads earn for singers a percentage of the wholesale price (after applicable exclusions) for 10 years, which is extended another 10 years if over one million downloads are sold within the first decade. Nonpermanent downloads pay in the same manner, but at a different percentage of the wholesale price, with the years of coverage determined by a separate agreement. Music videos are also paid as a percentage of wholesale, with one rate for the first 10 years from release and a different percentage for an additional five years. Singer payments are processed through the AFM/AFTRA Fund. AFTRA Health & Retirement (AFTRA H&R) contributions are also paid on all earnings.

With respect to the AFTRA Health & Retirement Funds, record companies are required to pay on behalf of AFTRA artists (royalty and nonroyalty) about 11.5% (the rate may vary) of their gross compensation for the recording. The term *gross compensation* is defined by the AFTRA code in this respect as including royalties paid AFTRA-covered artists by the record company. Payment into the fund is limited to the first $140,000 of gross compensation paid to the artist and $160,000 paid to an artist group of three or more by the record company in any calendar year. The payment into these funds is also required with respect to the contingent scale payments described above.

Because of the unique nature of royalty contracts, the AFTRA code also requires that H&R contributions be made on royalties earned, even if unrecouped. Therefore, if the artist has royalties earned and credited, even if unpaid because of recoupment, the artist receives his or her AFTRA H&R eligibility. Importantly, record labels are required to make a contribution on behalf of every royalty artist under contract to entitle that artist to a minimum of individual health insurance, regardless of earnings, if the artist enrolls in the AFTRA benefits plan.

Acquired Masters

When a singer records for an AFTRA signatory label, AFTRA has little difficulty controlling minimum wages and working conditions. But in a widespread practice, many recordings are made by very small companies and by independent record producers who later attempt to sell or lease their master tapes to a third party. Here full union control is difficult—often impossible—although AFTRA and the AFM do what they can to protect their members.

The AFTRA code requires that if a signatory record company acquires a master from a nonsignatory producer, that producer must have complied with the AFTRA code in effect at the time the recording was made. The purpose here is to ensure that no producer will be economically motivated to create a master for a nonsignatory as a way of avoiding minimum union payments.

When a signatory third party acquires interest in or ownership of a master recording that uses AFTRA members, it must comply with the obligations under the AFTRA code, including the making of H&R and contingent payments. The AFTRA code specifies that the original owner must require any successor to accept the terms and obligations of the code.

Artists' unions also endeavor to protect the interests of their members when master tapes recorded for one medium are licensed for use in another medium. Perhaps the most common occurrence of this kind involves a tape prepared for a commercial recording and then transferred for use on television, where the on-camera artist lip-synchs the performance. Whatever kind of secondary use is made of a recording (called a conversion, new use, or reuse), AFTRA requires the record company to get a warranty from the new user guaranteeing that the singers will receive no less than the appropriate scale payment for the new use. With respect to the music video field, AFTRA has a separate agreement with the producers.

Nonunion Recording

Even though AFTRA has agreements with all the major labels, the practice of non-union recording is widespread. Aspiring young performers, eager to jump-start their careers, often do not take time to learn established professional practices. Some artists never discover the advantages of collectivism, the foundation of all union activity. It is important to remember that there is typically a pronounced disparity of bargaining power between any one artist and an entertainment conglomerate. Unions, therefore, remain key players in the entertainment business, providing an important source of artists' rights protection.

Changing technologies provide more opportunity than ever before for artists who can't—or don't want to—sign with existing record labels. Young performers can inexpensively produce their own masters at home, then market themselves via their own Web sites, social networking sites, and Internet sales aggregators like CD Baby. They can also sell their wares electronically through iTunes and other digital sales sites. Rarely do such entrepreneurs adhere to AFTRA or AFM regulations or scales for themselves or supporting personnel. Many "self-produced" performers, at the start of their careers, are not even aware of the artists' unions and their traditions. Occasionally, the performer-producer-distributor-merchant experiences initial success in a limited geographic area. Some one-person record companies manage later to sell or lease their masters to an established label with national distribution. At that point, either the original entrepreneur or the lessee must meet the AFTRA obligations described above. Thus, the original entrepreneur saves no money in the long run by initially circumventing AFTRA and the AFM, for their members must ultimately be paid for any recording to take off in the mainstream national market.

AFM Agreements

Sound Recording Labor Agreement

Many labels that have agreements with AFTRA also have agreements with the AFM for the services of instrumentalists, conductors, arrangers, orchestrators, and copyists. Approximately every 3 years, the AFM, under the supervision of its president, designates a committee to negotiate a successor agreement with recording industry representatives. The current contract is known as the AFM Sound Recording Labor Agreement. It governs wages, benefits, and working conditions for the services of musicians working in the recording industry in the United States and Canada. The agreement also covers provisions for the production of music videos and concert DVDs.

In addition to wages paid for musicians' services, the contract also requires the employer to pay into the AFM Health and Welfare Fund (AFM **H&W**) to locals that have established them or directly to musicians, absent such a plan, and up to 12% of gross (scale) wages into the AFM-**EP**, the AFM Employers Pension Fund.

The contract provides 200% of sidemusicians' pay for the leader (musical director). Where a session calls for 12 or more musicians, an AFM contractor is required and receives double sidemusician's wages. Musicians doubling on a second instrument are paid, with some exceptions, 20% extra for the first **double**, then 15% for each additional double. The agreement contains many other provisions covering rest periods, meal breaks, and surcharges for work performed after midnight and on holidays, as well as special rates and conditions for work performed on electronic instruments. Even cartage fees for heavy instruments are stipulated.

As with AFTRA, AFM contracts control wages and working conditions for backup artists. But the acts whose names and sounds are used to sell records negotiate their own contracts, although the union contracts do set a floor for the individual agreements, along with many of the nonwage benefits. These performers are known as *royalty artists,* and the AFM defines such performers as an individual or self-contained group contracted to receive a record royalty of at least 3% of the suggested retail list price or a substantially equivalent royalty.

The AFM Sound Recording Labor Agreement provides that royalty artists receive one session payment for each song recorded on an album. The session payment may be part of recording costs that are recouped from artist royalties.

The agreement also requires that all music "prepared" for recording must be handled exclusively by arrangers, orchestrators, and copyists who are AFM members. Because the AFM claims no jurisdiction over the work of songwriters and other kinds of composers, the agreement does not cover their services.

Enforcement of union scales and working conditions generally goes smoothly with well-established, recognized labels when they produce their own masters. But as noted above, record companies frequently lease or buy "outside" masters. The agreement deals with this scenario in detail, but policing of these transactions is difficult, sometimes impossible. Record manufacturers are prohibited from using acquired masters unless the music was recorded under the AFM contract and scale wages were paid, or the musicians have been paid equivalent wages and the record company makes its required contribution to the AFM Pension Fund. The company may satisfy its obligation by securing a "representation of warranty" from the seller or licensor of the acquired master that the requirements of the AFM have been met.

Sound Recording Special Payments Fund

Phonograph Records. When a recording company becomes a signatory to the AFM Sound Recording Labor Agreement, it must simultaneously execute a Sound Recording Special Payments Fund Agreement.

Record companies make payments into the Sound Recording Special Payments Fund twice each year, based on the aggregate sale of recordings in the company's catalog. The "royalty" due the fund has changed over the years, but as of 2009 the record company payments averaged about $0.03 per physical unit sold and $0.005 per song downloaded.

Record labels pay all these royalties to the administrator of the fund. After administrative expenses are deducted, all funds are then paid to the musicians who, during the preceding 5-year period, performed on any of the recordings covered by the Special Payments Fund Agreement. Payments are based on the musician's earnings from overall record sales, not on the sale of particular recordings. Musicians who earned the same scale payments from work on sound recordings will receive the same amount from the Special Payments Fund, even if one musician worked on a multiplatinum album and the other worked on an album that sold only 5,000 copies.

The Sound Recording Special Payments Fund Agreement recognizes that during the 10-year royalty payment period, the ownership and control of a recording may change. Anticipating these changes, the agreement requires any such purchaser, assignee, lessee, licensee, transferee, or user to assume the original master or record producer's obligations to the AFM. Because of the frequent changes in the recording industry—companies and ownership come and go—the control and collection of these funds by the AFM is difficult and cannot always be accomplished.

Motion Pictures. The Film Musicians Secondary Markets Fund is collected from film companies and paid to musicians who have worked on sound tracks of films. Unlike the Sound Recording Special Payments Fund, payments to the Film Musicians Secondary Markets Fund reflect the relative success of each project. A musician who worked on a picture that made a lot of money will receive more than a musician who spent the same amount of time working on a commercially unsuccessful film. In both cases, musicians are also paid for the hours they actually work in the studio.

Music Performance Funds

The MPF, or Music Performance Fund, was established in 1948 as a nonprofit public service organization to help keep live music available to the public. From the beginning, the AFM recognized that the increasing impact of recording technology was devastating to the music profession except perhaps for the AFM members who earn at least part of their livelihood from recording. Knowing that nothing could stop the rapid technological growth, the AFM managed to negotiate agreements with record companies that return to union musicians at least a fraction of the income lost through the displacement of live performances by recordings. Signatory recording companies must enter into a Music Performance Fund Agreement with the AFM. Payments are made to the fund's trustee and are based on record sales.

The Music Performance Fund Agreement requires the trustee to use all monies collected, minus operational expenses, to schedule live music performances by AFM members. In actual practice, administration of these monies is shared by each of the AFM locals that parcel out jobs to their members, irrespective of whether they are recording musicians, and calls for prevailing local union scales. AFM locals may use some of the money to hire halls, finance publicity, print tickets, and so on. Cosponsors of concerts are generally required. The fund's purpose is to foster public understanding of and appreciation for live music. Most performances are for schools, hospitals, religious organizations, cultural events, and patriotic celebrations. If no admission is charged, the live performances may be broadcast. Established cultural organizations, such as symphony orchestras, opera, and ballet companies, often call on the fund to finance or partially finance live music performances.

The current phenomenon of digital downloading has adversely affected sales of physical product. This has had a negative impact on funds coming into the MPF, translating into fewer dollars for live performances sponsored by the Fund.

Nonunion Recording

AFM and AFTRA have tried to maintain strict union shops in recording studios for decades, with uneven results. Following enactment of the Taft-Hartley Act and right-to-work laws in various states, which allow employers wide latitude in setting wages and working conditions, the establishment and maintenance of a strict union shop concept has been difficult. The AFM oversees all professional symphony orchestra recording in the United States, along with most popular music recording in the major recording centers. Union control is less strong in the gospel, Christian, jazz, and country fields. The AFM, from time to time, implements a PR campaign to attract young players ("Young Sounds of the AFM") with reduced fees and dues. As young musicians gain professional experience, they usually discover that working under the protection of AFM membership offers financial advantages over participating in nonunion gigs.

Another kind of nonunion recording is the **spec** session. Producers will hire some musicians, pay them perhaps $50 per hour, then promise to make full payment later, "when the recording sells," in an amount equal to AFM scale. Still other producers pay the musicians (union or nonunion) nothing up front, promising to pay full union scale later when the producer can raise the money. Both these kinds of spec recording are disapproved of by the AFM, although the union contract does provide for a lower "demo" scale than its regular recording rates.

For more information about how the AFM helps musicians with record deals and recording contracts, go to www.afm.org/departments/electronic-media-services-division.

Royalty Artist Contracts

Many performers think the way to prosperity—the big money, the international reputation—largely depends on obtaining a recording contract. Until a performer becomes recognized as a recording artist, according to this outlook, it is almost impossible to attract enough notice to get gigs from concert promoters, major booking agencies, television, and film producers. Of course, an artist can develop a satisfactory career in one area—for example, on Broadway—without selling records. But most performers seek the prestige and potential income gained through recording.

Types of Deals

In earlier times it was simple: A record company signed an artist, instructed one of its house A&R (artist and repertoire) people to produce the record, and that was that. And that formula sometimes still applies. More often, though, the record company and the artist have a number of other options when they negotiate a contract. These options have come into play partly because of the decline in the clout of record companies, as well as the economic ascendance of other key industry participants, among them the independent producer.

Today, the most common deals placing an artist under contract include:

1. The label signs the artist, then has one of its producers handle the project **in-house.** The artist gets royalties; the staff producer receives a salary and perhaps a royalty override. The label pays all costs pursuant to a budget and may or may not pay advances to the artist. This deal is much less common than in the past.

2. The label already has the artist under contract. It retains an independent producer (or production company) to deliver a master tape. The record company assigns a production budget to the producer, and may pay a production fee up front, usually an advance on royalties. The producer also gets a royalty of 2% to 6%, based on the retail list price of records sold and on the prior success and negotiating strength of the producer.

3. The independent producer and an independent artist strike a deal, create a master tape, then try to induce a record company to acquire it. The label accepting the master pays the parties royalties based on units sold (the artist and the producer had previously arranged how they would share these royalties).

4. In a master lease deal, the artist or production company pays all recording costs and leases the master to the label in exchange for a royalty. The label may or may not pay an advance in the form of reimbursement of recording costs. Since the artist or production company as licensor assumes the risk of recording, the record company normally does not obtain ownership but merely distribution rights limited by time and territory.

5. An artist forms a production company to deliver a master tape to a label. The producer on the project might be on the production company's payroll or might be engaged freelance just for this project. The label pays the artist's company a royalty, and the artist then pays the producer a share of those royalties.

Negotiations

Currently, most record companies choose their talent more selectively than ever. Today's more conservative signing policies result largely from the prohibitive costs of "breaking" new pop artists, which could start in the range of $500,000 to $1 million or more for production and initial promotional and marketing expenses.

The negotiation process begins when the label executive sits down to discuss the terms of a contract with the artist's manager and/or lawyers. In the next step, the terms of the deal are determined, and then lawyers meet to hammer out the fine print. This scenario typically develops after an artist with savvy management has created a "buzz" among industry insiders. In the most desirable situation for an artist, several companies bid competitively to sign the artist.

If the artist lacks management and legal counsel, established labels will insist that an attorney represent the artist. Courts have set onerous contracts aside when it was learned that the artist had no attorney. A senior executive and the company's legal counsel handle the negotiations for the label. Sometimes a company's vice president for "business affairs" or the A&R head is empowered to negotiate an artist's contract.

Both parties see these negotiations as an opportunity to maximize self-interests. It stands to reason that the party getting more favorable terms is the one with greater clout. Compromise, however, is usually the key to an enduring, long-term relationship. Take, for example, one chief negotiating point—the advance. A large signing advance or recording budget might improve an artist's state of mind but substantially increase the record company's risk. An effective negotiation might satisfy both parties by providing royalty rate adjustments or bonuses as certain sales levels, sometimes called plateaus, are reached.

The Issues

Well-drawn recording contracts will cover the following issues:

Term. In the past, the standard length of an artist's recording contract was 1 year, with a specified number of 1-year options (usually three to five options) for the company to extend. More common today, at least with established artists, the contract duration is tied to the timing of master delivery release requirements and a period of evaluation by the record company. Experienced artists' lawyers often attempt to negotiate contracts on a multiple-album basis—for example, a "firm" three-album contract. If the first album does not sell well, the parties are still bound to each other for two follow-up releases. On the other hand, the record company prefers the commitment to be for an initial album with options for one or two more albums, based on the success of prior albums.

In a three-album contract, should the label decline to release all three albums, the artist's attorney often tries to stipulate that the contract provides a penalty (a "kill fee"), normally a sum of money ("liquidated damages") payable to the artist. The label, however, prefers the penalty to be a "pay or play" obligation, which means that the liquidated sum payable to the artist is only the minimum union scale payment for the unrecorded album. (Many deals are one-sided in that they may bind an artist for as many as seven albums, but also allow the label to exercise a series of options without giving the artist any right to opt out or obligate the label to release and promote a recording.) Fairly-drawn contracts provide guarantees of artist's delivery by a certain date and the company's release of the recordings. Experienced lawyers representing artists try to get the label to guarantee release within 90 to 120 days following delivery of the master to the company.

The holiday period of November and December is always excluded from these date specifications. During downturn periods in the recording business, or if the artist is unknown, companies sometimes commit only to singles and "EP (extended play) deals" that usually include five or six songs. In these circumstances, record companies may prefer to limit their risk and their initial recording expenses. They can produce an EP for, say, $5,000 per side or less, rather than the larger amount it would take to turn out a full album. This sort of deal occurs frequently in the urban and **alternative** music genres where there are many small indie labels.

Exclusivity. Almost all recording contracts require the artist to record, during the term of the contract, only for the label that has the artist under contract. But if the artist also records from time to time in a capacity other than as a solo artist or featured group—for instance, as a **session musician** or sidemusician on a jazz recording—the artist's lawyer will push for the contract to permit such outside services.

Royalties, Advances. Depending on the relative leverage of the record company and the artist, the royalty offer will generally be in the range of 10% to 15% of the retail price, with perhaps 3 percentage points of that going to the producer. Major stars have been known to get as high as 18% to 22% of retail. Sometimes a label will try to hold the initial royalty below 10% and then escalate the rate as sales rise. For example, the artist might receive 9% on the first 250,000 sales, 10% on the next 250,000, and 12% if the recording goes platinum. In this scenario, the artist's legal representative might persuade a label to compromise by upping the royalty rate on the second album, should sales of the first album turn out to be satisfactory.

There is no standard policy among record companies on royalty advances. An advance is really a prepayment of royalties, so the amount of an advance is based on an estimate of future sales. For instance, if an artist has a history of sales of approximately 100,000 albums and an average royalty is in the area of $1.00 per album, then an advance of $100,000 might seem reasonable. In practice, however, a prudent label might offer between $50,000 and $75,000, because at least some of those 100,000 records will be returned, and the manufacturer would establish a reserve against returns.

Production Budget Minimums. Major recording artists can negotiate big-budget commitments from a label to cover recording production costs, while less prominent artists generally cannot impose such demands. But a promising new artist is well advised, if negotiating with a label of limited resources, to demand a minimum budget commitment or risk being caught in a low-quality project that could hurt a developing career.

A recording budget is an estimate of the cost of the album production. If actual production or recording expenses come in under budget, the record company generally doesn't pay any more than actual recording expenses unless the contract provides for a recording fund rather than a recording budget. In that case, an agreed-on sum is set aside for a fund, with one third to perhaps one half of the amount being released to the artist (or the producer) at the commencement of recording. The balance is released from the fund following completion and satisfactory delivery of the master tape. Should the production expense total an amount smaller than the recording fund, some contracts allow the artist (or producer) to keep the difference, with the understanding that the entire sum is recoupable by the label from royalties earned by the artist on sales of the record.

Creative Control. The artist's track record and bargaining power will determine the amount of control an artist has over issues such as song selection, choice of producer, and style of album graphic art. Stars get lots of control, while less established artists generally have to accept the judgments of the record company. The parties usually decide together on selecting the producer. Labels usually want new artists to collaborate with producers having proven track records. As for the selection of songs, record companies rarely give up the final decision on which tracks to record, but few labels force their artists to record specific pieces of material.

Commitment to Promote. Strong-selling artists generally get their labels to commit sufficient money and personnel to fully exploit their releases. Even so, most artists, including the big stars, regularly complain that their label is not providing adequate promotion. Disagreement over promotion is one of the chief causes of artist-label tensions. If the music doesn't sell, the label blames the artist; the artist insists sales would have been just fine if the label had done its job promoting and marketing the release. Artists and their managers ideally seek label commitment for tour support, press coverage, interviews, independent radio promotion, retail in-store promotion, and TV, trade magazine, consumer magazine, and newspaper ads. (Often, half the money spent on promotion is recouped from the artist's royalty earnings, providing a disincentive for artists to go crazy with their demands.)

Chargebacks. Royalty contracts routinely stipulate that the record company does not have to pay the artist any royalties beyond whatever advances are negotiated, until the label has recovered, through a recoupment from the artist's royalties, its out-of-pocket production costs and advances. Production expenses that are considered legitimate to **chargeback** include studio rentals, the cost of blank tape, union wages to AFM and AFTRA members, music arranging and copying expense, producer costs, and any other expense directly or indirectly related to production of the album. Such costs can easily total $500,000 and more for a pop album. Upon completion of a project, all the artist gets are advances or the overage on the fund, if there is one. No more money comes to the artist until the label has recouped its recording costs. The record has to sell well just for the artist to break even.

Advances to artists are not returnable, but they are almost always recoupable. If album sales are not sufficient to recoup the advance through artist royalties, the artist is not obligated to return the money. When trying to determine how many albums must be sold before an artist has recouped advances, many attorneys use an estimate of 1 percentage point at retail being worth roughly 10 cents of royalty income to the artist per album sold. Therefore, 10 points would equal $1.00 per album sold. To recoup $100,000, the recording company would have to sell 100,000 albums.

Obviously, recoupment of an artist's recording account is not always necessary for the recording company to realize a satisfactory return on an artist's recordings. Although it is true that it would take 100,000 sales to recoup $100,000, the average wholesale price of a CD is close to $10.00, and so that same 100,000 sales will generate $1 million in gross income. Of course, there are costs involved with those sales, but it's likely that the record company in this situation sees profits long before the artist's royalty account is recouped.

It is not unusual for an artist to have fulfilled all recording obligations under a contract, have some recordings that sold well, and still not receive any royalties. Even with successful albums, the artist's overall royalty account may remain unrecouped. In fact, fewer than 15% of recordings recoup. Almost all record companies include a clause in the contract making costs accrued on all recordings recoupable out of royalties on all recordings (see the Royalty Discounts section, below). For example, if an artist makes three albums with each having recoupable costs of $100,000 and the albums sell very few copies but the artist makes a fourth album for $100,000, then the artist will not receive any royalties until the label has recouped $400,000. This concept, called *cross-collateralization,* makes it difficult, in the majority of cases, for the artist's royalty account to ever be recouped or "in the black."

Ownership of Masters. Initially, the recording company owns all rights to the masters. But when a contract is terminated, artists' attorneys often try to negotiate transfer of ownership to their clients. Record companies are rarely willing to give up ownership of masters, since master recordings of successful artists can have considerable residual value, particularly in the form of repackages and/or reissues. (Master tapes are often sold or leased to secondary labels for this purpose.)

Reissues of old recordings in new formats have contributed significantly to album sales. Most major record companies now have separate departments dedicated solely to "vaults," or reissues of their back catalogs. True superstars might, in some cases, be able to negotiate eventual return of their masters, but in general, if a label pays to record a master, the label will own it in perpetuity.

Publishing Rights, Controlled Compositions. When an artist composes original songs, many recording companies will try to persuade him or her to place them with a publishing company owned by or affiliated with the label. When this happens, the artist-writer may receive additional advances. If the label's publishing wing cannot obtain full publishing rights, it will probably offer to share the publishing revenue with the composer-performer in what is known as a copublishing arrangement. If the label or production company cannot share "in the publishing," it will almost always demand a reduced mechanical rate, commonly 25% below the current statutory rate, for all works owned or controlled by the recording artist. Such language is called *controlled composition* language, and the artist refusing to accept this language may not get signed.

Controlled composition language usually specifies that the label will pay a rate equal to 75% of the minimum statutory rate. It also provides that the maximum album rate for all compositions, controlled and noncontrolled, cannot exceed 10 times the per-composition rate. This can lead to disastrous results when the artist records both controlled and noncontrolled compositions. The publishers of the noncontrolled compositions are, of course, not going to abide by the 75% language and will demand full rate, which, in the case of longer works such as jazz recordings, could exceed the minimum rate applicable to works of 5 minutes or less. Since there is an album cap of 10 × 75% of the minimum, the artist's own rate will be reduced below 75%; in extreme cases it could go to zero or even be negative, meaning the artist could actually owe the label money. The statutory rate used in such calculations is the minimum rate in effect at the time the album was delivered or supposed to have been delivered. These contract provisions can rarely be avoided except by major stars.

Video Rights. Many labels demand the exclusive services of their contract artists for any and all performances on videos and DVDs (clips, compilations, and long forms such as concerts), offering to share the potential income from distributors. They also charge to the artist's recording royalty account all or part of video production costs.

A typical negotiated recording contract includes agreement on the following issues relating to videos:

1. Videos must be defined as "promotional" or "commercial." Promotional clips, compilations, and video "albums" (or "long-form" videos) are defined according to their lengths in order to clarify further the distinctions between promotional and commercial videos.

2. The label generally pays for production costs of the video. Video costs are recouped first from royalties on video sales. To the extent that video sales are insufficient for the recoupment of these costs, most recording contracts provide for recoupment of the balance of those costs from the artist's general audio royalty account. Contracts vary as to what percentage of video costs is recoupable from this account. Most labels initially insist on recouping 100%, although some will agree to limit video cost recoupment under the audio account to 50%.

3. If the artist owns or controls any of the music used on a video, the artist will be expected to waive licensing fees and royalties on that material, provided the video is for promotional purposes only. If the video is nonpromotional in nature, the artist-composer can argue for synchronization fees and mechanical royalties.

4. The artist should seek reasonable control over the selection of video directors, other production personnel, the budget, and storyline.

5. If the label refuses to produce a video, the artist may try to reserve the right to produce the video at the artist's own expense.

Foreign Releases. The artist's lawyer should try to persuade the recording company to specify the foreign territories in which the recording will be released. In addition, the attorney should try to get the label to effect these releases simultaneously with or shortly after the American release, to maximize the effectiveness of a promotion campaign and minimize the damage of both Internet piracy and imports into territories where cheaper records imported from Europe and the United States compete with the expensive domestic version. All major labels have their own foreign affiliates, but smaller labels work through licensees.

It is important for the artist to negotiate carefully how royalties are earned on sales in foreign territories. Many labels pay only 50% of the domestic rate for foreign sales, but this can often be increased through negotiation. When a sale takes place outside the United States, the artist is entitled to an accounting only after the licensee accounts to the U.S. label.

Overseas, recordings are rarely sold on consignment. Once a record has been purchased by a customer, it cannot generally be returned. In Europe, a sale is a sale; you get paid for what is purchased. This makes accounting simpler and obviates the need for the foreign licensee to hold back royalty reserves. The U.S. label might still take a reserve on foreign sales, though, because it would not differentiate these sales in terms of general reserve policies.

Assignment. Contracts normally specify the terms under which a label may assign a contract to another entity. When a contract is assigned, the new label owns all the recordings and artist services signed to the previous label. Record companies, especially smaller ones, often change ownership, leadership, or direction, and such circumstances may result in the label assigning its contract rights.

In negotiating an artist's contract, the artist's attorney should try to limit the label's right to assignment to the sale of the company's total business or assets. Generally speaking, the right to sell existing masters is permitted, while the right to require the artist to record for another company can be restricted to an affiliated entity.

Right to Audit. Royalty statements are rendered semiannually. The parties usually agree that the artist may, after proper written notice, audit the books of the label. In most states, a right to audit would be inferred by a court even if it weren't in the contract; therefore, labels write in a very restricted audit clause to avoid a much broader one being defined by a court.

Because most experienced auditors work by the hour rather than for a percentage of the recovery, audits for major stars are expensive. The artist's lawyer should seek a provision in the recording contract that requires the recording company to pay the entire cost of the examination if the amount found to be owed exceeds 10% of the amount actually paid. Although audits rarely reveal that the company has deliberately cheated an artist, discovery of royalties owed is a regular occurrence.

Default, Cure. If the parties have a fundamental disagreement, certain remedies are available to either side. If, for instance, the artist is scheduled to deliver an album but decides to take a 6-month vacation, the label may argue that the artist is not meeting contractual obligations. It can then either suspend the term of the agreement and its obligation to pay royalties, or terminate the agreement and possibly sue for damages.

Because recording contracts involve personal services, few courts will tell an artist to perform such services against the artist's will. If the recording company enjoins the artist from recording for a competitor during a dispute, the artist has three options: (a) not record at all, (b) attempt to renegotiate the contract, or (c) continue recording for the first company.

Sometimes a label agrees to renegotiate rather than pursuing legal remedies. Neither party wins, and good music rarely results, when a contract is viewed as inequitable or unfair.

Royalty Discounts. Record companies try to reduce the price on which royalties are calculated as much as possible despite protests from attorneys across the table. Here are commonly seen limitations on the royalty base:

1. *Breakage allowance.* Some labels still offer royalties based on 85% or 90% of sales, a practice justified decades ago by the fact that about 10% of the old 78-rpm records were damaged in transit. Although damages are nowhere near that percentage today, the practice of paying royalties on less than 100% of sales remains intact.

2. *Packaging discount.* Labels may deduct up to a quarter of the price to cover costs of tape or CD packaging materials. These materials don't approach these cost levels anymore, but the charge is assessed anyway—universally, 25% of retail on CDs and other digital formats and 20% on tapes.

3. *Free goods.* Companies usually discount royalties for free goods given to distributors and retailers as incentives and quantity discounts (e.g., "Buy 10 and we'll give you 12"). The royalty-based price is always reduced at least 15% to reflect this policy. Some labels believe they must give away nearly one half of their singles to sell the other half. Artists receive no royalties on these "free goods" or promo copies.

4. *CD rate discounts.* Artist royalty rates may be reduced 15% to 20% for CDs, payable on a reduced number of royalty-bearing units. In this instance, an artist royalty rate in a contract of 10% effectively becomes a net artist royalty rate of 7.5% to 8%.

5. *Record club sales.* Labels usually pay a tiny royalty on their net receipts from sales through record clubs, which in turn pay a very low royalty to the label.

6. *Merchandising.* Some record companies acquire these rights and make merchandising deals on behalf of the artist. Artists' attorneys should seek to retain rights in this area unless the label is in the merchandising business, which may or may not be the case.

7. *Cross-collateralization.* All recording companies attempt to **cross-collateralize** an artist's royalties. If one release sells well and earns royalties, those royalties are used by the label to recoup its production costs on the artist's other, less successful recordings. As noted above, labels will also recoup from artist's record royalties expenses incurred in producing videos. If the label has an interest in the artist's publishing, it will often try to cross-collateralize against the publishing income as well.

In most cases of contract negotiation with new artists, the record company bargains from a position of strength, creating a contract that is essentially one-sided and most likely will not yield significant royalties to the artist. As an artist's success grows, advances, recording budgets, and royalties go up and the balance of power begins to even out. When superstardom is achieved, the record company becomes more of a distributor, working for a relatively small "participation" to recoup an enormous investment.

360 deals

The growing phenomenon of the "360 deal" illustrates the power shift between artists and record companies as a result of the change in traditional methods of music distribution. With the sale of physical copies of recordings no longer the industry's growth engine, record companies want agreements under which they can earn income from a wide range of an artist's activities.

There are two basic types of 360 deals, also known as "artist brand" agreements. In the first, the record company receives traditional revenues from sales of the product, and simply gets a percentage of the artist's other income streams. These may include merchandise sales, endorsements, touring, ticketing, and, in a favored legalism, revenues coming from anywhere "now known or hereafter developed." When they meet resistance from artists, the labels argue that 360 deals are good for artists because these deals incentivize the labels to spend significant development and marketing resources on the artist's behalf—including dispersing free goods—so that everyone comes out ahead in the end.

The second kind of 360 deal goes beyond basic revenue sharing and finds the record company in a true partnership with the artist. Here both parties have to agree on major decisions, in addition to sharing income distribution. In a typical deal of this kind, the label's share of nonrecord fees would average around 10%. In some cases, where the label has leverage due to the artist's lack of a successful track record, the label's share has gone as high as 50%.

A 360 deal can also be structured as a traditional recording contract, but give the label an option to convert to a 360 arrangement based on certain criteria such as gross sales.

Trading on an artist's brand can be profitable for record labels, but the new environment is a double-edged sword. Artists that can afford it, or who want to take a chance, are increasingly abandoning their labels and exploiting themselves through the very same activities record labels are seeking to cash in on. If a label wants a piece of all the action, an artist with leverage has to ask if it's really a deal worth making. And traditional labels aren't the only potential partners. This deal structure has also lured other firms, with heritages ranging from artist management to concert promotion, to enter into 360 deals that otherwise might be signed by traditional labels.

New Use and Legacy Royalty Rates

Over the decades, the recording industry has absorbed dramatic changes in technology, and its standard recording artists agreement has been adjusted accordingly. Deals incorporating the long-playing album, the 45-rpm single, various configurations of tapes (including reel-to-reel, cassette, and eight track), and the CD all evolved out of contracts addressing the original 78-rpm, 10-inch shellac record. Then the digital age ushered in a whole new way of delivering music to the consumer.

Historically, recording contracts have incorporated new uses by fitting them into an existing category. For years, the CD was treated as if it were an LP, even though it had a retail price that was more than double that of the comparable vinyl LP. Royalties on CD sales are still lower than that for tape sales, despite the fact that CDs are the dominant (and in many cases the only) format in which records are sold through brick and mortar stores.

The standard recording artist agreement provides for payment to the artist at different rates depending on whether the record is sold, licensed, given away, or used as promotion. Direct sales by the label, as we have seen, provide a royalty payment to the artist that varies according to the type of sale. Licenses of masters for motion pictures, commercials, or television generate a license fee, either in the form of a royalty or a flat payment, which is usually shared with the artist on a 50–50 basis after deduction of out-of-pocket or third-party costs.

For royalty artists, digital downloads are basically treated as a record sale or license. It is a sale or license depending on whether the download is from the label's own site or whether it is licensed to a downloading site, such as iTunes. If there is a royalty payable to the artist, it will most often be at a reduced rate of 75% or less of the otherwise applicable CD rate, ignoring the fact that there are few of the manufacturing and distribution costs that helped justify the discount in the earlier medium. Promotional downloads are free of royalty even though the label may receive some compensation.

Another new use is the licensing of masters as telephone ringtones. Many telephones do not have the technology capable of reproducing actual recordings and they often use MIDI tracks, which don't involve a recording right at all, but only a license to the publisher of the underlying composition. If a master, in fact, were licensed for a ringtone use, the label would either treat it as a license and pay the artist a percentage of that fee or as a sale and pay a reduced royalty.

Yet another digital delivery use made possible by advances in technology is instant recording at live performance venues. It is now possible to make recordings of performances right on the spot, and the resulting MP3s are usually sold at specially equipped kiosks at the venue. This is often done with unsigned bands, where there is no record label involved. Labels have been reluctant to permit this type of delivery on the theory that it would negatively impact CD sales. If labels were to permit such a use, they would probably try to maintain that it was a promotional use since the recording is not CD quality. If the artist could negotiate any royalty at all, it would almost certainly be at a sharp discount from the regular CD royalty.

Chapter Takeaways

- Although many performers of recorded music are represented by unions, it is through separately negotiated artist's royalty contracts that truly lucrative deals are struck.

- Nonunion recording sessions are commonplace. A union signatory label wishing to release a recording acquired from a nonsignatory party must pay union scale to participants retroactively.

- Terms of royalty artist contracts vary significantly. An unknown artist must accept unfavorable terms; a superstar may be able to dictate many key contract provisions.

- Most recording deals are unrecouped— meaning the artists frequently sees no royalties beyond payment for delivering the master to the label.

- Though more lucrative for labels, 360 deals are actually a sign of the declining role of labels in powering the music industry economic engine.

Key Terms

- contingent scale payments (p. 149)
- cross-collateralization (p. 161)
- doubling (p. 151)
- EP deal (p. 156)
- gross compensation (p. 149)
- new use (p. 162)

- overdubbing (p. 148)
- pay or play (p. 155)
- recording fund (p. 156)
- recoupment (p. 157)
- reuse (p. 148)
- right-to-work laws (p. 153)
- royalty artist (p. 151)

- scale (wage) (p. 148)
- self-contained group (p. 151)
- side musicians (p. 151)
- spec session (p. 153)
- Taft-Hartley Act (p. 153)
- tracking (p. 148)
- union shop (p. 153)

CHAPTER 9

Unions and Guilds

Workers involved in the music and entertainment fields have developed numerous organizations to represent their interests.[1] The larger organizations related to music are discussed in this chapter. They are structured in a variety of ways. Some, such as the American Federation of Musicians (AFM) and the Screen Actors Guild (SAG), are trade unions, connected with the American Federation of Labor and Congress of Industrial Organizations (AFL-CIO). Others are more accurately described as **guilds**. Still others are simply associations of independent contractors. If this is not complicated enough, the list includes entertainment industry guilds (e.g., the Dramatists Guild), whose members may own the company with whom they are supposed to negotiate for their services.

Discussed below are the AFM, the American Federation of Television and Radio Artists (AFTRA), the American Guild of Musical Artists (AGMA), the American Guild of Variety Artists (AGVA), the Actors' Equity Association, and SAG. Other unions and guilds are described at the end of the chapter.

> *"Famous I don't know about. It's hard to be famous and alive. I just want to play music every day and hear someone say, 'Thanks, that was great, here's some money, same time tomorrow, okay?'"*
>
> *—Terry Pratchett*

Left: Photo © Gary S. Chapman.

When young artists start their careers, they are often reluctant to join the unions for their respective crafts because enlisting seems expensive and restrictive. But if a demand develops for the artist's services, opportunities will arise for which union affiliation is not only advantageous but imperative. Most employment available to artists above the small-time level is "union," meaning that if an individual wants to be a professional performer (or arranger, **copyist,** director, conductor, actor, dancer, etc.), those services will most likely be under the jurisdiction and control of a union contract.

The arts organizations and industries employing artists have recognized, often reluctantly, the bargaining rights of AFM, AFTRA, and the other unions. But artists' labor organizations have experienced, in recent years, the same problems affecting the labor movement as a whole: decreased bargaining power and loss of jobs through foreign competition and developing technologies.

American Federation of Musicians

The full name of the AFM is American Federation of Musicians of the United States and Canada. It is the oldest union in the United States representing individuals professionally active in the fields of entertainment and the arts, its history dating from the 19th century. AFM has always been the largest artists' labor organization and today has around 90,000 members. Through the decades, however, the AFM has been losing members and some of its power. Why? A number of reasons have been advanced: (a) difficulty in attracting many of the new, young professionals, (b) state and national laws restricting certain kinds of **collective bargaining,** (c) continuing displacement of live performances with recorded music, (d) increasing displacement of live musicians by electronic instruments, (e) importation of music recorded abroad, and (f) increasing prevalence of nonunion performances, live and recorded. In recent years, in at least some local branches, the trend toward lower AFM membership has started to reverse itself, and membership numbers have begun to rise.

AFM membership includes professional instrumentalists, conductors, arrangers, orchestrators, copyists, music librarians, orchestra contractors, and proofreaders, as well as some related fields, such as cartage people (or roadies) and, when there are no jurisdictional disputes, engineers. The union maintains no jurisdiction over the professional services of composers (although practically all composers professionally active in film, television, radio, commercials, and **syndication** are AFM members by virtue of their services as either conductors, instrumentalists, arrangers, or copyists).

If a musician sings professionally, it is not necessary to be an AFM member unless the musician also works professionally in one of the capacities listed for regular AFM membership.

Unlike a number of guilds and professional associations in the arts, the AFM is a bona fide labor union: Its members are employees, and the AFM represents the interests of its members to employers.

The AFM functions on two levels—local and federation (United States and Canada). The local offices of the union have jurisdiction over all union work for musicians that is not covered by federation-wide contracts. AFM federation contracts embrace all services of musicians in the fields of recording, network broadcasting, theatrical film, television film and tape, **live-on-tape** network television, home video, syndicated programs and services, subscription TV, commercial announcements, and contracts covering the taped music for certain traveling productions, such as circuses and ice shows.

Federation contracts are administered by the union's Electronic Media Services Division (EMSD), which is under the direct supervision of the AFM president. EMSD has resident representatives in New York City and Los Angeles.

AFM contracts, whether local or federation, generally include agreements on issues such as wages, hours, overtime, working conditions, instrument **doubling**, instrument cartage, type of venue (meaning different performance platforms such as a night club, symphony hall, or TV show), rehearsal fees, pay for leader and contractor, **tracking scale**, **reuse**, and new use of recorded material.

The AFM manages to negotiate reasonably satisfactory contracts, at least from the union's point of view, at the national level. But at the local level, union control over wages and benefits varies. This is largely because certain states invoke their **right-to-work laws** and, more significantly, because of the constraints on union jurisdictions imposed by the Taft-Hartley Act (1947). Under a National Labor Relations Board interpretation of this law, absent a collective bargaining agreement (CBA), musicians are considered independent contractors. As such, they are prohibited from compelling purchasers of musicians' services to recognize the AFM as the musicians' collective bargaining agent. As a consequence, these purchasers of musicians' services (such as club owners, hotels) are not required to contribute to employee benefits such as unemployment insurance, FICA, and pension funds. Under these circumstances, however, a bandleader may be considered the employer and therefore compelled to make benefit payments. Over many years, the AFM has urged Congress to modify the Taft-Hartley's limitations on musicians.

AFM Local 47 building, an industry landmark on Vine Street in Hollywood.

Photo by Gordon Carmadelle courtesy of Professional Musicians, Local 47.

Union Finance

The union finances its activities with new members' initiation fees, annual dues, and work dues. The amount assessed as work dues varies from local to local and generally ranges from 1% to about 5% of union scale wages earned by members.[2]

A share of these monies collected by the locals is forwarded to AFM's international headquarters in New York City to finance the union's activities throughout the United States and Canada.

Other Services

The AFM attempts to license and control booking agents through franchising them. This process is described in Chapter 7. The union also seeks to protect its members from employers who don't pay union musicians what they are due. Slow-paying or nonpaying employers are sometimes sued by the union. More often, they are simply blacklisted, in part through publication of the names of offenders in the musicians' monthly magazine, *International Musician.*

AFM contracts covering the record industry are described in Chapter 8. With respect to AFM employment in film scoring, see Chapter 21.

American Federation of Television and Radio Artists

The American Federation of Television and Radio Artists (AFTRA) represents 70,000 professional singers and other vocalists, actors, news broadcasters, dancers, talk show hosts, disc jockeys, announcers, and other television and radio personalities.[3] Among its membership are anonymous background singers and multimillionaire superstars.

Its jurisdiction includes live and taped television, radio, sound recordings, interactive media, and nonbroadcast material. The union has more than 30 regional offices, or locals. Like the AFM, AFTRA is affiliated with the AFL-CIO.

Also like AFM, AFTRA is a real labor union: Its members are employees, and AFTRA's main business is working out labor agreements with employers. As with most national labor unions, AFTRA's leadership negotiates its national and local contracts with industry associations representative of the major sectors of the entertainment industry—record companies, TV and radio networks and stations, TV producers, and producers of commercial **spots** intended for broadcast.

When a singer gets an opportunity to perform for the first time in a field where AFTRA has jurisdiction, the **gig** may be accepted without joining the union, because the Taft-Hartley Act initially excuses the performer from this obligation. But the artist must join the union within 30 days thereafter to continue accepting jobs under AFTRA jurisdiction. The fee varies and is comparable to other performer unions. Members' dues vary widely and are determined by the individual's annual gross earnings on AFTRA jobs.

With respect to AFTRA's jurisdiction over professional singers, the union's contracts classify nonroyalty artists as soloists, duos, or group singers. Scales are highest for soloists and duos; soloists who step out of an ensemble momentarily for a featured segment earn second-highest wages. Background singers are paid at a sliding scale in accordance with the size of the group. A group of three to eight singers is paid more than members of larger choral ensembles.

Of all the artists' performing unions, AFTRA has the most complicated schedule of wages. Particularly in the commercial spot field, **union stewards** must be able to tell a producer what the costs will be for singers relative to the intended market for the spots, whether they are for local, regional, or national broadcast. AFTRA wages rise according to the size of the market. So a commercial that runs in a big city generates a bigger fee for talent than if the same commercial runs in a small city.

In the commercial production industry, it is not unusual for large production companies and advertising agencies to have at least one full-time employee helping spot producers figure out the correct AFTRA scales. Commercial contracts are identical for AFTRA and SAG, because they are jointly negotiated and administered.

One of the most important components of AFTRA contracts is the provision for new use or **extended use**. As with most other artists' union contracts, when an AFTRA member performs on a recording intended for one medium, additional money is earned if that recording is later used in a different medium, such as when a commercial recording might be licensed for use in a movie or a television show. AFTRA artists also earn additional wages when the use of a broadcast commercial extends beyond the initial term (often limited to 13 weeks). Because many spot campaigns are broadcast for long periods of time, even years after the initial use, earnings of AFTRA members from this source can become very large.

As with the AFM, AFTRA requires a union steward on the job if there are three or more background singers, to make sure the producer meets all the obligations to the performers under contract. AFTRA is almost exclusively concerned with negotiating and implementing singers' activities covered by national contracts, particularly the recording, radio, and TV industries. The performers' union has minimal control over singers performing on local shows and commercials outside the recording centers of New York, Los Angeles, and Nashville.

AFTRA was the first talent union to provide its members with a pension and welfare plan. These benefits are funded by contributions made by employers.

For a discussion of AFTRA's involvement in the recording industry, see Chapter 8.

The 4As

AFTRA is a directly affiliated union of the AFL-CIO, and a member of a loose alliance known in the industry as "the 4As." The term stands for Associated Actors and Artistes of America; all unions under this banner are affiliated with the AFL-CIO. This group includes the Actors' Equity Association, AGVA, AGMA, SAG, and the Guild of Italian-American Actors (GIAA). The 4As have helped reduce jurisdictional disputes among performers' unions, although each 4A member organization requires performers to belong to its particular union when jurisdictions appear to overlap. The AFM also zealously guards its own turf. For example, a singer who also plays an instrument on a network TV show must belong to both the AFM and AFTRA. An actor who appears on a covered TV show must hold a SAG card as a film actor and an AFTRA card as a television performer.

AFTRA and SAG have worked together in defining their jurisdictions in the field of music videos: Those shot on tape fall under AFTRA's jurisdiction; those shot on film under SAG's. In the early history of this field, practically all videos were knocked out on shoestring budgets too small to permit the payment of union wages, particularly for singers, dancers, and actors. Small, independent labels and the smaller production companies may continue to produce their videos with nonunion (or partly union) artists and crews. Music videos produced or financed by companies that have signed the AFTRA Sound Recording Code will be produced under AFTRA's jurisdiction.

American Guild of Musical Artists

The American Guild of Musical Artists (AGMA) is one of the 4A unions (despite the word *guild* in its title). AGMA was organized in the 1930s to serve the interests of singers and dancers working in the opera, dance, concert, oratorio, and recital fields. AGMA employment agreements are often negotiated for a particular ensemble, such as the Met's **chorus** or the San Francisco Opera's corps de ballet. Such contracts cover the standard items in any labor agreement—wages, working conditions, and benefits. Most AGMA contract negotiations are with nonprofit arts organizations that own the performing groups—for example, the American Ballet Theatre Foundation, which owns and sponsors the American Ballet Theatre. The union negotiates several national Master Agreements for choristers, vocal soloists in opera and concert music, and dance corps members and dance soloists. Those agreements are used as a basis for individual agreements with particular companies.

American Guild of Variety Artists

The American Guild of Variety Artists (AGVA) represents singers, dancers, comedians, ice skaters, jugglers, magicians, and others who perform live, primarily in venues such as theaters, theme parks, clubs, casinos, resorts, and fairgrounds. AGVA includes in its membership not only the struggling regional performer but also world-famous artists drawing huge fees, performing live on Broadway, at the Radio City Music Hall, in Las Vegas, and elsewhere. AGVA negotiates national agreements with venues in which its members perform.

Actors' Equity Association

Professional actors and stage managers on the legitimate stage in the United States are represented by the Actors' Equity Association, which theater people refer to simply as "Equity." **Equity** is the oldest of the major actors' unions, founded in 1913. Equity is a trade union and is affiliated with the AFL-CIO.

For many years, Equity membership was made up mostly of personnel working in New York City. Today, Equity has members all over the country. This has come about with the growth of regional theaters, stock and dinner and small professional theaters, and acting companies in residence on college campuses.

There are more than 30 national and regional contracts, which Equity either negotiates with collective bargaining partners or promulgates on its own. Actors and stage managers employed on Broadway work under the Production Contract that Equity negotiates with the Broadway League (formerly known as League of American Theatres and Producers, Inc.). Other negotiated contracts include the **Off-Broadway** Contract, and the LORT (League of Resident Theatres) Contract, which governs employment in regional theaters.

Of all the artists' unions, Equity enjoys the best reputation with producers for its awareness of the economic variables within the theater industry: It knows that there are more members out of work than there are jobs for them to fill. While Equity will not permit the reduction of minimum salaries for Equity actors and stage managers, it may make other alterations (known as "concessions") in its agreement with a theater that can assist that theater in achieving financial stability.

One of Equity's primary benefits to its members is to require a bond, which protects the minimum guarantee of employment (usually 2 weeks), should a producer default on an obligation before or during rehearsal or during the performance period.

Equity also permits limited talent "showcases," called *Codes,* in New York, Chicago, Los Angeles, and San Francisco. These Codes are developed by and for members for the opportunity to gain experience, recognition, and, it is hoped, employment.

Screen Actors Guild

The Screen Actors Guild (SAG) is probably the most widely known artists' union in that so many of its members are world-famous performers. SAG's jurisdiction covers filmed entertainment—both movies and TV programs. Established in 1933, SAG has a rich history in the American labor movement, from negotiating with studios in Hollywood's "golden era" to asserting artists' rights amid the digital revolution of the 21st century. SAG has jurisdiction over all actors, singers, and on-screen instrumentalists who act in film; SAG shares jurisdiction with AFTRA over all actors, singers, and on-screen instrumentalists who act or appear in scripted TV, in commercials, in music videos, and in industrial films. SAG is classified as a trade union, in that its nearly 120,000 members are employees whose services are rendered to employers through contracts negotiated by the union (guild).

Again similar to AFM and AFTRA contracts, SAG agreements stipulate who is responsible for residual payments to actors when a production has multiple exhibitions.

International Alliance of Theatrical Stage Employes[4]

The International Alliance of Theatrical Stage Employes, Moving Picture Technicians, Artists and Allied Crafts of the United States, Its Territories and Canada (IATSE) is the union having jurisdiction over stagehands in the legitimate theater, and in the majority of motion picture and (filmed) television productions. Among the many jobs under IATSE jurisdiction are sound technicians, wardrobe, camera, and animators. In legitimate theater, jobs range from stage hands to ticket sellers.

Organizations with whom IATSE has agreements include the following:

- All the major motion picture studios
- All the networks as well as some local broadcasters in radio and television
- Most major opera, symphony, and ballet companies
- Most major arenas and civic centers
- Major producers of traveling theatrical productions

Other Unions and Guilds

National Association of Broadcast Employees and Technicians–Communications Workers of America

The National Association of Broadcast Employees and Technicians–Communications Workers of America (NABET-CWA) is another union that represents audio engineers and technicians and other workers in radio and TV, including makeup artists and some on-air talent.

Dramatists Guild of America, Inc.

The Dramatists Guild is a trade association, not a labor union. It represents composers, lyricists, and book writers active in the theater. The guild also includes, as members, playwrights who write plays without music or plays that use music only incidentally.

The Dramatists Guild is a corporate member of the Authors League of America, which has two branches: the Dramatists Guild and the Authors Guild. The latter is a trade association of authors of books other than dramatic works.

Royalty payments, maintenance of subsidiary rights, artistic control, and ownership of copyright have remained of paramount importance since the guild was established in 1919. The guild helps ensure that the ownership and control of the music, lyrics, and book of a show remain in the hands of its authors and composers—not the producers. Guild members retain copyright in their material, including the licensing of performances of dramatic rights (grand rights). The guild also helps its members preserve the integrity of their works, in that producers and directors are not allowed to alter music, lyrics, or the book to a show without the composers' and authors' consent.

Related Unions and Guilds

Other unions and guilds related to the music and/or entertainment fields are the Writers Guild of America (west and east), the Directors Guild of America, the Producers Guild of America, the National Conference of Personal Managers, and the Society of Stage Directors and Choreographers.

With respect to audio technicians working in recording studios and broadcasting, no one union has managed to gain complete jurisdiction. Many employers of these kinds of technicians have been able to avoid **union shop** status.

Open Shop Agreements

Some situations have both union and nonunion employees. Often in such a case an open shop agreement is established. Open shop agreements generally stipulate that individuals employed in such a situation are subject to the collective bargaining agreement in effect between the pertinent union and the employer, even if all employees are not union members. In the event of a dispute, the terms of the collective bargaining agreement govern the employment of the nonunion employee.

Other Issues

Additional concerns relating to unions and guilds have to do with the employment of minors and the issues of immigration and work permits, where one country seeks to limit foreign artists from displacing its own citizens from job opportunities. Individuals needing definitive information on these kinds of issues are advised to search out current regulations and statutes through attorneys experienced in labor or immigration law.

Notes

1. The following kinds of professionals are represented in some kind of organization: composers, arrangers, lyricists, instrumentalists, singers, playwrights, theatrical producers, directors, stage actors, screen actors, choreographers, dancers, scenic designers, scenery builders, stagehands, electricians, personal managers, record producers, audio technicians, and educators specializing in the fields of music management, merchandising, and recording technology.

2. As is frequently true in many entertainment job categories, employers of AFM musicians will often pay musicians through an artists' payroll service company. AFM contractors sometimes use this kind of company to handle wages, tax accounting, and benefit payments.

3. In Canada, the comparable union is the Association of Canadian Television and Radio Artists (ACTRA).

4. This organization does indeed spell "Employes" with only one "e."

Chapter Takeaways

- The two labor unions with the most influence in the music field are the American Federation of Musicians (AFM), mostly covering instrumentalists, and the American Federation of Television and Radio Artists (AFTRA), representing singers. They and other unions with smaller involvement in the sector have collective bargaining agreements with employers.

- A large proportion of work in the music industry is nonunion, usually by what are deemed as independent contractors.
- Guilds are organizations for a specific class of artists with similar creative interests and thus are different from unions that are focused on employer-labor relations. However, note that some true unions may have "guild" in their names.

Key Terms

- collective bargaining   (p. 166)
- doubling   (p. 167)
- extended use   (p. 169)
- open shop   (p. 172)

- right-to-work laws   (p. 167)
- tracking scale   (p. 167)
- union stewards   (p. 169)

CHAPTER 10

Artist Management

In Chapter 7, personal management was discussed only from the standpoint of regulation by state statutes and artists' unions. This chapter examines financial relationships and the manager's functions in advancing the artist's career.[1]

> "Management, too, is an art."
>
> —Mozart's father (and manager)

How important is a good manager? Ask a recording company. Labels today prefer an artist who has good management. They believe it is not cost-effective to invest time and money in an artist whose career, or even daily activities, are not thoughtfully planned. Good management is so important, in fact, that some labels will actually help certain artists find a good manager. However, undirected talent and unfocused careers remain commonplace in the music business. These performers may get lucky and land on the charts for a few weeks, but they quickly fade into oblivion, like thousands before them who lacked firm, knowledgeable management.

At what point do artists need a manager? About the time they discover they can earn more than union scale, suddenly they are in need of someone to handle their business affairs and develop their careers. This can be a difficult time, because they soon realize that many established managers are unwilling to take on a new, unproven act.

Left: Robert Plant and Alison Krauss perform in Oregon.

Photo © Chris Ryan/Corbis.

Discovering Each Other

An artist searching for a personal manager should look for a person who

- Believes in the talent of the artist
- Is well organized, systematic
- Is straightforward and honest and has a reputation to prove it
- Is an effective communicator, writes well, and is an articulate, persuasive speaker
- Won't try to fake expertise if lacking competence in certain fields; will hire outside experts when needed
- Has good industry contacts; if not, is busy developing them
- Shares the artist's long-term vision and career goals

Some managers have a strong creative side as well as good business skills. A manager might help to put an act together by advising about choice of artistic personnel. The manager may also help to make decisions regarding production of an album and choice of material to be included on the album.

Some managers are closely involved with the negotiation of business contracts; others are not. Some handle an artist's books as well as helping to make creative decisions; others do not. Each artist-manager relationship should be structured to best serve the client.

Successful personal managers have one other kind of expertise: They know how to spot a potential star. They cannot afford to invest their time and money in anyone who lacks what the manager views as the potential talent to reach the top. And until a manager's clients develop strong earnings, there won't be many dollars available to produce commissionable income—the manager's livelihood.

Experienced managers and artists all agree on one issue: The relationship depends on strong personal ties of friendship and trust. Although sometimes it may appear to be the other way around, the manager works for the artist, not vice versa. The manager is the extension of the artist and should act in ways appropriate to that artist. Behavior of the manager, both positive and negative, reflects on the artist and is ultimately the artist's responsibility.

Good communication skills on the part of the manager are paramount. Managers who raise their voices at personnel of record labels or those who come across as uninformed about how the business works tend to have their calls stuck in voice mail. The artist will suffer in this situation; record label personnel are less motivated to work for the artists whose managers have a reputation of being difficult or pushy. Good managers must strike the delicate balance between passivity and aggressiveness; they should motivate without stepping on toes and be congenial without being a pushover.

When a manager and artist are considering joining forces, they might well enter into a short-term "trial" or "honeymoon" agreement, usually 6 months to 1 year. If the manager achieves the objectives outlined in the trial agreement, the contract is generally extended to full **term**—3 or more years. A word of caution to the artist: Be sure that the management agreement is nontransferable—that is, the contract cannot be bought or sold.

The Financial Relationship

Established personal managers usually insist that the artist agrees in writing that the manager be authorized to handle all the artist's money—what comes in and what goes out. If an artist is fearful of granting the manager complete control over the money, the artist should not sign with that person.

As an alternative arrangement, a business manager selected by both parties could handle the responsibility for receipts and disbursements. Many artists of stature insist that the money be entirely handled by such an independent third party—usually a business management firm. When an act generates large sums of money, this is often a preferable arrangement.

Accounting

Whatever arrangements the parties agree on for business management, the personal manager's first responsibility in this regard is setting up the financial accounting. The astute personal manager will call in the accountants even in the formative stages of contract negotiations to make sure the parties agree on how they are going to control "the count" and report the taxes. The difficulty here is that even in the entertainment capitals of the world, there are few accounting firms fully knowledgeable in these specialized areas of entertainment and communications industries. For example, a major recording star requires a financial adviser who understands international tax treaties and the exchange of foreign currencies and fluctuating money markets. When accountants lack specialized knowledge, an act of international stature can have little confidence that the worldwide movement of royalties is sufficiently protected.

Although the personal manager should recruit a qualified accountant, the artist should approve the selection of that individual or firm. A major act may also need independent auditors to conduct periodic examinations of the books—not only those of the manager but of the publisher and recording company as well. Contracts with these parties must specify under what conditions audits will be acceptable and precisely who will be liable for the auditing expense.[2]

Controlling Expense

It is not generally understood that a large percentage of working artists incur expenses larger than their incomes. This may be true even of some of the artists the public considers rich and famous. Because the "successful" artist has to pay 10% to 25% of the gross to a manager, another 10% or so to a booking agency, and perhaps additional fees to a business manager, attorney, or accountant, the best hope of realizing a profit on what is left is to exert stringent control over all other expenses. Although a manager may make recommendations for expenditures, no expense over a certain dollar amount (agreed on by the artist and manager) is to be incurred without artist approval. The artist's attorney should include such spending constraints when the management contract is negotiated.[3]

However, many artists and managers have only a dim view of the realities of the rational business world. Many artists throw their money around, hoping that those earnings are going to keep rolling in forever. In such a case, a seasoned manager might persuade the artist to accept a weekly allowance and/or a tax savings plan. Show business stories abound of how former stars went through millions only to end up financially destitute. Submitting to a modest weekly expense account increases an artist's chances of surviving the late lean years when fame and income have faded.

Many personal managers also find it necessary to loan money to keep an act alive, at least in its developing stage. The management contract should state, however, that the manager is under no obligation to loan money or advance money to the artist, no matter how serious the crisis may be.

Manager's Commission

It is standard practice in the industry for personal managers to earn compensation for their services through commissions on the artist's gross income. The equity of this practice is open to question, but managers who know how the business has operated in the past will rarely accept any other arrangement. Their argument is a simple one—and persuasive: The manager may be the person principally responsible for the rise and fall of the client's income. The manager invests time (and often personal funds) in getting a career off the ground and is entitled to participate in the artist's prosperity, should it ever come.

The informed artist's point of view on this issue is set forth in the draft contract at the end of this chapter.

Going Rates

In recent years, certain "going rates" have become recognized in the industry for personal managers' commissions. They range from a low of 10% to a high of 25%. Factors influencing these rates include the following:

1. The stature and track record of the manager. A manager with powerful contacts in the industry—and who usually comes with a team and infrastructure that has its own overhead—may be worth 25% to an artist. A manager with little or no track record may earn a lower commission.

2. The income of the artist. If the artist has a high income, the manager will come out well even at a relatively low commission rate.

3. The extent of the manager's services. For example, if the manager farms out all business management, accounting services, and promotion services, top commission rates may not be appropriate.

An Argument for Reasonableness. A powerful manager can often get a very high commission even from an act that may be struggling to pay its rent. But if that artist later develops a high income, it may be tempting to renegotiate those commissions and reduce them to a reasonable level. More likely, the successful artist will be ready to dump the original manager and sign with a less expensive one. The manager who was greedy earlier in the relationship may well have lost an opportunity to come into really good earnings. Managers are well advised to keep their demands reasonable, because most artists are quick to discontinue association with support personnel, particularly personal managers, who fail to treat them fairly. Wise managers often volunteer to reduce or eliminate commissions on specific projects or concert dates. Such gestures go a long way in establishing long-term trust and goodwill between manager and artist.

Commission Base. Personal managers' commissions are usually based on the artist's gross income from all activity relating to the entertainment industry. In this context, "income" includes not only wages but also whatever is of value that comes to the artist from the entertainment industry, directly or indirectly, including sources such as royalties; an interest in, or ownership of, a production company, TV package, film, publishing, or recording company; stock in a corporation; interest in a partnership;

bonuses; merchandising; endorsements; tour sponsorship; commercials; video sales; and even gifts.

The commission *base* can be more important than the commission *level*. If the artist has a competent, aggressive attorney, and if the personal manager lacks the clout of the artist, the commission base can sometimes be limited to what can be called the adjusted gross income. An artist negotiating from strength should be able to convince the manager to accept a commission based on the artist's actual income, not on all the money simply passing through the accounts to support other persons and other activities. The artist will probably seek to exclude from commission items such as recording costs and **negative tour support** or tour shortfall (money the label has advanced to make up for deficits the artist incurred while on tour). The pros and cons of this fundamental issue are set forth in the draft contract later in this chapter.

The Money Flow

The artist and manager may work together successfully for many years. But one day that relationship could end. As difficult as it may be, they should anticipate the problems of disengagement even from the earliest point of the relationship. Like marriage, an artist-manager relationship is easier to enter into than to leave. When the artist and manager get divorced, not only will they suffer the wrenching experience of ending a close personal relationship, they will also have to negotiate some kind of "property settlement." A divorcing couple can eventually agree on "who gets the house, who gets the car," and so forth, but the artist and manager have a much more complicated set of financial problems.

The essential difficulty here is that an established act has money flowing in from contracts the manager negotiated, and when the couple disengage (for whatever reason) that money continues to flow. Should the departing manager continue to receive commissions on income from the contracts he or she has negotiated? Some lawyers make the argument that, unless negotiated otherwise, such commissions continue in perpetuity.

The richest source of these funds usually comes from publishing and recording contracts probably worked out during the period of service of the departing manager. Nearly all personal management contracts state that the manager is entitled to full commissions on this money, without diminution, for the full term of those contracts. Part of the problem this creates for the artist is encountered during the search for new management. If the artist's major source of income is already tapped for years hence by the old manager, what has a new manager to gain by signing on with an act so encumbered with prior commitments?

A Possible Compromise

If it is assumed the parties possess about equal bargaining strength, one of the simplest compromises available is an across-the-board de-escalation of commissions over a year or two following termination of the contract. This arrangement between artist and manager is often called the sunset clause. Figure 10.1 shows how this might work: The old manager continues to enjoy 100% of commissions for the first 6 months following disengagement from the artist. Then follows a 50% reduction for the next 6 months. At the start of the second year following disengagement, the artist pays the former manager only 25% of what would have otherwise been earned. After 12 months at this rate, all commissions to the former manager end.

If the manager is negotiating from greater strength than the artist, the same de-escalation formula might still be used, but the percentages could be set higher and stretched out over a longer time—up to 7 years. For instance, the old manager might earn a 100% commission indefinitely for deals he or she negotiated. The new manager might earn a 100% commission on all new deals set up for the artist. The new manager will also earn 100% commission on a holdover deal that changes.

One final advantage of a de-escalation formula: If the second manager accepts the plan suggested here, the parties should have little difficulty negotiating a similar de-escalation plan for the second manager as well when that relationship ends.

Figure 10.1 Artist's Money Flow to Managers

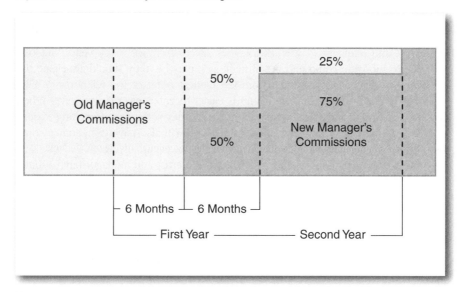

Note: Under this possible scenario, a new manager receives 100% commission from the outset on new business that the new manager generates.

The Manager's Role

Producing the Act

Once the artist and manager have negotiated their agreement, one of the first tasks they face is polishing the act—creating the presentation of the artist to the public. As we all know, the marketing of a commodity can be more valuable than the commodity itself. Many artists of modest talents seem to get by well in the marketplace largely because they are presented so attractively.

If an artist is already established with a defined public image and personal style, the new manager may not want to alter a presentation materially that has been working well. But when a manager signs on a relatively new act, both parties have a lot of work to do. Unless the manager is fully qualified, the best help the artist can afford must be engaged. An objective appraisal must be made at the outset on these basic questions: (a) Just what kind of performer or act do we have? (b) To what audience does the artist appeal? (c) Can that audience be expanded? (d) What must we do for the artist to fully exploit all the potential?

One useful tool for objective examination of an artist's performing strengths and weaknesses is video. The artist and coaches can use this medium to guide their work and measure progress toward the creation of truly polished performances.

The type of act tends to determine the type of presentation that is most appropriate in reaching that act's target audience. Although a pop act may be geared toward the slick performance and mass merchandising, an independent rock band may require a different look and personality.

In addition to engaging voice coaches, choreographers, wardrobe consultants, and more, the manager who takes the long view of the client's career will probably want to provide dramatic training, too. Nearly all musical performers who reach national prominence eventually receive opportunities to play dramatic roles.

Some managers provide important assistance when they have the ability to identify good musical material. Few artists—including those who write much of their own material—ever seem to have a sufficient supply of high-quality songs. The manager may have to take time listening to demos and helping search out usable songs. The act may also need **special material**—songs, patter, and routines created exclusively for that artist. Practically all stars booked into major venues such as in Las Vegas consider using special material that is essential to a big-time presentation.

Coordinating the Elements

Once the act has been fully prepared, the next move is to place it on stage, under flattering lighting, in an appropriate setting. Now, a theatrical producer is needed; if the manager can't handle this task, someone should be engaged who can. Major acts often tour with their own stage directors who supervise lighting, staging, and sound.

Student at console in Trebas Institute's multitrack recording studio.

Photo courtesy of Trebas Institute.

If cast in a touring Broadway show, the artist will be part of a company that travels, not only with its own sets, but its own lights, control board, audio system, even flooring.

Programming

Experienced managers representing powerful acts control the selection of opening and supporting acts, making sure that the headliner comes on at the best possible time and under the most advantageous circumstances. From the early days of vaudeville, headliners insisted on warm-up acts to preheat the audience. This sequencing of acts is called programming, and the manager must control it when possible. If the manager's client is to be introduced by a master of ceremonies (**MC**) or some other person, the manager must make sure the introducer says the right things and says them briefly.

Advancing the Career

The manager's main responsibility is advancing the career of the artist, whose reputation and income depend on how effectively this is done. A first-rate manager will design and execute a complete campaign for each artist, starting with people—with personalities, not organizations. Top managers develop extensive lists of key personnel in the industry. Most of these potential contacts will never be used. But when a manager must move quickly—which is most of the time—an up-to-date list of power brokers will prove useful.

Because the manager probably operates out of, or regularly travels to, one of the recording and publishing centers, it will become apparent who the decision makers are in the most active companies, as well as the important agents, promoters, and industry lawyers. The music industry is a giant, but only a few hundred individuals have positions of real power. When a manager is negotiating with one record company, the competing record companies for that contract have probably heard, privately, about what each side is offering. So the experienced manager knows there are few secrets in the business at the top level. This inner circle of powerful people knows who is a con artist, who will keep an agreement, who can deliver.

How does a new manager develop a network of contacts? By demonstrating credibility and competence.

The artist's manager must also develop good contacts wherever clients perform—the top music directors and programmers, retailers, distributors of recordings, media personnel, the important promoters, and agents. Given time, a network can be developed of key personnel in branch offices of record labels with whom clients are under contract.

Keep in mind, however, that the relationships between individuals are often not as significant as the relationship between corporations. Aspiring managers must not just cultivate relationships with individuals but must also keep abreast of corporate relations between labels and artists. A good manager will be on top of trends that influence the contracting, packaging, and sales of musical artists and how the corporate climate may affect business decisions.

Landing a Recording Contract

Most young performers today find it impossible to graduate to the big time without a recording contract. This has not always been true. Earlier in the last century, a performer might acquire a national following through media such as network radio, television, the movies, Broadway, even vaudeville. In general, though, building a following in the music business today revolves largely around recordings. A new act will find it difficult to get jobs, for example, in broadcasting or film before making it on records. Personal managers understand this and consider their most important responsibility to somehow land recording contracts for their clients. Many performers engage a manager primarily for this purpose. Occasionally, the artist's attorney will recommend that a personal manager be engaged only if the manager can, indeed, secure a recording deal. No recording contract, no personal management agreement. To most aspiring young performers, a personal manager has little to offer without delivering at this level.

Even if we assume the artist in question has great talent, the manager will usually find it difficult to gain the serious attention of an established recording company. The manager must somehow persuade a recording company to invest very big money for a debut album of this unknown artist—just to get the recording career started. In addition, knowing the right record label to attract is important. An artist who wants to maintain artistic vision may prefer to sign a contract with a smaller label that offers more artistic freedom rather than with a major label, even if that decision produces less income in the near term. Prospects for the manager's success in landing a record contract for a client will probably be determined by the answers to these kinds of questions:

How strong are the manager's contacts in the industry?

How strong is the manager's team (lawyer, accountant, support staff, etc.)?

How strong, how unique is the artist's talent? Is there star potential there?

Is the manager's approach timely? Is the label signing anyone at this time?

Is the recording company undersupplied or oversupplied with artists who perform somewhat in the vein of the manager's client?

Does the recording company believe in the manager? The label may love the artist but lack confidence in the manager's ability to deliver.

The Process. Let us assume that the manager is fully qualified, respected in the industry, and represents an artist/writer who has star potential. Here is the sequence of events that might lead to the securing of a record contract:

1. The manager makes a frontal attack on the label itself, almost always starting with the A&R (artist and repertoire) department. If unable to gain the attention of the top decision makers, the manager works on the next level down. Recording companies are populated with employees trying to make points with the boss. If a label employee, in whatever position, can participate in the company's discovery of a new star, that employee believes it will be a personal career boost. Among the lower-level contacts the manager might pursue are promotion people and field personnel for the label. The alert ones are on the lookout for new talent. Even A&R assistants can be valuable contacts.

2. The manager will try to work with the songwriter-client's publisher. If the client doesn't have a publishing deal, the manager will aggressively shop for one. Major publishing executives have excellent contacts with label executives and independent producers. It is, however, rare for an artist to get an attractive publishing deal without a recording deal.

3. The manager fails to reach the attention of record companies and focuses on independent producers and production companies. The best of these have direct contact with record labels. The manager may determine that an offer from a record production company looks more attractive than signing directly with a label; the production company may be able to present its services and the artist's services as a package to some label.

4. The manager arranges for third parties to catch the artist in a showcase performance or watch a video demo. If some respected individual in the industry tells a friend (who tells a friend . . .) about a great new talent, the word may get back to a decision maker at some recording company. Word of mouth may turn out to be as effective as knocking on doors.

The Result. If the manager should fail to get the client a recording contract after 1 or 2 years' effort, the artist may need to search for a place in some other sector of the entertainment industry. But let's assume the manager succeeds in persuading a recording company to negotiate a contract. What is a "good" contract? How much dare be asked? Is the label excited and ready to get behind the new act with strong promotion and lots of money?

Let's assume the next step: The contract is signed; everyone is happy. At the moment, that is. Now the manager must keep nudging—assertively, without being a pest—the label to promote the recordings. If the effort is halfhearted, the artist's recordings may never gain exposure such as radio and video airplay or reach the retailers. At this moment, the manager's greatest service will be prodding the label to perform on the contract, to deliver what was agreed. The manager must keep the artist a priority by talking to the label, the radio promo people, the marketing department—even checking to make sure distribution is correct in filling orders. Efforts in this direction can never stop.

Let's make one more assumption in this scenario: The record label fulfills its promises of promotion and the recordings sell very well. Now the artist has so much money rolling in, it seems time to say to the manager, "My friends tell me your commission is out of line. I want to renegotiate our contract. Your new rate is now 10%, not 25%. If that is unacceptable, I will sign with this other management company that will probably do more for me—and for a lower commission than I've been paying you." This kind of scenario is not uncommon. Personal managers may struggle for years establishing an act. Their biggest problem may turn out to be success. When their clients start coming into really big money, they may defect to a manager who had nothing to do with building the act to high-income status. A lawsuit could result if a contract is in place and the artist tries to break it.

Why do bright people go into the personal management field? Probably because the really competent managers continue to be in high demand, and they often seem able to develop sufficient loyalty among their clients to be in on the receiving end when careers prosper. These kinds of managers can easily become millionaires.

Care and Feeding of the Media

In executing a campaign to exploit an artist, the manager must develop contacts (and friends) with those who influence the audience through mass media as well as highly targeted information platforms. This would include influential music bloggers, video channels (e.g., MTV), networks, radio stations, wire service reporters, feature writers, syndicated columnists, syndicated radio programs, specialty Web sites, and the music press—the opinion-shapers focusing on personalities in the music and entertainment fields. They are not difficult to contact: They look to artists, managers, and publicists to feed them information.

Materials. When contact is made, the manager must feed these sources with appropriate material. This is usually done with press kits or **promo packs**. They are expensive to assemble but essential to a publicity campaign. Depending on budget and circumstances, promo packs often contain press releases, the artist's biography, news clips, previous media reviews, photographs (glossies suitable for reproduction), a disc containing digital artwork and electronic photos, and sample CDs or DVDs. If a recording company is involved, a major promotion will often include a material object (a novelty of some kind, sometimes called **swag**) that ties in with a new recording's release. The manager or the artist's publicist will help in getting these kits and trinkets to the press, disc jockeys, radio program directors, and perhaps to the employees of record distributors and retail outlets.

Interviews. Managers have learned that one of the most economical techniques to generate strong publicity for a touring artist is to set up audio interviews in advance of the artist's arrival. Telephone or broadcast-quality audio interviews can be used in large cities when an artist lacks time to visit all the major broadcasting stations.

As the artist travels across the country, the label's publicity staff will set up news conferences. Most reporters and camera people are dispatched to these events by their assignment editors; they will appear where they are assigned to cover a story. But freelancers and stringers can often be persuaded to cover a press conference if free food and drink are available following the press conference. When the budget allows, some press conferences are planned as press parties. Enterprising publicists can often induce the press to show up for these happy hours even when the artist is relatively unknown.

In addition to news conferences, a manager or publicist can arrange for exclusive interviews. One interview or guest shot with a syndicated columnist or network TV program can yield more good PR than many open press conferences.

Artists' managers rarely attempt to handle all the PR for their clients; instead they often try to convince the record label to handle public relations, either in-house or through a third-party firm. Services of these companies can run from $100-a-week retainers to perhaps $6,000 a month, depending on the services required and the track record of the supplier. Competition among publicists is keen. In their effort to produce maximum attention, professional **flacks** will sometimes resort to outrageous publicity schemes. The media and the public may actually enjoy a crazy hype for a while. But it is the personal manager's responsibility to rein in PR types when they try too often to substitute promotion gimmicks for campaigns based on something approximating reality.

Billing. From the early days of the entertainment industry, it has been standard practice for managers and promoters to control what professionals call *billing*. Billing has to do with the size, emphasis, and position of artists' names in print ads and screen credits. If an artist ranks as a "star," the name might be set above the name of the production—in large, bold type.[4] If the artist is a "costar," the name will appear below the name of the production and in type smaller than that used for the star. If the artist is a "featured" player, the billing will be much less prominent and relegated to an inferior position in the layout.

As the manager's client gains prestige, attention must be given to the possibilities of negotiating for increasingly prominent billing. An astute manager will occasionally accept a lower fee for the client if the billing is strong.[5] In rock shows, the second act is often called "special guest star" and may receive 75% of the billing that the main act receives for the show, depending on the contract.

Controlling Performances

One of the personal manager's most useful services is controlling the client's performance opportunities. Once a career gains momentum, it is not unusual for the artist to receive more offers to perform than can be accepted. Both the agent and the manager are tempted to maximize income and accept every gig in sight. But it is the manager's responsibility to limit the frequency of performances to avoid exhausting the artist's energies and to avoid overexposure of the act. The manager will be particularly concerned with travel times between engagements.

As important as determining the frequency of performances is the selection of the kinds of engagement offers. The sharp manager understands the artist's unique identity and the nature of the artist's audience. Insensitive talent agents and promoters will offer the manager job opportunities from time to time that are totally unsuitable. The money might appear attractive, but placing an artist on a bill where the audience might have different tastes can do more harm than good for a career. In considering potential concert dates for a rock performer, the manager will consider the importance of the market—for instance, record sales in that market, the artist's product presence in local record retail outlets, and whether local radio stations are playing the client's music.

A band performs on *Morning Becomes Eclectic,* KCRW Studio, Santa Monica College.
Photo courtesy of KCRW.

In addition to controlling the frequency and types of engagements, the manager must determine when the client is "ready." For example, if the performer is primarily a singer and the job opportunity also requires acting, the manager, in consultation with the client, should try to determine before they sign whether the artist can handle the role, whether the script is "right," and whether the production will be of respectable quality.

Negotiating for Appearances

Once a manager has developed a successful artist, other talent buyers fall into line, seeking to cash in on the performer's growing stature, and it is not uncommon for an artist to have more than one agent. For instance, some artists may have a separate agent who deals only with commercials.

The successful recording artist and concert performer attracts the attention of TV producers, who may engage the artist. The artist, now successful on records and television, may attract the interest of film producers and Broadway producers. The manager has a major star and high income. The big task now is to try to figure out how to keep all these good things happening. It should be noted that it is illegal for managers to directly contract talent engagements, unless they are licensed talent agents (see Chapter 7).

Developing Peripheral Income

Major stars receive additional opportunities to increase their incomes from sources such as product endorsements, broadcast commercials, and merchandising deals. It's up to the artist's manager to get those contracts and to know how to handle them to maximum advantage.

The field of product and service merchandising is bigger than most people realize. Major recording and touring stars may receive significant income from the sale of T-shirts, posters, and other concert souvenirs. Sponsorship fees from large companies may pay for the costs of an entire tour.

Each music souvenir merchandiser is licensed by the artist's manager to use the artist's name and image, then pays anywhere from 3% on up in royalties (at retail), depending in part on the clout of the individual artist, on each item sold. The manager may also receive invitations for clients to appear on broadcast commercials or endorse products and services. The manager, in consultation with the client, must determine whether these kinds of offers might help or hurt the artist's career.

In summary, it becomes evident that the personal manager is a key professional in the entertainment industry, often wielding more power and influence than any one person should be expected (or entitled) to handle. All that is asked of the manager is omniscience.

Personal Management Agreement

The artist and manager should both engage their own independent legal counselors and proceed to negotiate a contract. If their attorneys are well informed and aggressive, the artist and manager should negotiate for all they can get for themselves. Normal procedure is for one side to express demands—from a position, quite naturally, of maximum self-interest. The second party then counters with a position—similarly biased in that party's favor. At this juncture, the parties will need to negotiate compromises, with results being as satisfactory as possible to both parties.

To start negotiations, the manager will often issue a **deal memo** (a summary document that covers term, commission, and other major points of the potential contract).

The draft contract that follows assumes that the parties start their negotiations in the sequence just described. Where issues are particularly controversial, we articulate the opening position of each party. Then follows an articulation of a compromise position—what might be a fair resolution and balance of interests if the parties had equal bargaining strength.

The compromise positions expressed here are a consensus of opinion prevailing among a number of distinguished entertainment industry attorneys.

Draft Agreement

This draft agreement is for study purposes only. Its language should not necessarily be used verbatim in an actual contract. Each party involved in negotiations is urged to retain independent legal counsel to draft the actual language of a contract.

The body of the draft contract uses the pronouns *he* and *his* rather than *he/she* and *his/hers*. This usage is for simplicity and is meant to include both men and women.

AGREEMENT made (date) _____ by and between _____, the Artist, and _____, the Personal Manager (hereinafter called Manager).

WITNESSETH

Whereas the Artist wishes to obtain advice and direction in the advancement of his professional career, and

Whereas the Manager, by reason of his knowledge and experience, is qualified to render such advice and direction,

NOW THEREFORE, in consideration of the mutual promises set forth here, the Artist and Manager do agree:

DEFINITIONS

The "Artist"—the first party to this agreement—appoints the second party, the Personal Manager. The Artist may be one or more individuals comprising the professional performing group. If more than one individual signs this agreement as an Artist member of the performing group, then this Agreement shall be binding upon all such persons, individually and severally, and all of the representations, warranties, agreements, and obligations contained herein shall be deemed to be individual, joint, and several.[6]

This agreement covers all of the professional talents, activities, and services of the Artist in all sectors and media of the arts and entertainment industry, as an instrumentalist, singer, actor, entertainer, composer, writer, editor, arranger, orchestrator, publisher, executive, producer, manager, audio technician, promoter, and packager.

"Personal Manager" is used here to describe the individual who advises and counsels and directs the Artist's career and manages the Artist's business affairs.

"Third Party" is any individual, company, or corporation with whom the Artist and/or Manager do business relating to the agreement, such as talent agent, producer, publisher, record company, production company, promoter, business manager, accountant, auditor, union or guild, broadcaster, merchant, advertiser.

"Entertainment Industry" is used here, not only in its generally understood meaning, but also including all related aspects of literary activity, publishing, broadcasting, filming, telecommunications, promotion, merchandising, advertising, through all media of communication now known or later developed, of the arts and entertainment industry.

1.0. APPOINTMENT

Artist's Position: It is in the artist's interest to place strong language in the agreement setting forth precisely what the personal manager is obligated to do. To offer "advice and counsel" is ambiguous. The artist will seek a specific list of services to be rendered and require the manager to use the manager's "best efforts" to meet his responsibilities.

Manager's Position: The manager will seek only a general statement regarding his appointment. He may not accept the language committing him to his "best efforts," in that his commissions under such language might not be automatic.[7] The manager may prefer the expression "reasonable efforts."

Compromise Position:

The Artist appoints the Manager as his exclusive personal manager throughout the world in all fields related to the arts and entertainment industry. The Manager will offer the Artist advice and counsel and will use his best efforts to advance the Artist's career.

The Manager accepts the appointment as set forth here and agrees that, in fulfilling the appointment, he will (1) make himself available to the Artist at reasonable times and places; (2) devote his best efforts to the Artist's affairs; and (3) maintain an office and staff adequate to fulfill the appointment and his responsibilities thereunder.

1.1. Exclusivity. The Artist appoints the Manager as his exclusive personal manager and will engage no other personal manager during the term of this agreement. The Manager's services to the Artist are nonexclusive; he may manage other artists concurrently and carry on other business activities, at his sole discretion.[8]

1.2. Business Management. The Manager shall be in charge of the Artist's business affairs personally or, with the consent of the Artist, engage a Third Party as business manager.

1.3. Representation. The Manager shall represent the Artist's best interests with Third Parties and supervise agreements with them.

2.0. EMPLOYMENT

Artist's Position: Despite the language in most contracts of this kind, the artist expects the manager to actively procure employment in the form of a recording agreement. This is the very reason most artists sign on with a particular manager.

Manager's Position: The manager will insist that the agreement specifically excuse him from any obligation to procure employment for the artist. If the agreement is negotiated and "performed" in the state of California, the manager will require extra-strong language here disavowing any hint of even an attempt to procure employment or participation even indirectly in such activity.

Compromise Position:

The procurement of employment, or the attempt to procure employment, for the Artist is not an obligation of the Manager, and the Manager is not authorized, licensed, or expected to perform such services. But the Manager recognizes that the obtaining of employment is of the essence in advancing the Artist's career and that the Manager shall, after consultation with the Artist, engage, direct, and/or **discharge** persons such as talent agents, employment agents, as well as other persons and firms who may be retained for the purpose of securing engagement contracts for the Artist.

3.0. ASSIGNMENT

Artist's Position: The artist will attempt to deny the manager the right to transfer or assign the contract to another party. The artist enters into the agreement largely because of his feeling of confidence and trust in this particular manager. The artist could not be assured this same confidence and trust could be found in some other party who was allowed to take over the contract. To protect himself, the artist will seek a **key man clause** (below).

Manager's Position: The manager will seek to avoid inclusion of a key man clause, arguing that he may become disabled or otherwise unable to perform. He may develop different interests and want to be free to assign the contract. If the manager is employed by a management company, his company will probably insist it retain the right to assign the agreement.

Compromise Position:

The Manager is the key man in this agreement and is denied the option to assign this agreement without the prior written consent of the Artist. Any other party under consideration in this context shall agree to assume all the responsibilities assigned to the first Manager and be fully qualified, in the opinion of the Artist, to perform in a manner and at a level comparable to the first Manager.

4.0. TERM, TERMINATION

Artist's Position: Unless the artist is in an inferior negotiating position, he will seek an initial term of 1 to 2 years. He will try to avoid a longer first term on the possibility that the manager may do an inadequate job and it may become necessary to free up the commission for a new manager; or alternatively, the artist may want to negotiate more favorable terms at the end of the first term—or seek to terminate his manager and engage a new one willing to serve for a lower commission.

Manager's Position: It is in the manager's best interests to negotiate a maximum term allowed by state statute for personal services contracts. He seeks maximum assurance that he has the artist tied up and can enjoy high income for years to come. He wants to recover his investment made during the lean years of the artist's career.

Compromise Position:

The initial term of the Agreement shall be for 2 years, provided the parties satisfactorily fulfill their mutual obligations. If either party has substantial cause to claim the other party has failed to perform under this Agreement, the claimant must send a written notice by registered mail, return receipt requested, citing specific reasons for the complaint, allowing the recipient of the written notice 30 days to cure and reasonably satisfy the complaint. If the aggrieved party does not receive a response that is reasonably satisfactory to the claimant, the claimant may then terminate this Agreement by sending written notice 10 days in advance to the other party.[9]

The Manager may be given the right to exercise options to continue the Agreement beyond the initial term for additional 1-year periods, provided that certain performance criteria have been met, such as securing a recording agreement or generating a minimum amount of income as described below. The number of options should probably not exceed three.

4.1. Options. The Artist grants the Manager options to extend the initial term of this Agreement to a maximum aggregate total of _____ years,[10] provided the Artist has been offered opportunities for employment so that the Artist's gross income from the entertainment industry during the preceding year(s) aggregates these totals:

(A) First term:

$ _____

(B) First Optional Extension Period of One Year (total of (A) and (B)):

$ _____

(C) Second Optional Extension Period of One Year (total of (A) through (C)):

$ _____

(D) Third Optional Extension Period of One Year (total of (A) through (D)):

$ _____

The foregoing notwithstanding, the Artist grants these extension options only on the condition that the Manager fulfills, in the initial term and optional extensions thereof, all his responsibilities and obligations set forth herein.[11]

5.0. Power of Attorney

Manager's Position: The manager will attempt to get general **power of attorney**, including, among other powers, the complete and unrestricted right to (1) collect and disburse all the artist's money; (2) negotiate and sign contracts on behalf of the artist; (3) engage and discharge personnel; (4) exploit the artist's personality, name, likeness, photographs, which would include commitment of the artist to product endorsements and commercial announcements; and (5) exert "creative control," including the selection or rejection of musical and literary materials, record producers, staging, and costuming.

Artist's Position: An artist will seek to limit a grant of power of attorney. Grant of general power of attorney is all encompassing and affords exposure to conflicts of interest and abuse. The artist will probably be most resistant to extending power of attorney to creative control. Unless the manager is fully qualified to make artistic judgments, for example, the manager could impose poor decisions in sensitive areas such as selection of music to be recorded, the manner and style of presentation, and the selection of record producers. Whatever resolution the parties make in regard to creative control and constraints on decision making, the artist will probably demand that power of attorney be cancelable by the artist at any time.

Compromise Position:

The Artist agrees the Manager may need limited power of attorney from time to time for his convenience. Accordingly, the Artist grants limited power of attorney to the Manager to serve as the Artist's agent and **attorney-in-fact** in emergency situations only and denies the Manager this power without the prior written consent of the Artist (1) to accept any performing engagement on behalf of the Artist exceeding one week in duration; (2) to sign checks drawn upon the Artist-Manager's Trust Account with a face value greater than $1,000 and of an aggregate monthly amount in excess of $5,000 for all such draws; (3) to sign any agreement on behalf of the Artist that is of more than incidental importance or having a term longer than 1 month; (4) to engage or discharge support personnel; (5) to accept on the Artist's behalf any product or service endorsement; and (6) to limit the Artist's creative control over matters such as the selection of musical and literary material, and determination of the manner and style of performance, including staging and costuming. The Artist may terminate this power of attorney at any time, without notice, in the event that the Manager misuses, in the sole opinion of the Artist, this power.

The manager usually insists on the right to collect the artist's income early on in the artist's career to ensure reimbursement, payment of expenses, and the receipt of his commission. The artist should, however, make provision for a third-party business manager to handle all the money once income reaches a certain level, since abuses of artists' finances by personal managers are legendary in the music business.

6.0. ARTIST'S RESPONSIBILITIES, WARRANTIES

6.1. Encumbrance. The Artist warrants that he is under no restriction, disability, or prohibition in respect to the Artist's right to execute this Agreement and perform its terms and conditions. The Artist warrants that no act or omission by the Artist will violate, to the best of his knowledge, any right or interest of any person or firm or will subject the Manager to any liability or claim to any person.

6.2. Commitment. The Artist will devote his full time and attention to the advancement of his career.

6.3. Ownership. The Artist warrants that, to the best of his knowledge, he is the sole owner of his professional name,[12] _____, and that this warranty is restricted to adjudicated **breaches**.

6.4. Advice. The Artist will accept in good faith the advice and counsel of the Manager, in recognition of the Manager's special knowledge and experience in the entertainment industry.

6.5. Income. The Artist shall encourage all agents and employers to make payments of all monies due the Artist to the Manager, or to a Third Party approved by the Artist and Manager.

6.6. Employment. The Artist shall refer all offers of employment to the Manager, and the Artist shall not accept offers of employment without the consent of the Manager.

7.0. MANAGER'S COMPENSATION

Artist's Position: The artist will seek to sign the manager for a 10% to 15% commission. If this is unacceptable to the manager, the artist may offer to increase the rate as gross income rises.

Manager's Position: If the manager is new at the game and anxious to get into the field, he might accept a commission as low as 10%. An unknown manager will probably be able to attract only relatively unknown artists, so the parties must agree to struggle together in the early stages of their relationship. The astute manager who accepts a low starting income will seek commission increments when he can manage to increase his client's income substantially.

Compromise Position:

The Artist shall pay the Manager 15% of the Artist's gross income for the first year of this Agreement. "Gross income" shall include, without limitation, all fees, earnings, salaries, royalties, bonuses, shares of profit, stock, partnership interests, percentages, gifts of value, received directly or indirectly, by the Artist or his heirs, executors, administrators, or assigns, or by any other person, corporation, or firm on the Artist's behalf, from the arts and entertainment industry. The commission shall be 20% in the second year of this Agreement, provided the Artist's gross income for this second year increases _____ % over the first year. If this Agreement is extended to a third year, the commission shall rise to 25%, provided the Artist's gross income increases _____ % over the prior year.

In other circumstances, the parties may choose to decrease the percentage as income rises, thereby acknowledging that the Manager may be contributing less significantly to the generation of income but still resulting in more money for the Manager because the income is higher.

8.0. COMMISSION BASE

Artist's Position: An unknown artist may have to pay an established manager on the artist's unadjusted gross income. But an established artist with an aggressive lawyer may be able to obtain certain exclusions from that gross, such as those listed in the Compromise Position that follows.

Manager's Position: The manager will fight for the broadest possible commission base and seek to calculate his percentage on the artist's unadjusted gross income. But if the artist has any bargaining power, "gross income" will probably become an adjusted gross income.

Compromise Position:

The foregoing definition of the Artist's "gross income" notwithstanding, the following sums shall be deducted from the gross income for purposes of calculating the Manager's commission: (1) the first $25,000 aggregated income in any single year derived from the entertainment industry or $500 per calendar week, whichever is greater; (2) recording production expense where a Third Party provides same to the Artist; (3) record producers' fees, points, and percentages where a Third Party pays the Artist for same; (4) performance, production, and travel expense including salaries of support personnel connected thereto where a Third Party pays the Artist for same (often called "negative tour support"); (5) legal fees incurred by the Artist in dealings with the Manager and Third Parties in the negotiation and performance of agreements; and (6) passive income where the Artist receives money or other things of value from sources outside the entertainment industry or the Artist's income from investments inside or outside the entertainment industry.[13]

In any circumstances where the Manager has a financial interest with a Third Party or company with whom the Artist has any kind of business relationship, the Manager shall receive no commissions on any monies the Artist receives from such sources.[14]

When this Agreement and all extensions thereof terminate, the Artist shall pay the Manager 100% of his commissions for a period of 1 year from all income generated by contracts and agreements set up by the Manager during the term of the agreement. For the following 6 months, the Manager's commission is limited to 50% of the Artist's commissionable income. For the subsequent 6 months, the Manager's commission is limited to 25% of the Artist's commissionable income. Thereafter, all Manager's commissions on the Artist's commissionable income cease. The Manager is not entitled to any commissions on albums released after his tenure has expired.[15]

9.0. FINANCIAL ACCOUNTING

Within 30 days following the execution of this Agreement, the parties shall select, by mutual consent, a certified public accountant to provide accounting services for the Artist.

9.1. Records. The parties shall exchange informal financial records of all monies flowing through their hands that relate to this Agreement. The Manager's financial records shall account for all receipts, disbursements, commissions withheld, advances, loans, and investments, if any. Copies of the parties' financial reports shall be forwarded monthly to the accountant.

9.2. Audits. The Manager shall engage independent auditors, with the consent of the Artist, to conduct periodic audits of the Artist's publisher and record company to determine if these firms are fully paying royalties due the Artist and paying in a timely manner.

9.3. Limitations. The Manager may not incur any expense on behalf of the Artist in an amount larger than $ _____ for any one expense, without the consent of the Artist. The Manager may not incur monthly expenses on behalf of the Artist that exceed $ _____ without the consent of the Artist.

9.4. Loans. The Manager is not expected or required to make loans to the Artist or advance the Artist money. The Manager shall not make loans of the Artist's money to any other person or invest the Artist's money without the prior consent of the Artist.

If the Artist asks the Manager to loan him money, and if the Manager voluntarily agrees to do so, the Manager shall be entitled to recover when due such loaned money together with reasonable interest. If such repayments to the Manager are not made when due, the Manager may recover the amount outstanding from the Artist's current earnings from the entertainment industry.

9.5. Overhead. The Manager's office overhead is not recoupable from the Artist, nor is the Manager's travel expense within a 50-mile radius of his office. The Artist shall pay the Manager's travel expense outside this radius when the Manager is requested by the Artist to travel.

9.6. Liability. Neither party is liable to the other for debts and obligations they may incur that are not covered by the Agreement.

10.0. GENERAL ISSUES

The present Agreement constitutes the entire understanding between the parties, and no other agreement or commitment, oral or written, prevails between the parties. Neither party may change or modify any part of the present Agreement without the prior written consent of the other party.

If one or more parts of this Agreement are found to be illegal or unenforceable, for any reason or by any person, the same shall not affect the validity or enforceability of the remaining provisions of this Agreement.

10.1. Incorporation. If the Artist incorporates, he agrees to cause said corporation to sign an agreement with the Manager that provides no less favorable terms than the first agreement.

10.2. Default and Cure. If either party claims that the other is in default or breach of this agreement, the aggrieved party shall provide written notice setting forth the nature of the dispute. The accused party is then allowed 30 days to cure the alleged default, during which period no default or other grievances shall be deemed incurable.

10.3. Arbitration. The parties agree to submit all disputes to the American Arbitration Association and be bound by and perform any award rendered in such arbitration.[16]

10.4. This Agreement is made under the laws of the state of _____

IN WITNESS WHEREOF, the parties hereto have executed this Agreement as of the day and year first indicated above.

_____

Artist

_____

Personal Manager

Notes

1. In this chapter, the terms artists and stars refer not only to performers but also to other professionals who, from time to time, engage personal managers, such as writers, producers, directors, and choreographers.

2. When a major act audits a recording company, the expense can run from $30,000 to $100,000 or more.

3. Suppliers often try to overcharge entertainment business personalities, apparently assuming that such customers are not concerned enough to examine their bills critically.

4. Similar billings are used for producers, writers, directors, and others. In complex productions such as theatrical motion pictures, these participants may all joust for good billing, further complicated by the rules of competing unions. Some participants are so prestigious (or have invested so much money) that they receive star billing—their names positioned above the title of the production.

5. Contracts often specify billings in terms of relative percentages. For example, it might be required that an artist's name never be printed less than 50% as large as the production title—or that an artist's musical director's name appear 25% as large as the artist's name. These kinds of billings can be readily observed on Las Vegas hotel billboards.

6. The manager may require here that the members of the performing group are individually and severally liable for any claims against any other member of the group or the manager.

7. Joseph Taubman, *In Tune With the Music Business* (p. 80). New York: Law-Arts Publishers, 1980.

8. The artist may seek to limit the manager's freedom here by requiring a listing of current clients and agreement to limit future activity to those clients. This may help assure the artist that the manager will have sufficient time to serve the artist's best interests.

9. The parties may prefer that this option to terminate not be allowed and that all serious claims of failure to perform be referred to arbitration. But a powerful act may demand the right to terminate at any time, making the claim that the manager serves at the pleasure of the artist. But no prestigious manager would accept this, arguing possible vulnerability to a capriciously behaving artist.

10. States have statutes of limitation on contracts involving "personal services."

11. Whatever the circumstances of termination or disengagement, the lawyers will need to exchange notices of release. These releases may include **executory provisions**—requirements for performance, payments, and so forth following termination of the agreement.

12. Courts have held that the legal ownership of a trade name ultimately resides not with the person first using it, but with the person or persons identified with the name when it acquires a "secondary meaning."

13. A manager with a strong track record and powerful contacts will probably not accept these commission exclusions—or not without a higher commission rate. The author's rationale for suggesting these exclusions is simple: Most of these exclusions are not the artist's income; they are his overhead. The manager is entitled to commissions on income but not outflow.

14. The attorneys need to negotiate how commissions, if any, are to be paid where a corporation provides the artist's services. The commission will be adjusted to reflect whether the artist, in this circumstance, has a financial interest in the corporation, is only an employee, or both.

15. This compromise of entirely eliminating the manager's commission after a relatively short period of time may be unacceptable to a manager. If the manager is responsible for securing a beneficial recording agreement for the artist, it may be that even a successful artist has little or no commissionable income during the first few years of the agreement. The manager may have invested a great deal of time, energy, and money over that period and would see essentially no return at all. For this reason, managers may justifiably seek to receive some reduced commission in perpetuity for every album produced under the contract they arranged, or at the very least, for every album produced during their tenure.

16. Many contracts include a compulsory arbitration clause calling for the parties to submit disputes to the American Arbitration Association. Although rulings can be prompt through arbitration proceedings, their implementation may still result in lawsuits; if, for instance, one party refuses to abide by the decision of the arbitration board, the other party would file suit for breach of contract.

Chapter Takeaways

- A manager typically earns a commission of 10% to 25% of the artist's gross income, one of several major expenses for an artist.

- Managers may guide an on-stage persona for the performing artist in addition to overseeing the business of maximizing artist income throughout the entertainment industry.

- The music industry is a giant, but only a few hundred people have sustained positions of real power. A good manager knows how to tap the power network.

- Although a traditional record deal may not be as crucial to success as in earlier eras, a manager's main task often is to get and maintain a good label contract on behalf of the artist.

- Artist and manager should each engage experienced lawyers to negotiate a comprehensive artist management agreement.

Key Terms

- attorney-in-fact   (p. 192)
- deal memo   (p. 188)
- flack   (p. 185)

- master of ceremonies (MC) (p. 182)
- negative tour support (p. 179)

- promo pack   (p. 185)
- special material   (p. 181)
- swag   (p. 185)

Producing, Performing, and Merchandising

PART 4

CHAPTER 11

Record Production

Just as it is said that movie making is "the director's art," so one may say that creating sound recordings is "the producer's art." It is rare to hear a successful recording today that does not reveal the sure hand of a competent producer, backed by talented engineers who have worked their own brand of electronic artistry—whether in million-dollar suites in lush commercial studios or at low-cost computer-based workstations in cozy home setups. Even if the song is great and the performance outstanding, these elements must be brought together and presented to the ear as one artistic whole.

The record producer's number-one challenge is matching artist to repertoire, seeking a union of the performer and the material. An imaginative producer goes beyond this to devise ways of producing a good master even with material that is less than great, with an artist who may not always shake the earth. Under a savvy producer's capable control, the musical sum will always be greater than the parts. When the magic happens, it adds up to a hit.

> *"I can't record in the morning because I sound like Barry White."*
>
> *—Toni Braxton*

Record Producers

What is a record producer? The details of the role vary depending on the needs of a particular project, the artist's individual strengths and weaknesses, and the

Left: Miley Cyrus performs in her "Best of Both Worlds" tour.

Photo © Kevin Mazur/Wire Image.

producer's official job title. Some are big-picture organizers (**executive producers**), while others are detail people (engineer-producers), creative voices (artist-producers), or jacks-of-all-trades (producer). Different musical genres, too, present differing demands and challenges for a producer, from the beat-driven dance sector to vocals-focused pop to instrumental rock. Some productions—of jazz and classical recordings, for instance—emphasize skill in capturing live work in concert or in the studio, while others test a producer's technical artistry in the stitching of individual beats and tracks into a seamless whole. All producers, however, must be the objective, independent voice in the studio, the one who bridges the gap between commercial viability and artistic expression. He or she must analyze what is working (and, more delicately, what is not) and inspire the very best performances. The bottom line is that a music producer is responsible for doing whatever is needed to keep the recording session moving forward toward the desired outcome—that is, a commercially viable, marketable master.

Whether a producer will have creative control—the right to make artistic judgments—is another variable in the contemporary workday equation. Occasionally, the artist may have such high stature that creative control is relinquished to no one. In this case, the producer is charged with implementing the artist's ideas. More likely, the producer and the featured artist share in the making of creative decisions, with plenty of spirited give-and-take along the way.

Probably the most contentious creative call is in the selection of material to be recorded. Ideally, the producer and artist work together to winnow the choices down to the strongest songs. This process can be more difficult when the act composes its own songs, about which it surely feels possessive and protective. The producer has the tough task of selecting the best material and rejecting the weakest without offending the writers.

Matching Producer to Artist

Before song selection becomes an issue, of course, the producer and recording artist must first choose *one another*. A bad fit is in no one's best interest, and unless the producer is new to the field and hard up for work, selectivity in assignments is crucial. An experienced producer will meet with the act before signing up for the project. Preliminary meetings are particularly critical when working with a new artist or group; the artists probably have only a dim view of what lies ahead and are fearful of the outcome, but all jobs should include this step to ensure that producer and artist are compatible in working styles, expectations, and personalities.

That latter is of no small importance. Although you likely won't see it on the course list at music schools, "people skills" are a talent most working producers will tell aspiring students they need to develop. Producers say they find that at least half their time must be spent as resident psychologists, appraising the personality traits of the individuals, diplomatically delivering artistic criticism, learning whom they can pressure when necessary and who withdraws for hours when reproached. Producers skillful in human relationships also search for the group's resident comedian. Usually, the funny person in the group can be counted on to relieve tensions all around when it is 3 o'clock in the morning and everyone is getting surly.

Production Deals

How a producer and an artist come to work together, and under what terms, will vary depending on the production deal in effect. Over the years, employment practices concerning producers have varied widely. Until the advent of rock and roll, recording companies maintained a staff of full-time **house producers,** who had strong control over who was recorded and precisely what material the chosen few were to record. This setup began to shift in the 1960s with the rise of a new breed of rock acts that typically composed their own songs and wanted to control the selection of material. They achieved this either by sheer weight of their influence or by insisting they obtain creative control and hire their own producers. Since that time, most record companies, large and small, have used a mix of in-house and independent producers.

For the most frequent working arrangements for producers see Table 11.1.

Table 11.1 Types of Producers

Producer as label employee	A record company engages a producer as a full-time employee, provides a weekly salary, perhaps a royalty override. The label's head of A&R (artists and repertoire) assigns projects to the producer, who may have little to say about which artists or what music is recorded for the company.
Independent producer under label contract	The producer works as an independent contractor—as an entrepreneur or for a production company. Labels that employ the producer assign a budget, "deliver" the artist, and expect completion of a master. The producer will receive a portion of the recording advance and artist royalty.
Independent producer under artist contract	The producer's services are delivered by the artist, who has the producer under contract. This is sometimes called an "all-in" deal: Artist's representatives negotiate a package with a record company that involves a royalty and an advance on royalties. The artist then shares the advance and the royalties with the producer.
Independent producer/"spec" deal	The producer delivers the artist and a master. The producer and artist invest their time and money in the project and then try to sell the master to an established label. If they succeed, the parties negotiate a master purchase agreement that will provide the recoupment of all or part of the production costs, as well as a royalty that is shared by the producer and the artist. In some cases, the producer alone may pay for the cost of production of the master recording, which will then be shopped to record companies. This is known as a spec deal (short for speculation deal) and will generally occur when a producer believes very strongly in the potential of an artist. Although taking on all the risk, the producer also stands to gain more should such an arrangement lead to a contract with a label; the producer will get a larger portion of the advance and, in some cases, a promise to produce future projects with the artist.
Producer/label entrepreneur	Although the label-creation route has traditionally been the option of last resort for artists and producers when no buyer can be found for a finished master—"I'll show the big shots. I'll set up my own label!"—a growing number of producers, engineers, and studio owners explore the opportunities presented by releasing records on their own labels. The required investment, and thus the financial risk, has decreased significantly with the ever-expanding availability of low-cost, high-quality recording and replication equipment and the inexpensive avenues of promotion and sales offered via the Web, either through mail-order or digital downloads. Of course, a producer hoping to establish a full-scale independent label will still need sufficient funds for promotion, distribution, placing music on digital platforms and manufacture of physical CDs, and the knowledge to operate such a diverse enterprise. An established producer may have the track record and industry clout to line up investors and attract strong acts, raising the odds of success.

Royalties, Fees

Except perhaps on work turned out by a label's staff producers, virtually all independent production agreements today provide a royalty for the producer. In this sector of the business, people often refer to a producer's points, a term synonymous in this context with percentages. One point equals 1% (e.g., 1 point may equal 1% of retail or wholesale price of albums and singles). A point may also equal a percentage of a percentage (e.g., 1 point may equal 1% of retail of 90% of recordings sold). How many points can a producer earn? The party with clout prevails. A young producer just breaking in may get only 1 point. Most producers receive 2 to 4 points. A few superstar producers ask for and receive 5% or 6% on sales.

Some contracts treat the producer better than the featured artist, who must wait for royalties until the label has recouped its production costs. (Many releases fail to recoup their costs.) The artist will normally receive a royalty 2 to 5 times higher than the producer's, but there's a catch. The artist will only receive royalty payments once certain costs are recouped from sales, while the producer will generally have a contract that requires royalties from sale Number 1 (sometimes called "record one royalties"). This means that if an album sells poorly, the producer might get a small royalty payment while the artist receives no royalties at all (considered fair because the artist presumably received a big advance payment).

For top producers with negotiating clout, contracts may have escalators if their albums become best-sellers. The labels agree to such escalators because their upfront direct costs, such as recording expenses, will have been recouped when albums pass the contractually defined sales levels (such as 500,000 or 1 million unit sales). Of course, producers of lesser reputations are unable to negotiate such contingent bonuses.

In addition to royalties, it is standard practice for the label to pay a production fee. Some producers are fortunate to get a few thousand dollars in front as their fee, half of which is normally paid before the first session begins and the other half upon delivery of the master. Some fees are not extra payments but, may be minor advances deducted from the producer's royalties. Major producers can get tens of thousands of dollars or more in production fees, usually nonrecoupable by the label from royalties. Some artist's recording contracts call for the early payment of the producer to be recouped from the artist's future royalties.

In exchange for the "privilege" of choosing their producer, recording artists often pay the producer's points out of their own record royalty. The paperwork required between the producer, artist, and record label will be a few short pages and is referred to as a *letter of direction*. Typically, a letter of direction informs the record company of the fee that the artist will assign the record producer out of his or her advance and how many of the artist's royalty points the producer is to receive. In addition, the artist also grants permission to the record company to handle the accounting and pay the producer directly, which relieves the producer of worries that the artist may be hard to find and collect from in future years.

The Recording Studio: Operation and Selection ▪▬▬▬▬

Once a producer has aligned with an artist and struck a deal with the artist, a label, or both, another key early decision to be made is a basic one: Where will the music be recorded? There is no shortage of good options: The rise of the high-quality home or project studio, the contraction of the U.S. music market, and a resultant tightening of recording budgets by label executives have combined in recent years to put a squeeze on the commercial studio sector. Although this can work to the advantage of a producer and recording artist in potentially driving down fees and opening up slots, it makes it harder for the studios to make money and stay in business. To compete, commercial studios are stressing those factors that make them unique—from spacious room size to specialized staff and support, from properly designed acoustic environments to luxurious amenities.

Studio Operation

Except to industry insiders, the recording-studio sector is largely a hidden business—most of the best of them remain unknown to the public. Thousands of people are employed full-time in this unique industry, which requires cooperation between entrepreneurs, technicians, engineers, designers, acousticians, managers, and musicians. Here, art and technology must find accommodation. And while producers and engineers may never opt to open their own commercial studio operations, they can count on spending plenty of time in them over the courses of their careers. Having at least a general knowledge of the operations of the studio sector thus makes good sense for anyone interested in being a part of the music industry.

Although staffing levels fluctuate with the ebb and flow of good business times and bad, label-owned studios and the larger independent studios traditionally maintain a full-time staff of between 10 and 40 members, a smaller number than in the heyday of prior decades. With record label revenue declining in recent years, the recording studio business has likewise shrunk as labels economize on recording budgets.

The technology revolution has crimped the big multi-room studios by enabling medium- and small-sized recording businesses to proliferate. These smaller studios, often operating as a family business, may be equipped with semi-professional recording equipment that nevertheless delivers good audio quality. Modern recording equipment is compact and mobile. Small recording studios can offer remote recording services with high quality and low prices that would have been unthinkable a few decades ago.

One human impact from the cheap recording technology revolution is that the skill of engineering and production staff is now of paramount importance. Because the equipment provides so many options, the human decisions on which avenues to pursue—rather than the expense of the recording equipment—are larger factors in final product quality.

A key executive at the larger professional recording studios is the business manager, who is responsible for collecting delinquent accounts and determining to whom credit should be extended. A studio's staff also includes traffic managers, who book studio time and must sometimes contend with the feast-or-famine scenario of producers desperate for specific times, usually all at the *same* time. Traffic managers must sometimes schedule weeklong sessions months in advance, booking time for acts, for example, who will be coming off the road and who are determined to lay down an album at a specific time of the year. Besides these long-range booking problems, the studio traffic department must be adept at estimating when a session may run overtime.

Studio profit depends on how closely contiguous hours can be booked. When sessions fail to begin and end on schedule, both the studio and producer may experience serious financial losses. Major accounts planning to record an album often "block book" studio time. The producer estimates how many days or weeks are needed to lay down 10 or more songs and then requests the studio to reserve a particular room exclusively for that project. In block booking, the artists can leave equipment and microphones in place and not waste time trying to reinvent the setup that worked so well the previous day. Also, studios that block off a room for several days or weeks will offer the producer a much lower total price for the project than would have been charged on a per-hour basis.

In addition to the traffic manager and business manager, the staff of a full-line studio includes a chief engineer, a staff of house engineers, mixers, editors, **mastering** engineers/technicians, perhaps a video/film projectionist/technician, maintenance personnel, and people handling setups and the equipment movement. An office crew completes the staff of a full-line studio.

Few recording studios have sales departments or promotion people. Management finds that business comes or goes based largely on the word-of-mouth reputation of a studio. Ads generally do not help much. With the tougher recording environment of the last few years, however, savvy studio operators are working harder than ever to network in the industry, to help spark that all-important positive chatter.

Studio Design

A studio with even the latest hardware is in trouble if it lacks good acoustics in two critical areas: the control rooms and the studios themselves. Qualified engineers can predict how sounds will behave in a given space. But modern control rooms are difficult to design because the proper balance of stereo depends largely on where the **mixer** sits in the room; the producer, perhaps only 3 feet away from the mixer, hears a different balance. The interest in 5.1 surround sound compounds this problem, because sound is derived from six locations rather than two, putting a different spin on the entire process. The latest bells and whistles aside, studios ultimately often sink or swim on whether the performing musicians feel comfortable in them. One essential acoustical requirement for orchestras and ensembles is sound diffusion, which allows performers to hear a fair amount of the sounds occurring around them. However, the precise opposite occurs in tracking: Performers want very short reverberation times when using earphones, because they want to hear only themselves and the program coming over the earphones.

Selecting a Studio

A number of factors will play into a producer's selection of a studio, but the first filter will likely be cost: How much can the act spend to make its record? Those on extremely limited budgets will not have the luxury of even considering the highest-end studios, whose state-of-the-art equipment, top-tier staff, and luxurious accommodations come with an equally high-ticket price tag.

The next factor is where the act will be comfortable: Is a big city desirable? A small town where everyone can hang out after hours at a local bar? Although the industry is primarily based in New York, Los Angeles, Nashville, and to some extent, Chicago, professional studios can be found in countless other areas of the country, with affiliates around the world and creative resources everywhere. That a label bigwig is less likely to wander in during the sessions "just to see how things are going" is an added bonus to heading off the beaten path, some musicians say.

Photo by Elaine Maltezos, used by permission. Photo courtesy University of Miami.

The available equipment, the level of service, and the staffing provided will also be factored into the equation. The producer wants to select a studio in which a good sound can be achieved and where the maintenance of the hardware is reliable. One of a producer's biggest problems is **downtime** in the studio. When equipment is not working properly, the loss is not only in dollars but also in momentum. If a particular studio has a staff engineer who can keep the equipment working, that facility may be favored over one with more sophisticated equipment.

The producer who brings in a freelance engineer can expect an experienced mixer to adapt quickly to a new console. A producer who is particular about equalization (**EQ**) and **timbre** will usually go into a studio prior to the sessions with the engineer to check out the console, the monitoring system, and the acoustics. One who goes to this effort (not uncommon among pros) brings in a familiar recording. If the playback does not sound exactly as it should, the producer spends time with the engineer and a house engineer to adjust equalization of speakers and amplifiers. It is important to know precisely what sounds are coming over the monitors.

Another consideration for the producer is the range of equipment on offer. Some want **digital recording**; others insist on **analog** equipment. This, of course, presents a monetary challenge to already stretched studios: Only heavily capitalized operations can keep up with every innovation. Studios often start out by leasing leading-edge gear because of the lower capital outlay—and because they want to trade in outdated equipment as more sophisticated hardware becomes available. Some so-called digital recordings are not wholly digital; the recording machine may employ digital technology, but it can be hooked up to analog microphones and consoles. Some studios may use "automated" consoles interfaced with computers, and these consoles are used as a mixing and remixing aid. The computers "remember" previous sound settings, leaving the engineer free to perform other tasks.

Finally, a producer and the recording artist will consider intangibles such as a studio's hit-making reputation and overall "vibe." Many refuse to book time in a studio that has not produced successful or great-sounding records.

Types of Studios

With a checklist of desired attributes in hand and a budget in mind, the producer can consider the available options. Keep in mind that projects often encompass more than one studio. Rehearsals and demos may be done in one facility, for instance, while backing tracks could be laid down in another environment, and mixing and final mastering could occur in a third type of studio. The choices include the following:

Home/Project Studios. These are not the "converted garages" of old, where shaggy-haired guitarists rolled tape (among other things). Although hard-disc recording has existed in commercial products since the early 1980s, recent developments have made digital audio workstations (**DAW**) that combine recording, editing, mixing, and mastering functions in a single software/hardware package much more user-friendly and, equally important, much more affordable to a wide range of users. Leading the DAW revolution is the Pro Tools system, which in its basic form comprises hardware and sound cards connected to a computer on which digital music recording software is installed. Such systems now give even amateurs the means to achieve professional-sounding recordings in their own homes. These studios still serve their traditional role as a training ground for aspiring producers, engineers, and musicians, who can set up a versatile entry-level studio for around $1,000, but they are now also the professional playgrounds for established producing, engineering, and recording talents, who can choose among a significantly higher-end selection of professional-quality workstations and software. These types of studios are thus a viable, and increasingly popular, option to use for at least part of the recording process.

Preproduction/Demo Studios. The traditional entry-level commercial studio for musicians is one that specializes in rehearsal space and/or demo recordings. Nearly all of them offer 4- to 8-track tape equipment or some basic digital recording device, and room enough for a small ensemble. Because demo studios can offer hourly rates far lower than full commercial studios, they service the bulk of demo recording needs of writers and publishers, and are an efficient and cost-effective place for an act to work on its material for an upcoming recording. Well-managed demo studios can make a profit; however, financial difficulties may occur as the small operator attempts to keep up by purchasing all the latest equipment. Some demo studios live long and prosper by becoming headquarters for small production companies, small labels, beginning publishers, even artists' managers and agents trying to get established. Another kind of recording operation, which might be called the in-house studio, has become increasingly popular with publishers and advertising agencies. These are private operations, rarely open to the public, and intended to serve the host company and its business associates. They range in size from 8- to 16-track, and provide in-house production for everything from simple demos to master tapes to CDs.

Independent Studios. A big step above the demo studio is the full-line independent studio, which has at least 24-track tape recorders with multi-input consoles, and other **outboard equipment** sufficient to compete with plants operated by the major record labels. Digital equipment offers the capacity for even more audio tracks. A full-service independent studio will normally have one or two rooms capable of handling a studio orchestra or smaller groups, mixdown and editing, full musical instrument digital interface (MIDI) capabilities, equipment rack rooms, and possibly a maintenance shop, traffic control office, and lockers for equipment storage. Although these studios can pretty much be counted on to have the array of digital tools so pervasive in the recording business, they are also where producers and artists can usually find large-format analog tape recorders and consoles.

Label-Owned Studios. A carryover from the days when the major recording companies controlled all the links in the record-making chain, the label-owned studio still exists in large cities such as Los Angeles, Nashville, New York, and Miami. And although major-label consolidation has winnowed the list of music-business heavyweights down to a precious few behemoths, all still have a stable of studios—some of which are simply small, private setups—available to their various labels' artists, producers, and publishing groups. Many also operate as commercial recording studios, open to outside acts and producers, although label acts are usually given priority. Physical facilities and equipment are generally equal to, or superior to, those found in major independent studios.

The Five Stages of Record Production

Studio selection comes during the preproduction or planning stage of record production, when budgets are also being mapped out and set. The other four phases are basic tracking, overdubbing, mixing, and mastering (see Table 11.2). Each is a critical link in the music-making process.

Preproduction: Budgeting and Planning

The responsibility of developing and controlling budgets is a key part of the producer's job, whether the work is being done for a label or on a freelance basis. Preparing a production budget with precision is difficult because many of the expenses can be only roughly estimated. At budget-writing time, the producer may not even know in which city the recording will take place. Perhaps a rhythm section must be flown in from Nashville. Will some of the songs on the album require an expensive complement of string players? All the budget maker can do at the outset is identify expense parameters. After assembling all available data, costs must be specified in detail.

Budget Control

Well-organized producers work up budgets on some kind of summary sheet. Table 11.3 shows one kind of budget sheet, which may be used as is or tailored to a specific situation.

A budget control sheet must reflect careful research of current studio costs and the latest union wage scales and surcharges. Experienced producers often call in their American Federation of Musicians (AFM) and American Federation of Television and Radio Artists (AFTRA) contractors to help them pull together accurate figures, especially when they need to hire **session musicians.** These superb artists

Table 11.2   The Five Phases of Record Production

The following is a representative rundown of the many steps required along the route to a successful album production. The exact order may vary, particularly in the preproduction stage (this list, for instance, presumes that a producer initiates the project, as opposed to being assigned to it by a label or recording artist), depending on the project.

1. Preproduction: Budgeting and Planning

   - Create the concept
   - Prepare a budget, raise the money (or negotiate the budget with the label)
   - Locate and sign an artist (or sign on to an existing project with a label, artist)
   - Select the songs
   - Negotiate mechanical licenses
   - Lay out how each song is to be treated, engage arrangers to score the charts
   - Engage the musical director, union contractors
   - Book time in a studio
   - Engage an engineer, test studio equipment, acoustics
   - Confirm availability of any special equipment and instruments needed
   - Reconfirm all of the above
   - Rehearse the music

2. In the Studio: Basics and Tracking

   - Record the basic/backing tracks for each song
   - Maintain a tracking sheet, detailing what is laid down on each track
   - Execute punch ins as needed to fix/alter basic tracks

3. In the Studio: Overdubbing

   - Identify performances that still need to be fixed or fine-tuned
   - Add sweetener tracks
   - Record the vocals

4. In the Studio: Mixing and Final Preparations

   - Make decisions about levels, EQ
   - Prepare final mixdown to 2-track stereo or a multichannel format
   - Sequence album tracks
   - Pull out possible singles and edit for length
   - Make copies as needed
   - If songs are composed during recording, settle on composer credits immediately at end of session
   - Prepare union contracts for instrumentalists and vocalists

5. Postproduction: Mastering and Delivery to Label

   - Locate a mastering studio
   - Supervise mastering
   - Obtain clearances from graphic artist, photographer, liner notes writer
   - Turn over signed mechanical licenses to the record company
   - Obtain W-4 and I-9 forms and copies of identification from all employees
   - Deliver W-4 and I-9 forms, copies of identification, and union contracts to the company
   - Deliver lyric sheets and technical credit sheets to the company
   - Identify samples/interpolations and hire a sample clearinghouse
   - Deliver information on any samples/interpolations to the company
   - Confirm that all bills have been paid
   - Reconfirm everything
   - Deliver final master

sight-read the **charts** and are able to perform an acceptable take on the second or third reading.

In calculating the expense of recording an album, the producer potentially enters an arena of high finance and equally lofty risk. In some cases, the expense of recording a quality master for an album will start in the six-figure range. Other major-label budgets will be in the five figures, whereas still others for smaller independent companies or fledgling bands won't go far into four. Although the smaller budgets demand a much larger degree of creativity and flexibility in approach, all producers are charged with the task of turning in a quality master from the investment allotted, whatever its size.

Producers of rock albums often budget 10 to 20 hours of studio time per song. Some rock albums may clock 300 hours or more, including mixing, editing, and mastering. Producers and other recording executives worried about exorbitant recording costs might want to compare their figures with the studio time required by artists in other genres. Jazz album producers, for instance, may let the machines roll and catch great performances the first time, entirely unrehearsed—improvised. An even more impressive comparison of recording time for rock can be made with the classical field. A professional symphony orchestra of the second or third rank can record a 15- to 25-minute work, such as Stravinsky's *Rite of Spring,* in 6 to 9 hours! Of course, the orchestra would have learned the piece a few seasons back, but such an achievement is still remarkable.

Among the reasons that recording costs can exceed their budgets are these:

1. The group is poorly prepared; it uses the recording studio for rehearsal, even for composition.

2. The performers can't read music, can't mesh their performances, or can't come up with the right style.

3. The producer can't decide what is needed.

4. The engineer can't come up with the right sounds.

5. One or more of the participants is not qualified for the job, lacking the talent or the experience to compete professionally.

With these possible problems in mind, the experienced producer will "pad" the estimated recording budget so as to have access to additional funds without upsetting the record label; in effect, he or she "budgets" for budget overrides. A savvy producer will also attempt to head off as many potential budget-busting scenarios as possible; he or she may raise the subject of hiring a session musician or two to "ghost" some of the musician's parts that aren't coming out right, for instance, or ask the chief studio engineer or owner to be on hand for the first day or two to assist should there be any problems or questions about the equipment.

Recording expenses paid for by the record label are considered an advance against future earnings. As explained in Chapter 8, if the master is produced for an amount less than the fund, some contracts provide that the balance can be retained (by the artist or the producer, depending on their contract with each other) as an advance from the label against royalties.

Table 11.3   Recording Budget

Artist/Group _____   Date _____
Producer _____   Studio _____
Label/Client _____   Project No. _____
Contact _____   Engineer _____

	Cost Per Unit	No. of Units	Total Unit Cost	Subtotal	Extension
STUDIO					
Studio					
Basic Rate					
Outboard Equipment					
Set Up/Strike					
Basic Tracks					
Overdubs					
Vocals					
Mixing/Editing					
Tax					
ENGINEERS					
1st Engineer					
2nd Engineer					

ARRANGING/COPYING

Music Title	Arranging	Copying			
1.					
2.					
3.					
4.					
5.					
6.					
7.					
8.					
9.					
10.					
Union surcharges					

ARTISTS	Instrumentalists	Singers	Soloists		
Rehearsals					
Basic Tracks					
Sweetening					
Union surcharges					

EQUIPMENT					
Rentals					
Cartage					
Tax					

MISCELLANEOUS (payroll tax, etc.)

UNFORESEEN EXPENSE (15% of total)

TOTAL PRODUCTION COST

Not surprisingly, recording funds and budgets are more often overspent than underspent. Most record labels keep a sharp eye on the progress of the recording. They assign some individual to keep track of the money flow on a day-to-day basis, and the producer will be asked to keep this budget monitor informed whenever expense is incurred. When a project is nearing completion and has developed momentum, many labels permit reasonable budget overruns of around 10% or less. But a label might also include the equivalent of a "stop loss" order in its contract with a producer or artist, giving it the right to halt the recording process at any point if it believes the project is careening toward severe budget overrun. With the music industry in a prolonged period of belt-tightening, it is the rare artist today whose budget and expenses won't be carefully measured out and scrutinized by the label.

Arrangements and Rehearsals

After having set a budget and selected the songs to be recorded—a tough process, as discussed earlier—the producer and act must lay out how each song is to be treated. Does this need strings or horns? Is some of the material going to be most effective when presented with complete simplicity? When these kinds of decisions have been made, the producer engages arrangers to score the charts. Producers with strong musical backgrounds will probably work with arrangers in sketching out the arrangements, to increase the likelihood that the producer's conception will be implemented.

If the act and the producer have reached a working understanding on how the material is to be treated, preproduction rehearsals will follow, to make sure the music is prepared before going into the studio. Organized groups rehearse for free, of course. But if the charts call for added instruments such as horns and strings, established session musicians expect to be paid for rehearsals, often at straight recording scale.

If the charts call for outside session singers, the producer needs to know which AFTRA union contractors can deliver them.

Basics and Tracking

Now that the producer and the artist have begun recording, the second stage of the production process focuses on capturing the basic elements of each song, or the backing tracks. In most cases, this is when the rhythm section is recorded or, in the case of dance and hip-hop music, when the beat is built. For some genres, most everything that appears on the record is captured live. The producer will be looking for a steady rhythm that is appropriate for the song and has a good "feel" or "groove."

Practices vary, but most producers keep a written record of what is laid down on each **track**; this record is referred to as a tracking sheet. Tracking sheets cite the artist, the date, the studio, song titles, "take" numbers, timings, and footage counts for the start and end of takes. Of course, if the recording process is digital with search-and-find capability, location and level settings are readily recalled with the push of a button.

As the recording process goes forward through this stage, the producer can expect to be challenged from all sides. Although the first concern will be the music, the producer is supposed to know enough about recording technology to work effectively with the engineer. The self-confident producer will encourage the engineer to contribute creatively to the recording process. When the producer cannot come up with a solution to a problem, perhaps the engineer can save the day. Usually, the most successful producers will welcome and carefully weigh all the creative input they can find, whatever the source.

The rise of user-friendly digital recording technology has added a new challenge to producers during the recording process: the lure of having endless options. It is now all too easy to postpone a decision on the "best take" because a producer can record as many as desired—and retain them all. Likewise, some producers hear the siren call of the "undo" button, which allows experimentation without risk—and sometimes without end. An ability to know when they have got *the* take or achieved the best sound—and a willingness to commit to it—remains a big part of producers' jobs, whatever the technology being used.

Overdubbing

With the basic elements of the recording in the can, it is time to focus on those performances that need to be fixed or fine-tuned, to record the vocals, and to get creative and add any other instruments or effects to help "sweeten" the track. This process is known as overdubbing. Some producers may do some of the overdubbing

Associate Professor Reynaldo Sanchez and a student in a Music Business and Entertainment Industries class of the Frost School of Music, University of Miami.

Photo by Donna Victor courtesy University of Miami.

while laying down the basic tracks—for example, it is more efficient to fix the bass player's mistakes right away than to try to remember to do it later and have to find a time when the musician may be available. These fixes are called **punch ins**. In other instances, a separate track is immediately recorded instead.

The most important part of the overdubbing process for noninstrumental productions is the recording of the lead vocals, which will be the centerpiece of the recording. Vocals can be as hard to capture as they are critical to success, and the process will likely be equal parts trade craft (the right mike and correct placement) and skillful cajolery (knowing the ways in which to somehow elicit the best possible performance from the singer).

The producer must gauge the psychological and physical makeup of the lead vocalist: Does the vocalist need the session to be closed to nonessential people, for instance, or does he perform better with an audience on hand? Will several hours of singing push her voice too far, or is that much warm-up required before she hits her full vocal stride? Editing software, of course, provides plenty of opportunities to manipulate the vocals after the fact, from basic pitch correction or doubling to the more radical stitching together of pieces from multiple recording sessions.

Mixing

This stage in the recording process is when the decisions are made about what instruments should be at what level, which performances make the final mix from the sessions, what the tonal qualities and EQ should be, and where to place the instruments in the stereo mix. That last decision has been getting more interesting with the number of recordings mixed or remixed in multichannel sound as opposed to traditional two-channel stereo. Mixers have the option of creating various virtual experiences via the multiple channels, such as re-creating a live concert experience by placing the music upfront, as on a stage, and positioning audience ambience in the rear channels, for instance.

Whatever the technology, the human element—the mixer, or "mixing engineer"—will be the most important factor in success at this stage of production. Studios and record labels have had difficulty finding mixers and engineers who are thoroughly qualified and sufficiently versatile because obtaining adequate preparation is challenging: This group of professionals is expected to be fully educated in two different disciplines—electrical engineering and music. The aforementioned shrinkage of big multi-room recording studios with large staffs has even reduced the opportunities for newcomers to intern or serve as **gofers** at the hands of masters.

The mixers most in demand are those with "magic ears" for the current hot sound. They may not understand how to trace a short in an amp or adjust the azimuth on a recording head, but they do know how to piece together all of the tracks into a winning mix. They ride those **faders** with a sure touch, pulling from the console much more interesting sounds than what originally went into the microphones. In short, the top mixers are sensitive to sound and music, and they work their electronic wizardry like sound sorcerers—which they are. They have a good feel for the impact that a sound or musical sequence will have on the listener.

Besides the ability to ride a console with sensitivity and creativity, these artists have one additional attribute without which they would run screaming from the control room: Their temperament seems immune to high stress and tension. The mixer bears great responsibility for the final result. The top mixers feel the pressure, but they can handle it.

Although the industry is saturated with mixers, those who have "the ears" and a cool temperament are the individuals most likely to find regular employment and a high income. However talented the mixer and however good the mix sounds when piped through the studio's professional monitors and top-quality speakers, most producers won't OK it just yet. First, they want to hear how it sounds in a *real-world* environment—over the various types of low-end speakers, iPods, basic radio receivers, and car stereos that most music fans actually use.

Master Delivery Requirements

Even when the producer has survived the production and mixing of the master, the job is far from over. If a recording company has retained the producer, the firm now imposes specific delivery requirements that need to be completed prior to the company's acceptance of the master. For example:

1. The master tape must be mixed down to two-channel stereo or multichannel sound, as appropriate, on half-inch or quarter-inch tape, high-quality **CD-R**, or hard disk. The label will probably also expect the producer to pull out several tracks for possible release as singles. If so, the singles must be edited to appropriate lengths (usually under 4 minutes).

2. The producer must deliver letters of consent that were obtained earlier from all individuals involved in the project, allowing the label to use their names and photographs in promoting the music. Release letters must also state that the artists, musicians, and other creative personnel are unencumbered by conflicting recording agreements with any other firm. Should an artist on the recording be signed to an exclusive recording contract with another label, the producer must obtain permission in writing and alert the label as to any specific demands (i.e., the recording company must receive a courtesy credit in the liner notes, the artist's name cannot appear on the cover of the recording, among many other requirements).

3. The producer must deliver letters of consent from all photographers and graphic artists for the use of their works.

4. The producer must furnish evidence that all copyrights are clear and the owners have granted **mechanical licenses** for each cut on the album.

5. Lyric sheets must be submitted. Labels want to determine whether the song texts are acceptable for radio broadcast and the standards of some mass merchant chains, though presumably the label knows in advance whether to expect objectionable language. A decision must also be made as to whether the release will carry a parental-advisory label.

6. A technical credits summary sheet is required setting forth details such as the names of the engineers, side musicians, and background vocalists; where the master was recorded; who the arrangers and musical director were; the names of the union contractors; who mastered the tapes; and identities of artists' personal managers and booking agents.

7. A sign-off statement is required from the producer providing evidence that the bills have been paid and that there are no liens or encumbrances that might prevent the label from releasing the recording.

8. The producer must collect W-4 forms, I-9 forms, and union contracts for every individual involved on the project to whom wages were paid.

The smart producer won't mail in the master but will make an appointment with the person who set up the job, then walk in with the master and present it personally. At the same time, at least two or three CD transfer copies should be delivered so that the A&R people and other executives in the firm can hear the producer's work.

Assuming that the label accepts the master, the producer will then be paid the other half of the production fee or advance on royalties.

Mastering

Once the record is mixed and approved, it is sent to a mastering studio to prepare it for mass production. It is customary for the record company to pay for mastering and all subsequent steps leading to manufacture of the recordings; some companies seek to have mastering charged to the artist and producer's royalties, however. Although it is generally not part of the production agreement's requirements, a seasoned producer will be involved in the mastering process; decisions can be made at this point that will affect the sound of the final product.

The mastering engineer might do basic preparation work such as sequencing the album, adding the space between each song, and making sure that the track starts at the correct moment with regard to the corresponding track number. But this is also the last opportunity to make any sonic corrections to the recording. For example, the master might be too bass heavy, so the mastering engineer will "roll off" some lower EQ frequencies. The mastering engineer might also add some compression to the recording to make it sound fuller and more radio friendly. Once this process is finished, the producer's job is really, truly done, right? Well, almost. Some conscientious producers continue their postproduction services up to and including the checking of test pressings, to make sure all the effort invested in the project will be reflected in the ultimate sound of the music.

Getting Started as a Producer

So you have now studied the sector, assessed the challenges and opportunities, and decided that you do want to be a producer. How does one become a producer? The answer is simple: Start producing. Set up a studio at home or start going into a nearby studio and record your music, record your friend's music, or offer to help a local artist.

Many producers come from one of three entry points. Some start as a musician in a band that is recording. They find that they gravitate more toward the control room than the live room. They begin to take a leadership role in the recording session and become actively involved in all phases of the project. Some move from the engineer's chair into the producer's. They find that not only do they have the skills necessary to capture sound and make the band sound fantastic, but they also have an ear for what "takes" sound good and which ones should be done again. The third group begins its journey as passionate students of recordings. These people are usually critics, audiophiles, or both. They listen to a lot of music and can enunciate what makes one recording "better" than others.

Whatever the starting point, all young and ambitious producers will listen to, analyze, and critique many recordings, both current and classic. It would be wise to pay close attention to the works of legendary and successful producers such as John Hammond, George Martin, Teo Macero, Sam Phillips, Jerry Wexler, Quincy Jones, Dr. Dre, and Rick Rubin, to name just a few.

Key Requirements of a Producer

Before you get too far along with your pursuit, also ask these hard questions:

1. Have you got the will and the passion to succeed in a competitive, demanding discipline? Can you hang in there in the face of inevitable challenges and setbacks?

2. Are you gifted in locating artists with star potential? Neither you nor your acts will make a dime unless that potential is there. Can you persuade strong acts to work with you?

3. Do you have a talent for picking quality songs? Do you recognize commercial potential?

4. Can you evaluate the combined impact of the material, artist's delivery, and production sound?

5. Do you have access to money? Do you know how to present a convincing plan to potential investors?

6. Do you know how to present your artists to potential buyers of master tapes? You have three ways to do this: present live showcases, present demo tapes (audio, perhaps video), or present master tapes.

If you lack any of these abilities, you must locate collaborators who are strong in areas where you may be deficient. Translation: Form an independent production company. Few individuals are talented or fortunate enough to go it alone.

You may also wonder whether you need to be a technical wizard to make it as a producer. Although many producers have come up through the engineering route, the answer, as proven by the number of highly successful producers who have *not*, is no. But you will need to be able to communicate effectively with someone who does know the equipment. Particularly in an age in which it is rare for a commercial recording project to be untouched at some point by Pro Tools or another software-based platform, a producer at the very least wants to have a basic understanding of the terminology of both digital and analog recording and editing systems, as well as their options and functions.

Meeting Expectations

Aspiring engineers, of course, need to be technologically adept to work in today's studios. Increasingly complicated multitimbral synthesizers as well as digital and multimedia techniques challenge recording studio personnel. Keyboard players who play several electronic instruments simultaneously will expect the engineer to accommodate their recording needs. Engineers must also understand how to properly record synthesized percussion, various portable keyboards, and experimental instruments that defy classification.

The Do-It-Yourself Artist

For the musician or vocalist wanting to produce, the audio technology revolution has unshackled artists from the studio, allowing recordings to take place in spare bedrooms or even on rolling tour buses. There are many advantages of the do-it-yourself (DIY) ethic: the ability to record when inspiration hits, the artist's control of sound, the ability to be productive during in-between moments of life, and the opportunity to experiment with unusual sounds. But DIY also comes with some disadvantages.

Acoustics of the impromptu sound room are usually not ideal, for which the solution is to **close-mike** the audio source. Still, **slap** and invasion of external low-frequency noise, like the rumble of trucks on the street, can creep in. Another complaint is that low-cost digital equipment can produce a harsh, literal sound for tracks and overdubbing—prime activities of DIY recordings. Of course, a hard sound can often be softened in mixing when done on professional grade equipment with pro engineers, but only if the budget allows.

DIY also means working in a lonely world with little collaboration. The DIY artist cannot benefit from the insights and ideas of experienced, trained engineers and staff at a professional studio. Another drawback for artists intent on video recording their studio sessions for later promotion is the often bland and inappropriate visual setting of the DIY environment.

Experienced recording professionals say self-recording sounds easy, but when an artist gets stuck on a problem it can be maddening to resolve because of a lack experience. Indeed, good engineering skills require education and experience, difficult to acquire in a DIY-only environment. But recognizing that DIY is here to stay, some professional studios offer fee-based services to fulfill backend needs of the self-recording semi-pro artist. Besides mixing the artists' DIY tracks, these services can include on-site tech support; equipment repair; and CD mastering, duplication, and artwork design.

Professional Associations

Individuals who are serious about getting into sound recording may also want to become acquainted with the professional associations serving this sector of the industry, many of which offer educational workshops and forums.

The Audio Engineering Society (AES) holds annual conventions that feature seminars, technical paper presentations, and workshops on new recording technologies and displays of equipment manufacturers' latest audio products. AES has a committee dealing with the educational aspects of recording technology and career opportunities in audio.

The Society of Professional Audio Recording Services (SPARS) also concerns itself with educational standards for training audio technicians. Its programs include placement of interns, business conferences, educational seminars, networking, and consulting. SPARS membership includes postproduction recording studios, individual engineers and producers, production houses, postproduction facilities, manufacturers of professional audio recording equipment, schools, colleges, studio designers, leasing companies, and those who serve the audio recording industry. It increasingly offers services to members with small operations; such services may include insurance, advice on complying with local zoning regulations, and formulating financial business plans.

The National Academy of Recording Arts and Sciences (NARAS) is probably best known as the organization that administers the coveted Grammy Awards each year. It is also home to the Producers & Engineers Wing, which boasts thousands of producers, engineers, remixers, and other top audio professionals as members. Among the wing's activities are occasional professional education events and seminars.

Individuals believing they may want to work in the audio departments of TV and film studios can learn more about this field from SMPTE, the Society of Motion Picture and Television Engineers (see Chapter 21).

Chapter Takeaways

- The record producer takes charge in the studio with the responsibility of creating great music by meshing the talents of the lead artist, songs, accompanying instrumentalists and singers, and audio engineering.

- Besides getting creativity on track, the producer is typically responsible for scheduling all aspects of recording and keeping the project on budget.

- Top recording producers negotiate compensation that includes a percentage of music sales, which are called royalties and result in big payouts for hit records.

- With digital technology, relatively inexpensive home recording equipment can achieve high quality rendering of basic tracks. This tool is a big enabler of the DIY production approaches.

- The MIDI revolution enables simple recording systems to achieve a wide assortment of sounds.

- While some artists like to record tracks outside a studio with inexpensive mobile equipment, the final mix for top records with a polished sound is mostly done in studios with professional equipment.

- Producers often play back mixes on an assortment of consumer devices—such as car stereos and iPods—to test how the music sounds on equipment music buyers will actually use.

Key Terms

- "all in" deal   (p. 203)
- AES   (p. 219)
- analog   (p. 207)
- creative control   (p. 202)
- DAW   (p. 208)
- demos   (p. 208)
- equalization   (p. 207)
- home studios   (p. 208)
- house producers   (p. 203)
- independent contractor (p. 203)

- master purchase agreement (p. 203)
- master tapes   (p. 216)
- mastering   (p. 217)
- mechanical licenses   (p. 216)
- MIDI   (p. 209)
- mixer   (p. 215)
- NARAS   (p. 219)
- overdubbing   (p. 214)
- punch ins   (p. 215)

- royalties   (p. 204)
- session musicians   (p. 209)
- SMPTE   (p. 220)
- SPARS   (p. 219)
- synthesizers   (p. 218)
- timbre   (p. 207)
- tracks   (p. 213)

CHAPTER 12

Concert Production

While the recorded music business has struggled in recent years, it's a different story for live concerts. This part of the music industry has enjoyed growth, with box office sales in North America alone topping $4 billion a year. As a result, the music community is focusing more attention on live performance—one part of the industry that can't be pirated—including touring and its ancillary business.

Besides generating substantial revenue in themselves, live concerts boost record sales. Live concerts also increase demand for artist-related spin-offs, such as T-shirts, posters, jewelry, key chains, and books. Concerts and the sale of ancillary products are so critical that major recording companies are reluctant to sign an act that doesn't also have a compelling stage presence.

Three key players move and shake the concert promotion industry: the event promoter, the artist's manager, and the tour-booking agent. In Chapter 7, we detail the manager, agent, and attorney's roles; this chapter focuses on the promoters, the people who bring live events to the fans who flock to them.

> *"An artist, in giving a concert, should not demand an entrance fee but should ask the public to pay, just before leaving as much as they like. From the sum he would be able to judge what the world thinks of him—and we would have fewer mediocre concerts."*
>
> *—Kit Coleman*

Concert Promotion

Concert promotion looks easy: Rent a facility, hire a star, and collect the money. In fact, anyone who considers entering the field of concert promotion should have an aptitude for juggling a thousand details and managing all aspects of the production. Concert promoters take the risks, pay the acts, market the shows, and sell the tickets. They risk not making more money from ticket sales and other revenue sources than they will pay out in expenses.

National and Local Promoters

As is true with many industries, economies of scale and the ability to diversify risk can provide an operating advantage to large, sophisticated players. The best-known concert promoters are Anschutz Entertainment (including AEG, Concerts West, and Messina Group), Jam Productions, Live Nation, and Palace Sports & Entertainment. Music business stars prefer that national promoters (NPs) coordinate their tours—it just makes sense for continuity and effective organization. But NPs need local promoters with expertise to recommend appropriate venues, help determine seat prices, and arrange local promotional tie-ins with radio stations and record stores. National promoters quickly become aware of local promoters with good reputations.

National promoters usually negotiate a share of the net receipts—box office income minus expenses. Out of this, they pay the local promoter. Contracts between NPs, local promoters, and artists must be precisely drawn to make sure the expenses charged against gross income are allowable and accurate.

Key responsibilities of promoters include: orchestrating ticket sales, organizing sale of artist merchandise at the event, assisting in securing sponsorship deals to support a tour, arranging the stage setup, providing some of the event staff, financial accounting, and complying with a myriad of live-event safety regulations. All this is done by either the NP or local promoter in conjunction with the performing artist and venue operator.

Besides the big acts that are handled by the leading promoters, there are thousands of events mounted independently by smaller operators who make up an important part of the live-entertainment ecosystem. Small-scale concerts have low-entry barriers because venues are plentiful and up-and-coming acts constantly seek bookings.

Getting Started

As with many parts of the business world, competitive pressures have led to consolidation in the concert promotion industry, impacting artist representation and venue operations. But there is still room for the small start-up promotion venture.

How do aspiring concert promoters get their start? Some promoters have acts of their own that they book before professional promoters take an interest in them. Others break into the business as students by serving on their college campus's entertainment committee. Still others begin by putting together a performance to raise funds for a charity or other organization in need.

The Cost of Doing Business

Few start-up businesses run without an initial investment of cash, and concert promotion is no different. Promoters need cash to cover their expenses before the first ticket may be sold, and expenses may range from renting a concert hall to printing tickets, securing liability insurance, and hiring ushers. Is the act a big name? If so, the performers may demand a luxury trailer and six bottles of Dom Perignon before setting foot on stage. Is the act known to attract rowdy crowds? If so, the promoter may need cash for a hefty damage deposit before the hall can be booked.

Depending on the state or country in which the promoter does business, there may be fees associated with establishing a concert promotion company. Does the county need a business registration? Is a newspaper notice required? Has a business bank account been opened? For a general discussion of these kinds of challenges, see Chapter 26, "Starting Your Own Business."

Booking the Artist

Finding the Artist

Who do people want to hear in a live concert? Who will they pay money to hear? Chances are, people want to hear artists with heavy radio airplay or those who appear on TV. They are also the ones who are most likely already booked by major concert promoters.

Once acts sell thousands of CDs and downloads, and saturate the national media, it's probably too late to go after them. Many concert promoters start booking an act when it first comes together. Promoters who take risks with acts early on hope they are the same promoters who reap the benefits of the acts' eventual successes. These promoters are referred to in the industry as the **promoter of record**. Unless there is bad blood or historical conflicts between members of a group and their promoter that cause a break, promoters who establish personal relationships from the beginning with the artists, the agents, and the artists' managers have a chance to ensure loyalty as their collective careers progress.

How, then, do new promoters discover tomorrow's major acts?

Listening

Successful promoters love music and have an ear for potential popularity. Promoters should be cautious about listening for new sounds in only one genre, which may be their personal favorite. The Cuban band, Buena Vista Social Club, became a major concert attraction but was rarely played on commercial radio. National Public Radio (NPR), however, featured the band frequently. NPR's audience is educated, financially secure, and aware of world events; they expect and welcome different sounds that commercial radio considers too esoteric. The NPR audience helped make Buena Vista Social Club a hot ticket, and the promoters who also tuned in have shared in the act's success. Promoters looking for new acts must turn their ears to eclectic sounds from out-of-the-ordinary sources.

Observing

Promoters must know the audiences and have a sense of what sells tickets and to whom. Reading trade publications such as *Billboard* and *Pollstar* keeps promoters in touch with which acts are coming out with new recordings, what reviewers are saying about new efforts, and which acts record companies are pushing at the moment. Both publications offer printed periodicals and articles on their Web sites.

Developing Relationships

Promoters who develop friendships with people related to the music business often hear about talented new acts. Knowing people at radio stations and record companies as well as maintaining relationships with music critics and reviewers can give promoters the contacts that keep them poised for action.

Relationships with various ethnic communities can offer promoters new sounds to bring to people who will pay to hear them. Promoters who connect within ethnic media communities may very well sign foreign-language attractions that can fill all 20,000 seats at Madison Square Garden.

Assessing the Artists' Draw

If the artists' price is within their reach, some promoters permit themselves the luxury of booking the acts they personally prefer. Most experienced promoters favor their personal preferences but are more likely to follow the weekly fluctuations of the trade charts, regional sales, and airplay, and then do everything they can to book the acts that are the most recent successes in their concert territory. Booking artists who are on their way down—rather than up—the charts has hurt many a promoter.

Making an Offer

Booking the act is critical to the concert promotion process. There can't be a concert without a headliner. How do promoters book the artists? If the acts are just starting out, promoters may deal directly with the artists themselves. More likely, however, promoters begin with the artists' agents.

The Agent

As one of the three key players in the concert promotion industry, artists' agents bring offers to the attention of the artists they represent. Because agents work on commission, their job is to present the offers that reap the greatest possible fees. Promoters may find themselves dealing with a small talent agency or with one of the more prominent American agencies, such as William Morris Endeavor Entertainment (WME$_2$), Creative Artists Agency (CAA), or International Creative Management (ICM).

Who Represents Whom?

The simplest way to find out which agents represent which acts is through the Internet, where an abundance of fan-based Web sites list artist contact information. If an act has a recording contract, the record company will put promoters in touch with artists' agents. Trade publications such as *Pollstar* and *Billboard* also print talent and booking directories.

Promoters and agents often come together through conferences and meetings of performing arts administrators and university groups. Two examples of these opportunities to make agent contacts include the Association of Performing Arts Presenters (APAP) and the National Association of Campus Activities (NACA).

Preliminaries

What are the artists' fees and available dates? Once promoters have connected with the act's agent, they may make preliminary inquiries about the artists' usual fees and available dates. These inquiries can set in motion the preparatory steps necessary for a successful concert promotion, such as placing a hold on a particular concert hall for a particular date.

What are the possible venues? In many communities, the most attractive venues are booked months or years in advance. Securing open dates can be difficult, and open dates are useless without the coincidental availability of the featured acts. In selecting venues, promoters can usually rent the facility for a flat fee or a flat fee plus a percentage of the gross ticket sales.

What does the venue offer? Venue management generally furnishes the stage manager, box office manager, maintenance crew, and ushers. A facility may also provide security, or the city may require promoters to hire security personnel based on the reputation of the act's audiences. A venue may also offer promoters an option called **four-walling**, furnishing only the facility itself and a stage manager; promoters then bring all other personnel for the successful production of the show.

What is the venue's potential? Here, promoters must be cautious to estimate costs accurately. For example, a facility that seats 1,000 for a show with tickets at $20 each

Table 12.1   Seven Types of Concert Venues

Stadiums. The largest facilities for concerts, these multipurpose venues offer seating of 30,000+ and typically are configured for sports events. Since such facilities are not designed for live concerts, they require extensive setup/tear-down of concert stages.

Amphitheaters. Outdoor venues typically seat between 5,000 and 30,000, and are used primarily in good weather/summer seasons. These are specifically designed for concerts, with permanent stages.

Festival Sites. Outdoor locations used seasonally typically accommodate between 10,000 and 120,000 patrons for day-long or multi-day concerts. For operators, these venues are attractive because of low overhead costs, resulting in some of the industry's highest profit margins.

Arenas. Smaller than stadiums, these indoor venues typically seat between 5,000 and 20,000. Arenas often have luxury private suites—premium-priced seating areas that amphitheaters lack.

Theaters. Venues designed for legitimate theater can be adapted for concerts and typically have seating of under 5,000.

Mid-Sized Music Venues. Designed for concerts, these indoor facilities have ready-built stages and typically have capacity for between 1,000 and 6,500 persons. With this low-capacity seating, however, they don't offer potential for outsized profits, as do the larger venues, even in a sell-out.

Small-Sized Music Venues. Music and comedy clubs dominate this category of indoor venue, which sometimes provide beverage and/or meal service for patrons at their seats. Because seating is typically less than 1,000, capacity limits revenue potential. But these facilities have built-in stages, which reduces costs.

will obviously gross $20,000 if the show is a sellout. But few shows actually sell out, and even if every seat is sold, expenses that aren't anticipated may gobble up any profit. Promoters may more often come out ahead when they locate a 5,000-seat arena, book a headliner, and pull together enough money to finance an extensive promotional campaign. Regardless of a venue's potential number of ticket sales, experienced promoters don't budget for a concert that's standing room only (SRO) but for a *60% house,* meaning that 40% of the tickets just won't sell. Theater managers have used this 60% house figure since the 1800s in planning their concert promotion budgets.

After the promoter has worked out a preliminary budget based on all the information gathered, it's time to contact the artist's agent and make an offer.

The Offer

Very few acts will perform for a flat fee if they tour nationally. Most of the agents who represent these acts begin fee negotiations on the premise that the show will sell out.

Most of the promoters, on the other hand, want a protective cushion. If the show doesn't sell out, promoters want to know that they will, at the very least, earn back their expenses—including production, rent, and marketing costs—and that they will take home a profit before the main attraction and its agent get most of the money.

How these two deal makers come together is the subject of the next section.

The Art of the Deal

Negotiating Artists' Fees

Discussions usually begin with agents expecting for their clients a guaranteed fee plus a percentage of the ticket sales. If the event is free, or if tickets are subsidized by a charity or student activities fund, both parties expect to negotiate only a flat fee.

Promoters will want to negotiate a **split point**, which is a number based on ticket sales and at which point the act and the promoter divide the balance. See Table 12.2 for an example of a split point as well as an expense detail.

Preliminary Budgets

Agents will want to see all the estimated expenses associated with the event, including the artist's guaranteed fee, rent of the hall, labor for setting up and breaking down the stage, production costs (sound, lights, catering, and so on), and any other related expenses. Multiply the total expenses by a percentage—usually 15%—and this is the sum that agents traditionally allow the promoters as profit. Deduct the expenses and the promoters' allowed profit from the gross ticket sales, and this *back end*—or the balance of the revenue after the split point—is what the promoters and the artists split. Custom dictates that this percentage be divided in an 85% to 15% split, with the larger number going to the artists (although the trend for superstar acts is to take up to 90%). Promoters are free to argue for a higher percentage split.

Potential Versus Reality

The capacity of the venue (the number of seats that can be sold) multiplied by the value of an average ticket equals the *gross potential* of the event. A theater with

Table 12.2 **Sample of Expense Sheet**

Artist:			
Venue:			
Date:			
Expense Item	**Estimated Cost**		
Advertising	$20,000.00		
ASCAP/BMI	485.00		
Box office	100.00		
Catering	2,000.00		
Insurance	1,200.00		
Instrument rental	750.00		
Loaders	400.00		
Phones	100.00		
Rent	17,500.00		
Risers	600.00		
Runner	200.00		
Security	1,375.00		
Sound/lights	3,000.00		
Spotlights (2)	400.00		
Stage manager	500.00		
Stagehands (union)	4,800.00		
Piano tuning	125.00		
		Capacity: 3,000	
		Tickets	**Income**
Total production	$53,535.00	1,200 @ $50	$60,000.00
Headliner fee	15,000.00	900 @ $40	36,000.00
Support act fee	5,000.00	900 @ $30	27,000.00
		Gross potential	123,000.00
Total cost	73,535.00		
Promoter profit (15%)	11,030.25	Comp tix 100	5,000.00
Split point	84,565.25	(100 @ $50)	
		Net potential	118,000.00
Split: 85%–15%		Split point	84,565.25
		Overage	33,434.75
		Headliner share	28,419.54
		Promoter share	5,015.21

Offer based on 3-hour maximum show, 150-mile radius exclusivity, and local sound and lights; 8 a.m. load-in, stage dark 5 p.m. to 7 p.m.

2,000 reserved seats with a uniform ticket price of $25 has a gross potential of $50,000. Some of the tickets will be designated for the artists' guests, and some will be given to the press or to radio stations for giveaways that help promote the concert. Deduct the value of these tickets from the gross potential, and the resulting number is the *net potential.*

Before the act can take the stage, concert promoters must enter into a number of written agreements. Among others, promoters sign contracts with venue management, talent agents, merchandisers, lighting and sound suppliers, insurance companies, transportation firms, and caterers. They must also put in place clear agreements with the city's police and fire departments with respect to security arrangements. The costs of these contracts must be considered during the negotiation process or the promoter will end up with unexpected leaks in cash flow.

Control Sheets

As preparations for a performance unfold, promoters accumulate voluminous data: e-mails, written correspondence, telephone numbers, telephone messages. Experienced promoters may pull all the data together into a control sheet (see Table 12.3). This organizational tool lists all the details of the event.

The College Production Planning form (Table 12.4) lists the many tasks that must be *back-timed* so that preparations for a performance can unfold in orderly fashion. Anyone involved in the management of a production on a college campus should find this form helpful.

Contracts

Once agent and promoter agree on the broader points of the offer, it is time for a contract. Agents issue contracts, and contracts consist of two parts: the face page and the rider.

The face page defines the basic information: time, date, place, length of show, how the artists' names will be billed (how they will appear in advertising), the agreed-upon fees, and payment schedules.

The rider (or **technical rider**) is a document attached to the face page that details the artists' requirements. Riders may include the following: (a) travel arrangements; (b) hotels; (c) catering; (d) technical needs, such as band gear, sound, and light systems; (e) size and number of dressing rooms; (f) any other detail the artist finds critical for performance.

Most promoters will ask to see the rider prior to making an offer. They understand that there are sometimes rider requirements that can kill a deal. For example, if the artist needs the promoter to supply a backup string section of 20 musicians, this might add $5,000 or more to the promoter's expenses and can be the **deal breaker**.

The finer points of the rider can be open to negotiation and may depend on the star power of the act, whether there are multiple acts that must share in the billing and promotional campaign, and what sort of technical requirements the bigger names have requested and the smaller names will accept.

Table 12.3   **Production Control**

Performance facility (name/address/telephone/manager)

_____

_____

Performance date/time

_____

_____

Producer/promoter/agent(s)

_____

_____

Featured artist(s)

_____

_____

Road manager

_____

_____

Stage (size/risers/pit/stairs/curtains/exits, etc.)

_____

_____

Lighting (spots/borders/foots/dimmer/voltage/supplier/operator)

_____

_____

Sound (supplier/technician/description)

_____

_____

Dressing rooms (number/size/furnishings/condition/location)

_____

_____

Loading dock (access/parking/security)

_____

_____

Performance licenses

_____

_____

Union jurisdictions

_____

_____

Table 12.4   College Production Planning

Lead Time	Control Number	Responsibility
6–12 months	1.	Research history of college promotions in your area. What has worked well in the past?
3–6 months	2.	Formulate budget for forthcoming school year; appeal for funding.
	3.	Place tentative holds on performance facilities.
	4.	Make preliminary contact with talent agents to learn of tentative costs, available artists, and dates.
3 months	5.	Get school's approval of your plans. Submit bid for artist, specifying date and price.
	6.	Get acceptance, rejection, or counteroffer from agents.
	7.	Negotiate contracts with agents. Pending formal execution of contracts, exchange written confirmation.
	8.	Confirm your hold dates on facility, then formulate a written agreement with the facility management.
2 months	9.	Execute contracts with agencies, including technical riders.
	10.	Contact artists' record companies for help with promotion. Ask for press kits, promotional materials, money for block-ticket purchases, cooperative ads, and even services of promotion personnel.
	11.	Formulate promotion budget and campaign. Get print and broadcast ad costs (a local media-buying ad agency can provide estimates).
	12.	Contract for outside suppliers, as needed, for sound reinforcement, lighting, security, caterers, etc.
6 weeks	13.	Place printing orders for tickets, posters, banners, etc.
	14.	Line up cooperative ads with record stores, radio stations, etc.
4 weeks	15.	Contract for ticket-selling outlets.
	16.	Seek store displays of posters, albums, etc.
3 weeks	17.	Deliver printed tickets to outlets. Set strict controls for accounting.
	18.	Line up student volunteers for ushering, ticket takers, setting up/striking stage, publicity, gofers, box office, etc.
	19.	Clear plans with fire department: size of crowd, control of aisles, exits, etc.
	20.	Clear security plans with police, sheriff, rent-a-cop firm, and campus police. Discuss liabilities with school's legal counsel.
	21.	Distribute promotional materials to print and broadcast media. Schedule press conference, interviews. Mount banners and posters.
2 weeks	22.	Reconfirm arrangements with outside suppliers (sound, lighting, transport, caterers, etc.)
	23.	Check ticket sales. Adjust promotion budget accordingly.

Lead Time	Control Number	Responsibility
1 week	24.	Call a production planning meeting with facility manager, stage manager, production director, and student volunteers. Issue written instructions to everybody concerning their responsibilities, schedule, and contingency plans.
3 days	25.	Reconfirm everything! a. with artists' road managers regarding any changes in time of arrival of personnel, equipment b. with outside suppliers c. with facility stage manager d. with student crew chairpersons e. with ticket sellers (If sales are lagging, execute preconceived last-minute promotion campaign.)
Performance day	26.	Call production meeting 1 hour prior to scheduled arrival of equipment and roadies. Everyone charged with responsibilities relating to the production and performance attends this meeting and takes notes. Last-minute changes in plans discussed.
	27.	Set up. Confirm that all personnel and equipment are arriving per plan.
	28.	Pick up money and unsold tickets from outlets. Deposit money in bank, deliver unsold tickets to facility box office for sale there.
	29.	Welcome the performing artists and their entourage. Control issuing of backstage and auditorium passes. Save the best (free) seats for unexpected important guests.
Postproduction	30.	If agreed contractually, join the road manager for a count of receipts and unsold tickets shortly after the box office closes.
	31.	Make agreed payment, then arrange for secure place to store cash overnight.
	32.	Feed your people after the show, at least your volunteers. They've earned it!
	33.	Confirm facility cleanup is proceeding per plan. Did the place experience more-than-normal wear and tear? If so, discharge your contractual responsibilities.
	34.	Write a summary report, following a short meeting with your key personnel: What went wrong, what went well?
	35.	Thank the participants by telephone, e-mail, or letter for their cooperation, particularly those who worked as volunteers.

Marketing

How does the ticket-buying public know that tickets for an upcoming concert are on sale? Through marketing, or bringing all this pertinent information to the **market**.

Marketing can be divided into two categories: that which is paid and that which is not.

Multimedia Marketing

Print Media

Print media include newspapers and magazines. In major markets, print advertising can be costly and may be less effective in reaching the ticket buyers. If promoters want to sell tickets for a hip-hop concert or a heavy metal band, taking out ads in the city's daily newspaper may not translate into ticket sales because the audience may read alternative media. Many cities are home to free weekly newspapers that have less expensive ad rates than the mainstream daily city newspaper. These weeklies often list the cultural events in their cities and may cater to younger audiences. Examples include the *Village Voice* in New York City and *LA Weekly* in Los Angeles.

Advertisers purchase newspaper ads by an inch of column space. If a newspaper runs eight columns across a page and each page is 21 inches wide, the total number of column inches is 168 (21×8). If a big city newspaper sets its ad rates at $500 per column inch, it's easy to see why a full-page ad is out of the range for all but the deep-pocketed promoter.

Promoters who present ethnic music may find print media that cater to a slice of the ticket-buying public eager to support such music. Irish performances, for example, may sell more tickets through Irish publications than through the mainstream print channels.

Radio and Television

Like print media, radio and television stations appeal to the masses and to those with more varied preferences; different stations play music and run programs for all tastes and all audiences.

Radio stations sell air time in 30- or 60-second units, with fees based on the station's **rate card**, a list price based on estimates of how many listeners tune in and at what times of day. (For more on radio audience identification and market research, see Chapter 19, "Music in Radio.") Invariably, the most expensive time to advertise is the morning or evening drive time, when the greatest number of listeners tune in during commutes to and from work. The least expensive time is usually after midnight and before 5:00 a.m., when the smallest number of listeners play radio.

Broadcast television's most expensive time slot is prime time: those hours of programming that fall between the early-evening local news and late-night local news. But the desired demographic may be in a late night show or prime time series. Local cable television systems offer city and regional commercials on basic cable networks such as MTV, Fuse, and BET.

Direct Mail and E-Mail

Targeting a specific audience can be effective through direct mail advertising and promotional e-mails, but compiling the right mailing list is vital.

Mailing lists assembled by artists, promoters, and venues are valuable because they typically aggregate the most promising prospects to buy concert tickets. But such lists tend to be small—typically just a couple hundred or thousand contacts for a geographic area close to the concert venue. To cast a wider net, promoters can buy syndicated print mailing lists with thousands or tens of thousands of consumers, or mount tie-ins with third party organizations to gain access to mailing lists. For example, if promoters can obtain a list of concertgoers who bought tickets to see Joni Mitchell's most recent concert, they can target that audience when they're promoting a new artist who may have a few Joni Mitchell sounds.

E-mailing is attractive because there are no postage and paper costs, but blasting unsolicited e-mails is problematic. Gaining access to e-mail lists from third-party organizations can be appealing if names on their lists have opted-in, giving permission to receive e-mails. Deals to piggyback on third-party mailing lists can involve purchasing ads for cash or bartering in exchange for concert tickets. For example, concert ads can be placed on e-mail lists from radio stations, which would use the tickets as prizes in on-air promotion. Such tie-ins are often negotiated as part of paid advertising campaigns.

Advertising Production

Once promoters decide their media mixes—how much they want to spend on newspaper, radio, mail, online, and television ads—they need to produce the ads they want to run.

More and more, artists themselves control production of the commercials and print advertising that announce their performances. The industry term for reusable print materials is **ad mat**. Artists want to be certain that their names appear as specified, in their proper sizes, and that the photos always display the right image. (When Prince wanted to be billed as "The Artist Formerly Known as Prince," promoters complied.) Artists will often insist on ad mats as part of their contracts' riders. If the performance is sponsored, ads will feature the sponsors' names and will mention the acts' latest recordings.

Nationally touring acts typically employ one set of advertising materials that can be used for all their concerts with minor customizing for a local venue and date. For local bands just getting started, television and radio stations can create satisfactory ads, if provided with audio and video tracks. Promoters can also call on the services of professional production companies. Although these companies can be expensive, the quality of the commercials may outweigh the costs and ultimately result in higher ticket sales.

Publicity and Public Relations

Cheaper than advertising—and perhaps even free, publicity and public relations help promote live performances.

How can promoters generate publicity—or take advantage of the publicity already generated—for the acts that they book?

Web Sites

Internet Web sites are a great way to reach the public. An artists' site can list tour dates and venues for upcoming shows, offer fans the opportunity to sign up for e-mail newsletters, and collect data such as e-mail addresses from previous ticket buyers. An artist's site can also provide relevant links to venues' Web sites, fan sites, and a local calendar of events.

Christoph von Dohnani conducts the Los Angeles Philharmonic Orchestra.

Photo © Axel Koester/Corbis.

Foreign Interest

When presenting artists who are natives of foreign countries, promoters may contact the countries' consulates or embassies, where ministers of culture promote their own citizens who perform outside their countries. Both Canada and France, for example, enlist members of their cultural staffs to work with countries who feature Canadians or the French.

Press Releases

When reporters refer to upcoming concerts in their news stories, the promoter doesn't pay for air time, advertising space, or a radio spot. Promoters can keep in touch with reporters who write on culture, music, or the arts or who cover these events for their radio or television stations. Promoters who supply video footage, photos, or copies of the artists' latest CDs get the attention of the reporters who, in turn, provide free publicity.

Publicists

It may be worth promoters' efforts to hire professional publicists. A PR specialist has contacts in the press and devotes time when promoters cannot. Fees are usually negotiable, and a major feature story could be worth many dollars that promoters would otherwise pay to advertise.

Sponsorships

Many promoters find that the most efficient and profitable concert promotions are those with one or more sponsors backing the project.

Record Company Sponsorship

Recording-industry executives know that the successful promotion of a new album may depend on coordination with a concert tour. Record companies who help underwrite the costs of the concert production provide promotion materials, such as flyers, posters, and banners. Some will buy blocks of tickets and then give them away to people they believe might influence the ticket-buying public, such as disc jockeys or local media celebrities. In addition to spreading goodwill among influential people, giving away tickets helps fill the house and gives the audience the impression that the event is a huge success. Success sometimes generates more success, and **papering the house**, as the practice is known, has been used for many years on Broadway as well.

Recording companies may lend their own publicists or product managers to ensure a concert's success. Or they may pay for the advertising or share expenses with a local record retailer who wants a part of the promotion pie. Sometimes recording companies will organize and produce national tours for new acts, and there may be room for local promoters to work with labels as part of these national efforts.

Local Radio Station Sponsorship

Local radio stations frequently sponsor or cosponsor concerts in their listening area. Most regard these performances as excellent contacts with their broadcast audience. Concert promoters welcome broadcast sponsors because the people who listen to radio are the same who will come to the concert.

Venue and Corporate Sponsorship

Venues themselves cosponsor live events, especially when the venue is smaller and perhaps less known than the big arenas with frequent bookings. A smaller, more intimate venue can adapt quite well to major artists, and promoters expect the trend of venue sponsorship to increase.

From Nokia Theatre L.A. LIVE in Los Angeles to the Continental Airlines Arena in New Jersey to the Pepsi Arena in Albany, New York, major corporations want to tie in to the concert business, through links to venues or artists. Each year, hundreds of concert tours are supported by corporate sponsors. Electronics manufacturers, communication giants, computer companies, automakers, financial services, and beverage industries sponsor artists' tours, because big business knows these events reach their target audiences.

Promoters who attach sponsors to concerts must keep in mind that the artists may have the right to reject the sponsor or limit the sponsors' exposure. Artists may also ask for additional fees if products are to be identified with their shows.

Promoters should also watch for conflicts in corporate sponsorships. If Coca-Cola sponsors a tour, and the venue has an arrangement with PepsiCo that only Pepsi is sold in that venue, the promoter may need to book a different location.

College Sponsorship

Colleges and universities sponsor a large percentage of the live concerts in the United States. Student-run committees handle the school's annual budget for campus-sponsored entertainment, but because college students generally lack sufficient experience to promote or book on their own, schools often bring in professional promoters to assist. From this exposure, the promoters of tomorrow may be born.

Regional college promoters often band together and offer artists *block booking,* whereby the promoters take care of tour dates, venues, production, and promotion for a series of area concerts. Agents and artists appreciate this initiative to do much of the work for them, and the college block can also benefit through negotiating strength.

National Association for Campus Activities

The music industry has its own trade associations, and the college promotion side of the business has one of the strongest. The National Association for Campus Activities (NACA) represents more than 1,200 colleges. Successful concert promoters study NACA publications, particularly its magazine, *Programming,* and should be aware of annual NACA conventions, where college representatives, talent agents, performing artists, and recording companies come together for educational and showcasing opportunities.

Ticketing

The venue is booked, the artist is signed, the sponsors are on board, the promotion strategy is in place. All that's left for promoters now is to sell those tickets.

Ticket Purchasing

Centralized online ticket purchasing is a far cry from the long lines outside box offices that buyers had to face decades earlier. Now fans typically purchase their tickets online and arrange for pickup at the event, or simply print out a barcode on their home printer that is scanned at the event.

Online ticket purchasing has itself become a big business. In 2007, leading outfit Ticketmaster sold approximately 141 million tickets to concerts, sports events, museums, and other venues, valued at over $8.3 billion.

Ticket Terms

The term that promoters hate to hear most is deadwood, which is an unsold ticket. Promoters who ask, "How much deadwood did we have tonight?" clearly want this number to be low or, better yet, zero.

If it's obvious that ticket sales are slow and there will be a lot of deadwood, promoters might choose to paper the house. **Scaling the house** means pricing tickets differently depending on the location of the seat in the theater. Seats in the first few rows of each section are generally priced higher, although there may be venues in which the better seats are midsection, near the wings, or just outside the orchestra section.

Tickets for reserved seats guarantee their bearers a specified seat in a specified location. General admission (GA) tickets mean that whoever arrives first has the choice of seats. GA concerts may provoke more security concerns due to ticket holders pushing their ways to the better seats.

Ticket Scalping

Customers who purchase tickets in quantity the day they go on sale with the idea of selling these for higher prices when the best locations or the shows are sold out are called *scalpers*. This practice has been made easier with the growth of online ticket purchasing.

Ticket scalping is a problem for promoters because the artist, agent, and promoter share in none of the profits, and the scalper has taken advantage of a paying customer. The markups irk fans and have brought criticism from artists like Bruce Springsteen. Scalping is now illegal in many areas, but the practice continues. (On occasion, it's become known that certain tickets offered by resellers at inflated prices came from the performers and their associates.) The ticket scalping problem is driven by basic supply-and-demand: Top touring acts are in high demand but seating is limited. Some estimates put the resale of concert tickets as a $1.7 billion annual business.

Licensed Music Merchandise

The sale of licensed music merchandise is a $2 billion annual business, according to marketing researcher, *The Licensing Letter*. That makes this business nearly half the size of the concert ticket business. Growth in this market has come from innovations that go beyond the sale of traditional T-shirts and posters. Now, music stars promote leading fashion brands and license their persona for fragrances.

Vendors selling souvenirs at a concert.

Photo © Neal Preston/CORBIS.

In general, royalties received by music entities (whether headed by artists or artist managers) range from 8% to 14% of the wholesale price of merchandise—sometimes referred to as manufacturer's net revenue. For merchandise sold at concerts, royalty rates to artists are boosted to 15% to 22%, since they create foot traffic for vendors.

As recorded music sales decline, record labels increasingly negotiate to include other revenue-generating elements in their contracts. A recording contract that includes touring income, merchandise sales, and publishing revenue is referred to as a 360 deal. Artists have agreed to share such merchandising revenue with labels to help labels recoup advance payments.

Chapter Takeaways

- Concerts venues come in an array of configurations ranging from cavernous stadiums seating tens of thousands to intimate settings that can hold only hundreds of spectators.

- A handful of competitive national promoters handle big acts making national tours. Local promoters with lesser known acts account for the rest of the concert ecosystem.

- Concerts drum up ticket sales through a combination of publicity-generating news stories, paid advertising, short-term promotions where third parties such as radio stations get the word out, and long term sponsorships with partners such as cell phone carriers.

- Music artist-themed licensed merchandise is a $2 billion a year business, which makes it nearly half the size of the concert ticket business.

Key Terms

- deadwood (p. 238)
- four-walling (p. 227)
- papering the house (p. 237)
- promoter of record (p. 225)
- scaling the house (p. 238)
- split point (p. 228)
- sponsorships (p. 237)
- technical rider (p. 230)

CHAPTER 13

Arts Administration

The Classical Music Market

Precise definitions for general terms such as *popular, classical,* **art music,** and *serious music* can get slippery. Confusion prevailed long before the 1924 premiere of George Gershwin's symphonic jazz composition *Rhapsody in Blue,* and disputes about the correct way to classify music will continue. But to provide a framework for this chapter, the terms *classical music* and *art music* are used interchangeably to discuss the repertoire generally associated with the symphony orchestra, opera, ballet, recital, modern dance, choral music, chamber music, and church music.

Even though the pop field gets most of the publicity, a great many people are involved in the classical music field, and its production and consumption are big business involving thousands of jobs and millions of dollars every year.

> *"Life can't be all bad when for ten dollars you can buy all the Beethoven sonatas and listen to them for ten years."*
>
> —William F. Buckley, Jr.

The production and purveyance of serious music has traditionally been separate from pop. Though the artists and administrators often come from different backgrounds, they are, more often than not, engaged in very similar kinds of work. "Crossing the line" is an everyday occurrence. Individuals qualified to function in the world of "art music" often end up in "commercial music"; some who start their careers in one of the pop fields may find themselves working for a symphony orchestra or perhaps promoting classical artists.

Left: Photo © PNI.

It is customary to distinguish between pop and art music by describing the former as commercial or profit oriented and the latter as nonprofit, since the large performing groups, such as orchestras, ballet companies, and the like are legally formed as not-for-profit **501(c)3 organizations**. But in actuality, profit and nonprofit intersect, because many individuals in the serious music business make a very fine living from performing or producing classical music; for example, it isn't unheard of for starting wages of a major symphony orchestra musician to be in the neighborhood of $80,000 to $100,000 per annum. However, for the sake of clarity, this chapter uses the customary terms *nonprofit* or *not-for-profit* in discussing arts administration where accumulation of wealth is not the underlying purpose of the organization.

Perspective

Fueled in part by a healthy economy, the quarter century from the early 1960s to the mid-1980s saw an unprecedented growth in the arts in America. The number of professional symphony orchestras and opera or music theater companies nearly doubled, and ballet and modern dance companies burgeoned from 30 to more than 150. Those years also saw a dramatic increase in arts performances, employment of artists and arts administrators, and attendance at arts events. That encouraging picture, however, was changing by the end of the 1980s. In subsequent years, economic shocks and other upheavals stunted the growth of the arts generally, and music specifically. Arts organizations, especially orchestras, began aggressive marketing campaigns to increase audiences.

The exposure afforded by television viewing of the arts, particularly through the Public Broadcasting Service (PBS) and the Corporation for Public Broadcasting (**CPB**), and a number of cable channels, fueled the growth of interest in the symphony, opera, and dance. There have been sponsored weekly radio broadcasts of the Metropolitan Opera since 1931 (the longest running radio show to date), as well as of symphony orchestras (San Francisco, Seattle, Los Angeles, Chicago, among others). Telecasts of the Boston Pops and Boston Symphony have drawn audiences of millions. Imaginative producers such as Emmy Award winner Allan Miller found ways to make symphonic music look interesting on film and TV.

Despite these successes, a daunting fact remains: Only a small portion of the public has a serious interest in serious music. Classical music recordings have rarely sold in large quantities. In the 1960s, Stravinsky complained that sales of records of works he had written after 1920 rarely exceeded 5,000 copies. These pieces—even by the world-famous composer—lost money for record labels. However, record companies and arts organizations have worked together to create innovative ways to promote and package releases appealing to buyers who formerly limited their purchases to pop music.

The **crossover recording** in the classical field now reaches expanded markets worldwide, as evidenced by the success of artists such as Josh Groban and Sara Brightman. Another tactic was used in the case of *Chant* in the mid-1990s, a recording of traditional Gregorian chant brilliantly marketed to the pop audience. And, of course, one must mention the popularity of Paul Potts—an opera singer/overnight sensation as created by *Britain's Got Talent*. As pointed out in coverage of the recording industry, one of the strongest markets for crossover records is with movie music; sound track music appeals to both classical and pop music fans here and abroad.

Some serious music recordings, particularly the repertoire called *contemporary serious music,* often have difficulty making a profit. An important group of recordings of this repertoire is found on the CRI (Composers Recordings Inc.) label, now owned by New World Records, another nonprofit group whose mission is recording and distributing the music of contemporary American composers that might not otherwise be available for purchase.

How serious music organizations will weather the downturns of this or future eras is yet to be seen, but if history is a predictor, they will likely still be around for the next century and beyond. Arts organizations, especially orchestras, will always need to keep an eye toward growing audiences both in terms of numbers and demographic composition. With hardship, creativity is often born, and there are signs of creative health in the arts. Following are a few examples:

- Some orchestras that have had trouble in recent years attracting and/or making profits from recording deals have created their own record companies and produced their own products. The London Symphony has led the way with LSO Live recordings—offering conductors and musicians a stake in the profits as opposed to up-front payments. The Chicago Symphony's Resound Records is another example of an orchestra-controlled record company. This independent venture has been quite successful with various recordings available in both CD and Super Audio CD (SACD)—high-quality audio— versions. As with DIY popular artists, the orchestras retain the rights to these recordings for use in future projects.

- Other arts organizations, particularly smaller ones, are able to make short runs of recordings not to make a profit, but as a marketing tool—to increase the exposure and stature of the organization—often asking conductors and musicians to work gratis or to settle for a share of the profits rather than for an upfront fee.

- The Metropolitan Opera has been notably aggressive in embracing available technologies of the 21st century with initiatives such as its own media player available through a subscription service, partnerships with Rhapsody and SiriusXM, and a content-rich Web site. The Met has also experimented with **HD** performances in selected theaters around the country—and even posting selected performances live on the Web.

Representative Organizations

The world of classical music and arts administration includes a number of important organizations that represent the special interests of professionals in the field (see Chapter 9 on the unions and guilds representing artists in the classical field). A number of other important organizations—not necessarily "guilds," despite some of their names—are listed below.

- Organists—including students, professional organists, choir directors, teachers, organ builders, technicians, suppliers, amateur musicians, and dedicated supporters—are represented by the American Guild of Organists.

- The special interests of composers in the classical field have been served, since 1937, by the American Composers Alliance (ACA). Its American Composers Edition serves as a music publisher for its members, making scores and parts available through loans, rentals, and sales. One of ACA's member services is registering works with Broadcast Music Inc. (BMI). For many years, American composers have been active in the U.S. Section of the International Society for Contemporary Music (ISCM), founded in 1922 and formerly called the League of Composers. Founded by Aaron Copland and other distinguished American composers, this group has fostered public acceptance of contemporary serious music by offering concerts, goodwill, and publicity. The ISCM is active in 50 countries and sponsors the annual World Music Days.

- Another organization devoted to the promotion of contemporary music is the American Music Center, which provides composers and performers with assistance and information on career development, funding, performance and study opportunities, and numerous other concerns. It maintains a library of scores and recordings available for circulation worldwide and sponsors an American Music Week each year. The center pioneered one of the first music Web sites in the early 1990s at www.amc.net.

- The professional organization most representative of opera is Opera America. Its mission is to promote the creation, preservation, and enjoyment of opera in America. Through the Opera Fund, technical and financial support is provided to opera companies; the organization also provides consulting services on a wide range of topics for general directors of opera companies.

- Professional music critics have formed the Music Critics' Association of North America, which includes a large number of major critics in its membership.

- The organization Americans for the Arts (formerly Associated Councils for the Arts and the American Council for the Arts) forms a useful clearinghouse for information and ideas relating to state and regional arts council activities. It also provides extensive arts industry research, information, and professional development opportunities for community arts leaders nationwide, through a variety of programs and services.

- Arts administrators have organized the Association of Performing Arts Presenters (formerly Association of College, University and Community Arts Administrators). The Association of Arts Administration Educators represents educators in that field.

- An umbrella organization of broad scope is the National Music Council (NMC), chartered by Congress in 1956 to serve the interests of commercial and noncommercial music associations throughout the United States. It has some 45 member organizations that represent, in turn, an aggregate membership of more than 1 million. A partial list of its member organizations indicates the breadth of NMC: AFM, AGMA, AMC, ASCAP, BMI, CMA, MENC, MPA, NARAS, NMPA, RIAA, SAI, and SESAC.[1] The National Music Council has been designated the official U.S. representative to the International Music Council, a UNESCO-sponsored organization of national and international music committees. It holds a biennial general assembly and World Congress to discuss issues of musical importance. It began International Music Days, and it initiates a multitude of projects, including research into new media and technologies.

- Along with some of these larger organizations, almost every instrument represented in the orchestra has developed an association to develop performance, networking, and research-presentation opportunities for their members. Examples include the International Double Reed Society, International Trombone Association, and the International Trumpet Guild.

Symphonic Music

Although classical music has a much smaller market than popular music, a lot of money is generated by musical organizations performing this repertoire. The largest audience in this field is for symphonic music. There are about 2,000 symphony orchestras in the U.S., more than 50 of them claiming an annual budget of over a million dollars. These orchestras typically file with the IRS as 501(c)3 nonprofit organizations and are run by boards of directors. These symphonies employ thousands of musicians and require varying support positions including managers, booking agents, librarians, and venue management personnel.

Table 13.1   Symphony Orchestras in the U.S. With the Largest Budgets

Orchestras with budgets between $7 million and $15.4 million	Orchestras with budgets over $15.4 million
Alabama Symphony Orchestra	Los Angeles Philharmonic
Phoenix Symphony	San Francisco Symphony
Los Angeles Chamber Orchestra	National Symphony Orchestra
San Diego Symphony	Chicago Symphony Orchestra
Colorado Symphony Orchestra	Indianapolis Symphony Orchestra
Florida Orchestra	Baltimore Symphony Orchestra
Jacksonville Symphony Orchestra	Boston Symphony Orchestra
Louisville Orchestra	Detroit Symphony Orchestra
Grand Rapids Symphony	Minnesota Orchestra
Kansas City Symphony	Saint Paul Chamber Orchestra
Omaha Symphony	Saint Louis Symphony Orchestra
Buffalo Philharmonic Orchestra	New Jersey Symphony Orchestra
Orpheus Chamber Orchestra	New York Philharmonic
Rochester Philharmonic Orchestra	Cincinnati Symphony Orchestra
Syracuse Symphony Orchestra	The Cleveland Orchestra
Charlotte Symphony	Oregon Symphony
North Carolina Symphony	The Philadelphia Orchestra
Columbus Symphony Orchestra	Pittsburgh Symphony Orchestra
Toledo Symphony	Nashville Symphony
Tulsa Symphony Orchestra	Dallas Symphony Orchestra
Fort Worth Symphony Orchestra	Houston Symphony
San Antonio Symphony	Seattle Symphony
Utah Symphony & Utah Opera	Milwaukee Symphony Orchestra

Source: Member Directory: *Symphony Magazine* January/February 2008.

League of American Orchestras

Founded in 1942 and chartered by Congress in 1962, the League of American Orchestras (formerly the American Symphony Orchestra League) is the national nonprofit service and educational organization dedicated to strengthening symphony and chamber orchestras. The League's annual conventions draw enthusiastic delegates from all over the country. Its professional staff provides artistic, organizational, and financial leadership and service to the music directors, musicians, direct service and governance volunteers, managers, and staff who make up its member orchestras. Its work is made possible by grants from private and public institutions, contributions from individuals, and from members' dues; for member orchestras, these dues are scaled according to the size of the orchestra's annual budget. The League is research oriented and serves as a source of data for its members, who are interested in arts administration, audience building, and fund-raising.

Education is one of the most useful services provided by the League. Each year, the League staffs and sponsors regional workshops. Professional managers, symphony board members, conductors, and volunteer workers attend these meetings to learn from experts how to function more effectively in their own communities. The League offers annual workshops and symposia with leading orchestra conductors. Its Resource Center provides updated literature on governance. It also sponsors orchestra management seminars where current and aspiring orchestra managers attend classes for several days of intensive study. The League receives partial support of its educational activities from the National Endowment for the Arts.

Photo © Steve Niedorf.

Funding the Arts

The hard fact is that even the best-managed arts organization cannot expect to break even at the box office. All symphonies and opera and ballet companies, no matter how efficiently run, are unable to earn sufficient income to cover their expenses. Simply stated, all arts organizations are dependent on outside funding for survival. This has been true throughout history. Among the earliest patrons of the arts in the western world were the church and the nobility. Concurrent with patronage of this kind, artists occasionally earned part of their livelihood from municipal and national governments. When public theaters and concert halls increased in number in the 17th and 18th centuries, money generated by ticket sales to the middle class helped support musicians, as did persons with private wealth. In modern times, "arts societies" were formed by patrons to organize financial backing for orchestras and opera companies. For generations, U.S. arts organizations enjoyed large gifts from wealthy individuals. But in recent decades changes in federal tax laws have made it difficult for arts organizations to depend on large gifts from wealthy individuals.

Ticket Sales. Performing arts organizations typically earn anywhere between 30% and 65% of their costs of operation by ticket sales. If ticket prices were raised to cover all expenses, the resulting cost would be out of the range of all but the wealthiest patrons. Knowing this, arts organizations are always looking for strategies to maximize the revenue that does come in from this source. Tickets may sometimes be more easily sold for individual performances, but most major symphonies and opera and dance companies prefer that their energies are spent seeking sales of a full series of performances.

Subscriptions. Enthusiasts who buy season tickets not only commit themselves to more money, they are much more loyal and enthusiastic than those who attend only occasionally. The subscriber feels like a patron of the arts, a supporter of the performing group who takes pride in its health and progress. But selling subscriptions can be challenging, as audience members want flexibility to pick and choose. Successful organizations are redefining what subscription packages are and how to promote them.

Foundations, Corporate Giving

Foundations have been a major arts funding source; they still are, but of diminishing significance. When difficult times periodically hit organizations, as they invariably do, generous organizations such as the Ford and Rockefeller Foundations may find that their assets have dropped in value and they will be forced to cut grants accordingly. Nonetheless, hundreds of foundations still make important grants to the arts as they are able. Everyone in the field knows this, and these organizations spend much of their time receiving and processing pleas for money.

The Foundation Center is a clearinghouse for information about foundations and the grants they award. The organization publishes *Foundation Fundamentals: A Guide for Grantseekers,* which includes recommended procedures for locating information on foundations in specific areas and identifying their particular interests. Among its many targeted publications, the Foundation Center produces *The Grants for Arts, Culture and the Humanities.* (Most of the Foundation Center's research tools can be found online.)

Many businesses are interested and eager to support their local arts organizations. When arts groups complain about their lack of support from big corporations, the problem may not be lack of interest from the corporations as much as the absence of solicitation. Some of the big companies have never been asked—or asked correctly. And most of them will not give money until someone steps forth and helps them understand why they should. Companies want to know about audience demographics—are the people coming to the event the same people that are buying our goods and services? Many businesses are more likely to fund arts groups that have a direct impact on their own communities.

The Business Committee for the Arts, a division of Americans for the Arts, founded in 1967 by David Rockefeller and other prominent business leaders, is a national, not-for-profit organization that encourages businesses to support the arts and provides the resources necessary to develop effective business-arts alliances. BCA's more than 100 member companies have long-term commitments to developing partnerships with the arts that benefit business, the arts, and society.

Government Subsidy

In Europe, symphonies and opera companies have long enjoyed governmental subsidies. This is such a strong tradition that music lovers there have some assurance that their symphonies and opera companies will survive from year to year. In contrast, governmental support of the arts in the United States has been near zero throughout most of the history, but in the late 1960s, it increased measurably and continued to rise through the 1970s. In the early 1980s, federal funding for the arts was reduced, but there was an upswing in state funding in the mid-1990s only to fall again in the early part of the 21st century. It is likely that governmental support for the arts, either directly through grants or indirectly through tax benefits for donors, will continue to ebb and flow. While these funds are an important revenue source for many arts organizations, it appears likely that they will never be able to rely on government money as a reliable long-term subsidy.

National Endowment for the Arts

In 1965, Congress established the National Foundation for the Arts and Humanities. Within the foundation were established two agencies: the National Endowment for the Arts (NEA) and the National Endowment for the Humanities (NEH). In 1966, Congress appropriated $5 million for these agencies to "foster the arts." The appropriation for 2007 was $125 million. The enabling legislation provided that NEA funds were to be allocated upon the advice of the National Council on the Arts, a group of 14 private citizens appointed by the president and six (nonvoting) members of Congress to oversee the affairs of the NEA and NEH. Currently, the NEA receives several thousand applications a year, with nearly half of the music requests receiving grants. To be eligible an organization must be not-for-profit and have had at least 3 years of programming. On average, applications take 7 to 12 months to process.

State Arts Councils

According to the NEA, the number of community, regional, and state arts councils has been on the increase. Federal law requires the NEA to assign 40% of its programming funds to state and regional arts agencies.

Some state legislatures began support of the arts with great reluctance. Pressure on politicians from their constituents changed that. Many states assign tax dollars to help support artists and arts organizations, beyond those monies from the NEA. For example, New York began to appropriate far more (total) dollars for the arts than any other state years ago, after a wide-scale study of cultural and economic impact of the arts on the state. The study showed that the great majority of the electorate favored generous support of cultural enterprises from tax money and that money spent in these ways served to benefit the state's economy.

Arts enthusiasts in other states have used similar evidence to demonstrate the favorable economic impact of dollars paid out for symphonies, opera, and ballet companies. For example, the millions spent each year for the Boston Symphony Orchestra exert a strong influence on the economy of the Boston area. About one half of that huge budget will be spent around Boston through the wages paid the orchestra's artists and staff people. Other millions of that budget will be fed back into the local economy for transportation, utilities, advertising, and equipment. And hundreds of thousands of concertgoers further feed the Boston-area economy for things such as dinners out and taxicabs. One national estimate of the full economic impact of arts and culture is offered in Table 13.2.

Volunteer Support

There are many opportunities available to seek funding, but grant writing and soliciting donations takes a great deal of time and energy. Financially vibrant performing arts groups often have experienced development officers who also know how to solicit the support of volunteers who know how to ask for money. Boards of directors are comprised of individuals that have been asked to join the organization for a variety of reasons, but often some seats are reserved for individuals from the community who have connections to, and the respect of, wealthy community members. These individuals are expected to capitalize on their influence and connections to convince people of means to share their wealth with the organization. Arts organizations typically hope to enlist large numbers of socially conscious citizens to get out in the community and seek donations, large and small. Symphony, dance, and opera companies that can organize several dozen committees to get on the telephone and follow up with mail and e-mail solicitations generally find that this group of people becomes an irresistible force. The most effective campaigns of this kind are not only carefully timed and organized, but each solicitor undergoes training—how to talk to people, what to say, how to "close the sale."

Table 13.2   Economic Impact of U.S. Arts & Culture Industry

Nationally, the nonprofit arts and culture industry generates $166.2 billion in economic activity every year—$63.1 billion in spending by organizations and an additional $103.1 billion in event-related spending by their audiences. The $166.2 billion in total economic activity has a significant national impact, generating the following:

- 5.7 million full-time equivalent jobs
- $104.2 billion in household income
- $7.9 billion in local government tax revenues
- $9.1 billion in state government tax revenues
- $12.6 billion in federal income tax revenues

Source: Arts and Economic Prosperity III Study from Americans for the Arts, 2008.

In addition to their effective work in selling subscriptions, volunteer committees take on a great variety of fund-raising projects. Typical of such gala events are fashion shows, antique sales, and auctions. These projects raise millions for the arts. And to hear the volunteer workers tell it, taking part is also a lot of fun. No arts enterprise anywhere could function without the generous and enthusiastic efforts of its volunteer workers.

Any account of subsidies for the arts should include recognition of the generous contributions of the artists themselves—composers, conductors, and performers. In every community, these individuals subsidize the arts by either working without fee or for fees below professional levels. They donate their artistry to the cause because their love for music exceeds their desire for financial reward. Without these generous gifts of time and talent, the production and performance of the arts would suffer greatly.

Classical Artist Management

Just as popular musicians look for managers and talent agencies, the most well-known and sought-after artists need help finding and negotiating performances and scheduling tours. There are many agencies that specialize in classical artists, such as IMG Artists and Opus 3. One of the oldest and best known of these agencies is Columbia Artist Management Inc. (CAMI). Formed in the 1930's, CAMI serves artists in assisting with career development and concert touring. It boasts a roster of international artists from a broad range of genres including instrumental soloists, opera singers, conductors, classical music ensembles, orchestras, dance companies, popular and theatrical

The Walt Disney Concert Hall in Los Angeles.

Photo © Frazer Harrison/Getty Images.

attractions, and fine arts media productions. These artists play hundreds of gigs per year and some command impressive fees for their performances.

Administration

The Need

Training. Leading U.S. arts administrators define their work as "the art of losing money gracefully." Until recent years, their profession was unknown. The people who had the responsibility of managing an orchestra or opera company learned on the job and muddled through. This pattern still prevails too often today in hundreds of smaller arts organizations, which may be one reason many of them experience serious financial trouble.

Today, many quality educational programs in colleges and universities offer graduate degrees in arts administration or allied disciplines, ranging from Claremont College in California to the University of Miami. The Association of Arts Administration Educators keeps updated information available on current programs and how to contact them (www.artsadministration.org).

Although a few thousand graduates of various arts management training programs are currently employed in the field, there still is a shortage of individuals fully qualified to manage the affairs of arts groups, many of which have operating budgets in the millions. The League of American Orchestras states that there is an acute shortage of persons qualified to fill the job openings in this country for symphony orchestra management. William Dawson, former executive director of the Association of Performing Arts Presenters, has said that jobs await individuals possessing "professional skills" in the field. And fortunately, more and more resources are becoming available to hone the skills needed for success.

One way to gain a perspective on the need for professional arts administrators is to look at the staff of a major symphony orchestra. An organization with an annual budget in the range of $5 million to $10 million will have these professionals at work 50 weeks a year:

- General Manager or Executive Director
  - Assistant Manager
- Director of Development
  - Assistant Director of Development
  - Development Manager
- Special Projects Coordinator
  - Two to four additional professional money raisers
- Publications Director
- Director of Public Relations or Director of Press Relations
  - Assistant Public Relations Director
- Art Director
- Advertising Manager
- Volunteer Activities Coordinator
- Personnel Director
- Road Manager or Stage Director
  - Assistant Stage Director
- Property Manager
- Head Librarian
  - Assistant Librarian
- Controller or Accountant
  - Two to four assistants to the Controller (bookkeepers, etc.)
- Ticket Sales Manager
  - Assistant Ticket Manager
- Office Manager
  - Secretaries, Assistants

Responsibilities. The general manager ensures that the other individuals understand their responsibilities and discharge them properly. If the manager's associates function properly, this allows the manager time to operate at a strategic level—thinking, planning, budgeting, promoting, following directives from the board, raising money, handling finances, and creating an environment for the symphony that makes possible ever-finer artistic achievements, the reason this effort is expended in the first place.

Management, too, is an art, as Mozart's father once said. First of all, it is the art of working with people effectively. Arts organizations are remarkable in that they involve professionals and volunteers working side by side. The smooth cooperation of professionals and amateurs is not achieved easily, and some arts administrators never really get the hang of it. When individuals work for free, it's a good idea for the professional manager to treat them with respect. Armies of volunteers, essential to all arts organizations, just won't work unless they believe wholeheartedly in the artistic goals and the management of the ensembles and know that they are appreciated and important to the success of their organizations.

In addition to possessing the ability to organize and motivate large numbers of volunteer committees, the arts administrator must be responsive to the policies of and instructions from the board of directors. The League's Ralph Black was fond of saying that the number one problem of professional symphony orchestras is not money but weak boards. Helen M. Thompson, former staff head of the League, directed a study some years ago that showed that truly successful symphony orchestras enjoy the support of board members who really work at it. The second finding of the League's research demonstrated that the really well-run orchestras "had etched out a sound basic philosophy of the value of the orchestra as a permanent institution in the life of the community."

Assuming the manager and the board see eye to eye, the administrative head may have any or all of these responsibilities:

1. Supervise the work of the staff. Hire and fire.

2. Organize and supervise volunteers.

3. Direct long-range planning.

4. Raise money. This is a large part of the board's responsibility, but it needs direction and a lot of help.

5. Prepare budgets, including debt management, endowment funds, retirement plans, campaign funds, and operations budgets.

6. Work with the artistic director in the conception and implementation of programs—including casting, scheduling.

7. Negotiate contracts for professional services. The most difficult may be with the AFM, whose contracts normally run for 2 to 3 years. Dozens of contracts must also be negotiated with guest conductors and guest soloists. The manager who spends too much leads the organization deeper into debt. If too little is spent, artistic standards may drop.

8. Supervise technical matters relative to performances, the daily moving of artists and equipment; staging and lighting; and booking transportation, hotels, and meals for more than 100 artists. (Other staff members will generally handle many of these duties, but the director carries the ultimate responsibility for them.)

9. Handle press relations and public relations; keep the volunteers happy, the press happy, the politicians happy, the schoolchildren and their teachers happy, the National Endowment happy, the board happy, and above all, keep the audience happy.

Because no one individual knows how or has time and energy to accomplish all these things directly, it might be more instructive to list the specific skills and attributes required of a successful arts administrator.

The administrator:

- Doesn't just like music, *loves* it
- Has great energy and enthusiasm—the kind that makes others want to work, too
- Uses energy and time efficiently and knows how to organize the energies of others
- Knows how to run a meeting: starts on time, announces a specific agenda, manages the flow of conversation, prohibits digressions, encourages all points of view, summarizes decisions made, and adjourns on time
- Keeps in mind long-range goals but knows the most important thing to do on Monday morning
- Can prepare a sensible budget, present it clearly, and stay within it; although not a CPA, can count and is careful with other people's money

Financial Management

Management of arts organizations is difficult because there will never be enough money, so the administrators may limp along, improvising each day some kind of quick fix against impending disaster. Arts groups that survive must manage their finances astutely, starting with a well-conceived financial plan. This is a minimum requirement in avoiding serious fiscal difficulties but not an easy one. An arts organization's financial plan is not like a plan for a commercial business operation, because a symphony, opera, or dance company has no easy way of calculating what accountants like to call cost-benefit ratios. This is a way of asking, "If we spend $1,000 here, what benefits will that money produce?" Because arts groups are not-for-profit in nature, the decision about that $1,000 outlay must be calculated not on what profit it might yield but by what it might produce artistically—and artistic achievements cannot be listed on profit-and-loss statements. So the arts administrator must make many important financial decisions intuitively.

In many communities, experts in financial management, insurance, advertising, printing, graphic arts, and public relations volunteer their assistance without cost to arts organizations. These are significant contributions and help keep costs low. CPAs often tell arts administrators that their money problems don't particularly stem from a need for more frugality. Indeed, many arts groups can teach commercial concerns how to get things done at minimum cost. Rather, the accountants and other financial experts observe that lack of financial planning by boards and arts administrators for income, expense, and debt management is at the heart of many arts administration problems.

Audience Development

Between the "graying of America" and the decline of arts education in school systems, arts organizations are struggling to engage younger audiences. Consequently, audience development has become a major focus for arts administrators, especially in the classical music field. Arts organizations of all kinds have undertaken various new initiatives to build audiences and attract younger audiences. Notable amongst these efforts are special-interest concert and opera events, informal preconcert lectures, and performances incorporating film and other visual and electronic media. The now-common use of English supertitles for operas has made that art form more accessible to audiences of all ages. Programs undertaken by local symphony and chamber orchestras, such as active outreach to schools and instrument classes offered by orchestra musicians under the sponsorship of the orchestra, have made the organizations more visible in their communities, building broader bases of support. The decline of arts education in school systems over the years has impacted outreach programs for all arts organizations. But some organizations are fighting back with innovative programs, such as cut-rate tickets for the under-40 age group.

If an arts organization can learn good financial management and has a knack for audience development, the other essential component leading to success is a passion for the cause. Money and passion: a powerful combination.

Note

1. For a full list of professional organizations and their contact details, see Appendix C.

Chapter Takeaways

- The production and consumption of "serious" music is big business involving thousands of jobs and many millions of dollars.

- A wide variety of organizations promote the art and dissemination of classical music, including the League of American Orchestras, Opera America, Americans for the Arts, and the National Music Council.

- Even well-managed symphonies and opera and ballet companies require subsidies to cover all their expenses. Ticket sales, particularly subscriptions, are vital but not sufficient.

- Financial support for arts organizations comes from foundations, corporations, and various levels of government.

- Management of arts organizations—a key for success—has been improved in recent decades by a variety of education and training resources.

Key Terms

- 501(c)3 organizations   (p. 244)

- classical music   (p. 243)

- crossover recording   (p. 244)

- supertitles   (p. 256)

CHAPTER 14

Music Products

The music products industry is a major player in the overall music business, bringing in almost $8 billion annually in retail sales through music stores and related Web sites. In the United States, there are over 80 million amateur musicians in addition to the sizable number of professionals. These performers all need music, equipment, and **accessories,** and the music products industry sees to their needs.

> *"Playing this instrument brings out my soul."*
>
> *—Toots Thielemans*

For our purposes, the music products industry includes all musical hard goods and printed music. Musical hard goods have traditionally included acoustic and electronic keyboard equipment; wind, brass, percussion, and string instruments; and amplification and recording gear. With improvements in manufacturing technology and competition from off-shore factories, musical instruments are selling at lower prices than in the past, yet they now offer higher quality. There is also a growth of electronic and personal computer-based products producing a wide array of synthesized sounds. Video games in the mold of *Guitar Hero* and *Rock Band* have stepped beyond the traditional video game distribution system and are now also sold by musical instrument retailers, who see them as stepping stones to sales of conventional instruments. The industry also encompasses the services needed for customers to enjoy the products they purchase, such as repairs and lessons, and the merchandising and retailing of these products. (Chapter 16 covers merchandising of recorded music.)

Left: The NAMM Show.

Photo courtesy of NAMM.

Especially at the retail level, musicians often enter this field as a fallback option to performing full time but discover that careers in the music products industry become their number one choice for making a living.

Music Retailers

Full Line

Music stores come in all sizes, carry thousands of products from guitar picks to booming drum sets, and will gross anywhere from hundreds of thousands of dollars to $10 million annually. The big retailers, all with stores and mail order, include American Musical Supply, Sam Ash Music, Brook Mays, Guitar Center, Sweetwater Sound, and Full Compass.

Available products may include traditional and electronic instruments for rent, purchase, or lease; accessories such as cables; fretted instruments; electronic and recording equipment; DJ gear; recorded music; printed music scores; and publications from books to magazines. These stores serve as a one-stop service center for musicians and can be small "mom-and-pop" operations or the megabox stores that emerged in the 1990s.

It is often smart, and sometimes critical, for full-line music retail stores to give lessons to help their customers enjoy their instruments. For pianos and organs, it's customary for 6 months of lessons to be included in a rent-to-own contract. Along with teaching the customers to enjoy their purchases and creating a sense of community, the music school generates foot traffic, a vital ingredient for any retail store to keep its doors open. Another product line that generates foot traffic and also keeps mail order sellers at bay is the used instrument product line. Parents who are unsure of their child's commitment to music will often gravitate to used instruments, which are less expensive than new products. The ability to personally examine a used product is a crucial in-store advantage over online instrument sellers, who are mostly confined to new products.

A service frequently offered by full-line stores is instrument and equipment repair. These services can be hard to find and very costly if instruments need to be shipped out of town. Although it is becoming increasingly difficult for music storeowners to find and hire qualified repair technicians (and thus a good career opportunity!), this can be an important part of a store's offerings. Efficient, well-run repair departments help stores develop customer loyalty and, again, add to foot traffic as instruments are dropped off and picked up.

As in many fields of retailing, independent music retailers in the United States have been challenged by the "big box" operations—the musical equivalent of Wal-Mart. But the 2003 bankruptcy of MARS, the initial leader in the big box concept for music retail, gave investors second thoughts about too-rapid expansion in this retail category.

The Combo Store

Narrower in scope than the traditional full-line store, combo stores generally deal with drums, guitars, amplifiers, speaker systems, audio mixing panels, public address systems, and lighting equipment—and the accessory items that go with them all, such as microphones and stands, cabling, drumsticks, snares, and the like. Recording equipment can also be found in this group, and it has become very saleable, with the vast improvement in technology, the significant drop in price, and the advent of the home recording studio. With prices continuing to drop for this equipment while quality goes up, bands and individuals are now able to produce their own good-quality demos. It's a boon for music retailers, not to mention the increased opportunities for creative musicians, amateur and pro, to let their imaginations roam.

School Music

The market for band and orchestra instruments and equipment is made up of three groups of customers, the smallest being professional musicians. The next largest group includes amateurs, the individual music hobbyists—children and adults. The largest part—at least 75%—involves schools and colleges, which host multiple musical ensembles. These ensembles have an aggregate membership of several million young musicians (it has been estimated that 1 in 10 elementary school students joins a school band or orchestra). Their instruments, equipment, and music are acquired by individual musicians' families and by the schools themselves. The success of school music merchants depends on developing strong and loyal business relationships with the school band and orchestra directors in the area.

The instruments normally purchased or rented by students and families include flutes, clarinets, trumpets, alto and tenor saxes, trombones, violins, and violas. Often, retailers offer a rent-to-own (or lease-to-own) option where the rent or lease money can be used toward purchase, in whole or part. Merchants serving this community sometimes build up a large, lucrative rental business.

Many of these instruments are manufactured in three levels of quality and price that roughly correspond to the three groups of purchasers: student, step-up (i.e.,

Photo courtesy of NAMM.

midlevel), and professional musicians. The least expensive models are often recommended to beginners and their parents, since it's uncertain whether the youngsters will continue their musical activities. These instruments are ruggedly constructed, provide acceptable intonation, and are the type normally used for rentals. Some firms manufacture instruments and equipment "privately labeled," as well as their own name brands. This is becoming prevalent today with the influx of instruments being made in China and Taiwan. The Conn-Selmer Company, for example, has offered two lower-level instrument lines, the Prelude and the Aristocrat, that are made in Asia to the company's specifications.

Frequently, schools own background instruments (tuba, string bass, cello, baritone sax, French horn, euphonium, English horn, bassoon, oboe, piccolo, and lower-voiced clarinets) and the entire percussion section. These are obtained through a purchase order or bidding process with a local or national retailer. Also, many schools have discovered the advantages of a corporate or store lease as a way to obtain much-needed musical equipment immediately, with annual payments locked into a specific figure they can afford over a 3- to 5-year period.

To service schools, store reps pick up and return instruments for repair and carry along a good stock of accessory items such as reeds, mouthpieces, **ligatures,** valve oil, cork grease, and the like. Competent repair service for all customers, school based or otherwise, is critical. Free repair loaners are often available. And anyone working in the music products industry must know instrument nomenclature for all instruments they sell, such as "undercut tone holes," "diaphragmatic sound boards," and "draw knob combination preset actions."

Specialty Shops

As students make progress, some trade in their beginning instruments for step-up or professional instruments. These two levels of instruments cost at least twice as much as the economy student model. Some of the high-end professional instruments and gear have such a small market that most retailers cannot afford to carry them, and they are available only in stores that specialize in this very small niche market or by special order. A single person—often someone who plays or has experience with a given instrument—may run these retail operations.

These mini "meccas" often attract customers from around the country who travel great distances with checkbooks in hand to take advantage of merchandise available only through these shops. Other entrepreneurs have taken advantage of the Internet to market their offerings to customers at a greater distance. Still, for many professionals, the tactile experience of testing an instrument before it is purchased cannot be replaced.

Consumer Audio Equipment

There are three levels of audio equipment: professional, semiprofessional, and home use. Most audio equipment purchased for the home is sold through electronics retailing giants who stock the great variety of products on the market. Home-use music products can also be found in some electronics retailers (for example, Best Buy stocks both guitars and amplifiers). Stereo stores rarely sell professional audio equipment, the kind required for theaters and arenas. Professional systems of this kind are typically sold, installed, and serviced by sound companies specializing in this kind of business. An online search for "professional audio equipment" will provide a list of specialized sound companies in your area.

Keyboards

A well-rounded keyboard department or store offers a full line of vertical and grand acoustic pianos, to accommodate the full gamut of musicians, from the professional who needs a 9-foot concert grand to the student first learning to play. These stores also make vertical, student-grade pianos available through rent-to-own arrangements or other forms of financing. The entry-level product for this marketplace is the electronic keyboard, which comes in a range of models from grand piano configuration to small, easily portable instruments. They offer a wide variety of sound combinations to the player. The standardization of MIDI (musical instrument digital interface), developed in the early 1980s, allows different electronic musical instruments (usually keyboards) to communicate with each other. A simple patching job makes equipment **interface** easy and inexpensive. Several synthesizers can be played at once from a single keyboard, providing **multitrack** layers of sound. The principle behind the General MIDI is simply that any sequence should sound the same no matter what General MIDI instrument is used.

The development of the electronic organ has made it possible for the music merchant to be the major player in the church organ market. Pipe organs have priced themselves out of all but a small market, and they are fragile and take constant maintenance. The Allen Organ and Rogers Organs electronic instruments have become very acceptable instruments for serious concert and church performances. Competent repair service and technicians are a must in supporting keyboard sales. Acoustic pianos must be kept in tune. Electronic church organs must be ready for church services; to meet this need, some stores guarantee repair within 12 hours.

Print Music

Two types of retail outlets generally sell print. One is the music store that concentrates on instrument sales and stocks print as a service to its customers. A full-line store stocks pop folios, piano music to support serious piano study, and pedagogical vocal music, such as the Schirmer Library editions. This kind of retailer usually doesn't delve into the school and church music market.

The second type is the **institutional print** dealer. Institutional print music is purchased by schools, churches, and community groups for performance by choirs, bands, orchestras, and small (chamber) ensembles. The leader in this institutional sector is J.W. Pepper, headquartered in Chester County, Pennsylvania. Although founded back in 1876, J.W. Pepper is a 21st-century company offering sheet music via digital e-Print, which recipients print out on their own computer printers.

J.W. Pepper has two large music warehouses and multiple retail locations across the country. When shopping online, customers can hear and see the music offered for sale. The online store has broadened its customer base to include students, hobbyists, and musicians. Besides its main mail-order Web site, the company created a Web site exclusively for pianists at PianoAtPepper.com.

The profit margins for selling printed music are comparable to other parts of the industry, but it takes a lot more $25 and $50 sales to net the kind of profit generated by the sale of one Steinway piano. The biggest challenge for the institutional print retailer is how to make the buyers aware of new music which encourages school music directors and music teachers to visit their stores. This is done in a number of ways: new-materials reading sessions arranged through retail stores; direct-mail efforts of recordings of new material; descriptions in retail catalogs; and through people talking to people.

Books, Magazines, and Trade Journals

Music Books. The biggest market for books on music is in the elementary education field of school music. Perhaps the next biggest sellers are the popular accounts of the life and times of rock stars, followed by the next largest market share in music appreciation and music theory books. Jazz history books also sell well. The increase in record industry technology courses has generated a sizable market for textbooks in that field. Another popular type targets the amateur songwriter. Interest in textbooks in the music business is also growing. There are also certain scholarly books on music, of interest to musicologists and college students working on graduate degrees. W. W. Norton is the leading publisher in this field.

The merchandising of these products covers a broad range of outlets. Textbooks are naturally marketed through the bookstores of colleges offering pertinent courses. Some instrument stores carry books that might be interesting to their customers (e.g., some drum shops carry biographies of famous drummers and histories of particular kinds of drums). Bookstores market the more general-interest titles if their communities respond, and the Internet provides access to practically any title, no matter how esoteric.

Music Magazines and Trade Journals. The publication and sale of music-related magazines and trade journals are important facets of the music business, although print publications have declined as information moves to the Internet.

There are two basic categories of music magazines: popular (for music fans) and professional (for those who earn a living in music or aspire to do so). *Music Trades, Musical Merchandise Review, Instrumentalist,* and *Music, Inc.* are the primary journals for music product sellers. *Billboard* is the best known record industry publication, offered at select retailers, by individual subscription, or on newsstands in major recording centers.

Outside the professional trades are the "popular" music magazines. Probably the best known are *Rolling Stone, Spin, Mix,* and *Down Beat.* Established professional musicians receive *International Musician* each month if they are members of the American Federation of Musicians (AFM). Arts administrators value the League of American Orchestras' *Symphony* magazine. Another publication, *Campus Activities Programming,* is the journal for college concert promoters and talent agents. Two scholarly music journals should be mentioned: *Notes,* read by music librarians, and the *Journal of the American Musicological Society.*

For a more complete listing of the leading music magazines, see Selected Readings at the end of this book.

Sales Leaders

While each store proprietor needs to decide what type of store he or she is interested in—and what will work best in a given community—it is wise for these owners to keep track of current buying trends. According to NAMM,[1] the following categories of instruments top the best-seller chart in the U.S. music products industry. As shown in the following list, fretted products are the top leaders in sales (based on dollar volume), with the guitar proving once again to be the world's most popular instrument.

1. Fretted products

2. Sound reinforcement products

3. Printed music

4. Percussion

5. Wind instruments

6. Microphones

7. Acoustic pianos

8. General accessories

9. Computer music products

10. Instrument amplifiers

Data on the music products industry do not include figures on the used-instrument market, which is substantial but difficult to measure.

Growth Areas. Sales of computer and electronic instruments with synthesized sounds are booming. Instruments personalized for females have become popular, such as Daisy Rock guitars, which come in appealing colors and are designed to fit female body contours. Sales for sound reinforcement products, such as power amps, speaker enclosures, and powered mixers continue to improve, as does the electronic music market.

Promotion of Musical Products

The proprietor who has invested money in a music store is not really alone financially. The investment is backed up by the far larger resources of manufacturers of the lines sold. Manufacturers invest huge sums every year, not only in production but also in sales promotion and advertising.

One sales promotion device is the cooperative ad: The manufacturer and the merchant share the cost of Web site display ads, e-mailing, and radio and print advertisements. Another cooperative effort develops when the manufacturer supplies point-of-sale items for the merchant to display, such as signs, banners, streamers, show cards, special display racks, and window dressings. Some stores festoon their premises with these point-of-sale stimuli.

To pull floor traffic in slow periods, retailers temporarily lower prices on some items in heavily-advertised promotions that occur like clockwork at the same time each year. One major retailer schedules a Green Tag Sale every March, an Anniversary Sale in August, and a Sell-a-Thon in November.

Since school and college musical directors are among the biggest buyers of background instruments and equipment, manufacturers display these wares at professional educators' meetings and conventions. Manufacturers often employ well-known professional performers as goodwill ambassadors to attend conventions and music clinics, representing themselves as enthusiastic users of the firm's instruments. Some firms supply the services of these professionals to schools for benefit concerts and clinics with school bands or orchestras, further developing goodwill for the firm and its products.

Blending distribution and promotion, acoustic and electronic piano manufacturers have linked up with retailers to offer instrument loaner programs for colleges and universities. The retailer buys the instruments, loans them to the school (usually for the school year), offers them at sale prices at the end of the year, and then pays the manufacturer for them. In this kind of creative alliance, everyone benefits: The school has enough instruments for its students, the students have good instruments to learn and practice on, and the manufacturer and retailer have good opportunities to sell the instruments and, again, build name recognition.

Even more direct contact with potential customers occurs on the floor of the store when a family walks into the shop. The youngster of the family may have dropped in to get something repaired and left with a new Selmer alto sax. Many large sales develop through a store's offering music accessories, including instrument cases and equipment designed to enhance the performance of the musical instrument. Accessories offer high markup, draw a variety of customers into the store, and then cause them to return, since most accessories are expendable and need replacement.

Although many merchants cater to young musicians and schools, retailers also seek the business of professional musicians where feasible. They not only buy the higher-priced professional instruments and equipment, but they can be an effective sales force for the store—nearly all professionals, even semiprofessionals, have pupils who need recommendations on where to shop. Professionals who frequent music stores also use them for communication centers ("I need a drummer for Saturday night. Know anyone who can do the gig?" "John's rehearsal band is meeting Tuesday night this week. Will you help pass the word?").

New Trends in Music Retail

Mail Order and Online Sales

Not long ago, the brick-and-mortar music retail industry joined the rest of the retail world in fighting mail order sales that came with the Internet explosion. However, no single Web juggernaut has emerged for the music industry (as Amazon is to booksellers), because mail order Web commerce of music products is fragmented. The market is served by multiple specialists as well as by the Web divisions of several large retail chains.

Musical instrument stores typically carry several thousand different products and accessories, while mail order outlets stock tens of thousands. Benefitting from centralized warehousing, mail order tends to experience fewer out-of-stock items than stores whose capacities are limited to on-site storerooms, and it also escapes the burden of financing a broad inventory to support only a local market.

Mail order has boomed with the advent of broadband connections that bring full-featured catalog information via Web sites with audio, video, and multiple images, a big improvement from the static printed catalogs of the pre-Internet era. Music product sellers report that consumers tend to buy from both local stores and online mail order suppliers. It is common for a consumer's online supplier to be the Web site of their favorite local store.

Product Manufacturing: A New World

As economic globalization envelops the planet, the manufacturing of physical goods has increasingly become a contest in which only a few countries compete in a given product category. The never-ending quest is to turn out products faster and cheaper. The United States imports about $3 billion's worth of musical instruments a year—mostly from Asia, Mexico, and Canada—but also exports over $1 billion in music products around the world. Asia has become a hub of manufacturing because of low labor costs, which results in lower prices for consumers. One example is the South Korean-owned Sejung Musical Instrument Manufacturing Company, whose factory was built in Quingdao, China, in 2001. By 2004, the Sejung company had produced more than 1,000 grand pianos, 2,000 vertical pianos, and 1,500 fretted instruments each month. Today, the company employs several thousand workers in over 1 million square feet of modern production facilities.

In many cases, musical instruments produced in China and Taiwan now undercut prices of products made in Japan, just as the Japanese manufacturers had done to products made in the United States decades earlier.

Trade Associations

The music retail business has a number of trade associations that are active, vital, and dedicated to members of the industry. Among these associations are the

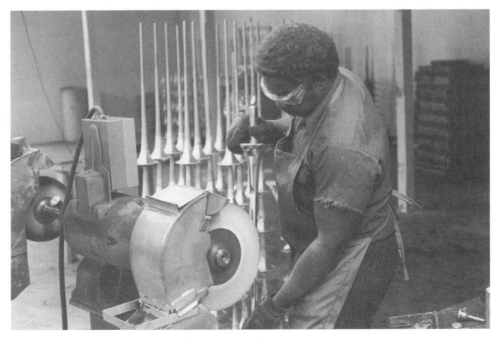

A technician works on a brass instrument.

Photo courtesy of Selmer Music Co.

International Music Products Association (formerly the National Association of Music Merchants and still known by its original acronym, NAMM), the, National Association of Professional Band Instrument Repair Technicians (NAPBIRT), and the Guitar and Accessories Marketing Association (GAMA).

The most representative trade association for people selling instruments, equipment, and accessories is NAMM. It is composed worldwide of more than 9,000 music retailers, manufacturers, and their representatives, wholesalers, and distributors. NAMM helps its members increase their business by providing training programs, supporting private and public music education, and generally promoting the benefits of music making.

The NAMM trade shows, held twice yearly, showcase musical instruments, professional audio equipment, and the latest in music electronics and software. NAMM provides educational sessions, sales and management seminars, industry publications, and market research studies to its members. NAMM's annual statistical review of the music products industry, *Global Report/Music USA,* is the most comprehensive summary available of market sales and trends in the musical instrument field.

Although not exactly a trade association, NAMM's education arm, NAMBI (NAMM Affiliated Music Business Institutions) is another organization worth mentioning. Its goal is to encourage college students to consider careers within the music products industry. Through this organization, students have the opportunity to attend the biannual trade shows, apply for scholarships given to qualifying schools, and learn from industry professionals. This organization also provides a forum for students to connect with and interview for jobs and internships with industry executives.

Opportunities for Employment

The music products industry is a dynamic field where music students often work part time. It can become a full-time career by design, or occasionally a career fallback for graduates struggling to find other jobs. Illustrating the field's size, the national retailing and mail-order chain Guitar Center, employs about 9,500 persons on both a part time and full-time salary basis. Opportunities in the music products sector range from entry-level retail positions to finance, marketing, or management for retailers, distributors, or manufacturers of musical instruments and accessories.

Through NAMBI and MEIEA (Music and Entertainment Industry Educators Association), music business curricula have been developed at the college and university level to train young people for careers in this industry. These degrees combine training in music and business since a solid background in both areas is beneficial. A degree in this field, combined with real-world experience, has led many individuals to fulfilling careers.

Note

1. As per NAMM's *Global Report/Music USA,* 2007 edition.

Chapter Takeaways

- The $8 billion musical products industry is dominated by specialty music stores. A few popular items such as guitars, amplifiers, and drums are stocked by mass merchants, but their product lines are limited.

- Brick-and-mortar specialty stores generally operate Web sites, extending their reach into the online sales market.

- Specialty stores have thrived with knowledgeable sales help that mass merchants don't match, instrument repair services (as well as providing loaners), the sale of used instruments (including purchasing instruments for resale), stocking niche accessories such as reeds and valve oil, and instructional lessons on-site.

- Sale of sheet music, to both individuals and institutions, is a steady business.

- Specialty stores are a source of employment opportunities, perhaps for students seeking part-time work in areas where they can be close to music.

- Some musical instruments are manufactured in the United States and Canada, while imported equipment comes mainly from Asia and Mexico.

Key Terms

- accessories   (p. 266)

- folios   (p. 263)

- full-line store   (p. 260)

- institutional print dealer   (p. 263)

- mail-order/online   (p. 266)

- music magazines/trade journals   (p. 264)

- rent-to-own   (p. 260)

The Recording Industry

PART 5

CHAPTER 15

Record Labels

The recording industry overwhelmingly dominates the art and business of music. Once a piece of music is composed, not much of importance can happen to it in the marketplace until it is recorded. The lives and fortunes of composers, performers, publishers, agents, and merchants rise and fall with the sale of recorded music. If **records** sell well, all other sectors of the business prosper. When they flop, other sectors struggle to fill the financial black hole.

For an understanding of how the recording industry functions today, some historical background will be helpful (see Table 15.1).

> *"I have learned from experience that it is easier to make a businessman out of a musician than a musician out of a businessman."*
>
> —*Goddard Lieberson*

Perspective

Numerous recognized record companies operate in the United States, with releases on more than 3,000 different labels. Probably the best way to gain a true picture of the record business is to analyze it in terms of *major* versus *independent* labels. It is probably best to define a major label as any label that is owned and/or distributed

Left: The Capitol Records building in Hollywood, California.

Photo courtesy of Capitol Records. The Capitol Tower is a trademark of Capitol Records, Inc. All rights reserved.

Table 15.1   Development of Recorded Music

1877:	Edison invents the cylinder phonograph.
1894:	The first commercial disc recordings appear in the U.S. market.
1900s:	The Victor Talking Machine Co. is incorporated in 1901, develops 10,000 dealers. At first, opera repertoire dominates. Then dance music begins to sell well (on Victor and Columbia labels).
1917:	The first jazz record is released.
1920s:	By 1921, 100 million records are produced in the United States. Large impetus from "commercial" jazz. Bell Laboratories develops an electrical process for recording in 1924, increasing audible range over the earlier acoustical recordings to 100–5,000 Hz. Bass instruments can be heard for the first time. Meteoric rise of radio popularity puts recording industry into a tailspin.
1930s:	The Great Depression hurts all business, particularly the record industry. Sales of discs and phonographs drop 90% compared with the 1927 peak year (total retail sales in 1933: $5.5 million). Jukebox industry grows large, helping to salvage the record business. By the late 1930s, the jukebox operators were buying 13 million discs to serve their machines. Decca starts marketing low-cost (35 cents) singles featuring artists such as Bing Crosby, the Mills Brothers, the Dorsey Brothers, Guy Lombardo; sells 19 million records in 1939. First albums appear by mid-1930s, each individual 78-rpm disc within the binder sells for 50 cents. Department stores introduce record and phonograph departments.
1940s:	Weekly volume of new records released in the early 1940s: 10 to 20 singles (78 rpm); by the end of the decade, 40 to 100 per week, depending on the season. American Federation of Musicians (AFM) strike against record companies paralyzes the industry 1942–1945, damages popularity of big band recordings, which, in turn, accelerates sales of records featuring pop singers. Airplay not yet a major promotion factor except big band remote broadcasts. Jukeboxes help break new hits, particularly in "race music" (as it was then called) and country fields. Late 1940s: One-stops (distributors handling all labels) come into being, mainly to accommodate jukebox operators. Rise of independent record labels, which begin to dominate the rhythm and blues (R&B) field. Proliferation of distributors into smaller markets. Average dealer markup: 38%. In 1948, Columbia introduces the 33 1/3-rpm LP, retailing for $5.79. This becomes the playback standard for decades. "Race records," country and western (C&W) diverge from pop records.
1950s:	Television rises rapidly, grabs a large share of the radio audience. To economize, radio stations drop most live music and turn to recorded music. Increasing popularity of TV also sharply reduces record sales from 1949 to 1954. R&B and C&W markets become dominated by independent labels. Interest in high-fidelity sound increases buyers of middle-of-the-road records. Rock and roll craze begins in the mid-1950s. "Cover record" concept initiated.
1955:	Record clubs begin. Columbia starts, soon followed by RCA and Capitol.
1957:	Rack jobbing begins.
1958:	Stereo is introduced. Record retailing changes. Proliferation of labels and products burdens retailers with huge inventories. Space demands force abandonment of listening booths. Record supermarkets begin concurrently with proliferation of the small-rack setups. Record retailing in chaos amid price cutting and expanding sales.

1959:	Classical music's first million seller: Van Cliburn's performance of Tchaikovsky's Piano Concerto No. 1.
1960s:	Social turmoil of the decade finds its "voice" in popular music, influences large sales increases of rock, R&B, soul, country records. Rock becomes the catalyst for Woodstock-type mass concerts.
	National Association of Recording Merchandisers (NARM) formed in early 1960s by record wholesalers.
	Rack jobbers cut heavily into "mom-and-pop" retailing and become dominant in the market; record clubs cut further into conventional retailing.
	Beatles craze accelerates worldwide interest in pop-rock music; sales boom ensues.
	Record supermarkets and retail chains proliferate in response to decreasing profit margins, growing inventories.
	Major labels recapture some markets lost earlier to independents.
1970s:	Independent record producers rise to greater importance.
	Singer-songwriters become the superstars. Crossover records become the superhits.
	Sophistication of technology increases: 16- and 24-track consoles; synthesizers, computer-assisted mixing, digital recording.
	Sophistication of music increases: rock softens, classical influences on polyphony, texture, instrumentation, form.
1980s:	Technological change advances sophistication of recording/reproducing equipment. Inexpensive keyboards and samplers enable a new generation of young producers to make records.
	Compact discs (CDs) gain market share.
	Video clips change record promotion methods, break new acts.
	Long-form videos develop as take-home consumer software.
1990s:	New technologies make high-quality home recording possible.
	Sophisticated in-store sampling units provide new vehicles for exposure and trial.
	DAT (digital audiotape) hardware is approved for consumer use in the United States.
	Electronic delivery of music arrives, in addition to traditional sales at record stores.
2000s:	Government clamps down on label co-op ad business practices, lowering CD prices.
	Consumer broadband growth spurs unauthorized peer-to-peer exchange of music files, reducing sales of cash-cow CDs.
	Web innovations such as MP3 and Napster scare labels with threat of piracy, eventually triggering new online label distribution approaches.
	As the rise of legal downloads only partly compensates for the fall-off of CD sales, the industry realigns to produce more revenue from sources such as publishing, licensing, concerts, and merchandise.
	Well-financed independent labels use 360 deals to infringe on major labels' turf.
	Some superstars, as well as newer artists, no longer see major label deals as the inevitable next career goal.

by one of the handful of major distribution companies. Conversely, an independent ("indie") label is any label lacking an affiliation with a major.

An understanding of this structure is important because the majors dominate the sales of records in the United States. Even though independents account for the overwhelming majority of the many thousands of different records released each year, majors account for a hefty majority of the records sold. Major labels are well funded, giving them the economic heft to sign the top artists, which leaves independents scrambling to fill niches and work with artists that that don't immediately interest the major labels.

Major Labels

The record business requires a tremendous investment in the areas of production, distribution, and marketing. A commonly quoted industry statistic is that only one of five records earns its money back. By being well financed, the major labels can ride out the frequent losses and wait for the big scores. Moreover, artists are attracted to the large advances and the prestige of being associated with a label such as Sony or Island Def Jam, the security of knowing there are sufficient funds for marketing, and the stability of an established company in a business where one of the greatest difficulties is getting paid. The major labels can also afford to fund more elaborate recordings with the best producers, musicians, and studios. Prominent artists are attracted to major labels primarily because of their powerful promotion departments and well-organized distribution networks. They would rather be known as a "Warner artist" than as a "Smith artist."

The advantages in economies of scale are also profound. When a big firm releases a new recording, it can assign much of its field force and merchandising personnel to that particular project. They can bring to bear 200 or more individuals actively working a particular release. Although major labels rarely assign their full energies to just one release, they can shift their field personnel whenever they find it necessary to push particular products. Because they sell more records, they can put much greater pressure on retailers to accept a lot of titles, particularly from new artists. And major labels offer stability and longevity. This can mean that they are more likely to maintain inventories and continue distribution of recordings long after their first release. Smaller labels may find it impossible to offer such ongoing service.

In contrast, independent labels are usually forced to stitch together a patchwork of different independent distributors and wholesalers to cover the entire country. Independent labels are the last to get paid by music retailers, and if an account is large enough for an independent label, the bankruptcy of a retailer or wholesaler can result in the failure of the label as well.

Last, the majors have a clear advantage in the costly marketing of records. Again, the structure of the majors allows a large staff to work together on distribution and marketing. Radio promotion can cost $100,000 or more per single. Video production costs range from $50,000 to $500,000 for one song. Retail placement and promotion can easily run into seven figures for a single album release. Add to this amount the cost of advertising, tour support, publicity, and the overhead for staff.

All this clout means that a major-label sales force can push to sales success even a weak recording. This issue is strongly disputed, some arguing that even heavily concentrated promotion cannot persuade the public to buy music that doesn't actually have it "in the grooves." But certainly, the powerful promotional forces of the major labels have much greater success with weak material than the smaller firms.

Independent Labels

Fortunately for the independents, the sheer size of the majors has built-in disadvantages. First, they are conservative companies that tend to be slow to catch up with changes in musical tastes. Most important developments in music have started at the independent level: rock and roll in the '50s and '60s; punk and modern rock in the '70s and '80s; alternative and "grunge" rock as well as rap and hip hop in the '80s and '90s. Knowledgeable music industry professionals have described independent labels as the "lifeblood of the business." To discover "the next big thing" in music, you need only look to the indies.

Of course, the natural evolution and goal of some independents is to become so successful that they are ultimately bought out and absorbed by the majors for many millions of dollars. Many of today's biggest major labels started out as independents, having lived through high-risk periods to develop into very profitable companies. Three English labels that started very small and grew very rich before being bought out by major labels are Island, Chrysalis, and Virgin. Three U.S. labels that did the same thing are Arista, Geffen, and Sire. From the outset, these companies exhibited creative leadership and determination—a winning combination.

However, developments in technology lessen the scale advantage of the majors. The affordability of recording equipment and the proliferation of home studios has brought the cost of recording down considerably. The refinements of CD replication and the number of competing factories have brought manufacturing costs down. Low cost equipment facilitating do-it-yourself recording, together with Internet distribution, has made it possible for almost anyone to promote and distribute music to the entire world.

With the their historic advantages in productivity and efficiency now blunted, majors now rely more heavily on their other differentiating characteristic—financial heft. More so than before, the majors concentrate their efforts on the most popular music with the best sales potential. This leaves many of the more modest-selling genres and artists to the independents.

Independent labels can also develop brand name awareness and consumer loyalty that is rare among the majors. Music fans will often purchase records from labels such as Alligator, Rounder, and Sub Pop Records ("Going out of business since 1988") on the basis of their trust in that label's taste.

Another fertile area for an independent label is at the local or regional level. An independent can make necessary connections with the radio stations, publicity outlets, and retailers in a limited geographical area. Relationships are the backbone of this industry, and if a group can earn the good favor of a few regional program directors, editors, and store managers, a modest success can begin and grow from there, especially if the acts can play in the area.

Specialty Labels

Some of the most successful independents are specialty labels, and a number of these are in the classical music field, for instance, Nonesuch, Deutsche Grammophon, Westminster, Odyssey, and Angel. The classics have been and are still being recorded by the world's greatest artists, and classical labels are largely concerned with selling known masterworks. Larger classical labels such as Columbia will, from time to time, record and market "new music," the works of "serious" contemporary composers.

Some specialty labels, particularly in the field of contemporary classical music, release their records "privately." They bypass more conventional distribution channels and seek to locate buyers of their sometimes-esoteric product through specialty markets or the Web, particularly to colleges and universities.

Other specialty labels limit their activities to certain demographic markets. They find ways to reach cultural enclaves or ethnic groups and work directly with retail outlets in those communities. Another kind of specialty label is Folkways, now administered by an affiliate of the Smithsonian Institute, which offers a variety of folk, blues, ethnic, and jazz music, selling mostly to schools and libraries.

One of the most successful types of specialty label sells gospel music. Among the most effective promotional methods used by gospel record companies are the many personal appearances of their contract artists. Touring gospel singers draw large audiences and sell lots of music.

Once again, these labels are successful because they do not compete directly with the mainstream music concentrated on by the majors and because they do not rely as heavily on traditional and expensive forms of promotion, such as radio and video.

Do-It-Yourself Labels

Beginning with the advent of compact discs, and accelerating with cheaper home recording equipment and the Internet, more and more artists have decided to take charge of their careers and release their recordings on their own. This is known as a "do it yourself" or DIY label. Some of these labels have progressed into full-time independent record companies, releasing albums by artists they admire and giving them the same creative control the founders enjoy. These labels are usually run by one or two of the band members or friends/volunteers who can handle many of the responsibilities that several people do at a larger label. Many DIY operations successfully gain mastery of inexpensive production, CD pressing, downloads, guerrilla promotion, and marketing—with or without distribution through brick-and-mortar retailers.

Photo courtesy of Trebas Institute.

Going it alone has a mixed track record. In 2007, Radiohead offered its album *In Rainbow* as downloads from the band's Web site months before a physical CD came out. Album download buyers were told to pay whatever amount they thought fair on a strictly voluntary basis. The band was not forthcoming with specifics afterwards, but it is believed money taken was a disappointment and that 6 out of every 10 downloaders paid nothing at all. Other big acts did not immediately follow. Supporters of the concept say it gave the album a promotional lift that paid off in subsequent CD sales, and that the concept drew good will and approving write-ups from fan-oriented media.

Record Company Structure

Record companies range in size from the multinational major to the modest, one-person DIY operation, and their structures vary accordingly. But whatever their structure, they must handle the kinds of tasks described, and certain generalizations can be made about how production, distribution, and marketing are organized and administered. Figure 15.1 gives an illustration of how a major record company (that is, a global distribution company with multiple affiliated labels) might be organized.

Executive Officers (CEO, COO, CFO, General Manager)

The CEO or president is often a strong entrepreneur who started the label and who had the vision it reflects. CEOs come from a variety of backgrounds, but two stand out. Lawyers often assume this position because the record business relies in large part on contracts and copyrights. Producers are also quite often in charge of labels because they know the music. This is particularly true in country music and urban music. Whether or not CEOs are lawyers or producers, they must have their respective abilities: They must know the "art of the deal" to negotiate favorable business arrangements, and they must have good "ears" to evaluate commercial recordings. They are often strong leaders, like David Geffen, Clive Davis, and Ahmet Ertegun.

Artist and Repertoire (A&R)

A&R executives are concerned first and foremost with finding and signing new talent. The A&R staff needs to keep informed—through a network of contacts, by evaluating demos, tracking the independent music scene, reading industry publications, and going to clubs to hear new music. After an act has been signed, the A&R professional remains involved on a number of different levels, including assisting artists in developing a particular project and/or their careers; administering the many production, budgetary, and other details of an album; or just acting as liaison between the artist and the label. If the label is large enough, separate departments may be established to handle these specific tasks, such as Artist Development, A&R Administration, Artist Relations, and Production on both the audio and video side. A major company incorporating multiple labels may house A&R executives under a particular label rather than under an all-encompassing A&R department, as illustrated in Figure 15.1.

Distribution/Sales

Whether a record company is a major or independent, it must have personnel who either oversee or are directly involved with convincing retailers to order and

Figure 15.1   **Major Record Company Structure**

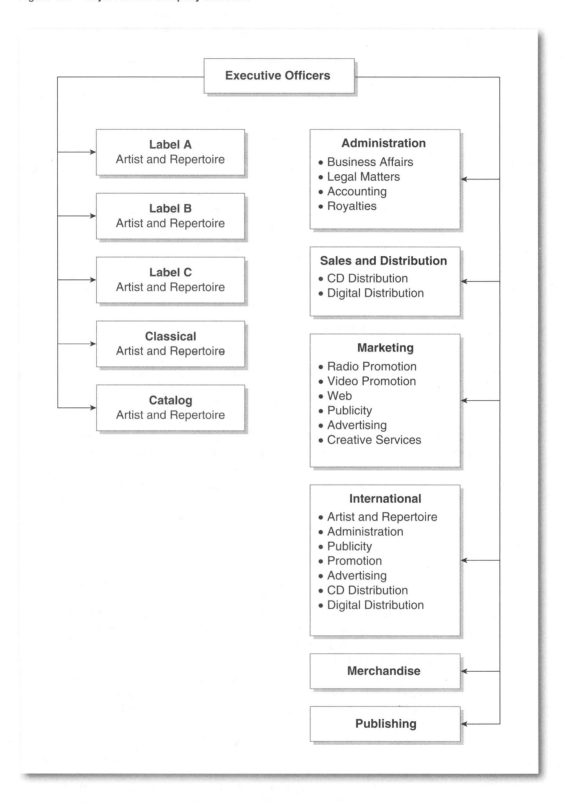

showcase in stores its CDs, and also get prominent "shelf space" at online stores. For physical CDs, it's a science in ordering sufficient quantities, because the label does not want excessive "returns" from retailers later, and at the same time doesn't want retail shelves to go bare while consumer interest is strongest.

Marketing

While sales and marketing are often linked, the marketing role is so distinct that it usually functions separately and is divided into several areas of specialization.

Product Management. Found in most medium and large record companies, product managers coordinate and oversee all aspects of a current release, including packaging, advertising, tours, publicity, promotion, and sales activities.

Radio Promotion. This is the very heart of the marketing of most records in most genres. The radio promotion department is in charge of getting radio airplay and charting. Some large labels subdivide this department by genre of music. In addition to effecting a strategy to gain airplay and chart position, the radio department works with stations to arrange promotional appearances, interviews, giveaways, and contests.

Video Promotion. This department attempts to get video airplay on TV and video streaming on the Web.

Publicity. In-house publicists manage media exposure through TV appearances, magazine and Web site articles, online social network promotions, e-mail campaigns, newspaper reviews, syndicated radio programs, and the like. Many labels are concentrating more and more on publicity because it is so much less expensive than promotion.

Advertising. This department arranges the advertising for a label and may be part of or work closely with the distribution and sales department since much of the consumer advertising cost is shared between label and retailer (co-op advertising). Ad departments also book trade publication ads that promote things such as the label's brand (and its relationship with artists) to distributors and retailers.

Creative Services. The creative services department is responsible for designing and producing any materials necessary to execute a marketing campaign such as posters, point-of-purchase materials, ads, Web site graphics, album artwork, and window displays.

Special Products (Catalog)

The special products department, which sometimes is called *catalog,* has two core responsibilities: (a) handling incoming requests to license masters of older product and (b) finding new ways to redesign or repackage the music that the company has previously released. Special products executives usually create "best of" packages, themed multi-artist compilations, or other reissue techniques, such as box sets or rereleases of a record, sometimes with new packaging, mastering, or unreleased recordings.

International Department

The global nature of the record business is such that most larger companies have international departments to oversee foreign sales and ensure effective communication between domestic and foreign affiliates. For many labels and many genres, foreign sales exceed domestic sales. The major labels often generate at least half their total revenue from local offices in the biggest 40 to 50 international territories. Typically, a major's significant foreign territories will maintain their own A&R operations to sign local talent (such as a French act for the French and Canadian market). (See Chapter 29 for a discussion of the international business.)

Business and Legal Affairs

Since this industry revolves around contracts and copyrights, record companies usually have legal departments to negotiate and draft agreements. These range from artist recording agreements to licenses issued by and to the record company for the use of copyrighted works. This department must also do its best to minimize litigation. Some larger companies have a separate department for business and legal affairs or smaller departments to handle specific tasks, such as licensing or copyright departments. These functions may all reside under a broad administration department, along with centralized functions such as accounting, purchasing, finance, and facilities.

Accounting

Record companies can require large and sophisticated accounting operations to handle a host of financial functions. Professionals with financial skills are involved in the development and administration of recording budgets, inventory, and manufacturing, with separate departments designed for each, such as operations and finance departments. Royalties are frequently handled in a separate department dedicated to that function. At very small labels all these tasks might be performed in a single, integrated department.

Merchandise

Some labels historically maintained departments to support concert tours of their artists. Nowadays, a critical function is handling artist-related merchandise, much of it distributed under license at concert venues. This function is particularly critical if the label has a 360 deal with an artist which gives it a direct stake in merchandise revenue.

Publishing Affiliates

Labels generally own or control at least two publishing companies—one connected with the American Society of Composers, Authors and Publishers (ASCAP) and one signed with Broadcast Music Inc. (BMI). Labels often seek to persuade their contract artists to grant them publishing rights to the music the artist records for the label. Although a publishing company may be owned by the same parent company as its affiliated record company, the publishing company is expected to show profit from its own operations and may sign artists who are not on the record company's roster. An exception may be found with publishing companies that are affiliated with very small labels. These companies may exist solely to handle the publishing of that label.

Trade Associations

A large number of associations represent individuals and companies in the recorded music business. Among the two more prominent groups are the Recording Industry Association of America (RIAA) and the National Academy of Recording Arts & Sciences (NARAS).

Recording Industry Association of America

The trade group representing the labels, major and minor, that account for the lion's share of sales, is the Recording Industry Association of America (RIAA). RIAA is well known for certifying best-selling records. In addition, the organization lobbies government for label-friendly regulations, represents industry to consumers, collects industry statistics, and battles online piracy and CD counterfeiting. RIAA is the most prominent force in the big music labels' drive to curb piracy.

National Academy of Recording Arts & Sciences

The National Academy of Recording Arts & Sciences (NARAS), commonly known as the Recording Academy, is best known to the public through annual telecasts of its Grammy Awards. NARAS has 12,000 voting members and 6,000 additional nonvoting members. NARAS's regular membership is limited to persons professionally active in the artistic, creative, or technical side of the industry (composers, performers, producers, **engineers,** etc.). Associate membership is open to those in the recording field who are only indirectly involved in record production. Some of the Recording Academy's associate members are students planning professional careers in recording. Applications are accepted at the academy's regional offices, located in major cities, or online at www.grammy.com.

Receipt of a Grammy Award is prized, not only for the prestige but because the attendant national publicity often helps boost record sales.

The Recording Academy sponsors several charitable endeavors, including a community outreach program called "Grammy in the Schools," a program to help musicians in need called "MusiCares," and various other grant and assistance programs to help further music and its preservation.

Chapter Takeaways

- Record labels are primarily in the distribution business. They also serve as music financiers when they advance funds to artists to create music.

- Although major labels command the bigger share of recorded music revenue, independent labels fill valuable niches and historically have been on the leading edge of creative trends.

- The segments of a label enterprise include: marketing focused on consumers, distribution that places product in retail outlets, artist & repertoire that oversees creative affairs, business affairs/accounting, music publishing (through an affiliate) and, in some cases, licensed merchandise.

- The first crude music recording device was invented in 1877. Record distribution tends to go through an upheaval with each subsequent invention of playback technologies—from vinyl discs of the prior century to today's downloads.

Key Terms

- Grammy   (p. 283)

- independent labels (Alligator, Rounder, Sub Pop Records)   (p. 276)

- major labels   (p. 276)

- special products (catalog)   (p. 281)

- specialty labels (classical music, gospel, jazz, etc.)   (p. 277)

CHAPTER 16

Record Promotion and Distribution

The Marketing Plan

To paraphrase an old adage: If you make a great recording and no one hears it, was it really great? Every participant from the largest label to the self-released independent artist will benefit by knowing the market, identifying the target audience, and planning an effective marketing and promotion strategy. After all, the artist and the label go to extreme lengths to record the best possible sounds.

It seems like it should be easy to sell recordings. Millions of music lovers purchase music every week. If the audience has the desire and the buying habit, why should such a detailed plan be required to compete in the marketplace? The answer is simple: In any given week there are many thousands of recordings (both new releases and not-so-new) fighting for the public's attention. Breaking through the noise is no easy task. To understand how recorded music is promoted, it is important to understand the elements of a marketing plan. Demand must be developed, not only nationally but also all over the world. Because of the significant costs, a label usually has to sell a lot of records— quickly—to be successful.

> *"It just seem like musicians want to sell a few records and put out a perfume line, and I think it's so sad that there are so many musicians who don't want to change the world . . . Music has been so much more."*
>
> —Moby

Left: Photo © Creasource/Corbis.

SWOT

An important early step in devising an effective plan of attack for marketing is to do a basic **SWOT analysis**. SWOT stands for "strengths, weaknesses, opportunities, and threats." This analysis gives a good perspective on what marketing concepts may be employed, what hurdles may be faced, and how those hurdles can be overcome.

Strengths. What does this project have working well in its favor? For example, if the artist has a successful history of radio airplay, it will be easier to get this artist's new single added to radio playlists. Perhaps the artist has built a loyal fan base through continuous touring, or maybe the artist possesses a sound or style currently in favor, or has cut a tremendous new recording that will be ground breaking. It's best to capitalize on what the project has going for it from the outset.

Weaknesses. Part of efficient marketing is avoiding tactics that aren't going to pay off. For example, if the artist will not be able to tour for health reasons, alternatives to personal appearances must be formulated.

Opportunities. Touring, TV appearances, and tie-ups with third parties (including other musical artists) are all potential avenues to exploit. If an artist has good relations with the media, fruitful TV appearances and journalist interviews can be expected.

Threats. It is equally important to identify possible forces that may be working against marketing efforts. Such conditions might include a crowded month of high-profile releases that will be competing for airplay and press attention, or the release of a big video game that drains the wallets of teenagers who are the target demographic. By identifying threats, the marketing team can chart a course that will both address these threats and find other ways to achieve exposure.

The Concept

Crafting an effective marketing plan can mean the difference between a hit and a flop. Sometimes the target market is obvious—such as selling a record in the young children's category to parents and teachers. In less obvious cases, labels may enlist market research to help understand and identify the target groups most likely to buy. Narrowing the marketing aim to a target audience means marketing sources are focused on the demographic most likely to respond, which results in less wastage of resources on unresponsive consumers.

At this early stage, the company's marketing people try to come up with a **hook** that will bait potential audiences, which market research may later explore in greater detail. Those invited to help formulate the hook and the resulting marketing plan might include the artist's manager, the producer, the head of marketing, the art director, the heads of promotion and publicity for the label, and the A&R (artist and repertoire) representative.

The Marketing Team

Larger labels may include in their marketing departments the following personnel:

- Marketing executives. Responsible for conception and execution of sales campaigns and providing sales aids to distributors and retailers

- Radio promoters. Responsible for gaining exposure on the radio
- Publicists. Responsible for getting stories, reviews, and news releases to print and broadcast media
- Advertising managers. Responsible for the conception, production, and placement of ads in print, digital media, radio, and TV

Campaign Management. Most labels assign one individual—the **product manager**—to manage a marketing campaign. These managers receive a budget from the company and are expected to oversee a promotion strategy, coordinate the various departments (marketing, radio promotion, publicity, and advertising) and execute the marketing plan. They may also have the responsibility of assigning promotion personnel to certain geographic areas and coordinating the efforts of staff promoters working out of the label's branch offices. Product managers designate timing of the campaign and how much attention and emphasis it is to receive.

Product managers also keep track of which radio and TV outlets are adding or dropping the new release. If they observe good airplay developing in a particular geographic area, they may double efforts there in an attempt to develop a regional hit. They then alert the marketing and distribution departments of the new regional radio acceptance to ensure that sufficient product is in retail **channels** to meet the possible demand caused by the airplay. The sales team documents airplay popularity that is in turn presented to retailers to convince them to stock and promote the music product.

Product managers follow the progress of a new release on the trade charts and collect point-of-sale (POS) reports for CDs and sales of digital downloads. Information on the entry, rise, and fall of a recording via these metrics provides guidance on how to spend (or withdraw) the money available for a campaign.

The Elements of a Marketing Plan

The Strategy

A marketing plan is a broad strategy to convince a target audience to buy. It can contain many elements, depending on the concept, the nature of the target market, and the budget. One element is promotions, which are one-time special efforts that communicate marketing messages, typically in conjunction with other parties. Promotions can include temporary in-store displays marking an album's release; events mounted with media outlets such as a music magazine, record store, soft drink company, or cellular phone provider; and "street teams" of hired staff creating awareness in public places of urban areas. Another element is publicity, aimed at nudging journalists in radio, TV, magazines, newspapers, and Web sites to create editorial content discussing artists and their music. A third element is paid advertising, which tends to be a relatively small effort for music. Paid ads may appear in magazines, radio, cable TV, and digital media.

Once the label crafts the marketing concept, certain basic steps follow, regardless of budget: The art (or creative services) department renders sketches for cover art and one-sheet promotion pieces, a photographer or other artist is engaged, the copy is written, and the **mechanical** (assembled graphic elements—not to be confused with *mechanical royalties*) is rendered. But that's just the beginning.

Radio Promotion

Although radio is no longer as dominant an influence on record sales as it was a half-century ago, it is still a heavyweight medium for promotion. Every day radio exposes millions of potential music buyers to countless musical experiences. But radio is no easy challenge for promoters vying for airplay. Fearful that unfamiliar artists and their music will turn listeners away, radio outlets restrict their playlists and are cautious about new and untested sounds. Out of hundreds of new songs available each week, many stations will only add two or three, if that many.

Large record companies employ a staff of full-time people to handle promotion in-house. Outside (independent) promoters may also be used; however, this type of promotion is so expensive that record companies may negotiate recoupment of some or all independent promotion expenses against future artist royalties.

Promoters must decide on the station musical styles or formats that would be most appropriate in promoting the recording. Station formats are either singles-based or album-based. For example, a singles-based format such as Top 40 radio requires the label to choose a specific song from the album to promote to the panel of stations in that format. If the format is album-based, such as for college radio, the panel of stations wants the whole album delivered, and each station chooses the track or tracks it prefers to program.

Reporting Stations. Promoters focus nearly all their attention on reporting stations—that is, outlets that the trade papers, electronic song-tracking services, and tip sheets monitor to learn which songs have been programmed. Note: Although all reporting radio stations are monitored, not all monitored stations are considered reporting stations, mostly because the music they play is not considered current enough to be useful for charts (e.g., "oldies" stations, adult contemporary stations, some country stations). Tip sheets are e-mails or faxed commentaries of interest to programmers from independent analysts about trends and specific songs. Years ago, some tip sheets were highly influential, but as available music research data improved the value of such third-party analysis has declined.

If an unheralded new release lands in the midrange of a national chart, the promotion people more often than not have a hit on their hands. At this point, most record companies accelerate their efforts, instructing their label's regional promotion staff to intensify their campaigns for airplay. The promotion staff is now in a position to prove the claim that the new release, which is starting to break nationally, has strong hit potential. At this point, radio station programmers who were too timid weeks ago to take a chance on the new release may now be persuaded to jump on this potential hit. Sometimes there is a catch to this. Occasionally, the broadcast successes yield only **turntable hits**: A recording manages to get good airplay, but audiences just don't buy it. No one has come up with a satisfactory explanation for the turntable hit phenomenon.

To gain the confidence of radio program directors (PDs), promoters must establish a reputation for credibility. What the PD needs most is useful information—research, not fast talk. The station needs to know whether a new release fits its programming and whether it is gaining airplay elsewhere. It also wants to know a release's overall ranking with the rest of the records getting researched; it wants to know the release's "burn factor"—do people really want to hear it more?

If a promoter cannot provide these assurances to the station, there is one other hope: The music might appeal to the personal tastes of the PD or musical director. Occasionally, these decision makers will program a new release just because they like it, but few outlets permit personal tastes to have too much influence on these important decisions. That influence is now even more limited with the advent of the group PD—a single PD responsible for a group of stations in a format or clustered geographically.

Mailings, Telephone Follow-Ups. Because only a small number of stations can be reached by personal contacts, promoters mail and e-mail free promotional copies to a larger number of outlets. The risk of this approach is the scant attention mailings from labels and promoters receive, as PDs are inundated with such airplay requests.

Mail campaigns need to be followed up by telephone calls ("Hello, Frank. Did you get my e-mail? How'd you like the song? What did you find time to listen to? What have you added? No? How about next week? So-and-so is breaking big in Toledo; you won't want to miss out on it. How can I help you . . . ?" and so on). The success of this kind of telephone call follow-up depends not only on the suitability of the recordings mailed but also on the rapport between the caller and the station programmer.

Payola. The correlation between record sales and radio play has led to many eras of abuse. The first well-known cases of employees of a radio station taking money or favors in exchange for airplay or chart position surfaced in the 1950s. Although there was a very public trial and condemnation of the practice of "pay for play," new ways of corrupting the air ensued.

Using a third-party independent promoter tended to insulate the client record label from direct involvement in seamy practices, and third parties might presumably be more willing to stretch the rules than staff employees of labels. But using such third parties hasn't always protected labels from liability. For example, in 2005 and 2006, three major record companies agreed to pay the New York attorney general a total of $27 million to resolve payola charges. Some of the abuses involved individuals who portrayed themselves as music consultants to radio stations, but in fact were also getting consideration from record labels for programming their product. Unfortunately, the practice muddies the waters for honest radio consultants who operate without conflicts of interest.

Beyond Terrestrial Radio

As AM and FM radio have become more difficult to break into in recent decades, other media have emerged as promotion platforms for new music. Satellite radio—typically a monthly subscription service with relatively deep playlists—boasts many genre-specific channels that must be filled with music. Digital cable music channels and Internet radio also add promotional punch. Cable video music channels are another key target for promotion, where an attention-grabbing video can support a new audio release.

Sometimes dance clubs have been effective places to test or showcase new recordings. Prior to commercial release, labels may remix a single into a longer version favored by dancers, and then get it into clubs to test patrons' reactions. If the clubs report a strong response, the label will be encouraged to launch a general commercial release.

Publicity

Many record companies handle their publicity activities in-house; others have only a small resident staff and engage publicists and public relations (**PR**) firms to help out. A small label may depend totally on an outside firm or independent publicist for PR.

The publicity campaign attempts to create a buzz that convinces magazines, newspapers, and Web sites to publish content on a record release, a process that may begin when the artist gives an interview. The campaign also includes booking personal appearances on TV, radio, and Webcasts. In a technique known as the "satellite tour," the artist conducts a series of interviews with different stations back to back over several hours, all the while sitting in a single studio with a satellite uplink.

Among the more desired media outlets are the traditional media—the print magazines—and their associated Web sites. Monthly print magazines have a lead time of 3 to 4 months, (for example, stories for the June issue are written in February or March), so any hope of securing a cover or feature story starts well before an album hits stores and download platforms.

Dailies and weeklies (newspapers and the weekly arts publications) are other types of publications available. These publications tend to focus on local artists and artists playing concerts in the area.

Fanzines are publications with a relatively small consumer base, usually written and published by a fan of an artist or style of music. Although not as widely circulated, the readership includes more proactive consumers.

Internet sites represent a wide spectrum of publications from polished professional content to from-the-gut blogs.

Advertising

While publicity is desirable because the cost to the label is relatively low, paid advertising has the potential advantage of yielding a large number of controlled **impressions**. Large labels find it profitable, from time to time, to place ads in mass print media—mostly magazines and newspapers. But in general the music industry has not found multi-million dollar ad campaigns to be cost-effective. So while movie distributors buy ads in TV's most expensive platform—the Super Bowl telecast—music labels do not (although top acts may get free exposure in the half-time show).

Most consumer advertising is either paid for by the label (and doesn't mention a specific retailer carrying the release) or is **cooperative,** in which case the cooperating retailer is listed in the ad and either pays part of the ad cost directly with cash or indirectly by meeting certain inventory ordering requirements.

Another type of advertising is trade advertising. The label places an ad in publications and Web sites aimed at companies within the industry—not consumers. It could be as all-encompassing of the music industry as *Billboard* or as specific as *Pollstar* for the live entertainment industry. These ads help in both promoting the release and confirming to the music industry community the label's commitment to its artist. Marketers use the expression *pull-through* to describe advertising or promotion that induces consumers to buy, and *push-through* to describe advertising that induces retailers or distributors to order merchandise to put on sale.

Digital Marketing

Promotion, publicity, and advertising efforts are typically handled by different professionals who are specialists in each discipline. But these efforts often converge under a multi-prong approach that we might call *digital marketing*. First, there's the standard publicity outreach by press releases to Web sites. A second push places content—such as videos—in digital media where the labels can generate money in return. Labels sometimes have revenue-sharing deals for ads placed in and around their content, which means they earn a trickle of revenue even as the content publicizes a new release. In a third prong, labels might buy some digital media ads on platforms with which they have formal, but noncash, promotional tie-ins.

The publicity, promotion, and paid ads are usually part of a grand plan, and this deliberate interlocking of elements is called *marketing integration.* The belief is that interconnected efforts will drive traffic to digital media placements that might otherwise be ignored, and this integration—elements feeding off each other—is far better than a broadly focused, scatter-shot approach. Integration can combine traditional and digital media—for example, a paid ad placement in a print magazine that directs readers to a Web site.

Another of the plan's goals is to make digital media interactive. The media may be seeded with content that users can customize through modification: Consumers may e-mail to friends music content that they've altered, which serves as a form of viral media. Since the activity of Web site and e-mail users can often be counted, labels and artists can measure the popularity of individual elements, such as various types of merchandise. Another type of interaction is the forum in which consumers can post comments. "Fans want to chime in," says one music marketing executive. "They no longer just want to listen passively. They want to be an active part of the culture of their bands."

Labels and DIY artists are constantly coming up with new digital marketing approaches. Table 16.1 summarizes common techniques.

International Promotion

Multinational recording companies may spend more money and effort promoting releases abroad than they do domestically because the foreign market is a patchwork of territories, each requiring individualized—and often costly—attention. A multinational label must determine whether to have a foreign release occur simultaneously with the U.S. release or whether to test the audience response in the United States (or in another territory) before rolling it out globally. With pervasive record piracy, the trend for some time has been to release simultaneously so that legitimate music is available as an alternative to unauthorized versions. In fact, the artist's recording contract may specify the countries where the label is to make recordings available simultaneously with domestic release.

Foreign promotions cannot be handled like those in the United States. The big record companies have staffed affiliates in 40 to 50 foreign territories that have the responsibility of releasing and promoting the firm's product. In all these territories, differences in the radio landscape, satellite and cable availability, law, language, culture, and buying power require different approaches. Among the strongest foreign markets for breaking new U.S. recordings are the Netherlands, the United Kingdom, Germany, Japan, Australia, and France (see Chapter 29).

Record Distribution

Once the master is at a replication facility and the promotion and advertising teams have sparked interest in a new release, the label must find a way to get the product to potential customers—wherever they may be, at the right time, and through the most effective distribution channels. Distribution of physical product has become increasingly challenging with the decline of traditional record retailers. This

Table 16.1   A Dozen Digital Marketing Opportunities

E-mail lists assembled by label. E-mails are most useful if the label's music is focused by genre, because the audience is then potentially predisposed to all the music offered. E-mails usually contain multiple hyperlinks to third-party pages related to the label's acts. To spur consumer interest to actually open the e-mail, contests and prizes are often offered.

E-mail lists assembled by the artist. Because they are associated with the talent, these are opened far more often than e-mails from labels or corporate entities and are less likely to get caught in users' spam filters. Artist e-mails can be a jumping-off point for powerful viral buzz if forwarded to a user's acquaintances because the endorsement comes from a personal friend. These e-mails can carry photos, touring news, snippets of songs, and links to radio stations where fans can ask for songs to be added to playlists. Artists often let labels step in to manage and market to these lists because labels may have greater expertise and resources.

Label Web sites: These tend to present brief explanations of albums and bands in a brochure-like format. Links to related third-party Web sites are essential to get users more deeply immersed.

Artist Web sites: Fans demand to voice their views, so an essential element is the capability to host discussions where users can post comments and band members provide blog commentaries. Content such as news and photos should be more personal than that found on a label or third-party Web site.

Third-party Web sites. These run the gamut from music sections of general portals like Yahoo, to music fan Web sites, to Web sites of music publications. Artists get exposure through "news" about live appearances, upcoming albums, touring, and lifestyle tidbits such as travel and recording activities. Well-known artists and their labels want to strike promotion partnerships with high-traffic Web sites which allow them to broaden their Web circulation, since label and artist Web sites have limited audiences.

Blogs. Many music bloggers have established Web traffic that makes them useful for publicity and promotions. Journalists and DJs tend to be prolific bloggers.

Video Web sites. The typical starting point is to place videos on YouTube, MTV, and/or AOL, and then to drive traffic to them via links. This raises music video rankings in search engine popularity lists. These lists are based on user clicks and activity from user-posted commentaries. The ad-revenue sharing deals offered by hosts help shape label decisions about where to concentrate promotion for label videos.

Online music stores. Many download retailers like iTunes closely manage their environment, so few opportunities exist to barge in with ad hoc publicity. The only real publicity options come through formal joint promotion deals. Emerging bands can make headway with The Orchard, ioda, Tune Core, SirGroovy, and others, which usually work with emerging bands and independent labels lacking significant in-house digital operations to circulate music on cyberspace.

Social Web sites. Most artists have official presence on MySpace, Facebook, and Twitter, which are prized because they have huge built-in audiences. The ability to feed a stream of personal comments gives Twitter a blog-like capability. Content is usually a mixture of professional and personal news that fits the social atmosphere.

Search engine marketing. Labels optimize Web sites to pull traffic and will buy key words if a new release has potential to attract a new audience.

Cellular phones. Providers tightly control their online music stores and Web page environments, leaving formal promotions the best avenue. Labels can provide exclusive content like songs or negotiate for artist appearances in phone ads or promotions.

Virtual worlds. The publicity platforms of online worlds have an uneven track record in pulling in consumers.

once-dominant channel was buffeted toward the end of the 20th century by mass merchants and giant bookstores with music sections. And it only got tougher from there. In recent years, brick-and-mortar retailers have had to compete not only with illegally streamed or downloaded music, but also with the rise of legal online services offered by new entrants.

In general distribution efforts, labels distribute CDs and other offline products in specialty record/DVD/game stores, supermarkets, mass merchants, and discount stores. Distribution and wholesaling is a challenging business because a great deal of capital can be tied up in massive inventory, profit margins tend to be slim, and there are many thousands of unique products (called stock-keeping units, or **SKU**s) that must be provided to retailers quickly and efficiently. Several kinds of distribution and wholesaling organizations may serve as intermediaries to get merchandise to those who actually sell the product to consumers. After many years of trial and error, even major labels are still trying to figure out a better distribution system. (Figure 16.1 illustrates several pathways for merchandise to reach the end user.)

Types of Distributors

Majors. A handful of major multinational distributors are integrated with the biggest record companies (as outlined in Chapter 15). These behemoths serve as umbrella organizations for a large number of labels, collectively accounting for the lion's share of records sold in the United States. These majors offer merchandise through their own far-flung distribution organizations, historically characterized by large staffs located in branch offices. Major distributor branch offices normally have two divisions. One handles regional promotion; the other concerns itself with distribution and sales. The distributor's promotion staff coordinates with the promotion staff of each label.

Figure 16.1   Record Distribution and Retailing

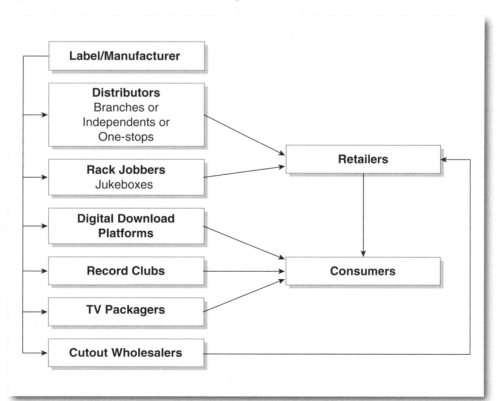

Independents. The majors don't do it all. A small but significant share of the business is in the hands of independent distributors who provide services for hundreds of independent labels and artists who release their own recordings. Independents, who don't handle product sourced from the majors, usually provide promotion services as well. Most have a staff that calls or visits retailers, delivers merchandise, sets up store displays, makes deals with Web sites for music downloads, and operates online music sales operations—much like the major label branch offices do.

One-Stops. In the 1940s, distributors called **one-stops** formed to offer a full music product line to jukebox operators and small retailers that could not get the attention of the big labels or big wholesalers. They handled merchandise delivery and setup of in-store promotions to mom-and-pop stores. One-stops typically sold product (sourced from major labels and some independents) in low volume at high unit prices. In recent years, they declined as their customer base shrank.

Rack Jobbers. This is a service business that selects titles and places shelves in stores. Consumers patronizing the stores don't realize that the music racks are the property and responsibility of an unseen third party that is either subleasing the space or otherwise splitting the revenue with the host merchant. Rack jobbers historically have serviced retail categories where music is ancillary to the host merchant's main business—such as department stores, convenience stores, and car washes. Today rack jobbers are more common in specialized niches, such as offering Latin product to retailers catering to Hispanic clientele.

Retail Merchandising

From the distributor or label warehouse, the physical goods flow to retailers. Retail competition is bruising, and nimble retail managers are constantly juggling the dollars set aside to buy inventory (called "open to buy"), scrambling to advertise and build excitement in the store, and setting prices that will allow them to protect market share (by being low enough) and profit margins (by being high enough). Winning is by no means guaranteed. The categories of retailers that dominate the business have shifted dramatically over the years (see Figure 16.2 for sales by type of outlet).

Mass Merchant Chain Stores

The same "big box" transformation in retail that has swept over many kinds of merchandise has remade the landscape of music retailing. As recently as the 1990s, the majority of CDs and pre-recorded cassettes were purchased at independent or chain record stores. Since then, mass merchants such as Wal-Mart, Best Buy, and bookstores have commanded the lion's share of the business. Iconic record retail brands such as Tower Records, Sam Goody, and Virgin Megastore shriveled away under the pressure.

The mass merchants—which are now the masters of retailing in the brick-and-mortar arena—have amassed such clout that in many cases they can dictate prices. They can even demand changes in the music itself to meet the objections of their core middle-market audience, such as revised versions of CDs that don't contain crude lyrics. The major labels tend to sell direct to the mass merchants, thereby eliminating the expense of a middleman wholesaler.

Reflecting this transfer of marketplace clout, some big acts agree to release their CDs only through a single mass merchant, or to give the mass merchant an exclusive

Figure 16.2 Record Distribution and Retailing

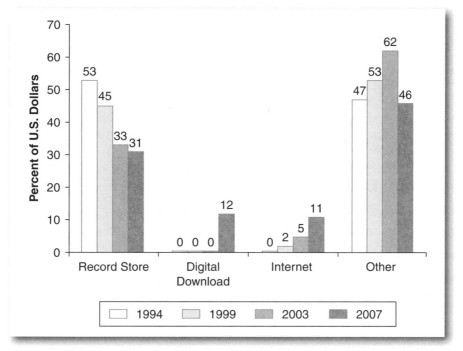

Note: Internet includes online retailers like Amazon. *Other* includes mass merchants, mail order, clubs, and other minor categories.

Source: Analysis of Recording Industry Association of America data from telephone surveys of past-month music buyers.

early window. In exchange, the mass merchant agrees to accept a large quantity of CDs with no or limited returns of unsold merchandise. (Under normal circumstances, returns might run to 20% or more of the original orders.) Irrespective of marketing requirements specified in contracts, retailers are under pressure to give such albums heavy promotion to make sure they aren't stuck with unsold quantities. Sometimes, the exclusivity is for CDs only and the same music is widely available for downloading at the same time.

Top acts that have mounted exclusive CD retailing deals with Wal-Mart include Bruce Springsteen, the Eagles, AC/DC, Garth Brooks, and Journey. Springsteen later expressed regret because of Wal-Mart's labor practices, but not its sales clout. Target snared Christine Aguilera and Prince for exclusive CD deals. The Guns N' Roses agreement with Best Buy was said not to have been a success.

From time to time, labels have tried special tie-ups with other kinds of retailers, such as a coffee chain. Though in some instances these deals have paid off, such outlets can stock only a limited number of titles and provide at best only a small boost to the overall music industry.

Entertainment Retailers

The type of retailer that once fueled the recorded music business—the record store—has been on a long slide toward obsolescence. The surviving specialty record stores of yore have largely evolved into mass merchants of another stripe—broader-based entertainment software chains with DVD, game, and music product on their shelves. This kind of retailer may be categorized in industry statistics as a record store, but recorded music might not constitute the majority of its sales. One reason traditional record-only specialty stores declined is that they cannot buy enough stock to receive an adequate discount from distributors. In turn, this means they cannot discount their retail prices to compete with mass merchants.

One type of relatively small record store may prosper when it is well managed: the proprietor who earns the confidence of a small but loyal clientele, and stocks the particular kind of music that appeals to that community—such as blues, urban, Asian, or classical. Some such battles for retail survival are being won, but the war to preserve the traditional neighborhood record retailer is largely lost.

Digital Distribution

Once perceived as only a threat to the legitimate business, online music has evolved to become a significant channel for legitimate distribution. Whether downloaded or streamed, sold by subscription or by track or by album, experienced through a handheld device or a desktop computer, online music commands a respectable share of total recorded music revenue. Subscriptions offer unlimited access to a specified pool of music for a flat monthly fee.

In another variation on the business model, the access may be free to the user, with the labels receiving a share of the advertising revenue generated by the Web site hosting the service. Over the years several pioneering entrepreneurs offered such services, but success has been elusive. Services have experimented with custom Web players/browsers that expose users to advertising, and have employed DRM technology to induce the cooperation of major labels. None of these advertising-supported approaches have come close to filling the revenue gap triggered by the decline in brick-and-mortar sales.

Some digital media outlets also sell physical CDs and thus follow in the steps of yesteryear's mail order (when orders were made by phone or mail instead of via a Web site). Digital media outlets include iTunes, Napster, Rhapsody, Zune, Yahoo, T-mobile, Verizon Wireless, YouTube, MySpace Music, and Amazon.com. Traditional brick-and-mortar retailers, including mass merchants, have also got into the act by offering an online service to complement their storefronts.

Music Clubs

The traditional record and book clubs historically offered physical media at low prices to "members" who agreed to buy a certain quantity. Pioneering the music club sector was Columbia House Records, which launched in 1955 when it was owned by broadcaster CBS. RCA and then Capitol Records quickly followed in establishing record clubs. When record clubs began, retailers threatened court action, arguing that a big company pushing sales of only its own label through the mail constituted unfair competition and restraint of trade. Columbia responded by expanding its club offerings to include products from other labels. Today, the traditional music club model incorporating expensive direct mail solicitations has been largely eclipsed by other distribution channels, including downloads and physical CDs sold via the Web.

Parent Advisory Label

Labeling music to identify crude content is an on-and-off hot-button issue for the music industry. The Recording Industry Association of America (RIAA) created the Parent Advisory Label (PAL) as "a notice to consumers that recordings identified by this logo may contain strong language or depictions of violence, sex or substance abuse. Parental discretion is advised."

The Web site of RIAA states that in some instances, record companies ask an artist to rerecord certain songs or to revise lyrics because a creative and responsible view of the music demands such a revision. Sometimes songs are simply removed from an album altogether. In other instances, the artist and the record company agree that there is musical and artistic credibility in the whole of the work even when the lyrics may be too explicit for mainstream distribution.

When lyrics are flagged, the RIAA's PAL logo is typically applied prominently to the outside of the permanent packaging. The logo or a similar PAL notice may also appear in advertising for the sound recording, and throughout online

Photo by Robert P. Marich.

and mobile products or services that allow consumers to receive and play a sound recording on their personal computer or mobile device.

Labeling to advise parents began in 1985 under pressure from a consumer group and U.S. Senate hearings on songs with crude lyrics. These days, it is estimated that less than 5% of albums carry PAL warnings. While the music industry addressed the issue, in general the music industry exerts less self-restraint than the movie/DVD and video game industries. Indeed, while labels work out content problems with acts *after* albums are recorded, film director employment contracts routinely specify that directors deliver a movie that will achieve a specified audience classification. In addition, the movie industry goes to great lengths to "grade" all its releases with audience ratings.

Cutouts and Repackaging

Consumers are always looking for bargains, and so there is a lively niche market selling deeply discounted music, known as **cutouts**. These can include excess CDs from current titles and also familiar oldies with low or no royalties payable to the artists (thereby facilitating the low pricing). Cutout middlemen buy discounted music at warehouses which they sell at low prices to stores or place on rack job displays. The retail outlets include discount dollar stores, regular convenience stores, restaurants, car washes, and truck stops.

For years, cutout merchants and repackagers have been able to sell "rereleases" or "new" releases of the big name band hits of the 1940s and genre compilations such as *Monster Metal Ballads of the 1980s.* Perennial repertoire also comes from early rock-and-roll hits and reissues of country music. Direct response marketers buy relatively cheap ad inventory and typically acquire merchandise at a discount from normal wholesale pricing. The resulting commercials are well known to TV viewers who suffer from insomnia.

Retail Terms and Inducements

The industry has generally offered retailers generous returns policies, allowing the return of a substantial portion of purchases for credit, ranging up to 100%, if the goods don't sell. This practice is expensive for labels but does tend to keep bins stocked. By federal law, distributors cannot give individual direct accounts special discounts. All must get the same discount offer, though the value of that discount will vary depending mostly on volume. Labels can, however, offer more co-op advertising or prerelease exclusivity to selected retailers.

Record companies, of course, always want eye-catching placement within the store. Once a recording is out of a routine location such as alphabetical bins, labels believe a consumer is more apt to make an impulse purchase—the same principle that leads to a candy display at the supermarket checkout counter. Many retailers offer a variety of opportunities for a label to purchase what is referred to as "price and positioning." Most of these programs include having CDs both on sale and in a special location. Some examples of store-level price and positioning are listening stations or kiosks and the **end caps**, or racks at the end of aisles or in prominent locations in the store where a SKU will be on display at a sale price. Sometimes these end caps promote multiple SKUs and have a theme, such as "music of the holidays" or "June is blues month."

In addition to price and positioning, record companies may try to have point-of-purchase (POP) displays set up in the retail store, announcing the availability of product. POP displays might include one-sheet posters, banners, cardboard stand-ups, special display racks, window displays, flags and streamers, and perhaps souvenir items (nicknamed "swag") that the merchant can give away. POP displays can be costly to distribute, and thus the technique isn't universally employed. Some retailers view POP displays as a distraction, and won't accept them from manufacturers even if they are free.

Sometimes a retailer gives a release better positioning in exchange for free or discounted CDs to sell. These CDs are referred to as "cleans" because they are "clean" of any of the markings they would have if they were for promotional use only. "Promos" are altered or labeled in some other way, indicating that they are not for sale to the public.

In 2000, major labels were forced to loosen a restrictive policy known as MAP (minimum advertised pricing). MAP had been used by the labels to protect smaller retailers from a rapid erosion in market share. MAP had restricted large discount retailers from undercutting smaller merchants by threatening those outlets that broke MAP policies (such as price floors) with a temporary suspension of co-op advertising funds. With the threat of MAP sanctions softened, smaller retailers continued to decline.

National Association of Recording Merchandisers

The National Association of Recording Merchandisers (NARM) is the trade association that represents the recorded music distribution industry. Key activities include lobbying local, state, and federal authorities on legislative matters, and providing a myriad of information resources to members.

Benefits of membership include an annual convention and other events, marketing research, an online database of product releases, and a Web site listing upcoming titles.

There are three broad categories of membership:

1. *General members:* This category includes retailers, direct mailers, telecommunications carriers that resell entertainment, and wholesalers such as rack jobbers, one-stops, and independent distributors.

2. *Associate members:* This category includes labels and other vendors, software and hardware manufacturers, and various service providers such as operators of digital distribution platforms.

3. *Individual members:* Anyone whose business activity, client, or consultative relationship is involved with the music retailing community may join. In addition, any current full-time college student or educator in an accredited institution of education whose primary area of study includes music, business, marketing, research, or recording technology is eligible for membership.

Chapter Takeaways

- When planning a campaign, label marketers should employ a SWOT analysis—examining strengths, weaknesses, opportunities, and threats.

- Promoters spend considerable effort to convince radio stations to add new records to playlists, hoping to alert music lovers to a new title's availability.

- Successful publicity campaigns, prized because they can be inexpensive to execute, often hinge on getting artist interviews in print and electronic media.

- Paid advertising can augment a marketing campaign, but often is secondary to promotion and publicity.

- Multinational record companies dominate distribution of music, but independent distributors and other wholesalers fill vital roles in feeding product to retailers.

- Over the years "big box" mass merchants and entertainment software chains have eclipsed the role of the once-common neighborhood record store.

Key Terms

- airplay (p. 289)
- cleans (p. 300)
- co-op (p. 300)
- cutouts (p. 299)
- end cap (p. 300)
- MAP (p. 300)
- marketing hook (p. 288)
- marketing integration (p. 293)
- NARM (p. 300)

- open to buy (p. 296)
- Parent Advisory Label (p. 299)
- payola (p. 291)
- playlist (p. 290)
- price and positioning (p. 300)
- product manager (p. 289)
- pull-through (p. 292)
- push-through (p. 292)
- returns (p. 297)

- satellite tour (p. 292)
- SKU (p. 295)
- SWOT (p. 288)
- turntable hit (p. 290)

CHAPTER 17

Record Markets

Understanding the Consumer

For decades, recorded music was strictly a creative-driven business where the emphasis was on the song and artist. The philosophy was if a label got those two things right, music sales would surely follow. Labels treated radio stations as their most relevant customer, with little interest or understanding of the identity of music buyers—the folks who actually plunked down the money to purchase their products.

Technology has changed all that, for two reasons. First, the art and science of market research became more sophisticated, enabling stakeholders to ask and receive better answers to questions about consumer behavior and attitudes. And second, new distribution technology threatened the business model of selling physical media, forcing labels especially to fight harder, and smarter, for every dollar.

> *"Music critics get their records for free so their opinions usually don't matter."*
>
> *—Marilyn Manson*

Until the 1990s, research of record "sales" data was generally imprecise and too often failed to make clear the distinctions between the figures for merchandise actually sold and the huge amounts of unsold stock returned by retailers. Whole genres and stylistic trends were under- or over-reported, questionable "hits" climbed the charts in mysterious ways, and misleading manipulation of the crude methodology was commonplace. Part of the problem was that the estimates were projected from a retail sample that was neither randomized nor big enough.

Left: Grammy Award ®© NARAS.

Photo used with permission of the National Academy of Recording Arts & Sciences, Inc.

But research tools and sample bases improved steadily. In the first decade of the 21st century, labels under financial pressure were forced to better understand music consumers. This meant not only catering to active record buyers but also looking for niches where new demand could be spurred by a combination of delivering to specific kinds of fans the right kind of music, pricing, promotion, and retailing.

Most consumer research in music falls into three general categories. First, there are sales surveys measuring unit sales (such as a count of albums or singles) and/or revenue (expressed in dollars). This information is delivered on a corporate subscription basis so industry players receive a steady stream of data. Second, there are consumer attitude research reports that may be **one-off** or infrequent (such as quarterly) that typically mesh findings from consumer interviews with sales data.

The final category is "custom research" where an entity such as a trade group or record label (or in some cases a small consortium) picks a topic and then hires a research company for the project. The report won't be sold to others. Sometimes, a custom research report interviews new consumers or analyzes census behavior. It can also be a "special sort," pulling out a narrow slice from an existing database. For example, a sort might compile a report on R&B/urban album sales at specialty record stores in the Midwest over the past 10 years. Another might be on cities where country music accounts for more than 15% of all music sales. In essence, the special sort is tailored to illuminate whatever initiative the custom-report buyer is pursuing.

Methodologies vary. Techniques include tracking transactions at the point of sale (POS)—such as scanning a bar code at a cash register or counting an iTunes download—interviewing consumers individually in a mall, gathering several consumers in one place for a focus group, having consumers fill out an online survey, or interrupting the evening meal with an intrusive telephone call.

Users of consumer research include record labels, music wholesalers, music distributors, performing artists, personal managers, booking agents, retail stores, new media commerce outfits, concert promoters, concert venue operators, and the investment community. A key point of contention is who sets the research agenda and who owns and controls the data, often determined by who owns the customer relationship.

Research Topics

The Charts

The growing music industry interest in consumer research replaces a fixation for decades on measuring music popularity solely by *the charts,* which are lists of most popular music typically associated with trade publications. *Billboard* publishes the most widely quoted charts. Nearly every category of music has its own chart, some more than one. Even foreign sales get the chart treatment. Some charts indicate only **airplay**; others list only estimates of sales. Some charts combine this data and formulate overall rankings.

In 1991, *Billboard* began producing catalog title charts featuring older music. This was soon followed by the Heatseekers chart, devoted to new and developing artists who have never reached the top of *Billboard*'s 200, R&B, or country charts. In 2004, the magazine introduced the *Billboard* Buzz Top 25, which is based not on sales or airplay but on Internet surveys of music fans. Other charts rank ringtones, concerts, music videos, and digital downloads.

When the popularity of pay-per-download services such as Apple's iTunes and Napster 2.0 helped revive the single in 2003, *Billboard* introduced the Hot Digital Songs chart to monitor sales of downloads.

Demographics

The most important yardstick for analyzing the marketplace is the characteristics of consumers—age, gender, ethnicity, income, geographical location, etc. This is called **demographic** information, referred to in research as "demos" (and is in no way related to "demos" that are demonstration recordings shopped to labels by acts seeking recording contracts!). For example, the Recording Industry Association of America (RIAA) will sometimes conduct surveys on the buying activity of specific age groups. In this case, their research indicates that the biggest buying age blocs are 15–19 years, 35–39 years, and 10–14 years. Music buying falls off after age 40. (See Figure 17.1.)

By putting a microscope on the different demographic segments, marketers glean insights into slices of music buyers to target them efficiently. This represents a major mind-shift from the music industry's traditional mass-market approach. If labels can identify and sell effectively to the consumer niches, perhaps niches can be piled up on a brick-by-brick basis to increase overall music sales. It sounds simple to target consumer segments. But the trick is to understand consumers and their behavior in order to minimize marketing and distribution waste when selling music, otherwise the smallish consumer niches are too expensive to address.

Record Categorization

It's easier to describe something, and thus to sell it, if it fits into a neat category. That's one reason music industry charts tend to put music into genre categories. When

Figure 17.1 Recorded Music Purchases by Age: Percent of Dollar Volume

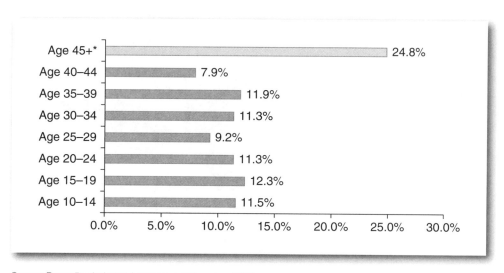

Source: Recording Industry Association of America, 2007.

*Age 45+ is a wider age range than other bars, and thus is not directly comparable.

categorizing an album for playlists or retail, a primary genre is initially assumed, and the music is placed on the corresponding chart. This is done, in part, so that media outlets playing that particular type of music can feel ownership of the album. However, if the album gains popularity on outlets featuring other genres, the album is then "crossed over" to one or more additional charts. If a recording is crossing over from one category to another, it might rank Number 5 on the Hot 100 chart, Number 10 on Adult Contemporary, and perhaps Number 40 on the Country chart.

Regardless of the category selected for a particular song or recording, one thing is certain: The public does not really care. For many years, the record-buying public has repeatedly demonstrated that it is attracted by the sound of the music, not its type, and the clearest evidence of the public's disinterest in categories is the crossover recording. Many superhits today are crossover—or *multiformat*—recordings, achieving multimillion-selling status by picking up listeners crossing traditional lines.

New categories of recordings are always finding new markets to exploit. A good example of this would be children's recordings, which used to be one of the smaller markets but has grown to be very important, as seen in Figure 17.2.

Stylistic Preferences

Because pop music is in a state of constant development and change, acts—particularly in the pop, rock, and hip-hop fields—can go from star to has-been status, sometimes within the same year. Artists who attach themselves to musical trends (or who are marketed that way by their recording companies) are often washed up once the public tires of the trend. Those artists who show the ability to transcend trends tend to have the longest and most successful careers.

Figure 17.2 Consumer Music Preferences by Genre: Percent of Dollar Volume

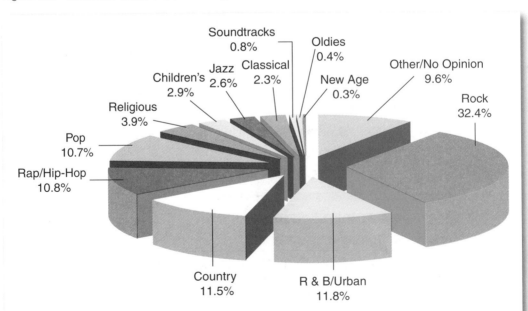

Source: Recording Industry Association of America, 2007.

Sometimes, however, shifts in the musical climate are too dramatic for artists to significantly navigate. For example, when Beatlemania hit America in the mid-1960s, pop crooners such as Bobby Darin and the Four Seasons saw their fan base virtually disappear overnight. Similarly in the early 1990s, Nirvana's punk-influenced grunge sound made the slick pop-metal of bands like Poison and Warrant immediately passé. While musical trends come and go, some show such staying power that they are absorbed into the culture. For example, when rap music first hit the scene in the early 1980s, many pundits wrote it off as nothing more than a passing trend. Decades later, hip-hop continues to be a popular musical genre.

Changing Research Topics

Today, charts, demographics, and stylistic preferences are only a small part of the research story. With new-century shifts in the industry, the research spotlight shines on areas neglected in an earlier era.

A big area of research is music consumption in new media, a field that allows companies to determine where to make music available in the digital world and how to price it to maximize revenue and profit. Advances in technology allow many actions of a Web surfer to be monitored so, in the online area at least, it is possible to build a vast historical record of detailed consumer activity. One drawback is that identities of Web surfers might not be known, so activity can't always be matched up with consumer demographics. (Of course, for privacy advocates, this drawback is a safeguard against abuse.)

College students make up an audience segment of particular interest. They are big consumers of music and have a propensity to use the latest media technology, which makes them trendsetters. Yet, they are a difficult audience to research as access to university e-mails is restricted and students are usually just seasonal residents at their schools.

Pricing and what consumers value in terms of product offers form another field of keen study. In the digital era, a lot can be bundled in a music product purchase: coupons for ringtones, coupons for free or discounted digital music downloads, online fan club subscriptions tied to artists, online commerce selling band and album merchandise, discounts to concert tickets, and, of course, CDs.

Data Sources

The recording industry uses a variety of methods to elicit data. Below are the often-used research services noted for their music-specific data. Additionally, the music industry buys consumer research from BigChampagne, comScore, Forrester Research (which acquired JupiterResearch), Gartner, Hitwise, and Yankee Group. Also, comprehensive market research is conducted (or commissioned) by the labels' trade group, the Recording Industry Association of America (RIAA), whose members account for the vast majority of prerecorded music sales.

Nielsen's Broadcast Data System

Nielsen's Broadcast Data System (**Nielsen BDS**) electronically "listens" to selected radio stations and TV channels 24 hours a day in the United States and Canada. The Nielsen BDS service monitors broadcasts and recognizes songs and commercials.

This methodology is far more accurate than having human researchers listen/log music manually or relying on playlists supplied by outlets, which aren't necessarily eager for the outside world to dissect their programming moves. The Nielsen BDS electronic monitoring compares audio from outlets with music and other audio in its memory, and then recognizes the "fingerprint" of that audio.

By detecting actual airplay, Nielsen BDS's computer-based technology prevents programmers from giving false airplay reports. However, even Nielsen BDS is not beyond manipulation. In 2003 and 2004, several labels attempted to influence chart positions by buying cheap overnight radio advertising in small and medium markets, where the songs in ads could be misidentified as airplay.

Mediabase 24/7

Radio airplay/programming is also monitored across the United States and Canada by Mediabase 24/7, a unit of Premiere Radio Networks that, in turn, is owned by radio group broadcaster Clear Channel. Besides logging airplay, the service originates charts ranking music popularity and provides subscribers with analytic tools to understand data. Mediabase 24/7 also provides monitoring of a host of other programming elements—promotions, contests, and morning-show components, for example—that go beyond the identification capabilities of computer-based-only airplay monitoring. Mediabase 24/7 also operates the consumer music-testing Web site, www.ratethemusic.com.

Mediaguide

The performance rights organization ASCAP helped bankroll the monitoring service Mediaguide, which catalogs music on commercial, noncommercial, and Internet radio, and also verifies that radio commercials actually run. Further, it generates charts ranking music popularity. ASCAP'S primary goal is to use Mediaguide's monitoring to more accurately apportion ASCAP royalties, although Mediaguide is also set up to serve other clients.

Music Xray

Harnessing computer power, some researchers try to quantitatively analyze new recordings to evaluate their marketplace appeal and also point out possible tweaks to improve their sales potential. One such independent service is Music Xray, which produces a numerical snapshot comparing new songs to past hits by analyzing acoustic wave forms, lyrical content, melody, harmony, beat, rhythm, octave, pitch, chord progression, and fullness of sound. Such analysis may rub artists the wrong way, but researchers say their report is just another tool that provides an unbiased opinion.

NPD Group

Another leading supplier of music research reports is NPD Group, which also provides consumer information on an array of industries within media/entertainment, such as toys, movies, personal computers and video games, in addition to music. NPD pays special attention to consumer activity at point of sale (POS) and some of its findings come from interviewing consumers to discover their attitudes. Among NPD's many clients has been the retailer trade group NARM.

RingScan

RingScan, another Nielsen service, compiles mobile ringtone sales that include ringback, voice, polyphonic, and mastertones. The RingScan service gathers data from U.S. mobile carriers, aggregators, and other mobile entertainment retailers.

SoundScan

SoundScan—which like BDS and RingScan is owned by research giant Nielsen—tabulates unit sales of recorded music in the United States and Canada, both physical product such as CDs and downloads. The SoundScan sales trackers are linked to download platforms and bar codes from brick-and-mortar retail outlets representing more than 90% of the nation's record sales. SoundScan uses that big base to project unit sales estimates for the full marketplace.

SoundScan's sales tabulations are offered to the music industry on a subscription basis. Many media outlets reprint the SoundScan lists and thus the service has high visibility in the consumer market. Founded in 1991, SoundScan was acquired a few years later by what is now Nielsen, and began supplying data to Nielsen-owned *Billboard,* which previously relied on sales rankings provided each week by select retailers.

Before SoundScan, record companies were forced to estimate sales based on the number of records they manufactured and shipped to retailers. Even approximate net sales figures were not available until the retailer had shipped unsold product back to the label. Known as *returns,* this product sometimes wasn't received until months after the initial shipment. Stores previously provided no exact sales figures, only a listing of the top sellers in an approximate order and amount. Some retailers neglected to include country, rhythm and blues, and other genre product in their lists of the top 200 albums sold, relegating those releases to specialty charts, even though they might be outselling more mainstream titles. What's more, the old system was subject to manipulation by recording companies that targeted certain stores for extra promotion and by bribable store managers and radio programmers. SoundScan eliminated much of the potential for inaccuracies in reporting by tracking bar-coded POS activity.

Web-Based Research

The digital realm is fertile ground for music companies to track consumer activity stealthily for insights in how to become better marketers to multiple specialized audiences. It's a vast landscape because consumers operate over 1 billion Internet devices globally.

Research outfits leading the digital world include **Arbitron**, comScore, Compete Inc., Google, Harris Interactive, Hitwise, Ipsos, Nielsen/Nielsen Online, Omniture, Quantcast, Visual Sciences, Web Trends, and WPP. To easily aggregate many kinds of data on behavior, preferences, and demographics, audience tracking firms set up big consumer samples—which are larger than ever possible in analog media. Just one vendor, for example, may have millions of media users in its global consumer panel.

Chapter Takeaways

- Market research is much more sophisticated than in earlier eras, when the only question was whether a record was climbing "the charts."

- Today's research includes point-of-sale transaction censuses, consumer attitude surveys, plus custom research on behavior or demography.

- Researching stylistic preferences isn't always useful, as tastes and the genre categories themselves are permanently fluid.

- An array of independent research organizations are in the field, constantly spewing forth torrents of data.

Key Terms

- airplay reports   (p. 308)
- demographics   (p. 305)
- point of sale (POS)   (p. 304)
- SoundScan   (p. 309)

CHAPTER 18

The Digital Age

For nearly a century the modern music industry was forged by two then-new technologies—the phonograph record and broadcasting. In the late 20th century, a third force—digital technology—emerged to shake the industry's foundations. Digital technology radically altered not only the business of music but also its creation, manufacture, and distribution. Furthermore, it changed the very culture of how music is created, with inexpensive technologies to record, present, distribute, promote, and play music, fashioning a unique artistic and commercial digital democracy, which drew music artist and music consumer closer even as it blurred the boundary between them.

> *"The future is here. It's just not widely distributed yet."*
> —William Gibson

Digital's power was most graphically illustrated in the arena of distribution. The unauthorized digital distribution of music via peer-to-peer (P2P) networks like Napster and Grokster was often cited as the primary force behind the music industry sales slump that began in 2001. Ironically, although these P2P networks also presented a method for legitimate digital distribution via the Internet, record labels, which had reaped a fortune from the sales of CDs for two decades, perceived digital distribution as a threat rather than an opportunity. When Philips and Sony collaborated on the development of the compact disc (CD) in the early 1980s, no one could have predicted the extent to which digital technology, in combination with the Internet (which was still gestating at the time), would revolutionize the music industry.

Left: Steve Jobs unveils Apple's iPod Mini, 2004.

Photo © Frederic Larsen/San Francisco Chronicle/Corbis.

The Double-Edged Sword

From the onset, digital recording and distribution created a quagmire of conflicting benefits and disadvantages for the recording industry. On one hand, those making the actual recordings—performers, producers, and engineers—found in the digital medium freedom from the technical constraints of analog tape, including tape noise and limited dynamic range. Furthermore, as digital audio technology progressed, musicians and producers were given powerful new tools, such as digital signal processing systems (DSP)—digital reverbs, delays, samplers, looping, and editing capability—that vastly enhanced their ability to create and assemble sounds.

Record labels equally benefited. The CD was initially an expensive proposition to manufacture and replication was concentrated in factories owned mainly by major record labels. But the cost of a manufactured, packaged CD dropped quickly, from an estimated $2 per disc in 1988 to less than $1 by 2000. Thanks to sustained demand for CDs, however, these record labels managed to maintain their retail prices to a large extent throughout this period, thus steadily increasing the profit margin on each disc. At the same time, the labels' marketing strategy of releasing popular album titles from their vast catalogs was encouraging consumers to replace entire vinyl and cassette tape collections with the CD version, further stimulating sales of CDs and CD players (some companies, such as Sony and Philips, which owned both record labels and consumer electronics divisions, derived double benefit). Furthermore, when the CD was introduced but was still untested as a successful consumer format, major record labels were able to demand royalty rate reductions from recording artists, ostensibly to help mitigate the legitimate cost of fostering the new technology but simultaneously increasing label profits.

However, digital's dark side quickly became apparent. While cassette tapes could be copied fewer than a dozen times before generational fidelity loss rendered them unusable, digital music, on a CD or in the form of an electronic file, could be copied—"cloned"—infinitely.

Internet Synergy

The growth of the Internet in the 1990s created a volatile proposition, providing a virtually unregulatable and broadly accessible channel to distribute digitized music files between computers. Music piracy mushroomed, buttressed further by the proliferation around the world of CD plants, some of which dabbled in unlicensed content, engendering financial losses assertedly in the hundreds of millions of dollars for record labels, music publishers, and the artists, producers, musicians, and songwriters who depended on music sales for their livelihood.

But even as labels fought piracy on CDs, less obvious to them, initially, was the growing underground phenomenon of file-sharing on the Internet. That combination of technologies—digital audio technology and the Internet—became devastating.

MP3.com—the commercial Web site built on the **MPEG** software-based protocol that enabled recordings to be compressed into files easily transferable over the Internet—became a lightning rod in 1999 when the general news media began to widely report on what had by then become a massive global subculture. It was quickly followed by Napster, which used a P2P protocol that significantly hindered tracing who sent files and to whom they were sent. As a result, millions of users traded or sold millions of music files—*per day.*

A lengthy series of legal battles and buyouts left the major recording corporations in control of both MP3 and Napster but with little in the way of innate corporate organizational or cultural capability of turning them to their own advantage.

Labels Lay Seeds of Self-Destruction

As the digital Pandora's box began to open, the music industry fought back using legislation, litigation, and market propaganda. Several key pieces of digital technology legislation were passed in the United States. The Audio Home Recording Act (AHRA) of 1992 stipulated by whom and for what purposes digital copies could be legitimately made. The Digital Millennium Copyright Act (1998) was more comprehensive, particularly in establishing a mechanism for securing copyrighted music online.

But it wasn't enough. As file sharing overtook the pirating of CDs as the record industry's main problem, the Record Industry Association of America (RIAA) turned to mass litigation. It sued colleges, universities (their central servers had become a popular file-sharing nexus among students, the largest cohort of early illicit downloaders), and many individuals. The civil litigations were tactically successful, but strategically dubious, causing far greater public relations damage. The RIAA countered with publicity campaigns to raise awareness about the implications of illegal music distribution, but CD sales continued the relentless decline that had begun at the dawn of the 21st century.

Ultimately, many in the traditional music industry came to acknowledge the futility of the consumer litigation. The former chairman of the International Federation of Phonographic Industries (IFPI, the consortium of label trade associations including the RIAA) and ex-director of EMI Records, Per Eirik Johansen, stated in a 2009 interview that he came to believe that the music industry's fight against piracy has been useless. Johansen even questioned whether illicit file-sharing is actually the same as theft and concluded that with copyright violation so widespread, the only recourse is to find better solutions. In that same year the RIAA announced an end to its 5-year mass litigation campaign, in which more than 30,000 individuals had been sued for file sharing, saying it would instead seek to work with Internet Service Providers (ISPs) to suspend file sharing copyright scofflaws.

The RIAA's efforts may have gone as far as they could: digital rights management (**DRM**), file encryption, and the threat of litigation were deterrents to casual P2P file sharers, but they did little to affect an apparent hard core of P2P users who were likely continue to download illicitly. This legislative/litigious game of technological cat-and-mouse made one thing clear: The mechanisms of law and regulation simply could not keep up with the rapid innovation that digital technology brought to music. An on-demand mindset was fostered among music consumers, who now wanted music whenever and wherever they decided, and ultimately changed the economic structure of the music industry.

Smaller, Cheaper, Faster, Better (?)

At the heart of the digital music revolution is how digital technology changed the process of making music, from the relative confines of analog tape to the potentially infinite realm of digital's nonlinear universe.

In the late 1980s, computer-based multitrack recording and editing platforms began to proliferate, from companies including Cakewalk, Propellerhead, and Digidesign (whose Pro Tools system eventually came to dominate the field). Within a decade, hard-disk-based audio recording became ubiquitous. Analog tape, on which modern music recording had been founded, had become an expensive niche.

This had serious implications for the music industry. For one thing, it lessened the need for conventional recording studios. Records that once had to be made in multi-million-dollar facilities with costly acoustical designs and complicated equipment could now be made in spare bedrooms, using an expanding universe of inexpensive software-based recording and processing systems. Lower production costs should have been a boon to the music industry. In reality, the affordability of digital recording equipment began to reduce the need for large corporations to capitalize productions. Simultaneously, the ability to distribute and promote independent records using the Internet was greatly enhanced. This chipped away at the major labels' other putative advantage—their promotion, manufacturing, and distribution infrastructure. The independent record sector of the music business, which by the turn of the century accounted for nearly a quarter of all reported sales, began to threaten the power of the larger labels. Digital democracy, indeed.

The Economics of Digital Distribution: Change and Evolution

The rise of pop music as a multi-million-dollar enterprise and the transformation of record production into a months- or even years-long process created an economically

Students mixing sound tracks on Pro Tools HD Pro Control recording system in Post Production lab at Trebas Institute.

Photo courtesy of Trebas Institute.

distorted landscape. As rock music and later hip-hop genres became a larger force in popular culture, recordings were transformed into artistic sojourns, and the now lightly supervised recording process sometimes stretched into months and even years. Costs spiraled upward. But with a larger array of technologically advanced and geographically diverse recording facilities, and a growing cadre of independent record producers to guide them, rock and pop music artists gained more autonomy over the making of their records. Record label A&R departments, which once routinely assigned producers to artists and chose their recording studios, transitioned to advancing artists lump sum amounts to pay for their choice of producer and recording location(s) and as an advance on royalties (they hoped) to be earned from the sale of those records.

The numbers game of music production evolved into one that seems, in retrospect, odd, to say the least: Most of the thousands of recording artists signed by what were once a dozen or so major labels in the last 40 years never recouped their costs. However, contracts almost always stipulated that the advanced monies could be recouped only from the sales of artists' records; that is, if an artist was dropped from a label, the debt remained with the recording, not the artist, who was free to sign with another label, if he or she could, and start the process all over again.

In a very real sense, record labels were acting as banks which, when they made "bad loans" (advanced for failed albums), forgave the debt; when they made successful products, the artists found themselves relegated to a sort of decently-paid sharecropper status (in a typical recording contract earning between 10% and 15% of gross sales). Nonetheless, despite the fact that record budgets continued to increase—particularly after the music video (which could sometimes cost as much as the album to produce) became an accepted part of artist promotion in the 1980s—the system worked. That is, until music file sharing undermined it with its own undeniable logic: The more successful a recording was, the more it became the target of illicit downloading.

The New Economic Order

Digital technology and the Internet created a new paradigm for recording artists, one that enables far more artists to actually earn a living from making and selling music as independents outside the framework of the traditional business architecture.

Twenty years ago, a recording artist or band might have incurred a debt to a record label of $1 million or more for a first album, video, and related costs, before the first record could be sold. To show for it, they would have had the record and the video, the copyrights to both of which would be retained by the label unless a reversion clause had been negotiated—a rarity with unproven artists the first time out.

Twenty years later, that same artist or band can invest a fraction of that amount in recording equipment and have not only the same creative output but also the means of production for the next album and video—and the next and the next. Instead of paying over $100,000 of fully recoupable dollars for 2 months in a traditional recording studio, they can pay less than $20,000 for a comprehensive computer-based recording system. Instead of over a quarter-million dollars for a music video, they can purchase affordable video editing software and a high-definition video camera for well under $2,000. Instead of the high-overhead workings of major corporation publicity and marketing materials for the record release, they can use powerful graphics/word processing/Web site creation software suites costing only several hundred dollars. In addition, they can choose from any number of Internet-based services that provide promotional services for independent artists and record labels, such as CD Baby and Taxi.com. At the end of the day, the independent artists not only own the equipment—possibly already amortized and ready to do the next project—but they can also retain the rights to their recordings and are thus able to repurpose and remonetize them. A tidal wave of social networking Web sites that offers access to millions of potential customers has transformed the marketing of music. (See "Music in Social Networking" sidebar.) This transformation radically changed the economics of music. The lower capital costs of this new economic order enable artists to sell their music for less, yet retain a higher percentage of the revenues.

Digital democracy comes at a price, however. While the power implicit in the software tools of digital music and the unprecedented reach of the Internet have created a "backstage pass" past the music industry's traditional gatekeepers—like A&R executives and managers—some argue that what has been lost is the filtering process that the "old-school" record industry offered. In the previous era, bands and artists had to run a gamut of self-financed steps—demos, club gigs, etc.—in order to attract initial record label interest. From there, artists had to prove themselves to successive levels of label hierarchy, at the same time pursuing business management, agency representation, and other necessities. As economically unstable and inflexible as the old record industry business model had become, it had also served as a development ground for several generations of well-trained "ears" who knew what it took to make a hit record and recognize talent—executives like Doug Morris, who once sold records for his independent label from the trunk of his car and later became chairman and CEO of Universal Music Group; or Clive Davis, former president of Columbia Records and later founder of Arista Records. As gatekeepers have receded, vastly greater numbers of records have been released into the market even as overall unit sales decline—the flip side of digital democracy.

iTunes Arrives

Near the turn of the century, the most robust new business model for the music industry emerged from a computer company, perhaps both appropriate and ironic, given the computer's central place in the upheaval of the music business. Apple's iTunes was a way to legitimize and monetize music downloads: Consumers would pay 99 cents per downloaded song and would own the file.

The economics were cut and dried: Labels received a fixed amount from each sale, approximately two-thirds of 99-cent single-song downloads, with that formula extrapolated for complete digital album sales. However, the labels lobbied vigorously for Apple to raise its prices, a move which Apple's CEO Steve Jobs resisted until 2008, when a reformulated agreement between iTunes and the labels resulted in both sides compromising on two key points: Apple would for the first time permit a variable pricing scheme, keeping the 99-cent 128-KB-resolution single-song download and adding a $1.29 price point for higher-quality downloads at 256 KB, as well as a 69-cent price for back-catalog songs, applicable at the labels' discretion. For their part, the record labels agreed to let Apple remove embedded DRM code from the song files.

The single-song download far outstripped entire album downloads, and that phenomenon began to effect its own changes on the new landscape of digital music. For the purpose of certifying gold, platinum, and multiplatinum awards, the RIAA would now count 10 single-song downloads as equivalent to one album sale.[1] But a more significant change was taking place as recording artists began to focus on individual songs rather than albums as their primary products. The decline of the

Music in Social Networking

Social networking is perhaps the most significant digital phenomenon of recent years. Web sites like MySpace, Facebook, Buzznet, and Twitter host interactions between millions of users every day. Music is an integral part of this social interaction—a fact that has come to the attention of those in the music business. A MySpace page is considered critical to marketing music by new and established artists alike, as well as record labels, music venues, and other business entities.

However, not much has changed in one sense: Though new artists can leap the "cultural noise" barrier to become known, it's established artists that still dominate the 24/7 world of digital media. With fewer gatekeepers to control the volume or quality of new digital-only releases, an artist with a reputation (a "brand") has a decided edge in making a splash. With hundreds of thousands of albums in commercial release, it's clear that most of the music being released independently is flying well under the radar of both fans and the bulk of the music industry itself.

Filtering the Noise

Many tools have emerged to do battle against obscurity. Web sites like Taxi.com, which seeks to connect its membership with an array of placement possibilities for their music, and AirPlay Direct, which offers online promotional materials, purport to help music artists differentiate themselves in an increasingly crowded market.

Listeners, too, can be overwhelmed, and they turn to a slew of music blogs, review Web sites, and taste-making enterprises that apply collaborative filtering techniques to steer consumers toward more music they might enjoy based on what they already know they like. At Pandora.com, music has been deconstructed, song by song, bit by bit, reduced to elements that can be matched by Pandora's algorithms to similar elements in other songs that the service then recommends to users. Major digital distributors, such as Amazon.com, have integrated collaborative filtering into their customer interfaces. Apple's iTunes includes a feature called Genius Sidebar, which selects and suggests new songs from the iTunes online store that complement what the user is playing from a personal song library, with the added benefit of not recommending any song the user already owns.

When fans find new favorites, they have any number of ways to let the world know about it, from posting a music file on their MySpace page to linking it to their Web sites or blogs. This in turn may link to more literate sites, like Pitchfork Media, that have become influential in determining what music people acquire. Web sites like iLike.com and iMeem.com create online communities whose members discover new music through sharing.

Communities for Musicians

Musicians themselves have their own specialized networked communities that have become so plentiful and diverse that they can be categorized by state (www.texaasmusicians.net), belief (www.christianmusician-network.net), gender (www.femmuse.com), genre (www.jazzchicago.net), and ethnicity, as the Vietnamese Musicians Network (www.vmnusa.blogspot.com) illustrates. Musicians made seemingly redundant by developments such as sequencing, sampling synthesizers, and drum machines might find some comfort in eSession.com, which allows musicians to list their credits and services and make them accessible to anyone. If a band in Iowa decides it just has to have the former drummer for Peter Gabriel play on one of its tracks, it can contact the musician via the Web site, send him the file for evaluation, agree on an artistic direction and a fee, and the musician performs his part, sending it back to the band, ready to be mixed.

Online social networking has taken the last of the levers from the hands of the traditional music business by eliminating the engineered smoke and mirrors of conventional music marketing. It's connected music artists to their fans in an immersive manner and allowed fans to determine their own level of engagement. If social networking is the manner in which people connect in the future, what music has done with digital technology has provided the soundtrack for those lives.

vinyl single record had begun in the 1980s, as CDs solidified the album concept as music's main shelf item. Labels viewed singles primarily as promotional tools to sell the album. But the advent of downloading began the reversal of that process, and iTunes hastened it significantly.

Mobile: On the Go

The iPhone was the vanguard of a wave of cross-pollination between music and mobile phones and other devices that continues unabated, generating billions of dollars annually for a web of stakeholders including device makers, operating system developers, labels, video producers, and music creators. In 2005, mobile handset maker Ericsson joined forces with Napster to offer the music service to phone users; AT&T launched its own music service jointly with emusic.com in 2007; in 2008, Nokia launched its *Comes With Music* unlimited downloads service in the U.S. In fact, as the number of mobile phone distribution channels proliferate, some industry observers believe that those streaming music—so-called "all you can eat" service plans that offer unlimited streamed music for a monthly fee—are the inevitable eventual winners.

The Digital Future

Since digital technology became a factor, the rate of change that the music industry has experienced is enormous. New technologies, formats, and business models appear constantly. In fact, the only reliable component of music business future is that over time it will continue to change. However, certain outcomes are reasonably predictable, based both on ongoing large-scale trends and the history of techno-economics in general.

Every new technology of the last two centuries—railroads, telephones, electricity, the Internet—experienced similar stages of evolution: an embryonic, high-tech stage (limited accessibility, technology rapidly evolving), an entrepreneurial stage (technology stabilizes and attracts capital), an explosive growth stage (numerous commercial start-ups and multiple business models appear), and a consolidation phase (the participants are fewer but the entities are larger because of mergers and acquisitions).

What happens to technology industries after that depends.[2] In the case of buggy whips for horses, demand evaporated and the industry disappeared, replaced by a cottage industry model of artisans with low product outputs and higher unit pricing. In the case of the telephone, the underlying technology constantly reapplies itself in new ways, pushing the resulting more diverse array of products and services further into the realm of low-unit-priced commodities. The music industry in the digital era will likely be an interesting combination of both evolutionary paths.

Consolidation

Merger and acquisition activity has been common within the music industry throughout its history. It accelerated in the 1970s as existing larger major labels acquired smaller ones to increase their market penetration (such as Sony Corporation's buy of

Columbia Records in 1988), acquire its catalog assets (such as the sale of Motown to MCA that same year) or as a creative resource (a role David Geffen's Asylum Records played for Warner Bros. in the 1970s). This trend continued into the 21st century, though it was fuelled more by the need to reduce costs in the face of the digitally driven music business. In 1998 there were six majors: Warner Music Group, EMI, Sony Music, BMG Music, Universal Music Group, and PolyGram. By 2004, Universal had absorbed PolyGram; 4 years later, Sony had merged with BMG. Given the state of the global economy at the end of the century's first decade, the consolidation trend will likely continue.

It seems likely that this highly consolidated core of old-school companies will remain a force in the music industry, though less as an engine for new creative directions than exploiters of catalogs built up over decades. From the early days of the digital paradigm shift, the majors fell well behind other companies such as Apple, Microsoft, and RealNetworks in creating viable download revenue systems like Apple's iTunes. It's worth noting that the latter set of companies all have digital origins, compared with the analog origins of remaining major labels. That causal relationship may be inferential, but it's difficult to deny: Music—its creation, realization, and distribution—is now a digital entity. Companies and individuals who understand the dynamics of digital commerce are poised to exploit the change.

Price Versus Value

The digitization of music and distribution channels has also created more music than ever before, because the means of producing it are more widely accessible and affordable. The history of economics informs us that commodities rarely increase in unit price when the means of producing and obtaining them remain prodigious. However, economies of scale do not necessarily mean that higher-value products cannot be created in a stagnant or declining price environment. For instance, ringtones of popular songs, which are comprised of about 30 seconds of music and often at lower resolution than the complete MP3 or iTunes track, continue to command prices as high as $2.99, even though the full song in a higher resolution can cost as little as 69 cents. Underscoring how a popular application can add premium value to an otherwise mass-market product, iTunes offers a utility that lets purchasers of a track pick a 30-second portion of it to convert into a ringtone. At 99 cents, the service effectively doubles the revenue for the same product.

Streaming Versus Downloads

The downloaded music file, the foot soldier of the digital music revolution, may itself be headed for a diminished role in the industry it transformed. Early attempts to create music subscription services using streaming media failed to gain much consumer interest and the concept was overshadowed by the success of iTunes. However, within a few years, services such as Rhapsody and Napster To Go began to see subscriptions increase, particularly when offered as part of a larger package (such as Rhapsody's whole-house digital audio systems bundling with companies like Sonos and Nokia's *Comes With Music* streaming service). What may well relegate the download to second-tier status is the growth of "cloud" computing and the popularity of netbook computers whose users increasingly rely on online storage and access services.

Digital has also changed the attitude of a generation of music consumers, perhaps irrevocably. The ease with which digital distribution made music freely accessible also created a culture in which music is often perceived as being free of cost, as well. This attitude was hardened in many minds by the adversarial relationship that evolved between record labels fighting digital piracy with litigation against individual downloaders. The public often perceived the conflict as one between corporate hegemony and individual rights, a situation that encouraged a widely held perception that the cost of music product was out of proportion to the cost of making it.

Ultimately, as the corporate shell of the old music business disintegrates, digital technology has made the music business an entrepreneurial one once again. With access to affordable production of music and digital distribution unencumbered by the capital and logistical requirements of manufacturing and physical distribution, the music industry has become less mythical and more accessible to more people. As a result of digital, the music business may have shed some of its mystique and glamour, but in the process, it has become a viable career choice for more people than ever before.

Notes

1. RIAA certifies bestselling recordings as Gold (500,000 units), Platinum (1 million), Multi-platinum (2 million or more), and Diamond (10 million). In addition, it issues Digital Sales and Master Ringtone Sales awards. When a label believes its sales justify such a certification, RIAA has an independent audit conducted. RIAA awards are based on manufacturers' unit shipments and dollar value, net after returns.

2. For two provocative viewpoints on the impact of disruptive change on an existing order, examine Clayton M. Christensen's *The Innovator's Dilemma* (HarperBusiness, 2000) and Carl Shapiro's and Hal Varian's *Information Rules: A Strategic Guide to the Network Economy* (Harvard Business School Press, 1999).

Chapter Takeaways

- Digital technology has been a double-edged sword, improving the ability to produce new sounds, but threatening the established order of distributing recorded music.

- Overwhelmed by the free-on-demand mindset sweeping cyberspace, record labels eventually backed away from anti-piracy mass litigation and digital rights management as enforcement tools.

- The democratization of the music business has diminished the importance of the gatekeeper function of key record label personnel.

- "All you can eat" digital subscription services rose in importance in the early years of the 21st century.

- The major labels were largely caught flat-footed in the digital age, watching with alarm as technology companies such as Apple, Microsoft, and RealNetworks pioneered disruptive business paths.

Key Terms

- collaborative filtering   (p. 319)
- digital rights management (DRM)   (p. 315)
- Internet Service Providers (ISPs)   (p. 315)
- MP3   (p. 314)

- Pro Tools   (p. 316)
- recoupable   (p. 317)
- social networking   (p. 318)

PART 6

Music in Broadcasting, Film, and Theater

CHAPTER 19

Music in Radio

For decades, record labels aggressively pursued radio airplay because it was the surest path to increased retail music sales. There was no doubt radio was the best medium to introduce new songs to vast audiences. However, the dawn of the digital media explosion in the early 1990s diminished the supremacy of broadcast radio. A succession of digital music platforms carved out slices of today's music-consuming market—portable CD players made popular by the Sony Walkman, Apple's iPod and iTunes, Microsoft's Zune, MTV: Music Television and other 24-hour music TV channels, Internet radio and satellite audio.

Yet it all started with broadcast radio. The early radio broadcasts were all live, of course, often featuring opera stars and other artists in the classical field. The audio quality was poor, and the broadcast signals were filled with static, but audiences loved the novelty of radio and rushed out to buy the new crystal sets to receive the broadcasts in their homes.

The first commercially licensed station went on the air in 1920. Entrepreneurs saw the potential of the medium, and within 3 years, more than 500 stations were licensed and the first radio network had been formed. Radio grew, as

> "For a long time I wasn't listening to music, to the rock and roll stuff on the radio, because it would cause me to get sweaty—it would bring back memories I didn't want to know about, or I would get that feeling that I'm not alive 'cause I'm not making it. And if it was good, I hated it 'cause I wasn't doing it. And if it was bad, I was furious 'cause I could've done it better...."
>
> —John Lennon

Left: Photo © Nick Koudis/Royalty Free/Getty Images.

did the popularity of phonograph records, and these two industries formed the first mass media for sound. Music could now be delivered to audiences of millions—at the speed of light. In the early 1940s, the *Make Believe Ballroom* made its appearance and attracted a big following—it was the first radio show to use only recorded music. Stations throughout the country quickly followed suit, spurred by the realization that they didn't need live orchestras to attract listeners.

It seemed radio was headed for near extinction in the late 1940s, as the emergence of television not only siphoned audiences but also drained radio of its programming, which at the time consisted of scripted comedies, dramas, and variety shows, in addition to music. Radio stars such as comedian Jack Benny, baritone narrator and drama actor William Conrad, and comedian/actor George Burns departed for TV. A legendary Texas broadcaster, the late Gordon McLendon, perfected radio's salvation in the early 1950s with a then-revolutionary concept of broadcasting genre-specific programming instead of a broad mix of general entertainment. His most famous creation was Top 40 radio on Dallas radio station KLIF. The format called for a tight playlist of hit songs, on-air contests, goofy promotions, and banter from "personality" disc jockeys. Though derided over the years for slavish conformity to current hit songs, Top 40 was an innovation at the time.

Today, as digital media captures consumer fancy, radio is struggling as an advertisement-supported medium. Yet, although no longer dominant, radio is still potent. According to Arbitron, Inc., 234 million persons ages 12 and older in the United States listen to an average of 18 and one half hours of radio a week. That is a lot of consumer consumption and represents 93% of the age 12+ population. To get a picture of how the phenomenon has developed historically, see Table 19.1.

Types of Stations

One way to classify stations is by their carrier waves. **AM** stands for amplitude modulation, where the power or amplitude of the carrier wave varies, but the wave frequency remains constant. **FM** stands for frequency modulation, where the carrier wave frequency varies but its amplitude remains constant. In the beginning, AM stations dominated radio broadcasting. Although FM stations have been around since the 1940s, in the early 1970s they increased their share of the audience dramatically. Today, FM stations generally are music stations, and AM is the home of news, talk, and sports.

Another way to classify stations is by their call letters. The earliest U.S. radio stations selected their own three- or four-letter call letters beginning with either a W or a K. Stations in Mexico and Canada were required to use an X and C, respectively. The letters K and W had been in use worldwide as part of an index for ship radio stations, with K standing for ships on the East Coast and W standing for ships in the Pacific. For some reason, however, the letters were reversed when it came to land-based radio stations. In the late 1920s, the Federal Radio Commission devised rules that required stations east of the Mississippi to adopt call letters beginning with a W, while stations west of the Mississippi had to begin their handles with a K.

Audience Identification and Market Research

Most radio stations adopt a supremely simple programming philosophy: to attract a particular segment of the radio audience, broadcast its favorite music. As an

Table 19.1 Historical Development of Music in Radio

1864:	The basic theory of electromagnetism is set down by British scientist James C. Maxwell.
1865:	Italian inventor Guglielmo Marconi develops the first radio.
1920:	The first commercially licensed radio station goes on the air (KDKA, Pittsburgh), broadcasting the presidential election returns (Harding vs. Cox).
1922:	The novelty of radio quickly attracts larger audiences. Sixty stations are on the air.
1923:	Radio broadcasting booms. AT&T inaugurates the first radio network.
1926:	Radio rapidly becomes "show business." Stars of the Metropolitan Opera and other classical artists are featured. Vaudeville headliners begin to be programmed.
1930s:	Over 600 stations are on the air by 1931. In 1934, the Federal Communications Commission (FCC) is set up by the Federal Communications Act. Broadcasting is turned over to "free enterprise" with minimum federal control. During the Great Depression, when people cannot afford to buy records or tickets to the movies, radio offers "free" entertainment to mass audiences. Network shows feature vaudeville headliners, movie stars, and name bands. Advertising revenue soars.
1941:	The FCC authorizes commercial FM stations, but development is delayed until after World War II.
1945:	By the end of World War II, 950 stations are on the air.
1946:	The postwar boom is on—many additional stations, AM and FM, go on the air.
1950s:	The rapid growth of television nearly kills network radio, quickly wiping out most live music and radio staff orchestras. Radio stations narrow their programming to one type of music, pulling impressive audiences. The personality-oriented disc jockey begins to dominate. Payola scandals bring national attention to the way music is selected for airplay.
1960s:	The FCC authorizes multiplex broadcasting. The record business booms, largely due to the promotional medium of radio. FM stations increase in number and begin to attract specialized audiences.
1970s:	FM stations turn more toward the "middle" audience in quest of a larger market share. Most AM and FM programming becomes predictable, with few programmers risking innovation. But the medium continues to earn good money.
1980s:	The FCC relaxes controls over programming. FM stations gain larger audiences. Stations continue their search for that magic music format that will beat the competition. Radio's once-dominant power to influence record sales is now shared by music video.
1990s:	Formats split into tighter niches. Digital audio reaches radio stations in the form of digital workstations in production rooms and control rooms. Number of stations individual owners can hold increases, radically changing management and staffing patterns and greatly speeding up the spread of successful formats.
2000s:	Traditional radio stations continue to face new competition from commercial-free, newly launched subscription-based satellite radio and streaming Internet audio stations. Spanish-language outlets pull in large ratings and are among the most popular stations in certain U.S. markets. Cable TV and digital media siphon audiences and advertising dollars with their segmented programming, depressing radio profitability and bringing financial strain to station groups and program syndicators. In congressional hearings, critics charge that radio ownership consolidation has negatively affected diversity of programming and political discourse. The birth of HD radio brings improved audio quality as traditional radio stations simulcast their main signals in digital format.

advertisement-supported medium, radio station managers start by identifying audience segments in a given metropolitan area which have appeal to advertisers. They then select a program format expected to attract that audience in that competitive environment.

Demography. Audience research is based on demographic studies which deal with the distribution, density, and vital statistics of populations. Stations and their advertisers are interested in the location, ages, gender, education, economic status, and races of their potential audience—and above all, how many people listen to the station at various times during the day.

Research Methods. Radio market research largely depends on polling samples of its audience or potential audience. Companies sampling broadcast audiences assert that their figures are in the 3% to 5% accuracy range. But not all market research is this good or this useful to broadcasters and their advertisers. Research methods range from casual to scientific. The most trustworthy, systematic methods used for broadcasters attempt to determine three basic sets of statistics:

- Station rating. This is determined by counting the percentage of the potential audience that is listening to a particular station at a particular time. For example, if a station has a rating of 5.2 at noon on weekdays, that means that of every 1,000 households surveyed, 52 were listening to that station at noon on a weekday.
- Sets in use. This is a count of the actual number of homes with sets turned on. If the market had 100,000 households and 62.4% of the sampled homes had radios turned on, then sets in use would be projected at 62,400.
- **Audience share.** This is a statistic indicating the comparative popularity of a program being broadcast at a particular time. For example, if a show has a 10.1 share, that means that, of the homes that had their sets turned on, 10.1% were listening to that particular program at that particular time.

Radio operators conduct their own music popularity research in addition to buying *syndicated* research (reports and data sold to multiple clients). To estimate the audience size that drives the placement of billions of dollars annually in radio advertising, Arbitron, Inc. measures over 80 metropolitan areas four times a year and over 200 markets two times a year. Separately, the Nielsen company, which dominates TV audience measurement, is a big player in monitoring music in the radio sector. Nielsen Broadcast Data Systems (Nielsen BDS) electronically catalogs over 100 million song performances annually. These songs originate from 1,800 broadcast radio stations, satellite radio, and video and cable music channels in over 140 markets in the U.S., and more than 30 Canadian markets. Airplay information provides insights to radio operators on trends around the country as well as local competitors' programming.

Nielsen also owns *Billboard*, whose airplay and sales charts utilize information from Nielsen BDS and SoundScan. Prior to automated electronic measurement from Nielsen BDS and others, airplay lists were largely compiled by asking radios stations what music they played, a methodology subject to manipulation since stations were under no obligation to provide accurate answers.

Data Interpretation

It is one thing to accumulate research data. It is quite another matter to interpret their meaning. The accuracy and usefulness of audience research information is widely disputed. The following questions are commonly raised:

1. How good was the sample? Did it typify the market?

2. How weak, how strong was the program preceding/following the program being measured?

3. How strong, how clear was the station's signal at the time the sampled audience was listening?

4. How strong were the competing programs?

5. What was the influence of publicity?

6. What was it that most attracted listeners (the music, the disc jockey, the talk show host, a prize contest)?

Influence on Music Sales. There is abundant evidence that radio exposure helps sell recordings. But it's also true that a radio station's audience size for a particular kind of music programming does not necessarily translate into sales of recordings. For example, "adult" radio listeners often favor the music of adult artists, but usually they do not buy as much music as the size of their radio audience would suggest. However, on occasion, an artist who appeals to adults (e.g., Norah Jones, Sarah McLachlan) will strike a chord with adult music buyers and radio listeners.

Spectrum of Formats

Commercial broadcasters have one common goal: making money. Although most early stations served in the public's interest and offered a wide variety of information and entertainment, stations survived on how well the programming attracted advertisers—and that remains the bedrock of this business. The development of specific formats is a direct result of a wider variety of musical choices coupled with the broadcaster's desire to reach a lucrative segment of the audience. If a station gains listeners, it can attract new advertisers, adjust rates accordingly, and make a hefty profit. In an age of **narrowcasting**, formats constantly emerge, evolve, and recede.

CHR/Top 40

CHR or contemporary hit radio, also known as Top 40, plays the most popular current hits of the day and focuses on attracting teen listeners. Although the roots of CHR are the Top 40, often its playlists feature 25 or fewer songs in rotation, allowing for repetition and maximum exposure of the songs its audience wants to hear.

Adult Contemporary

Adult contemporary (AC) is a broad category containing subgroupings such as hot AC (a more current-driven and upbeat version of the format), adult Top 40, and mainstream and modern rock tracks. More traditional AC stations draw on oldies, but usually no older than a decade.

Country

Country music stations initially programmed the type of popular music associated with Nashville, what is often referred to as traditional country. This has been enlarged to include pop-country or country-rock, a more polished variety of music. Though associated with the South and West, the format is found in markets all over the nation in all categories of stations—AM and FM, commercial and noncommercial.

Urban Contemporary

While historically these stations sought a predominantly black, inner-city audience, that changed dramatically with the rise of rap music as a significant sales force. As a result, suburban youths weren't only buying recordings by hip-hop artists, they were tuning into urban stations, which at one time shunned rap but were forced to embrace the music because of its popularity. However, rap music, or hip-hop, does continue to divide some radio stations. Often, adult urban stations will focus solely on the more accessible and smooth sounds of R&B and lure an older more mature listener with the promise of "no rap."

Alternative

Prior to the early 1990s, the alternative genre, also called modern rock, was made up of a variety of music that did not fit elsewhere on the commercial radio dial, such as alternative rock, some world music, reggae, and techno styles. Alternative acts such as R.E.M. and U2, and later the grunge explosion of the mid-'90s with Nirvana and Pearl Jam, became mainstream rock.

AOR

AOR or album-oriented rock rose to prominence in the late 1960s, as rock musicians began to embrace the concept of recording an album rather than a series of hit singles. In part a reaction to the tightly formatted Top 40 sounds on the AM dial, a new brand of radio personalities shunned hit singles and instead focused on album cuts and lengthy songs that would never receive airplay on a Top 40 station. Core artists included Led Zeppelin, known for the AOR staple "Stairway to Heaven," Yes, Pink Floyd, and the Who.

Oldies

The oldies format strives to capture the excitement and nostalgia of early Top 40 by programming the hits of yesteryear for those who want to be reminded of their youth. Initially, the format focused on rock 'n' roll hits from the 1950s and 1960s, but as time passed, the format expanded to include hits from later decades.

NAC

This format, also known as new adult contemporary or smooth jazz, rose to prominence in the 1990s as sort of a new version of **easy listening** or Muzak. It favors light instrumentals or soft vocals that are not intrusive. Core artists include saxophonist Kenny G and New Age keyboardist Yanni.

Non-English Stations

Spanish-language stations make up the bulk of non-English-speaking radio stations. As with English-speaking stations, the Spanish stations embrace specific genres of music or formats. And in areas with large enough populations speaking other languages, particularly Asian communities, radio stations have emerged to serve them, as well.

Others

National Public Radio. The **FCC** sets aside a segment of the FM broadcast band (88 to 92 megahertz) for schools, colleges, civic entities, and others who devote all or part of their programming to education, the arts, and other kinds of nonprofit enterprise. Most public radio stations are low powered, 10 watts or less. Each station addresses a limited geographic area, and they do not accept commercial advertising. Their audiences are generally smaller than those of commercial stations.

Stations located on college campuses are often connected with one or more campus departments, such as music, broadcasting, or theater. Programming tends to lean to the personal tastes of the current group of station managers. Alternative music and lesser-known recording artists are sometimes featured. Promoters and agents for the artists are well received by campus stations, and promoters from recording companies say that pushing alternative discs to college radio stations has had an impact on sales. Most public radio stations are receptive to special programming that might include chamber music, opera, electronic music, avant-garde, ethnic and world music, campus recitals, and concerts featuring faculty and students. These stations also sometimes broadcast educational music programs, such as "Music Appreciation" or "Understanding Jazz." Noncommercial programs like "Morning Becomes Eclectic" on KCRW in Santa Monica, California, are legendary as a platform for promoting new music through both in-studio performances and recordings.

Many public radio stations are affiliated with National Public Radio (**NPR**), which was incorporated in 1970. The network and its affiliates receive financial support from the Corporation for Public Broadcasting, the National Endowment for the Arts, cities, state arts councils, and private donations. Some public radio stations receive support from American Federation of Musicians (AFM) locals, which use this medium to foster "live" broadcasts of music and musicians. NPR has a long-standing agreement with the AFM, not only to pay union wages but also to protect AFM members from unauthorized new uses of music originally cleared only for NPR broadcasts.

Christian Stations. Many stations addressing an audience attracted by music oriented toward religious faith and church activities are located in midwestern and southern states, and big cities elsewhere. Most of these stations have no difficulty holding almost exclusively to the great supply of recordings available in this style.

How Commercial Radio Stations Work

Operations

As a result of the 1996 Telecommunications Act and the resulting consolidation of ownership of stations, the management structure of the majority of commercial stations has shifted over the years. Where it had been common to see one general manager, program director, and marketing and promotions director for one or two radio stations, it soon became clear that a company that owned eight stations in one market could manage them all with one manager. It's now common to find

NBC Radio, 1949.

Photo courtesy of Roberta Baskerville archive.

Live Music Then and Now: In the Golden Age of network radio, live music predominated, such as on this 1949 musical quiz show broadcast nationally from NBC studios in Hollywood (above). Today, live radio music is a rarity, but still exists. This NPR station (below) features live music from bands seeking to promote themselves and their local club dates.

Band performing on *Morning Becomes Eclectic*, KCRW Studio, Santa Monica College.

Photo courtesy of KCRW.

one market manager running six stations in a given city, a promotions manager in charge of those six, and one sales manager selling them, either individually or in combination. Program directors (PDs) and engineers often perform their functions for several sister stations, as well. (For a description of music-related careers in radio, see Chapter 25, Career Options.)

Programming

Once a station has settled on a format, there's the ongoing work of putting together the week's playlist, the day-to-day programming, including which new songs to fold into the current playlist and which older ones to drop. The consolidation of radio stations has made it more difficult for songs to make it on the air, because the decisions about what gets aired rest in the hands of fewer people. For many years, songs landed on a station's playlist based on three criteria: local sales figures, requests, and the music director's gut instinct. Today, music selections often come from a radio group's corporate brass—which typically is in a distant city. Still, many stations, particularly CHR outlets, like to play up the audience's perceived participation in shaping its playlist.

Recording companies spend lots of money promoting their major artists, from magazine ads promoting a new single or album, to visits to radio stations, to occasional billboard campaigns. They know that as important as it is to promote their new wares directly to the public, it's getting them airtime that will often make the difference.

Until the late 1950s, most of the records that got on the air were selected by the disc jockeys, who were prime targets for the blandishments and bribes of music business promoters, which led to **payola** scandals that hit the national news. Since then, there have been occasional scandals involving independent recording promoters, but for the most part, stations have kept a careful eye out to prevent them happening again. However, controversy still exists over some stations' allegedly strong-arming artists to play station-sponsored events in exchange for airplay. In a typical week, 10 to 15 songs may be up for consideration as "adds" of new songs for the station's playlist. However, usually only 3 will be chosen for the choice spots.

Reverse Programming. Most radio stations have discovered that radio audiences tend to leave a particular station on, provided they don't hear a song they dislike. Many listeners will explore the radio dial, not for a particular station but for a style of music they like. Studies repeatedly show that the listener will not move off a station unless a recording comes on that is different in musical style, inconsistent with the other music the station typically programs. When the listener notices the station is playing a song different from what is familiar or pleasing, that listener may then punch out and search for another station that is more consistent, less disturbing. Radio programmers therefore do everything they can to avoid upsetting their audience, which has led to what's known as "the blanding of radio."

Song Clustering, Pacing. Whatever the dominant type of music programmed, stations often cluster their songs, then cluster their commercials. Some studies show that this pattern of grouping tends to hold an audience more effectively than a pattern of announcement-song-commercial, announcement-song-commercial, and so on. A typical example of clustering is the playing of *sets,* such as six songs in a row or 30 minutes of nonstop music.

There are different views on how to pace recordings. Some believe that in a three-song cluster, audiences will favor a sequence of tempos, say, slow–medium–fast. Others prefer to alternate solo artists with groups. Over the years, radio increased the **commercial load** in response to booming advertising demand, reducing music. But then radio as an industry reduced commercial time in 2005 after listeners and advertisers complained of oversaturation. Radio was forced to accommodate listeners, who increasingly have alternatives with handheld audio devices such as iPods, subscription satellite radio and Internet radio.

Stations using **cluster programming** and **back-announcing** allow a span of airtime for the disc jockey to speak, thus affording the station an opportunity to invest some personality into an otherwise canned program.

Networks and Syndication

The original concept of a radio network as defined by the Federal Communications Act—linked stations broadcasting the same programs simultaneously—dominated the industry until about 1950. At that time, the national networks were NBC, CBS, ABC, and MBS (Mutual Broadcasting System).

Today networks and independent production companies package complete programs, then license or sell them to stations. Such programs are said to be in syndication; their packagers are called syndicators. The producer of syndicated programs determines a format for a show or series of shows, engages the announcers, then lays in the elements—music tracks, interviews, whatever is to go into the programs.

A radio station or a radio chain can order prepackaged programs delivered on digital audiotape, CDs, phone line, the Internet, or by satellite transmission. The shows provide time for insertion or addition of commercial messages by the local station. Syndicated program material can range in length from 30 seconds to a full **day part** or more. It can be an individual, one-time program, or a series.

For many years, syndicated programs were mainly once-a-week countdown programs, say, of the Top 40 pop or country songs, and talk shows. In the early 1990s, a few companies such as Westwood One began to take talent from a wide variety of successful radio stations and offer their shows to stations in other markets, no matter what size they were. Soon, Howard Stern could be heard every morning in Las Vegas, Albany, San Jose, and Miami. Rush Limbaugh and Dr. Laura Schlessinger became national talk superstars, airing in just about every city in the United States. One of the consequences of syndication has been that the air talent displaced by syndicated shows has grown in number, and opportunities have greatly diminished for up-and-coming talent to land positions in smaller markets and hone their skill before moving up to the larger markets—the traditional route that disc jockeys in the past took to become high-profile, well-paid successes. An example of a popular syndicated format is The Jack, which programs 1960s through 1990s rock hits. The format package is so complete that stations can use the same signature DJ, thus reducing local on-air talent.

Satellite Subscription Radio

Satellite radio, offering a subscription service, was launched in 2001. The two national players, Sirius and XM, later merged after a ruinous bidding war for nonmusic programming resulted in financial losses. In a costly bid to jump-start subscription sales, automobile makers were paid to install satellite radio equipment in cars at the factory and were given bonuses for their car buyers who became subscribers. Satellite radio expanded distribution to satellite TV, other third-party platforms, and the Internet, but came into conflict with the music industry after introducing portable receiver/recorders dubbed XM+MP3. Music labels filed a lawsuit against XM which reached settlements in 2007 and 2008 by agreeing to an expanded music royalty deal covering consumer recording.

Satellite radio services offer an abundance of music channels. These include niche programming focused on specific music groups or eras as well as mainstream music formats such as hip-hop, blues, country, Latin, and classical. However, music is considered the "bulk" of the satellite radio program offer and is not a vital point of differentiation with *terrestrial radio* (AM and FM). Rather, it is exclusively the talk formats—such as shock jock Howard Stern and play-by-play sports event coverage—that historically have driven significant sales of satellite radio subscriptions.

Internet Radio

Streaming audio programming, which marked the beginning of Internet radio, started in the early 1990s as a novelty and today is an established media business. Internet radio—also called **Webcasting**—benefitted from the arrival of broadband Internet connections which replaced the often-erratic signals of dial-up narrowband connections.

Traditional radio stations usually simulcast their signals via the Internet, thus serving out-of-town audiences and achieving global reach at a low cost. Measuring listenership is superior to broadcast measurement because each consumer's listening device can be identified when it hooks into an Internet server and the length of connection is known. Over-the-air radio stations routinely place a link to their Internet radio stream on their stations' Web sites, which carry advertising, content, and promotion.

In the early days of Internet radio, music performance royalties were small. But in 2006, sound recording performance rates were raised by the United States Copyright Royalty Board (CRB), a federal government agency created by Congress. This triggered an outcry from Internet radio which asserted its music performance royalties were disproportionally high relative to other media. The performance rights organization SoundExchange negotiated with Internet radio outlets on the issue and in some cases offered alternatives to the CRB statutory rate.

There is rapid growth and development in this field. Internet radio operators view mobile wireless broadband as the next frontier from which to stream their signals.

HD Radio™[1]

The traditional terrestrial broadcast radio sector introduced HD Radio™ technology in 2003, allowing AM and FM stations to **simulcast** their main signals in a digital format, offering improved audio quality. In addition, FM stations are able to squeeze more audio channels in their allocated spectrum via HD Radio™ technology through what is called **multicasting**. (AM stations cannot insert multicast channels because of their spectrum limitations.) The FM multicasting helps close the gap with satellite radio's vast channel offerings.

A consortium of radio broadcasters known as the HD Digital Radio Alliance pushes the technology by organizing radio stations to transmit digital signals and promoting sales of compatible radios for consumers.

▪ Note

1. HD Radio™ is a proprietary trademark of iBiquity Digital Corp.

Chapter Takeaways

- Commercial radio stations orient their programming toward a specific audience demographic. This concentration on audience types is attractive to advertisers.

- A proliferation of music platforms—ranging from the portable iTunes to music audio channels in subscription entertainment— siphon audiences from broadcast radio.

- Due to changes in ownership rules, much of the radio industry has consolidated, frequently leading to multiple stations in a market being run by the same management team. Among the effects: tight playlists.

- Satellite radio, which launched in 2001 and is heavily geared to the car radio market, is offered as a subscription service for a monthly fee.

- Internet radio, which is also called Webcasting, streams continuous audio around the globe.

- Regular ("terrestrial") radio stations, which broadcast in analog, offer digital programming via HD Radio™.

Key Terms

- back-announcing (p. 336)
- cluster programming (p. 336)
- day part (p. 336)
- HD radio (p. 337)
- Internet radio (p. 337)

- multicasting (p. 337)
- narrowcasting (p. 331)
- network (p. 336)
- payola (p. 335)
- rating (p. 330)

- satellite radio (p. 336)
- share (p. 330)
- station formats (p. 331)
- syndication (p. 336)

CHAPTER 20

Music in Television and Video

For a full understanding of the present chapter, refer to Chapters 5 and 6 (video copyright and licensing), Chapter 8 (video issues in recording contracts), Chapter 16 (promotion, distribution, and retailing), and Chapter 21 (dramatic scoring).

> *"If you had lived 2,000 years ago and sung like that, I think they would have stoned you."*
>
> —Simon Cowell, American Idol *Judge*

Long before MTV made "music television" into a corporate brand and pop-culture catchphrase, the two entertainment industry sectors were deeply intertwined. From *The Ed Sullivan Show* piped into a 13-inch black-and-white console to *Soul Train* strutting through a 27-inch color set to *American Idol* blasting out of an expansive 50-inch LCD HDTV screen, music has always been part of the broadcasting picture, however fuzzy the image or sharp the sound. It's sometimes the star of the show (on music specials and variety shows, for instance) and often a bit player (piped softly into the background during a dramatic scene, perhaps), but it's always there, *somewhere*, occupying a vital role. Any full discussion of the music business, therefore, must include a look at TV.

Left: Ne-Yo's video shoot for "Closer."

Photo © Matthew Simmons/WireImage.

Why is it so important? Because for the music industry, the broadcast TV networks, cable networks, and satellite services represent the following:

- A key income source (via licensing for performance rights and commercial uses)
- A prime marketing vehicle (via spotlight placement in specials, series, and high-profile commercials)
- A national stage for exposure (via band bookings on talk shows and other entertainment programs)
- A means of selling music directly to a targeted audience (via promotional programming or commercials bought by labels or direct-response marketers)

In recent years, the broadcasting arena has also become a populist **A&R** mechanism—letting TV audiences select the next record label signings through reality show talent competitions in genres including pop, country, and hip-hop. New technology, meanwhile, is opening doors to interactive music programming and direct impulse purchases by viewers, enhanced by the popularity of handheld devices such as iPods and cellular phones. The emergence of home theater systems and DVD hardware has created a thriving market for the sale of music video programming designed for home or on-the-go viewing on devices that increasingly blur the lines between TVs, radios, stereos, telephones, and PCs.

For its part, the TV industry gets a source of mood-setting background music, as well as high-profile programming fodder that promises to bring in big audiences in key age groups so cherished by many advertisers—such as the 18 to 34s.

Although important to both sides, the music industry/TV pairing has not always been without static, and this too is something as old as the broadcast medium itself. Janet Jackson's infamous "wardrobe malfunction" during the 2004 Super Bowl halftime show may have sent shockwaves through the halls of the Federal Communications Commission (FCC), but Elvis Presley, the Beatles, and the Rolling Stones long before her had caused their own headaches for TV programmers worried about breaching the broadcast standards of the time.

Table 20.1 provides a brief timeline of some of the significant moments in the evolution of music on television. On the following pages is a more detailed guide to common types of music/TV tie-ins past and present, as well as an exploration of the changing broadcasting industry picture, the technological shifts in TV hardware and music-themed home video software, and the rise of MTV and the short-form music video format.

Variety and Talk Shows

The music variety show was one of the most popular types of programming in the first two decades of TV, especially during the 1950s "Golden Age of Television," after the American Federation of Musicians (AFM) negotiated a system of new payments from TV producers to musicians. Variety shows employed live orchestras, backup singers and dancers, arrangers, and the leading stars of the day. "High-culture" performances of classical music, opera, and theater were showcased on all three networks throughout the 1950s and into the 1960s, but high production costs and poor ratings killed more than one series with high aspirations.

By the early 1960s, another type of show had begun to emerge. Aimed at a youth audience, it often took its cues from the Top 40 charts in terms of popular artists and featured a throng of dancing teenagers. *American Bandstand* is the best known, but others included *Hullabaloo, Where the Action Is,* and the long-standing syndicated favorite, *Soul Train.* In the 1970s, *In Concert* offered a live rock concert every weekend and set the stage for later series such as *Austin City Limits.*

Table 20.1 Historical Development of Music in Television

1930s	First television broadcasts available in London in 1936.
	The 1939 New York City's World's Fair demonstrates the first TV broadcast to the American public, although WWII delays its roll-out.
1940s	The AFM tightens control of the music industry by banning live music on TV and prohibiting members from recording for television programs until 1950.
	Kraft Television Theatre brings Broadway-quality live theater to TV.
	The Ed Sullivan Show debuts and becomes TV's longest-running and most successful variety show (1948–1971).
	Bandleader Lawrence Welk begins broadcasting performances of "champagne music" that appeals to traditional tastes.
1950s	TV set penetration balloons from fewer than 4 million U.S. households in 1950 to over 40 million by decade's end.
	Variety shows, amateur talent shows, and classical performances dominate the "Golden Age of Television."
	Omnibus, hosted by Alistair Cooke, launches to become a revered cultural series and provides inspiration for American public television.
	Classics birthed: *Name That Tune, So You Want to Lead a Band, The Tonight Show, Musical Chairs.*
	ABC's *Rock 'n' Roll Show,* hosted by Alan Freed, is the first prime-time network special devoted to rock music.
1960s	ABC's *Hootenanny* is the first regularly scheduled folk music program on network television, followed by CBS's country music and comedy series, *Hee Haw.*
	73 million viewers watch the Beatles perform on *The Ed Sullivan Show.*
	ABC produces the youth musical comedy series *The Monkees* as an American answer to The Beatles.
1970s	A Coca-Cola commercial makes the ad's song "I'd Like to Teach the World to Sing" into a worldwide hit.
	Soul Train debuts and is syndicated in 1971.
	TV shows based on musical personalities abound: *The Partridge Family, The Sonny & Cher Comedy Hour, The Captain & Tennille Show, Donny & Marie Show,* and *The Jacksons.*
	The late-night slot becomes a showcase for musical performers with *Midnight Special, In Concert, Don Kirshner's Rock Concert,* and *Saturday Night Live.*
	PBS's *Great Performances* series debuts.
1980s	The Black Entertainment Television and Country Music Television networks debut.
	Chart-based music show *Solid Gold* debuts in syndication.
	MTV signs on cable TV with the Buggles' "Video Killed the Radio Star."
	Pepsi fuels the trend of high-profile music marketing by hiring Michael Jackson as pitchman; his hair famously catches fire during the commercial's production.
	Viacom targets older music fans with VH1 and then launches the European version of MTV.
	The growth of prerecorded videocassettes creates a new market for long-form music video.
1990s	MTV spreads its music channel programming formula abroad, becoming a global cultural force.
	MTV diversifies by moving beyond compilations of video clips into program production that introduces an MTV lifestyle with *The Real World,* spawning a cultural fascination with reality TV.
	Enter *Beavis & Butthead,* an animated show about two heavy-metal music fans doing stupid things, designed to keep young male viewers from channel hopping.

(Continued)

Table 20.1 (Continued)

2000s	Nearly 3 billion people worldwide tune in to TV or Internet telecasts of the 2005 "Live 8" global poverty benefit concert series with 1,000 musicians performing in nine countries.
	American Idol, a format adaption of the U.K. show *Pop Idol,* debuts on Fox Broadcasting, eventually making recording stars of many of the winners and runners-up who were selected by viewers.
	Janet Jackson's "wardrobe malfunction" during the 2004 Super Bowl halftime show raises an outcry over television and decency standards; the FCC eventually fines CBS-owned affiliates a total of $550,000.
	The popularity of DVDs with their high audio and visual quality expands the allure of music videos.
	Music videos get posted on the Internet, allowing consumers with broadband connections to select titles at will, ending decades of viewing being dictated by TV schedules.
	Video piracy sparks industry fears that rights holders will lose control of distribution, just as they did with audio P2P file sharing.

In terms of sheer significance, however, no music variety program can match the prime time weekly series *The Ed Sullivan Show* for breaking new ground. It presented Elvis to the American mainstream (while censoring his gyrating hips), first televised the Rolling Stones and the Doors, and launched the British Invasion with its historic showcase of the Beatles in 1964.

While schedules can change quickly with audience tastes, the era of these classic "music variety" shows would seem to have passed, although various concert series are still going strong, primarily on public television, supplanted at least for a time by music talent contests such as *American Idol.*

Taking up the live-music showcase mantle for established acts, in large part, are an expanding slate of morning, daytime, and late-night news/entertainment/talk shows that regularly feature performances by the hottest bands from that week's charts. Particularly coveted by the labels for their promotional power are bookings on the major late-night shows and morning programs. Daytime talk shows are less likely to feature musical performances on a regular basis, but when they do, they can offer an opening for artists outside the pop music mainstream, including classical and show music performers. The long-running comedy sketch show *Saturday Night Live* has remained for many years the most sought-after TV-series booking, guaranteeing watercooler conversation on the Monday morning after a performance and a potential record sales boost in the days beyond.

Music Specials/Events/Awards Shows

Although "music variety shows" have faded out as a series format on mainstream English-language TV, the prime-time live-music special or event on TV has continued to thrive. Just as it once wasn't Christmas until Bing Crosby or Andy Williams sang about the season with other sweater-clad stars on TV, the holidays today still inevitably bring forth a range of special musical programming, in multiple genres and various show formats. Particularly high-profile concerts (such as "farewell" performances or lavishly staged spectacles) also find their way onto the small screen, as do "mini" concerts keyed to other events, such as the Super Bowl. A small number of stars still get their own telecast specials on occasion.

The most abundant source of music event programming comes from an array of music awards shows, which now cover the gamut from pop to country to hip-hop to Latin music to "people's choice" picks across the musical spectrum. The main music awards shows are The Grammys, the MTV Music Awards, the CMA Awards (from the

Country Music Association), the Rock and Roll Hall of Fame Induction Ceremony, and American Music Awards. Even nonmusic shows such as the Emmy Awards, the Oscars, and theater's Tony Awards have carved out airtime for musical performances of nominated show songs or musicals. (The Emmys, of course, have long honored the many music contributions to TV with awards in numerous categories from outstanding title theme music to outstanding music direction.)

Figure 20.1   TV and Video Production

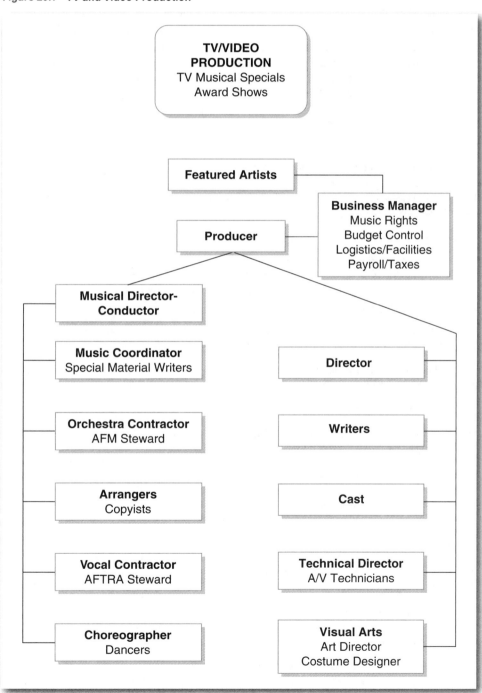

Performing slots on the highest-profile of these shows are valued as much as, or more than, the trophies themselves. The power of an award to boost a winner's album sales can vary from greatly to hardly, but sales upticks are easily measured in the catalogs of acts that performed live during the shows.

As one might expect, music specials are major productions to pull off. Figure 20.1 represents graphically how musicians and other personnel work together in this genre. This flowchart for a *recorded* music special (a process similar to, but in some ways quite distinct from, a *live* program) exhibits a huge payroll; productions on this scale are economically feasible only for network shows and cable TV specials. It is probable that part of the cost of such productions is borne through exploitation of **aftermarkets**—home videos, Web video downloads, or foreign exhibitions, for instance. On the plus side, these programs offer employment opportunities for a wide array of creative individuals, from studio musicians to background singers to copyists. Table 20.2 runs down the many steps required to put together a music special, and the many people required to make one successful.

Table 20.2   Production of a TV Music Special

A program of this kind requires the services of a large number of talented artists and businesspeople. The following is a typical sequence of activity.

1. The producer contracts with the director, writers, and performers.

2. The producer schedules a series of meetings to decide what music is to be programmed (original or preexisting; live or prerecorded) and who is to perform it. These decisions are made in consultation with the musical director, writers, choreographer, featured performers, and art director. Star performers' personal musical directors and/or personal managers may also provide input.

3. The musical director meets with the special material writers, music coordinator, and featured artists to set music routines—style, key, sequence, etc. The music is sketched for full scoring later.

4. The music coordinator, often doubling as the rehearsal pianist, rehearses the featured performers, using musical sketches, confirming keys, routines, and more.

5. The musical director hires arrangers to score the music for the orchestra.

6. If background singers are to be used, the musical director will probably hire a choral director to prepare the music for the singers, hire the singers, and rehearse them separately from the orchestra.

7. The arrangers hire copyists or a music preparation firm to extract the individual parts for the instrumentalists and singers, run off copies as needed, bind the scores, set up the books, and deliver them to the studio for rehearsal and recording. The supervising copyist attends the recording sessions, acts as music librarian, and corrects mistakes in the parts, reorchestrating passages if needed.

8. Meanwhile, the musical director has hired an AFM contractor to engage the individual musicians for the studio orchestra. The contractor and supervising copyist develop a list of doublers—the musicians in the orchestra required to play more than one instrument. The contractor notifies the doublers what additional instruments to bring to the sessions.

9. The orchestra prerecords most, if not all, of the show. Prerecording may be done to provide accompanying music for dancers. Featured singers might prerecord their voices, too, particularly if they are called on to dance when they sing.

10. After preliminary rehearsal, the background singers join the orchestra to record their tracks. Meanwhile, the audio engineers have been busy recording the best possible orchestra-choral sounds and coordinating live recording with prerecorded tracks. They are assisted by music cutters or editors. Final master tapes are produced that now include music, dialogue, and sound effects.

Theme Songs

Many TV theme songs (e.g., the country whistling tune of *The Andy Griffith Show,* the organ heavy *The Addams Family* theme, the hopeful piano lilt of *Hill Street Blues,* and the techno-sound throb from *Miami Vice*) have claimed a place in the pages of American music history. A select few, such as the *Miami Vice* theme and the Rembrandts' rendition of the *Friends* theme ("I'll Be There for You"), have even taken up residence for a time on the pop music charts. Today, fewer shows have full-scale opening theme songs (networks fear viewers will channel-surf away during a long introduction), and others use existing pop songs in place of original material. Still, the TV theme song remains a vital part of the TV scene.

Background Music and Foreground Spotlights

Like film music (see Chapter 21), the majority of TV music serves as "background," added during editing to create mood, to fill gaps, and to provide cultural context. As noted earlier, this type of music use is a significant one for the music business because it brings in licensing revenues.

Although the use of background music for TV shows has been a constant since the medium debuted, the prominence given to that music has been on the rise over the years. Background music, in effect, has come increasingly to the *foreground* in some shows. Teen-targeted programs have led this trend, using large excerpts of current songs during each episode in what is called a "back sell": telling viewers at the end of the show what music was featured, displaying the album cover, and sending viewers to the network's Web site to buy the album.

Another innovation is the "club" set added into the regular environment for some TV shows, into which popular bands are booked to perform in the background while the TV characters carry on the plotline in the foreground, making a point to mention the band's name once or twice. *Beverly Hills 90210* led this pack with its Peach Pit After Dark, but *Buffy the Vampire Slayer* (The Bronze), *Charmed* (P3), and other teen-skewed shows followed. Acts that have played these TV "venues" include the Flaming Lips, Cibo Matto, Aimee Mann, and Blink-182.

The Singer/Actors

Sometimes the "band" and the TV show characters are one and the same. Classic sitcoms like *The Monkees* and *The Partridge Family* produced popular television fare as well as numerous hit records and often included performances by the band during the shows. Now, as in the past, recording stars turn up as actors on TV series, although most often in nonperforming roles; likewise, young TV stars can occasionally translate their popularity on the small screen into recording contracts and careers.

The Commercials

Ultimately, the function of the entertainment programming on broadcast or basic-cable TV is to lure the viewer to watch the commercials that bring in revenue. Any couch potato could argue, however, that these spots can sometimes be entertainment themselves, and music has played a large role in making them so. From classics of the ad jingle business such as the Alka-Seltzer "plop plop fizz fizz" rhythmic rhyme, the Oscar Meyer hotdog song, and the Meow Mix feline sing-along to the lush,

Television station control room.

Photo © Bob Cunningham.

pop-fueled approach of contemporary campaigns for car and clothing companies, songwriters and musicians have been star players in the TV commercial sector.

Although product-specific jingles are still commissioned from songwriters and used in TV spots, there has been an increased emphasis in recent years on **licensing** existing popular songs for commercial use. The dividends for the music business are twofold. The company pays the record label and music publisher for the right to use the music, of course, and these fees can be significant. But recording acts have also found that they can reap retail rewards through the exposure a major TV ad campaign can bring; the payoff is particularly valuable when the act is new, lesser known, or has faded from the spotlight. One example among many is the group Trio, which fell off the radar after scoring a pop hit in the early 1980s but hit the charts again after Volkswagen used the band's "Da Da Da" in a commercial, sparking an influx of calls and e-mails to the car company asking for information on how to purchase the song (Volkswagen once distributed a CD that compiled popular music from its commercials). For a fuller discussion of music in advertising, see Chapter 22.

The Evolving TV Picture

Why has TV become such a vital medium for the music industry, as outlined above? Just consider the numbers: 99% of American households have at least one TV set, making television's potential programming reach enticing. More than that, however, is the opportunity that TV programs present to connect with audiences who might not otherwise be exposed to music[1]—those not inclined to tune into a radio station, for instance, or to pop on a pair of headphones in a listening post at a mall record store.

Not all programming reaches that wide audience—"mainstream America"—anymore, of course, because hundreds of channels have arisen to target viewers with specific interests.

Four major commercial networks (NBC, CBS, ABC, and Fox) dominate conventional broadcasting, with the CW Network also a national player. The more frequently viewed local TV stations tend to be affiliated with one of the networks. Local station program production is normally limited to news programs, low-budget children's shows, talk shows, perhaps an occasional local talent show, and public service shows; the use of music in local station programming is minimal. If music is needed in connection with locally produced shows, library music tracks are most often used.

Although NBC, CBS, and ABC claimed 80% of the viewing audience in 1980, network-affiliated TV stations—the leading purveyors of "free TV"—have seen their share of the overall audience pie steadily slip to under 40% in prime time. This has posed challenges to the traditional business model for TV networks, which is built on selling high-priced "mass-market" commercial spots to advertisers with the promise that they will be seen by a large number of viewers enticed by the "free" network programming.

Claiming more and more of those viewer eyeballs now are the ever-expanding slate of cable channels, which offer "narrowcast" programming centered on everything from food to sports to gardening to soap operas to game shows to science fiction to, of course, music (more on this segment—and the pioneering MTV—a little later on). The revenue model for a basic cable network has typically been a dual-revenue stream, including both ad sales and subscriber fees paid by cable operator systems, satellite TV, and other multichannel platforms. Faced with this new environment, the networks/cable distinction is blurring into a new "conglomerate" model, with networks, cable companies, and/or program producers being brought under single corporate umbrellas. This allows for the sharing of programming and costs, such as ABC Television and cable sibling ABC Family's joint buying of the TV rights to *The Sound of Music*.

Competing with both conventional broadcast TV and cable are direct broadcast satellite (**DBS**) and Internet protocol television (**IPTV**) platforms, which deliver digital TV programming directly into homes. Arriving on the scene in 1994, DBS has claimed a big chunk of the audience.

Besides traditional linear TV channels, consumers now have TV options that they can call up whenever they desire, which puts consumers "in charge" in the digital media revolution:

- Pay-per-view (PPV): A variation on traditional cable pay-TV, PPV delivers events such as concerts, movies, and sports at a scheduled time.
- Video-on-demand (VOD) programming: Unlike PPV, where viewers cannot control when they view movies or programs, on-demand programming allows the user to choose precise viewing times, as well as to rewind and pause programming. On-demand choices are offered over digital cable and IPTV either for a one-time fee, free with preroll advertisement, or as part of a subscription service. The digital video recorder (**DVR**), typically offered through cable and DBS services, is a successful variant, allowing users to record regular programming for playback at any time.
- Interactive programming: This form of programming exists primarily as a so-called two-screen experience, where viewers use their PCs with Internet

access to interact with a program via quizzes, contests, or voting; the aim is to increase the amount of time that a viewer "sticks" with a program and thus make it more appealing to advertisers.

On-demand programming and DVRs have put pressure on advertisers to develop commercials or promotional programming that viewers might *choose* to watch, since hard-sell and abrasive commercials will lead to tune-out now that viewers have plenty of options. And that, of course, is opening new doors for the entertainment industry to work with the ad sector.

The Home Theater Impetus

Part of what has spurred interest in new music programming for television is the evolution of the TV set itself, which has become a home entertainment center. The home theater boom itself was initially driven by the dramatic growth of the DVD format in the 1990s, as consumers migrated away from VHS movies to the new digital entertainment format. Music-related DVD software titles—featuring concerts, backstage footage, artist commentary, interviews, and more—have proved to be a popular sales niche for the music industry.

Where once stereo sound was hailed as a breakthrough, the ultimate home experience now includes high definition (HD), big screen TVs, HD DVD players, and DVRs. The result is a living room with stunning sound and visually spectacular effects like that experienced in movie theaters—or in concert halls and nightclubs. Cable and satellite operators have exploited this opening, offering commercial-free digital music programming through TV sets.

MTV and the Rise of the Music Video ▮▮▮▮▮▮▮▮

Any exploration of the role of music on TV must include some discussion of MTV, the pioneer and champion of "music television." Although not the first to air music videos—the broadcast of minimovies of the Beatles' "Strawberry Fields Forever" and "Penny Lane" in the 1960s broke ground for the concept, and other clips shows followed over the years—MTV *was* the first to build an entire commercial channel around the concept. It signed on August 1, 1981, with a clip of the Buggles' "Video Killed the Radio Star," and although that prophecy did not come to pass, the music video channel did permanently alter the promotion and marketing equation for record labels and bands, putting a new premium on presentation and visual image. In the years since its debut, MTV has shifted its programming focus to include fewer videos and more original shows while also spinning off a host of new channels and subchannels focused on music segments, including music for **baby boomers** and college students as well as alternative music. Competition has also arisen from Country Music Television, Black Entertainment Television, Fuse, and others.[2]

The rise of MTV also sparked the growth of a relatively new industry: the music video production business. Once a rarity, a music video quickly became a standard promotional tool for major-label acts in the 1980s and 1990s after marketing executives realized the power of the broadcast medium to captivate fans—and motivate album buyers. Although tighter budgets at the labels have trimmed production levels, many major acts still produce at least one clip for an album. But it is unlikely today that a short-form video will clock in at the estimated $7 million spent for Michael Jackson and Janet Jackson's *Scream* or the 14-plus minutes used for Michael's *Thriller*. With youth culture's embrace of the Internet and hand-held devices such as iPods, music videos on cable and satellite TV are less preeminent, although still a major force.

Producing Short-Form Videos

The production of music videos, or short-form videos, demands many of the same sets of skills and cast of professionals needed to make long-form projects: directors, producers, editors, special-effects experts, and so on. Many of the directors working in the field, therefore, have backgrounds directing films or commercials. Unique to the video clip process is the role of the record company, which most often produces the music videos (either sharing costs or charging all of the costs to the artists).

Most recording companies do not have in-house video directors; instead, they generally have someone in charge of overseeing video assignments for the label's acts. This person is commonly called a "video commissioner."

In a typical scenario, the artist and/or label executives overseeing music videos will approach a number of directors; generally, they will do this by going through the executive producer or director's rep at one of the many video production companies, which often boast rosters of 5 to 20 directors. Sometimes, they may also consider someone unaffiliated with a production company who has made a strong impression via a music video reel sent in to the label, unsolicited.

Each of the selected candidate directors will then come up with a concept for the video, incorporating into it any style/thematic preferences that the artist or label has put forth (oftentimes, they leave the creative end entirely to the director; other times, they have a specific idea in mind). In most situations, directors come up with their own concepts and thus perform double-duty as writers as well, although a few do work with third-party writers.

In pitching the director's concepts to the label/artist, the production company's producer will hand over the director's treatment (typically a one-to-three page script of how the director sees the video), design aids (photos or scenes from movies or other things to explain or demonstrate the vision), and a budget based on the elements of the treatment. This budget should fit within the monetary guidelines originally put forth by the commissioner. (For a sample music video budget worksheet, see Table 20.3.)

The commissioner will then narrow down the pitches and go to the artist and the rest of the management and creative team at the label to choose the one that best fits their needs. At this stage, a few of the directors may be asked to fine-tune certain parts of their treatment, before they choose the one they want to go with.

The organization most representative of short-form video producers is the Music Video Production Association (MVPA). MVPA's major goals are to exchange technical information, standardize production-bidding procedures, and formulate guidelines for fees and payment schedules.

Once a video director has been selected, he or she will want to engage, early on, a production designer, and possibly a choreographer. A video **storyboard** is sometimes created, when the budget is sufficient, similar to the storyboards created for TV commercials (see Chapter 22), and a shooting schedule is set. Many music videos are now shot on location because it is less expensive than building sets (and budgets have been decreasing). Table 20.4 shows the three phases characterizing most short-form video production.

Table 20.3   Music Video Budget Summary Worksheet

Production/song title _____   Date _____

Video commissioner/label _____

_____

Director _____

_____

Principal photography begins _____   No. of days _____

Above-the-Line Expenses

Production	Cost
Director	
Producer	
Above-the-line subtotal	

Below-the-Line Expenses

Production assistants	
Extra talent	
Set operations	
Property	
Wardrobe	
Makeup and hair	
Electrical	
Camera	
Sound (playback, sound package, walkie-talkies)	
Transportation	
Location (rental, permits, catering)	
Film, tape, and lab	
Other	
Subtotal production	
Postproduction	
Off-line editing	
On-line editing	
Stock, dubs, transfers	
Other	
Subtotal postproduction	
General and administrative	
Insurance	
Office and miscellaneous	
Contingency	
Subtotal general and administrative	
Below-the-line subtotal	
Grand Total	

Note: Production budgets for music videos range all the way from a few hundred dollars ("let's grab a camera and shoot in the park"), to $1 million and up ("Madonna wants another 50 medieval extras for the night banquet scene at the castle"). The bigger variables include size of the crew and number of shooting days.

Table 20.4 Short-Form Video Production: The Three Phases

<table>
<tr><td colspan="1" align="center">**Preproduction phase**</td></tr>
</table>

1. Audio master tape is completed. Record company negotiates a synchronization license with the music publisher for the video.

2. Label determines a production budget, negotiates with the artist for possible sharing of costs.

3. Budget is set, and label engages a freelance video director.

4. Director, label, and artist develop a concept for the video.

5. Director engages a producer, possibly a choreographer, supporting cast, director of photography.

6. Director and production designer lay out a storyboard.

7. Sets are designed, then constructed or rented; locations are scouted and secured.

8. Costumes are designed, then executed or rented.

9. Soundstage is booked; production manager engages production personnel (gaffers, stagehands, etc.).

10. Producer rents equipment as needed (cameras, lights, dollies).

11. Director orders audio click tracks to aid rehearsals.

12. Producer arranges accident, health, and liability insurance.

13. All of the foregoing are reconfirmed.

<table>
<tr><td colspan="1" align="center">**Shooting phase**</td></tr>
</table>

1. Director rehearses the performers' lip-synching, stage movements. Choreographer rehearses dancers.

2. Director rehearses camera movements, approves lighting, and plans special effects.

3. The production is shot.

<table>
<tr><td colspan="1" align="center">**Postproduction phase**</td></tr>
</table>

1. Producer orders return of all rented equipment, sets, costumes; orders sets struck, soundstage cleared, locations cleaned up.

2. Director supervises all postproduction work, including editing, processing of visual effects, computer graphics, opticals; edits final master, orders copies made.

3. Producer (a) obtains releases from all performers, artists, and creative personnel; (b) gets signed W-4 forms from all personnel; (c) satisfies all union contracts; and (d) authorizes payments to all personnel.

4. Director delivers video master to the recording company.

5. Director and producer confirm that all bills have been paid.

6. All concerned look for their next job!

7. Record company seeks airplay for promotional purposes and hopes to recoup producion costs through other revenue streams, including home video release.

During production, differences may arise over "artistic control." The director may want one thing, the artist something else. The artist's recording contract, when properly drawn, will articulate who decides how the videos are to be handled, particularly in respect to style, content, and choice of director. Smart artists will usually defer to the judgments of directors of proven ability. It should be noted, however, that the final product belongs to the record label and that it retains the final approval on edits. Occasionally, directors who are highly respected will be awarded "final cut," but such occurrences are rare.

Notes

1. Consider the case of Ken Burns's *JAZZ,* a 10-part PBS documentary series that ran in 2001 and created an immediate surge of sales for jazz titles both directly tied to the broadcast and others simply featuring acts showcased in the series. There are many other examples throughout the years of sales spikes for music in genres with few other wide means of exposure.
2. Both CMT and BET were later acquired by MTV parent company Viacom.

Chapter Takeaways

- Music was prominent in TV's early days with regularly scheduled music-oriented series and variety shows.

- The first 24-hour music TV channel launched in 1981 and spurred demand for promotional videos made by artists to market their songs.

- Handheld devices with video capability, ranging from cell phones to DVD players, have expanded the realm of music TV.

- Televised music awards shows that have proliferated are useful promotion platforms for selling songs and artists.

- Theme songs of TV programs are usually original tunes that are created to set a mood, helping establish a show's brand image with the audience.

- TV commercials utilize music—both original compositions and licensed existing songs—in what is a huge industry offering employment opportunities for musicians.

Key Terms

- affiliates (p. 344)
- aftermarkets (p. 346)
- digital video recorders (DVRs) (p. 349)
- licensing (p. 348)
- MTV (p. 350)
- posted on the Internet (p. 344)
- short-form video (p. 351)
- storyboard (p. 351)
- theme songs (p. 347)
- treatment (p. 351)
- video commissioner (p. 351)

CHAPTER 21

Dramatic Scoring for Movies, TV, and Games

Many musicians have a common ambition on their multifaceted career "to do" lists—to score the music for a movie, TV show, or video game. Others in the industry make a good living by crafting such creative works as their only pursuit.

Though scoring is most often associated with music for the blockbuster theatrical release or the hit TV series, much of the work in the field is performed with other markets in mind. Business, educational, training, and documentary films and videos offer potential employment opportunities because they, too, require film scoring. Under the term *scoring,* we include composition, orchestration, copying, and recording. Professionals use the expression *film scoring* in reference to the preparation and recording of **dramatic music** intended to synchronize with and augment the action on the screen.

> "[An intellectual] is someone who can listen to the "William Tell Overture" without thinking of the Lone Ranger."
>
> —John Chesson

According to one American Society of Composers, Authors and Publishers (ASCAP) source, "The musical score is the glue that holds much of a movie together." Music evokes human emotional response. The action on screen can be intensified, made humorous, or relaxed (or trivialized) by what happens in the musical score. Sometimes, it functions as background; other times, the music is definitely in the conscious foreground. Film composers have saved many a weak scene. The artistic contributions of our best movie composers often match those of the actors observed

Left: Actress Jodie Foster on a scoring stage.

Photo © Michael Tighe/Getty Images.

on the screen. As for public acceptance, it is not unusual for a movie sound track album to turn a profit rivaling the film itself, and some of the music scored for TV dramas will probably be remembered longer than the programs.

Background

From the very first days, music has been an integral part of the movie experience. Silent films were accompanied by small orchestras, or if that was too expensive, by piano players, or in the big movie palaces, organists, who improvised to suit the action (at least, the first time they saw a film).

The first music heard by the public on a movie sound track occurred in 1927, when vaudevillian Al Jolson broke into song in the middle of a film titled *The Jazz Singer*. The public loved it, and very quickly producers began adding music and audible dialogue to their movies. At first, they simply borrowed music from other sources—Broadway, Beethoven, Liszt, **Tin Pan Alley,** just what the musicians for silent films had done. But soon, producers turned to classical composers to score original music. These included many prestigious composers of the early 20th century: Satie, Milhaud, Honegger, Hindemith, Shostakovich, Stravinsky, Schoenberg, Prokofiev, Castelnuovo-Tedesco, Thomson, Vaughan Williams, Toch, Copland, and Bernstein. These composers scored films only sporadically; composers who work in the field full-time have scored most movies.

The period of the 1930s and 1940s is known to film music buffs as the Golden Age. All the major studios in Hollywood—MGM, 20th Century Fox, Paramount, Columbia, Universal, Disney, Warner Bros., and RKO—had composers on salary full-time. Each major studio had a staff orchestra of almost symphonic proportions, required because the preferred musical style was **neo-romantic**. Producers would explain that they wanted music that sounded like Tchaikovsky, Rachmaninoff, or Debussy. Leaders in the neo-romantic style were Alfred Newman, Franz Waxman, Bronislau Kaper, and Miklos Rozsa (although Rozsa broke 19th-century bonds with period pictures such as *Ben Hur*). These scores sounded European because most of these composers were either from Europe or trained in European styles.

Changing Styles

Tastes began to change after World War II. In the 1950s, a number of first-rate film composers began to abandon the musical clichés to experiment with more contemporary American sounds (jazz, big bands, etc.). The leaders in this break from European romanticism included Hugo Friedhofer, David Raksin, Jerome Morros, and later, Bernard Herrmann, Alex North, and Henry Mancini.

Composers were influenced, until the 1960s, by techniques used for movie cartoons, such as Popeye the Sailor and Mortimer (later changed to Mickey) Mouse. Producers wanted their composers to **catch the action**: If Mickey Mouse slipped on a banana peel, the composer was expected to **underscore** the action with a trombone **glissando.** When the Good Guy discovered the Bad Guy lurking in the shadows, the orchestra was expected to play what is still known in the business as a **stinger,** a **sforzando** chord. Remnants of the old Mickey Mouse style remain here and there, but a film score using it today can sound silly, because audiences have long since memorized these clichés from watching old programming on TV.

In many of the early comedies, the entire movie was underscored with a popular song droning in the background, even under dialogue. Of a higher artistic order was the practice in the 1930s of hiring Broadway and Tin Pan Alley composers to write songs for feature films. Some of these early Hollywood musicals spawned a fair share of the standards we know today.

The discovery by film producers of the value of a good popular song occurred in 1949, when the main theme from *The Third Man* film, featuring a zither, hit the pop record charts. The message was not lost on other film producers, who searched for film composers who could turn out hits that could be incorporated into their feature films. Many of these songs had little to do with the film itself. Nevertheless, producers continue to include seemingly pointless songs in their films in the hope that if the movie bombs at the box office, they might recover some of their production losses with a pop sound track recording. By the 1950s, movie composers could be classified into one of two categories: (a) those able to underscore drama on film and (b) the pop songwriters, most of whom were unfamiliar with techniques for writing for sound tracks or background music. By the 1960s, a third group had emerged, artists who could not only underscore film drama appropriately but who could also invent attractive melodies that could be pulled from a sound track and popularized on hit records and sheet music. This kind of versatility was new to the movies but hardly unknown in traditional music—Mozart, Verdi, Bizet, and many other theater music composers knew how to underscore drama, then follow with a popular-type song as the occasion might demand.

Jazz found its place in the movie-scoring business, too, and was given further impetus from television. In 1959, film composer Henry Mancini wrote the score for the television mystery series *Peter Gunn*. It was agreed that Mancini would use a "big band" playing driving jazz. It was particularly appropriate for this series, because the big-city chase scenes seemed to call for the frenetic energy of jazz. It worked so well it became one of the great classics of TV scoring. A new generation of film composers emerged who could do both dramatic, classical-based underscoring and contemporary jazz. Some left concert touring with name bands and found new homes (big ones) in Hollywood. Lalo Schifrin, European trained but very creative in jazz styles, could not only handle dramatic underscoring but would occasionally score an entire film using improvised jazz, such as in the National Geographic TV series, *The Hidden World of Insects*. For this series, he brought to the scoring stage just some sketches, tone clusters, and 12-tone rows, then instructed his small chamber orchestra to improvise freely on these fragments.

After some experimentation with synthesizers when they first hit the scene, the industry turned again to late-19th-century neo-romantic music with full orchestra as the basic foundation for film music, even the thrillers. Into this, themes, styles, and instrumentation from the whole world of music are integrated, in the service of enhancing the films. For films with a strong ethnic element, native instruments are folded into more standard orchestration, and musical clichés and phony ethnic music are carefully avoided. Moviegoers (and directors) have developed sophisticated ears.

Emergence of Sound Tracks

Including potential hit songs in sound tracks has evolved to the point where song scores are now quite prominent. Many of these songs and sound track albums have been gigantic hits, netting tremendous profits for the films' producers and the composers (see Table 21.1 for a hypothetical example).

Table 21.1   Hypothetical Revenue Streams for a Successful Movie Song

Synchronization and video buyout	$40,000
U.S. radio and TV performances	800,000
U.S. album sales (CDs and downloads)	150,000
U.S. single sales (CDs and downloads)	78,000
Academy Awards telecast	1,600
Grammy telecast	1,600
Sheet music and folios	18,000
Ringtones and ringbacks	52,000
Foreign performances: radio, TV, and theatrical	300,000
Foreign album sales (CDs and downloads)	112,000
Foreign single sales (CD and downloads)	33,000
Miscellaneous royalties	30,000
TV and radio commercials	35,000
Video games	0
Total combined songwriter and publisher receipts	**$1,651,200**

Source: 2009 estimate based on multiple industry sources.

The Craft

Those who underscore films use many of the techniques employed for centuries by opera composers, and most film composers are classically trained and fluent in many musical dialects. But the unique time-lapse illusions in cinema art challenge the creative powers of film composers well beyond the more familiar techniques of scoring music for the theater.

The Process

The film is first shot completely and taken through at least one edit, often more. At this point, a *temp score,* a mock-up of the score to come, is put together by a music editor (also called a **cutter**), gleaning from existing music. Sometimes, the temp score is so appropriate, the director prefers it to the finished score. There have been many cases where the temp score was used and an original score thrown out, such as in *2001: A Space Odyssey* and *The Exorcist.*

Spotting the Film

The first time the composer views the movie, it is usually in the company of the producer, director, film editor, and music editor. The director and composer watch the film roll by and spot the film, identifying the turning points, the changes in mood. Just as important, they also discuss where music should not be used. The music editor listens to this conversation and makes notes and comments on what the other two have decided. When the spotting is complete, the composer generally receives the first part of the agreed-on fee.

Spotting Notes. The music editor gives the composer **spotting notes**, which specify where each cue will happen when in the movie. An example of the shorthand follows:

1M1	(reel #1, Music, location of cue on reel #1)
02:40:20:00	(SMPTE time code—see next paragraph)
39 + 12	(film footage of start)
46	(timing or length of cue)

Scene Break Downs. For several decades music editors have used video/SMPTE (Society of Motion Picture and Television Engineers) technology to gather the timing information needed to write scene break downs for each reel of film. Most contain the name of each scene calling for music, net film footage, and timings to 1/10 (or even 1/100) of a second. Another column provides space for indication of **click tracks**. The "click" is simply a steady beat that can be made to go faster or slower, depending on the needs of the picture. The click track enables the composer to sync music to film with mathematical precision.

Theatrical film moves through the projector at a rate of 24 frames per second, or 1,440 frames per minute; video moves at 30 frames per second. To create a film music *tempo,* the editor or composer divides the metronome (M.M.) tempo into 1,440; the result is known as a *frame-click tempo.* Let's say the tempo is M.M. 144; dividing 1,440 by 144 gives 10, which means the cutter must prepare a 10-frame click track. Click tracks are generated by computer, and they can even determine clicks for *rubato* (speeding up/slowing down) passages. This is called a *variable click track,* and it can identify those split seconds in the score when the music must catch the action precisely. During recording sessions, the sound of the clicks will be conveyed to the conductor and musicians in the orchestra via **headsets**.

Composers on major films will usually want to view a picture several times before starting to score it, and they use video to do so. A music-editing system is used almost universally to transfer the film to a digital recorder, using a synchronization scheme that transfers film feet and frames to the standard SMPTE time code. The picture is electronically synchronized with multitrack recorders. The video copy of the film normally has a sequencing program, a time code, and a feet and/or frames reference for film footage conversion burned into the picture; in addition, the tape is "striped" with SMPTE code so that the code numbers can be read on a synchronizer/SMPTE code reader. This time code provides precise reference points to the composer for critical timings. The code appears this way: "00:10:23:18" and translates as follows: 0 hours, 10 minutes, 23 seconds, and 18 frames.

In recent years, the film composer often receives the film on a DVD. It can then be opened as a Quicktime movie on the computer and **slaved** while running a computer sequencer program.

Composition

Having become familiar with the film, the composer composes the new score. When the score is complete, another installment of the salary fee is paid. Many contracts for full-length feature films provide that the composer shall write the music and have it recorded in 10 weeks. In actual practice, the producer is more likely to give the composer 3 to 4 weeks to complete the job. Some composers work under 6-week deadlines, which may or may not include recording. In Europe, the composer has traditionally been expected to present a completed score to the copyists. In the United States, film composers may compose orchestral sketches, perhaps three to eight **staves** per system (system being a grouping of staves), then give the sketch, with indications for instrumentation, to an orchestrator to render the full score. This practice developed because producers were always in a hurry—and still are. They have been willing to pay the extra costs of dividing the writing of movie scores between two persons. A few unschooled but highly gifted composers also hire orchestrators to write out their scores.

Film scoring today is done electronically as well as acoustically, and often, both are used for the same project. A number of computer synchronization methods are now available, as well as service companies that can aid composers in laying out whole movie scores with appropriate clicks, meters, bars, and tempos.

Recording to Film

Then it's time to record the music; when that's accomplished, the final installment of the fee is paid. Whether a film composer uses an optical click-track system or computer methods, it should be pointed out that many composers prefer to conduct to film by free timing, using a system of "streamers and punches" as timing guideposts. A streamer is a straight line that takes 2 seconds to traverse the screen from left to right, and a punch is the flash of light produced by punching a hole in the film, usually every three frames. Such composer-conductors leave precise synchronizations to the ingenuity of their music cutters.

Many films combine synthesizers, samplers, and orchestra and require multitrack recording and **mixing.** Feature films are commonly recorded all at once, "live," with the full orchestra present, often including an extensive arsenal of electronic (MIDI, or musical instrument digital interface) instruments as a significant section of the big studio orchestra. Most feature films are recorded on movie "scoring stages." These facilities are huge. Soundstages are attended during recording sessions not only by a half-acre of musicians, but also by scoring **mixers,** a music librarian, the music editor, the composer's agent, and the head copyist.

Occasionally, a film director will throw out a complete score, fire the composer, and engage another one to redo the job. But these instances are rare. However, producers and/or directors often require music changes on the scoring stage, placing everyone under tremendous pressure. Usually, this high-tension environment proceeds with efficiency—because the stage is inhabited by pros. As a rule, the only delays in scoring movies are similar to the ones afflicting most other recording sessions—mistakes in the orchestra parts or equipment malfunction.

The Final Mix

Following the music recording sessions, which last for several days on major films, the music is combined with dialogue and sound effects in dubbing sessions. This final

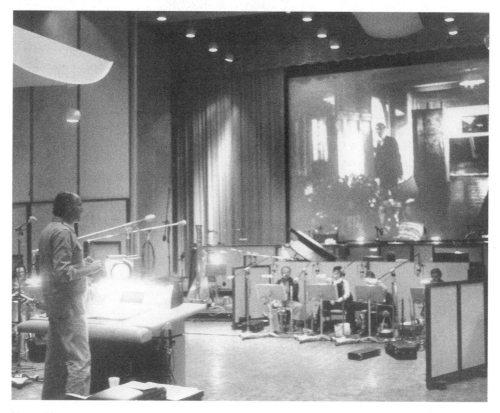

Henry Mancini conducting on a scoring stage.

Photo courtesy of Mancini Family.

phase of sound synchronization, called rerecording, is mostly concerned with setting relative sound levels and making final choices regarding the music and sound, including whether some segments need to be recut. The composer, music cutter, sound effects person, and one to three engineers or mixers attend these dubbing sessions. At elaborate dubbing facilities, the remixing setup may call for up to seven mixers at a huge console. Film directors attend these sessions to make sure the sounds they require are sufficiently prominent. Not infrequently, the composer approaches despair when music gets lost behind shouting dialogue or screaming sirens.

Music Scoring for TV

Movies produced for television employ the same stylistic approach as for feature films, but the time frame is much faster, and the person who makes the music decisions is often the producer of the show, not the director. Composers often work in both media.

TV drama series (including soap operas and sitcoms) also use original music along with their libraries of prerecorded themes and melodic fragments. The amount of music varies from show to show—one might record new music three times a week; another, once every 2 or 3 years. Composers for new shows often compose 2 or 3 weeks' worth of new material to establish the "feel"; for later shows, the music editors cut the bits they want from the show's library, which has been created from the new music.

Styles incorporate the same wide range as feature films; one multiple Emmy Award winner, for instance, orchestrated a Beethoven string quartet to underscore a chase scene! It has been the task of the music cutter over the years to lay in the various musical sources as appropriately as possible in subsequent shows in a series, trying to make them fit not only new timings but different dramatic situations. A TV series' composer is sometimes required to become, literally, a one-person band—composing, conducting, and playing the music, perhaps joined by a few other instrumentalists. The composer usually has one or two assistants, along with a music engineer, and occasionally may assign orchestration to nonstaff personnel.

An organization to be aware of is the Society of Composers and Lyricists, whose members work exclusively in TV and films.

Music Scoring for Video Games

The process of scoring for video games is very similar to film and TV. Indeed, a number of renowned film and TV composers have lent their talents to video games, among them Bill Conti, Sean Callery, Mike Giacchino, Steve Jablonsky, Chris Lennertz, Mark Mothersbaugh, Paul Oakenfold, and Hans Zimmer.

The composer's objective is to capture a game's personality and emotional heart in music. Games are interactive—the screen action is unpredictable. Despite that difference from linear content, game composers say there is no special twist to scoring video games other than to be true to the title's spirit. Games are electronic products, so it helps if composers are game aficionados and have a tech orientation, but this is not mandatory.

Much of the audio content of video games is original since signature music further embeds the "brand" of the game in the minds of consumers. Branding is important to game companies because game content passes through various media; they can be played on consoles, portable hand-held players, wireless devices, and can be adapted into movies and TV programs.

Composers are hired on a freelance basis, although game companies have staff music supervisors to manage each project. With hit video games out-grossing most movies, a game's creative content is becoming increasingly valuable. Composing fees have escalated from the early days and licensing of game music to other media—such as soundtracks—is on the rise. Some music has been created specifically for release through video games: Rise Again's 2009 track "Death Blossoms" was written for *Guitar Hero: World Tour,* and Motley Crüe released the single, "Saints of Los Angeles," in 2008 as a download through *Rock Band.*

Not all game music is originally written for the medium, of course. When popular music is used, labels, artists, composers, and publishers derive royalty payments from licenses negotiated by game developers. Importantly for the licensors, these are non-linear synchronization rights that do not cannibalize revenues from other channels like CD sales or online distribution.

When a video game has music at the heart of the game, it provides another profitable avenue for game licensing. Music-based games act as aggregators of music, such as *Guitar Hero: Greatest Hits,* which featured tracks from Alice In Chains, Queen, Poison, Rage Against The Machine, Twisted Sister, and Heart.

Game music is increasingly being added as a category to industry awards, or qualifying for soundtrack awards along with film and TV. With this evolution, game audio has advanced from the rudimentary beeps and bleeps of the medium's earliest years to CD quality music that in some cases is recorded by symphonic orchestras.

Library Music

Beyond the glitter of Hollywood, thousands of educational films, documentaries, and movies are produced for business and industry every year, and practically all of them use only library music tracks. The reason is simple: low cost. Purchase of music from a library for prerecorded music includes all necessary clearances and licenses for use of the music. A producer can underscore complete productions with **cues** (or **bridges**) lifted from the music library.

Library services classify cues in predictable ways (you can buy the whole catalog or pay for individual **needle drops**). Even "neutral" bridges are available. The lengths of these fragments are rarely critical. The director can instruct the mixer to fade out the music whenever necessary. Library-type material is often prepared by composers with MIDI studios. See Chapter 24 for more information about production music libraries.

Hiring Practices

The pathway to movie jobs is often a connection to the film's director, who oversees hiring of all creative workers. Professionals recommend that scorers have a competent attorney and music publisher to negotiate deals that leave composers with some rights to their music, instead of signing away everything to the producer. A good agent is also useful.

AFM Contracts

The musicians' union does not set scales for composition, leaving that issue to be negotiated between the composer and the producer. But the American Federation of Musicians (AFM) does set minimums for other persons engaged in music preparation—arrangers, orchestrators, copyists, proofreaders, and librarians. Union musicians earn premium rates for services performed after 12 a.m. and on holidays, and music preparation workers earn the same fringe benefits as instrumentalists.

Musicians working in film receive additional income once a year from the AFM Film Musicians Secondary Markets Fund. This fund derives its income from producers and movie studios that sell exhibition rights to their movies in additional marketplaces.

Package Deals

In the film-scoring field, producers and directors require the services of composers, orchestrators, arrangers, music editors, supervisors, copyists, librarians, and instrumentalists, as well as recording and mixing engineers. At one time, all these services could be provided by the major film studios, which retained these artists and technicians on staff, most of them full-time. But after 1957, when the staff musicians were let go by the film studios, producers had to engage all their musicians on a freelance basis. To make this situation manageable, producers would often negotiate package deals with independent contractors. This practice prevails today in many aspects of the field. For instance, almost all TV shows are packaged. Some composers of electronic scores agree to package deals because their compositional skills combined with their computer skills allow them to function as the composer, orchestrator, copyist, instrumentalist, and scoring mixer.

Producers like package deals because the system transfers their financial risk to the independent contractor. The production company usually budgets a set figure for music. That money must cover all music production costs—composition, orchestration, arranging, copying, proofreading, library services, conducting, instrumentalists, instrument cartage, studio or soundstage rental, tape, mixing, and editing. The producer will contract with a composer to assume all these responsibilities and expenses for a lump sum.

Many composers learn how to budget their time and expenses and come out well on these deals. Many manage to pay full AFM scale and have enough left over for themselves to compensate for several grueling weeks of composition and orchestration. Recognizing that some independent pictures are produced for a total cost that's less than the music budget for a blockbuster, the AFM has come up with a two-tier scale for motion picture work. Producers of music for low-budget films are allowed to hire musicians at a significantly lower scale than that required for a high-budget film.

Composers

In the field of underscoring movies and TV drama, there are many employment opportunities for the fully qualified professional. Although some feature films are still recorded in New York, most American-made movies are recorded in Los Angeles. Well-known composers say they get their picture assignments because of their reputations; their agents do not actually find them jobs but assist in drawing up contracts with producers and help in keeping their business affairs in order. Producers are accustomed to negotiating with composers' agents.

For many years, only a few agents have dominated the scene, and the young composer often finds it extremely difficult to acquire the services of an established agent. The composer must thus function as the agent and contact directors, producers, and anyone else who might be a potential employer. A composer has a better chance of securing an agent and influential music lawyers after achieving several scoring credits. Some composers rely on building and maintaining good relationships with particular filmmakers to land their projects, and use the services of attorneys for the contract negotiation rather than agents.

Top film composers sometimes get so busy they find it necessary to call in helpers to meet deadlines. These assistants include not only arrangers, orchestrators, and copyists but composers as well. Under pressure of time, or possibly because the producer has provided funds to pay for orchestration in addition to composition, studio composers will entrust completion of their sketches to arrangers and orchestrators who understand how the composer wants the music to sound. The composer, not the producer or director, selects all arrangers and orchestrators used in these secondary capacities.

The use of orchestrators is much more common in feature film work than in television. They are paid by the musician whose name goes on the screen credits. Purists may be bothered by the **ghost-writing** phenomenon, but this is the route many hopefuls have found for breaking into TV and film scoring. Yet another way of cracking these high-paying media is to be an advanced student of a busy composer. Not infrequently, teachers farm out some of their work to their best students, who later begin to locate scoring jobs in their own names. Sometimes, composers take on composer assistants, a form of apprenticeship of benefit to both parties.

Several excellent books have been written about music in the movies. For example, Fred Karlin's *Listening to Movies: The Film Lover's Guide to Film Music* is an authoritative and readable survey of movie music.

Music Supervisors

With the rise to prominence of song scores, many film producers now hire a music supervisor. In some situations, this individual finds songs and music to support and enhance the video or film image. Such responsibilities are much like those of a record producer or an A&R (artist and repertoire) executive with a recording company. Sometimes, the music supervisor is responsible for putting together only the songs used in the sound track but in other instances is in charge of every facet of the score, including hiring a composer for dramatic scoring.

Music supervisors may have various duties, depending on the type of production and the size of budget of a film or video project. A music supervisor may be asked to

1. Make up a budget, make deals, and act as a music department for an independent film company.

2. Place existing songs in appropriate spots of the movie.

3. Oversee a musical movie, picking songs from a certain period or place to match the action and plot of the movie.

4. Be in the studio when a performer from the movie is recording a song that will be used in the movie.

5. Prepare people for the set, deciding on those who can do their own vocals and those who will need to lip-synch over someone else's singing voice.

6. Assist the director and choreographer in designing shots that will work with the music. This can be very creative work, much like directing.

7. Explain "score design" to investors and other interested parties. Some investors in film properties are quite knowledgeable, but others are new to the business or lack the experience necessary to make responsible budgetary decisions during the making of the movie. These investors often want to see evidence of progress during the movie-making process, so music supervisors make the temp tracks available for a showing of a movie preview.

The music supervisor may also help make the transition from the temp track to the music track that is eventually composed for the movie. This can involve hiring a person who can take an MIDI file—a score or cue that does not exist on paper but instead has been created in a computer sequencing program—and translate it into a conventional sketch that then goes to the orchestrator.

Copyists

Copyists are engaged by the composer or sometimes by the orchestrator. In the film and TV fields, it has been traditional to schedule composition and recording sessions within a time frame calculated to produce a maximum level of panic in all concerned. Last-minute recording sessions are the rule. Also standard in the business is the tendency for composers to begin their assignments several hours beyond the last possible minute. Thus, the copyists consistently work under intolerable time pressures. Because an individual cannot copy many scores in the time available, it is common practice for head copyists to turn over some or all of the work to a music preparation service. Although some copyists still manually write notes in musical parts, others are adept at using the various computer programs that exist for this purpose, such as Finale. Most computer music programs allow the copyist or arranger to make instant changes of key and time signature if such changes are required to suit the picture.

When television shows or films are being recorded, the **supervising copyist** is expected to attend the sessions to serve as music librarian and, more important, to be available to correct errors in the extracted parts during the recording.

Orchestra Musicians

Instrumentalists hired to play film and video scores produced in the United States are most often members of the AFM. Despite this dominance, the number of movies produced in the United States that are scored and recorded by nonunion musicians has increased through the application of MIDI studios and computer one-person bands. When large groups of union musicians are called for, they are engaged by the orchestra contractor. The contractor and the composer together prepare a **first-call** list of players, with a supplemental list of second- and third-choice players, should their favorite musicians not be available. Many composers conduct as well, but some prefer to hire conductors so they themselves can oversee in the sound booth, conferring with the mixer and the film's producer or director.

In New York and Los Angeles since the 1930s, the artists getting this high-paying work have been selected from a relatively small pool of musicians. These musicians have earned reputations over the years for being able to play almost anything placed before them perfectly at sight, and they often make the music sound better than it is on paper.

Musicians who play in major symphony orchestras have successfully completed a series of demanding and highly competitive auditions, but musicians who work in recording studios rarely audition for those jobs. Instead, they prove their worth and bring themselves to the favorable attention of music contractors by a variety of other methods.

Musicians who want to break into the studios are rarely accepted before they've spent the time necessary to prove their abilities to the inside pool of players. When a new player earns credentials by establishing a good reputation, not just with contractors or conductors but with the players themselves, there will be a much better chance of being recommended for recording sessions. The inside players are always alert to evaluate the newcomers.

Another pipeline to the inside is through players who are also teachers. Musicians too busy to accept all the offers they receive may recommend their most advanced students for studio and symphony jobs.

String players, almost without exception, are current members or alumni of symphony orchestras. A high percentage of them are former **concertmasters** or **first-desk** players. Besides competence in standard orchestral playing, these string players must understand jazz phrasing and the kind of style sometimes called "the Hollywood sound"—beautiful tone, romantically expressive, perfect intonation, entirely relaxed. As for double bass, many studio players have, in addition to extensive traditional backgrounds, the ability to play jazz—and often the electric bass. But when a really hot bass line is required, specialists in the rock or rhythm and blues fields are added.

Brass players making it in the studios originally came from theater orchestras and symphonies. In the 1940 to 1960 period, many brass players came off the road from name bands. In more recent years, some brass players have come from the nation's leading university concert bands. All brass players, whatever their backgrounds, are expected to handle not only **legit** music but any other style, from country to rock. When brass players take their chairs in the studio or on the scoring stage, they already know who is expected to play lead; which chair, if any, is "the jazz chair"; what horn player will play the lyrical solos. Even among this prestigious clique of superb artists, some players enjoy a special additional prestige. Most trumpet players are expected to play trumpets in B, C, or perhaps even the piccolo trumpet in D. Most **double** on flügelhorn. Trombone and French horn players are sometimes called on in big film scores to double on Wagner tuba, euphonium, or tenor tuba, even contrabass trombone.

Many studio woodwind players have backgrounds in professional symphony orchestras, and many are graduates of university concert bands and orchestras.

It is generally known that woodwind and saxophone players are expected to be competent doublers on clarinet and flute, perhaps even double reeds. But this demand for doubling is less common for feature films and TV movies, where the composers may prefer to engage specialists on each instrument.

Many woodwind and brass players now double on MIDI controllers. Composers are asking for these instruments more and more because of their versatility and the seemingly infinite number of colors and effects that are possible. They are particularly popular in TV scoring.

Studio percussionists usually come from wide backgrounds that would include extensive study and experience in styles ranging from jazz and Latin to symphonic and rock. When a particularly authentic rock or "urban" sound is wanted, sometimes specialists are brought in. The use of electronic drum sets and MIDI percussion has become widespread, and most working commercial drummers own electronic setups. If the timpani work is extensive, many contractors will engage a player with solid experience in symphony work. Even though nearly all studio percussionists play mallet instruments, contractors will sometimes hire special artists to handle elaborate solos.

Keyboard players are expected to be able to play traditional and current styles, sight-read, and improvise. The use of MIDI keyboard controllers has become so prevalent that it is now rare to find a working studio keyboard player who does not own an extensive collection of synthesizers, samplers, and related gear.

Guitarists must be competent in several musical styles. Not only are they expected to be excellent sight readers, they must also be able to improvise, to play music by ear, or even to compose music on the spot, to suit the style of music being recorded.

Music Editors

Music editing can make or break a film's score. The editor often must make copies of cues in order to use pieces of them again in the film and cut down existing cues when the picture is recut after it has been scored. Many low-budget films provide no budget at all for music cutters and expect composers to deliver a fully synchronous score, whatever system is used for timing music to picture. Composers just breaking into the profession must often function as the music editor on their projects.

The job of the music editor is to make sure the music is cued to exactly the right spots in the action. An understanding of SMPTE code, click tracks, and Pro Tools—a digital editing software program—is essential. The music editor must be completely literate and fluent in music.

Although some schools have emerged with good training programs, film music editors often acquire their skills on the job. Some start out as film editors who then turn to music cutting. Others are composers or orchestrators, then switch to music editing. The best music cutters are amazingly versatile, possessing great musical sensitivity, a keen ear for balance, and an awareness of how music can make or break a scene, all combined with knowledge of the special technology used in synchronizing music tracks to film or tape.

Society of Motion Picture and Television Engineers

Professionals seeking greater knowledge about recording techniques in film and TV often participate in the Society of Motion Picture and Television Engineers (SMPTE). In addition to serving as an information exchange, SMPTE attempts to standardize recording and synchronization techniques to enable its members to move comfortably to jobs in either medium. SMPTE has its headquarters in White Plains, New York.

Chapter Takeaways

- Although not as celebrated as the visuals, music in movies, TV programs, and video games is crucial in creating an atmosphere that advances the overall creative objective for the project.

- Scoring increasingly requires computer software skills in addition to the traditional attributes of creativity, ability to work under severe time pressure, and ease in collaborating with other professionals.

- Library music—available for easy licensing with usage rights already cleared—is financially attractive content for producers of film, TV, and video game productions.

Key Terms

- click tracks   (p. 361)
- cues   (p. 365)
- library service   (p. 365)
- music supervisor   (p. 367)
- package deals   (p. 365)
- spotting notes   (p. 361)
- supervising copyist   (p. 368)
- temp score   (p. 360)
- underscore   (p. 358)

CHAPTER 22

Music in Advertising

One of the first memorable uses of "commercial music" was the radio **jingle**, "Pepsi-Cola hits the spot/Twelve full ounces/That's a lot." The early jingles jangled, and the "jingle" label stayed on long after the maturation of the first-generation advertisers who created the monotonous promotions in the early days of broadcasting. The public simply calls them commercials, of course. Advertising agencies and broadcasters call them **spots.** As the media world expanded, campaigns also spread across the Internet, cell phones, in video games, radio, and TV. The unique vocals and orchestration of the music in a given advertising campaign remains constant across media types, keeping ads on message and reinforcing a brand in the consumer's mind.

"Give me a laundry list and I'll set it to music."
—Gioacchino Antonio Rossini

As pointed out in the chapters on radio and television, it would be difficult to exaggerate the importance of broadcast commercials in the field of advertising. With radio, it is sounds, creating a "theater of the mind," that sell. In TV, it is pictures and sounds together that move the goods and services, and musical sounds can often be more effective sellers than strictly verbal ones. With online video, music can become the signature for an interactive media experience.

Although music without lyrics can be effective, it's often true that ad copy that is sung is easier to remember than copy that is spoken. Music also enhances the pictures and acts as a "**clutter**-breaker" to sort out the jumble of spots. Advertisers continue to pay for music in commercials, knowing that it is money well spent.

Photo © Comstock/Royalty Free/Getty Images.

Influences on Style

Ad agencies and their clients expect the musicians they hire to be capable of performing in current styles. The most effective spots often copy the music trend that is selling well commercially, especially if that music is receiving a lot of airplay. However, the decision to use a certain type of music should spring, ideally, from the concept that shapes the particular spot. Many television commercials employ the visual effects pioneered by music videos. These high-energy, fast-paced, audacious production styles hold viewers' attention, especially in this day and age when society itself is fast-paced. However, a slower-paced spot sometimes makes a very effective contrast, with the added benefit of still being coherent when fast-forwarded on digital video recorders, unlike quick-cut ads.

Advertisers experiment with shaky handheld camerawork and flashing visuals to grab the attention of viewers who may skip or fast-forward through a block of commercials. One advertising agency executive said that his clients are searching for unusual sounds to put in their spots that will "rivet the ear and stop the zap." In fact, he said, the line between music and sound effects has blurred so that sounds made by musical instruments are now being combined with those from many other sources. In response to this new emphasis on unusual sounds, "sound design" and "sound specialists" have sprung up in creative centers across the country for advertisers who want a distinctive sound to go with their pictures and words. Today, to capture the public's attention, sound must go beyond reality, merging organic and synthetic sounds.

Studies show that viewers tend to forget the commercials that run in the middle of a long string, called a pod, thereby limiting the effectiveness of those spots. In smaller markets where limited budgets may dictate that "talent" is composed of the local radio or television personnel, the wise advertiser will spend a few more dollars and use an "outside" voice, someone less familiar to the audience.

Jobs

Writing music and lyrics for commercials is an exciting combination of composition and commerce and, in the larger markets, is one of the most lucrative forms of music employment available; the competition for jobs is therefore ferocious. At the national level, advertisers and agencies are willing to pay fees large enough to attract hit songwriters and alumni from Broadway. Commercials were a starting point for successful musicians such as Barry Manilow, Paul Williams, and punk rocker Iggy Pop. In addition, the spot field at the local level affords good opportunities for talented but unknown writers to break into the commercial field.

Music Uses

In the musical commercial, the composer's goal is to form in the listener's mind a memorable association of the music with the product. A good musical theme and underscoring will establish immediate identity with the product; if it includes words identifying the product name, it is even more memorable, often inseparable in the listener's mind.

Another use of music with commercials involves underscoring dramatic action in a manner similar to the way films are scored. Many commercials are conceived as little plays, and music is used to help create the appropriate mood or perhaps to **punch up** action. If the minidrama is comedic, the music may be scored in a style associated with movie cartoons or television situation comedies, because the thematic treatments from these shows are already familiar to the audience.

Sometimes commercials will simply borrow music from another source. The melody may already be familiar to the listener, but the original words are discarded and new language is written to convey the advertising message. If the producer wants to borrow a copyrighted melody, permission must be obtained from the copyright owner to alter the material and use it for advertising purposes.

Another type of musical commercial might be called "star based." A well-known person offers, by acting or singing or dancing, a "testimonial" for the advertiser. The advertiser assumes the audience will be persuaded to buy the same product the star "uses." Original music is composed for the star, but if the artist has a pop, rock, or country hit, that recognizable tune might be sung with modified lyrics, as mentioned above.

Budgets

Music budgets range from several thousand dollars for a local spot to the high six figures and sometimes even seven with licensing and performance rights included (for well-known celebrity music) for an elaborate national campaign with a multiple-year contract. Microsoft reportedly paid millions of dollars to use the Rolling Stones tune "Start Me Up" in the multi-spot Windows 95 ad campaign, and Ford later licensed the same song for vehicle ads. These days, the most expensive individual TV commercials reach $1.5 million for 30 seconds.

One of the reasons the spot business is so good for musicians is that even hometown, local advertisers like to promote their products by purchasing their own theme music or aural product **logo.** Many composer-directors of limited experience break into the music spot business through low-budget advertising jobs financed by the local furniture store or car dealership.

The small-budget TV advertiser may try to save money by using music from a stock **music house** that supplies radio, TV, and films with **canned tracks.** If an advertiser also uses local radio spots, portions of the audio tracks may be **lifted** and transferred to video use, thus drawing extra mileage from the money originally invested in custom music for the radio campaign.

Nearly all local broadcast spots have limited budgets for music. National campaigns, however, often spend huge sums for custom music. New York remains the biggest advertising production center. Other hot creative centers include Boulder, Chicago, Dallas, Miami, Portland, and San Francisco.

Station Branding Logos

One of the most widely used types of musical commercial is the **station logo** or **ID**, which gives an outlet a "brand" image or identity to standout as the media landscape fragments. Most radio and television stations hire an independent production company to create a musical "trademark" or fragment of sound that is used whenever the station announces (or shows on the screen) its call letters. Many station logos feature a small vocal ensemble. Electronically synthesized sounds are primarily used (at a cost far less than a full orchestra) and are often supplemented by "real" or acoustic instruments (live drums, guitar, flute, saxophone, or strings). Logos vary in length from a few seconds to thematic types of extended duration. The latter, sometimes called "image-type" logos, function more as theme songs and can be broadcast full-up or in the background for announcements. Wealthy TV, radio, and new media outlets often use a whole series of musical IDs, played frequently enough for the listener to learn to associate the music with the outlet.

The Agency Role

Most advertising is handled through advertising agencies. These firms range in size from one-person, office-in-your-hat operations to global supergiants such as Havas, Interpublic Group, Omnicom, and WPP, whose annual billings in broadcast and production media alone total in the billions of dollars. Most advertisers prefer to place their radio and TV spots through ad agencies for two reasons: The agencies negotiate low ad rates by aggregating buying for many clients, and, as large centralized media buying entities, they can better support overhead costs such as personnel salaries and office space leasing.

Compensation for ad agencies used to generally be a simple 15% to 20% of ad buying which covered the cost of conceiving ad messages, but not physically producing the ads. These days, ad agency contracts can vary from an hourly billing for work performed to a negotiated flat fee for specific services over a specific time frame, to having escalators based on higher product sales. Under the traditional 15% fee, if the agency buys $1 million in advertising on CBS Television, for example, the network takes just $850,000, leaving $150,000, or 15% of the buy, for the agency's commission. In addition, for the same ad buy, the agency may spend $100,000 in direct costs (studio rental, actors, composers, etc.) to create the advertisement, which is billed to the advertiser. The advertiser and agency may agree in advance that some agency expenses will not be the responsibility of the advertiser.

The larger agencies tend to offer their wide array of services on an à la carte basis. This allows an advertiser to engage an ad agency for its media buying, consumer research, publicity, and/or promotional marketing services, but to use commercials created somewhere else. Advertising buying is a particularly compartmentalized service, made increasingly complex by media fragmentation from the Internet and other new media. Some small and specialized agencies, called creative boutiques, offer single services, such as only creating ads. Such creative boutiques are particularly common in the movie business for theatrical campaigns.

Advertisers retain ad agencies on the theory that companies specializing in marketing know more about how to sell things than the advertisers. Some small and medium-sized advertisers maintain in-house "advertising agencies" where their own employees conceive, produce, and place the company's advertising. But even **house agencies** will often retain an external agency to assist it in spot production and media buying.

An advertiser determines what can be spent in one year for advertising, then retains an ad agency to offer advice on what part of that ad pie should be allocated for various media buys—print, TV, search marketing, flash ads on Web sites, etc. Once the budget for TV, radio, and new media ads (such as Web banners), is agreed on, the agency uses that money to implement the campaign. If the ad agency is very large, it will have on its staff a production department and its own in-house staff of writers. Large agencies also often have their own small recording studios in-house. Although it is rare for even the largest agencies to attempt to record masters involving music in-house, they will often use their own facilities to produce demos and voice tracks.

The ad agency's next task is to farm out what it cannot handle in-house. This would normally include rental of production studios, set design, acting, music composition and performing, and editing. Even the largest agencies will normally go outside their own shops for music. Many agencies do retain individuals on their creative staffs with some competence in music, particularly in the composition of lyrics and other kinds of copy intended for musical setting.

The ability to send production content over the Internet has speeded up and smoothed out the process enormously. And it has broken down any barriers to working with artists worldwide. A composer in London can post music securely on the Web, the agency in Chicago that has requested it can hear it within minutes, and a technician in Los Angeles can be mixing it, practically simultaneously.

After the production work is completed, the agency has the responsibility of recommending to its client how and when the spots should be placed. Once the client and the agency agree on these matters, the agency instructs its **media buyer** to purchase advertising and the campaign launches. If the campaign appears to be selling effectively, the advertiser will be advised to stay with whatever happens to be working. If the results of the broadcasting campaign are disappointing, the advertiser may change the creative message—or it may fire the agency. Alliances in advertising survive only as long as the advertiser is satisfied with the results.

In addition to serving their advertising clients in traditional ways, some large agencies are involved in outside work—for example, the production of music videos for record companies. Because videos have reenergized commercial TV music, they offer a fertile field for ad agencies' creative talent to explore. Increasingly, ad agencies create long-form content for the clients, which can include "infomercials" up to 1 hour in length, entertainment content that subtly pitches advertisers, sponsored Web content, and Web sites promoting client products or services. The expanding media world provides vast potential for such sponsored content.

Advertising, Music, and the Age of Social Networking

For years advertisers and agencies have been vexed by the declining impact of traditional broadcast spots in a world increasingly dominated by more interactive media such as online video. A months-long promotion from Sprite soft drink was a fitting example of how a multinational brand can become a willing partner with even an unknown musical artist—who got a global stage out of the association.

(Continued)

(Continued)

Aspiring British songwriter and singer Katie Vogel was showcased in a series of 5-minute videos that were subtly sponsored by the soft drink on YouTube and had a tie in with the social networking Web site, Facebook. A marketing team from Sprite selected Vogel—who then lived with her parents in London—from an open audition to re-locate to New York in her pursuit of pop music stardom as cameras tagged along.

"I was told they were looking for someone who was ready to have their whole life recorded, rewound, and remixed," Vogel said in a Web video that aimed to be compelling reality TV for a youth audience. Sprite, a Coca-Cola brand, drove traffic to the videos via online promotions, TV spots, special packaging on Sprite cans in some countries, and live events featuring Vogel.

Vogel got to keep rights to her songs. Unlike in a typical label deal, the financial support from Coca-Cola in this case was designed to produce marketing fizz, not back-end royalties for the advertiser. Vogel performed her music in parts of the videos, and her own personal remix included the tearful on-camera breakup with her boyfriend as she headed off for New York.

Katie Vogel.

Photo © C Brandon/Redferns/Getty Images.

Sprite's involvement was subdued to make Vogel's life story seem authentic. Vogel played a green guitar and the video series was titled "Green Eyed World"—both in nods to the lemon-lime soft drink. The Sprite name popped up only at the end of each video, with the voiceover tag line, "Powered by Sprite."

Spot Production

All advertising is concerned with persuasion. Because most TV spots are now 30 seconds or less in length, skill is required to make the "sale"—fast!

Writing Copy

Top writers make these recommendations:

1. Mention the advertiser's name as often as you dare.

2. Be economical with words. In radio, let the music say it; in TV, let the pictures "talk."

3. Use simple language.

4. Express one idea—again and again.

Another school of thought, born of this age of clutter, is that the body of the commercial should interest the viewer and pique curiosity, but the name of the advertiser is shown or mentioned only once at the end of the spot. Sometimes less is more.

One of the things done least well by advertising agencies is writing copy to be set to music. It is astonishing how often even **national accounts** will accept music that is almost halted in its flow by the awkwardness of the words being sung. In preparing ad copy or lyrics for singers, the minimum requirement is to come up with language that permits a natural rhythm.

Scoring Music

Clients are not always articulate when it comes to musical sounds. The smart composer will arrive for a briefing session armed with examples, usually actual sample **tracks,** either original or taken from current on-air notables.

Instrumentation was once determined largely by budget constraints. Synthesizers changed that somewhat, but the amount of instrumentation is still determined by budget. Synthesized music is more economical, but as always, more tracks cost more money. Unlike much popular music making, just about everything for commercials is written out. Improvisation is limited to appropriate liberties taken by the rhythm section. The arranger's main goal is to have the **front line** stay out of the way of the singers or speakers.

The advertiser wants to hear the text, not the background. The cardinal rule for all arrangers scoring backgrounds is, Stay out of the way of the words. Modern technology helps, because each vocal line is often recorded on a different track. During mixing, when the final sounds are selected, the main track is mixed farther forward (made to sound much louder) than the background music, allowing the listener to hear the words. The important rule for arrangers is to score backgrounds in a range different from the main vocal line.

Production Companies

Although commercial production companies once specialized in either radio or television, a common practice these days is to put TV and radio under one roof, separate from Internet advertising. The TV/radio production firms are typically staffed by a producer (or producer-director), a director (or director-cameraperson), office personnel, and sales staff. The production company will sometimes contract for audio and video technicians through a technical production house. An art director and perhaps a graphic artist will be engaged freelance, as will musicians.

Television production companies lease or own their own studios, which must provide room for at least single-camera film, sophisticated lighting, scenery/prop/graphics production, and film- and tape-recording facilities. Almost all commercials today are edited on videotape at a video postproduction facility. Wages and rental of facilities run to hundreds, sometimes thousands, of dollars per day, depending on the extent to which the production company farms out part of the work.

Companies outside the major production centers are typically smaller operations that serve local, regional, and occasionally, national accounts. They usually have an in-house staff of two to five persons. Companies with small staffs may have modest TV shooting studios, or more likely, they will rent shooting stages. Audio is usually recorded in recording studios and, later, synchronized with tape or film.

Small production companies offering radio commercial services have studios big enough to handle small choral/instrumental sessions. When an advertiser wants something on a grander scale, producers rent independent recording studios. In smaller markets, there is often a close relationship between the local radio stations and production companies. In fact, very often the local radio station *is* the production studio for local producers.

Going beyond basic commercial spots, firms involved in production often offer their clients complete programming services in whatever musical format the station wants—CHR (contemporary hit radio), adult contemporary, country, rap, and so on. They write original music tracks for the client. In addition, full-production houses also offer their clients music library services that include "commercial **beds.**" These are 30- or 60-second music tracks arranged for use with whatever ad copy the station or advertiser wants. For example, the library may contain solid, dignified-sounding music for sponsors such as banks and insurance companies. When a station needs music background for a store advertising clothing for teenagers, it can select any number of CHR-type beds from the library. The necessity of keeping music beds up to date with changing musical styles opens up another avenue for employment opportunities in music (see Chapter 24). Library services also include a selection of "neutral" tracks for advertisers not seeking a particular musical trademark or association. These commercial beds are often arranged in three segments: A 60-second bed might open with a 20-second front that establishes the tone of the commercial. A **bridge** follows, where the music is less full in orchestration and less active in texture. This provides a musical background (bed) that makes it easier for the listener to understand the ad copy. This copy can be read live by the disc jockey or it can be prerecorded. Following this middle section, the remaining time, perhaps 10 seconds, is where the bed rises up, so to speak, offering a musical reprise of the front. This end section is often called the tag, a term borrowed from vaudeville. Tags return to the "**up full**" sound of the front.

Production companies can be engaged to add singers and custom copy to the front and tag sections of canned tracks of this kind. This radio commercial format was widely used in the 1950s and beyond. Because the format became so predictable, more imaginative producers and advertisers now prefer a less pat format and have experimented with a variety of sequences of copy, music, reprises, **cold** copy, and musical trademarks.

Commercial producers, whether supplying custom spots or library services, regularly offer their clients lifts. These are usually 10-second extrapolations from 60-second spots that were initially scored in anticipation of a short section being lifted from the full-length commercial. These lifts provide the sponsor with the option of buying 10-second time segments and having available spots of the appropriate length—with minimal additional production cost.

Artists and Fees

Advertisers and agencies are accustomed to paying creative fees for music and texts. Although some composers charge no creative fee—only for their arranging, copying, and conducting—it is not uncommon for a spot composer to get paid a creative fee (for one piece of material) of $500 or more for a local campaign. At the national level, creative fees vary widely, from thousands to tens of thousands (or even more) if using a "star" composer.

Composers generally work for ad agencies on a buyout basis: As employees performing "work for hire," they give up all copyrights in their work. For a while, increasing numbers of agencies had contracts with their creative people that provided that the composer retained copyright in the music and assigned rights for use into perpetuity to the agency or the advertiser for advertising purposes only. This kind of contract left the composer free to seek exploitation of the material in other media, particularly the pop song field. But agencies began to realize that there is gold in publishing and now try to procure the publishing rights to music. The composer with enough clout doesn't let them do that. The lesser-known composer has no choice. Some ad agencies that "buy out" a composer's copyright may still allow the composer to collect the writer's share of performance income.

Fees are paid in a number of ways. There is usually a partial payment when the contract is signed and final payment when the material is completed. Sometimes, however, the creative fee is paid up front; then the commercial is written. If the client approves the spot, the rest of the fee is then paid upon the completion of the project after everything (orchestration, recording, etc.) is finished.

Returning for a moment to budgets for small markets, advertisers will often seek **package deals.** A composer-arranger scratches around for an assignment and discovers a prospective client who has, say, $7,500 for a musical spot. The musician agrees to take on the complete package for that fee and composes the music, perhaps also the text, scores the arrangement, extracts the parts, rents the studio, engages the performers—and delivers the master tape to the client. If this packager could get away with using just one singer and a three-piece band, or better yet, one synthesist who sounds like a three-piece band, there might be a few hundred dollars left for the 2 weeks of labor. Or if the job was budgeted carelessly and ran overtime in the studio, the packager could end up in the hole.

In national campaigns, package deals are less common. But here, instead of one individual taking on the whole project, an ad agency will engage a music production house for a flat fee. This kind of company often figures its budgets on two levels: **above-the-line** costs (creative fees, "talent") and **below-the-line** costs (expenses such as studio rentals, scale payments to union artists, music copying, tape).

Some music production firms are owned or partly owned by the composer. Such houses will offer a client, for one lump fee, composition, text, arranging, orchestration, and musical direction. Such fees for national accounts are in the tens of thousands of dollars.

A producer or agency may locate a naturally gifted songwriter to do the creative work for a campaign. Some of these individuals may have attracted the attention of producers through their songwriting success on pop records. Some are musical illiterates and are helpless without the aid of competent arrangers. They will often sing their tunes into a tape recorder, then hire an arranger to pull the music off the tape and render it in correct music notation. The **leadsheet** thus produced is then turned over to the arranger-orchestrator-director who is hired to score the music for the recording session.

Artists' Contracts

Singers, instrumentalists, arrangers, and copyists employed on national spots are members of their respective unions. The total dollars earned by AFM members working in the spot field rivals the amount earned by union musicians scoring TV movies and theatrical motion pictures. The national contract covering AFM members in this field covers employment in radio and TV commercials, as well as their use on commercials for in-store videos, movie theaters, and online.

The contract also governs the employment of AFM instrumentalists, leaders, **contractors,** orchestrators, music librarians, and copyists—not composers. As with certain other AFM contracts, "leaders" generally receive double scale. A leader may be a conductor or an instrumentalist who has some extra responsibility during a recording session. Instrument **doublers** make extra wages of varying percentages for the first double, then in many cases extra fees for additional doubles. If the orchestra contractor is an individual other than the leader, the contractor earns double scale.

The use of synthesizers is treated not as instrument doubling but as **overdubbing**: The musician charges scale for each of the different parts that are played, although the number of parts for which a synthesist will be paid will probably be negotiated up front, before the session begins.

If the employer is a signatory to the AFM contract, the employer agrees to abide by the terms of that contract, which includes using AFM musicians and music preparation employees paid at contract scale. The employer (who may be the advertising agency or the spot producer) must also pay into the AFM-EP (Employers Pension Fund). The AFM contract stipulates that the employer is responsible for additional payments to the musicians for uses of the music following the initial 13-week period covered by the basic fees for national spots. For such extended use (starting with the 14th week) or for each spot dubbed into a new commercial or used in a new medium, each AFM member who was employed on the original project receives an additional payment per 13-week cycle. National advertising agencies and their clients are accustomed to paying these extended use (or **new use**) payments, as well as sideline payments for any appearances on camera. Musicians who perform on national spot sessions can sometimes earn big money over the years, if their spots have long runs. Spots usually just run one or two cycles.

Local spots under union jurisdiction are paid at a lower wage scale than national spots. At the local and regional levels, circumvention of extended use and **reuse** payments is common. Many local spots are produced for straight buyouts by the advertiser or the ad agency for all services creative and artistic. Many are nonunion.

The American Federation of Television and Radio Artists (AFTRA) claims jurisdiction over professional singers on radio and most of television, and the Screen Actors Guild (SAG) has jurisdiction for some television. Signatory agencies and advertisers are obligated to adhere to union scales for national campaigns and most regional campaigns. As with standard recordings prepared for commercial release to the public, AFTRA and SAG have set, in the spot business, special scales for solo, duo, and group (three or more) singers.

One of AFTRA's important tasks is obtaining payments for each use of its members' recorded work. On one hand, rates for singers are per use of the singer's recorded work: Each use requires a new payment. On the other hand, AFM members are paid per 13-week cycle for all use, not for each use. Responsibility for payment of fees may rest with different entities or their successors, depending on the terms of the initial contract for the union artists. As with the AFM, AFTRA artists may well receive more income via reuse payments than they do from the initial recording sessions. When singers receive conflicting calls for jobs, they will opt for the work that appears most likely to stay on the air beyond 13 weeks. Top jingle singers in the major production centers can earn huge incomes through extended-use payments across multiple commercials just at AFTRA and SAG scale.

The singers who get hired to record national spots are usually drawn from a select pool of vocal artists. In addition to being able to sing almost any style and sight-read like demons, spot singers must excel at clear diction. The advertiser's first concern is not an "operatic" voice quality—**bel canto**—but clarity of language. The composer may have scored music comparable to the "Hallelujah Chorus," but the **account executive** may demand it be discarded in favor of a voiceover if the listener can't make out the words.

OPEN ON A SERIES OF FAST MOVING
SPLIT-SCREEN FRAMES OF
VARIOUS HONDA GRILLES, FOLLOWED
BY A MONTAGE OF OTHER
SPLIT-SCREEN SHOTS OF VARIOUS
ANGLES AND CLOSE UPS OF

DRAMATICALLY LIT HONDA VEHICLES.
THE PACE OF EDITING IS ALL DEPENDANT
ON A VERY ENERGETIC
HARD-DRIVING MUSIC TRACK.

AS THE MUSICAL RHYTHMS CONTINUE,
CUT TO A LOW ANGLE
SHOT OF THE FRONT OF A PILOT.
THE LIGHT TRAVELS FROM REAR
TO FRONT, AS IT RIM LIGHTS ITS
SCULPTURAL FEATURES.

THE CAMERA PULLS BACK AND
VARIOUS FEATURES OF OTHER
TRUCKS SLIDE INTO FRAME.

THE SCREEN DIVIDES INTO
THIRDS AS THE GRILLE OF A
RIDGELINE AND THE FRONT OF
AN ELEMENT SLIDE IN.

THE BOTTOM THIRD OPENS UP
TO REVEAL THE FRONT OF THE
RIDGELINE.

RP Alpha group

Figure 22.1   Storyboard for TV Commercial

Source: Courtesy of Rubin Postaer and Associates.

Production Sequence

The process of producing a broadcast commercial is very involved. Here is how the events might fall in place for a network television commercial where the budget for music is large. In this hypothetical case, the advertiser instructs its advertising agency to come up with a TV campaign for a new soap product. Also, we will assume the advertising agency retains a production company to assist. Events might occur in a different order than the sequence listed here.

1. The agency, through its **creative director**, decides on a concept and calls a production meeting. Agency staff members attending are the creative director (chairperson), writers, TV producer, art director, and account executive.

2. The creative department creates a **storyboard** for the advertiser's approval. A TV storyboard is a visual representation, either rough drawings of the sequence of events scheduled to occur on the screen, or in some cases crude animation. If the storyboard is presented as still frames, the aural components (dialogue, music) are indicated below each picture as captions, enabling the stakeholders to perceive an approximation of how the eyes and ears are engaged in the 30-second spot. (See Figure 22.1.) The advertiser accepts the advertising concept for the campaign.

3. The agency develops a detailed budget to cover the cost of production.

4. The agency's creative director or **house producer** contacts two or three music houses (production companies) and/or recognized commercial music composers and invites them to submit appropriate music, from which it will make its selection. Composers and houses will compose soap-selling music—good, clean sounds—on a demo tape, on **spec.** Some ad agencies will pay for costs of demo production, typically passing on the cost to the advertiser. The agency creative group selects its favorite from the spec demos submitted.

5. The agency contacts a casting agent or casting director, who may issue what is known in the trade as a **cattle call** for actors and actresses, according to the specifications that the agency supplies. Or the agent may simply select from casting books half a dozen pictures or videos of actors and actresses who might look right for the cast. If a casting session is held, it is usually videotaped. The advertiser approves the casting.

6. The producer notifies the music house/composer of which track on the demo the advertiser and agency people liked best, and they settle on a creative fee for music. The music house/composer accepts the fee and asks to retain all publishing rights exclusive of the advertiser's uses of the music. The agency, well aware of the value of holding on to music publishing rights, balks on this point and further negotiations ensue, resulting in a contract price high enough to convince the composer to give up the publishing rights.

7. The producer tells the music director or business manager of the music house that there is a production budget for a 20-piece orchestra and five singers, and a recording date is set.

8. The composer reserves a studio for the recording and is guaranteed a favorite engineer.

9. The business manager/musical director calls up an AFM and a SAG contractor to engage the performers, telling the AFM contractor that the musicians will be expected to bring an array of musical instruments.

10. Before the recording date, the music director instructs the **music preparation** service to deliver copies of the score to Studio A for the orchestral recording session at 9 a.m., and the vocal recording session at 10 a.m. in Studio B.

11. The morning of the date, the orchestra reads through the chart and records **Take** 1. Takes continue for the hour budgeted.

12. As the orchestra is finishing the final takes, the singers arrive. The AFTRA contractor-vocal director rehearses the singers. For the rest of the hour budgeted, the artists record takes with the prerecorded orchestral music.

13. The final mix, attended by the producer and the music director, may be done that day or another day.

14. The musical director, producer, and account executive select the best take and instruct the studio to deliver three **DATs**, CDs, or an MP3 file to the agency by 5 p.m. that same day.

15. The producer meanwhile has filmed all the visuals, created a final edit, and proceeded to lip-synch the actors with the musical track. Following adjustments in the picture transfer, the complete commercial is ready for duplication and distribution to broadcasters.

16. The agency files work reports with all the unions representing the singers and musicians. The agency, working through a talent payroll service familiar with all the current rates, issues the payroll checks for distribution.

Postscript. In rare instances, the wise and/or powerful composer who has been able to retain publishing rights to the music (limiting the advertiser's music rights to use in advertising) finds a lyricist to set new words to the music, then submits it to a publisher. A publisher accepts the song in the hope that it can get a free ride based on the current popularity of the music generated by the broadcast campaign. Everyone is happy, even the advertiser, who now enjoys additional identity through the popularity of the pop song version of the theme music.

Chapter Takeaways

- Advertising music can be lucrative, particularly with national or big-market campaigns.

- Agencies are often engaged by advertisers to both create spots and buy media advertising time to run them.

- Independent production companies are frequently subcontracted to produce an entire spot or just the music for the spot.

- The Internet allows some professionals in the advertising-music production chain to work remotely—uploading their parts of the work-product to others for approval or mixing.

- Composers generally write advertising music for a flat fee or "buy out" of all rights. In some cases, they retain publishing rights to benefit from later exploitation of the work.

Key Terms

- above-the-line (p. 381)
- account executive (p. 382)
- below-the-line (p. 381)
- canned track (p. 375)
- commercial bed (p. 380)
- creative boutique (p. 376)

- doubling (p. 382)
- lifts (p. 380)
- media buyer (p. 377)
- national account (p. 379)
- over-dubbing (p. 382)
- package deal (p. 381)

- pod (p. 374)
- spot (p. 373)
- station logo (p. 375)
- tag (p. 380)
- testimonial (p. 375)
- voiceover (p. 382)

CHAPTER 23

Music and Theater

Music has played an integral part in the theater for centuries. Many of the master composers experienced their greatest success in the theater: Wagner, Stravinsky, Gershwin. In Western civilization, musical theater can be said to have started in the Jewish synagogue and the Roman Catholic Church; most religious ceremony would be unthinkable without music. Much religious pageantry, of itself, is choreographed music.

Musical theater's earliest patronage, in addition to organized religion, came from the aristocracy who built and operated theaters right on their own premises. Later, men of wealth—for example, the merchants of Venice, the Medici family of Florence—became enthusiastic patrons of the arts. By the 17th century, public opera houses began operating, selling tickets (at the current equivalent of about 50 cents each) to cover production costs. In the 18th century, years before he scored his biggest hit with *Messiah,* Handel was hustling around London, buying and managing theaters, booking talent, scoring, producing, conducting operas, even doubling as a **pit** musician (keyboards) in his own theater. Competing musical shows, particularly *The Beggar's Opera,* eventually drove impresario Handel out of the musical theater business, while other producers, whose ears were more in tune with current taste, established a musical theater tradition in London that flourishes to this day.

By the 19th century, musical theater in Europe and this country, including everything from grand opera to minstrel shows, was prospering, selling tickets, and

> *"Extraordinary how potent cheap music is."*
> *—Noel Coward*

Left: Tony Award®.

Photo by Souders Studios and courtesy of Tony Award Productions.

turning a profit. Early in the 20th century, opera and ballet production costs began to exceed box office income, and the musical *patron,* the big giver, reappeared to keep these art forms alive. Meanwhile, imported European operetta was being transformed in this country into forms such as the musical revue, musical comedy, light opera, and, since *Show Boat* (1927), the musical play. In our own time, it is musical theater that keeps Broadway and most regional theater going.

Types of Musical Theater

Broadway Musicals

That piece of territory in New York known as Broadway has seen the production of contemporary musical theater's most treasured repertoire; it has been the working place for dozens of America's most gifted composers, lyricists, playwrights, producers, directors, and performers. Broadway would have collapsed had it not been for the musicals that kept it alive after 1945. Some Broadway musicals have produced more profit through recorded music sales and publishing income than they ever generated through ticket sales. Royalties from successful Broadway musicals have earned substantial sums of money for the composers, lyricists, and book writers (the term "book" is used in the musical theater to describe the scenario and dialogue of the musical drama; it excludes music and lyrics). Broadway musicals have always been the most expensive kind of production to mount. In 1950, a sumptuous production cost $200,000. Today, a producer may have to raise $7 million or more to mount a first-class Broadway musical, and for most shows, the investors could not expect to break even with a 52-week run: Many musical plays do not start turning a profit until they have run 2 or even 3 years.

Costs are now daunting because of theater rental expenses and high wages for Broadway's heavily-unionized skilled workers. No matter how carefully a show is budgeted, a producer cannot increase the "efficiency" of live singers, dancers, and musicians. The live audience may total only 1,000 per performance, not the millions available on television. Investors have risked their money partly in anticipation that the Broadway run is but a preliminary phase of the potential profitable life of a musical through original cast recordings, performance licensing, national tours, and perhaps even movie rights. Broadway producers with track records (such as Harold Prince and Andrew Lloyd Webber) can raise money more easily than others. Some of them have a consortium of investors waiting to risk their money.

The death of Broadway has been predicted since the 1930s, but this lively tradition refuses to attend its own funeral. Encouraged by the amount of money to be made by a hit, investors have been more than willing to take risks.

Off-Broadway Theater

As rising costs began to reduce the number of shows mounted on Broadway, producers in the 1950s began to develop a theatrical movement that came to be known as **off-Broadway**. This movement away from New York's 10-block theater district centered on drama, particularly experimental theater. It had minimal impact on musical theater until 1967, when the late Joe Papp, noted producer of the New York Shakespeare Festival, purchased an about-to-be-demolished library and reopened it as the Public Theater. Dedicated to the production of new plays by American writers, the Public's first presentation was *Hair,* which became the first successful rock musical and moved to Broadway after its premiere. Going the same route some years later was *Two Gentlemen of Verona.* Unquestionably, the Public's most spectacular success came with *A Chorus Line,* which opened in 1975 and became one of Broadway's longest-running musicals ever. The income from *A Chorus Line* was undoubtedly the single most significant factor in keeping the New York Shakespeare Festival running. Because of the rising costs of musical theater production, even off-Broadway has become financially prohibitive for many small shows in New York City and elsewhere. For this reason, some shows are first presented in small theaters that are known as *off-off Broadway* productions.

School Productions

Concurrent with the off-Broadway movement, American universities began to increase their musical show production. Before a musical show can be performed at a school, the school must first get a license from an amateur performance licensing agent, typically a publishing house such as Samuel French, Inc. As described in Chapter 6, such an agent will license the right to present the show and will also rent the script and the musical parts. The agent traditionally gets 10% of the license fee. The other 90% of the license fee goes to the authors and their overall agent.

Regional Theater

Also around the same time as the off-Broadway movement, indigenous theater began to develop and became known as regional theater. At last, Broadway lost its monopoly on professional musical production. Regional theater includes amateur, semiprofessional, and fully professional productions, often functioning in that gray area between the fully professional and the semiprofessional worlds. Actors' Equity regularly negotiates agreements with regional and community theaters that permit Equity members to perform in the same cast with non-Equity members. Actors, singers, and dancers now use university and regional theaters to learn their craft. These establishments help fill the void left by the death of live-stage national variety circuit vaudeville in the 1930s where, as the show business expression has it, a performer found "a place to be bad."

Regional theaters find particularly strong public acceptance for plays, dances, and shows designed for children. Some children's theaters will break even at the box office. Regional theaters that focus on the classics or on experimental, noncommercial productions may receive financial support from the National Endowment for the Arts to help them stay alive and well. They also depend on grants and funding from private donors and foundations, city governments, light opera associations, and regional arts councils. Earned income through the sale of tickets is often insufficient for survival.

A particular kind of regional theater—dinner theater—finds that its biggest draws are productions of hit Broadway musicals. The public does not seem to tire of yet another production of *Camelot* or *Carousel.* Only very rarely do dinner theaters invest in the production of original musical plays, a common policy with many non-dinner theaters as well. Many dinner theaters cast leading roles with established performers, stars of lesser stature, or talented college students. But the students get paid, and in this sense, dinner theaters can be considered part of the professional theater as well as a valuable training venue. These establishments rarely have a

proscenium stage; they mount their productions in the round, use **blackouts** instead of curtains, employ a minimum number of dancers on their small stages, and make do with duo-piano accompaniment or a tiny pit band. Despite these limitations, some dinner theaters turn out attractive shows.

Summer Theater

Another component of musical theater is summer theater, popular across the country. Cities with particularly successful summer theaters are Chicago, Kansas City, Houston, Sacramento, New York, and Dallas as well as the Berkshires region in Massachusetts. They mount proven Broadway musicals almost exclusively. Many of these productions are quite good. They usually hire name artists for the leads, support them with the best local talent (professional and semiprofessional singers-actors-dancers), and employ a pit orchestra of AFM (American Federation of Musicians) musicians. Many summer theaters break even, perhaps even turn a profit, at the box office during their seasons, which may run from 2 to 6 weeks. Productions are mounted in old movie houses, community arts centers, parks, theaters, and even tents. These productions offer short-term professional employment, and some of their performing alumni go on to careers on Broadway, television, music, and film.

National Tours

An important part of musical theater is touring shows. Most Broadway hit musicals develop at least one road company that begins touring as soon as the investors believe the public has heard about its New York success. Major hits have more than one New York-mounted road company that not only prosper on tour but also produce a lot of employment for singers, dancers, and musicians. Road companies generally tour with their own musical conductor, perhaps a percussionist, and one or two lead players, then fill in the pit orchestras with a dozen to three dozen local AFM members. The producer or musical director uses local AFM contractors, perhaps through the local promoter, to engage the pit musicians. These "casual" jobs provide considerable supplemental income for musicians across the country, many of whom are otherwise employed as music educators, members of local symphony orchestras, or studio musicians. There are "first-class tours" in so-called first-class cities, which are defined by tradition rather than other characteristics, such as size of the city or venue. There are also so-called bus-and-truck tours that go into the smaller venues.

Classical and modern dance are a part of American musical theater. Resident and touring companies offer at least seasonal employment for dancers and the musicians who are engaged to accompany them. Many dance companies perform to recorded music, which limits live employment of union musicians despite the AFM's efforts to reduce this practice. But the bottom line is as important for theaters as it is for any business, and recorded music is much less expensive than hiring an orchestra or even a small combo.

Las Vegas and Other Entertainment Centers

A significant part of musical theater in this country is found in Las Vegas and other entertainment centers, such as Atlantic City, New Jersey, and Branson, Missouri. The quality of the arrangers and players working in Las Vegas ranks with the best anywhere. A number of them were first drawn westward in search of work in

Hollywood, then moved to Las Vegas and accepted steady employment there in preference to intermittent jobs in the Los Angeles area.

Revues are popular in Vegas, although headliners also continue to perform with their own music directors and nucleus of musicians, augmented by local instrumentalists.

Industrial Shows

Another component of American musical theater is the industrial show. When new products are introduced or national sales campaigns are being organized, companies such as Toyota and IBM hire a producer or a production company to create commercial entertainment packages designed to motivate and instruct their sales staffs and to show appreciation to customers. These kinds of shows are not open to the public and are scheduled in major cities where the corporation might pull in its regional sales force. Industrial shows often have big budgets and offer seasonal employment for composers, arrangers, copyists, singers, dancers, and instrumentalists. Writers and producers of industrial shows are usually found among the group that also produces broadcast commercials. Several major cities—including Detroit, Chicago, Los Angeles, New York, and Philadelphia—have production companies set up to turn out the kind of shows major corporations want.

Amusement Parks and Cruise Ships

Many amusement parks around the country present musical stage revues, particularly during the peak summer and holiday seasons. These are usually original shows themed to each individual setting but can also feature Broadway or contemporary hit songs. Cruise ships also offer original musicals and abridged versions of Broadway shows.

Theater Associations

The League of Resident Theatres (LORT) is a multiemployer bargaining association representing individual, not-for-profit theaters. LORT represents member theaters in negotiation with three **collective bargaining** units: Actors' Equity Association (AEA), the Society of Stage Directors and Choreographers (SSDC), and the United Scenic Artists (USA). Member benefits include centralized collective bargaining and legal advice.

The Broadway League (formerly known as The League of American Theatres and Producers) is the national trade association for the Broadway industry. Their 600-plus members include theater owners and operators, producers, presenters, and general managers. The League supports its members through an array of programs and events designed to promote Broadway as a vibrant national entertainment medium. Other key services include overseeing government regulations for the Broadway industry, maintaining extensive research archives and databases, and investing in audience development programs. Due to the costs of employing live orchestras, the Broadway League has sought to eliminate the minimum guarantee of orchestra players altogether, which by 2009 had shrunk to 18 or 19 musicians.

An organization that produces new works as well as the "standard" musicals both on- and off-Broadway is the Nederlander Producing Company of America, Inc.

Nederlander, based in New York City, owns more than 35 theaters throughout the United States, as well as several theaters in London.

Also interested in the creation of new musicals is the National Alliance for Musical Theatre, an association of about 150 producing organizations that present theater on a cooperative basis. Any number of member companies pool their artistic and financial resources for one production of a show rather than stage several separate productions of that same show.

Production Components

The Producer

For almost every theatrical production, everything begins and ends with one individual: the producer. Usually, all employment and all income are initially generated through the producer's vision and resources. In musical theater, the producer's work begins with acquisition of a property. Broadway's musicals are either original or based on an underlying property, such as a novel or dramatic play. The producer enters into an option agreement with the owner of the property (usually the playwright) providing that the producer will pay a nonreturnable advance against royalties to have the right for a period of time to develop and subsequently present the play. Sometimes, subsequent option periods are conditioned on certain additional requirements, such as the producer's engaging a composer, a book writer, lyricist, or well-known director. If option conditions are met, the option period can be

Actors Ryan Steele, Kyle Coffman, George Akram, Karen Olivo, Matt Cavenaugh, and Josefina Scaglione attend the "West Side Story" Broadway revival opening night at The Palace Theatre, New York.

Photo © Jim Spellman/WireImage/Getty Images.

extended with the payment of additional money. The same concept is applied in the producer's contracts with the show's composer, lyricist, and book writer: The producer gets the exclusive right to create and present the show, which must happen during the option period(s) or the producer loses all such rights.

Producers are not always the only individuals seeking musical show properties. An influential director or aggressive agent can also put together a package, then seek out a producer to assume the overall responsibility of pulling the production together and mounting the show. Composers afflicted by the Broadway itch continually search various sources—novels, plays, even movies—for properties that they believe might form the basis for musical treatment. If they are successful in securing an option on a property, they can then take it to a producer.

Sometimes the authors put the shows together without a producer. In that instance, a collaboration agreement is first entered into among the authors that spells out the parties' respective rights and obligations and contains options and elements, similar to the ones in the agreement between the producer and the authors described earlier.

If the musical is heading for Broadway, the producer must negotiate contracts with the book writer, the composer, and lyricist. The Dramatists Guild of America has developed standards and procedures contained in the document known as the Approved Production Contract (APC). Its membership includes numerous playwrights and musical show book writers, composers, and lyricists active on Broadway.

Subsidiary Rights

The producer negotiates contracts with the show's book writer, composer, and lyricist that specify what these authors are to receive in advances, royalties, and credit and what the producer will receive from the authors' exploitation of subsidiary rights. Once the show has completed its first run, the authors have the right to exploit the valuable subsidiary rights; the producer may receive a part of the income but has no control over the exploitation or disposition of these rights. Examples of subsidiary rights include movie rights, stock and amateur rights, touring rights (to the extent that the producer doesn't exercise the producer's option with respect to them), and rights to do different productions and derivative works (e.g., the right to have a dramatic play turned into a musical or vice versa). The book publishing rights of a play are usually retained by the book writer and not shared by the producer or the other authors. Separate rights to the music and lyrics are normally carved out by contract and retained only by the composer and lyricist and/or their music publisher.

Original Cast Album

The original cast album right is neither an author's subsidiary right nor exclusively a producer's right but a hybrid right involving both. Generally, the producer negotiates for the right to make the cast album deal, providing certain conditions favorable to the author, such as a minimum royalty. Conditions might typically include an agreement about the division of recording company royalties that will be payable to the producer and to the author. An author might agree, for example, to allow the producer to make the cast album deal with a recording company if the recording company pays a royalty of at least 14% of the retail price of the album.

Option and Royalty Payments

The typical producer-writer contract provides for the writer to receive an option payment during the period the show is being created, with an additional advance payment to be made during rehearsals. With the APC contract, the writer gets significant advances, but the "royalty pool" concept also has been added; so after the advance payment, the writer may not receive a significant amount of money beyond a guarantee in the early days of a show while the pool is in effect.

Approvals

These contracts also provide that when the show's director, cast, conductor, dance director, and designers for costumes, scenery, lighting, and sound are engaged, approval for these artists must first be obtained from the book writer, composer, and lyricist (such approval is either by unanimous or majority vote, depending on the arrangement made by the particular individuals involved). Furthermore, the producer cannot delete or add a song without the approval of the authors. The producer cannot make any changes at all to the authors' work without their approval, and the author involved owns all the changes. This is different from the movie industry, where the writer has no ultimate control.

Costs

Concurrent with the effort to raise money for the show and sign the writers, the producer employs a general manager who prepares a preliminary budget and negotiates many of the creative contracts. One of the largest components of weekly running costs will be a combination of theater rental and labor-related expenses. Rent is generally a flat amount, but theater owners frequently negotiate a percentage of the adjusted gross box office receipts. There is no standard percentage amount on this revenue sharing.

A producer schedules production time after estimating the date for opening on Broadway, then tries to locate a suitable theater that will be available. Most Broadway theaters are relatively small; the producer of a Broadway musical must locate a house that provides more than 1,000 seats in order to have sufficient capacity to generate adequate weekly box office revenue to be able to recoup the large costs of mounting and running a musical.

Broadway theater owners know from long experience that the life expectancy of a new musical ranges from one performance to several years. They, too, must gamble with the show. A theater owner is reluctant to sign a rental agreement with any but a reliable producer and will be more willing to risk tying up the theater if the producer has a good track record, if the show's writers are well known, or if the cast includes a star. The rental agreement calls for the producer to reimburse the theater owner for all the theater's operating expenses—fixed costs, such as utilities, heat, and air conditioning, and the salaries of ushers, box office staff, and other personnel—plus a rental fee that may be a percentage of the weekly gross box office receipts. All theater rental agreements have a "stop" clause that gives the theater owner and the producer the right to terminate, in the event that the show receipts fall below a certain negotiated amount. It is evident that a Broadway musical must do near-capacity business to stay alive.

The investors have a contract with the producer that says if there is any money left after the producer has paid the costs of mounting and running the show, the investors will next receive all the money that's left until they've recouped their investments. After recoupment has been achieved, the investors split the show's receipts, normally 50–50 with the producer, depending on the producer's share as outlined in the investment contract. The production company's receipts include the net receipts from the production company's presentation of the show and any portion of the subsidiary rights income to which the production company becomes entitled.

Typical weekly running costs of a full-line musical show will include most, possibly all, of the following:

1. Royalty payments of from 6% to 9% of the box office gross, divided among the writer, composer, lyricist, director, choreographer, and designers, drawn from a *royalty pool*. This pool is a complicated method of figuring that allocates a certain number of percentage points to each individual involved, with a minimum guarantee per point plus an allotment of the profits.

2. Salary (plus a possible weekly royalty) for the star.

3. Salaries for leading players (actors, singers, dancers).

4. Salaries for the stage manager and assistant stage manager.

5. Salaries (based on Actors' Equity scale) for supporting actors, dancers, singers.

6. AFM scale for the pit musicians and any musicians who might appear on stage.

7. Salaries for union stagehands, electricians (including audio technicians), carpenters, wardrobe personnel, hair and wig stylists, and other theater personnel, such as treasurers.

8. Producer expenses. The producer's "cash office charge" (usually a fixed amount per week) is provided in the agreement that defines the producer's rights in relation to the investors' rights. This agreement, although negotiable, often says that in addition to the cash office charge, the producer (who raised the money) will receive a producer's royalty each week equal to 1.5% to 2% of the gross weekly box office receipts before the investors get their money back and before the promoter-producer or the investors share net profits. The producer may also receive income for providing electrical, sound, or other equipment for the production. There is usually a fee to the general manager of the show as well. This is normally a weekly dollar amount commencing a few weeks prior to rehearsals and ending a couple of weeks after the closing of the show. The general manager is the person who is knowledgeable about budgets and about how to negotiate an appropriate lease with the theater owner. A good general manager is crucial if the producer is good at raising money but doesn't know the nuts and bolts of producing.

9. Salaries for production assistants, retainers to public relations personnel, fees (or percentages) to theater party promoters who are part of the public relations efforts.

10. The rental payments under the theater lease.

Even if the show is a hit, the investors will not begin to get any of their investment returned until these weekly running costs are met, and the producer and investors will not receive any net profits until the investors' outlays have been returned. One of the reasons investors continue to put their money into this high-risk field is that income from subsidiary rights sometimes will not only help cover production costs but will greatly exceed box office revenue.

Grand and Small Rights

After the initial run, subsequent producers wishing to reproduce musical plays and operas are required to pay royalties to the copyright owners for performance of the show. When such producers license the rights to an existing show from the authors' agents, the producer has to negotiate for these **grand rights.** These kinds of performance licenses (see Chapter 6) are required for both amateur and professional productions.

If a song from a musical is performed separately (not as a part of the musical show), on radio, TV, or in live performance, the rights to nondramatic performance become part of the **small rights** that are licensed by the performing rights organizations, which collect a performance royalty from the music user and distribute that royalty to the composer, the lyricist, and the publisher of that song.

Chapter Takeaways

- Elaborately staged musicals enjoy enduring popularity in live theater. The famed Broadway circuit in New York would likely have suffered economic collapse in the television era without loyal audiences that support music-oriented stage productions.

- Music in theater is more diverse than what plays under the bright lights of Broadway. It encompasses song-oriented performances in regional theater, dinner theater, Las Vegas and other entertainment centers, summer theater, industrial shows, amusement parks, and cruise ships.

- Obtaining the right to and making rights payments for musicals in theater requires navigating a complex contractual thicket. Producers, lyricists, composers, stage-play authors, performers, and directors make varying proportional claims to revenue streams generated by stage performances, original cast record albums, and touring versions.

Key Terms

- Approved Production Contract (APC) (p. 395)

- book writer (p. 390)

- grand rights/small rights (p. 398)

- national tour (p. 392)

- off-Broadway (p. 390)

- pit (p. 392)

- proscenium (p. 392)

- revue (p. 392)

- royalty pool (p. 397)

- subsidiary rights (p. 395)

CHAPTER 24

Business Music and Production Libraries

Foreground and Background Music

A substantial portion of music produced today is not really meant for active listening. Rather, it is intended to remain on the edge of consciousness, providing an "extramusical" service, affecting people's moods and energy levels. Background music murmurs on, as we all know, just about everywhere people can be found: in many places of business—including restaurants, malls, supermarkets, airports, elevators, sometimes even in restrooms—and during "hold" time on the phone.

"I worry that the person who thought up Muzak may be thinking up something else."

—Lily Tomlin

Considering the sheer frequency of exposure to music, the "business music" audience is by far the largest in the world. For years, business owners have looked to music as a means to attract more customers, motivate employees, and sell more. Over time, methods and motivations for using music have changed, and business music moved from data-driven consumer behavioral analysis focused mainly on productivity to a greater focus on music's direct impact on the customer's experience and its support of marketing objectives for businesses' brands.

Traditionally, business music has been separated into two basic categories: foreground and background. *Foreground* music is usually described as music designed specifically for the business in which it is used and played for very particular

---

Left: Weeks Recording Studio, Frost School of Music, University of Miami.

Photo by Elaine Maltezos, used by permission. Photo courtesy of University of Miami.

purposes, such as drawing in targeted customers and keeping them in stores, entertaining telephone callers on hold so that they will be less likely to hang up, or helping airline passengers stay calm and relaxed. Foreground music tends to be played at a higher volume than background music.

Although as carefully designed for its particular setting, *background* music is intended to go largely unnoticed in a conscious way, an unobtrusive accompaniment to work, shopping, conversation, dining, and relaxation. In health care, it's used to reduce stress and even to make the hearers more likely to stay healthy.

The lines between foreground and background music have become blurred with the greater emphasis on music as a design and branding medium. Using traditional definitions, businesses have moved toward foreground music.

Research has demonstrated that the controlled application of music can modify mood, energy level, and behavior. Studies of manufacturing plants, for example, have shown that workers exposed to music are more productive and happier than when working in silence or with nothing but the drone of machines in the background. Psychologists and music therapists consult with companies offering music services so that the selections heard are programmed to fit specific environments. Hospitals use it to help doctors as well as patients. Many studies have shown that music has an unusual power to help patients' recovery from physical or mental trauma.

Service Companies

The business music industry in the United States has been dominated by two companies: Muzak, LLC, the largest and oldest firm, founded in 1934, and DMX Inc., founded in 1971. Service companies not only offer the music, they also create proprietary product platforms that deliver the music and they design, install, and service the sound systems. The companies contract with businesses nationwide through an extensive integrated network of sales and service offices or through in-house project management and field technician teams and a wide network of affiliates.

Transmission. Service companies use delivery transmission systems that include digital streaming via satellite, disk delivery, and IP multicast file transfer via wide area networks, depending on individual clients' needs. Satellite transmissions enable large numbers of locations to be served with an economical amount of bandwidth. Most of the satellite receivers used can be controlled remotely, which allows companies to control which music program is playing and which advertisements (if used) are aired. All systems are designed to protect the music assets by encrypting the source and running on proprietary software systems.

Companies that contract with business music services have a broad choice of music programs from content libraries covering all genres and eras of music, from classical to pop.

Musical Production. In its early days, Muzak used to face copyright and licensing restrictions that limited its access to original artists' music, so it produced its own versions. For many years, this music did not incorporate vocals, and the instrumental music became ingrained in the American pop culture lexicon as "elevator music." Material was drawn from music already published, ranging from standards to current hits, and musicians were hired to record it. Although some of these recordings were made in the United States, others were made in Europe, where musicians were sometimes willing to work for lower rates than AFM (American Federation of Musicians) scale in the United States.

Licensing and Copy Protection. In the early 1980s, companies gained access to music by original artists—the same music heard on the radio. They addressed the licensing and copy protection laws that previously limited access to original music by establishing new-use licensing agreements with performing rights societies such as ASCAP and BMI, which protect the rights of artists and record labels and control the illegal use of music for commercial benefit. Business music libraries now mostly contain music by original artists.

Airline Music. One specialized field within this already specialized field is supplying music to airlines for the in-flight entertainment of travelers. More than a dozen companies compete for this market nationally and internationally. Spafax, founded in 1985, services over 60 international airline clients worldwide, providing audio- and video-on-demand (AVOD) channels, as well as original content such as boarding and safety videos. The focus of this industry has shifted to flexibility and freedom of choice by the customer. Airlines choose up to 100 full-length CDs featuring music formats such as classical, opera, pop, jazz, rock, New Age, easy listening, country, children's, Broadway, sound tracks, showcase, and regional music. In addition to the on-demand CDs, airlines can also select preprogrammed audio (radio) channels, mostly featuring news and sport. The length of the transcriptions is chosen by the airline and ranges from 60 to 120 minutes. Each airline also chooses how often to change the programs and CD selection; every month is usual, with all new radio programs and up to a 30% refreshing of the CD selection. As with other business music, the programs are designed to enhance the airline's image—and also to ensure that the passengers recognize a majority of the selections on their chosen channels and on-board CD libraries.

Production Music Libraries

Production music libraries offer music and sound effects that are original rather than covers of already existing songs and music. Musicians record original music that is then sold or licensed for specific use, such as theme music for a news broadcast. Before 1980, the AFM and AFTRA (American Federation of Television and Radio Artists) required that musicians who recorded production music be paid each time the music was used, so production libraries and music users bought their music from Great Britain, Germany, and France, where such **reuse** payments were not required. In the 1980s, AFTRA and AFM were unable to maintain this stance, so U.S. production music libraries began to gain prominence in this field.

Killer Tracks, a production music library that opened its doors in 1990, serves as a good example of a successful, modern music production company. Its catalog, available in the form of over 20 unique libraries, has been a source for music used in feature films, commercials, and corporate productions and by TV shows, networks, cable stations, and CD-ROM producers. The service is inexpensive and allows music users to easily obtain the appropriate license to meet their needs. Material is licensed in perpetuity for a fee based on the type and scope of the clearance required for a specific project. Each use of music, referred to as a **needle drop** or cue, requires licensing. For instance, if a music user licensed a piece of music for a 30-second use as background music in a newscast, a separate license would be required if the licensee wanted to use that same music in a 30-second ad spot for television. The exception to the rule would be the **production blanket**, which allows an unlimited use of music in one production for a capped or flat fee. This fee is based upon the length of the total production and the clearance category required.

Production music companies offer libraries of CDs of diverse categories and musical styles. Some CDs feature compositions in 30- and 60-second lengths. Others contain full-length cuts, in addition to 30-, 60-, and a variety of 10- and 15-second lengths. Each cut may feature a variety of mixes, such as "full," "narration," and "alternate." The narration version deletes the lead or melody instrument so as not to compete with a narrator's voice. The alternate version may offer additional instrumentation, a "lite" rhythm mix, or something unexpected. Also, many compositions feature live vocal effects. Software is available that allows the user to retrieve, sort, cross-reference, and log use of the music that has been chosen. Digitally recorded libraries of thousands of sound effects are also available. Production music libraries offer employment for experienced musicians as well as newer composers, who can use this experience as a springboard for work in films and television.

Chapter Takeaways

- Recorded music helps businesses improve the productivity of workers and the attitudes of patrons.

- Production music libraries offer musical snippets that customers can put to use for specific production purposes, such as a station identification jingle for a radio station.

Key Terms

- background music   (p. 402)

- foreground music   (p. 401)

- needle drop   (p. 403)

- production blanket   (p. 404)

Career Planning and
Development

PART 7

CHAPTER 25

Career Options

Tell people that you intend to work in the music industry and they will probably imagine that you have one of two goals in mind: rock star or record label mogul. While those are two perfectly fine—and potentially attainable—career options, the reality is that music-related occupations run an extremely wide gamut, offering a diverse array of choices to individuals with equally diverse talents, training, and interests. When you consider the many points at which music intersects with the wider entertainment industry—from films to TV shows to radio to video games to the Internet—the potential opportunities expand still further. There are careers to be made both onstage and backstage, in the spotlight and behind the scenes, in big-city offices and small-town schools. Some offer steady paychecks and structured workweeks, while others hold out the promise of rich rewards without providing any guarantees of making next month's rent.

"And they sit at the bar and put bread in my jar And say, 'Man, what are you doin' here?'"

—Billy Joel "Piano Man"

The U.S. Bureau of Labor Statistics' *Occupational Outlook Handbook* forecasts that overall employment in the category of musicians, singers, and related workers will grow in line with the general economy for the 10-year period to 2016, although it also notes that competition for full-time jobs will be intense. Other business sectors for music-minded job seekers offer varying prospects for growth, ranging from

Left: Bono of U2.

Photo © Jeff Brass/Getty Images.

flat to robust for teachers specializing in "self-enrichment" that includes music. There is always room in *any* field, however, for new talent and well-qualified aspirants. Most successful people in the business have a strong spirit of drive and entrepreneurship. They stay alert to trends and try to predict new areas of interest in the marketplace.

Reflecting the border-crossing nature of the entertainment industry, many jobs (such as songwriter, music supervisor, or composer) will have value in multiple industry sectors. To provide a perspective of the various career options, however, we group them broadly as follows:

Creative Careers	Broadcasting/Film/Video Game Careers
Directing/Producing Careers	Music-Related Careers
Performing Careers	Entrepreneurs/Starting Your Own Business
Teaching Careers	

Choosing the right career can be one of the most important decisions in a person's life. Before proceeding to examine the options available, look at the summary in Table 25.1, which outlines the stages the prudent individual could go through in planning and developing a career.

Creative Careers

Professional Songwriter	Composer of Classical Music
Lyricist	Arranger-Orchestrator
Composer of Show Music	Music Editor
Composer of Educational Materials	Music Copyist
Composer of Children's Music	

Professional Songwriter

Career Description. Typically, the professional songwriter spends about half of his or her time composing, focusing creative energy on one market—the record industry. (Writers will also find work in the advertising, broadcasting, and videogame sectors, which are addressed later in this chapter.) The other half of the songwriter's workweek is usually spent promoting—trying to persuade performers and producers to actually record the material. This is a highly competitive field, and thus most beginning songwriters find it necessary to support themselves with other kinds of employment that may or may not relate to music. Once genuinely talented songwriters gain an initial degree of success, they may be able to discontinue moonlighting and devote their full attention to writing and promoting their songs. When this happens, they often find themselves increasingly involved in related activities such as music publishing, record production, and even artist management or show production. The real pros write not just dozens of songs but hundreds, knowing that prolific activity is required to sustain a full-time songwriter career.

Table 25.1   Career Planning and Development

Discovering yourself
Self-appraisal of temperament, talent
Professional assessment of your temperament, talent
Defining goals
Personal needs, preferences
Investigation of career options
Short-term employment objectives
Long-term career goals
Getting prepared
Education, training
Apprenticeship, work experience
Diplomas, degrees, licenses, union affiliations
Finding work
Surveying the job market: current, potential
Predicting entry: time, place, pay, status
Breaking in: auditions, demos, e-mails, letters, résumés, interviews
Self-employment options
Climbing the ladder
Planning advancement: status, income, power
Vertical vs. horizontal job change
Quitting vs. hanging on
Attainment of career goals
Realization of personal goals
Periodic reassessment of goals
Retirement
When, how
Estimated financial requirements

Professional songwriters generally find it helpful to live and work in a major recording center, where they can make direct personal contacts with publishers, record producers, and recording artists. Working conditions are ideal: The song-writer sets the hours and vacation periods, usually writes at home, and can limit professional contacts to the kinds of individuals desirable to be around—musicians and show people.

Qualifications and Preparation. Because the publishing/recording business requires hundreds of new songs every week, even untalented, poorly prepared songwriters may sometimes get heard—initially. But those songwriters who hope to build a *lasting career* will need to possess true talent and genuine skills. How can one honestly assess these attributes? Aspiring writers may want to start by soliciting informal feedback from as many objective sources as possible. But it is the marketplace itself that will ultimately offer the most realistic career guide: Aspiring songwriters should offer their songs to as many producers and performers as possible over time; they will then learn, with persistent effort, whether these professionals—the actual song users—judge their work good enough to merit a possible recording. If aspirants find no acceptance after 2 or 3 years' effort, the marketplace message becomes clear: They do not have what song users want.

Assuming that the aspirant has demonstrable creative talent, a second key requirement is to learn the craft. Chapter 3 treats this topic at length. Songwriters who tend to make it have a strong sense of curiosity. They may start out ignorant of both their craft and their profession, but they study, observe, and ask questions.

Unless the aspirant is so creatively gifted that song users beat a path to the door, certain personal traits will also be required to survive in the field. The essential one is determination. The writer must be strongly motivated to write songs and then more songs, and then get out on the street and push the material unrelentingly, day after day, persevering until he or she gains acceptance. Even established pros rarely enjoy the luxury of sitting at home waiting for the telephone to ring. Songwriters learn that the world must be continuously reminded that they are still alive, still producing.

In selling songs, as in life, there also is a certain "right place at the right time" factor. A sense of anticipation of those ideas that capture the cultural imagination is a plus; similarly, the ability to spot and react quickly to a developing musical trend can increase a songwriter's odds of finding favor with record producers and artists who are looking to capitalize on a hot sound.

Employment Prospects. As in all creative careers, there are no guarantees of success. That said, there is also no reason an aspiring songwriter *can't* succeed if he or she is genuinely talented, is professionally competent, has the temperament described, and is persistent.

Most songwriters do not hold traditional salaried positions but, rather, earn money based on their creative output; *how much* depends largely on how popular those songs are in the marketplace, since income derives from performance and mechanical royalties. Writers may, however, strike employment arrangements with music publishers under which the publisher will normally contract for the writer's services for a year or more on an exclusive basis, meaning that the individual can write only for that particular publisher. These deals typically give the writer a monetary advance in return for the publishing company's taking a large percentage of the royalties earned from the songs. Most such writers receive a weekly "salary," but this is most often really an advance on future royalties earned by the writer; the standard contract provides that all royalty advances and salaries based on potential royalties are fully recoupable by the publisher. In many cases, these staff deals allow a songwriter to work full-time on his or her songs, at least for a period of a few years, without having to hold an outside job to pay the bills. Less established songwriters will usually strike "single-song" publishing deals, which may include an advance on royalties but do not offer a guarantee of a steady income provided by the publisher.

Employers often prefer to contract for writers' services on a work-made-for-hire basis. In short, work-for-hire means that, by law, the employer, not the writer, is legally considered the author of any creative work resulting from their relationship. A creative work is considered work-for-hire when it is prepared by an employee within the scope of employment, or it is specifically ordered or commissioned for use in one of several categories, the most relevant for composers perhaps being "as part of a motion picture or other audiovisual work." Both parties must sign an agreement saying the work is made for hire. For further information on these contracts, review Chapter 5.

Lyricist

A subset of the "songwriter" career option is that of the "lyricist," who writes words to songs. The first difficulty in attempting to make it as a lyricist is the same one confronting the pop singer: Almost all of us think we can do it. Employment prospects of lyricists aspiring to full-time careers are not promising for anyone lacking a distinctive creative talent. Unless writers are richly endowed, their careers may continue to support them only if they become active also as composers or in some other music-related work, such as publishing, producing, or artist management. A lyricist who is able to team up with a talented musical collaborator to form a strong songwriting team stands better odds. Talented wordsmiths may also find a welcome in the advertising business, which is addressed later in this chapter.

Lyricists who want to write for the musical theater must have a genuine sense of theater and a love for what takes place there. They will probably associate themselves with other composers and creative talents of similar tastes and professional goals. This often occurs, as it did with Cole Porter, Richard Rodgers, and others, when the writer is still in college, where student-written shows provide vehicles for novices to learn their craft.

When a writer has a feeling for how a song can contribute to the progress of the drama on stage, the writer will probably take the next step and become involved in collaborating with others in writing the **book** for shows, a term used on Broadway for the text of a musical play. Among the most distinguished (and wealthy) lyricists who also wrote (or helped write) books for successful Broadway shows were Ira Gershwin, Oscar Hammerstein II, and Alan Jay Lerner. The field of writing for the professional musical theater is very difficult to break into, but the rewards, artistic and financial, can be rich indeed.

Composer of Show Music

Career Description. A small group of professional composers devotes most of its creative efforts to writing music for shows. Years ago, this would have meant only the kind of creative work involved in mounting a Broadway production. Today, additional show-writing opportunities can be found off-Broadway and "off-off-Broadway," as well as in regional theaters, children's theater, and industrial shows throughout the country.

Show music composers work differently than do pop songwriters. The latter are free to invent whatever material they think might appeal to record producers. But show music composers normally start work only after a producer or writer has presented them with a script defining the nature of the show, the scenario, dialogue, and early on, the book for the production. The composer works sometimes on a daily basis with the show writers and producers, searching for music and lyrics that enhance the show and move it forward. Show music composers often work steadily on a project for several months, even a year or more, shaping and reshaping the music to fit the script—which is also probably undergoing constant rewriting. Completed, polished songs may have to be thrown out and new ones hastily inserted. Casting may change, and the composer may have to rethink the type of material that will best suit the new performer. Show music composers may be handed a lyric and be asked to come up with the music in 2 or 3 days, even overnight. Some great standards that were composed overnight have emerged from Broadway hits; Stephen Sondheim wrote the music and lyrics to *Send in the Clowns* in just one evening! On the other hand, Rodgers and Hammerstein (*Oklahoma!, South Pacific, Carousel, The Sound of Music,* etc.) were known for working and reworking music and lyrics on just a handful of songs for a year or more until they attained their artistic goal. Composers and lyricists of stature are almost always called on to serve as consultants to the producer in matters such as casting, dialogue, staging, and orchestrations. Show music composers/lyricists are, then, men and women "of the theater," and their work starts and ends with what works on stage.

Some show music composers are occasionally called on to write not just show songs, but also instrumental music, dance music, even dramatic music to underscore stage action. For example, the master show music composer Richard Rodgers was called on to compose dramatic ballet music, *Slaughter on Tenth Avenue,* for one of his Broadway shows. A composer able to handle diverse assignments of these kinds rises above the ranks of "songwriter" and becomes a "composer's composer." It is more common in most shows, however, to expect the composer-lyricists working on the project to be engaged only for songs, not dramatic music.

Qualifications and Preparation. Show music composers must possess the same qualifications cited for songwriters plus a sense of theater. Show composers are often expected to work well with collaborators, particularly lyricists. Although Broadway has had a few masters who could write words and music—Cole Porter, Irving Berlin, and Stephen Sondheim, for example—most shows are created by a kind of committee involving composers, lyricists, playwrights, and directors. Choreographers and lighting directors also help shape the final composition. The creative artist who is comfortable only when working alone is better off staying away from the theater.

How does a person prepare for this level of composition? Unless gifted with bountiful natural talent and polished with private instruction, such a composer would have to spend at least 4 to 6 years beyond high school studying music, probably in a university. The aspirant might major in composition and minor in theater—getting experience in campus or local productions, as did Stephen Sondheim, Oscar Hammerstein, Cole Porter, Richard Rodgers, and many others. The "complete" show music composer would not only become immersed in the Broadway repertoire but also study the great "show music" composed by earlier masters, such as Mozart and Wagner, not to mention Stravinsky and Copland in the 20th century.

What kind of temperament must a composer have to work professionally in the theater? Already mentioned was the need for an ability to collaborate artistically; a "loner" cannot make it in this environment. Also, the show music composer must be able to endure the sudden rejection of material without experiencing collapse of ego. The aspirant must have unlimited patience—be willing to work on one project for a year or two, then see the show fold after one performance and be willing to go through the whole process again. The person must also possess sufficient aggressiveness to search for show backers and producers. Creative musicians working in the theater must hustle their own financial support and convince investors that the project is as good as the composers believe it is. In this aspect of a theater composer's career, there is little room for modesty. Self-confidence and drive are as important to professional success as the musician's creative prowess.

Employment Prospects. There is no such thing as an "employer" or a "job" for show music composers. Rather, they work on projects, perhaps for long periods without compensation, in the hope that they can locate a financial backer along the way. Despite the daunting ratio of flops to hits among musical shows, every season financial benefactors, or **angels**, emerge with money in hand, ready to sink up to several million dollars into an untried, unproved musical dream. A show composer may struggle for years and never find financial backing or a receptive producer. Still, writers new and old continue to make their way in the theater.

Potential income sources for show music are described elsewhere in this volume. Because royalties for show music from records and print media can be significant, every year this pot of gold attracts still more show music composers determined to follow the rainbow. Because the rewards can be great, composers always seem willing to endure long periods of starvation waiting for that hit. Individuals engaged in this long-odds game must have outside income of some kind.

Trebas Institute students in Sound Design lab.

Photo courtesy of Trebas Institute.

Composer of Educational Materials

Career Description. When schools and colleges accelerated their music education programs following World War II, publishers became increasingly involved in attempting to supply the print music needs of school bands, orchestras, and choruses, as well as the requirements of the individual student in search of learning materials. This print music market expanded in the 1960s to involve several hundred composers/arrangers/editors in the publication of music education materials. Today, many composers of educational materials are educators themselves; of those, most are affiliated with a college or university.

The most successful composers of educational materials usually concentrate on the particular medium that they know best: Band directors tend to compose mostly band pieces; choral directors tend mostly to create choral repertoire; orchestral directors compose and arrange orchestral literature. Occasionally, composers of educational material extend their talents beyond grade school– and university-level literature and compose works for professional ensembles such as symphony orchestras, ballet and opera companies, and military bands.

Qualifications and Preparation. Most composers and arrangers of educational music have a degree in music; most have an advanced degree in composition and several years of experience with school ensembles.

Employment Prospects. It can be tricky to get a foot into the educational-music door. Composers, arrangers, and transcribers who are not affiliated with a major publishing company but who wish to have their works published should shop their material to a smaller, independent publisher or consider self-publishing their material. Those submitting to a small firm that accepts unsolicited work will help their prospects if they strictly follow submission guidelines. And all aspirants should be sure their music addresses a specific market (such as a high school marching band).

Composer of Children's Music

Career Description. Anyone with a child at home can testify to the power, the popularity, and the pervasiveness of children's music, which can be found on albums, TV shows, DVDs, Web sites, and films. Disney led the way in marketing such specialized music, eventually discovering that sound tracks and videos are extremely lucrative reminders of a pleasant viewing experience, but today numerous record labels and video companies specifically target little eyes and ears with a wide variety of releases.

A composer seeking a professional career writing children's music must understand how to score ideas in a simple style yet avoid the simplistic. Competition in the field is strong, and even the simplest songs should reveal at least a hint of charm, if not originality. Song texts are essential to most music appealing to children—the sing-along factor is often key. If not adept at composing lyrics, the composer will need to locate a strong collaborator. Also, the aspiring composer in this field needs to know how limited in range melodies must be for young voices.

One aspect of composing music for kids spills over into the educational field, particularly through children's television programming and educational DVDs. This market includes material that helps young children learn to count, to spell, to recognize the names of animals, and so forth, sometimes correlated to music books with sound recordings. Composers interested in this kind of writing and production are involved not just in entertainment but in education as well.

Qualifications and Preparation. Aspirants may find work in this field with the qualifications cited above for writers of popular songs—natural creative gifts. An arranger can always be called in to bail out the illiterate composer who is not skilled in the craft. But it is more likely that publishers and record producers, given a choice, will prefer to look at the music submitted by musicians who know how to score what they create. Serious children's writers also need a good grasp of children's age-level characteristics and would be well advised to make themselves knowledgeable in areas such as child development and keep current in trends within children's entertainment.

Employment Prospects. Most income in this field derives from recordings and printed music that follow the release of a successful musical film or TV program. Some of this work is rendered by songwriters hired by the film producers. Music publishers and recording companies then follow up the film with special editions. The qualified composer aspiring to work in the children's music field should contact publishers within this market who accept unsolicited work.

Composer of Classical Music

Career Description. Musicians who aspire to professional careers as composers of classical music generally view themselves as functioning outside the music "business," believing they can spare themselves confrontation with the commercial world. But most composers in the field bump up against the rude realities of the marketplace just like their counterparts in popular music. If gifted with both abundant talent and the right temperament for such a career, the serious music composer should become acquainted with the professional lives of Bach, Handel, or Chopin—not to mention Schoenberg and Bartók. Each of these composers discovered that he had to devote much of his time to hustling for jobs, commissions, and students. Nowadays, only a handful of composers devote their full workweek to composing. Either through choice or financial necessity, nearly all composers divide their time among composing, teaching, performing—and job hustling.

Practically all serious music composers find that about the only place they can find steady employment is on the teaching staff of a conservatory or university (in the last century, Schoenberg, Bartók, Harris, Piston, Hindemith, Persichetti, Crumb, Foss, Schuller). Once a composer starts to acquire a good reputation, commissions follow. A composer of national and international reputation could live fully off commissions alone, for musicians of this stature receive more requests to compose than they can accept. But the composer aspiring to this high station may have to wait a lifetime to reach these heights.

Composers of even modest reputation enter composing contests. These come along all the time, and an energetic composer can often earn several cash awards a year this way. Certain contests of this kind can lead to a national reputation; through them, composers can receive commission offers, even teaching jobs.

Qualifications and Preparation. To find employment, the aspirant must be highly motivated and determined. Let us hope for talent as well. But how can the first-rate serious music composer be identified today? There is no consensus on this question.

As it turns out, the composers who manage to achieve more than regional reputations are those who attract media and critical attention. Sometimes this attention is generated by using outlandish tricks (quartet for strings and cement mixer)—or "composing" pieces that are silent musically (John Cage). Or a composer may attract attention through tricking critics (garnering rave reviews for a piece that was deliberately performed backwards). Other serious music composers get their music played because they appear as soloists or conductors. If they are really good at either, they give the impression of being first-rate at anything musical.

How does a serious music composer prepare for a career? Practically all of them today who get teaching jobs must have an earned terminal degree from an accredited university. Of these, the most useful is the doctor of musical arts (DMA) in composition, the degree now most often awarded to musicians planning professional careers as composer-teachers. Some colleges and universities award the doctor of music, doctor of philosophy, or master of music as the terminal degree, also with a specialization in composition. Most advanced-degree candidates serve as teaching assistants to the faculty under which they are studying or teach music in a school to support themselves financially during the arduous period of graduate study. Whatever the work/study combination the degree candidate can set up, advanced study focuses on developing the student's craft—through extensive exercises, performances, and study of master works.

Employment Prospects. The musician aspiring to employment as a composer of serious music cannot expect to earn a living scoring masterpieces. The aspirant will almost certainly find work, early on, primarily as a teacher of theory and composition in a college or university. As a potential pedagogue, the aspirant should know that the supply of qualified, certified teachers has often exceeded demand. Still, those who are sufficiently motivated will continue their quest for employment as serious composer-teachers.

How does the aspiring composer-teacher land the first job? In these ways:

(a) developing a good reputation with influential musician-teachers;

(b) joining the College Music Society and following up its job-opening notices;

(c) registering with the alma mater's placement bureau;

(d) attending professional meetings and making contacts, setting up performances of new work, seeking publicity;

(e) registering with teacher employment services; and

(f) persevering for at least 5 years.

Arranger-Orchestrator

Career Description. Many creative musicians earn most of their incomes as arrangers. They take music written by someone else and arrange or add voices to suit the needs of the artist or film company. They accomplish this in diverse ways, ranging from writing leadsheets to scoring motion pictures. Hundreds of arrangers make their living working for songwriters and publishers, turning out leadsheets and song copies. The American Federation of Musicians (AFM) has pay scales covering this kind of work, but they are often ignored because the union has few opportunities to police this kind of employment.

Publishers engage arrangers to score various editions, particularly for the educational field. Astute publishers hire only specialists for this kind of work—choral arrangers for vocal editions, jazz specialists for jazz charts, and so on.

The largest segment of professional arrangers work for performers. Most professional performers use custom arrangements exclusively. Nearly all arrangers are employed freelance; few are retained on regular salaries. Their services are considered, under copyright law, as work made for hire; they receive one flat fee, up front, and do not receive royalties on copies or recordings sold.

Orchestrators take music that has been written by someone else and write or score the music for instruments. Arrangers and orchestrators usually work under tight deadlines, largely because composers and producers are also working under tight deadlines. It is a high-pressure field. Panic-type time schedules are regularly relieved, however, with intermittent periods of idleness. But musicians attracted to the arranging field appear to love their work and manage to survive careers that are a mix of great artistic satisfaction and trips to the unemployment office.

Many musicians work as part-time arrangers, dividing their professional efforts among related fields such as composition, directing, producing, and performing. Others are working at least part-time in fields such as publishing and management.

Qualifications and Preparation. To qualify as a professional arranger, the individual should have thorough training in music theory, sight singing, and ear training. An arranger's ear must be as finely tuned as that of a composer, and many professional arrangers qualify as composers, too. An arranger is expected to work quickly and be able to knock out a score overnight when necessary.

Besides schooling in music theory, the best training for aspirants is to write—and write and write—then hear the score in rehearsal. Then rewrite. Then rehearse the revision—and on and on over several years of experimentation, trial, and error. All good writers, whether they create prose, poetry, or music, recommend two basic activities: Read a lot and write constantly.

Employment Prospects. The aspiring professional arranger need not starve throughout the learning experience. All arrangers who eventually make it as pros begin to pick up small jobs early on—first for free, then maybe for a few dollars for one of their charts—if they'll copy off the parts and run the rehearsal. Really talented arrangers attract attention quickly, and they begin receiving requests for their work, often from those not able to pay much. But outstanding talents can break in. Employment prospects for them are generally good, provided they are prepared, at least early in their careers, to fill out their workweeks with other jobs. Top arrangers working in the recording field for stars or busy record producers earn big money. If they manage to keep abreast of ever-changing musical styles, their careers can last longer than those of the artists for whom they write.

Music Editor

Career Description. There are several kinds of music editors, some of which will be described elsewhere in this chapter. Here we discuss the kind of music editor who prepares music manuscripts for publication.

All publishers of printed music require professional editors, because even skilled composers and arrangers are rarely knowledgeable concerning precisely how scores and parts must be edited before the music is printed. In the popular field, most publishers contract with one of the major print houses to handle their music editing and paper publishing.

Music print publishers of classical music engage editors to rewrite the composers' or arrangers' scores so that they conform in content and style to the standards this country inherited centuries ago from master European engravers and printers. Most modern printed versions of musical notation are produced on computers and then printed in quantity. Prospective music editors are advised to gain substantial knowledge of music-editing traditions as well as computer software skills.

The music editor must first correct and proofread music that has been submitted to the publisher. Part of this work can involve actual rescoring, arranging, and even original composition. The music editors who are most in demand are almost always qualified as composers and arrangers, too. Many editors specialize in just one field, such as choral music or piano music.

Editorial staff often contribute to judgment on acquisitions in respect to musical quality, style, and market suitability. Publishing decisions will be based on those judgments.

Qualifications and Preparation. To qualify for a job as a music editor, the individual should undertake a complete musical education in theory, history, literature, and performance practices. This broad background is most readily available in universities with strong music departments.

Employment Prospects. For many musicians, particularly composers and arrangers with good educational backgrounds, music editing is a fallback position; they enter the field as a second career choice, or more commonly, as one component of a combination career.

Nearly all freelance editors earn part of their incomes from composing, arranging, copying, performing, or teaching.

Music Copyist

Career Description. Many musicians break into the composing and arranging fields as music copyists, who transcribe musical parts onto staff paper from a score. The tasks may include copying various parts for different instruments or voices. Other musicians develop well-paying careers in the copying field itself.

Qualifications and Preparation. Many professional copyists are also arrangers, for the two professions have much in common. Aspirants must be highly skilled in notation and transposition, have music theory training, and be extremely accurate. Professional copyists are expected to make no mistakes, and they are also expected to correct the errors in the scores they work on. The experienced professional copyist may not be able to reach the composer-arranger to answer questions about illegible notes or incomplete sections. The copyist must then have sufficient skill and knowledge to correct and complete the score without guidance. Computer-generated scores and parts are commonplace, and the aspiring music calligrapher must become proficient in using these tools.

Employment Prospects. There is an actual shortage of fully qualified musicians who have the knowledge and skill required of professional copyists, and copying jobs exist everywhere. But the aspirant must sniff such out opportunities and make sure his or her talents are known to every composer-arranger who can be located. Most copyists supplement their income in other branches of music. Combination careers can often yield satisfactory incomes.

Directing/Producing Careers

Music Director-Conductor

Record Producer

Music Director-Conductor

Career Description. Most musical performers require musical direction of some sort.

The conductors best known by the public are those engaged as music directors of symphony orchestras and opera companies. Some are called "artistic director." It is customary for musicians holding these posts to assist management in contracting guest conductors and guest soloists, selecting programs, working with orchestra managers in planning operating budgets, and hiring and firing musicians.

Artistic directors also become involved with the major orchestras in negotiating recording contracts for their ensembles. Because of the heavy responsibilities assumed by these kinds of musical directors, they require at least one assistant conductor. Some of the major orchestras have two or more assistant conductors who help the artistic director by conducting performances for school children and pop concerts.

Musicians who serve time as assistant conductors often graduate to roles of principal conductors and music directors of orchestras and opera companies.

Music directors and assistant directors have such heavy responsibilities that they rarely find time for any other professional employment, save for guest conducting other symphony orchestras. In addition to their directing, they must meet with the various committees charged with raising money for operations. An important part of this aspect of the work is fostering goodwill among the individuals and corporations and foundations that pledge money to support the artistic goals of the ensemble.

Some music directors are engaged by arts centers and community centers as artistic directors. They not only may conduct rehearsals and performances but are also likely to function as organizers and supervisors of artistic and educational programs for these entities.

Thousands of music directors are employed by churches. These professionals may be organists or other performers, many of whom serve double duty as choir directors. Large churches sometimes call their music directors "ministers of music." A person serving in such a capacity may direct choral and other musical groups for the institution. While the largest churches pay their music directors full-time salaries, smaller institutions do not, expecting them to fill out their incomes through other activities.

Music directors for movies and TV can be hired first as composer-arrangers and be expected to conduct their own music when their scores are recorded (more information on the film/TV music sector can be found later in this chapter). This same pattern prevails in the field of music library services: Music directors usually serve the producers as triple-threat artists—composers-arrangers-directors.

In the pop field, the individual serving as music director may not be a conductor but simply a performer in the group who assumes a leadership role. Musical direction of groups of this kind is sometimes shared. As for soloists, when an artist reaches star status, he or she usually finds it necessary to employ a music director, at least for appearances on tour. These individuals are almost invariably rehearsal pianists-accompanists who assist the artist by selecting material, arranging it, and conducting rehearsals and live performances. Many of these pianist-conductors are not trained baton twirlers but manage to make sufficient gestures from their position at the piano keyboard to cue the musicians.

Some jobs for music directors in the pop field are found in major cities, conducting shows. Other musical directing jobs are available in the field of industrial shows. Broadway, off-Broadway, and regional theaters employ music directors.

Qualifications and Preparation. All successful music directors share a common attribute: a commanding presence. They know how to lead, either intuitively or through training. This leadership quality is not limited to musical matters but extends to relationships with the variety of human personalities they work with in rehearsal and performance.

Nearly all successful music directors have had extensive schooling, often a combination of formal education and private instruction. Because music directors must be well informed on all aspects of music, their education, at least through the baccalaureate degree level, will be broad. Postbaccalaureate study may include emphasis in performance, composition, or conducting.

In the pop field, directors are often performers, and they are usually involved in composition and arranging, perhaps rehearsing and directing performances of the music they themselves have scored.

The best environment for an aspiring music director is a first-rate university with a strong faculty and a variety of performance groups. In addition, most conductors start early, usually while still in college, to direct a church choir or jazz band or pop chorus or whatever group they can get their hands on; some major cities, such as Los Angeles and New York, also have youth or training orchestras that can offer the talented novice conductor opportunities to practice the craft.

Employment Prospects. Job prospects for music directors can be compared with those found in other aspects of the arts and business: Work is available for top people. Symphony and opera conductors of repute often hold down at least two conducting posts. Other fine musicians prefer to serve smaller communities where the salaries are lower, but the pressures are too.

Music directors in the popular field rise or fall less on their abilities as conductors or leaders than on their abilities to please their employers as writers. A music director who is a really competent composer and arranger can usually find work—and the ability to rehearse and conduct groups is a minor consideration. Employers may tolerate weak leadership qualities and baton techniques when the music director is a whiz at writing music.

In the pop field, young music directors usually start out earning no more than the other performers in the group they direct. When the group goes union, AFM scales generally call for the leader to receive double sideman's scale. When a record producer or music library service (syndicator) production house hires a music director, the director will probably be paid AFM scale (double sideman's wages), then be paid again for any arranging.

Record Producer

Career Description. The work of the various kinds of record producers is described in more detail in Chapter 11 of this book. Some producers are successful largely because they are very good at locating the right musical material, then matching it to the right artists. This is why the old label for these practitioners was "artist and repertoire producers." Some producers are masters of the control room and may have started out as recording engineers. Others know how to raise money, then hire outside experts to arrange the music, mix the sound, and supervise postproduction. Still other producers are master musicians who succeed because they are creative and capture artistic performances on disc. No matter the point of entry, the producer must always be the bridge between artistic integrity and commercial potential.

The majority of the work is performed freelance. The nearest thing approaching steady employment is found with major labels, although label jobs have been in decline for decades. The majority of producers float from job to job pretty much like recording artists; they get return engagements when their music sells and their reputations grow. If they produce a string of flops or are difficult to work with, their telephones stop ringing. Income can keep coming in from past hits, though: In addition to upfront fees, producers are paid royalties on the records they produce.

Independent producers often own their own production companies, and some launch their own independent record labels.

Qualifications and Preparation. An individual aspiring to a career in record production should not expect to follow an orderly path; each producer has his or her own unique story to tell. Nearly all producers who make it discover that they must first become recognized in an allied field—such as songwriting, arranging, sound mixing, criticism, musical direction, or other related experience. In addition to competence in one or more of these facets of music, the record producer usually possesses some kind of leadership ability and a temperament that mixes well with artists, technicians, and executives. The producer must remain stable when others on the project are disintegrating through frustration or fatigue.

The producer has the additional worry of staying within budget. So the record producer must be a kind of miracle person—possessing strong musical ability, technological know-how, magic ears, a psychologist's mentality, the stability to remain rational under great pressures, *and* business acumen.

The producer of classical music must possess many of the same qualifications as the pop record producer, plus a few more. This professional has to be as good a score reader as the conductor and know details of the score being recorded. Ideally, the producer in the booth should be the twin of the conductor on the podium, so closely must they understand each other and the musical interpretation the literature requires.

To qualify to produce classical music recordings, the musician must have training identical to the kind described for classical music conductors. In addition, the producer must have knowledge of technology, perhaps even acoustics, sufficient to give direction to the mixing and mastering technicians.

Employment Prospects. Because no one possesses all the talents outlined above, those who come close find themselves in high demand. Although record production budgets have been tightening and competition for slots increasing, labels and artists are always searching for those record producers who can pull all the elements together in the studio to create a chart-worthy hit. Producers possessing the essentials of the art *and* craft will work and prosper.

Because of the absence of employment continuity, nearly all record producers have other irons in the fire, just as most musicians do. They may write songs, own part of a publishing company, manage artists, function as agents, write arrangements, produce shows—whatever works.

As noted above, staff producers earn regular salaries; some of them also have contracts providing royalties based on sales. Some contracts provide that although royalties are earned on all of the producer's recordings, royalties are not actually paid until they exceed the amount of the accumulated salary. Some producers do not start receiving royalties until the label has recovered its out-of-pocket production costs. Some independent producers are given all their production expenses by a recording label and receive a flat production fee plus royalties, or possibly no fee, just royalty income.

Performing Careers

> Singer
>
> Instrumentalist

Singer

Career Description. This is one of the more open-ended career categories, because it can encompass a wide range of professional possibilities. In the field of popular

Band performing on *Morning Becomes Eclectic,* KCRW Studio, Santa Monica College.

Photo courtesy of KCRW.

music, singers find careers not only as soloists and recording artists but also as group singers, background vocalists on commercials, and "production" singers, singing actors, or singing dancers. As most singers have already discovered, a career often starts at school, college, or local clubs where the individual can learn quite early whether audiences respond well. In the pop field, these amateur and semiprofessional beginnings are often combined with instrumental performance or songwriting, sometimes both.

Steady employment depends on the performer's skill. Successful singing careers involve a mix of live appearances and recordings. Established recording stars also appear on television, sometimes in commercials and film. Professional singers' lives are filled with almost incessant travel. The longest engagements occur when an artist remains in one location for a month or two to complete recording an album. Stars who play Las Vegas may be booked in for a few weeks, but most other singing jobs in the pop field are strings of one-nighters or weeklong engagements. Few experiences are more exhausting than constant traveling, and a professional singer's first concern, under these strains, is to stay healthy despite the rigors of the road. The second concern is, or should be, finding a competent personal manager. The third priority is the ongoing search for good material.

Even singers who write most of their own songs must somehow find outside sources to feed their acts. Nonwriting singers never stop searching for good songs. Writers and publishers know this and follow singers around, leadsheets in hand. Successful singers are also plagued with enthusiastic, even overbearing fans. These multiple pressures can debilitate a performer, and only the hardy can survive. But those attracted to the field seem to sustain themselves on the applause and adulation of their audiences—not to mention the money.

Qualifications and Preparation. To qualify for a successful career as a professional singer, it is helpful for the aspirant to be able to sing. But any audit of the field will reveal that dozens of nonsingers manage to make a living as "singers." Individuals with only modest musical talent sometimes win an audience. This occurs when the public becomes attracted to a performer not for singing ability, but because of the individual's personality or acting ability. Those performers who have made a successful career for themselves do, however, share some important characteristics: some musical talent, charisma, self-discipline, physical stamina, versatility, creative ability, and poise.

In classical music, most artists who qualify for work have spent several years studying voice in college or with outside teachers. College music majors often pursue the master's degree, majoring in voice or perhaps choral music. Should the "legitimate" singer aspire to opera, the performer may opt for a music conservatory diploma rather than a university degree. The former provides concentrated training in performance. Opera students must acquire facility in several foreign languages, with French, Italian, and German being the most important.

Employment Prospects. The job outlook for singers ranges from grim to excellent. Naturally, the fewest opportunities lie in the musical arenas that attract the smallest audiences and, therefore, bring in the least amount of money. These would include the solo recital and concert fields, especially for singers with only classical training. Some employment is available with symphony orchestras and in community concert series, but these engagements are mainly seasonal.

In the field of opera, artist managers arrange some engagements; other artists are in such demand, they book themselves—opera companies outbid each other for their services. Unfortunately, only a few trained singers qualify for leading roles with good companies. Thousands of university graduates aspiring to careers in their fields are disappointed each year, and turn to Broadway, teaching, voice coaching, or church choir jobs.

Churches offer many jobs to trained singers who can also direct choirs. Some singers who are unable to develop the performing careers they had planned turn to schoolteaching, then pick up singing jobs at business events, night clubs, weddings and funerals. Practically all of this work is nonunion.

Musical theater sometimes offers an employment option for trained singers, particularly if the auditioners are young, of the right physical size and shape, and able to act and/or dance. Although New York producers audition and hire many new singing actors each season, more extensive job opportunities are found in regional theaters, theme parks, and cruise lines. Aspiring singers sometimes begin their professional careers as supporting players, then graduate to leading roles.

Another source of fairly steady employment can be found by crackerjack singers willing to locate near centers of commercial and film and TV music production. These versatile singers need to be expert sight readers in any musical genre and be able to perform with minimal rehearsal.

When it comes to job prospects for pop singers, there is yet another set of conditions. Here, *image* matters, and record labels likely will be looking for an entire "package"—an appealing personality to market and sell to admiring audiences. Pop singers who write their own songs will find their chances of catching the ears of label executives and audiences alike greatly improved. Since the Beatles in the mid-1960s, the preponderant number of new singing artists breaking big in the business have been performing composers. These artists may not be either great singers or top composers, but the combination enchants audiences, and these versatile artists sell a lot of music.

Instrumentalist

Career Description. The working hours of a full-time instrumentalist may average only 3 hours a day, but most musicians are busy at least 40 hours a week. Practically all professional instrumentalists do at least some teaching. These accomplished musicians often have more students waiting for openings than they can accept. Student fees not only offer income to supplement playing jobs, but they can often provide at least minimum sustenance during periods when musicians cannot find playing jobs. Besides setting hours aside for teaching, professionals usually engage in regular daily practice, continuing throughout their careers to polish their skills and expand their repertoire.

In addition to these musical activities, a large percentage of professional instrumentalists are actively employed outside of music. From choice or necessity, many pros moonlight (more often, daylight) at jobs with flexible hours, thus providing release time for them to accept whatever music jobs come along.

Many professional musicians manage a different kind of moonlighting: They accept every attractive playing job that comes along, then fill in the balance of their workweek in music-related employment such as composition, arranging, copying, perhaps artist management or record production. Many professional musicians work fairly regularly as instrumentalists, while filling their daytime hours as music merchants—selling instruments, equipment, and so forth. Many work in "casuals"— club dates, one-night performances—and events such as conventions, bar mitzvahs, awards banquets, and the like. Others still put together packages of musicians for casuals and work as one part musician, one part producer, and one part talent agent.

An important consideration for those planning careers as performers is the matter of travel. Most musicians must move around a lot—which can be fun when they are young but which becomes intolerable after several years of the gypsy life. Another important concern is the seasonal aspect of most performing careers. Many symphony, opera, and dance company musicians are laid off in the summer months. Broadway pit musicians know only seasonal employment, which generally means the life of a particular show. Instrumentalists working clubs on so-called steady engagements are delighted when a job extends beyond a few weeks.

Qualifications and Preparation. The young instrumentalist who has ambitions for a full-time, fully professional playing career must be endowed with outstanding musical talent. Instrumental study should begin in childhood and continue throughout the career.

To qualify for the concert and symphonic field, students today will usually complete at least a master's degree, often a doctorate, in performance (some graduates complete a "diploma" program). Whatever amount of formal training the musician might undergo, the working professional must be familiar with performance practices of both classical and popular music. Practically all symphony orchestras have a pops series where traveling artists bring in charts ranging in style from blues to country. And musicians in the theater and recording fields are expected to be able to perform any musical idiom in the correct style. The old days of the sharply delineated "classical" and "jazz" musician are nearly gone. Almost all pros now must cross the line.

The great majority of full-time professional instrumentalists are expected to be musically literate and read at sight what is placed before them. Nonreaders can be financially and artistically successful, but their success is often based more on their personality, composing, or strong natural talent.

Besides having a personality that works well with others, the real pro must be willing to work very hard for long years and persevere during periods of disappointment. Just "liking music" is not enough. Most truly accomplished professional artists reach their goal through a love, even a passion, for music making.

Yet another personal attribute is essential for the instrumentalist who strives for the highest-paying fields, particularly symphony and studio work: strong nerves. Young musicians shooting for the big time are generally unaware of the working atmosphere in the recording field particularly, which is one not just of high tension but of sheer terror. Those jobs demand perfection in performance. There is minimum tolerance for error and none whatever for carelessness. A top studio player is allowed an occasional flub but is subject to being quickly displaced, sometimes forever, by a competitor who can demonstrate even greater reliability. Nerves of steel come in handy, but before the faint-of-heart abandon their dreams of the big time, it should be reassuring to remember that artists of international stature—musicians, dancers, actors—have said that controlled tension aids artistic performance.

Employment Prospects. Even though there are thousands of unemployed and underemployed instrumentalists, the truth is that there is a scarcity in some areas. Employment prospects depend on the particular instrument as well as the musician's talent and training. The best advice is to be around music a lot and get to know

Photo courtesy NAMM.

successful people in the field who will in turn recommend you for different projects. Practice makes perfect, and the more musicians the aspirant can "sit in" with, the better.

Keyboard Players

There is a daunting oversupply of first-rate concert pianists and recitalists. Conservatories and colleges continue to turn out thousands of these artists, but their employment prospects are poor. Most communities have an abundance of restaurant, club, and lounge pianists.

In the theater music field, there is a shortage in most communities of keyboard artists who can sight-read a traveling Broadway show book, handle the written-out parts, and also play **comp style**. In the recording field, there are brilliant keyboard artists but an actual shortage in most cities of musicians who can handle diverse styles such as jazz, pop, and rock. Even more scarce are those pianists who can handle these styles plus Mozart or Chopin or Gershwin's concert pieces. If a keyboard artist seeks work in the recording field (and even in pit orchestras), employability will be increased by facility in performance synthesizers. Many keyboard players specialize in the electronic realm.

Finally, keyboardists can often find employment as accompanists. Some pianists consider accompanying second-class employment, but truly competent performers are often in demand.

Guitarists

There is a huge oversupply of amateur and semiprofessional guitarists who want to become full-time professionals. Many of these individuals do not understand the difference between an amateur and a truly professional performing artist.

Any guitarist who is a good reader and who can perform artistically in the basic idioms of jazz, blues, rock, and country will probably need help in juggling job offers. This kind of competence and versatility is in demand everywhere.

Percussionists

Even before rock and roll, the world was oversupplied with drummers. Nevertheless, in most communities today there is an undersupply of fully competent, versatile percussionists. Directors and contractors can rarely find a drummer/percussionist who can really read well and who can handle not only conventional percussion but also mallet instruments and timpani. Many drummers play great jazz or rock or Latin rhythms but don't really know how to play concert or show music.

Few percussionists take the time to study seriously the art of timpani tuning and playing or to learn much about non-Western music. Percussionists who can do most or all the basic musical styles well, and who are good readers, are rare in most areas and in high demand. Percussionists in the next most active group are those who come close to the prowess and versatility of the "complete professional percussionist." Drummers who are unwilling to undertake this level of training will continue to compete with thousands of other drummers of comparable skill. Competition among "average" musicians will always be great.

Wind Instrument Players

The school band programs of recent decades have produced a large supply of good wind instrument performers. There is even an oversupply of fully qualified wind players with master's, even doctoral, degrees. When an opening is advertised by a professional symphony orchestra on, say, clarinet or trumpet, it is not unusual to see several hundred applicants. A respectable percentage of that group would have ability that would qualify them for serious consideration. In recording studios, a great abundance of wind players compete for those high-paying jobs. Extensive woodwind doubling is expected in the show music field and in recording. Because it takes a lifetime to master even one instrument, it is understandable why top doublers are so scarce. Those who come closest to really playing several winds get a lot of work—and when they do, they earn, through their doubling ability, 20% to 100% above basic scale.

In any discussion of career opportunities for wind players, mention must be made of the hundreds of jobs open for them in military bands.

String Players

Hundreds of string players find full- to part-time employment in America's many symphony orchestras. For details, review Chapter 13. Performers heading for careers as soloists in the classical field will find it difficult to break in without the aid of an agent or manager. The most active concert agents and management companies are listed in directory service Musical America, which also includes the names and addresses of symphony orchestras and opera companies here and in Europe.

The most direct route for an instrumentalist in any field to find work is through establishing a reputation for being able to handle whatever opportunities come along—and a reputation for being better qualified than the competition. An instrumentalist of genuine ability becomes known throughout the musical community very quickly. Jobs can be scarce, but when they come along the really good players are in demand.

A musical reputation can work even more quickly the other way around: Less talented performers, weak readers, and undependable musicians earn overnight reputations, too.

Teaching Careers

Studio Teacher	College Music Instructor
School Music Educator	Music Therapist

Studio Teacher

Career Description. Studio teachers are private instructors who give individualized or group lessons, setting their own fees and developing their own lesson plans. Some teachers are contracted by music stores and may work on-site, but most operate out of their own homes or offices.

Qualifications and Preparation. The studio teacher most in demand is the professional who is an active performer engaged in teaching as a sideline. However, performers who moonlight as teachers can possibly do more harm than good to their prospective students—if they are not actively engaged in the *teaching* process, the instructor can end up just performing for students and not actually teaching them. To teach, one must be more than just a good musician. The job requires patience and an ability to impart information in a way that can be understood by children and adults. The teacher must be able to relate to the student on his or her age level and level of aptitude. Especially when working with children and adolescents, winning the trust of the student is half the battle. A sense of humor is also invaluable.

Genuinely qualified music teachers have completed 4 to 8 years of college-level music study, are competent performers themselves, possess sound pedagogical techniques, and know how to inspire students. All the schooling in the world will not prepare one for the challenging job of working with, and motivating, sometimes reluctant students.

Employment Prospects. How does a qualified musician build up a student clientele? By building a strong reputation in the community—first as a musician, and second as a teacher. Advertising can bring in many students, along with good word of mouth. School music educators can be counted on to make recommendations to their pupils.

Many active professionals teach at least part-time. The best of them fill every vacant hour in 40- to 60-hour workweeks and experience excellent income. Others, unable to stand an unending stream of kids passing through their studios, will accept only a limited number of pupils. Because most studio teachers work for themselves, small business skills are necessary for this career.

School Music Educator

Career Description. Music educators work in public, private, or parochial schools. Duties vary depending on the ages taught and the guidelines often set by state or district supervisors. Music teachers employed in Grades K (kindergarten) through 6 have responsibilities different from those working in junior and senior high schools. Many school districts try to finance a sufficient number of general music teachers for the lower grades to provide at least some music listening and participation for every child: singing, movement to music, and improvised performance on simple rhythm instruments and toys.

Teachers in junior and senior high schools are usually hired for specific duties. One director may be in charge of brass, wind, and string ensembles while another has responsibilities for the choral groups; either of these—or both—may be involved in the production of musical plays. The number of teachers and the division of responsibilities are usually determined by the size and financial commitment of the school.

Bands seem to dominate music education, and most senior high schools have an assortment: concert band, marching band, pep band, stage band. From August through November, high school band directors' lives are generally consumed by rehearsing their football bands. During these frantic weeks, music educators often feel they are not so much musical directors as drill sergeants, arrangers, copyists, and entertainment directors for the school's athletic department. Following football season, these teachers must hastily prepare a holiday program, then come springtime music festivals involving their concert bands and stage bands. When summer vacation finally arrives, they usually spend some of their time off trying to get equipment repaired and shows planned for the fall football season. High school music educators are accustomed to 60-hour workweeks, but many appear to thrive on their heavy loads.

Music Education Supervisor

Most school districts employ at least one "music supervisor" to direct and coordinate activities of all vocal and instrumental music teachers. The role of the supervisor is to guide formulation of educational policy, assist school principals in hiring new teachers, fight for and control music budgets, and offer pedagogical guidance to the music educators employed in their districts. Music supervisors also administer acquisition and circulation of central music lending libraries for their districts. These individuals are also involved in organizing music festivals, reading clinics, and contests. Many also teach. Some supervisors are employed on 12-month contracts.

Qualifications and Preparation. Except for the field of music therapy, school music teaching is the only kind of employment where applicants are required to have a college degree in music. School music teachers (Grades K through 12) in practically all states are also required to have a teaching certificate or teaching credential. Some states will automatically certify a teacher in a particular music teaching field if the teacher holds a baccalaureate degree in music from a state-accredited college or university. Other states require that college graduates in music also successfully pass a state-administered certifying examination. Types of teaching certificates vary from state to state.

In addition to a college degree and teaching license, those who do most of the music teacher hiring (school principals, usually) look for one or more of these qualifications or attributes: a good reputation as a teacher, high grades in college and on the certifying examination, and an outgoing personality.

Employment Prospects. For many years, a reasonably talented college student majoring in music education could expect to find a full-time teaching position after graduation. But more recently, the employment prospects for school music teachers have diminished. Top universities with distinguished track records of turning out fine teachers continue to place most of their graduates. But decreasing employment opportunities for individuals seeking teaching jobs in music and the other arts in most cities will probably continue because of downward pressure on school budgets. Music programs are often the first to be trimmed when money is tight.

College Music Instructor

Career Description. Before describing careers in college and university music teaching, the junior colleges should be discussed. Most junior or community colleges offer courses such as music appreciation, music theory, class piano, perhaps class guitar, band, and stage band. Junior colleges that offer a 2-year associate in arts degree in music may also offer courses such as music arranging, music history, and music business. Individuals aspiring to employment in one of these junior colleges are usually required to teach about 20 hours a week, almost double the teaching load of music instructors in 4-year colleges and universities. Because of this extremely burdensome schedule, few junior college music teachers have adequate time to prepare for their classes as well as for rehearsals, and they are among the most overworked teachers in the music education field.

Quite a different kind of employment is found at 4-year colleges and universities, where full-time music faculty members usually teach between 12 and 16 hours a week. Practically all music instructors at this level specialize in one particular aspect of music, and most, if not all, of their teaching and directing responsibilities relate to that specialty—for example, theory, choral music, instrumental music, applied music instruction, music history, and perhaps jazz education. They may teach only three or four different classes or ensembles a week, but their "off time" is filled with preparation for their hours in the classroom or rehearsal hall. Most university-level music teachers claim to have a workweek that averages well above 48 hours. Teachers who have attained higher academic rank, such as associate or full professor, are normally assigned somewhat lighter teaching loads. But the senior professors may be even busier than their colleagues of lower academic rank—engaged in research and other creative activities such as writing music, articles, and books.

Qualifications and Preparation. Practically all states require that their junior college teachers have not only a master's degree in music from an accredited institution but, in addition, a junior college teaching certificate. Musicians applying for "the choral job" or "the band job" at a particular junior college are expected to have established reputations in their field of specialization. Such reputations are usually acquired first at the high school level before the aspirant is considered for a faculty position in a junior college. Prospective faculty members are normally hired by the junior college president, on recommendation of the resident music faculty.

Four-year colleges and universities normally hire only those individuals who have earned a terminal degree in music—DMA, DM, or PhD, for example. Some prestigious schools occasionally hire faculty members who lack a terminal degree but whose reputations as performers, composers, or scholars are equal in prestige to a doctoral degree. Many colleges and universities will not consider prospective faculty who lack publications; either music compositions/arrangements or writings about music or music-related topics are considered "publications." These same institutions tend to waive this requirement when they are evaluating prospective members for their "applied music" faculty.

Employment Prospects. In some colleges and universities, funding for new faculty positions has been difficult to find. The number of music majors in American colleges has been influenced by the increasing awareness that many college-level music studies appeared to lead to no job. But the individual aspiring to college-level music teaching would be mistaken to conclude that no career opportunities exist. Although we are oversupplied with aspirants holding even doctoral degrees in theory, history, musicology, piano, and choral directing, some colleges and universities have difficulty finding fully qualified instructors (with doctorates) in certain specialties, such as ethnomusicology, music therapy, jazz education, electronic music, pop choral music, improvisation, sound synthesis, recording, and the music business.

Music Therapist

Career Description. Music therapy is the prescribed use of music by a qualified person to effect positive changes in the psychological, physical, cognitive, or social functioning of individuals with health or educational problems. Music therapists assess the emotional well-being, physical health, social functioning, communication abilities, and cognitive skills of their clients through musical responses. They then design therapeutic music sessions using techniques such as music improvisation, receptive music listening, songwriting, lyric discussion, music and imagery, music performance, and learning through music. Interdisciplinary treatment offered by music therapists can be used for a variety of populations, such as people with developmental and learning disabilities, mental health needs, Alzheimer's disease and other aging-related conditions, and brain injuries. It can also be of use to those seeking therapy to cope with everyday stressors and for personal growth.

Qualifications and Preparation. To qualify as a professional music therapist, the aspirant must graduate from an approved college degree program—offered at universities around the country—which requires completion of a clinical internship with a 6-month minimum. These individuals are then eligible to sit for the national examination offered by the Certification Board for Music Therapists. Music therapists who successfully complete the independently administered examination hold the music therapist-board certified credential (MT-BC). The curricula offer a thorough study of music, along with coursework in psychology and the biological, social, and behavioral sciences. Graduate degrees are offered at several universities in music therapy and related disciplines.

Employment Prospects. Music therapists are finding employment in record numbers in psychiatric hospitals, rehabilitative facilities, medical hospitals, outpatient clinics, day care treatment centers, agencies serving developmentally disabled persons, community mental health centers, drug and alcohol programs, senior centers, nursing homes, hospice programs, correctional facilities, mental health residential treatment centers, schools, and private practice. The job outlook is promising, especially in terms of job opportunities related to our aging population and a growing interest in integrative forms of treatment.

Students produce and edit original music at a recording studio designed by Michael Green at SUNY Oneonta.

Photo by Nick Keish, courtesy of State University of New York, College at Oneonta.

Broadcasting/Film/Video Game Careers

Radio Broadcasting

Film/TV Broadcasting

Music Video/Music Special
Producer-Director

Video Game Scorer/Audio Programmer

Advertising Jingle Writer

Radio Broadcasting

Disc Jockey

Career Description. The individual who masters the ceremony of getting recordings identified and on the air is a key figure in radio broadcasting. Disc jockeys in major markets are often confined to introducing recordings and making commercial announcements, these proceedings interrupted by ad-lib comments by the jock about the entertainment, the performers, or most anything that might engage the listeners. In addition to time on the air, the DJ is usually occupied in a variety of tasks related to the operation of the station. Most station managers try to increase community visibility by encouraging their air personalities to become involved in activities such as being master of ceremonies (MC) for civic affairs such as nonprofit fundraisers, shopping center openings, and judging beauty contests. Many jocks are involved in promoting, even sometimes acting as MC for, rock concerts. Disc jockeys in smaller markets are often called on to perform every conceivable task at their stations, from making up playlists to sweeping out the studio. A station with a limited budget will also require its DJs to run the audio engineering board concurrently with physically handing the discs and tapes.

Qualifications and Preparation. Some disc jockeys get started with little or no professional training—instead, connecting with employers and audiences by virtue of their outsize personalities and radio-friendly voices. Some self-taught DJs (or on-the-job apprentices) rise to the top of their profession. But the life expectancy of a disc jockey can be short, comparable to that of a professional athlete. Audience tastes change and stations may seek bigger ratings through a new DJ; stations may also switch formats, often necessitating a new group of air personalities; DJs experience burnout from the drain of constantly appearing to be bubbly and entertaining.

Although it is not difficult to get some kind of modest start as a disc jockey, individuals planning a career in broadcasting should take time out to earn a college degree or two in broadcasting, communication, or an allied field such as music, theater, or perhaps even journalism. Those who qualify themselves with a good education will almost certainly rise faster in their broadcasting careers than others whose backgrounds may limit their potential for leadership roles.

Employment Prospects. The consolidation of the radio business has put pressure on DJ employment. Most jobs are landed through the submission of airchecks accompanied by the individual's résumé. A home tape recording won't do: A station manager wants to hear how the individual sounds on the air during an actual broadcast. Airchecks submitted for audition should have most of the music edited out, retaining only a few seconds to enable the auditor to hear how the performer gets in and out of the music. Those seeking their first job and those changing jobs can learn of available openings by word-of-mouth, and through trade magazines and job boards. Jocks often change jobs as frequently as musicians do. The disc jockey just starting may find opportunities in very small stations for some kind of tryout, partly because such stations (even some larger ones) pay their inexperienced DJs only minimal wages. By job hopping to bigger markets, DJs can eventually work their way up to big-city gigs. Of course, top DJs in major markets (and syndicates or networks) can earn celebrity incomes. Aspirants should also explore opportunities at online music companies, some of which produce radio programming specifically for Internet broadcast, and satellite radio companies, which supply a range of music programming to subscribers.

Program Director

Career Description. As discussed in Chapter 19, program directors (PDs) hold a leadership role at radio stations, including working in consultation with the station's (or station group's) general manager to hire and fire disc jockeys. On some stations, the PD may also participate in engaging and disengaging other on-air types such as news reporters. He or she may also help determine the station's playlist and show lineups; in some cases, the PD will also handle the duties of a music director.

Qualifications and Preparation. Some radio PDs gain their background as DJs, and may continue as on-the-air personalities with reduced schedules. Radio PDs can perform their jobs well without strong musical backgrounds, depending on their musical intuition. PDs who demonstrate strong leadership qualities may eventually grow into the role of group PD (managing operations at multiple stations) or radio station general manager.

Employment Prospects. As with DJs, competition is most intense in the major radio markets in larger cities. Salaries will rise along with the size of the market in which a PD lands.

Music Director

Career Description. As radio stations have consolidated, their programming decisions have become more centralized. The result is a decline in music director jobs at individual radio stations. Where such a job remains, the specialist is responsible for listening to promotional copies of upcoming releases, exchanging information with record promoters, conducting research about listener preferences, and compiling the station music playlist.

Qualifications and Preparation. To qualify for a job as a radio station music director, the aspirant should be knowledgeable about recorded music, recording artists, demographic research methods, and the vagaries of public taste. Most will have extensive hands-on experience in radio broadcasting. Aspirants possessing some of these qualities may perform in the job quite well without any special music training. The individuals who accept these jobs should have one additional personal attribute: the ability to handle continuous pressure from record promoters.

Employment Prospects. Competition for the available slots is keen, particularly in the major markets.

Film/TV Broadcasting

Composer of Dramatic Music

Career Description. Large numbers of musicians develop full-time careers composing what is generally referred to as "background music" for television and movies but which professionals working in this career prefer to call "the underscore." These composers screen the assigned film or other broadcast project and then confer with the film or TV director and/or producer, the music cutter, and sometimes the music supervisor (see below) to determine where music should be underscored and just what kind of music would be appropriate for the dramatic situation. Underscoring composers must write at top speed. Producers may demand a score for a 30-minute TV episode, even a 1-hour show, in 1 week or less. Movie producers may require the music score be written and recorded for a feature film within 4 to 6 weeks and sometimes in periods as short as 2 weeks. Even well-established composers in this field experience feast and famine; they live on beans and rice for a while, then suddenly are called on to turn out a 13-week TV series in 3 months and work on a film score concurrently. Hot and cold, rich and poor, that is the pattern.

Generally, TV and film composers must locate in Los Angeles, New York, or a major foreign production center to find work in TV and the movies. Within the field, there is an array of specialization. Some composers specialize in writing musical themes for films and TV series. Others find opportunities writing music for music libraries, which are collections of themes and musical "feels" ranging from **stingers** to longer pieces of a minute or more. These "needle drop" music libraries are used extensively in television in place of original underscoring.

Qualifications and Preparation. The musician aspiring to a professional career scoring dramatic music must possess outstanding creative talent. The aspirant must also be highly sensitive to dramatic values, tone painting, and how music can enhance theatrical experience. To have the best competitive edge, film and TV composers should have strong backgrounds in symphonic music and be able to draw from all styles available. They also need to be fluent in current styles, such as hip-hop, ambient, or electronic. Successful film composers today use electronic instruments and computers in all phases of their work, from demos for directors to the final recording itself.

Employment Prospects. The pool of potential TV work has expanded as cable TV shows proliferate. Independent films have also increased, which further creates job opportunities, although many such films don't get theatrical release but instead go direct to DVD, become TV premieres, or surface only online. The most readily employable composers of dramatic music today are those adept at scoring for electronic instruments as well as acoustic instruments. One way composers can break into the film world is by first working as orchestrators or apprentices for established composers. For additional kinds of employment prospects in scoring drama, review Chapter 21.

Music Supervisor

Career Description. Starting with the heyday of blockbuster movie soundtracks and continuing through the proliferating channels of cable and satellite TV, music supervision has become an important part of the production process. Album tie-ins are a major marketing item for many movies and television series, and the pressure is on the music supervisor to land promising upcoming artists and established hit makers to pump up the soundtrack and the bottom line. A music supervisor for a feature film or television program can have many, or few, duties on a production, depending on how the role is viewed by the producers, studio (if applicable), and/or director. In general, the music supervisor is a liaison between the music ("creative") and the business interests on a project. The music supervisor, who is sometimes called the *music director,* may be charged with all, some, or none of the following: preparing a music budget for a project, studio, or production company; hiring a composer, soundtrack producer, music clearance house, and music contractor; clearing recorded music to be used as underscore, source music, or on a soundtrack product; making deals for title songs, end-credit songs, and "special appearances" of current hit bands and artists; overseeing recording sessions; facilitating the composing, prerecording, and technical preparation of source music that will be needed for on-camera use during production ("production music"); securing the services of side musicians and vocalists for on-camera appearances; and preparing music for DVD and other posttheatrical use. (Music supervisors will also find work in the video game industry; see that section in this chapter for more on this field.)

Qualifications and Preparation. Music supervisors' academic credentials range from BFAs in music to no degree at all. Since the job entails a lot of negotiating—for rights and clearances, publishing and performance deals, etc.—many music supervisors have a legal background; some are ex-producers, production assistants, or development personnel who are familiar with the needs of the production process. There are few actual musicians working as music supervisors. Artist-music supervisors (Don Was, David Byrne, T-Bone Burnett) often also function as composers of underscore and/or source music, and are usually chosen for the like-minded artists they can attract to a project. There are also ex–rock band side musicians, music agents, and managers. Music supervision courses are available in university extension departments (often as part of a music business certificate program), and studios and large music supervision companies often have internships available. Internships lead to assistant positions, which then lead to music supervisor positions. The problem for the musician who seeks to become a music supervisor is that actual musical knowledge—the ability to read, write, perform, and interpret music—is not really needed to do the job, although these abilities certainly can't hurt. Familiarity with popular music styles and artists, knowledge of the production process, extensive contacts in the music and production industries, and the ability to sense a "hit" are all assets.

Employment Prospects. This is one of the few production specialties that has almost unlimited growth potential, because there are no technical qualifications at all and no universally accepted job description. The field remains wide open to people with connections and the ability to get the job done. Virtually every feature film, no matter how low the budget, and every TV series now has a music supervisor on staff (and probably a soundtrack album in production). In addition, most major studios and television networks, as well as large production companies, have staff music supervisors who function as overseers of all the individual projects' music needs. These staff jobs offer more security (in exchange for less money and recognition) because they are not tied to the success of any one hit film or TV series. Staff music supervisors often move into management positions such as music department vice president. Many ex-staffers leave a studio or production company and use the extensive contacts they have built to go into business as independent music supervisors or producers.

Music Editor/Music Cutter

Career Description. Music editors are sometimes called music cutters, referring to the days when an editor's job actually included splicing pieces of audiotape or film together. As explained in Chapter 3, music editors are the individuals who are responsible for selection, timing, and synchronization of recorded music to a TV show or a film. Editors also work with music for radio and TV commercials and for music videos. Although many videos hold entirely to the audio master tape, others call for music editors to change the sound tracks to fit the action called for in the script.

Qualifications and Preparation. Those qualified to work as music editor have usually acquired their craft and art as apprentices, working alongside other, more experienced, editors who themselves learned in a master-apprentice relationship over many years. Many good editors are expert musicians. Others are simply very sensitive to how music can enhance dramatic events and do expert work without having acquired formal musical training.

Employment Prospects. The individual seeking a career as a music editor should expect to follow the time-honored apprenticeship training, perhaps getting started on amateur movies, or educational or sales films. For further information on music editing careers, contact the Motion Picture Editors Guild.

Music Video/Music Special Producer-Director

Career Description. The popularity of music videos spiked in the 1980s with the debut of MTV, and they have since become part of the standard marketing arsenal for some recording artists. An industry arose around this business, with teams of directors who specialize in work on music videos, but independent contractors also work in the field. In addition to overseeing the filming, a director's job description can include formulating the "vision" for the video production in consultation with the recording artist. TV music specials are another sector where broadcast-minded music aspirants are employed. Roles here include everything from executive producers and directors to music coordinators, audio technicians, arrangers, and copyists.

Qualifications and Preparation. Versatile artists who aspire to direct music videos or other filmed/broadcast musical productions will have spent years in related activities such as songwriting, live musicals, record production, and commercials. Conversely, directors may enter the field from the other direction: They are trained in the production arts first and foremost and pick up what musical knowledge they have as they go along. Both paths are equally valid.

For broadcast newcomers, a good way to learn the craft is directing low-budget videos. Developing a respectable track record in this arena may lead to opportunities for more elaborate projects.

Good preparation can also come from college film/TV programs. Directors sometimes come from the ranks of editors as well as writers. Work on low-budget commercials in local markets could be training for videos, which in turn can lead to longer-form work.

Employment Prospects. Although supply exceeds demand, there is always room for a hustling, talented music video director in tune with contemporary tastes. Opportunities to work on music specials are available for qualified aspirants in many different career categories, although the number of such productions is limited.

Video Game Scorer/Audio Programmer

Career Description. This is a relatively new career sector for music-minded job aspirants, and one with parallels to the film/TV music arena in terms of the need for qualified composers, music supervisors, and sound engineers. Increasingly sophisticated video game platforms have allowed for music on games to move from the "bleeps and blips" of long ago into today's high-quality songs and scores that have been released as popular album soundtracks and performed by major symphony orchestras. Respect for this medium has grown. The Grammy Awards recognizes game soundtracks, and the MTV Music Video Awards includes a category for Best Video Game Soundtrack. Although a good deal of music is simply licensed from record labels for use on the games, there is also a need for composers to create original game music and for audio professionals to provide an array of sound design and sound effects needs. These individuals can work on staff or on a freelance basis for large video game companies and independent game producers.

Qualifications and Preparation. The background required for work in this field will vary widely depending on one's position. Scorers of original game music must possess the creative traits required of all composers and songwriters (see the "Creative Careers" section) but must also be able to write in a style that is based on the need of the games and that reflects the overall setting, emotions, and action of the games. Games are an interactive platform, and thus, game music requires sensitivity to the unique demands of writing for the medium. Game composers need not be gaming addicts, but it doesn't hurt to enjoy—or at the very least understand—the videogame business. In addition to composers/scorers, more technically skewed aspirants can work in this sector as audio programmers and audio directors; these fields usually require a degree in computer science or extensive on-the-job training. Music supervisors and music directors, who may hire composers and supervise programmers, should possess both creative and technical savvy, as well as project management skills.

Employment Prospects. Video games have posted impressive sales for a number of years, outshining the revenue of audio-only music at retail. The increasing crossover promotions between record labels and film companies and big game releases has produced rewards for all participants. The downside in the music industry's heightened interest in video games is the trend toward licensing existing recordings for use on game soundtracks rather than commissioning original music, a maneuver that helps the label if not the composer shut out from a new assignment. Nonetheless, there is an appetite for talented, qualified composers, and those who excel in this field can become stars in their own right. Audio programmers and directors who have a passion for games, a head for technology, and a good feel for music will find themselves with real opportunities.

Advertising Jingle Writer

Career Description. A jingle writer is a songwriter/composer/lyricist who specializes in writing music for radio, TV, and online video commercials. These professionals are assigned a product or service and must then craft a composition or song that "fits" with the message/brand identity the client is hoping to convey. Not all jingle writers work exclusively in the field: Some songwriters of popular music write jingles occasionally.

Qualifications and Preparation. Jingle writers must take direction well, since they are responsible for pleasing a client with very specific goals in mind. They should be skilled in many musical styles and be strong arrangers. Needless to say, they must also be able to compose well for a very short form. Lyricists will need to be strong wordsmiths with a knack for conveying a message or concept in an accessible, memorable way—and in as few words as possible.

Employment Prospects. There is plenty of work in the advertising field, but there are also plenty of people vying for assignments. Even hit songwriters have competed to compose jingles for major consumer-product brands, such as Coke. The rewards can be lucrative. Smaller ad agencies with smaller businesses for clients provide an opening for newcomers.

Music-Related Careers

Critic/Journalist/Editor   Sales

Music Librarian   Legal Services

Science and Technology   Visual Arts/Graphics

Managerial/Executive

Some of the careers listed here relate directly to music, others only indirectly (see Table 25.2). Some are open to trained musicians; others offer employment opportunities to nonmusicians. The more prevalent music-related careers are discussed in this section.

Critic/Journalist/Editor

Career Description. Some of history's most distinguished musicians have used their creative energies not just for composing but also to write about music. Although few musicians have managed to perform these two tasks as well as Richard Wagner, today hundreds of creative persons have fashioned rewarding careers as music critics, journalists, and editors. Each job title entails a different set of responsibilities. Critics will find their work schedules filled with attending concerts and writing up reviews on deadline, and their workdays will be occupied in reviewing endless stacks of new recordings and books on music. Journalists may also act as critics of recordings and shows, but their mandate will probably also include writing news and feature articles about recording artists, industry trends, and events. Editors are often responsible for assigning reviews and articles to other critics and journalists and editing their copy but may also write articles and review music. Those who have both a love of music and a way with words may also find opportunities in other arenas, such as writing liner notes for album releases or music news for broadcast outlets and online music sites.

Qualifications and Preparation. To qualify as a music critic in the classical field, an individual should have a thorough musical education acquired through formalized university-level study or individual effort. Most distinguished critics have grown into their work after long years of observation, study, and publishing commentaries. They not only develop penetrating insights on compositions and performances but manage to write in a style that communicates effectively with a broad general readership. Not all critics meet these criteria, of course; it is not unusual for a newspaper to ask a general-assignment reporter to cover concerts and review recordings.

Critics in other forms of music, including pop and rock, are less likely to have formal music educations, although most will have a passion for music developed from their earliest years and an endless enthusiasm for hearing new bands and fresh material. Many are at least amateur musicians, although this is not a prerequisite. Nonmusicians who work as critics may tend to focus more on the lyrics of a composition or on the personalities of the performers than on the music itself.

Music journalists need at least basic reporting skills—the ability to conduct interviews with multiple sources, to assemble and check facts, to write a compelling narrative. Editors should also have those journalistic chops, along with knowledge of the newspaper, magazine or Web site production process, and the ability to set and enforce deadlines.

Employment Prospects. Due to the deteriorating finances of traditional media, staff jobs for music critics at traditional media are dwindling as more of the work goes to freelancers. There are fewer full-time jobs for music editors as well. TV, radio and print media find the value of their professional critic reviews diminished as cyberspace is jammed with postings from amateur observers. Aspiring freelancers should contact the appropriate editor (e.g., the music editor, reviews editor, entertainment editor) for submission requirements. The Internet also presents a host of new outlets for writers and editors, including writing up local concert reviews for online city guides, music-news sites, and other types of Web sites with dedicated music sections, such as social Web sites.

Those with little previous writing experience would be advised to start by approaching smaller outlets and publications, such as college and neighborhood newspapers, city guides, local magazines, or even local access television. The pay will be low (or nonexistent), but the work will build up a writer's all-important "clips file" and possibly lead to better-paying opportunities.

The great majority of critics and music reporters earn salaries comparable to most other journalists, which are not high, although those who get jobs at major newspapers or magazines can be well compensated. Freelance rates will depend on the size of the publication, ranging from a free CD in exchange for a review (commonplace) all the way up to a few dollars per word for a feature article (a rarity).

Individuals wishing to pursue the various kinds of employment available in writing about music can obtain further information from the Music Critics Association of North America.

Music Librarian

Career Description. Librarians are employed in a variety of settings. The most familiar are individuals working in college and public libraries as music specialists. Some of these jobs involve little more than clerking. At the other end of the scale are the trained music catalogers and researchers who apply knowledgeable judgments and perform sophisticated, occasionally even scholarly tasks.

Qualifications and Preparation. All but the smallest libraries employ paraprofessionals and professionals. For the former, college degrees are sometimes required. Individuals aspiring to careers as fully professional music librarians should plan to acquire a baccalaureate degree in music, preferably with a concentration in music history and literature. Then they should plan to go on to a master's degree in library science, preferably from a university with a well-respected curriculum. Few libraries will consider applicants lacking these credentials. Another kind of music librarian is employed by production music libraries. For these jobs, the qualifications are a solid and broad knowledge of musical styles, both contemporary and historical; a terrific musical memory; and an affinity for detail work. No degree is required, but those with degrees in musicology may have an edge.

Table 25.2   A Sampling of Music-Related Careers

Records and music

Composer
Historian
Librettist
Lyricist
Critic/journalist
Playwright
Publisher

Writer/editor

Music services
Music coordinator
Music copyist
Music cutter/editor
Music librarian
Music therapist
Talent coordinator
Transcriber

Managerial/executive

Advance person
Artist and repertoire
Administrator/coordinator
Agent (talent agent)
Arts administrator
Artists' union officer
Audience research director
Broadcasting executive
Business manager
Company manager (TV, theater)
Concert promoter
Development director (arts)
Educational director
Entertainment director
Market research director
Nightclub manager
Orchestra manager
Personal manager
Personnel director
Product manager (recordings)
Production manager
Professional manager

Program director
Programming consultant
Project director
Recording company executive
Recording studio manager
Road manager
Stage manager
Studio manager
Talent agency manager
Talent coordinator
Tour coordinator
Traffic manager

Broadcasting/advertising

Account executive
Consumer researcher
Creative director
Disc jockey
Jingle writer
Musical director
Program supervisor
Promotional staffer
Research director
Spot producer/director

Business/merchandising

Broadcasting station broker
Concert promoter
Music merchant/salesperson
Music rights manager
Music wholesaler/distributor
Publicist
Salesperson
Ticket sales manager/agent

Arts/graphics

Commercial artist
Graphic artist
Scenic designer
Music calligrapher
Music engraver
Web site designer

(Continued)

Table 25.2 (Continued)

Music production (theater, film, TV)	Theme specialist
Arranger	Variety artist
Audio technician/engineer	Visual synthesist
Choreographer/dancer	**Science and technology**
Conductor	Audio engineer/technician
Church music director	Computer music programmer
Costume designer	Digital audio editor
Director/supervisor	Digital remastering engineer
Floor manager	Equipment designer
Instrumentalist	Equipment maintenance technician
Lighting designer	Instrument designer/manufacturer/ repairer
Music coordinator	Mastering technician
Orchestra contractor	Multimedia developer
Producer/executive producer	Music/rerecording mixer
Property master	Piano tuner/technician
Scenic designer	Recording engineer
Singer/actor	Sound engineer/technician
Special material writer	Studio designer/acoustician
Stage director	**Legal services**
Stage manager	Copyright researcher
Studio musician	Copyright lawyer
Synthesis specialist	Entertainment business lawyer
Talent coordinator	Paralegal
Technical director	

Science and Technology

Sound Engineer/Technician

Career Description. Individuals employed in the technical aspects of sound reinforcement, recording, and broadcasting are generally referred to as *engineers.* Many in the field are more properly called *technicians.* The appellation *audio engineer* is more accurately reserved for university graduates who hold degrees in electrical engineering or, perhaps, physics, audiology, acoustics, or computer science. These engineers engage in work such as research and development of audio equipment, studio and equipment design, record mastering, equipment maintenance, and sound mixing. Most of these engineers are employed full-time by equipment manufacturers, sound reinforcement companies, recording studios, radio and TV stations, and film studios. Some engineers are assigned only one type of work, such as design or maintenance or audio mixing. In smaller firms, audio engineers perform a variety of tasks.

Employers also hire audio technicians, who may or may not have a university-level education. Many audio technicians and mixers are simply talented, self-taught handypersons who, through years of apprenticeship, earn job assignments that involve sophisticated technology. Most engineers and technicians are attracted to these music-related jobs by their love for music, and some of them hold college degrees in music or have studied music informally. The art of sound mixing demands considerable musical knowledge and the ability to make sensitive aural judgments.

Qualifications and Preparation. To qualify for employment as a sound engineer, university degrees in both electrical engineering and music would be ideal, but few professionals are so prepared. With the increasing sophistication of audio equipment, employers more and more require not just audio technicians but sound engineers and computer scientists as well. Engineers believing they may find employment in broadcasting will have to qualify for an FCC (Federal Communications Commission) operator's license. Individuals who want to go to the top in recording technology and sound engineering should not only study as much music as they can, but they should go on to at least some studies in acoustics. Such persons might be called on to design and build state-of-the-art recording studios. All engineers will be expected to keep up with the latest trends in recording technology.

Employment Prospects. Although there are many people jockeying for engineering positions, those professionals who have demonstrated the qualities outlined above will be in demand and can enjoy good earnings. Those who want to establish long-term careers in this business will also have another qualification not found on any résumé: a high tolerance for stress and tension, required when dealing with unpredictable equipment problems.

Instrument Design/Maintenance

Career Description/Qualifications/Prospects. From early times, the inventors and designers of musical instruments have held a distinguished place in the history of the art. Although the basic design of most acoustic musical instruments was set centuries ago, scientists and technicians continue not only to improve instruments but also to invent new ones. Persons interested in the physics of sound, acoustics, and electronics manage to develop music-related careers. It cannot be said that there is a big demand for instrument designers, but positions can be found for qualified persons with manufacturing companies, particularly those involved in developing ever-newer electronic instruments.

As for careers in the field of instrument maintenance, there is a shortage in most communities of competent instrument repair technicians. Qualified repair technicians can just about choose where they want to live, then knock on the door of the nearest instrument repair shop and go to work the same day.

Other jobs await qualified maintenance personnel in school systems, colleges, and universities, not to mention the armed services. Persons aspiring to such careers can acquire their training in some junior colleges and some universities. It is more common, however, for aspirants to learn their craft as apprentices to masters.

Repair technicians often specialize in keyboard instruments. Many communities lack fully qualified piano technicians/tuners. The best of them have been factory trained or learned their craft as apprentices. Fortunately, piano tuners today do not even have to have a true sense of pitch. Tuning can be accurately handled with the use of electronic pitch-measuring machines that are readily available with piano repair kits. Piano technicians are almost always independent contractors working out of their homes; they set their own hours and vacation periods. The competent ones are in demand and make a good living.

There is also a shortage of electronic keyboard maintenance personnel. Those who acquire competence in repairing electronic keyboard instruments will be able to find steady employment at good pay. And those with musical backgrounds will, on most jobs, be able to do a better job than just straight technicians.

With the proliferation of lower-cost electronic musical equipment of all kinds, it is safe to predict that steady employment at good pay will be available to those who take the time to educate themselves in electronics and music.

Online Music Developer/Operator

Career Description. Those with a love of both music and technology have many career options these days, thanks to the rapid growth of the new-media music business. Large companies such as AOL, Apple, Yahoo, Microsoft, Nokia, RealNetworks, Verizon, and many others have set up music-related businesses online, as have countless smaller firms, ranging from music retailers to Webcasters. The major record labels and almost all indies have their own Web sites. All need talented individuals to do everything from setting up and maintaining Web sites to coding music, designing new site features and promotions, and handling technical problems. In addition, tech-savvy creative types can carve out a business sideline developing sites for fellow artists hoping to promote and sell their music online.

Qualifications and Preparation. Although there are many opportunities for creative people in the online medium, these positions put the emphasis on technical know-how over music-industry savvy. Candidates in some cases can be self-taught, but a degree in computer science may be required to open doors for other more technical positions. For software developers particularly, knowledge of multiple computer languages and operating systems is highly desirable. One way to break into the market is to start with exposure through social networking sites and build from there.

Employment Prospects. There is no shortage of people with new media skills, but candidates with a combination of both advanced technical chops *and* music smarts will find themselves in demand.

Managerial/Executive

Career Description. Individuals not involved directly in music making can develop successful careers in the business and managerial sectors of the arts and entertainment industry. Countless options await them in areas including record labels, artist management firms, publicity companies, music publishers, music video networks, and royalty-collecting societies, among many others. Career patterns are often circuitous. The person who aspires to become an artists' manager may start out in music publishing and end up in record production. The individual who initially wants to run a talent agency may experience greater success as a TV executive. Fast learners who are quick on their feet will seize career opportunities as they develop. The most creative executives won't wait for job offers; they will create their own opportunities.

Qualifications and Preparation. The college or university graduate who has gone through an educational program that integrates music and business and the recording arts has the advantage in breaking into the field. These graduates often have experience with college radio stations or college concert boards. Dozens of colleges and universities in the United States and Canada now offer these kinds of curricula, and their graduates are finding places in the arts and entertainment industry.

Two of the best forms of educational preparation for careers in management are a law degree or a Master of Business Administration. The higher someone climbs in business, the more valuable those kinds of underpinnings prove.

Of all the music-related career options available, arts administration may present one of the greatest challenges to an individual's versatility and imagination. Educational institutions with degree programs leading to professional employment in that area include Yale University and New York University.

How does one qualify as an arts administrator? A master's degree will probably help. For a fuller answer to this question, review Chapter 13.

Employment Prospects. Those who take the time to prepare themselves in business and music will be among the most sought-after executives. A clear indication of this is the track record of schools offering music business studies. The good ones are placing an impressive percentage of their graduates in beginning and middle management positions. Although record labels have been undergoing consolidation and belt-tightening in recent years, they are still large, complicated operations with an ongoing need for new employees and fresh executive-track talent. Other industry sectors are similarly open to the best prospects.

Sales

Career Description. No matter how polished the musician or well produced the album, the music business couldn't function without the too-often-unsung talents of another group of individuals: the salespeople. Thousands of careers in the music business are available for individuals who prefer to involve themselves in the marketing or sales of goods and services relating to the industry—the "business" end of the music business equation. Jobs in this sector run the gamut from record store clerks and managers to music merchandisers and distributors to top label sales and marketing executives and everything in between. Live music, too, is a "product" that must be advertised, packaged, and sold by savvy specialists.

Qualifications and Preparation. Until recent years, a music merchant or talented salesperson did not require a university degree to succeed in the music business. Such a person could often make it, at least for a while, just being "street smart." But as the music business has become increasingly dominated by career migration across many branches of a diverse industry, the person who wants to rise to the top may find an edge in a strong academic background. Jobs are now going to the merchants and agents and promoters with expertise in fields such as market research, brand marketing, advertising, accounting, and finance.

Employment Prospects. Individuals who are fully prepared and motivated for work in the sales and marketing side of contemporary business will find good career opportunities. Even in periods of economic downturn, employers will usually take on an employee who can sell—if not on salary, at least on commission. While local retailers offer an entry-level opportunity for music-business job seekers, those with strong university training in music and business will find many more doors opened for them in multiple business sectors. Whatever the educational background, a musician-businessperson's ultimate achievements will probably be governed more by imagination and drive. Armed with these two attributes, the aspirant will create "luck." As more than one person of achievement has expressed it, "The harder I work, the luckier I get."

Legal Services

Career Description. Each year, the music business requires the services of more and more legal experts, because nearly every aspect of the industry involves copyright law and the negotiation of contracts. Even though all law schools train their students in contracts, it is often difficult for an attorney in general practice to be sufficiently well informed to handle certain kinds of music business agreements. In the field of copyright, the attorney lacking expertise may be unable to counsel clients adequately. For these reasons, increasing numbers of lawyers now specialize in entertainment law and copyright.

Qualifications and Preparation. Law students who believe that they will want to practice entertainment law should focus their studies on intellectual property, including copyright, patent and trademark, contract, and agency law and on unfair competition, privacy, and publicity rights. The individual who is attracted to the law but lacks the means or opportunity to attend law school may be able to carve a career track as a copyright researcher, music rights agent, or paralegal with the appropriate professional training.

Employment Prospects. In society as a whole, garnering a law degree is no guarantee of a successful legal career. But the brightest, best-informed, best-connected entertainment attorneys have plenty of clients and high incomes. Those of considerable experience often get full-time positions as legal counsel for firms such as publishers, recording companies, and film studios; some may rise up the ranks to senior executive positions in their companies. Others go into artist management. Because the rise of new technologies such as digital downloading and online music streaming have created a host of complicated copyright and contracts issues (not to mention lawsuits), attorneys familiar with such new-media issues will be viewed as particularly attractive employment prospects. In addition, those who have already established careers in some aspect of the music industry before attending law school (or who attend concurrently while holding down their day job) may have a leg up on other applicants for music-business legal positions. For an extensive treatment of the role of lawyers in the music business, review Chapter 7.

Visual Arts/Graphics

Career Description. Creative persons in the aural and visual arts have often worked in close alliance. Some have been talented in both fields. For example, Schoenberg and Gershwin were good painters; Stravinsky worked closely with Picasso in stage design and costuming. Today, musical performers must be attractively staged and costumed. Music merchandise must be packaged to sell. These demands create many career opportunities for talented individuals interested in graphics and other visual arts. Job descriptions include designing the covers and packaging for albums and creating promotional posters, advertising layouts, and in-store fliers for marketing and sales efforts. In the music video sector, opportunities exist for scenic artists and production designers.

Qualifications and Preparation. Aspirants to positions as art directors or graphic designers should have a good working knowledge of computer graphics and an artistic "eye." Formal training is strongly preferred. Some professionals study commercial art and graphics, whereas others enter the field from a fine arts background. A sensitivity to music and an ability to bridge the sometimes conflicting demands from the "creative" and "sales" sides of a project are also key to success in serving record labels, concert promoters, retail chains, and the industry's many other sophisticated users of good visual design.

Employment Prospects. Recording companies alone require the services of many graphic artists, whom they employ on staff or on a freelance basis. Commercial art companies contracted to do work for music firms also offer employment opportunities for individuals skilled in creating the striking packaging and displays that are all-important in catching a customer's eye. Self-employment is a realistic goal for the truly talented who have a "serve the client" mentality.

Entrepreneurs/Starting Your Own Business

Many persons of independent mind choose not to work as an employee, preferring to "go it alone." The rapid changes in the music industry that began in the 1990s and continue today have expanded the ranks of entrepreneurs considerably. This is partly because some people were squeezed out of positions in the traditional business by industry cutbacks and cutthroat competition but largely because new technologies and changing mind-sets have made striking out on one's own easier, less costly, and less intimidating. In the independent-label field, for example, the online realm now offers low-cost promotion and distribution mechanisms; recording costs can be slashed by making use of home-studio-based professional-quality recording and duplication equipment at ever-more-accessible prices. While the odds of success for any new business are probably the same as they ever were, the monetary risks of failure have often lessened as the required capital investment for a startup has dropped.

Some entrepreneurs choose to launch their own independent businesses in traditional music-industry sectors, such as with production firms, concert promotion organizations, management companies, or music publishing businesses. Others are innovators, seeking out new music market niches to tap and services to offer, either online or offline.

However one decides to proceed, the establishment of a business can be a daunting undertaking and should be approached with professional advice and intensive research. See Chapter 26 for more information about establishing a new company.

Chapter Takeaways

- The music industry is populated by more than a small group of household names hauling down rich paydays.

- Numerous fulfilling music or music-related careers exist in the realms of composing, directing/producing, performing, education, radio, music video, advertising, journalism criticism, library science, merchandising, technology, equipment design or maintenance, management, distribution, and legal affairs.

- To succeed, "liking" music isn't enough. Winning professionals need full preparation, hard work, and luck.

Key Terms

- aircheck   (p. 435)

- angels   (p. 415)

- clips file   (p. 442)

- combination career   (p. 420)

- comp style   (p. 428)

- master-apprentice   (p. 438)

- terminal degree   (p. 418, 432)

CHAPTER 26

Starting Your Own Business

In the United States, 20 million people are in business for themselves, and many more operate as small partnerships or in guerrilla-style small corporations. Examples in music are everywhere: Classical musicians are redefining performance careers by working as independent contractors—playing for a variety of small orchestras—or starting their own ensembles, playing the music they want to play with the musicians they want to work with. Composers are contracting to create and perform complex underscores—the kind of work that in another era was performed by union workers employed by studios or networks. And inventors of innovative musical products and services aren't waiting for a large company to employ them or license their creations. Instead, the Internet and other distribution channels often make the one-man-band venture a realistic alternative. All across the music industry, people have broken away from the traditional mold, running businesses the way they want.

Technology has had a huge influence. Because of the availability of digital technology, unprecedented opportunities have opened up for small businesses. And with ever-cheaper recording equipment, coupled with the far reach of the Internet, it is now possible for artists to record and promote their own work. Some may choose to

> *"Hell is full of musical amateurs."*
>
> —*George Bernard Shaw*

Left: Weeks Technology Center, Frost School of Music, University of Miami.

Photo by Elaine Maltezos, used by permission. Photo courtesy University of Miami.

stay independent throughout their careers; others will leverage their successes from self-promotion into signing that first major record deal.

Self-employment requires energy, enthusiasm, motivation, and more than the average 40-hour week. On top of this, no matter how great an idea is, if it is not accompanied by skills in diverse disciplines such as accounting, marketing, operations, and salesmanship, the company will not survive. Still, the means are available to help entrepreneurs succeed.

Getting the Process Started

Getting a business started is often the hardest part for many would-be entrepreneurs. Fortunately, there are some good resources available, including the Small Business Administration (SBA) government program, as well as a significant number of Internet resources full of practical information. (Table 26.1 outlines a step-by-step approach for starting a music publishing business.)

The first thing any aspiring entrepreneur needs is a business plan. This plan can be a few pages long or a lengthy document, depending on the scope and scale of the project. One can choose from several different types of business plans, but whatever the format used, the following questions should be answered:

What product or service is being offered?

Who will own/run the company?

What resources will be needed?

Who are the customers and how will they be reached?

How will the product or service be distributed?

How will the profits be made?

Choosing a Name

When choosing a name for a new company, both aesthetic and practical considerations are important. First of all, the name should fit with the company's offerings, as well as the image the company wants to put forward. Secondly, the name should appeal to the target customer. A memorable name is key, and nothing should be finalized without careful consideration; once a name has been chosen, and once an investment has been made to market that name—building brand recognition and loyalty—it will be hard to change it. It also might be a good idea to trademark the name of the company or its products. The application can be found at the U.S. Patent and Trademark Office, or online at www.uspto.gov/ebc/indexebc.html. Engaging the services of an attorney specializing in intellectual property, although expensive, can be a good insurance policy against future problems.

Forms of Ownership

In the United States, a business enterprise is generally organized in one of three basic ways: sole proprietorship, partnership, or corporation. Each form of ownership has certain advantages and disadvantages.

Table 26.1   Starting a Music Publishing Company

One of the music businesses that is easiest to get started and least expensive to finance is publishing. This fact is reconfirmed all the time by hundreds of new firms being set up, usually by songwriters frustrated after repeated turndowns of their material by others.

Here is a step-by-step approach to setting up a publishing company in the popular music field.

1. **Research.** Study this book and publications concerning business management found in most libraries.

2. **Acquisitions.** You have to acquire copyrights (property interests in musical compositions) before you can start publishing. The easiest way to acquire copyrights is to write your own music. In addition to your own copyrights, search out other qualified writers and gain their confidence and assistance in your publishing plans. Retain a lawyer to assist in drawing up contracts. Use the guidelines listed in Chapter 4.

3. **Structure your financing and business entity.** Once you have determined whether you will be organized as a sole proprietorship, partnership, or corporation, you can estimate and solicit the working capital you will need.

4. **Contact ASCAP, BMI, or SESAC.** Tentatively choose a company name and ask whether it is already being used by someone else. The licensing organization may ask you to supply your first choice as well as alternate choices for your firm name. At this point, a prudent move might be to initiate a trademark search to see whether your name is being used anywhere else in the United States. Affiliate with one of these organizations after deciding upon a name that is not in use by another company (see Chapter 6).

5. **Register your firm name.** If your company is a sole proprietorship or partnership, call on your county clerk and recorder's office and search the records to learn if your choice of firm name has been previously registered in the county. Duplications will not be accepted. Unless you identify the company with your own full, legal name, you will be required to register a fictitious firm name (some counties use the term *trade name*). For example, if your name is John Doe, the county will record your firm as "John Doe DBA Hit Publishing Company" ("DBA" is the abbreviation for "doing business as"). Procedures and applicable fees vary from county to county.

   If your firm is to be a corporation, you must meet the requirements for incorporation in the state in which you are doing business.

6. **Establish your company bank account.** Your bank will not open your account until your firm name has been established as described above. Do not commingle personal funds with your company account, even if you are the sole proprietor.

7. **Business license.** If you limit your firm's activities just to publishing, you may not need a business license. But if your company should branch out into artists' agency work, most states would consider that as a kind of employment agency, and nearly all states license and regulate employment agencies.

8. **Arrange outside services.** Because most new publishing companies start very small, proprietors generally do not attempt, at the outset, to handle everything themselves. Vendors are available to handle just about any service a business needs—mail, telephone answering, secretarial, bookkeeping, accounting, and more.

9. **Prepare your materials.** A songwriter sometimes manages with leadsheets and demos prepared by amateurs. But now that you are a publisher trying to exploit your properties, everything you present to a producer or artist for consideration must be suitably prepared.

10. **Your first success.** The essence of the publishing business in the pop field is getting material recorded and released. The first release of any recording requires the manufacturer to receive a mechanical license from the publisher. Many publishers use their own mechanical license forms and negotiate directly with the recording companies, settling on mutually agreeable terms. If your first recorded song hits, you may want to publish it in printed form. You will probably license a music printing company to handle this for you (see Chapter 4). Also, reread in Chapter 4 how to set up subpublishing deals abroad through licensing agreements with firms active internationally.

11. **Forms, contracts.** Copyright forms are readily available, without cost, from the U.S. Copyright Office (www.copyright.gov). When you negotiate writers' publishing contracts, retain a qualified music business attorney—or use the draft contract discussed in Chapter 4 as a basis for your discussions with an attorney less experienced in the music field.

(Continued)

Table 26.1 (Continued)

12. **Your second company.** Performing rights organizations won't accept a publisher imprint already affiliated with a competitor. Just as soon as your first company gets under way, establish a second one so that you can accommodate properties from writers affiliated with ASCAP, BMI, or SESAC. Except for the preliminaries outlined here, the procedures for setting up a second firm are the same as for your first venture.

13. **Persistence and continued success.** Once your new firm starts to get its copyrights licensed, don't sit waiting for royalty checks. Real profitability comes along when a firm can achieve continuity year to year, building catalogs of hundreds, eventually thousands, of songs and exploiting those copyrights. So the search for new writers and new properties goes on and on. That is the publishing business.

Sole Proprietorship

The principal advantage of a sole proprietorship is that it is easy to set up and get under way. All the entrepreneur needs is some money (personal or borrowed funds), a great amount of energy—and a lot of nerve. The sole proprietor who wants to fold the venture can do that, too; there is no need to call a meeting of the board to make decisions.

That's the good news. The bad news is that the sole proprietor is personally responsible for all financial losses the business may experience. If the company cannot pay the bills, the creditors can take possession of all personal property, including a home, car, pet parakeet—whatever is of value. The sole proprietorship has the challenge of limited capital. Even if the business is going well, the single operator may find it difficult to raise enough money to move the business forward. A proprietor may employ many others, although typically, the team is small. As the business grows, the operator will often need to add employees to fill gaps in capabilities, or perhaps retain the services of other companies or individuals. Finally, the sole proprietorship may have to cease operations suddenly if the owner-manager becomes physically or mentally disabled, gets divorced, or moves away.

Partnership

The Uniform Partnership Act defines partnerships as "associations of two or more persons who operate a business as co-owners by voluntary legal agreement." General partnerships are established when all partners involved carry on the business as co-owners. Limited partnerships (not permitted in some states) are composed of one or more general partners and one or more limited partners. A limited partner is one whose liability to the company is restricted to the amount that person has invested in it. Joint ventures are a third type of partnership and are popular with investors who come together temporarily to undertake a short-term business enterprise, such as producing a show.

Partnerships offer certain advantages of ownership. First, they are easy to form. All that is required is a written agreement that defines shares of ownership and spells out each partner's responsibilities. Second, partnerships are likely to have more **working capital** than sole proprietorships. Third, a firm where two or more individuals are active in management will probably have people with complementary skills (one partner may be tops in sales, and another may be adept at accounting, for example).

The principal disadvantage of this form of organization is that the partners may disagree on how to run the business; disputes may arise over disposition of inventory and how outstanding debts are going to be paid. There is also the possibility that the partners may develop personality conflicts. And if an impasse is reached, it may be difficult for the company to be dissolved.

Corporation

Sole proprietors and partners are people, whereas a corporation is an entity. To shareholders, the most obvious advantage of a corporation is that their liability is usually limited to the value they contribute, even if the losses of the company exceed that capital. Management may have more money with which to work, particularly in the rare event that the corporation some day goes public, meaning its ownership shares may be sold through a mechanism such as a stock market. Corporations may also have a diversity of managerial talents and the financial capability to buy in large quantities, thus reducing costs per unit of doing business. On the downside, of the three types of business ownership, the corporate structure is the most difficult to set up and the slowest and most expensive to get into operation. Each state charters corporations according to its own laws, and state and federal regulatory agencies can burden management with costly paperwork.

Another disadvantage for investors in corporations is that some forms of corporations experience double taxation: Not only does the enterprise pay corporate taxes, but the investors also pay personal income taxes on dividends received from the corporation.

A comparison of advantages and disadvantages of the different forms of ownership is shown in Table 26.2.

Table 26.2 Types of Business Ownership

Sole Proprietorship	Partnership	Corporation
Typical Advantages		
1. You are the boss	1. Simple to organize	1. Limited personal liability
2. Easy to form, easy to dissolve	2. Complementary management skills	2. Perhaps more capital
3. You retain all profits		3. Lower cost per unit of doing business
Typical Disadvantages		
1. Very hard work	1. Unlimited financial responsibility	1. Expensive, complicated
2. Unlimited financial liability	2. Strategy conflicts	2. Legal restrictions
3. Management deficiencies	3. Personality conflicts	3. Double taxation
4. Limited working capital		
5. Potential lack of continuity of operation		

Permits and Legalities

To legally start a business, paperwork must be filled out, and fees must be paid to various government bodies. What is needed varies widely from state to state and town to town and depends on the type of service offered. A good starting point is often to file a "DBA"—Doing Business As form. These are obtained and filed at the county clerk's office. The intent of this process is to alert the public about a new enterprise; often, it is required to give public notice through a local newspaper. Once the paperwork has been filled out and processed, the next step is to obtain a business license from the city or county.

A number of other permits may also be required, such as health department permits, professional licenses, and so on. The best place to get advice on what exactly is needed is the local Small Business Development Center. Appointments with counselors there are free of charge and offer invaluable assistance.

Even a small, part-time operation must charge (and remit) sales tax for taxable products or services. To do this, a tax number must be obtained, and filing must be done on a periodic basis, sending in a check on taxed purchases. At the moment, products sold over the Internet out of state are not taxable, but this is likely to change, so it is important to keep current on local tax laws. Failure to collect and file quarterly tax returns could result in significant fines and penalties.

Some people are tempted to think this paperwork step is too complicated and expensive, and that they can bypass it and stay under the radar. Don't do it. The music industry is particularly fussy about copyright issues, and working through all the legalities of using prerecorded music is not for the faint of heart. The Internet is particularly visible—open to any browsing eyes—so extra care must be taken to avoid any use of copyrighted material—visual or aural—in Web site promotions. Keep in mind that many people have had great ideas and put a good deal of effort into starting something, only to be shut down—sometimes permanently—because they failed to obtain the right permits and permissions.

Raising Funds

Some small businesses do not require much start-up capital. Many *service* offerings—where the customer is paying primarily for human labor as opposed to a tangible product—fall into this category. However, the majority of companies will need some working capital, often more than the owners themselves can provide.

There is a lot of hype on the Internet about free money and grants to start small businesses. Unfortunately, the money never seems to really materialize. Once again, if it sounds too good to be true, it probably is. This leaves the time-honored tradition of going to the bank to seek a loan. Banks can be a difficult source to tap, setting high barriers to get a loan. Even with a great business plan, commercial banks will still likely insist on collateral to secure the loan. If a car, house, or other tangible property cannot be provided, the government—through the SBA—offers loan guarantees (not free money) for some well-planned ventures. The stark reality is that the most common sources of funding for a small business are the pockets of the entrepreneur, or perhaps the contribution of friends and family.

Marketing

Contrary to popular belief, marketing and advertising are two very different things. Advertising is paid media coverage. Marketing is a more in-depth process, covering all the many aspects involved in getting people interested in a business and its services. One of the simplest ways to get an overview of this concept is through the four Ps of marketing model developed by William D. Perreault, Jr. and E. Jerome McCarthy (*Basic Marketing: A Global Managerial Approach,* McGraw-Hill, 2004): *product, price, place,* and *promotion.*

Product

The first step in the marketing process is to examine the products or services being offered. Will the offering satisfy an important need or desire? Why will customers part with their hard-earned cash? By answering these questions, an offering can be designed that customers are looking for—not one that will need to be pushed on them. Many consumers are interested in more than just a purchase; they are looking for support after the sale, good directions included with the order, and so on.

Price

What is the service worth? Many entrepreneurs initially think of a markup strategy that simply tacks a percentage on over the cost of production. However, this is rarely the best strategy, because there are too many other factors to consider when setting a price. Although many theoretical models are involved in price setting, one of the most practical is to decide what the customer is willing to pay. Then, working backward, the cost of production can be considered. Can a sufficient profit be made at that price? If not, both service and business goals should be reconsidered.

Place

This is also known as distribution and is a tricky part of the marketing plan. The Internet has rewritten most of the traditional rules about distribution, and one company, eBay, has made it possible for almost anyone to sell almost anything for a very small charge. Although large companies take advantage of the Web to varying degrees, the real benefit has been to the small entrepreneur. With the click of a mouse, customers from thousands of miles away can reach a virtual storefront easier than they could drive downtown. This is particularly helpful for entrepreneurs who have chosen a specialty niche. The important thing is to match the channels of distribution with the product and the audience, and that matching requires careful analysis.

Promotion

This term is often used interchangeably with marketing; it means getting the word out about a company and its services. There are many ways to do this, and these ways are often split into two categories: advertising and publicity. Advertising is media coverage that one pays for. This may involve ads in local newspapers, on TV, on radio, by direct mail, and on the Internet. Publicity, on the other hand, involves getting local or specialty media interested in the company's "story," without having to pay them to print it. The music industry, of course, is famous for taking advantage of this. Any news that gets an artist on a cover—good or bad—can equal money for the company. Clever entrepreneurs will make friends with media outlets and provide them with material to secure that "free" press.

The Internet is a good promotional tool for new businesses—especially for companies that specialize in a small niche market and need to reach a wide geographic area. To attract—and particularly to keep—online customers, a site must offer something (usually information) for nothing. The most successful Web sites have embraced this idea and offer their customers dynamic, ever-changing content that provides some form of useful information. In addition, a site could provide special offers, affiliated newsletters, and customer support—anything to keep its users satisfied and eager to return. (See "Music in Social Networking" sidebar in Chapter 18.)

Accounting and Finance

Although accounting software can do calculations, there are some decisions where the manager (and perhaps the accountant) will need to decide how to keep track of the money. Among the key decisions is how to record the "when" and "how" of an individual transaction.

When to Record a Transaction

There are two basic methods of recording a transaction. The "cash" method involves entering the record of a transaction when the money is received (or disbursed). The other way to record a transaction is called the "accrual" method. In this case, money is listed in the accounts receivable so the business can better see what funds are "in the pipeline." This also holds true for bills that are owed. In cash accounting, a bill that is owed (say, a credit card bill) does not exist in the books until the check is written. In an accrual system, the expense is incurred when it is due—even if the check isn't paid on time.

How to Record a Transaction

With cash accounting, the money received and spent is entered into an accounting journal. Income and expenses for a given period of time (day, week, month, year) can be calculated at the bottom of the page and should show how much money is in the bank. This system works well for small companies with limited resources. However, the more accurate and sophisticated method of accounting involves a double-entry system. Everything is entered into the books twice, which provides a built-in checks-and-balances system helpful in avoiding errors. There is no question that this method is more complicated, but many accounting programs will help walk a novice through the system.

Keeping Track of the Money

Three financial statements can be done quite easily and may provide useful information to even the smallest of operations.

Balance Sheet

The balance sheet is particularly valuable in understanding exactly what a company is worth at a specific, given point in time. The balance sheet always includes three categories—assets, liabilities, and equity.

Assets: Among other things, will always include cash, accounts receivable, and value of inventory

Liabilities: Includes accounts payable (bills owed), interest charges, taxes due, and loans

Equity: The sum of invested capital and retained earnings

This "snapshot" of the business is labeled the balance sheet because of the well-known accountant's formula: assets = liabilities + equity. This formula is used to create a trial balance that helps accountants make sure that all money has been "accounted" for. Although professionals in the field will tell you this isn't helpful to their work, a little algebraic contortion may help put this formula into a more understandable format.

Assets (what a company has) – **Liabilities** (what a company owes)
= **Equity** (what a company is worth)

Income Statement

This statement shows (in a simplified format) where the money came from, what was spent, and what was left over after all expenses were paid. Unlike the balance sheet, the income statement always applies to a period of time, such as a month or a year. A typical income statement might look like the following:

Acme Musical Products

Income Statement (in thousands)

Sales revenues	30,000
Cost of goods sold	10,000
Gross margin	**20,000**
Sales, administration, & general expenses	5,000
Depreciation expenses	2,000
Income before interest and taxes (EBIT)	**13,000**
Interest expenses	600
Earnings before income tax	**12,400**
Income tax expense	4,000
Net income	**8,000**

Cash Flow Statement

A cash flow statement is derived from the income statement and balance sheet, and shows the cash and cash equivalent entering and leaving a company over a specific period of time. The money coming into the business is called cash inflow, and the money going out from the business is called cash outflow. Cash can come from three avenues: core operations (sale of products or services), investing, and financing. The cash flow statement is different from the balance sheet and income statement in that it does not include the amount of future incoming and outgoing cash that has been recorded on credit. The cash flow statement is useful in determining the short-term viability of a company—particularly its ability to pay bills—and how much cash it generates, particularly from its core operations. This would be of particular interest to investors.

Pop Sounds Musical Products

Cash Flow Statement (for the period 01/01/2008–12/31/2008)

Cash flow from operations	40,000
Cash flow from investing	(20,000)
Cash flow from financing	5,000
Cash Flow for FY ending 12/31/2008	**25,000**

With or without such statements, an independent businessperson will need to know how much money he or she is making. This may seem like a simple task, but as seasoned professionals will tell you, it is sometimes difficult to know where and how the money travels through a business. Once this information is acquired, the best decisions can be made—and that can make the difference between a healthy profit and an unexpected bankruptcy.

Operations Management

Many people get into a business because they are already giving a service away and see the potential to sell it for a profit. If this is the case, it is relatively easy to expand the service and begin to charge for it. Although the business is small, it will be easy for a single person—or a small team of individuals—to provide the service. However, as the business grows, it may get harder to meet demand—especially in the time each person has to give to the company. Although this problem is the sign of a healthy, growing company, it can create logistical difficulties. The academic subject of operations management offers many ways in which a business can overcome these problems and effectively meet demand. A few of these concepts can be particularly helpful for small companies facing production issues.

Gantt Charts

Organization is a key component for people in business, whether in a one-person operation or a larger company. Planning is also important. One simple aid used frequently in business is the Gantt chart. The idea behind this organizational tool is to provide a clear outline of the steps needed to complete a project within a given time frame. These charts can be set up in fancy formats using computer programs, with standard word processing programs, or even done by hand. It might look something like Figure 26.1.

Figure 26.1   Gantt Chart

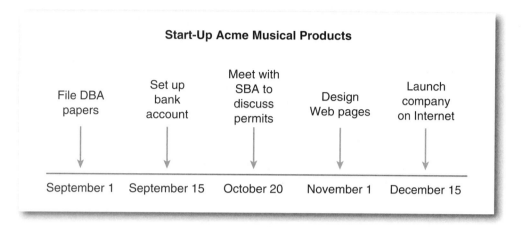

The example in Figure 26.1 highlights each event and gives it a corresponding date. Taking the time to do this makes the project manager consider all steps in the process and provides everyone involved with realistic, well-defined goals.

Management

Authoritative studies have shown time and time again that some 90% of business failures result from poor management. Individuals planning careers in the music business as, for instance, agents, managers, attorneys, or entrepreneurs will probably increase their chances of success by studying business management.

Dozens of books and hundreds of college courses treat the subject. Although they differ in approach, the most respected writers and teachers on the subject generally agree with this summary of what good management entails: planning, organizing, staffing, leading, and controlling.

Any discussion involving management should probably start with the boss. Effective leaders come with lots of different attributes. Some are authoritarian—making all the decisions themselves—whereas others prefer to involve employees in the decision-making process. Some lead by making expectations known and clearly outlining tasks for employees to accomplish. These transactional leaders can be very effective at getting the job done and are often best placed in middle management positions. Another kind of leader, a transformational leader, is one who inspires employees through enthusiasm and vision. These leaders can, and do, really make a difference for their companies and employees—just as long as their creativity does not totally eclipse the need for taking care of details.

Motivating Employees

If a new business ends up being successful, chances are that sooner or later (or maybe from the start) employees will have to be hired. Many entrepreneurs find that it is not easy to work with employees because they are likely to have different backgrounds and varying commitments to the company.

Companies can use numerous incentives to encourage employees to do their best, but deciding on the most effective methods is the challenge. One key to designing a reward system is to truly understand one's employees. Abraham Maslow, an early 20th-century psychologist, developed the need-satisfaction model (see Figure 26.2) in an attempt to explain what motivates people's (in this case, employees') behavior.

In this theory, the bottom of the pyramid shows people's need for food, shelter, clothing, and the like. If people are concerned about meeting these basic needs, they are likely to be motivated by incentives that will enable them to obtain these necessities, most likely taking the form of hourly pay increases or cash incentives. Some jobs (e.g., many summer jobs for students) may even include housing and a food allowance to cover the short-term needs of these employees. Once the basic needs are met, Maslow believed the employee would next be concerned with safety and the desire for order, followed by the need for socialization and belonging. An employer in this case can focus on social events, team projects, and any activities that will foster a sense of belonging. This is especially important for employees working from home or who spend a lot of time on the road.

The next rung up the scale deals with issues of self-esteem. If this is a primary motivator for employees, managers will want to design reward programs that recognize exceptional work. This might be as simple as an e-mail outlining someone's recent success or a specially designated parking place—or as elaborate as a trip to the Bahamas or a pink Cadillac.

The very top of the pyramid addresses self-actualization. This is probably the hardest step to understand and harder yet to foster. This concept involves fulfilling inner desires and feeling that one has accomplished all he or she was created to do. Bosses who oversee world-renowned scientists and academics, for example, may want to support their employees by giving them the time to write the book they've always wanted to, or by funding an experiment that will further their careers.

Figure 26.2 Maslow's Hierarchy of Needs

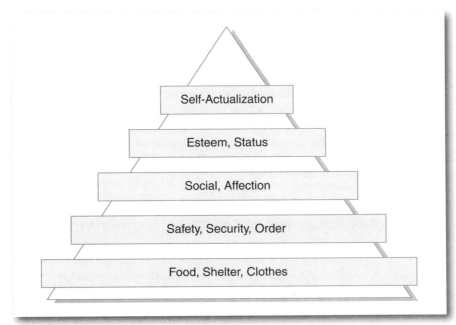

Although some academics find this model too simplistic, it does provide some good insights into possible motivators for employees. However, once again, the music industry provides a notable exception—and points out a weakness in this theory. The succession of steps in the pyramid fails to account for the "starving artist" syndrome. This is an all-too-familiar phenomenon in an industry where people are willing to forgo all the rungs of the ladder (including, but not limited to, the basic needs of food and shelter) to focus on the apex—self-actualization, or the achievement of their dreams. However, Maslow's main concept—that all employees are different and are motivated by different incentives—is still valid and worthy of consideration. By getting to know his or her employees, the successful manager will find the right combination of incentive plans to fully engage the workforce.

Where To From Here?

Statistics tell us that people entering the workforce today will have, on average, at least seven different careers. It just goes to show that planning for the unexpected is always a good idea (think about this if you are just starting college). Landing a job right out of school and spending 40 years there (the stereotype of earlier generations) is just not conceivable in today's world. Workers must be ready to adjust to change. Many opportunities will be presented during a career, one of which may very well be to escape the corporate world and make a go of it on one's own. Entrepreneurship is certainly not for everyone, but for those individuals who crave freedom and creativity over everything else, it can be a healthy alternative. In fact, for some it may be the only way to go.

Chapter Takeaways

- Many songwriters establish their own publishing companies, a type of business typically requiring less capital than most.

- A business plan is essential, outlining strategy, resources, and financial requirements.

- In the initial stage the entrepreneur must decide whether to establish a sole proprietorship, partnership, or corporation.

- Investigate and acquire all the necessary licenses and permits, saving headaches later.

- To finance a small business, often the most realistic source of funds is friends and family.

- Financial statements (balance sheet, income statement, and cash flow statement) are important to monitoring performance and staying out of financial hot water.

Key Terms

- Abraham Maslow   (p. 464)
- DBA   (p. 458)
- fictitious firm name   (p. 455)
- Gantt chart   (p. 462)

- general partner   (p. 456)
- product, price, place, promotion   (p. 459)
- SBA   (p. 454)

CHAPTER 27

Career Development

Recent studies reveal that involvement in some aspect of music is one of the most frequently named career goals. Millions of young people are drawn to music and want somehow to become part of the profession. But many of these dreams are poorly defined. Aspirants can be attracted by the "glamour" and big money of the music and entertainment fields but have no clear idea of how they might break in.

The world of music and entertainment has always had a certain mystique. The most visible people in these fields seem to be rich and famous. Producing and selling music can be enjoyable and profitable, but there's another whole world concerned with what goes on backstage, off-camera. Here, we uncover thousands of individuals no one has ever heard of, most of them employed quite regularly, earning respectable incomes—and enjoying what they are doing.

> *"Eighty percent of success is showing up."*
>
> —*Woody Allen*

Landing a Job Versus Building a Career. It is important to distinguish between a "job" and a "career." To borrow from Gertrude Stein, a job is a job (is a job). But a career, properly defined, is more likely an ongoing series of related jobs that add up to an employment sequence that has continuity and development.

Using Counselors. Although employment counselors may not be able to address everything a person may need, they are probably the most competent persons in the

---

Left: The Beatles.

Photo © John Launois/Black Star/PNI.

community to offer professional help, or what can be called structured intervention. Most counselors have information concerning career options and statistical projections of employment prospects. One of the useful services a qualified counselor can offer is assisting aspirants in finding out who they are. Counselors can offer a battery of aptitude tests, interest measurements, and temperament tests. The objectivity and value of these tests and measurements remain in dispute, but they are almost always somewhat helpful, and career seekers should avail themselves of every possible opportunity to find out where they may excel and just what makes them tick.

For people out of high school and college, counselors are available through state employment services. In larger communities, professional career counselors, independent of the government, are available, with payment of a fee. People who are still in high school or college can, of course, generally avail themselves of well-trained advisers and career placement and development staff.

Discovering Yourself. Concurrently with defining career goals, you should try to define *yourself*—analyze not only your interests but also your particular temperament and personality. Along with this personal discovery should come measurement of aptitudes and talents. In addition to doing all you can to discover who and what you are, you should obtain outside appraisals from qualified professionals.

A large part of the workforce is probably miscast. Whole lifetimes can be spent in frustration and failure. Although many different reasons may be identified for these unsuccessful lives, very often they got started off wrong, before they knew who they were or measured their talents or considered whether they could meet the competition. Well-planned careers do not always work out. But if you proceed sensibly, with all available information, at the very least you will have reduced the probability of failing in a chosen field.

Many students have used the "Discovering Yourself" form (see Table 27.1), devised particularly for people interested in careers in the arts and the music business. There is no "passing" or "failing" score. Rather, the answers should be interpreted and evaluated in light of the information set forth in these pages concerning music-related careers and the kinds of talents and personalities that have been found appropriate in pursuing certain careers. For example, if your answers show a dislike for travel and fear of not always having a steady job, you might be unhappy and unsuccessful in attempting to build a career as a performing musician. On the other hand, if your highest priority is being free to create and there is little concern about job security, you might be a strong candidate for building a career as a composer or record producer.

Besides seeking to understand your own interests and value system, it is equally important at this early stage to conduct an inventory of personal strengths, weaknesses, and talents. The accompanying form (Table 27.2) can assist you in these assessments; to be useful, they must be rendered as objectively as possible.

Inaccurate talent appraisals are readily available. For example, a musician who works every Saturday night at the local American Legion Hall can offer a "professional" opinion but may have no idea what level of talent or what type of specific musical skill is required in the recording studios. The local singing teacher may hold an advanced degree in music but not know what would be expected of voice students seeking work in broadcast commercials. Many of our university professors of music composition do not know the level of talent (and craft) demanded of film composers. Seek the opinion of such people because they have valuable knowledge, but also seek the advice, when possible, of people who have achieved some level of success in the specific career in which you are interested.

Table 27.1 **Discovering Yourself**

Effective career planning should begin with careful self-appraisal. What is important to you? What makes you most effective? What kinds of talents do you have? Place a number from 1 to 10 in the appropriate spaces below. Think of the number 1 as "low," "little" or "poor," depending on the nature of the category. Use the number 5 for "average." Number 10 means of "high," "a lot," or "very important." After you have indicated your own appraisals, seek an outside professional opinion to learn if others view you as you see yourself.

MY VALUE SYSTEM	My Estimate	Outside Estimate
Need for respect from others		
Need for prestige, status		
Need for audience approval		
Desire for peace of mind		
Need to be liked		
Desire to be loved		
Need for artistic freedom		
Concern for health		
Desire for leisure time		
Desire to have children		
Importance of artistic achievement		
Importance of job security		
Importance of money		
Tolerance for jobs demanding travel		
Desire for personal development		
Desire for artistic development		

If, through systematic appraisal of temperament and talent, the aspiring musician discovers a love of music but no desire to perform, there still are scores of career options in music-related fields. Many musicians are surprised to find that they can be successful in the business world. Many of the same qualities that make a good musician are also important to a music business person: perseverance, a willingness to work as much time as it takes to get the job done well, and a strong belief in one's own abilities. Of course, it is also helpful to have a "good ear" and to love music.

Climbing the Ladder

No two people hold the same views on just what constitutes "success." To many, the professional who earns a good living has achieved success. But in the arts, many individuals place a higher value on personal fulfillment or artistic idealism. They refuse to be seduced by the dollar; they won't "go commercial," preferring to hold to their conception of artistic integrity, whatever the consequences. Psychologists would describe this kind of idealist as one who is more concerned with "psychic rewards" than financial security.

How many people in the working world are happy with what they do for a living? Many surveys have been made; most of them indicate that *more than half* of those interviewed stated they were unhappy with their jobs. Unhappiness over low pay was rarely the number-one concern. Those interviewed have most often complained they felt trapped in their jobs and that they had little confidence they had a chance to "get ahead." A majority of those asked stated that, if they had the opportunity, they would change their line of work. Those planning a career related to the arts have to know at the outset that they are engaging in a high-risk enterprise. But even though careers in the arts, particularly music, often provide only minimum security, many aspirants would not give up the personal rewards the field offers in exchange for more stable employment.

For those who contemplate climbing the music career ladder, it will be helpful to be aware of the following:

1. Most music-related careers are combination careers. For example, many performers also teach music students in schools or in private studios.

2. Most people experience serial careers; they move from job to job, not necessarily because they quit or get fired but because of the nature of the profession. A typical example is a person who starts out as a gofer; then begins to get a few music copying jobs; and may then progress to arranging, composing, perhaps getting into the publishing business; and eventually becomes involved in artist management and record production. Each job helps the individual prepare for the next step.

3. The music business offers decreasing opportunities for the poorly prepared. The jobs offering the best potential for advancement go more and more to well-educated, genuinely competent individuals.

4. Men still dominate the business. Women, with some notable exceptions, are underrecognized, underused, and underpaid at some levels of the business.

5. Young people tend to dominate the creative and performing aspects of popular music. Persons of more mature years tend to dominate the field of serious music, music teaching, and the business and managerial facets of both popular and serious music.

6. All professions within all fields are characterized by rapid change. But in music, career opportunities change every day. New jobs and new opportunities keep coming along.

Table 27.2   **My Strengths, Weaknesses, Talent**

This Form can be revealing for both musicians and people in business. Use the 1–10 numbering system described in Table 27.1

	Today		When Fully Developed	
	My Estimate	Outside Estimate	My Estimate	Outside Estimate
Motivation, ambition				
Self-confidence				
Creative talent				
Performing ability				
Musical knowledge				
Business sense				
Effectiveness as an oral communicator				
Ability as an organizer				
General leadership ability				
Musical leadership ability				
Capacity to accept direction				
Ability to work with others				
Understanding of the music profession				
Understanding of the music business				
Emotional stability, health				
Intelligence				
Capacity for musical growth				
Capacity for personal growth				
Personal habits				
Ability to adjust to change				
My strongest personal attribute				
My strongest talent				

Finding Work

Career counselors and research experts declare that at any given moment during stable economic times in the United States, there are at least 1 million job openings of all kinds. The person pounding the pavement searching for work scoffs at such a figure when unable to discover even one opening. The 1-million figure, although a rough estimate, can be understood in part by polling several hundred music and entertainment industry employers. Most complain they cannot find really qualified employees and insist the openings are there for individuals of demonstrated ability. Surveys show that many companies would either offer jobs or create new positions for people who could produce more, sell more, write better, work harder, or manage more efficiently.

Networking. Most career counselors urge job hunters to develop what is often called a "network" of personal and professional contacts. It takes time to develop a strong supportive group of people who will speak well of you, but nothing could be more valuable in building a career. An effective network need not be limited to persons of high influence; the best contact could turn out to be a casual acquaintance in a Laundromat who mentions that so-and-so's band is looking for new people.

Most jobs in the music business are never advertised or made known to outsiders. In this field, there is often no need to place ads in the trades for help. Applicants line up immediately when word hits the street that some job may be coming up. So who gets the call? As with most fields of endeavor, what really counts in the music business is word of mouth. In short, "Who do you know who could cut it? Who might be ready for this job?" The individual who is prepared has built a good reputation and has a network of supportive contacts—that person wins in the end. Of course, once your network has helped you to get an interview or a job, you also need the specific skills or knowledge required for that job. If you are able to get a job without these skills, you'll still have a chance to succeed if you have a good, basic knowledge of the business you're entering so that you can build on the understanding you already have. When you become part of the music business, you'll still need to build on what you've learned through classes and texts like this one, but you'll have a good foundation on which to build.

Internships. Many college music industry programs require or strongly recommend that the student serve an internship as part of the degree requirements. Internships can provide valuable, practical examples of concepts learned in school. They can also help in two other very important ways:

1. They can give you actual experience in the industry. This experience can look very good on your résumé.

2. They can help you build your network of contacts. If you do good work during your internship, the professionals with whom you have worked are more likely to offer you a job or help you find employment after you've graduated. They may also give you permission to use their names as references. A successful intern understands that the internship can act as an audition for a job and will show up early for work and stay late, looking for ways to be useful and things to learn.

Personality, Work Habits. Another major influence on career development is the matter of human personality. Many jobs are won or lost not so much on intelligence and skill as on personal considerations such as dependability, flexibility, and congeniality. Research in the field of counseling has revealed that career problems are usually "people problems." Can you be counted on? Can you work effectively with others, or does your network of contacts report back that you are difficult to get along with, that you are not always dependable? People, then—their word about you—can thrust you forward or hold you back.

The Value of Research. If your network of contacts is working for you, not against you, job opportunities are bound to come up. Before trying to get an interview, carefully research your prospective employer. Focus your fact-finding on trying to discover what the employer needs most. Present yourself as a solution to the problem. An employer, perhaps having just fired your predecessor, is really searching for a replacement who will solve problems the other person left behind. For example, your chances of getting hired might hinge largely on your perceived ability to follow through—filling the shoes of the person fired whose most annoying shortcoming, perhaps, was never finishing an assignment. Individuals who get hired, get promoted, and earn the most generally appear to have their egos under control and expend their energies trying to make the boss look good.

The Résumé. Job hunters automatically assume that they must mail out a lot of résumés to gain the interest of prospective employers. But the usefulness of circulating dozens, perhaps hundreds, of résumés is very limited: Many studies show that only a few jobs are landed through the submission of such documents. Dozens of books on the subject are readily available; one of the best is Richard Bolles's *What Color Is Your Parachute?* Résumé-writing techniques are covered in other books, so here, information on that subject is limited to what might be especially useful in seeking music business-related employment.

Gaining Interviews. All résumés should be accompanied by a cover letter requesting an interview or audition. Again, you must "translate" your aspirations to solving your potential employer's perceived needs:

1. Address your résumé and letter only to the individual with the authority to hire you.

2. Everything you put in the documents should focus on one thing: helping attain the reader's goals.

3. Keep in mind that all the résumé and letter can really do is describe your past. The reader must guess what your past might indicate for your future and your usefulness to the company tomorrow.

4. Cite no negatives; don't use words and phrases such as "fired," "didn't like my boss."

5. Use colorful terms to describe jobs you have performed. If you ran errands, don't say you were a "gofer." Try "production assistant."

6. Don't list references, but be sure to state they are available.

7. Emphasize "you," not "I." The first sentence in your letter, or at least one in your first paragraph, should state precisely what you can do to help fulfill the employer's needs.

8. The résumé and letter should be perfectly typed, with correct spelling, grammar, and punctuation.

9. Your résumé and cover letter should each be only one page. The reader is too busy to read your life story.

10. The final sentence should specify just what next step you want the reader to take.

If your résumé and cover letter hit the prospective employer right, you may be invited for an interview. In that case, intensify your research on what the company is looking for and what you might expect from the particular interviewer. Don't go in cold. The best books on how to handle yourself in job interviews generally agree on the following:

1. Dress appropriately, in line with other employees at the firm working at levels near the one you might be assigned.

2. Your interviewer may not know how to conduct a job interview properly. Be helpful; raise appropriate questions, if necessary, to deliver useful information about yourself and what you might do for the firm.

3. Don't get too cozy, too breezy—or too formal. Be respectful yet congenial.

4. Learn what the job normally pays, then ask for a little more (not a lot more).

5. Focus on how you believe you can help solve the interviewer's needs.

6. Immediately following the interview—the same day—mail a thank-you letter to the interviewer for the opportunity provided for you to learn more about the firm. Your thoughtfulness might favorably impress the interviewer.

7. Attend as many job interviews as you can; such experiences often tend to reduce nervousness and increase effectiveness.

Applying these suggestions should be helpful, but successful interviews often depend on intangibles. For example, if the conversation affords you an opportunity to suggest a new idea for the company (usually hard to do), that one contribution might yield a job offer. Or if you and the prospective employer get into discussing a mutual acquaintance, a personal consideration of this kind might help create an atmosphere of trust. A job offer could follow.

It makes little difference in the music business at just what level of entry the newcomer breaks into the field. Associates will quickly assess competence, and that person's career will rise or fall accordingly. As has been stressed time and again here, artistic and financial success in the music business are possible, even likely, when you, the aspirant, can present this package to the world:

- You have genuine talent.
- You have the right temperament.
- You get the important information.
- You work with qualified associates.
- You have the will to win.

Hang in there.

Chapter Takeaways

- To chart career success, use counselors, self-assessment tests, and other resources to determine strengths and weaknesses, likes and dislikes.

- Picking the right career path is crucial: More than half the population is unhappy at work.

- Your reputation for competence within a strong network of contacts can be the ticket to getting a good job.

Key Terms

- artistic freedom   (p. 469)
- combination careers   (p. 470)
- job security   (p. 468)
- internship   (p. 472)
- résumé   (p. 473)
- success   (p. 470)

The Global View

PART 8

CHAPTER 28

Understanding Canada's Music Scene

Richard Flohil

Quick fact of life: Most Americans know almost nothing about one of the most vibrant music scenes in the world that's furiously active right next door.

That's okay: Americans know very little about Canada anyway, and it's not their fault. No U.S. news organizations or television networks have offices in Canada, and the only time the country's neighbor even gets a mention is when the president pays a flying visit, or there's another nasty winter storm blowing in from the north.

Despite this, the world—and most particularly the U.S.—consumes billions of dollars' worth of Canadian music. A partial artist roster: Celine Dion, Nickelback, Michael Bublé, Shania Twain, Feist, Gordon Lightfoot, Avril Lavigne, Joni Mitchell, Anne Murray, Nelly Furtado, Alanis Morissette, and Neil Young.

And, to some extent or other, they—and hundreds more artists in every musical genre you can think of—have been the beneficiaries of a cultural attitude that provides a wide range of direct and indirect government support for Canadian artists and Canadian music.

In turn, all this stems directly from this Canada's different historical background, Canada's geography, and Canada's physical proximity to the United States.

> *"I hate show business."*
> —Joni Mitchell

Left: Singer k.d. lang attends Canada's Walk of Fame at the Four Seasons Performing Arts Centre in Toronto, Canada.

Photo © George Pimentel/WireImages.

So, a tiny handful of quick facts:

- The population of Canada is about 10% of that of the U.S.
- Almost 90% of Canadians live within 200 miles of the American border.
- The east-west border between Canada and the U.S. is 3,145 miles long.
- Canada is the United States' largest single trading partner (way ahead of China and Mexico).
- Almost one quarter (23%) of Canadians speak French as their mother tongue.
- Canada is becoming increasingly multicultural, now home to 200 different ethnic groups.
- While exchange rates vary, in recent years the Canadian dollar has been worth about 20% less than the U.S. dollar.

All these factors have their impact on Canada's music industry, and should be considered when musicians and industry people outside the country want to deal with the Canadian music business.

Most importantly, however, Americans should understand Canadian attitudes—particularly those involving our relationship to the United States. Canadians know far more about the U.S. than Americans know about Canada. We live, after all, in the lap of the U.S.; we read American books and magazines, we watch American television, we go to see American movies, and we avidly consume American music.

Most Canadians express their nationality in terms of who they are *not* rather than in terms of who they *are*. Canadians tend to accept (and endorse) a greater degree of government involvement in their lives than do Americans; they tend to be less assertive and more reflective than Americans; and the majority of Canadians have a strongly negative response to hand guns, capital punishment, urban decay, and other things they see as symptomatic of the "American way of life."

Most of all, Canadians hate being taken for granted, and they figure that Americans do that all the time. At the same time, however, Canadian achievements are usually seen in the light of foreign approval of them; Canadians who may be unaware of artists from their own backyard will offer them star status once they have been successful in the U.S. or Europe.

Would You Believe a Government That Makes Pop Music a Priority?

Canadian governments (at federal, provincial—state—and local levels) take the position that it is desirable to support the Canadian "cultural industries" (including the domestic music industry as well as film, TV, theater, and the visual arts). It follows this course to offer a balance to what is seen as the danger of domination by foreign (i.e., U.S.) culture.

Domestic Music Quotas

With this in mind, the regulatory body that parallels the Federal Communications Commission (FCC), the Canadian Radio-Television and Telecommunications Commission (CRTC), instituted the "Canadian content" (CanCon) regulations.

Starting in 1971, Canadian radio stations were required to ensure that 25% (as of 2008, 40%) of all music played was either written or performed by Canadians and produced in Canada. Thus, the components of each musical piece are broken down: Music, Artist, Production, Lyrics (the acronym MAPL neatly indicates the maple leaf, Canada's national symbol). Two or more of those four elements were enough to gain a piece status as "Canadian."

Back in 1970, there were few established Canadian artists, and without radio play it was difficult to build anything like a national hit. Most bands performed in their immediate home markets, with word of mouth building a sufficient fan base to support local gigs. Because there was no radio play, and therefore no hits, there were no facilities in which to make good records. Catch 22 indeed. Many artists, hampered by lack of opportunity, left for greener pastures in the U.S.

But almost overnight, the regulations began to work. The major multinational companies operating in Canada decided to release music by Canadian artists; high quality recording studios were built, equipped, and opened; and some early independent record companies eased their way into business. An industry infrastructure—agency, management, concert promotion, and publicity companies—was established in short order.

Canadian songwriters began to earn a significantly larger share of domestic performing rights income. More and more Canadian artists discovered that they could perform outside their own cities and towns; one booking agency estimated that, prior to the regulations, it had half a dozen acts on its books that could tour across the country; only 2 years later, there were more than 50. Today, there are probably more than 3,000 Canadian artists who can tour nationally in their own country.

In turn, Canadian exposure gave more artists access to American and European markets—and performing rights income from abroad for Canadian songwriters and publishers skyrocketed from some $100,000 (Canadian) in 1970 to well over $39 million today.

The idea of domestic music quotas, pioneered in Canada, has spread to a number of other territories, including Australia and France. Artists in those countries, too, have shared the Canadian experience—more domestic exposure leads to more international exposure for domestic artists, which leads to exponentially increased opportunities and income.

Other Government Support

Government support for the arts is expressed in a number of other ways. The country's senior funding body, the Canada Council for the Arts, supplies grants that help individual artists, provides financial support for tours, and supports programming initiatives at festivals and theater venues. In fact, the Canada Council's annual budget, funded by the federal government, is only slightly less than that of the National Endowment for the Arts in the United States.

All the various provincial governments offer a variety of support programs, as do some of the larger municipalities.

The music industry earns considerable financial support—over $14 million a year—from FACTOR, the Foundation to Assist Canadian Talent on Records. Funded by the federal government and to a lesser extent by radio stations, which are required to contribute under the terms of the licenses they earn from the CRTC, FACTOR distributes this money through grants or loans to individual musicians, bands, or record labels. Canadian artists can apply for tour support in foreign countries (yes, that includes the U.S.), and for half the costs to participate in foreign showcases, including SXSW in Austin, CMJ in New York, Popkomm in Berlin, Folk Alliance in Memphis, MIDEM in France, or Music in the City in the United Kingdom.

A more recent funding source is the Radio Starmaker Fund, established by the Canadian Association of Broadcasters to "support emerging artists with star potential in such a way that it has a direct impact on their marketing and touring initiatives in Canada and abroad in a way that will make a difference." In recent years some $20 million has been distributed to artists and independent record companies.

The Record Industry in Canada

Recent changes in Canada's record industry have been a gut-wrenching experience—and not only for the remaining handful of major labels, but for the rapidly growing number of independent record companies, and the hardy retailers that still exist.

All the major multinational record companies still operate in Canada, and despite the fact that they distribute most of the stronger independent labels, they face brutally challenging times.

CD sales continue to collapse in freefall—close to 20% down in 2008 from the previous year, according to Nielsen Soundscan, for a total of 35.9 million units, compared to 41.8 million the previous year. There was a more troubling fact hidden in the statistics: The 58% increase in digital sales did not begin to make up the declining sales of physical product. That they would do, or will do, seems at present to be wishful thinking. As the Canadian Recording Industry Association put it in 2007: "Digital sales in Canada fall far short of making up for the sharp, long-term decline in sales of physical formats." In Canada's relatively undeveloped digital market, downloads, digital subscription services, and mobile music comprised just 12% of total sales in 2007, lagging far behind the market share in the U.S.

The major labels have also drastically cut back on the number of Canadian artists they are signing. Increasing marketing costs and the assumed need to present their parent companies with a minimal amount of red ink have encouraged the majors to leave talent development (with its associated costs) to the independents. The majors are signing occasional Canadian artists in Canada, but artists looking for a major label deal know that the U.S. market is 10 times the size of the domestic one, and given the opportunity, usually prefer to sign with the company in the U.S. as a way to secure American commitment.

Canada's independent labels do everything they can to carve a path through the jungle. Independent labels—and more than 100 are members of the Canadian Independent Record Production Association—are often artist owned. Anthem is owned by the band Rush; Quinlan Road by singer Loreena McKennitt; while others specialize in various niche markets—Stony Plain markets roots music, Borealis is a folk label, ElectriFi and NorthernBlues are blues labels, Marquis sells classical crossover artists, Arbor Records serves Aboriginal performers, and Alma markets Canadian jazz artists.

Most Canadian independent labels, however, market pop music, often concentrating on edgier variants. The largest of these is Nettwerk, based in Vancouver, which combines its label with a major management company; Sarah McLachlan is their signature artist. At the other end, is Six Shooter Records, a Toronto company run by two women that, in addition to a flourishing label with half a dozen artists, has a powerhouse management company, a concert promotion firm, and a retail outlet that sells Canadian CDs, music books, jewelry, and painted cowboy boots.

As in the U.S., big box retailers (Wal-Mart, Best Buy) command a huge share of overall unit sales, using deep discounts to merchandise a limited number of titles.

With retail in disarray, the majors losing sales, and independent labels (dependent on major label distribution support) amounting to some 20% of sales, the old ways are surely passing. The CD itself, for most independent labels, now represents either a calling card for the label or the artist, or a souvenir of a live performance.

Live Music Opportunities in Canada

Canada is not only a small market, it is one complicated by its geography. There are only a dozen music centers in the country, and they are in most cases hundreds of miles apart from each other. Travel costs are high—and there's a theory that Canada has always produced good singer-songwriters because they are able to crisscross the country economically, as opposed to a four- or six-piece band in a van.

Donnie Walsh, leader of the Downchild Blues Band, for four decades Canada's best-known band in the idiom (and the original inspiration for fellow-Canadian Dan Aykroyd's Blues Brothers project), struck a chord with musicians when he explained his band's success: "Once we made a record, and once we got some airplay," he said, "then we had to deal with the geography."

And the geography will certainly challenge any U.S. musician who's used to working in the population-rich areas of the stateside music scene. There are, basically, half a dozen major urban centers in Canada: Halifax, Montreal (with its own peculiarities), Toronto (the music business capital of the country), Winnipeg, Calgary, Edmonton, and Vancouver. Domestic airfares within Canada are high, gas is expensive, and the destinations frequently 2 or 3 day's drive from each other. Touring in Canada is not for the faint-hearted or for those without deep pockets.

Crossing the Border

Geography aside, touring in Canada is not helped by Customs and Immigration, which levies a fee for musicians (and other entertainers, from strippers to opera singers to sports teams) to cross the border in the first place. Permission in advance must be obtained by employers from Human Resources and Skills Development Canada, and forwarded to those who plan to cross the border.

With permission granted (usually a formality) and your contracts in hand—and there's no way you're getting in without both—you may be charged (as of 2008) $150.00 (Canadian) if you're an individual performer, and $450.00 if you're in a group of between 2 and 14 members, if you cross at the same border point at the same time. This applies to gigs in bars and clubs; if you are playing a concert hall, you will still need the paperwork, but you may not be charged. However, individual customs offices, as confused by the rules as visiting musicians, often levy the fees anyway. Therefore a new band making its first foray into the bar scene will probably earn $400 for a gig, less 15%, and less the border fee. It is no consolation to know that Canadian artists wanting to perform in the United States have even higher regulatory and financial hurdles to leap over.

On your arrival, you'd better have—in addition to your contract—a valid passport as well as cash to pay duties on merchandise you may be bringing in to sell in Canada, and a list of all your instruments and gear (including the original cost and the serial numbers).

Add to all this the value of the Canadian dollar, and the lesson is obvious: Performing in Canada, for foreign artists, is something only for the rich or for those with rich record companies behind them! (For complete information on working in Canada, check with the Canadian consulate nearest you.)

Given all that, the live music scene in Canada is surprisingly strong. Toronto probably has more club shows and concerts than New York and Los Angeles put together—the city's two entertainment weeklies, *Now Magazine* and *Eye Weekly* carry ads and listings each week for hundreds of shows. Vancouver has a healthy scene, limited only by its relatively small number of venues, and Montreal, Edmonton, Calgary, and Halifax also host a wide range of shows by local artists, acts from across the country, and international groups.

A booming music festival scene offers a way into the market for a wide variety of music; major folk festivals (and the definition of the F-word is broader than you may think) in Vancouver, Edmonton, Calgary, and Winnipeg have helped launch many artists in Canada. Ontario has more than 30 annual summer festivals; there are numerous smaller but similar events in the Atlantic provinces.

What Doesn't Make It Across

It should be pointed out, however, that certain styles of music that are popular in the U.S. have little relevance in Canada. Latin music has only limited popularity north of the border, and rap and hip-hop styles, while popular in a small handful of markets, earn little airplay, and are not popular in live settings. The various genres of gospel music gains hardly any airplay or sales.

However, a variety of **alternative country** and "folk" styles are popular in western Canada, while Celtic music retains its popularity in the Atlantic provinces. Most importantly, Canada remains a strong (if small) market for current forms of mainstream and alternative rock, much as in the U.S.

Quebec: Vive la Différence

For slightly under one of every four Canadians, French is the mother tongue, and nowhere else in the world (and that includes France) is the language more promoted and protected than in Quebec. In addition to Canadian content rules, broadcasters in the province with French-language licenses must play 65% French-language music.

Although Montreal, the province's capital, is thoroughly bilingual, there are still people surviving in the city whose knowledge of French is less than that of an average grade school child in Omaha. Traditionally, Montreal, a sophisticated, European-style city, has acted as a breaking-in point for many international acts—Pink Floyd and Dire Straits among them—in North America. For all that, the rest of this part of Canada remains an island of "francophonie" in an English-speaking continent, and as a result, the music scene in Quebec is dramatically different.

Demographically, Quebecers buy more records than anyone else in North America, and they also buy records far longer into their life cycles. English-speaking North Americans, as a rule, stop being major record purchasers when they have acquired spouses, homes, cars, and children—but this isn't the case in Quebec, where people go on buying records well into their fifties and later. The meltdown in record sales is now happening in Quebec, but it took a lot longer to take effect than it did in the rest of Canada.

The results of this demographic quirk is that Quebec has an entirely separate French-speaking music industry, with dozens of artists at any given time who may sell platinum (80,000 copies) or more and yet who are almost totally unknown in Toronto, only 350 miles down the highway from Montreal, and as a result never venture near the place. Francophone artists, including their superstars, see Europe, rather than the rest of Canada or the U.S., as the logical market to expand into.

It's also worth noting that the highest-selling female artist of all time, Celine Dion, had more than a half-dozen best-selling albums in Quebec and in Europe long before she learned to speak and sing in English. Two hundred million records later, she regards her language lessons as the best investment she ever made.

Promoting Music in Canada

The old media are failing. And it's not news to add that the new media are complex, confusing, and present far too many ways of promoting music, none of them with the erstwhile strength of the former triumvirate of print, radio, and television.

Music Videos and Television

Just as American "music" channels (MTV, VH1, and CMT) no longer program anywhere near as much music as they did even a few years ago, their counterparts in Canada are now concentrating on reruns of TV sitcoms and low-rent "reality" shows. However, CMT Canada, MuchMusic, MuchMoreMusic, and Bravo all offer financial support to artists and domestic record labels so they can make videos—they are forced to provide this support as a condition of their licenses. And while they may give such videos limited airplay (and sometimes not at all), the videos have continuing life on YouTube and other Web-based outlets.

Once again, there is a Canadian content requirement on Canadian television and cable channels, although the average Canadian can also see a host of channels from across the border. Both of Canada's major TV networks, CBC and CTV, have spotty records as producers of music specials, although smaller channels like Bravo do air music series from time to time. But the public network, CBC, broadcasts the Canadian Country Music Awards; the East Coast Music Awards and The Juno Awards (Canada's equivalent of the Grammys) are aired by the largest privately owned network, CTV, and draw diminishing audiences each year. Even *Canadian Idol*, after a successful run, was dropped by CTV in 2009.[1]

Music Publications

Canada also only has a small handful of music publications. The longest running is *Canadian Musician,* aimed toward players. An exhaustive Web site (www.fyi music.ca) works to fill the role once occupied by defunct publications.

Radio

Commercial radio—with the obvious difference caused by Canadian content requirements—follows American patterns, with ownership consolidating rapidly in recent years. College, campus, and community stations in major markets fill the left-hand end of the dial with eclectic programming. Two CBC radio channels provide a wide variety of regional and national music programs, including thoughtful, well-crafted specialist shows covering classical, blues, jazz, and alternative pop/rock. In addition, the CBC succeeds in topping a 60% CanCon level.

Christian radio, a force in the U.S., is almost nonexistent in Canada, and the noisy right-wing talk shows so familiar to American listeners simply do not exist north of the border.

Digital media

With disappearing opportunities in mainstream media (particularly for independent labels) new digital media are vital to create an awareness of active artists. Social networks are the way to promote music. YouTube carries more Canadian music videos than all the TV channels combined.

Royalty Collection in Canada

Canada manages its royalty collection process quite differently from the U.S. Performing rights are handled by a single organization rather than the three that operate in the United States. The Society of Composers, Authors and Music Publishers of Canada (SOCAN) is based in Toronto, with major offices in Montreal and Vancouver, and regional offices in Edmonton and Halifax.

Songwriters and publishers in Canada join SOCAN and may then elect which of the three U.S. organizations (ASCAP, BMI, or SESAC) will represent them in the United States. If they do not make a choice, ASCAP will collect their royalties and pass them to SOCAN for distribution. Meanwhile, SOCAN administers performing rights in Canada for all the members of all three American organizations, plus, of course, the members of all other foreign societies.

In Canada, performing rights income on a per capita basis is considerably higher than it is in the United States. Total SOCAN revenues are now close to $250 million (Canadian) per year, with some 55% delivered to performing rights organizations outside the country (the overhead is some 16%, and the remainder is distributed to Canadian members).

Mechanical royalties and synchronization rights in Canada are administered by the Canadian Musical Reproduction Rights Agency (CMRRA), owned and operated by the Canadian Music Publishers Association, which operates parallel to the Harry Fox Agency.

Canada: A Hothouse for Talent—And a Challenge for U.S. Musicians

Ambitious, focused, and dedicated artists with a unique sound and good songs do rise like cream to the top, and Canada's current crop of star-bright talent is strong indeed.

Whether or not the idea of government involvement in the arts—which was raised at the beginning of this chapter—makes sense to you, there is little doubt that the system seems to work. It has helped build international reputations for dozens of Canadian artists as well as a diverse, active, workmanlike, and profitable industry in a country where little existed, musically, 40 years ago.

One paramount fact remains: Audiences north of the border have always extended a warm welcome and encouraging applause to artists from around the world, with a particular regard for our friends from the United States. Nothing—from government support of domestic artists and music to the increased difficulty of physically crossing the border—is ever going to change that.

Table 28.1   Twenty-Three Organizations to Help You Access the Canadian Music Scene

Rights Organizations

Audio-Visual Licensing Agency (AVLA). Administers licensing for the reproduction of sound recordings and reproduction and broadcast of music videos. Victoria Shepherd, Program Manager; Ph: (416) 922-8727; E-Mail: info@avla.ca; URL: www.avla.ca

Canadian Musical Reproduction Rights Agency (CMRRA). Roughly equivalent to the Harry Fox Agency. David Basskin, President; Ph: (416) 926-1966; E-mail: inquiries@cmrra.ca; URL: www.cmrra.ca

Neighbouring Rights Collective of Canada (NRCC). Administers rights of performers, musicians and producers of sound recordings. Ian MacKay, President; Ph: (416) 968-8870; E-mail: info@nrdv.ca; URL: www.nrdv.ca

Society of Composers, Authors and Music Publishers of Canada (SOCAN). The equivalent of ASCAP, BMI and SESAC. André LeBel, Chief Executive Officer; Ph: (416) 445-8700; URL: www.socan.ca

Industry Associations

Canadian Academy of Recording Arts & Sciences (CARAS). Equivalent of NARAS. Melanie Berry, President; Ph: (416) 485-3135; E-mail: info@carasonline.ca; URL: www.carasonline.ca

Canadian Country Music Association (CCMA). Equivalent of Country Music Association. Ph: (416) 947-1331; E-mail: country@ccma.org; URL: www.ccma.org

Canadian Independent Record Production Association (CIRPA). Represents independent music organizations. Duncan McKie, President and Chief Executive Officer; Ph: (416) 485-3152; E-mail: admin@cirpa.ca; URL: www .cirpa.ca

Canadian Recording Industry Association. Equivalent of the Recording Industry Association of America. Graham Henderson, President; Ph: (416) 967-7272; E-mail: info@cria.ca; URL: www.cria.ca

l'Association quebecoise de l'industrie du disque, du spectacle et de la vidéo (ADISQ). This group represents all aspects of music in Quebec. Paul Dupont-Hébert, President; Ph: (514) 842-5147; E-mail: info@adisq.com; URL: www .adisq.com

Songwriters Association of Canada (SAC). Don Quarles, Executive Director; Ph: (416) 961-1588; E-mail: admin@songwriters.ca; URL: www.songwriters.ca

Urban Music Association of Canada Ph: (416) 916-2874; www.umacunited.com

Funding Organizations

Canada Council for the Arts. The Canadian Equivalent of the National Endowment for the Arts. Russell Kelley, Music Officer; Ph: (613) 566-4414 ext. 4240; E-mail: russell.kelley@canadacouncil.ca; URL: www.canadacouncil.ca

Foundation to Assist Canadian Talent on Records (FACTOR). Provides funding for Canadian recording initiatives. Heather Ostertag, President and Chief Executive Officer; Ph: (416) 696-2215; E-mail: genersal.info@factor.ca; URL: www.factor.ca

Industry Conventions

Canadian Music Week (CMW). Canada's major industry gathering, trade show, and showcase event held annually in March. Neill Dixon, President; Ph: (905) 858-4747; E-mail: neill@cmw.net; URL: www.cmw.net

East Coast Music Awards. Conference and showcases held annually in various cities in the Atlantic provinces, usually toward the end of February. Ph: (902) 892-9040; E-mail: ecma@ecma.ca; URL: www.ecma.ca

(Continued)

Table 28.1   (Continued)

Industry Conventions

North By North East (NXNE). This event, held each June, parallels Austin's famed SXSW.
Andy McLean, Managing Director; Ph: (416) 863-6963; E-mail: info@nxne.com; URL: www.nxne.com

Ontario Council of Folk Festivals Conference. Conference and showcases held annually in Ottawa.
Peter MacDonald, Executive Director ; Ph: (613) 560-5997; E-mail: info@ocff.ca; URL: www.ocff.ca

Western Canadian Music Awards & Conference. Held each year in September in varying western Canadian cities.
Ph: (204) 943-8485; E-mail: info@wcmw.ca; URL: www.westerncanadianmusicawards.ca

Talent Booking Agencies

Live Tour Artists. Agency which handles wide variety of music artists, and theatrical and corporate shows.
Joan Kirby, President; Ph: (866) 400-1003; E-mail: info@livetourartists.com; URL: www.livetourartists.com

Paquin Entertainment Group. Handles adult contemporary, rock, folk and family artists.
Gilles Paquin, President & Chief Executive Officer; Julien Paquin, President, Agency Division
Ph: (204) 988-1124 (Winnipeg), (416) 962-8885 (Toronto); E-mail: info@paquinentertainment.com;
URL: www.paquinentertainment.com

S.L. Feldman & Associates. The largest talent agency in the country, working in music, film, TV, and artist
management.
Sam Feldman, Chief Executive Officer; Ph: (604) 734-5945 or (416) 598-0067; E-mail:feldman@slfa.com;
URL: www.slfa.com

The Agency Group. Canadian office of major UK-based agency; handles rock, blues, and pop artists.
Ralph James, President; Ph: (416) 368-5599; E-mail: ralphjames@theagencygroup.com;
URL: www.theagencygroup.com

Industry Web Site

FYI Music News. Only major industry news web portal in Canada.
David Farrell, Editor/Publisher; Ph: (416) 534-0607 ext. 21; E-mail: david@fyimusic.ca; URL: www.fyimusic.ca

Richard Flohil is a Toronto-based music industry veteran who works as a writer, publicist, and music event promoter. The artists he has worked with include k.d. lang, Loreena McKennitt, Serena Ryder, Ian Tyson, The Chieftains, Eric Idle, Billy Connolly, and countless others. He is a member of numerous Canadian music industry organizations, and has lectured on music and media topics at several schools in Ontario.

Note

1. In Quebec, however, there are several daily TV shows that feature music and which actively promote local artists in a way that local and national channels in English Canada cannot possibly match.

Chapter Takeaways

- Since 1971 Canada has established quotas for the proportion of broadcast music that must be Canadian in origin—a policy that has fueled significant growth in the industry.

- Canada Council for the Arts pumps Canadian federal government money into the arts at about 10 times the per capita rate as occurs in the U.S.

- Many Canadian artists prefer to sign record deal with the U.S. arm of multinational distributors because the Canadian counterpart organization represents such a small portion of North American sales.

- Canada is afflicted by the same problems as the rest of the global business: declining CD sales, struggling retailers, and a small downloads business.

- Touring in Canada is expensive and difficult, whether an act is Canadian or from outside the country.

- Quebec's music industry is somewhat separate from the rest of the country, and enforces strict French-language quotas for broadcast music.

Key terms

- CanCon   (p. 480)
- CBC   (p. 485)
- CMRRA   (p. 486)
- CRTC   (p. 480)

- CTV   (p. 485)
- FACTOR   (p. 481)
- SOCAN   (p. 486)

CHAPTER 29

The World Outside the United States

Phil Hardy

The international music industry has experienced a sea change as opportunities for global exposure and sales have emerged—opportunities that would have been unimaginable only a few years ago. A confluence of factors—the digital revolution, the Internet, increased globalization, the opening up of huge markets like China and Russia, and the continued consolidation of music companies—have significantly altered the landscape for artists, record companies, music publishers, and other music-related entities, from the largest conglomerate with offices around the globe to the lone musician doing it all in the basement. The digital revolution has been a mixed blessing, spawning a new set of challenges, as we'll see later in this chapter.

> *"You can never get silence anywhere nowadays, have you noticed?"*
>
> *—Bryan Ferry*

The vital importance of the "global" aspect of the global music business makes it imperative for artists and companies to rethink everything from touring to the myriad means of marketing and sales via the Internet (including online sales, digital downloads, streaming music subscription services, ringtones, Web sites, blogs, and social networking). The reduced costs of recording, marketing, and distribution (the distribution and transportation of online song files costs virtually nothing), along with the lightning speed of digital international commerce have made it possible not

---

Left: Paul Simon and Art Garfunkel perform in Hyde Park, London.

Photo © Jo Hale/Getty Images.

only for superstars to brand themselves throughout the world but also for independent and genre artists to develop micro-brands and market their products to specific locales and to dispersed niche audiences.

Globalization has wrought many changes in the way music is consumed in various countries, creating more cross-cultural opportunities than ever before. For example, MTV, which has established indigenous networks in many territories, can give exposure to the local music of, say, Israel in the U.S., and vice versa. In terms of revenue, a genre like rockabilly might sell well in Germany while being largely ignored in the U.S., its home country.

Live performances in markets outside the U.S. are more important than ever in developing careers for recording artists. Fans in Europe, Australia, and Japan are much more open to new artists than those in the U.S. Having acts get on the international road to play clubs, concerts, and festivals is perhaps the single most productive way to develop or broaden a fan base, which in turn propels sales and other forms of revenue for both new and established acts.

The International Scene

Challenges

Because the global economy is so intertwined, key challenges facing the international music business mirror those in the U.S. The most pressing issues for the recorded music industry worldwide have been a continuing decline in sales and the opportunities and threats posed by the Internet and the digital revolution.

The dramatic decline in **soundcarrier** sales has various causes, and it affects regions around the world in different ways. After years of benefiting from the success of DVD-format concert films and music videos, record companies worldwide have been hurt by a slowdown in the overall DVD market.

Despite an improvement of living standards in many parts of Asia, Africa, and Latin America, counterfeiting of CDs and DVDs in those regions remains a problem. In more affluent regions such as Western Europe, Japan, and the United States, declining sales principally stem from unlawful P2P (peer-to-peer) file sharing and competition for disposable income from many sources, including legal digital formats, electronic games, mobile telephones, and streaming audio services. Exasperated by rampant unauthorized P2P file sharing in China, the world's major labels partnered with Google affiliate Top100.cn to monetize music through authorized streaming and downloading. The only label revenue from the China initiative comes from sharing modest advertising receipts, not consumer payments.

In the late 1990s, many experts forecast that online music sales would quickly come to represent a large proportion of record industry income. These predictions were soon shown to have been premature, in part because the necessary infrastructure was not in place, especially in Europe (see below), and in part because of only a tentative commitment by the major international record companies, who feared the Internet would reduce their degree of control over their productions. However, within a few years, the digital revolution, which now included mobile as well as online recorded music sales, was firmly established. According to the International Federation of the Phonographic Industry (IFPI), digital recorded music sales in 2008 accounted for more than 20% of recorded music sales globally ($3.8 billion trade value and growing).

Performance Rights

Despite global integration, there remain important cultural and legal differences between the music industries of the United States and most other countries. For example, record companies and recording artists outside the U.S. often enjoy relatively lucrative performance rights for recordings themselves (not just the songs), permitting these stakeholders to collect significant copyright fees from radio and television stations. Historically, the strength of the broadcasting lobby in the U.S. has led to the U.S. lagging far behind the rest of the world in generating this kind of income for music-makers (see Chapter 5).

Performing rights for songwriters and publishers are also generally stronger in Europe, where royalties from broadcasters, concert promoters, and other music users are greater per capita than in the U.S. At the same time, representatives of U.S. composers and publishers (and those of the United Kingdom) have become increasingly critical of the large deductions made by European copyright societies for spending on cultural activities and welfare payments to their members. Organizations like ASCAP and BMI retort that a large proportion of these deductions come from royalties earned by American music in Europe but that U.S. songwriters do not benefit from the resulting cultural spending. In response, European societies maintain that it is only because they fund such cultural subsidies that they have the ear of their governments and are able to ensure that songwriters, including those from the U.S., are fairly rewarded for their efforts.

The tension between the Anglo-Saxon (North American and British) and European approaches led to a dispute in the mid-1990s between music publishers, notably those owned by the major international record companies, and the European copyright collection societies. The publishers won a reduction in the societies' commission rates on mechanical royalties under an agreement generally known as the Cannes Accord. Another attack on the societies and their joint body BIEM (see Chapter 30) came from the international division of the behemoth Universal Music Group (UMG). Claiming that BIEM had an unfairly dominant position, UMG requested that European societies reduce the mechanical royalty rate previously agreed upon by BIEM and the record companies' organization, IFPI (Chapter 30).

More recently, as intellectual property has grown in economic importance, regulators have taken a closer look at its administration. The European Commission (EC) has overseen both aborted and successful mergers of major record companies, challenged the administration of copyrights by the European authors' societies, and recommended new ways of administering digital rights. A number of leading publishers have formed partnerships with selected societies to more efficiently exploit their rights. The projected merger of EMI and Warner Music Group (WMG) was aborted by the parties in 2000, when the EC made its disapproval clear. The merger of the majority of the recorded music interests of Sony and Bertelsmann was successfully challenged in the courts after it was initially approved; this led to a re-examination of the merger by the Commission and a further approval, in 2008, for Bertelsmann to sell its interests (BMG) to Sony, resulting in the creation of Sony Music Entertainment (SME) in 2009.

In a separate action, RTL, Europe's largest TV, radio, and production company (majority-owned by Bertelsmann), filed a complaint stating that as a Europe-wide broadcaster it wanted to license music rights from one society rather than have to go to each national society and seek individual licenses. Seeing the way the wind was blowing, major publishers of Anglo-American repertoires have struck individual deals with authors' societies providing for regional representation.

These developments are especially important for U.S. rights holders because over the past half-century, foreign markets, especially Europe, have become more significant to the U.S. music industry. There are two reasons for this: Since the 1950s, American pop music has found bigger and bigger audiences around the globe; and since the 1960s, the proportion of world record sales generated in the U.S. has been slowly declining as first the European and then the Asian and Latin American markets have matured. Sales of U.S. repertoire are particularly strong in Europe and Australasia, where they represent between 20% and 40% of each market. In fact, some American artists sell more albums overseas than at home. Similarly, a growing proportion of the royalties collected by ASCAP, BMI, and SESAC, the U.S. performance rights organizations, comes from abroad. These organizations receive monies for the use of American music overseas through bilateral contracts with other national societies.

U.S. copyright owners have also benefited in recent years from the proliferation of foreign music radio and television stations. In many countries, this is the result of the abolition of state-owned broadcasting monopolies, while the spread of satellite and digital technologies has encouraged the launch of regional music channels in Asia, Europe, and Latin America by MTV and other network owners. The increased use of music on the world's airwaves has naturally increased the performance royalties collected by the various copyright societies.

In the 1970s, record sales in the United States accounted for roughly half the world market by value. This share has steadily declined, and in 2008 comprised 28%. Nevertheless, the United States remains by far the largest national soundcarrier market. The next largest is Japan, followed by the United Kingdom, Germany, and France. Outside Japan and Western Europe, the most important foreign markets are Canada (sixth largest), Australia (seventh), Russia (eleventh), and Brazil (twelfth). Table 29.1 lists the top 10 territories for recorded music in 2007. The global trend is consistent: key world markets have seen a decline in soundcarrier sales and a rise in digital distribution revenue. And while royalties paid by broadcasters and others for sound recording performance rights (*neighboring rights*) grew a hefty 16% globally in 2008, the U.S. lagged seriously behind other countries in this revenue category because of the U.S. regulatory framework (see Table 29.1).

Figure 29.1 lists the revenues of music publishers from 2002–2007.

Even as recorded music sales have fallen, the revenues of music publishers have risen as new revenue streams have emerged. A prime example is ringtones on mobile phones, which, along with mastertones (actual recordings), generated billions of dollars in music publishing revenue in the early years of the 21st century. While the once-dependable growth of music publishers' mechanical royalties faltered, publishers have benefited worldwide from the use of music in movies, television, commercials, and video games.

New Patterns Around the World

In Europe, the pressure on profits has been mitigated by the blossoming of the long-awaited efficiencies of the European Union's single market. Although most major record companies maintain national offices for A&R (artist and repertoire), promotion, and marketing, in recent years European manufacturing and production has become more centralized as record companies no longer see such activities as part of their "core business." The major labels also alleviate some administrative costs by

Table 29.1   The Trade Value of the Top 10 Recorded Music Markets in 2007(in Millions of Dollars)

Country	Physical	Digital	Neighboring Rights	Total
United States	4,559.1	1,476.0	23.4	6,058.6
Japan	2,942.2	572.8	61.7	3,576.7
UK	1,743.8	169.5	128.3	2,041.6
Germany	1,392.1	86.5	85.8	1,564.4
France	935.2	78.6	72.3	1,086.1
Canada	424.0	53.0	19.5	496.4
Australia	369.7	33.0	11.3	413.9
Italy	317.2	26.3	21.2	364.7
Spain	252.4	25.0	28.1	305.5
Netherlands	227.2	11.6	42.4	281.2
World	15,873.0	2,873.0	660.0	19,405.0

Source: International Federation of the Phonographic Industry (IFPI), 2008.

Figure 29.1   World Music Publishing Revenues 2002–2007 (in Billions of Dollars)

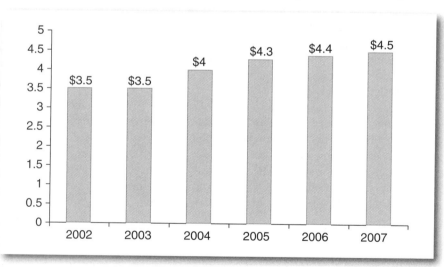

Source: THEVIEW.

routing much of their mechanical royalty payments through central licensing agreements covering several (or all) European nations.

The digital revolution has dramatically changed the regional patterns of recorded music sales throughout the world. In Southeast Asia, for example, indications are that markets previously dominated by music cassette sales, such as China and India, have leapfrogged the move to CDs and headed directly to the digital market. In 2007, the trade value of physical sales in China was $37.7m (a fall of 24%), but the value of digital sales was $31.8m (an increase of 13%); in South Korea, digital recorded music sales at $87.5m were higher than physical sales ($56.3m).

In the digital sector, there are also marked regional differences. Generally in Southeast Asia, mobile phone sales represent a greater proportion of overall digital sales than in Europe or the United States. However, the pattern is slowly changing as mobile phone companies turn to music to differentiate themselves and seek new subscribers. The pioneer in this has been Nokia. Its *Comes With Music* service gives subscribers access to virtually unlimited downloads from the four major labels and a host of independents, and subscribers can keep the downloads when their subscription ends. The service, launched in 2008, was first made available in the UK and Australia, with competitors quickly drawn to develop similar offerings.

Steps Against File-Sharing and Piracy

The growth of P2P file sharing has led to tensions between Internet Service Providers (ISPs) and rights owners. Rights owners seek to hold ISPs responsible for the actions of their subscribers, while ISPs maintain that how their service is used is not their responsibility. Two strategies have emerged in Europe to deal with this: government regulation and commercial agreements.

Government Regulations

An ongoing battleground is France, which in 2009 adopted the "Internet and Creation" bill that established HADOPI as an independent authority to monitor Internet infringement. At the request of rights holders, HADOPI was intended to force ISPs to assist in revealing the identities of alleged infringers, leading to an enforcement process. But the law was immediately challenged for provisions that would have imposed sanctions on those only accused of infringement, not just those formerly determined to be violators.

Other countries have adopted a variety of strategies. Swedish authorities rejected a recommendation that ISPs be made legally responsible for terminating the subscriptions of persistent copyright infringers. In 2007, a Belgian Court ordered the ISP Scarlet to use filtering technology to remove infringing content in a case brought by Belgian authors' society SABAM (Société d'Auteurs Belge—Belgische Auteurs Maatschappij). The Court also ordered Scarlet to end the unauthorized sharing of electronic files containing music in SABAM's repertoire.

Commercial Agreements

With the threat of government action in the background, a number of ISPs have changed their relationships with content providers. In 2009, Irish ISP Eircom agreed to implement a graduated response program; the record companies have endeavored to strike similar agreements with all other ISPs in Ireland.

In 2008, Japan's National Police Agency (NPA) proposed a system whereby ISPs are to send alert messages to infringing users and then terminate the accounts of repeat users. Also, rights holders may seek payment for damages and/or the NPA can investigate and bring criminal charges against infringing users.

In the UK, ISPs and the music industry reached a voluntary Memorandum of Understanding (MOU) under which ISPs agreed to send warning letters to alleged copyright infringers when notified by content owners. The MOU was signed by the country's six largest ISPs.

In many cases, content owners and ISPs have struck their own agreements under the Access to Music Charge (AMC) concept, which holds that the only viable means of monetizing the online music user is at the user's point of access through the ISP. Here, users would get access to music with no DRM restrictions and would be able to exchange downloaded files. An early offering of this sort was Turkish ISP's popular TTNET, which allowed its broadband subscribers to download 10 tracks per month. If they upgraded to the unlimited service option, they could download 500 DRM-protected tracks per month, copy them three times to other devices such as an iPod, and keep the tracks if they end their subscription.

Danish telecom company TDC implemented a similar plan with TDC's PLAY, a free, unlimited download service available to existing mobile, online, and cable subscribers. All licensing fees are paid to rights holders by TDC PLAY, which carries a catalogue of over 1 million tracks.

Worldwide Piracy

Markets in China, India, and Russia have boomed over the past decade, though the worldwide recession beginning in 2008 slowed their growth. China has continued to provide more capitalistic opportunities after a long period of centralized state control, and despite widespread piracy, the major record companies have pursued joint-venture labels with Chinese partners. The same is true of India and Russia,

Google launches an ad-supported legal music search site in China, 2009.

Photo by ChinaFotoPress/Getty Images.

where many in growing middle classes take pride in buying legitimate products or patronizing legal download Web sites.

The market in counterfeit and pirated copies of foreign as well as local recordings is still a major barrier to sales growth throughout much of the world. A 2009 report from the International Intellectual Property Association (a U.S.-based lobbying coalition of American copyright-based industry groups) detailed some $1.97 billion in estimated losses to U.S. companies from piracy of music. The piracy problem remains particularly acute in Africa where meager disposable incomes and political instability in many countries have hampered the development of a legitimate music industry. The situation is somewhat better in Latin America. In Europe, as in North America, music piracy skyrocketed due to the ease of unauthorized file sharing via P2P networks and the copying of CDs onto blank CD-Rs.

Breaking Artists

The size of the U.S. music market has made it a prime target for foreign pop and rock acts ever since the Beatles led the "British Invasion" of the 1960s. Although overseas artists account for a small portion of U.S. soundcarrier sales, this dollar value is greater than sales in most other markets around the world. However, only a small percentage of successful acts from abroad achieve success in the U.S.—due partly to differences in national musical tastes and partly to the different methods of marketing and promotion in North America as compared with Europe or Australia. Foreign artists are therefore highly dependent on the local knowledge of their U.S. labels and promoters; it follows that independent labels in Europe and elsewhere prefer to work with partners familiar with the U.S. industry. (Graduates of music business programs in the U.S. might find it useful to seek employment abroad in this capacity.)

On the other hand, U.S. artists who can't get signed domestically frequently seek deals in other countries or territories. Both recording artists and songwriters sometimes break through in a territory like France, and then either make their careers there or eventually also do well in the U.S.

Live Performance. Revenues from international performances and tours have remained strong even as sales of recorded music stagnate. A study by UK society PRS for Music revealed that in 2008, for the first time in memory, live music in the UK generated more revenue ($1.79 billion) than the record business ($1.74 billion). Big acts sell out regularly and command higher ticket prices, while mid-level artists and their managers have had to become more creative in promoting their live appearances.

For American artists, managers, booking agents, and record labels, international tours are a crucial way to provide exposure to a worldwide audience while capitalizing on one of the few growth areas of the business. Labels entering into 360 deals with their artists (see Chapter 8) have a particular incentive to pursue lucrative foreign as well as domestic live performances. (U.S. artists frequently engage different booking agents in various foreign territories, rather than using their domestic agents.)

Just as the major world record companies sought to expand their cross-border control in the 20th century, the rise of global promoters for live events promises to be an important force for consolidation in the coming era. More and more domestic and foreign companies are seeking to combine concert promotion with business functions such as artist management, booking shows, and brokering sponsorship deals.

The Beatles are commemorated by replicas of their equipment cases in front of the Liverpool Institute for the Performing Arts. Seated are David Leonard, President, Trebas; and David Price, Director of Learning, LIPA. Standing right is George Hood, Director, Trebas.

Photo courtesy of Trebas Institute.

Conferences and Contests

A number of regularly held international conferences and contests provide attendees with the opportunity to make deals, share information, hear some live music, network, and get tips on how to "break" artists in the international market.

Billboard, the world's leading music industry trade magazine whose subscribers and visitors to billboard.com span the globe, holds several conferences each year that focus at least in part on international developments. Subjects include Latin American music, touring, and mobile entertainment.

MIDEM, held annually in Cannes, is the leading worldwide music publisher's convention, attended by publishers, lawyers, and artists from all over the world. Independent publishers and subpublishers dominate the activities at MIDEM, making deals to buy or administer catalogues in various territories.

Another leading conference is hosted every other year by The Institute of Popular Music (IPM). The IASPM conference, held in Liverpool, focuses more on the history of pop music, but business-related activities are also a major theme.

There are also myriad song competitions, including the Eurovision and Intervision Song Contests, in which both unknowns and successful writers can break through to international exposure.

Phil Hardy was the founding editor of MUSIC & COPYRIGHT. He is now the editor and publisher of THEVIEWFROMTHEBOUNDARY.COM, the online newsletter about the international music industry, which is published from Norfolk, UK.

Chapter Takeaways

- Over the last half-century the non-U.S. share of the global business has risen, presenting business opportunities to both local players and the multinational majors.

- Global digital music sales (downloads, streams, subscriptions) accounted for about one-fifth of recorded music sales in 2008.

- Piracy and counterfeiting of recorded music remain a serious problem in many world territories, stunting legal commerce.

- In a dual "carrot and stick" approach, ISPs are being urged to battle infringers who are their customers, as well as offer legitimate music subscriptions.

- In some countries, ticket sales to live performances now rival record sales.

Key Terms

- Access to Music Charge (AMC) (p. 497)

- Cannes Accord (p. 493)

- MIDEM (p. 499)

- neighboring rights (p. 494)

- soundcarrier (p. 492)

CHAPTER 30

International Copyright

Phil Hardy

Issues of copyright protection and enforcement are complicated on the world stage as each country or regional authority has its own laws and policing methods. In an effort to forge cooperation among nations so that rights holders can be compensated, a number of major international copyright agreements have been reached and modified over the decades.

International copyright agreements fall into two categories. First, there is a series of *copyright conventions* whose membership is open to all nations willing to accept their terms. The conventions (or treaties) are administered by U.N. organizations, principally the World Intellectual Property Organization (WIPO). Second, there are also *bilateral or multilateral agreements* on levels of copyright protection between trading partners in different countries or groups of countries.

> *"Music can change the world because it can change people."*
>
> —Bono

Copyright Conventions

Copyright owners are affected by six important international conventions. Three (the Berne Convention, the International Copyright Convention, and the WIPO Copyright Convention) concern the rights of authors and composers, and the other three (the Geneva or Phonograms Convention, the Rome Convention, and the WIPO

Left: World Intellectual Property Organization, Switzerland.

Photo by Fancois Lachon/Time & Life Pictures/Getty Images.

Performances and Phonogram Treaty) deal with the interests of neighboring rights owners such as performers, record producers, and broadcasters. The United States is also a member of the Buenos Aires Convention, a regional agreement.

Berne Convention

The Berne Convention for the Protection of Literary and Artistic Works was signed in 1886 and has been amended six times since. The amendments have endeavored to enable authors' rights to keep pace with new uses of their works brought about by technological change. The Berlin revision of 1908 incorporated references to photography, cinema film, and sound recording. The Rome Act of 1928 extended authors' control of their work to sound broadcasting, and television was brought within the scope of the convention at Brussels in 1948.

The concept of an author's **moral rights** was first included in 1928. Later revisions in Stockholm (1967) and Paris (1971) concentrated on issues such as the *compulsory licensing* of films. The most recent addition to Berne is the WIPO Copyright Treaty of 1996, which provides for copyright protection in relation to the Internet and other digital platforms (see below).

Nine countries signed the original Berne document, seven of them European. Today there are more than 150 signatories. There are significant limits to the protection a Berne signatory can provide for works of citizens of other Berne states, and nations have to rely on their own national laws for further protection.

A number of Berne's provisions are optional—for example, the granting of moral rights (such as the right of an author to be properly identified and to insist that any editing of a work preserves its integrity). When the United States finally joined the Convention in 1989, pressure from the film industry ensured that it did not accede to the moral rights part of the treaty.

Reciprocal Treatment. The purpose of the Berne Convention is for each country to provide protection for foreign authors within its own copyright laws, and these rights can be adopted into national law in two distinct ways. *National treatment* for foreign authors means that these copyright owners will receive the same level of protection as domestic authors. But a Berne Convention member can also decide to grant *reciprocal treatment,* in which case foreign authors will get only the level of protection granted in their own country. The most prominent example of reciprocal treatment for authors concerns the private copying or home-taping levies that exist in a number of European countries. The only foreign composers entitled to share in the distribution of these levies are those from countries that also have a private copying levy in place—thus excluding U.S. authors.

Broadcasting Rights Options. Another "opt-out" written into the Berne Convention's broadcasting clause permits the general rights of authors granted by the convention to include the power to "authorize or prohibit" the use of their work. By the late 1920s, the radio industry had itself become a powerful force in Europe, and music was one of its most important sources of program material.

When the issue of broadcasting rights for composers was considered by the Berne Convention nations, a strong lobby favored substituting a compulsory license for the prohibition right. Under this system, the copyright owner is compelled to allow works to be used, subject to appropriate payment from the user. Rather than codifying this, the Berne Convention signatories provided that each national government could make its own decision. The compulsory license procedure ensured a constant supply of music for radio, even when there was a dispute over royalty payments. What constitutes "equitable remuneration" is determined in most countries by a government-appointed tribunal or special court.

Film Authorship. The definition of *authorship* itself came into question in 1928 when the nature of cinematographic works was under discussion. Prior to this, the Berne Convention had accepted that an author of a book, play, or song was a single individual or a partnership of named individuals. But the collaborative nature of filmmaking made it more difficult to determine an individual author; it was decided that definition of film author(s) should be decided by each member of the convention.

Buenos Aires Convention

As noted above, the Berne Convention at its outset comprised a majority of European countries. Subsequent to its adoption, various countries in both North and South America, including the U.S., came together to fashion a similar agreement, the Buenos Aires Convention of 1910. Under this convention, compliance with the copyright law of the country of first publication qualifies the work for protection in the other member countries. Each work must also carry a notice indicating that the property rights in the work are reserved, which is generally satisfied with the inclusion of the words "all rights reserved" in the copyright notice.

Universal Copyright Convention

Although the Buenos Aires Convention governs U.S. copyright relations with most American nations, it is unlikely to attract additional members because of adoption of the Universal Copyright Convention (UCC) of 1955, of which the United States was a founding member.

Because the sponsor of the UCC, the United Nations, wished to attract a maximum number of participants, the exclusive rights granted under this convention are held to a minimum level of "adequate and effective protection." According to the UCC, such protection includes "basic rights ensuring the author's economic interests, including the exclusive right to authorize reproduction by any means, public performance and broadcasting." Formal notification of copyright protections should be indicated by having all relevant copies bear the copyright symbol (©), the name of the copyright proprietor, and the year of first publication.

One goal of the UCC was to avoid competition with other prevailing agreements, particularly Berne and Buenos Aires. Where provisions differ, the UCC provides that "the most recently formulated convention" shall prevail.

Rome Convention

The 1961 Rome Convention for the Protection of Performers, Producers of Phonograms, and Broadcasting Organizations put record companies and performers on the international map as rights *owners* as opposed to merely rights *users*.

The Rome Convention confirmed the rights of both performers of music and record companies to control the reproduction and public performance of their work. It set a minimum period of copyright protection at 20 years. Today, most national laws protect sound recordings for 50 years, a figure included in the 1996 Performances and Phonograms Treaty agreed to by a committee of WIPO (see below).

Broadcasting Rights. The Rome Convention followed Berne and provided for a compulsory broadcasting license. Both the compulsory license and the 20-year minimum represented concessions to broadcasters who wished to see recordings fall into the **public domain** and become free of copyright royalties as quickly as possible.

Signatories to the Rome Convention could also opt out of granting broadcasting rights to producers and performers. Monaco and Luxembourg both exercised this option, and partly as a result they now have powerful music radio stations broadcasting to neighboring countries. The Rome Convention left it to each nation to determine how broadcasting royalties should be shared between record producers and performers.

The relationship between "contracting" and "noncontracting" states is complex when it comes to broadcasting royalties. As with Berne, Rome provides a fundamental national treatment for performers, producers, and broadcasters of other contracting states.

Rights owners from noncontracting states may also share in royalties if the recording in question received "simultaneous publication" in the contracting state. *Simultaneous* is defined here as within 30 days of the recording's release in its country of origin. Any contracting country may, however, drop the criterion of "publication" of a recording and replace it with one of *first fixation,* which refers to the location of the studio where the recording was created.

At the time of this writing, the United States was not a signatory to the Rome Convention.

Adopting the criterion of first fixation, as several European countries have done, means that performers and producers of U.S. recordings cannot benefit from airplay of their works in those countries—although under the Berne Convention, royalties must be paid to U.S. songwriters.

Geneva Phonograms Convention

The Rome Convention provided broad protection against copyright infringement, but it was drafted at a time when the piracy of sound recordings was still a relatively minor occurrence. With the arrival of the compact tape cassette in 1963, however, music piracy became big business. By the end of the 1960s piracy and counterfeiting of prerecorded cassettes were becoming endemic, and the music industry, along with some national governments, saw the need for a new international treaty specifically designed to deal with piracy.

The result was the 1971 Convention for the Protection of Producers of Phonograms Against Unauthorized Duplication of Their Phonograms, known as the Phonograms Convention. This treaty added new import and distribution rights to those in the Rome Convention. Record producers could now stop illegal imports and take action against wholesalers and retailers as well as those who manufactured illegal copies.

WIPO Copyright Treaty and Performances and Phonograms Treaty

In 1996, two new international treaties were established to update the Berne and Rome Conventions, principally regarding the use of music on the Internet. The WIPO Copyright Treaty (WCT), which has the status of a "special agreement" under the Berne Convention, provides additional protection for authors when their works are used on the Internet and via other digital services, including downloads and streaming.

The WIPO Performances and Phonograms Treaty (WPPT) extended similar protection for neighboring rights owners in relation to the Internet and other digital platforms. The new author's right with respect to downloads and streaming is paralleled by a similar right for performers and record companies.

Other elements of the 1996 treaties include the outlawing of devices designed to circumvent electronic protection systems linked to digital recordings, stronger protection against illegal copying, and confirmation that Berne Convention and Rome Convention provisions on the reproduction of works or recordings apply to the digital domain.

Multilateral and Bilateral Agreements

The economic importance of the music business and other copyright-based industries has caused the inclusion of copyright protection in many trade agreements between nations. The most far-reaching to date is TRIPS (Trade Related Aspects of Intellectual Property Rights, Including Trade in Counterfeit Goods), which was accepted by more than 120 countries at the conclusion of the Uruguay Round of the General Agreement on Tariffs and Trade (GATT) in 1993. First negotiated in 1948, GATT is an international treaty designed to promote and enforce free trade worldwide. GATT is renegotiated about every 10 years; the 1986 changes incorporated trade in intellectual property for the first time.

Many of the TRIPS treaty's provisions echoed the Berne and Rome Conventions in providing fundamental rights for authors, performers, and producers. The treaty makes allowances for developing countries, permitting them to phase in the TRIPS provisions over 5 or 10 years. The treaty has helped Western copyright owners by further opening up Third World markets.

Other multilateral copyright treaties have grown out of free trade issues. Here, the principle is that each country that is a member of a free trade area or "single market" must apply the same standards of copyright protection as its fellow members. The North American Free Trade Agreement (NAFTA) and the European Union are the most important of these accords. Implemented in 1994, NAFTA's intent is to end trade barriers among its members, Mexico, the United States, and Canada. Under NAFTA, the three countries give reciprocal treatment to each other's copyright owners. (But NAFTA hasn't stopped Canada from legally favoring its own musicians, as explained in Chapter 28.)

The EU program, dating from the late 1980s, includes a provision to **harmonize** the copyright laws of its member countries and other countries associated with the European Union. A number of directives were issued to all members, and those affecting the music industry centered on rental, private copying, the trans-border aspects of cable and satellite broadcasting, the equalization of the duration of copyright protection at 70 years for authors and 50 years from publication for neighboring rights owners, and the enforcement of intellectual property rights.

Bilateral Treaties

Copyright protection has also been enhanced via bilateral treaties. The United States has made the greatest use of this strategy through the 1988 Omnibus Trade and Competitiveness Act. This permits the United States Trade Representative (USTR) to nominate "Priority Foreign Countries" whose trading practices are alleged to be harmful to U.S. industries that are dependent on the protection of intellectual property, such as the music industry. Once designated, nations may be subject to trade sanctions if they fail to implement fair commercial and trading rules.

Two Chinese policemen walk past a street stall selling pirated movie DVDs and music CDs in Shanghai.

Photo by MARK RALSTON/AFP/Getty Images.

In 1989 the USTR set up a Watch List and a Priority Watch List of countries perceived as unfair trading partners of the United States. Two years later, Thailand, China, and India were the first to become Priority Foreign Countries for their failure to protect U.S. copyright material adequately. China and India eventually agreed to ease restrictions on the operations of foreign companies. Since then, the Priority Foreign Countries list has included a number of countries.

Table 30.1 lists foreign affiliates of the Harry Fox Agency (HFA), which aids clients with licensing, collection, and distribution of music. As explained in Chapter 4, HFA grants licensees the rights to reproduce and distribute copyrighted musical compositions (songs), including uses on CDs, records, tapes, and certain digital configurations.

Intergovernmental Bodies and International Industry Organizations

World Intellectual Property Organization

The World Intellectual Property Organization (WIPO) is an organ of the United Nations, with headquarters in Geneva, Switzerland. WIPO is charged with administering the Berne and Rome Conventions as well as other conventions dealing with non-music-related items. WIPO's meetings facilitate discussions about updating or redrafting of copyright conventions in response to technological developments.

Table 30.1 Foreign Affiliates of the Harry Fox Agency, Inc.

Society/Agency	Territories of Control
ACUM Authors, Composers and Music Publishers Assoc.	Israel
AEPI Hellenic Society for the Protection of Intellectual Property S.A.	Greece
AMCOS Australasian Mechanical Copyright Owners Society, Ltd.	Australia, Fiji, New Zealand, Pacific Island Territories, Papua New Guinea
ARTISJUS Magyar Szerzoi Jogvedo Iroda Egyesulet	Hungary
AUSTRO-MECHANA[a]	Austria
CASH The Composers and Authors Society of Hong Kong, Ltd.	Hong Kong, Macau
COMPASS Composers and Authors Society of Singapore, Ltd.	Republic of Singapore
COSCAP Copyright Society of Composers, Authors and Publishers, Inc.	Barbados
COTT Copyright Organisation of Trinidad and Tobago	Trinidad and Tobago
FILSCAP Filipino Society of Composers, Authors and Publishers, Inc.	Republic of the Philippines
GEMA Gesellschaft Fuer Musikalische Auffuehrungs Und Mechanische Vervielfaeltigungsrechte	Bulgaria, Germany, Poland, Romania, Turkey
HDS Croatian Composers' Society	Croatia
ICS International Copyright Services, Inc.	Republic of Liberia
JASCAP Jamaican Association of Composers, Authors, and Publishers, Ltd.	Jamaica
JASRAC Japanese Society for Rights of Authors, Composers and Publishers	Japan
KCI Yayasan Karya Cipta Indonesia	Republic of Indonesia
KOMCA Korea Music Copyright Association	Republic of Korea
MACP Music Authors' Copyright Protection Berhad	Malaysia

(Continued)

Table 30.1 (Continued)

Society/Agency	Territories of Control
MCPS/The Music Alliance Mechanical Copyright Protection Society	Bahamas, Bermuda, British Virgin Islands, India, Ireland (Eire), Kenya, Nigeria, Uganda, United Kingdom, Northern Ireland, Zimbabwe
MCSC Music Copyright Society of China	People's Republic of China
MESAM Turkiye Musiki Eseri Sahipleri Meslek Birlige	Turkey
NCB Nordisk Copyright Bureau	Denmark, Estonia, Finland, Iceland, Latvia, Lithuania, Norway, Sweden
OSA Ochranny Svaz Autorsky	Czech Republic
RAO Russia Authors' Society	Russia
SABAM Société Belge des Auteurs, Compositeurs et Editeurs	Belgium
SADAIC La Sociedad Argentina de Autores & Compositores de Musica	Argentina
SAMRO Southern Africa Music Rights Organisation	South Africa
SDRM/SACEM Société pour l'Administration du Droit de Reproduction Mécanique des Auteurs, Compositeurs et Editeurs de Musique	Andorra, Luxembourg, Monaco, Republic of France, Algeria, Benin, Burkina Faso, Cameroon, Central African Republic, Chad, Congo, Cote d'Ivoire, Djibouti, Egypt, Gabon, Gambia, Guinea, Lebanon, Madagascar, Mali, Mauritania, Morocco, Niger, Senegal, Togo, Tunisia, Zaire
SGAE Sociedad General de Autores de Espana	Spain
SIAE Societa Italiana degli Autori ed Editori	Italy, San Marino, Vatican City
SOZA Slovensky Ochranny Zvaz Autorsky	Slovak Republic
SPA Sociedade Portuguesa de Autores	Azores, Madeira, Portugal
STEMRA	Aruba, Dutch Antilles, Irian Barat, Netherlands, Surinam
SUISA Schweizerische Gesellschaft fuer die Rechte der Urheber Musikalischer Werke	Liechtenstein, Switzerland

(Continued)

Table 30.1 (Continued)

Society/Agency	Territories of Control
In addition to its relations with the foreign affiliates listed above, the Harry Fox Agency (HFA) also coordinates representation in certain foreign territories through its wholly owned subsidiary, the Fox Agency International, Inc., as follows:	
Fox Agency International	Hong Kong
	Indonesia
	Malaysia
	The Philippines
	People's Republic of China
	Singapore
	South Korea
	Taiwan
	Thailand

Source: The Harry Fox Agency, 2009
a. Although the Austro-Mechana repertoire is represented in the United States by HFA, the HFA repertoire is represented in Austria by GEMA.

World Trade Organization

The World Trade Organization (WTO) is tasked with implementing and policing the GATT and TRIPS agreements. The similarity between the TRIPS agreement on enforcement and that proposed by WIPO demonstrates the convergence of the international trade organization and the international copyright bodies.

In relation to the TRIPS agreement, the WTO must ensure that developing countries upgrade their copyright laws to TRIPS standards within certain time limits. The WTO is also responsible for resolving bilateral disputes or complaints concerning noncompliance. The United States was adjudged to be guilty in the first copyright dispute dealt with by the WTO. The European Union, supported by several developing countries, was concerned about a provision in U.S. copyright law included in the 1998 Fairness in Music Licensing Act that exempted bars, restaurants, and stores from paying to use copyrighted music when the music was sourced from radio or television programs. In 2001, a WTO disputes panel agreed with the European Union that this was a breach of the obligations of the United States as a Berne Convention member. The panel ordered the payment of compensation by the U.S. government, and, with Congressional approval, payment was made.

International Confederation of Societies of Authors and Composers

The International Confederation of Societies of Authors and Composers (CISAC) groups together organizations from more than 60 countries. CISAC has a small secretariat based in Paris, and an executive board composed of representatives from many affiliated societies runs the confederation. In addition to convening a world congress every two years, CISAC's main role is to encourage cooperation between its members and to help form new authors' societies, particularly in developing countries and in the former communist nations.

The key issues for CISAC include evolving a common policy for protecting copyright in the face of advancing technologies and the harmonizing of documentation so musical works can be more easily identified worldwide and payments can thus be allocated more efficiently.

To help new societies, CISAC maintains a regional office in Singapore that in recent years has worked closely with composers in Vietnam, Indonesia, and the People's Republic of China. There is also a "twinning" process whereby established authors' societies advise and train officials of new organizations.

The American Society of Composers, Authors and Publishers (ASCAP) and Broadcast Music Inc. (BMI), America's leading performance rights organizations, work with CISAC on issues of international significance and contribute to each others' events and conferences. Both PROs traditionally have seats on CISAC's Board.

Bureau International des Sociétés Gérant les Droits d'Enregistrement et de Reproduction Mécanique

Founded in 1929, the Bureau International des Sociétés Gérant les Droits d'Enregistrement et de Reproduction Mécanique (BIEM) also represents the interests of composers and music publishers. In regular negotiations with IFPI (International Federation of the Phonographic Industry, the global recording industry body; see below), BIEM sets the standard mechanical royalty rate for most of Europe and Latin America; the BIEM-IFPI rate does not apply in the United States, Canada, Australia, or the United Kingdom.

At the time of this writing, the BIEM-IFPI contract stipulated a standard rate of 9.1% of the "published price to dealers" of all disc and tape formats. The standard figure is subject to only slight variations at national levels, based on local agreements about packaging deductions, including television-advertised albums, the number of tracks on an album, and other factors.

International Federation of the Phonographic Industry

The need to find a common position in relation to BIEM was the major motivation for the 1933 formation of the International Federation of the Phonographic Industry (IFPI), an international organization representing record companies. The federation endeavors to defend in the international domain the interests of its members by preserving their existing rights, statutory or otherwise. IFPI works to safeguard the welfare of its members via representation as a federated body in negotiations with and representations to governments and other interested parties. Over the years, IFPI has become one of the most skilled lobbyists for copyright reform at the international level. It has NGO (nongovernmental organization) status with the International Labor Organization (ILO), UNESCO, and WIPO. IFPI has also established itself as a consultative body with the European Commission.

IFPI has more than 1,500 member companies in 76 countries. In almost 50 countries, there is a trade organization that constitutes an IFPI National Group. The Recording Industry Association of America (RIAA) is the U.S. affiliate of IFPI.

The policy-making arm of IFPI comprises four regional boards in Europe, the Pacific Rim, Latin America, and the Confederation of Independent States (the former Soviet Union). Each board has representatives from the major international record companies as well as leading independent labels. The IFPI Secretariat, based in London, provides the industry's official statistics for soundcarrier sales as well as for global piracy. It also coordinates lobbying for copyright reform and provides logistical support for negotiations on mechanical royalties with BIEM.

International Federation of Musicians and International Federation of Actors

The two international unions of performers, the International Federation of Musicians (FIM) and the International Federation of Actors (FIA), also have NGO status with WIPO and with the ILO, another U.N. body. The American Federation of Musicians (AFM) is a member of FIM; Actors' Equity is a member of FIA.

The principal impact of FIM and FIA on the world music business is through their long-standing agreement with IFPI on the distribution of broadcasting royalties between neighboring rights owners. Under this agreement, the two parties agree to divide equally any broadcasting royalties collected on their joint behalf. In most European countries as well as in Japan, there is a single collecting society for performers and producers.

Chapter Takeaways

- A series of international conventions (treaties) governs copyright. Conventions concerning the rights of authors and composers include the Berne Convention, the International Copyright Convention, and the WIPO Copyright Convention.

- Other treaties, focused on issues related to labels, artists, broadcasters, and

piracy, include the Geneva or Phonograms Convention, the Rome Convention, and the WIPO Performances and Phonogram Treaty.

- Reciprocal treatment provisions of the Berne Convention block U.S. songwriters from receiving a share of foreign levies on blank media.

Key Terms

- BIEM   (p. 512)

- copyright conventions   (p. 503)

- CISAC   (p. 511)

- first fixation   (p. 506)

- harmonize   (p. 507)

- moral rights   (p. 504)

- public domain   (p. 505)

- reciprocal treatment   (p. 504)

- WCT   (p. 506)

- WIPO   (p. 508)

- WPPT   (p. 506)

- WTO   (p. 511)

Appendix A

Membership and Copyright Forms

Membership and copyright forms can be downloaded from the Internet at the following Web sites.

ASCAP

At the American Society of Composers, Authors and Publishers (ASCAP) Web site, you can download the ASCAP Writer Application, the ASCAP Publisher Application, and the membership agreement form, which appears at the end of both the Writer Application form and the Publisher application form. At the ASCAP home page (www.ascap.com), click on the Join ASCAP link, or go directly to that page using this URL: www.ascap.com/about/howjoin.asp.

BMI

Go to the Broadcast Music Inc. (BMI) Web site (www.bmi.com) and click on the "join" link to determine if you are eligible to join BMI as a publisher or writer/composer. To join online, you must meet several requirements: (a) Technical requirements have to do with your computer operating system, ability to read pdf files, and ability to print the application. (b) Professional requirements include having your work commercially recorded and released or having written/co-written or composed a song that is likely to be performed on radio, TV, the Internet, and the like. (c) Legal requirements have to do with age and affiliation or past affiliation with a performing rights organization.

Copyright Forms

Paper copies of the U.S. Copyright Forms PA (for a work of the performing arts) and SR (for a sound recording) are being phased out. To file an electronic application through the Copyright Office online system, go to www.copyright.gov/eco. There you will find links to eCO Tips, eCO FAQ, and the eCO Tutorial. Alternatively, to register basic claims use the new fill-in Form CO, which replaces Forms PA and SR. The form, along with Tips, FAQs, and a Tutorial, can be found at www.copyright.gov/forms

Patent and Trademark Forms

All information and forms relating to patents and trademarks can be accessed at www.uspto.gov/ebc/indexebc.html

Appendix B

Selected Readings

Books

2007 NAMM Global Report, Music USA. Carlsbad, CA: NAMM, 2007.

Anderson, Chris. *The Long Tail: Why the Future of Business Is Selling Less of More.* New York: Hyperion, 2006.

Barrow, T. *Inside the Music Business.* New York: Chapman & Hall, 1995.

Billboard Staff. *Billboard International Buyers Guide 2008.* Garner, Bryan A., ed. New York: Nielsen Company, 2008. [Annual]

Black, Henry C., et al. *Black's Law Dictionary.* 8th ed. St. Paul, MN: West, 2004.

Blume, Jason. *Six Steps to Songwriting Success.* Rev. ed. Watson-Guptill, 2008.

Bolles, Richard Nelson. *What Color Is Your Parachute? A Practical Manual for Job-Hunters & Career Changers.* Rev. and updated. Berkeley, CA: Ten Speed, 2008.

Brabec, Jeffrey, and Brabec, Todd. *Music, Money, and Success: The Insider's Guide to the Music Industry.* 6th ed., updated and expanded. New York: Schirmer, 2008.

Christensen, Clayton M. *The Innovator's Dilemma.* New York: HarperCollins, 2003.

Counseling Clients in the Entertainment Industry 2005. New York: Practising Law Institute, 2004. [Annual]

Dannen, Fredric. *Hit Men: Power Brokers & Fast Money Inside the Music Business.* New York: Random House, 1991.

Denisoff, R. Serge. *Inside MTV.* New Brunswick, NJ: Transaction, 1990.

Eargle, John M. *Handbook of Recording Engineering.* 4th ed. Boston: Kluwer Academic, 2005.

Eargle, John M. *Music, Sound and Technology.* 2nd ed. New York: Van Nostrand Reinhold, 1995.

Elias, Stephen, and Levinkind, Susan. *Legal Research: How to Find & Understand the Law.* 12th ed. Berkeley, CA: Nolo, 2007.

Eliot, Marc. *Rockonomics: The Money Behind the Music.* Secaucus, NJ: Carol Publishing Group, 1993.

Entertainment Law Institute. [Various titles and authors]. Los Angeles: University of Southern California. [Annual]

Fair, Ron, and Perry, Megan. *How To Be a Record Producer in the Digital Era.* Watson-Guptill, 2008.

Faulkner, Robert R. *Hollywood Studio Musicians: Their Work and Careers in the Recording Industry.* Lanham, MD: University Press of America, 2002.

Faulkner, Robert R. *Music on Demand: Composers and Careers in the Hollywood Film Industry.* New Brunswick, NJ: Transaction, 2003.

Feist, Leonard. *Popular Music Publishing in America.* New York: National Music Publishers Association, 1980.

Fink, Michael. *Inside the Music Industry: Creativity, Process, and Business.* 2nd ed. New York: Schirmer, 1996.

Frascogna, Xavier M., and Hetherington, H. Lee. *Successful Artist Management.* Enl. rev. ed. New York: Watson-Guptill, 1990.

Friedman Group Staff. *No Thanks, I'm Just Looking: Professional Retail Sales Techniques for Turning Shoppers Into Buyers.* Reprint ed. Dubuque, IA: Kendall/Hunt, 2002.

Gaar, Gillian G. *She's a Rebel: The History of Women in Rock & Roll.* Preface by Yoko Ono. Exp. 2nd ed. Seattle, WA: Seal, 2002.

Gallagher, Mitch, and Mandell, Jim. *The Studio Business Book.* Jewett, Andy, ed. 3rd rev. ed. Milwaukee, WI: Hal Leonard, 2006.

Goldstein, Jeri. *How to Be Your Own Booking Agent: The Musician's & Performing Artist's Guide to a Successful Touring Career.* Estrin, Kari, ed. 3rd rev. ed. Palmyra, VA: New Music Times, 2008.

Halloran, Mark, ed. and comp. *The Musician's Business and Legal Guide.* 4th rev. ed. Paramus, NJ: Prentice Hall, 2007.

Karlin, Fred. *Listening to Movies: The Film Lover's Guide to Film Music.* New York: Schirmer, 2000.

Karlin, Fred, and Wright, Rayburn. *On the Track: A Guide to Contemporary Film Scoring.* 2nd ed. New York: Routledge, 2004.

Karmen, Steve. *Through the Jingle Jungle.* New York: Billboard Books, 1989.

Knopper, Steve. *Appetite for Self-Destruction.* New York: Free Press, 2009.

Kohn, Al, and Kohn, Bob. *Kohn on Music Licensing.* 3rd ed. New York: Aspen Law & Business, 2002. [Also periodic supplements]

Koontz, Harold D., and Weihrich, Heinz. *Essentials of Management.* 6th ed. New York: McGraw-Hill, 2004.

Krasilovsky, M. William, and Shemel, Sidney. *This Business of Music.* 10th ed. New York: Watson-Guptill, 2007.

Lathrop, Tad. *This Business of Music Marketing and Promotion.* 2nd ed. New York: Billboard Books, 2003.

Leikin, Molly Ann. *How to Be a Hit Songwriter: Polishing and Marketing Your Lyrics and Music* (3rd ed.). Milwaukee, WI: Hal Leonard, 2003.

Lindey, Alexander, and Landau, Michael. *Lindey on Entertainment, Publishing and the Arts: Agreement and the Law.* 3rd ed. St. Paul, MN: Thomson/West, 2004.

Marcone, Stephen. *Managing Your Band: Artist Management: The Ultimate Responsibility.* 4th ed. Wayne, NJ: HiMarks, 2006.

Marich, Robert. *Marketing to Moviegoers: A Handbook of Strategies and Tactics.* 2nd ed. Carbondale, IL: Southern Illinois University Press, 2009.

Martin, George, and Hornsby, Jeremy. *All You Need Is Ears: The Inside Personal Story of the Genius Who Created the Beatles.* New York: St. Martin's, 1994.

McPherson, Brian. *Get It in Writing.* Milwaukee, WI: Hal Leonard, 1999.

Musical America International Directory of the Performing Arts, 2009. New York: Musical America Publications. [Annual]

Nimmer, Melville B. *Nimmer on Copyright.* 11 vols. New York: Matthew Bender, 1997.

Passman, Donald S. *All You Need to Know About the Music Business.* 6th ed. New York: Free Press, 2008.

Perreault, William D. Jr., McCarthy, E. Jerome, and Perreault, William D. *Basic Marketing: A Global Managerial Approach.* 17th ed. New York: McGraw Hill, 2009.

Pettigrew, Jim, Jr. *The Billboard Guide to Music Publicity.* New York: Watson-Guptill, 1997.

Pleasants, Henry. *Serious Music—And All That Jazz.* New York: Simon & Schuster, 1969.

Rachlin, Harvey. *The TV and Movie Business: An Encyclopedia of Careers, Technologies, and Practices.* New York: Crown, 1991.

Rapaport, Diane S. *How to Make and Sell Your Own Recording: The Complete Guide to Independent Recording.* 5th ed. Paramus, NJ: Prentice Hall, 1999.

Raugust, Karen. *The Licensing Business Handbook.* 7th rev. ed. New York: EPM Communications, 2008.

Sanjek, Russell, and Sanjek, David. *Pennies From Heaven: The American Popular Music Business in the Twentieth Century.* New York: Da Capo, 1996.

Schladweiler, Kief, ed. *Foundation Fundamentals: A Guide for Grantseekers.* 7th ed. New York: Foundation Center, 2004.

Scott, Michael D. *Multimedia: Law & Practice*. Englewood Cliffs, NJ: Prentice Hall Law & Business, 1993.

Shapiro, Carl, and Varian, Hal. *Information Rules: A Strategic Guide to the Network Economy*. Harvard Business School Press, 1999.

Siegel, Alan H. *Breaking Into the Music Business*. Rev. ed. New York: Simon & Schuster, 1990.

Simon, Deke, and Wiese, Michael. *Film & Video Budgets*. 4th ed. Studio City: Michael Wiese Productions, 2006.

So You Want to Open a Music Store. Rev. ed. Carlsbad, CA: NAMM, 2000.

Steinberg, Irwin, and Greenblatt, Harmon. *Understanding the Music Business: A Comprehensive View*. Needham Heights, MA: Simon & Schuster, 1998.

Stim, Richard. *Music Law: How to Run Your Band's Business*. 5th ed. Berkeley, CA: Nolo, 2006.

Suisman, David. *Selling Sounds*. Harvard University Press, 2009.

Voelz, Susan. *The Musician's Guide to the Road*. Watson-Guptill, 2007.

Vogel, Harold L. *Entertainment Industry Economics: A Guide for Financial Analysts*. 7th ed. New York: Cambridge University Press, 2007.

Volunteer Council of the League of American Orchestras. *The Gold Book: A Sourcebook of Successful Fund-Raising, Education, Ticket Sales, and Service Projects*. American Symphony Orchestra League. [Annual]

Wadhams, Wayne. *Dictionary of Music Production and Engineering Terminology*. New York: Schirmer, 1988.

Wadhams, Wayne. *Sound Advice: The Musician's Guide to the Record Industry*. New York: Schirmer, 1990.

Weissman, Dick. *Making a Living in Your Local Music Market: How to Survive and Prosper*. 3rd ed. Milwaukee, WI: Hal Leonard, 2006.

Whitsett, Tim. *The Dictionary of Music Business Terms*. Emeryville, CA: MixBooks, 1999.

Wilder, Alec. *American Popular Song: The Great Innovators, 1900–1950*. Reprint ed. New York: Oxford University Press, 1990.

Woram, John, and Kefauver, Alan P. *The New Recording Studio Handbook*. Rev. ed. New York: Elar, 1989.

Journals, Magazines, Newspapers, Newsletters

Advertising Age   Weekly trade publication covering agency, media and advertising, news and trends

Billboard   Professional international news weekly for members of music and video and home entertainment industries and related fields

Broadcast Engineering   Technical monthly covering digital television technology, systems, installation, management, and maintenance

Broadcasting & Cable   Weekly business publication for broadcast and cable TV

Campus Activities Programming Magazine   Trade magazine covering college campus programming for the student and professional

College Music Symposium   Interdisciplinary quarterly

Columbia Journal of Law & the Arts   Scholarly quarterly with articles concerning timely art law topics

Copyright Law Reporter   Monthly with articles about today's rules, new and proposed regulations, current case law activity, and views of the regulators

Country Music   Bimonthly consumer magazine covering country music artists and the recording industry

Daily Variety   Daily tabloid newspaper of the entertainment industry

DJ Times   Business monthly with the latest technology, trends, music, and business information for DJs

Down Beat   Monthly consumer magazine covering contemporary music and aimed at the seriously involved player and listener

Electronic Musician   Monthly business magazine covering electronics and computers in the creation and recording of music

Facilities   Monthly trade magazine for the public assembly industry

Film Score Monthly   Publication providing film music reviews and composer interviews

Hit Parader   Consumer monthly with news of the heavy metal music industry

Hollywood Reporter   Daily business news and reviews of all phases of the entertainment, theatrical, and new media fields

Instrumentalist   Monthly with practical, professional information for school band and orchestra directors

International Musician   Monthly journal for members of the American Federation of Musicians

Journal of the American Musicological Society   Scholarly articles on diversified branches of musicology, published three times a year

Journal of the Copyright Society of the U.S.A.   Quarterly dealing with domestic and foreign copyright laws, revisions, and court decisions

Journal of Music Therapy   Research-oriented quarterly for practitioners and others

Licensing Letter   Semimonthly tip sheet offering detailed industry sales data

Mix, the Recording Industry Magazine   Monthly business magazine focusing on contemporary music arts and audio and video music production

Modern Drummer   Monthly for the student, semipro, and pro drummer

Music & Copyright   Publication providing global reporting on the commercial aspects of the music industry, published semimonthly by Informa Telecoms & Media

Music & Sound Retailer   Monthly serving owners, managers, and sales personnel in retail musical instrument and sound product dealerships

Music Educators Journal   Quarterly dealing with all facets of study and teaching methods at all levels

Music Inc.   Business monthly providing newest trends in product merchandising, new products, industry news, and dealer and manufacturer profiles

Music Trades   Business monthly for music stores selling instruments, accessories, music, and electronic music and home equipment

Musical Merchandise Review   Monthly trade magazine and weekly eNewsletter for the musical instrument market

Notes   Quarterly journal covering developments in music librarianship and activities of the Music Library Association

Post   Monthly serving the field of TV, film, and video production and postproduction

Radio Business Report   Monthly publication covering business issues, inside news on people, and company controversies

Recording   Consumer monthly focusing on all aspects of home and small studio recording

Rolling Stone Magazine   Weekly coverage of American culture

Spin Magazine   Consumer monthly covering trendsetters in music world

Sound and Communications   Business monthly for sound contractors, engineers, consultants, and system managers

Sound & Vision   Monthly service magazine offering guidance to buyers of all types of audio equipment and the discs and tapes to be played with it

Soundtrack!   Quarterly magazine covering film music and other entertainment personalities

Symphony Magazine   Bimonthly publication with news and articles for symphony orchestra managers, trustees, volunteers, and musicians

Variety   Business weekly reporting on the entertainment industry worldwide

Wall Street Journal   Daily newspaper focusing on the business and investment communities

Appendix C

Professional Organizations

Academy of Country Music (ACM)
5500 Balboa Blvd., Ste. 200,
Encino, CA 91316
(818) 788-8000
Web site: www.acmcountry.com

Acoustical Society of America (ASA)
2 Huntington Quadrangle, Ste. 1N01,
Melville, NY 11747-4502
(516) 576-2360
Web site: http://asa.aip.org

Actors' Equity Association (AEA)
165 West 46th St., 15th Fl., New York,
NY 10036
(212) 869-8530
Web site: www.actorsequity.org

Alliance of Artists and Recording
Companies (AARC)
700 N. Fairfax St., Ste. 601, Alexandria,
VA 22314
(703) 535-8101
Web site: www.aarcroyalties.com

Alliance of Motion Picture and Television
Producers (AMPTP)
15501 Ventura Blvd., Sherman Oaks,
CA 91403
(818) 995-3600
Web site: www.amptp.org

American Choral Directors Association
(ACDA)
545 Couch Drive, Oklahoma City, OK
73102
(405) 232-8161
Web site: www.acda.org

American Composers Alliance (ACA)
648 Broadway, Rm. 803, New York,
NY 10012
(212) 925-0458
Web site: www.composers.com

American Federation of Labor and Congress
of Industrial Organizations (AFL-CIO)
815 16th St., NW, Washington, DC 20006
(202) 637-5000
Web site: www.aflcio.org

American Federation of Musicians of the
United States and Canada (AFM)
1501 Broadway, Ste. 600, New York,
NY 10036
(212) 869-1330
Web site: www.afm.org

American Federation of Television and
Radio Artists (AFTRA)
260 Madison Ave., New York,
NY 10016-2402
(212) 532-0800
5757 Wilshire Blvd., 9th Fl., Los
Angeles, CA 90036-3689
(323) 634-8100
Web site: www.aftra.com

American Guild of Musical Artists (AGMA)
1430 Broadway, 14th Fl., New York,
NY 10018
(212) 265-3687
Web site: www.musicalartists.org

American Guild of Organists
475 Riverside Dr., Ste. 1260, New York,
NY 10115
(212) 870-2310
Web site: www.agohq.org

American Guild of Variety Artists (AGVA)
184 5th Ave., 6th Fl., New York,
NY 10010
(212) 675-1003

American Mechanical Rights Agency, Inc.
(AMRA) (formerly American
Mechanical Rights Association)
149 S. Barrington Ave., Ste. 810, Los
Angeles, CA 90049
(310) 440-8778
Web site: www.amermechrights.com

American Music Center (AMC)
30 W. 26th St., Ste. 1001, New York,
NY 10010-2011
(212) 366-5260
Web site: www.amc.net

American Music Therapy Association, Inc.
(AMTA) (formerly American
Association for Music Therapy/National
Association for Music Therapy)
8455 Colesville Rd., Ste. 1000, Silver
Spring, MD 20910
(301) 589–3300
Web site: www.musictherapy.org

American Musicological Society (AMS)
6010 College Station, Brunswick,
ME 04011-8451
(203) 798-4243
Web site: www.ams-net.org

American Society of Composers, Authors
and Publishers (ASCAP)
1 Lincoln Plaza, New York, NY 10023
(212) 621-6000
Web site: www.ascap.com

American Theatre Wing
570 Seventh Ave., Ste. 501, New York,
NY 10018
(212) 765-0606
Web site: www.americantheatrewing
.org

American Women in Radio and Television
(AWRT)
The Emma L. Bowen Foundation for
Minority Interests in Media
1760 Old Meadow Rd., Ste. 500,
McLean, VA 22102
(703) 506-3290
Web site: www.awrt.org

Americans for the Arts (formerly American
Council for the Arts)
1000 Vermont Ave., NW, 6th Fl.,
Washington, DC 20005
(202) 371-2830
Web site: www.artsusa.org

Amusement and Music Operators
Association (AMOA)
33 W. Higgins Rd., Ste. 830, South
Barrington, IL 60010
(847) 428-7699
Web site: www.amoa.com

Archive of Contemporary Music
54 White St., New York, NY 10013
(212) 226-6967
Web site: www.arcmusic.org

Associated Actors and Artistes of
America (4As)
165 W. 46th St., Ste. 500, New York,
NY 10036-2501
(212) 869-0358

Association of Arts Administration
Educators (AAAE)
c/o Bolz Center for Arts
Administration
975 University Ave., Madison, WI 53706
Web site: www.artsadministration.org

Association of Independent Music
Publishers (AIMP)
5 W. 37th St., 6th Fl., New York,
NY 10018
(212) 391-2532
Web site: www.aimp.org

Association of Performing Arts Presenters
1211 Connecticut Ave., NW, Ste. 200,
Washington, DC 20036
(202) 833-2787
Web site: www.artspresenters.org

Audio Engineering Society, Inc. (AES)
60 E. 42nd St., Rm. 2520, New York, NY
10165-2520
(212) 661-8528
Web site: www.aes.org

Authors Guild (AG)
31 E. 32nd St., 7th Fl., New York,
NY 10016
(212) 563-5904
Web site: www.authorsguild.org

Authors League of America, Inc. (ALA)
330 W. 42nd St., 29th Fl., New York, NY
10036-6902
(212) 564-8350

Broadcast Music Inc. (BMI)
320 W. 57th St., New York, NY 10019-3790
(212) 586-2000
Web site: www.bmi.com

The Broadway League (formerly League of
American Theatres and Producers, Inc.)
226 W. 47th St., New York, NY 10036
(212) 764-1122
Web site: www.broadwayleague.com

Bureau international des sociétés gérant les
droits d'enregistrement et de
reproduction mécanique (BIEM)
20–26 Boulevard du Parc, 92200
Neuilly-sur-Seine, France
+(33) (1) 55 62 0840
Web site: www.biem.org

Business Committee for the Arts, Inc. (BCA)
29–27 Queens Plaza North, 4th Floor,
Long Island City, NY 11101
(718) 482-9900
Web site: www.bcainc.org

California Copyright Conference (CCC)
P.O. Box 57962, Sherman Oaks,
CA 91413
(818) 379-3312
Web site: www.theccc.org

Certification Board for Music Therapists
506 E Lancaster Ave., Ste. 102,
Downingtown, PA 19335
(610) 269-8900
Web site: www.cbmt.org

Chamber Music America (CMA)
305 Seventh Ave., New York,
NY 10001
(212) 244-2022
Web site: www.chamber-music.org

College Music Society (CMS)
312 East Pine, Missoula, MT 59802
(406) 721-9616
Web site: www.music.org

Columbia Artists Management Inc.
1790 Broadway, New York, NY
10019-1412
(212) 814-9500
Web site: www.cami.com

Content Delivery and Storage Association
(formally International Recording Media
Association, International Tape/Disc
Association)
182 Nassau St., Ste. 204, Princeton, NJ
08542-7005
(609) 279-1700
Web site: www
.contentdeliveryandstorage.org

Copyright Society of the U.S.A. (CSUSA)
352 Seventh Ave., Ste. 739, New York,
NY 10001
(212) 354-6401
Web site: www.csusa.org

Country Music Association (CMA)
1 Music Cir. S., Nashville, TN 37203
(615) 244-2840
Web site: www.cmaworld.com

Country Music Foundation (CMF)
222 Fifth Ave. S., Nashville, TN 37203
(615) 416-2001
Web site: www.countrymusichalloffame
.com

Directors Guild of America (DGA)
7920 Sunset Blvd., Los Angeles, CA
90046
(310) 289-2000
Web site: www.dga.org

Dramatists Guild of America
1501 Broadway, Ste. 701, New York,
NY 10036
(212) 398-9366
Web site: www.dramatistsguild.com

Early Music America
2366 Eastlake Ave., E. #429, Seattle,
WA. 98102
(206) 720-6270
Web site: www.earlymusic.org

Electronic Industries Alliance (EIA) (formerly
Electronic Industries Association)
2500 Wilson Blvd., Arlington,
VA 22201-3834
(703) 907-7500
Web site: www.eia.org

Entertainment Merchants Association
(EMA) (formerly Video Software Dealers
Association)
16530 Ventura Blvd., Ste. 400, Encino,
CA 91436-4551
(818) 385-1500
Web site: www.vsda.org

Entertainment Services and Technology
Association (ESTA)
875 Sixth Ave., Ste. 1005, New York,
NY 10001
(212) 244-1505
Web site: www.esta.org

Entertainment Software Association
575 7th St., NW, Ste. 300, Washington,
DC 20004
(202) 223-2400
Web site: www.theesa.com

Film Musicians Secondary Markets Fund
12001 Ventura Pl., 5th Fl., Studio City,
CA 91604
(818) 755-7777
Web site: www.fmsmf.org

Foundation Center
79 Fifth Ave./16th St., New York, NY
10003-3076
(212) 620-4230
Web site: www.foundationcenter.org

Gospel Music Association (GMA)
1205 Division St., Nashville, TN 37203
(615) 242-0303
Web site: www.gospelmusic.org

Guild of Italian-American Actors (GIAA)
(formerly Italian Actors Union)
352 W. 44th St., New York, NY 10036
(212) 262-7300
Web site: http://giaa.us

Guitar and Accessories Marketing
Association
P.O. Box 757, New York, NY 10033
(718) 274-3210
Web site: www.discoverguitar.com

Harry Fox Agency, Inc. (HFA)
601 W. 26th St., Ste. 500, New York,
NY 10017
(212) 834-0100
Web site: www.harryfox.com

International Alliance for Women in
Music (IAWM)
For further membership information:
Hayesd@colorado.edu
Box 2731, Rollins College 1000 Holt
Avenue, Winter Park, FL 32789-449
Web site: www.iawm.org

International Alliance of Theatrical Stage
Employes, Moving Picture Technicians,
Artists and Allied Crafts of the United
States, Its Territories and Canada (IATSE)
1430 Broadway, 20th Fl., New York,
NY 10018
(212) 730-1770
Web site: www.iatse-intl.org

International Association of Assembly
Managers (IAAM) (formerly International
Association of Auditorium Managers)
635 Fritz Dr., Ste. 100, Coppell, TX
75019-4442
(972) 906-7441
Web site: www.iaam.org

International Confederation of Societies of
Authors and Composers (CISAC)
20–26 Boulevard du Parc, 92200
Neuilly-sur-Sein, France
+(33) (1) 55 62 08 50
Web site: www.cisac.org

International Federation of Actors (FIA)
Guild House, Upper St. Martin's Lane
London WC2H 9EG,
United Kingdom
+(44) 207-379-0900
Web site: www.fia-actors.com

International Federation of Musicians (FIM)
21 bis, rue Victor Massé, F-75009,
Paris, France
+(33) (1) 45 26 3123
Web site: www.fim-musicians.com/eng

International Federation of the
Phonographic Industry (IFPI)
IFPI Secretariat, 10 Piccadilly, London
W1J 0DD, United Kingdom
+(44) 207-878-7900
Web site: www.ifpi.org

International Music Products Association
(NAMM) (formerly National Association
of Music Merchants)
5790 Armada Dr., Carlsbad, CA 92008
(760) 438–8001/(800) 767-6266
Web site: www.namm.com

International Society for Contemporary
Music
ISCM Secretariat, c/o Muziek Centrum
Nederland, ROKIN 111, 1012 KN
Amsterdam,
The Netherlands
+31-20-344-6060
Web site: www.iscm.org

Jukebox License Office
1700 Hayes St., Ste. 201, Nashville, TN
37203
(800) 955-5853
Web site: www.jukeboxlicense.com

League of American Orchestras (formerly
American Symphony Orchestra League)
33 W. 60th St., 5th Fl., New York, NY
10023
(212) 262-5161
Web site: www.symphony.org

League of Resident Theatres (LORT)
1501 Broadway, Ste. 2401, New York,
NY 10036
(212) 944-1501
Web site: www.lort.org

Los Angeles Copyright
Society (LACS)
(310) 859-0434
Web site: www.copr.org

Metropolitan Opera Guild (MOG)
70 Lincoln Center Plaza, 6th Fl., New
York, NY 10023
(212) 769-7000
Web site: www.metguild.org

Motion Picture Association of America
(MPAA)
15301 Ventura Blvd., Building E,
Sherman Oaks, CA 91403
(818) 995-6600
Web site: www.mpaa.org

Motion Picture Editors Guild
7715 Sunset Blvd., Ste. 200, Hollywood,
CA 90046
(323) 876-4770
Web site: www.editorsguild.com

Mu Phi Epsilon (International Music
Fraternity)
International Executive Office, 4705 N.
Sonora Ave., Ste. 114, Fresno, CA
93722-3947
(559) 277-1898 /(888) 259-1471
Web site: http://home.muphiepsilon
.org

Music and Entertainment Industry
Educators Association (MEIEA)
1900 Belmont Blvd., Nashville,
TN 37212
(615) 460-6946
Web site: www.meiea.org

Music Critics Association of North America,
Inc. (MCA) (formerly Music Critics
Association)
722 Dulaney Valley Rd., Rm. 259,
Baltimore, MD 21204
(410) 435-3881
Web site: www.mcana.org

Music Educators National Conference
(MENC)
1806 Robert Fulton Dr., Reston,
VA 20191
(703) 860-4000/(800) 336-3768
Web site: www.menc.org

Music Library Association, Inc. (MLA)
8551 Research Way, Suite 180,
Middleton, WI 53562
(608) 836-5825
Web site: www.musiclibraryassoc.org

Music Performance Fund (formerly Music
Performance Trust Funds of the the
Recording Industry)
1501 Broadway, Ste. 518, New York, NY
10036-5501
(212) 391-3950
Web site: www.musicpf.org

Music Publishers' Association of the United
States (MPA)
243 5th Ave., Ste. 236, New York, NY
10016
(212) 327-4044
Web site: www.mpa.org

Music Teachers National Association
(MTNA)
441 Vine St., Ste. 3100, Cincinnati, OH
45202-3004
(513) 421-1420/(888) 512-5278
Web site: www.mtna.org

Music Video Production Association (MVPA)
201 N. Occidental St., Bldg. 7, Unit B,
Los Angeles, CA 90026
(213) 387-1590
Web site: www.mvpa.com

Musical America
400 Windsor Corporate Park, 50
Millstone Rd., Ste. 200, East Windsor,
NJ 08520
(800) 221-5488 ext. 7877
Web site: www.musicalamerica.com

National Association of Band Instrument
Manufacturers (NABIM)
38–44 W. 21st St., 5th Fl., New York,
NY 10010
(212) 924-9175 or (866)-49-MUSIC
Web site: www.nabim.org

NAMM Affiliated Music Business Institutions
(NAMBI)
Dr. James Payne, Dept. of Music and
Performing Arts,
University of Nebraska at Kearney,
Kearney, NE 68849
(308) 865-8606
Web site: www.nambi.org

Nashville Songwriters Association
International (NSAI)
1701 Roy Acuff Pl., Nashville, TN 37201
(615) 256-3354/(800) 321-6008
Web site: www.nashvillesongwriters
.com

National Academy of Popular Music
(NAPM)/Songwriters Hall of Fame
330 West 58th St., Ste. 411, New York,
NY 10019
(212) 957-9230
Web site: www.songhall.org

National Academy of Recording Arts &
Sciences, Inc. (NARAS)
3402 Pico Blvd., Santa Monica, CA
90405
(310) 392-3777
Web site: www.grammy.org

National Academy of Television Arts &
Sciences (NATAS)
111 W. 57th St., Ste. 600, New York,
NY 10019
(212) 586-8424
Web site: www.emmyonline.org

National Alliance for Musical Theatre
520 Eighth Ave., Ste. 301, New York,
NY 10018
(212) 714-6668
Web site: www.namt.org

National Assembly of State
Arts Agencies
1029 Vermont Ave. NW, 2nd Fl.,
Washington, DC 20005
(202) 347-6352
Web site: www.nasaa-arts.org

National Association for Campus Activities
(NACA)
13 Harbison Way, Columbia,
SC 29212-3401
(803) 732-6222
Web site: www.naca.org

National Association of Broadcast
Employees and Technicians–
Communications
Workers of America (NABET-CWA)
501 3rd St. NW, 8th Fl., Washington,
DC 20001
(202) 434-1254
Web site: http://nabetcwa.org

National Association of Broadcasters
(NAB)
1771 N St. NW, Washington,
DC 20036
(202) 429-5300
Web site: www.nab.org

National Association of Negro Musicians,
Inc. (NANM)
P.O. Box 43053, 11551 S. Laflin St.,
Chicago, IL 60643
(773) 568-3818
Web site: www.nanm.org

National Association of Professional
Band Instrument Repair Technicians, Inc.
(NAPBIRT)
P.O. Box 51, Normal, IL 61761
(309) 452-4257
Web site: www.napbirt.org

National Association of Recording
Merchandisers (NARM)
9 Eves Dr., Ste. 120, Marlton, NJ 08053
(856) 596-2221
Web site: www.narm.com

National Association of Schools of Music
(NASM)
11250 Roger Bacon Dr., Ste. 21, Reston,
VA 20190-5248
(703) 437-0700
Web site: http://nasm.arts-accredit.org

National Association of Teachers of Singing
9957 Moorings Dr., Ste. 401,
Jacksonville, FL 32257
(904) 992–9101/(888) 262-2065
Web site: www.nats.org

National Conference of Personal Managers,
Inc. (NCOPM)
P.O. Box 50008, Henderson, NV 89016
(866) 91-NCOPM
Web site: www.ncopm.com

National Endowment for the Arts (NEA)
1100 Pennsylvania Ave., NW,
Washington, DC 20506
(202) 682-5400
Web site: http://arts.endow.gov

National Federation of Music
Clubs (NFMC)
1336 N. Delaware St., Indianapolis, IN
46202-2481
(317) 638-4003
Web site: www.nfmc-music.org

National Music Council of the United States
(NMC)
425 Park St., Upper Montclair, NJ 07043
(973) 655-7974
Web site: www.musiccouncil.org

National Music Publishers' Association
(NMPA)
101 Constitution Ave., NW, Ste. 705, East
Washington, DC 20001
(202) 742-4375
Web site: www.nmpa.org

National Music Theatre Network (NMTN)
(also known as Broadway Dozen)
P.O. Box 2639, New York, NY 10108
(212) 664-0979
Web site: www.broadwayusa.org

National Opera Association (NOA)
Robert Hansen, Executive Director, P.O.
Box 60869, Canyon, TX 79016-0869
(806) 651-2857
Web site: www.noa.org

Opera America (absorbed Central Opera
Service)
330 Seventh Ave., 16th Fl., New York,
NY 10001
(212) 796-8620
Web site: www.operaamerica.org

Phi Mu Alpha-Sinfonia Fraternity of
America, Inc.
10600 Old State Rd., Evansville,
IN 47711-1399
(812) 867-2433/(800) 473-2649
Web site: www.sinfonia.org

Piano Technicians Guild (PTG)
4444 Forest Ave., Kansas City,
MO 66106
(913) 432 9975
Web site: www.ptg.org

Producers Guild of America (PGA)
8530 Wilshire Blvd., Ste. 450, Beverly
Hills, CA 90211
(310) 358-9020
Web site: www.producersguild.org

PRS for Music
Copyright House, 29/33 Berners St.,
London W1T 3AB, United Kingdom
+(44) 207-580-5544
Web site: www.prsformusic.com

Radio Music License Committee
1616 Westgate Cir., Brentwood, TN
37027
(615) 844-6260
Web site: www.radiomlc.com

Recording Artist Royalties
AFM/AFTRA Fund, 1200 Ventura Pl.,
Ste. 500, Studio City, CA 91604
(818) 755-7780
Web site: www.raroyalties.org

Recording Industry Association of America,
Inc. (RIAA)
1025 F St., NW, 10th Fl., Washington,
DC 20004 (202) 775-0101
Web site: www.riaa.com

Recording Musicians Association
817 Vine St., Ste. 209, Los Angeles,
CA 90038-3716
(323) 462-4762
Web site: www.rmala.org

Screen Actors Guild (SAG)
5757 Wilshire Blvd., 7th Fl., Los Angeles,
CA 90036-3600
(323) 954-1600
Web site: www.sag.org

SESAC, Inc.
55 Music Sq. East, Nashville, TN 37203
(615) 320-0055/(800) 826-9996
Web site: www.sesac.com

Society of Composers, Inc.
P.O. Box 540, New York City,
NY 10113-0450
(212) 989-6764
Web site: www.societyofcomposers.org

Society of Composers & Lyricists
8447 Wilshire Blvd., Ste. 401, Beverley
Hills, CA 90211
(310) 281-2812
Web site: www.thescl.com

Society of Motion Picture and Television
Engineers, Inc. (SMPTE)
3 Barker Ave., 5th Fl., White Palms,
NY 10601
(914) 761-1100
Web site: www.smpte.org

Society of Professional Audio Recording
   Services (SPARS) (formerly Society
   of Professional Audio Recording Studios)
   9 Music Sq. South, Suite 222, Nashville,
      TN 37203
   (800) 771-7727
   Web site: www.spars.com

Society of Singers, Inc.
   15456 Ventura Blvd., Ste. 304, Sherman
      Oaks, CA 91403
   (818) 995-7100
   Web site: www.singers.org

Society of Stage Directors and
   Choreographers (SSDC)
   1501 Broadway, Ste. 1701, New York,
      NY 10036-5653
   (212) 391-1070/(800) 541-5204
   Web site: www.ssdc.org

Songwriters Guild of America (SGA)
   1560 Broadway, Ste. 408, New York,
      NY 10036
   (212) 768-7902
   Web site: www.songwritersguild.com

SoundExchange
   1121 Fourteenth St., NW, Ste. 700,
      Washington DC 20005
   (202) 640-5858
   Web site: www.soundexchange.com

United Scenic Artists, Local 829
   29 West 38th St., 15th Fl., New York,
      NY 10018
   (212) 581-0300
   Web site: www.usa829.org

Volunteer Lawyers for the Arts (VLA)
   1 E. 53rd St., 6th Fl., New York,
      NY 10022-4201
   (212) 319-2787
   Web site: www.vlany.org

Women in Film (WIF)
   8857 W. Olympic Blvd., Suite 201,
      Beverly Hills, CA 90211
   (310) 657-5144
   Web site: www.wif.org

World Intellectual Property Organization
   (WIPO)
   34, chemin des Colombettes, P.O.
      Box 18, CH-1211 Geneva 20,
      Switzerland
   +(41) 22 338-9111
   Web site: www.wipo.int

World Trade Organization
   Centre William Rappard, rue de
      Lausanne 154, CH-1211, Geneva 21,
      Switzerland
   +(41) 22 739-5111
   Web site: www.wto.org

Writers Guild of America, East, Inc.
   555 W. 57th St., Suite 1230 New York,
      NY 10019
   (212) 767-7800
   Web site: www.wgaeast.org

Writers Guild of America, Inc. (west)
   7000 W. Third St., Los Angeles,
      CA 90048
   (323) 951-4000
   Web site: www.wga.org

Young Audiences, Inc. (YA)
   115 E. 92nd St., New York,
      NY 10128–1688
   (212) 831-8110
   Web site: www.youngaudiences
      .org

Glossary

360 deal. A contract in which a record label, which traditionally acquired only recording rights, gains a share of other artist revenue streams such as touring, publishing, and merchandise.

501(c)3 organization. A provision of the United States Internal Revenue Code, listing types of non-profit organizations exempt from some federal income taxes. Many states reference Section 501(c) for definitions of organizations exempt from state taxation as well.

A&R producer. Artist and repertoire (record) producer.

Above-the-line (expense). Special production expenses—for example, salaries for featured artists, creative fees, above-scale wages. Contrasts with below-the-line expense.

Accessory. Item, usually relatively inexpensive, used to enhance the musical effect of an instrument or musical experience.

Account executive. Liaison person between an advertising agency or medium and one of its clients; salesperson.

Acoustic instrument. An instrument that is not electronic and is not amplified.

Ad mat. Reusable advertising artwork suitable for print media such as newspapers.

Adult contemporary. Broad music genre made up of mainstream and modern rock and classic hits from the past.

Affiliate. Broadcasting: A station that airs programming from a specific network.

Aftermarket. Income sources available for exploitation following first exposure. The broadcasting of a theatrical motion picture is an aftermarket of theatrical release.

Airplay. Radio broadcast of a commercially released music recording.

Alternative country. Any country music subgenre that tend to differ from mainstream or pop country music. The term is sometimes known as **Alt. country** and has included country music bands that have incorporated influences ranging from American roots music, bluegrass, rock & roll, rockabilly, acoustic music, americana, honky-tonk, and punk rock.

Alternative music. Youth-based, active music incorporating new wave, punk, "grunge," and techno styles.

AM station. Radio station using an amplitude modulation signal.

Analog. An electrical signal or wave form in which the amplitude and/or frequency vary continuously. Frequently contrasted with "digital."

Angel.   Individual financial backer of a Broadway show or other business venture.

Annual billing.   Amount invoiced time buyers for the calendar year by broadcasters.

Approved Production Contract (APC).   Developed by the Dramatists Guild of America, this model contract sets standards and procedures for creative rights in Broadway shows.

AOR.   Album-oriented rock.

Arbitration clause.   Provision in a contract requiring the parties to submit disputes to an impartial arbiter, often administered through the American Arbitration Association.

Arbitron.   (1) The Arbitron Company, supplier of radio and television ratings research. (2) Home Electronic device monitoring consumer media usage.

Arm's length.   Refers to a transaction between parties who act in their own self-interest rather than one party's being under the control or influence of the other.

Art music.   Repertoire associated with opera, ballet, symphony, and chamber music. Often used interchangeably with classical music or serious music.

Assignment.   Turning over of a contract or copyright to another person's control or ownership.

Attorney-at-law.   "An advocate, counsel, or official agent employed in preparing, managing, and trying cases in the courts" (Black's Law Dictionary). Compare **lawyer**.

Attorney-in-fact.   "A private attorney authorized by another to act in his place and stead, either for some particular purpose, as to do a particular act, or for the transaction of business in general, not of a legal character" (Black's Law Dictionary).

Audience share.   Comparative popularity of broadcast program, determined by dividing the program rating (expressed as a percentage) by the percent of sets in use at a particular time.

Audiovisual work.   Work that consists of a series of related images intended to be shown by the use of projectors, viewers, or electronic equipment, together with accompanying sounds, if any.

Baby boomers.   Americans born between 1946 and 1965, courted by entertainment media and advertisers because of their large discretionary incomes.

Back-announce.   In radio broadcasting, the accumulation of a group of announcements following several uninterrupted playings of recorded music.

Bed.   Advertising: Musical background for a commercial announcement.

Bel canto.   Fine singing; the Italian tradition of classical vocal production.

Below-the-line (expense).   Costs in production budgeting, such as union scale wages for technicians, equipment, and facilities rentals. Contrasts with above-the-line expense.

Best edition.   For purposes of copyright: The edition of a work that the Library of Congress determines to be the most suitable for its purposes.

Bio. Biography—a written summary of an individual's professional background.

Blackout. A turning off of stage lighting.

Board. Recording or mixing console.

Boilerplate. Time-tested language that may be found in most contracts but does not require a great deal of negotiation.

Book. In a musical play, the scenario and dialogue for a production.

Breach. "The breaking or violating of a law, right, or duty, either by commission or omission" (Black's Law Dictionary).

Breach of contract. "Failure, without legal excuse, to perform any promise which forms the whole or part of a contract" (Black's Law Dictionary).

Bridge. Musical phrase in a song following the hook, sometimes called "release" or "B phrase."

Bundle of rights. The six exclusive rights in copyright ownership vested initially and exclusively in the author of a work.

Buyout. The purchase of rights in a property (usually for a lump sum), rather than the payment of royalties for the use of the property.

Cable network (channel). A provider of a stream of programming on a specific channel, e.g. HBO, ESPN. Compare MSO.

Canned track. A prerecorded segment of music that has not been written for the particular work for which it may be used.

CARP. Copyright Arbitration Royalty Panel, phased out from 2005 and replaced by the Copyright Royalty Board. (See **CRB**.)

Cartage. The act of moving heavy or bulky equipment, particularly musical instruments; the union scale reimbursement for same.

Carve outs. Exceptions in legal contracts and other agreements, such as excluding music publishing rights that an artist creates from a broader artist recording contract.

Catch action. Compose a musical cue to synchronize with specific action on the screen.

Cattle call. Producer's announcement of open auditions.

CATV. Community Antenna Television, or cable television.

CD. Compact audio disc.

CD-R. A blank disc that can be loaded with sound recordings by means of a personal computer.

Channel. (1) The frequency of transmission for a broadcaster. (2) A program service feeding programming to one or more stations, cable systems, satellite services or Web sites. (3) A mode of product distribution—e.g., rack jobber channel.

Chargeback. An expense assessment, e.g., a charge by a recording company against an artist's royalties.

Chart. (1) Musical arrangement. (2) List of recordings currently most popular on radio or at retail.

Chorus. (1) The refrain section of a song that includes a phrase repeated at intervals. (2) A group of persons singing or speaking something simultaneously.

Clam. Wrong note in the copied parts or a note performed incorrectly.

Classic jazz. The "pure," traditional jazz sound: predominantly instrumental, rarely vocal, largely improvised rather than arranged, performed primarily on acoustic, not electronic, instruments.

Classic rock. The enduring music of such rock-and-roll trendsetters as Elvis Presley and the Beatles, originating in the 1950s and 1960s.

Classical music. The repertoire associated with symphony, opera, ballet, chamber, and some choral music.

Click path. A report on specific user Web actions which may be aggregated to draw conclusions about consumer behavior.

Click track. Audible guide used by musicians scoring music to aid synchronization with film.

Close-miking. Recording with a microphone close to the sound source.

Cluster programming. Radio broadcast of several recordings uninterrupted by announcements.

Clutter. The airing in rapid succession of many short spots during a television or radio commercial break; the proportion of a program period, such as an hour, consisting of interruptions.

Cold. (1) Advertising copy read without musical introduction or background. (2) A performance without rehearsal.

Collective bargaining. Negotiation between an employer or group of employers and representatives of union employees in order to reach agreement on terms of employment such as wages, work hours, and conditions.

Collective work. For purposes of copyright: A work, such as a periodical issue, anthology, or encyclopedia, in which a number of contributions, constituting separate and independent works in themselves, are assembled into a collective whole.

Commercial bed. See Bed.

Commercial load. The proportion of a broadcast station's or program's time that is given to spot announcements.

Common law. A body of law, written or unwritten, that originated in England and that derives its authority from tradition or from judgments and decrees of the courts recognizing such tradition.

Comp style. An improvised piano accompaniment often characterized by syncopated, block chords.

Competent party. Of sound mind and body; not demented or otherwise unable to act responsibly.

Compilation. For purposes of copyright: A work formed by the collection and assembling of preexisting materials or of data that are selected, coordinated, or arranged in such a way that the resulting work as a whole constitutes an original work of authorship. The term *compilation* includes collective works.

Compressor. Electronic sound device that limits the dynamic response to create a more constant, even dynamic level.

Compulsory license. In copyright law, a right determined by statute rather than negotiation between licensor and licensee. For example, copyright owners of nondramatic music have complete control over recording rights of their properties until they license the material for the first recording. But after this first recording is distributed to the public, they are compelled by law to license any other person to produce and distribute recordings of the copyrighted music in exchange for a fixed statutory royalty.

Concertmaster. Leader of the first violin section of an orchestra who has special authority and consults with the conductor about musical matters more than other musicians do.

Consent Decree. A judicial ruling expressing a voluntary agreement between parties to a suit.

Consideration. "The inducement to a contract, the cause, motive, price, or impelling influence which induces a contracting party to enter into a contract. The reason or material cause of a contract" (Black's Law Dictionary).

Contingent fee, contingency fee. A fee that is often a percentage of the money received from a certain contract. An attorney, for example, might charge a fee of 5% of the money received by his or her client as a result of a contract negotiated by the attorney.

Contingent scale payment. Royalties on sales of recordings paid to certain AFTRA members.

Contractor. In unions, the steward who hires performers, supervises their working conditions, and confirms they are properly paid.

Controlled Composition Clause. Language in a contract between a recording label and a composer-performer, in which the label demands to pay a reduced mechanical royalty for works owned or controlled by the recording artist.

Cooperative advertising. Form of product-specific advertising or promotion placed by the retailer, but funded in whole or in part by the manufacturer.

Copublishing. Act of two or more entities sharing publishing income but not necessarily the publishing responsibilities.

Copyist. A person who copies music or parts of a musical score.

Copyright. The legal right to reproduce, adapt, distribute, perform publicly, and display a work of intellectual property.

Copyright proprietor. Same as copyright owner.

Cost-per-thousand (CPM). The fee for delivering a commercial message to 1,000 readers, listeners, or viewers.

Coterminous.   Two or more conditions or contracts that end on the same date.

Country.   Music genre traditionally associated with Nashville, now ranging from traditional country/western and bluegrass to pop-flavored styles.

Cover, cover record.   Song that has been rerecorded by other artists after a first recording by the artist who introduced it.

CPB.   Corporation for Public Broadcasting.

CRB.   The Copyright Royalty Board comprises three Copyright Royalty Judges who determine rates and terms for copyright statutory licenses and make determinations on distribution of statutory license royalties collected by the United States Copyright Office of the Library of Congress.

Creative director.   (1) In an advertising agency, the individual in charge of creative advertising concepts; supervises writers, graphic artists, and audio-video producers. (2) For a production company or recording label, the person in charge of creative services.

Creative fee.   Money paid a composer or copywriter by an advertising agency, producer, or production company.

Creative services.   Division of a recording company that provides marketing concepts, graphic art, sales aids, editorial services, and advertising materials.

Cross-collateralize.   Shift of royalties earned by one property to the credit or debit of another property, resulting in a net total of royalties earned by all of them.

Crossover recording.   A recording focused on one market segment that achieves sales in one or more additional markets.

Cue.   Short musical passage composed to accompany dramatic action or underscore dialogue.

Cure.   Satisfy a complaint or resolve a dispute concerning a contract.

Cut.   In recorded music, a recording that is part of a whole, as in one cut from an album.

Cut-in.   Owner of a property shares ownership or the financial benefits of ownership.

Cutouts.   Surplus record inventory sold at bargain prices.

Cutter.   An editor, e.g., a film editor of music recorded for synchronization with pictures.

DAT.   Digital audiotape.

DAW.   Digital audio workstation.

Day parting.   Radio programming that divides the broadcast day into segments, such as "morning drive," "midday," and so forth.

DBS.   Direct broadcast satellite.

Deal breaker.   Issue that, if not settled, terminates contract negotiations.

Deal memo.   A summary document that covers term, commission, and other major points of the contract, often prepared before the full contract is drawn up.

Decay.   Diminution of sound pressure (audible volume).

Default.   Failure to perform under a legal contract.

Demo. (1) Demonstration recording. (2) Demography, demographic group.

Demography, demographics. The study and measurement of the characteristics of populations including distribution, density, and vital statistics such as age, income, and gender.

Derivative work. For purposes of copyright: A work based on one or more preexisting works, such as a translation, musical arrangement, dramatization, fictionalization, motion picture version, sound recording, art reproduction, abridgment, condensation, or any other form in which a work may be recast, transformed, or adapted.

Digital recording. Audio or video recording made with the analog signal converted into a stream of discrete numbers, thus producing an abstract template for the original sound or moving image.

Digital transmission. The transfer of music encoded as digital data. This transfer occurs by means of the Internet, satellites, cables, phone lines, or other means.

Discharge. To void a contract, cause it to be nonbinding.

Display. To show a copy of a work.

Distributor. Wholesale source of a retailer's goods, often an intermediary between the manufacturer and the retailer.

DIY. Do-it-yourself. A DIY label is a record company in which one person (or very few persons) performs most functions.

Double. The second (sometimes third) instrument a musician is called on to play. For example, a flute is a common double required of saxophonists.

Doubling. Act of playing more than one instrument in a performance.

Downtime. A period when recording or filming equipment is not functioning properly, thus unusable.

Dramatic music, dramatico-musical. Music closely related to drama or a scenario, particularly opera, a musical play, ballet, narration.

DRM. Digital rights management. DRM protects intellectual property either by encrypting the data so that only authorized users can access is, or by embedding a digital watermark so that the content cannot be freely distributed.

Drop ship. Fulfillment of a customer's order by shipment from an entity other than the one from which the customer ordered.

DVR. Digital video recorder.

Easy listening. Primarily instrumental music genre, gentler in sound than adult contemporary and notably popular in elevators.

End cap. Retail display at the end of an aisle.

Engineer. An audio mixer or sound technician.

EP. (1) Employers Pension Fund of the AFM. (2) Extended-play record.

EQ. Equalization.

Equity. Actors' Equity Association.

Executive producer. Top administrator and/or financier of a production.

Executory, executory provision. A requirement of performance to be rendered following disengagement from (termination of) a contract.

Exploit. In the entertainment field, to promote, advertise, publicize, display, distribute, license, sell, or advance an artist or a property.

Extended use. A prerecorded tape or film used for a period longer than the one initially paid for.

Fader. A recording console control used to effect changes in sound level.

Fair use doctrine. Legal defense to a copyright infringement claim, allowing minimal takings of copyrighted material for purposes such as scholarship, research, and news reporting.

Fake book. A collection of musical lead sheets intended to help a performer quickly learn new songs.

FCC. Federal Communications Commission.

Fiduciary. (1) A person who manages money or other things of value for another person and in whom the second party has a right to place trust. (2) A situation or relationship between persons where one acts for another in a position of trust. Example: a lawyer or agent acting on behalf of an artist.

Find. To decide and declare.

Finding. "The result of the deliberations of a jury or a court" (Black's Law Dictionary).

First-call musician. Performer a contractor prefers to hire above others available.

First desk/first chair. The lead instrumentalist in a section of an orchestra.

Flack. A publicist.

Flat. A natural sound, without coloration or alteration of highs and lows.

FM radio. Radio broadcasting using a frequency modulation signal.

Four-walling. Rental of a performance facility where the landlord offers only the venue—no stagehands, ushers, or box office help.

Franchised agent. A talent agent or booker licensed by an artists' union or guild.

Front line. Melodic instruments in a band or orchestra, as opposed to the rhythm section.

Gaffer. Lighting technician on a video, television, or motion picture set.

Ghost writer. A writer or composer who does work for hire under the name of another writer or composer.

Genre. A category of musical composition characterized by a particular style, form, or content (e.g., blues, jazz, country, rap, classical, easy listening).

Gig. Job; engagement of a musician or entertainer for a specified time.

Glissando. The musical effect produced by playing a series of instrumental notes in quick succession without performing each individually.

Gofer. An assistant who may run errands and "goes for" whatever is requested.

Grand right. Performance right in dramatic music.

Graphic equalizer. A sound control that provides adjustment of a signal over a broad range of frequencies.

Guild. An association of professional persons with similar interests (sometimes used synonymously with trade union).

Harmonize. Legal: To rewrite or amend statutes or regulations so that they are in agreement or accordance with other statutes or treaties.

Harmonizer. A signal-processing device that creates delay effects and changes the pitch of a sound without affecting its tempo.

HD. High definition.

Head. Start of a tape or film reel.

Headset. Earphones.

Hook. (1) Song: Memorable melodic (or lyrical) phrase. (2) Advertising: Campaign slogan or concept.

House agency. Advertising department within a company, as distinct from an independent agency.

House producer. One of the company's salaried staff production employees.

H&W Fund. AFM's Health and Welfare Fund.

Hyphenate. Artist providing multiple services—e.g., producer-director, singer-songwriter.

ID. Station: See Station logo.

Immaterial. "Not material, essential, or necessary; not important or pertinent" (Black's Law Dictionary).

Impressions. Advertising: The number of perceptions of a message—e.g., 1000 people viewing a single TV commercial would equal 1000 impressions.

In-house. Done within a company itself; not hired out.

Institutional ad (or spot). Promotion intended to impress the public with a firm's or organization's merit (as opposed to that of a specific product).

Institutional print. Music used by schools and churches for bands, choruses, choirs, and orchestras.

Intellectual property. Ideas translated from creators' minds to tangible expressions such as songs, writing, and other forms.

Interactive TV. A form of television that permits viewer to change the picture or add to it.

Interface. To connect by means of a machine or specific software protocol.

i.p.s. Inches per second, referring to tape-reel speed.

IPTV. Internet protocol television.

Jingle. Original term for a broadcast commercial (spot) containing music, or the music in the spot.

Joint venture. A business partnership of limited duration set up for a limited purpose.

Key man clause. Artists' contracts: Contractual provision that if an artist's manager, agent, or producer leaves a particular company, the artist may follow that individual without legal or financial reprisals.

Label. A brand of commercial recordings, usually issued under a trademarked name; a record manufacturer-distributor.

Lawyer. "A person learned in the law; as an attorney, counsel, or solicitor; a person licensed to practice law" (Black's Law Dictionary). Compare attorney-at-law.

Leadsheet. Music manuscript containing a song's melody, text, and chord symbols.

Legal consideration. "One recognized or permitted by the law as valid and lawful; as distinguished from such as are illegal or immoral" (Black's Law Dictionary). The term is sometimes used as equivalent for "good" or "sufficient" consideration.

Legit. Slang for legitimate. Style of music or theatrical performance in the classical, formal tradition.

Library service. A collection of a large quantity and variety of recorded passages that are available for use in productions not using original or "custom" music.

Licensing. The awarding of rights to perform, reproduce, distribute, or transmit a copyrighted work.

Lift. In broadcast commercials, a short recorded segment drawn from a longer one.

Ligature. (1) A slur indicating a group of notes sung or played as a connected phrase. (2) The group of notes thus indicated. (3) The device on a clarinet or saxophone mouthpiece holding the reed in place.

Limiter. Signal-processing device that reduces peaks but affects overall dynamics less than a compressor.

Live-on-tape. A television production performed live, with TV recording occurring at the same time for later editing prior to broadcast.

Local. (1) Branch office of a national union or guild. (2) A market or audience contained within one city or area.

Local marketing agreements. Agreement whereby a broadcast station owner may "lease" programming and sales to another station owner.

Logo. A musical or visual symbol used repeatedly in an effort to reinforce public recognition of a product or organization.

LV. Laser video, an early analog videodisc format.

Market. A particular group of buyers (or a type of audience) that can be identified by demographic research and/or analyses of preferences; a geographically distinct region.

Master use license. A license granting the right to use the recorded master, not just the underlying song.

Master purchase agreement.   A contract used by a recording company to obtain exclusive rights in a master tape recording that has been produced by another person, such as an independent producer.

Mastering.   The process by which album tracks are equalized and balanced in relation to each other, then transferred to a master storage device (DAT, CD, cassette, or lacquer disc) to be used as a duplicating master for the purpose of manufacturing recordings.

Material.   "Important; more or less necessarily; having influence or effect; going to the merits; having to do with matter, as distinguished from form" (Black's Law Dictionary).

MC (or Emcee).   Master of ceremonies.

MD.   Music director.

Mechanical license.   Legal permission given by the copyright owner (either through negotiation or a compulsory license) to make a commercial recording of copyrighted music.

Mechanicals.   (1) Royalties paid by a record manufacturer to the owner of a music copyright. (2) Elements of graphic art assembled for printing.

Mediabase 24/7.   A data collection service that monitors airplay through a combination of technological and human identification.

Media buyer.   Salaried employee who contracts for print ad space or broadcast time buys.

MIDI.   Musical instrument digital interface. (1) Technology that allows a composition to be transcribed into musical notation by playing it on the keyboard. MIDI notation prepared for one instrument can be used to reproduce similar performances with other MIDI instruments. (2) Standard for exchanging musical information for musical devices including instruments.

Mix.   To combine and equalize, into one or more channels, a larger number of separate tracks of recorded sounds.

Mixer.   (1) Recording technician who operates a console. Often referred to (incorrectly) as an engineer. (2) Electronic equipment that enables the mixing of sounds.

MOR.   Middle-of-the-road type of music, now more commonly referred to as "nostalgia/big band," that favors instrumentals over vocals and is somewhat similar to easy listening music.

Moral rights.   The right of an author to be properly identified and to insist that any editing of a work preserves its integrity, without alteration, distortion, or mutilation of the work.

MPA.   Music Publishers Association of the United States.

MPEG.   The family of digital video compression standards and file formats developed by the group Moving Pictures Experts Group.

MSO.   Multiple system operator, a cable TV infrastructure company owning more than one system. Compare with Cable Network (channel).

Multicast.   System for the simultaneous transmission of two or more signals over the same wire or radio frequency channel. Compare simulcast.

Multiplex.   System for the simultaneous transmission of two or more signals over the same wire or radio frequency channel.

Multitrack.   The recording device or tape on which parallel tracks can be recorded. Each track has separate music or information that can be mixed or edited separately.

Music coordinator.   Production assistant keeping track of musical elements.

Music cue.   Short musical fragment used to bridge dramatic scenes or provide musical background.

Music cutter.   Same as film music editor.

Music house (or music supply house).   A company of composers and arrangers offering creative services (and recording) for buyers of "custom" music.

Music preparation.   Music manuscript proofreading, extraction of parts from the score, collation, reproduction, score binding, and delivery.

Music supervisor.   A person primarily responsible for selecting and licensing music for film, TV, and new media productions.

Music supplier.   See Music house.

Narrowcasting.   Contrasts with broadcasting: program material produced and delivered to audiences of special tastes.

National account.   Advertising: Customer of an agency or production company that advertises nationwide.

Needle drop.   Brief recorded passage (orchestral or a sound effect) drawn from a transcription library that a producer uses for a dramatic program or broadcast commercial.

Negative cost.   Expense of producing a movie or TV show before incurring costs of distribution or promotion.

Negative tour support.   The advance a recording company may make to pay the difference between the touring costs and touring income, if a band's touring does not break even or make a profit.

Negotiated license.   In the recording industry, a right to record worked out between a music publisher and a record producer. Contrasts with a statutory compulsory license.

Neighboring rights (or related rights).   The rights in a work that don't belong to the author. There are three general categories of neighboring rights: those of performers, producers, and broadcasters.

Neo-romantic.   Any of various movements in the arts considered as representing a return to the artistic styles associated with the romantic period of the 19th century.

Network.   Broadcast service usually distributed simultaneously through more than one station or outlet.

New Age music.   Mellow, mostly acoustic instrumental music with an ethereal, soothing quality, popularized in the 1980s.

New country music. Music genre that combines elements of country and rock and roll.

New use. Application of recorded music tape or film to a medium different from the one originally intended—e.g., a record album to be used in a film.

Nielsen BDS. Nielsen Broadcast Data Systems. A data collection service whose technology monitors broadcasts and recognizes songs and/or commercials aired by radio and TV stations.

Nielsen rating. Percentage of the potential broadcast audience watching a particular program or network, according to Nielsen Media Research. A household rating of 10.0 would indicate one in ten homes watched the program.

Nondramatic music. Musical works, such as pop singles, not incorporated and performed in the context of a story, such as an opera or stage play.

NPR. National Public Radio.

NTSC. Abbreviation for a standard for TV transmission used primarily in North America and Japan.

O&O station. A radio or TV station owned and operated by a commercial broadcasting network.

Off-Broadway. Low-budget, often experimental, professional theater, produced in New York City venues but outside its Times Square theater district.

One-off. Something that is not repeated or reproduced.

One-stop. Record distributor/wholesaler offering a variety of recording companies' merchandise to retailers and jukebox operators.

Open to buy. The budget (such as monthly dollar amounts) for new merchandise purchases by a retailer or distributor.

Opticals. Visual effects created for film or videotape.

Orchestrator. One who takes music written by someone else and writes or scores the music for the various instruments that play it.

Outboard equipment. Recording hardware external to the recording console that is patched into it to enhance the mixer's options of controlling sounds.

Overcall album. Recording requested by label but that was not covered by initial contract.

Overdubbing. Adding music or sounds to a previously recorded tape.

Overtracking. (1) Adding sounds to a previously recorded tape. (2) The use of one voice several times or recording one voice several times, then playing them simultaneously on a recording to produce the sound of a larger ensemble.

Package deal. Combined goods and/or services delivered under one price tag.

Pan pot. Recording console control (fader) used to place a signal to the left, right, or center of the stereo image.

Paper business. Printed-editions sector of a music publishing company.

Papering the house. Concert promotion: Issuing free tickets to ensure a full audience for a performance.

Pass.   Make a negative judgment; to turn down, reject.

Pay TV.   Television delivery business model for specific channels for which an extra fee is paid, contrasting with basic TV (at a lower cost to the viewer) and free TV (no cost to the viewer).

Payola.   Money or other compensation illicitly given radio station personnel in return for playing particular recordings.

PD.   (1) Program director. (2) Public domain.

Performance.   A performance occurs any time music is played publicly, whether at a live concert or broadcast over radio, TV, Internet, or other means of transmission.

Performance license.   Legal permission granted by the copyright owner or his or her representative for the public performance of copyrighted music in exchange for a fee. These are generally granted in the form of blanket licenses, offering access to a large catalog of copyrights.

Performance right, performing right.   Exclusive right given to the creator of copyrighted material to authorize the use of the work in public.

Performance royalty.   Payment for the broadcast or performance of a writer or composer's work.

Phonorecord.   Any physical medium carrying recorded music, such as a phonograph record, CD, or prerecorded tape.

Piracy.   Illegal duplication and distribution of sound recordings.

Pit.   Area occupied by the orchestra in a theater, often below the floor level of the audience.

Playlist.   Radio station's recorded music schedule for broadcast.

Points.   Royalties: Synonymous with percentages.

P.O.P.   Point-of-purchase (merchandising aids).

POS.   Point-of-sale.

Power of attorney.   "An instrument authorizing another to act as one's agent or attorney; a letter of attorney" (Black's Law Dictionary).

PR.   Public relations.

Print.   Music in printed form.

PRO.   Performing rights organization. An intermediary collecting license fees on behalf of rights owners.

Product manager.   Person in charge of a promotional or marketing campaign.

Production blanket.   A means of using unlimited amounts of music in one production for a capped or flat fee.

Production manager.   Business affairs head for a production.

Promo kit.   See **Promo pack.**

Promo pack.   Package of promotional materials.

Promoter of record.   Promoter who first produces an artist's or group's public appearances.

Proscenium.   Wall arch that separates the stage from the auditorium.

Public domain.   Material, such as music or other intellectual property, available for unrestricted use on which the copyright or patent right has expired or that has no copyright.

Publishing.   In the music industry, publishing is the distribution of printed copies or phonorecords for sale, or the control of the exploitation of a work in a print or nonprint medium (such as recordings or broadcasting).

Punch in.   Augment taping or filming with insertion of new (or additional) material.

Punch up.   Add emphasis to music or script.

Rack jobber.   A merchant paying a rental fee or commission to maintain and sell inventory within the retailer's store.

Rack up.   TV film and tape presets that may then be called up by a technician for broadcast.

Rap.   Lyrics spoken in rhyme to rhythmic music.

Rate card.   Summary of advertising rates for a specific medium (radio stations, TV network, etc.) given to ad agencies, clients, and prospective clients.

Record (album, single).   Generic term for a distributed copyright recording, e.g., a digital download, compact disc, audiocassette, or vinyl recording.

Record label.   The company that coordinates the production, manufacture, distribution, marketing and promotion, and enforcement of copyright protection of sound recordings and music videos; maintains contracts with recording artists and their managers; and manages brands and trademarks associated with the marketing of music recordings and music videos. Also called a record company or recording company.

Release phrase.   See **Bridge.**

Remedy.   Solve a problem or cure a default under a contract.

Reuse.   (1) Use of a recorded performance after an initial time period is over. (2) Use of a recorded performance in a medium that is different from the medium for which the performance was first used.

Rhythm and blues.   Predominantly black music genre featuring a lead vocalist backed with harmonizing singers, piano, bass, and drums, with harmonic structure adapted from popular and blues forms.

Rhythm section.   The "motor element" of a band or orchestra, normally composed of piano, bass, drums, and guitar.

Right-to-work law.   A state law that makes a closed shop, where union membership is a condition of employment, illegal.

Sampling.   (1) Music performances: Technique used by music rights organizations to estimate total performances by examining a limited number of performances. (2) Music recording: The digital taping of a sound or series of sounds from already recorded material, for insertion into a new recording so as to enhance that recording's sound; the source sound can be inserted unchanged or transformed by synthesizer or other electronic equipment.

Scale.   Specified minimum union wage.

Scaling the house.   Determining what quantity of available seats in a performance facility are to be priced the least expensive, the next least expensive, and so on.

Score (a film).   Compose, perform, and record music to synchronize with a motion picture.

Second engineer.   Assistant to the head audio engineer (technician).

Secondary transmission.   Cable TV broadcast of an originating program source, such as from a commercial television station.

Sel sync.   The ability of a tape recorder to record on one track at a time in synchrony with previously recorded tracks.

Self-contained group.   (1) Small ensemble that writes its own material. (2) An organized ensemble that performs together regularly without outside members.

Selling agent.   Person or firm offering printed music or merchandise for sale at the retail level, under a royalty contract or for commission.

Serialism.   The method or practice of composing with tone rows.

Session musician.   Instrumentalist employed in recording studios and usually paid union scale.

Sforzando.   "Stinger" note or chord that brings special attention to specific dramatic action—e.g., to identify a villain, emphasize the sounds of a fight, or suggest the sounds of a beating heart.

Sheet music.   Musical composition printed on unbound sheets of paper.

Shop tapes.   Submit audition tapes to potential buyers.

Side.   (1) One side of a recording. (2) One song on a recording.

Sidemusician.   An instrumentalist other than the leader or contractor.

Simulcast.   To transmit the identical programming at the same time on different channels. Compare multicast.

SKU.   Stock keeping unit. A uniquely-configured offering at retail. A vinyl LP of an album would be a different SKU than a CD of the same recording.

Slap.   The "tony" or buzzing sound that is produced by plucked/fingered bass when vibrating strings come into contact with the metal frets.

Slate.   Chalkboard ID (or visual equivalent) of a filmed or videotaped segment, or a spoken recitation of a description of the take, to aid in the editing process.

Slaved.   To be made directly responsive to another mechanism.

Small right.   Performance right in nondramatic music.

Song score.   A film sound track composed primarily of songs that have the potential to be hits.

Soundcarrier.   A phonorecord.

SoundScan.   A data collection service that tabulates sales of recorded product through POS devices. SoundScan's sales tabulations are generated by a computer network linked to retail outlets and rack jobbers nationwide.

Spec, speculation. Employed without assurance of getting paid.

Special material. Music, lyrics, dialogue, and patter specially written for a particular artist's performance.

Split copyright. Copyright proprietor shares his or her ownership with one or more persons.

Split point. Point of cumulative revenue at which the artist and the promoter divide any net income from a concert.

Split publishing. One party shares his or her publishing rights with one or more persons.

Spot. (1) A broadcast commercial announcement. (2) Theatrical spotlight. (3) To place in a particular position, as in "spotting" a film—deciding precisely where a film should be underscored.

Spotting notes. Notes given to a composer of motion picture music by the music editor to specify where each cue will happen in the movie.

SRO. Standing room only, meaning "sold out."

Staff paper. A set of horizontal lines and intermediate spaces used in notation to represent a sequence of pitches, in modern notation normally consisting of five lines and four spaces. Also called a stave.

Station. In radio or television, a station is generally a broadcaster that transmits on one frequency and from one locality. A group of stations is frequently referred to as a *broadcast network*.

Station logo. Broadcast station's musical or visual signature, identification.

Statutory license. An exception to copyright provided by law to use a copyrighted work without the explicit permission of its owner. In the U.S. it often specifically refers to the license to broadcast digital music and audio over the Internet.

Statutory rate. For a mechanical royalty, the government-established maximum rate paid by the label for the recorded use of intellectual property on a consumer-distributed phonogram such as a CD. Paid on a per-unit basis, the rate is tied to the individual song, or for longer works (such as classical compositions), to the work's length. The rate is periodically adjusted.

Stave. See **staff paper**.

Steward. Hires performers and supervises enforcement of their union contract with the producer.

Stick. (1) Music: A baton. (2) Broadcasting: A transmission tower.

Stinger. Accented chord played by an orchestra to underscore a dramatic moment on the screen.

Stock arrangement. Published edition; not a custom chart.

Storyboard. A series of sketches showing the sequence of events for a film or video.

Strip show. A series of broadcasts scheduled several times a week at the same hour each day.

Studio musician. Same as session musician.

Subpublisher. Firm affiliated with a prime publisher in providing publishing services, usually abroad.

Subsisting. Now in existence, as in subsisting copyrights.

Sunset clause. A provision in a contract specifying that an agreement, regulation, or law will end or be modified in a predetermined way at a future point in time.

Supervising copyist. Copyist who directs the services of additional copyists working on the same job.

Swag. Give-aways—posters, novelties, souvenir items, and the like—as part of a promotion.

Sweeps. Period of the year during which research firms collect data concerning broadcast audience size.

Sweeten. Record additional sounds by overdubbing.

SWOT analysis. Tool for identifying strengths, weaknesses, opportunities, and threats when, for example, developing a marketing or strategic plan.

Synchronization license. The right to synchronize a composition in timed relation with visual images on film or tape.

Synchronization rights. The right to use music in such a way that it is timed to synchronize with, or relate to, action on film or video.

Synclavier. Keyboard synthesizer incorporating a computer terminal, digital processor, and storage unit, with which an operator can create, store, retrieve, and re-create musical sounds.

Syncopated. Rhythmic placement of musical tones so that their accent does not coincide with the metric accent.

Syndication. Broadcasts of programs (produced by a network or syndicator) that individual stations air simultaneously or at times convenient to them.

Tail. End of a tape or film reel.

Take. One version of a recorded performance, as in "The second take was best."

Technical rider. Addendum to a performance contract stipulating requirements for staging, sound reinforcement, equipment, etc.

Telecommunications. Production and delivery of all modes of entertainment and information.

Term. The time interval embraced by a legal agreement.

Tessitura. Prevailing pitch and range of a melodic line.

Tight. Slang for a well-rehearsed, cohesive performance.

Timbre. Quality, tone color distinguishing one voice or musical instrument from another.

Time buyer. Advertising agency employee who purchases time on a broadcast station or network for an advertiser.

Time shift.   Capacity of a VCR or personal video recorder (DVR) to record a TV program off the air and move its playback to a time more convenient for the viewer.

Tin Pan Alley.   The business of popular music most prevalent in the 1920s in New York. Also, style of popular song of that era, usually sentimental, with a verse and chorus form in which chorus predominated.

Tour support.   Financial resources, such as those provided contractually by a record label, that help underwrite the costs associated with touring a given act.

Track.   (1) One recorded portion of combined tracks, as in "24-track" recording; the sound on one track, as in "the bass track." (2) A single selection on an album.

Tracker.   Label employee following the progress of a record release—airplay, chart action, sales, etc.

Tracking.   (1) An AFM and AFTRA payment category in which performers tape the same notes more than once and the producer or engineer uses each recording simultaneously to produce the sound of a larger ensemble. AFM and AFTRA performers are supposed to be paid for each taped use of their work. (2) A promotion practice of record companies in which the company has employees call radio stations and record stores to see how often a song is played or a recording is sold.

Tracking scale.   Union wage scale for tracking sessions.

Tracking session.   Taping session following the recording of basic tracks; overdubbing.

Trading fours.   Jazz musicians taking turns improvising alternate four-bar phrases.

Transcription.   A copy of recorded music made for purposes other than direct sale to consumers (such as Muzak, in-flight entertainment, and radio syndication).

Turntable hit.   A song which is successful in the airplay charts but not so strong in sales.

Underscore.   To place recorded music behind a movie or TV program.

Unencumbered.   Of or relating to an owned asset that does not have a claim against it.

Union shop.   An establishment that hires only members of a labor union or those who promise to join a union within a specified time.

Union steward.   An agent who supervises the employment of union artists and provides liaison for them with their employer.

Unison.   Music played or sung by two or more people in which instruments or voices perform identical parts simultaneously in the same or different octaves; the interval formed by two tones of the same pitch.

Up-front payment.   Money advanced prior to completion of a job or production.

Up full.   Background music crescendo to foreground.

VCR.   Videocassette recorder.

VDP.   Video disc player.

Venue.   Place of performance or trial.

Verse.   A section or stanza of a hymn or song; a section preceding the refrain or chorus of a song.

Videocaster.   One who broadcasts, cablecasts, or telecasts videos.

Videogram.   Any audiovisual physical medium, such as videocassettes and DVDs, that contains musical compositions.

VJ.   Video jockey, analogous to DJ.

VOD.   Video on demand. A form of per-program electronic delivery requested by an individual viewer.

Voiceover.   Words spoken by an actor or announcer who is not seen on the screen.

Webcasting.   Broadcasting over the Internet; the distribution of media files over the Internet via streaming media technology.

Weighting formula.   Evaluations by a performing rights organization used in determining the relative value of various kinds of music performances in order to judge what royalties are due a writer or publisher.

Work made for hire.   (1) A work prepared by an employee within the scope of his or her employment. (2) A work specially ordered or commissioned for use as a contribution to a collective work.

Working capital.   The assets of a business that can be applied to its operation; the amount of current assets that exceeds current liabilities.

Index

About the Author

Author David Baskerville (right) receiving ASCAP's Deems Taylor Award, given each year for outstanding books on music. The presentation is by Academy Award–winning songwriter Hal David, representing ASCAP.

Author **David Baskerville** received a Ph.D. in music from UCLA. His background included staff composer-conductor for NBC-Hollywood; arranger for Nelson Riddle, Paramount Pictures, and 20th Century Fox; television producer for BBC-London; conductor at Radio City Music Hall; trombonist with the Seattle Symphony, Los Angeles Philharmonic, and NBC-Hollywood orchestra; Executive Vice President of Ad-Staff, Inc.; producer of award-winning broadcast commercials; Executive Editor of Tor Music Publishing Company; and President of Sherwood Recording Studios, Los Angeles (subsequently operated by Warner Bros. Records).

He also served as a consultant to companies in the entertainment industry, such as Walt Disney Productions, and to research and marketing firms, such as Vidmar Communications, Los Angeles.

As an educator, Dr. Baskerville created and directed the music management program at the University of Colorado at Denver, where he became professor emeritus. He was a guest lecturer, consultant, or clinician at USC, UCLA, Chicago Musical College, Hartt School of Music, the Ohio State University, University of Miami, and Trebas Institute, Canada.

He was a featured speaker at national conventions of the Music Educators National Conference, College Music Society, National Association of Jazz Educators, and the National Association of Schools of Music.

About the Co-Author

Co-author **Tim Baskerville** has a diverse background in entertainment and media. He began his career in broadcasting after receiving a B.A. in theater arts from UCLA. Early affiliations included CBS and Cox Broadcasting, where he served as a writer-producer. The first TV documentary he created for CBS stations was nominated for an Emmy.

As a publisher and entrepreneur, he launched business periodicals on the home video software industry, global film distribution, and multinational broadcasting. Today, a publishing company he founded in London in the 1990s is one of the world's leading providers of data on mobile entertainment (www.informatm.com).

In recent years he served as President of Kagan Research, the leading provider of financial analysis on the media industry, and CEO of JupiterResearch (acquired by Forrester Research), a key source of consumer research on Web behavior.

As a consultant, Baskerville's clients have included the Motion Picture Association of America, *Variety*, Time Warner, IBM, International Data Corp., Young & Rubicam, JVC America, Apple, and The Rockefeller Foundation. He has been both a strategy consultant and weekly columnist for *Billboard*.

Baskerville was Vice President of the Music and Entertainment Industry Educators Association (MEIEA), member of the Writers Guild of America, west, and chapter founder of the Overseas Press Club of America.

Supporting researchers for more than 40 years

Research methods have always been at the core of SAGE's publishing program. Founder Sara Miller McCune published SAGE's first methods book, *Public Policy Evaluation*, in 1970. Soon after, she launched the *Quantitative Applications in the Social Sciences* series—affectionately known as the "little green books."

Always at the forefront of developing and supporting new approaches in methods, SAGE published early groundbreaking texts and journals in the fields of qualitative methods and evaluation.

Today, more than 40 years and two million little green books later, SAGE continues to push the boundaries with a growing list of more than 1,200 research methods books, journals, and reference works across the social, behavioral, and health sciences. Its imprints—Pine Forge Press, home of innovative textbooks in sociology, and Corwin, publisher of PreK–12 resources for teachers and administrators—broaden SAGE's range of offerings in methods. SAGE further extended its impact in 2008 when it acquired CQ Press and its best-selling and highly respected political science research methods list.

From qualitative, quantitative, and mixed methods to evaluation, SAGE is the essential resource for academics and practitioners looking for the latest methods by leading scholars.

For more information, visit **www.sagepub.com**.